Downtown America

HISTORICAL STUDIES OF URBAN AMERICA

Edited by Kathleen N. Conzen, Timothy J. Gilfoyle, and James R. Grossman

Also in the series:

The Creative Destruction of Manhattan, 1900–1940
  by Max Page

Brownsville, Brooklyn: Blacks, Jews, and the Changing Face of the Ghetto
  by Wendell Pritchett

My Blue Heaven: Life and Politics in the
Working-Class Suburbs of Los Angeles, 1920–1965
  by Becky M. Nicolaides

In the Shadow of Slavery: African Americans in New York City, 1626–1863
  by Leslie M. Harris

Building the South Side:
Urban Space and Civic Culture in Chicago, 1890–1919
  by Robin F. Bachin

Places of Their Own:
African American Suburbanization in the Twentieth Century
  by Andrew Wiese

Downtown

ALISON ISENBERG

America

The University of Chicago Press *Chicago & London*

Alison

Isenberg

is associate

professor of

history at

Rutgers

University.

The University of Chicago Press, Chicago 60637

The University of Chicago Press, Ltd., London

© 2004 by The University of Chicago

All rights reserved. Published 2004

Printed in the United States of America

13 12 11 10 09 08 07 06 05 04   1 2 3 4 5

ISBN: 0-226-38507-8 (cloth)

Library of Congress Cataloging-in-Publication Data

Isenberg, Alison.

   Downtown America : a history of the place and the people who
made it / Alison Isenberg.

      p. cm. — (Historical studies of urban America)

   Includes bibliographical references (p.) and index.

   ISBN 0-226-38507-8 (cloth : alk. paper)

   1. Cities and towns—United States—History.   2. Central business
districts—United States—History.   3. City and town life—United
States—History.   4. Community life—United States—History.
5. Inner cities—United States—History.   6. Urban renewal—
United States—History.   7. City planning—United States—History.
I. Title.   II. Series.

   HT123.I74 2004

   307.76′0973—dc22   2003024058

This book is printed on acid-free paper.

For my parents

Marian Ellenbogen Isenberg

Lee E. Isenberg

in loving memory

CONTENTS

ILLUSTRATIONS

Plates (following page 46)

ACKNOWLEDGMENTS

One of the major satisfactions of finishing this book is being able to thank the individuals and institutions that have made this publication possible. The intellectual engagement, advice, and skepticism of countless people have sustained this project. For their thoughtful responses to chapter drafts, I am especially indebted to Robin Bachin, Susan Bickford, Peter Coclanis, Steven Conn, Mona Domosh, Howard Gillette, Will Jones, Steven Lawson, Guian McKee, Martha McNamara, Max Page, Gail Radford, Erika Rappaport, Marc Stein, John Stuart, and Carla Yanni. Numerous conferences, invited talks, and seminars have enabled me to sharpen my arguments over the years in dialogue with colleagues and friends. For their helpful commentary and pointed questions in such venues, I would particularly like to thank Ruth Alexander, Rose Beiler, Stan Chojnacki, Lizabeth Cohen, Robert Fairbanks, Leon Fink, Robert Fishman, Robert Fogelson, Carolyn Goldstein, Nancy Hewitt, Joel Hoffman, Helen Horowitz, Lara Iglitzin, Temma Kaplan, John Kasson, Sallyann Kluz, T. J. Jackson Lears, Alex Lichtenstein, David Nasaw, Kathy Newman, Gunther Peck, Barb Ryan, Mary Ryan, David Schuyler, Diane Shaw, Mary Corbin Sies, Amy Slaton, Bonnie Smith, Mark Szuchman, Joel Tarr, Joe Trotter, Victor Uribe, Harry Watson, and Deborah Gray White. The participants in the 1999–2000 Charles Warren Center Seminar at Harvard University provided an especially wide-ranging critique along the workshop themes of economy and culture, while an audience of historians, urban design professionals, and policymakers at the 1999 conference "Reframing the 1945–1965 Suburb" hosted by the Design Center for American Urban Landscape gave me spirited interdisciplinary feedback.

I have long been grateful to my dissertation adviser, Michael Katz, for the freedom I had to find my own way and for his astute, supportive critiques and balanced advice over the years. I was very fortunate that Tom Sugrue arrived to teach at the University of Pennsylvania just as I launched this project. His comments on the dissertation helped me articulate key implications of my research, and his own work is a model for interweaving the history of cities with the broader, essential questions facing postwar America. From Michael and Tom, and from Mary Frances Berry, I learned a great deal about understanding and building the connections between history and policy. Other faculty members of the University of Pennsylvania history department, especially

Lynn Hollen Lees and Walter Licht, took a strong interest in this project from its beginnings and offered suggestions and encouragement.

A series of remarkable academic communities have improved this book greatly. My graduate school colleagues early on demonstrated that scholarship did not have to be a lonely task, and the lively exchanges have happily continued over the years. I have been fortunate to benefit from the rich insights of colleagues too numerous to list, within the unique intellectual environments of three outstanding history departments — at Florida International University, the University of North Carolina at Chapel Hill, and Rutgers University. My students in two graduate courses, "Historical Perspectives on the Built Environment" at UNC and "Urbanism Unclothed: Gender and the Built Environment" at Rutgers, proved to be ideal coinvestigators in the exploration of urban form. At Radcliffe's Schlesinger Library, where I spent a year as a visiting scholar, I was able to research and refine the gendered themes of this book in the company of the terrific historians affiliated with that institution. While teaching in Miami I fell in with a crowd that blended friendship, scholarship on the built environment, and an interest in public history — Robin Bachin, Joel Hoffman, John Stuart, and Erika Rappaport — in a fun and productive Floridian mix. Finally, fellow members of the Society for American City and Regional Planning History, drawn from many disciplines, have shared their scholarship and commentary at the organization's stimulating conferences.

In writing this book I have often relied upon the skills of graduate students and benefited from a steady flow of newspaper clippings from friends, relatives, and colleagues. Barbara Hahn undertook a research foray into chain stores, Jennifer Nardone pursued several key questions, and Daniel Wherley assisted with gathering permissions. Matthew Andrews, Rachel Wilson, and Melissa Stein helped with last-minute fact-checking, and Pablo Toral provided research assistance during the project's earlier stages. Maire Murphy's investigation into St. Louis's Gaslight Square on my behalf deeply enriched my understanding of that fascinating commercial district. Special thanks also to Jon Farnham for sharing with me the cartoon that became figure 1.5, to Barbara Hahn for her discovery of figure 2.16, and to Martha McNamara for bringing figure 7.1 to my attention.

I owe a special debt to Kathleen Conzen, who in her capacity as series editor read the dissertation and later the book manuscript, both times providing remarkably perceptive comments. The press's anonymous reader also made many useful suggestions. It has been a pleasure to work with the editors at the

University of Chicago Press, first Doug Mitchell and then Robert Devens, on all of the aspects of bringing the book to fruition. Elizabeth Branch Dyson, editorial associate, handled an amazing number of details with enviable speed. Thanks also to Christine Schwab, senior production editor; to Lois Crum for her patient editing and close attention to straightening out the notes; and to Rich Hendel and the press's design department for their care with the visual dimensions of a book that addresses the significance of what downtowns have looked like.

This book has benefited from the financial support of many institutions. The Graham Foundation for Advanced Studies in the Fine Arts provided a generous publication subvention, and grants from Rutgers University and the University of North Carolina helped defray the costs involved in including so many illustrations. The junior faculty leave policies of both the University of North Carolina and Rutgers University allowed me crucial time to write, while the Schlesinger Library gave me a uniquely hospitable base and a peaceful office for the year that I spent there. Travel grants from Cornell University and the Hagley Library and Museum facilitated extended research trips to those archives. The FIU Foundation of Florida International University awarded the project a summer research grant, as did the Center for the Study of the American South at the University of North Carolina. Funding from the Mellon Foundation permitted me to complete in a timely manner the dissertation from which this book evolved.

Numerous archivists have given generously of their time and expertise. For their unusual interest in this project, and extra help to its author, I would especially like to thank Debra Gust, Christine Pyle, and Katherine Hamilton-Smith of the Curt Teich Postcard Archives; Mary Daniels of Harvard University's Frances Loeb Library; William Fischetti of the Western Historical Manuscript Collection of the University of Missouri, St. Louis; Jim Baggett of the Department of Archives and Manuscripts in the Birmingham Public Library; Linda Drake of the Chapin Planning Library at the University of North Carolina; Dana Twersky of the National Building Museum; and Barbara Kellner of the Columbia Association Archives. The directors of several private organizations allowed me to peruse historical company and association records, and the results of that research fundamentally shaped my thinking. Kenneth Riggs Jr., CEO of the Real Estate Research Corporation, set me up with a microfiche reader to examine decades-old appraisal reports, welcoming several of my visits over the years. Rich Bradley of the International Downtown

Association found a few boxes of "old stuff," and it was in reading that organization's conference transcripts from the mid-1950s that I first began to puzzle over unexpected references to housewives amid discussions of urban renewal. Billy Barnes and Jim Appel were both generous in sharing and discussing their respective private collections.

I have done my best to work creatively with the multifaceted contributions of so many individuals, and I hope that they will recognize their imprint on the pages that follow. Responsibility for the book, of course, remains my own. Finally, numerous friends, new and old, have provided me with places to stay and have joined me for meals and conversations on my research trips over the years. This has added enormously to the pleasures of writing. For this special brand of hospitality I would especially like to thank Tracy Bach and Brian Lombardo, Maria Murray Riemann and Neil Riemann, Susan Swider and Colin Davis, Carrie Struble Horsey and Revell Horsey, Et-tsu Chen and Gordon Yu, and Rose Beiler.

It is through family that I first learned, and have frequently relearned, the importance of history and the fascinating ways in which it is forgotten, remembered, and rewritten. In their rich lives, my parents have always been an inspiration, and my greatest debt is to them. Since my mother was an architect, you could say that I observed and even commented upon gendered aspects of the built environment at a young age. Upon meeting a new partner in my mother's firm about 1970, I reportedly whispered, "Hee hee, a man architect." My father, who worked for the Retail Trade Board of the Hartford (Conn.) Chamber of Commerce from the late 1940s to the mid-1950s, also took an interest in my research. I can only imagine how delighted my parents would be. My brother Neil Isenberg, Nicole Gartland and Natalie, Ruth Flaxman, Ed and Aileen Isenberg, Caroline Hirasawa, Laura Flaxman, Kenny Purser, Gary Flaxman, Rich Isenberg, Holly Sternberg, Lisa Isenberg, and Paolo Trapanese have for many years shared the longest laughs and the deepest sorrows, a history that holds us together despite geographical distance. Bert and Lynette Wailoo and my Lewis and Wailoo relatives have for twenty years extended strength and friendship and made me feel at home. My husband, Keith Wailoo, brought his superb skills as a historian to bear on virtually every dimension of this book, helping me achieve my goals for it. For this, and for an impossibly long list of other things, I am deeply grateful. Our children, little Elliot and Myla, always up for a walk to Main Street, keep me pointed toward the future, while they still ask for new stories about the past.

In September 1992, yet another community was about to lose its last
Main Street department store. The May Company announced that it
would close G. Fox & Co. in downtown Hartford, Connecticut, and
familiar scenes unfolded in the local newspapers. White-haired patrons of the luncheonette who had come for hot dogs or coffee over
the years and even decades were on the verge of tears. A local reporter
confirmed that, indeed, "many of the shoppers mourning the passing of the G. Fox store downtown were elderly." The store had been
such a downtown fixture that two eighty-year-old customers could
not remember a time when they did not shop there. Articles wistfully
recalled the city's retail "heydays" earlier in the century and method-
ically ticked off all the landmark stores that had closed since the
1950s.[1]

Hartford's history of slow commercial decline, along with decades
of competition from suburban malls, lent legitimacy to the May
Company's simple explanation that "economics dictated the decision
to close the store." The firm's spokesman pointed to a projected annual loss of $1.5 million. One G. Fox executive said the closing was
merely a response to "the message delivered by the consumer about
the future of a store downtown." Customers preferred to shop in the
malls, he noted. Retailing trends had claimed another victim.[2]

Hartford happens to be my hometown. But stories of the downtown's twentieth-century rise, fall, and possible resurrection have become ubiquitous in America. The explanatory frameworks employed
by journalists, retailers, and scholars to make sense of this history
have become nearly universal as well. Main Streets everywhere have
been portrayed as living organisms facing the end of eventful lives. A
1996 *Wall Street Journal* story on Newberry, South Carolina, read,
"Downtown wasn't dead, but it was on the gurney headed toward the
morgue." A year later, the *New York Times* compared a closing Woolworth to an "elderly uncle who hangs around the house and tells

well-worn stories to impatient children." At the same time, Main Streets were widely believed to stand helplessly in the path of inevitable, objective economic forces. Downtown experts Bernard Frieden and Lynne Sagalyn blended these metaphors in their 1989 book: "With downtown business districts crumbling, cities faced fiscal ruin. Forces beyond anyone's control were pushing them into an economic back alley where they could die quietly."[3] Either way — as organic being or product of market forces — the downtown's history is usually portrayed as a process whose trajectory has been out of the control of human hands.

In an effort to contextualize the "rise and fall" story of the downtown, and in certain ways move beyond it, this book identifies quite a large cast of human actors who have set the frameworks of urban economic development. Despite the obvious appeal of living-organism and free-market metaphors, Main Street has been neither a dying relative nor the victim of objective economic forces.[4] Not that these narratives should be brushed aside; they reveal a great deal about the cultural assumptions that have guided late-twentieth-century downtown investment trends. Those who relied upon natural life cycles or economic forces to explain the G. Fox decision, for example, would resign themselves to the store's closing and the city's decline. Most models of urban transformation are driven by the theme of decline. Such theories constrain our understanding of the urban past and similarly limit current and future policy choices in ways that contribute further to disinvestment.

Throughout the twentieth century, most downtown real estate decisions were propelled by interested individuals — concerned about the future — who envisioned the possibilities of urban commercial life and tried to create value where buildings and people came together. Put another way, varied downtown investors endeavored to make their own markets and to chart Main Street's future in order to protect and enhance their stakes. The hands of many participants — consumers and protestors as well as businesspeople, government leaders, design consultants, and real estate professionals — have been evident in this history, negotiating the nature of, and the standards for, urban commerce.

Rarely has inevitability, passivity, or death captured the realities of downtown development. Even facing the Great Depression's economic collapse, real estate investors did not suffer paralysis. Rather, Main Street experimented with demolition and storefront modernization, and professionals recast the appraisal field to solve the nation's crisis of confidence in the field's ability to foresee and judge values. These and other depression innovations signaled a redefinition of wise investment practices, particularly a reorientation toward recycling and rebuilding rather than freewheeling metropolitan growth. The violence of the 1960s riots and looting, perhaps most emblematic of urban "death," induced many people to abandon their stake in cities. Yet others saw the potential for new commercial forms, new consumers, and new investors to galvanize promising relationships among fragmented and discouraged people. Key investors, including James W. Rouse, believed that a reinvigorated urban commerce might heal the country's racial rifts, since commercial sites had played a central role in the inflammatory racial conflicts of the 1960s. One goal of this book is to reconceptualize the downtown's history to incorporate more of these creative efforts to reinvent urban commercial values, even while accounting for uncertainty and fears of decline.

Some of the attempts to transform downtown commerce, such as urban renewal and the Civil Rights movement, were greeted with controversy and resistance. Other strategies, like Reilly's Law of Retail Gravitation and the concept of the 100% district (key ideas guiding investment in the 1920s), were equally influential in another way — quietly making their way into executive board rooms and confidential investment newsletters. Those two concepts seemed at the time to be neutral scientific formulas, yet they expressed and supported particular cultural values: they promoted the belief that women's shopping activities underpinned peak downtown land values, and they boosted the contributions of chain stores to the Main Street economy at a time when the chains' status was openly questioned. Still other improvement agendas, such as the goal of a "dignified" Main Street envisioned during the Progressive era, were hammered out and refined over decades of innovation and conflict, as leadership in downtown beautification shifted from women's clubs to Main Street businesses and the expanding design professions, including city planning.

Even though newspapers continue to announce, even today, that "economics dictated the decision to close the store," such decisions have not occurred out of a dry commercial logic removed from the rest of society. Economic anxieties have long intertwined with core cultural ideals to make Main Streets resonant and symbolic locations, and downtown participants have manipulated and mobilized cultural values for their own purposes. In the 1910s city planners ridiculed the idea of a feminized commercial landscape ("it's not like we're going to tie pink ribbons on the lampposts"), in order to distance themselves from the female downtown housekeepers whose Main Street civic agenda the planners had in part adopted and commercialized. In contrast, between the 1920s and the 1960s, executives did everything in their power to make the downtown appealing to the white, middle-class shoppers, mostly housewives, whose actions (they firmly believed) seemed to determine the future of downtown real estate. Civil rights protestors understood Main Street's cultural and economic interdependence when they selected Woolworth, Kress, and the downtown generally for their sit-ins and boycotts in the 1950s and 1960s. Attention to such features in the history of Main Street necessarily alters our view of the interplay of culture, politics, and economics in investment and disinvestment choices.

Since the 1970s the mourning and nostalgia evoked by store closings have suggested something about the complex attitudes underlying the downtown's history. These sentiments themselves compel us to look beyond the cold declarations by market analysts who universally dismiss chain stores as "dinosaurs" facing inevitable extinction — outmoded commercial forms without any appeal. Occasionally, consumers in the news accounts claim not to understand all the funereal imagery and emotion. A college student in Ithaca, New York, responded sarcastically to the 1997 closing of the local Woolworth (and all remaining Woolworths, for that matter): "It's tough for mankind. Where are you going to get flip-flops and stuff?"[5] For him, Woolworth was simply another business. However, many Americans would have understood better the sentiment of the Woolworth employee who posted "Closed Forever" on the door of the empty Charleston, South Carolina, store and the passer-by who wrote in lipstick "We miss you Woolworths!" (fig. 1).

But what exactly did people miss? The nostalgia flowed both from strong personal memories and from a collective, community-wide sense of loss. In Hartford, one journalist wrote: "It's not just the lights going out in a struggling Main Street store. For longtime Connecticut residents, the closing of G. Fox & Co.'s Hartford store marks the passing of a hallowed tradition, a once-grand building that was the setting of some of their warmest remembrances." When Woolworth shuttered its Durham, North Carolina, location in 1994, a local reporter described the somber mood during the closeout sale. He found the shoppers to be "almost reverent" as they waited in line. "It is as if they realize they are at a funeral, which, essentially, they are. This Woolworth's, after nearly 90 years of serving as a community gathering spot, a civil-rights era landmark — and yes, a wistfully remembered five-and-dime — has reached the final checkout."[6]

One explanation for the mourning lies in the fact that the downtown has been not only the linchpin of urban real estate and conspicuous consumption

Figure 1. In July 1997, Woolworth announced that it would close its remaining four hundred or so variety stores. Market analysts declared good riddance to a "dead" retailing concept, but a torrent of nostalgic commentary poured forth from the public. Emptied of the crowds that had given them meaning and value a hundred years earlier, what did vacant downtown stores represent at the end of the twentieth century? (Photograph by the author, January 1, 1998.)

but also an idealized public place and thus a powerful symbol. Like so many aspects of American culture, the downtown meant business, but it was also invested with civic meaning. In the divided city (microcosm of a divided nation), the downtown has served as a potential place of interaction and negotiation of difference — a place of community gathering as well as all kinds of conflict. A dominant theme of twentieth-century urban life was the division of the city and the emergence of worlds inhabited by separate races, classes, genders, and ethnic groups, but the democratic ideal of the downtown has optimistically suggested otherwise.[7] Little wonder, then, that scholars and public officials repeatedly debate whether urban commercial spaces were truly public, democratic, and inclusive. The downtown as a twentieth-century cultural and economic artifact illuminates how a nonpolitical entity (in fact the downright crass business street) came to represent the heights of democratic hopes and the depths of democracy's failures.

For some, the sense of loss stems not from businesses closing but from the conviction that the democratic nature of commercial life declined over the twentieth century. Historian Jon Teaford's description of the early-twentieth-century city, for example, suggests that the downtown was once a true melting pot: "In the downtown area the diverse ethnic, economic, and social strains of urban life were bound together, working, spending, speculating, and investing. Along the downtown thoroughfares wealthy financiers passed by grubby beggars, rubbed shoulders with horny-handed porters and draymen, and jostled for space with clerks and stenographers. In the socially and culturally fragmented city, the central business district was the one bit of turf common to all."[8] This compelling romanticization of a "turf common to all" (in which physically bumping into one another roughly equaled democracy) has many adherents among influential urbanists. Michael Sorkin, in *Variations on a Theme Park,* paid tribute to a similar ideal. "This book," he wrote, "pleads for a return to a more authentic urbanity, a city based on physical proximity and free movement and a sense that the city is our best expression of a desire for collectivity. . . . The effort to reclaim the city is the struggle of democracy itself." Mike Davis too, in his popular book on Los Angeles, *City of Quartz,* yearned for a lost "demi-paradise" of "democratic space," and David Goldfield and Blaine Brownell described the downtown street and department store as "a metaphor of American democracy" in their historical survey of urban America.[9]

This study suggests that democratic inclusion *was* often an important theme in the formulations of downtown development, but so too was exclusion — a duality revealed in the competing efforts of downtown interests (including property owners, businesspeople, civic leaders, design professionals, and consumers) to control and manage downtown commercial life. Economic investment decisions have been firmly underpinned by evolving cultural preferences about who should be downtown and why. Improvement strategies of beautification, modernization, or renewal have gone hand in hand with policies designed to attract certain types of people downtown while ignoring or explicitly rejecting others. Race played an important role in Main Street plans, as did gender, class, and age. Segregationists in the early twentieth century believed that racial separation and boundaries in urban commerce were one way to protect property investment. By the late 1950s, the desperate-sounding belief that suburban women shoppers could save downtown property values stood in stark contrast to the neglect of the more proximate audience of African American consumers. Black shoppers had become generous downtown spenders, but their presence was still construed narrowly by Main Street businesses. Blacks were expected to keep a low profile in bargain basements, in the "low-end" fringes of the business district, and in segregated commercial facilities. Among other things, the Civil Rights movement rejected this vision of urban commerce, using lunch counter sit-ins and boycotts to propose instead that Main Street could be revived (morally and economically) through integration. When market analysts in the 1980s and 1990s concluded that the downtown five-and-dimes were no longer viable, that judgment also devalued the largely elderly, nonwhite, and low-income variety store customers, along with their often frugal ways of living and spending. Throughout the twentieth century, the tensions between democratic rhetoric and exclusionary practices continually redefined and transformed urban commercial life.

Most of the participants who appear in this book, in promoting their own downtown values, helped create this decidedly ambiguous space — democratic yet exclusionary, public yet also private. As the municipal housekeepers of the 1890s plunged into scrubbing Main Street and setting new standards of commercial aesthetics, they encountered many who believed the women did not belong there. But the latter successfully manipulated widely held beliefs about public and private realms in order to cross the gendered boundaries separating women's housekeeping work from men's business. In doing so, they redefined civic involvement and paved the way for a new generation of Main Street businesses to embrace urban improvement without the taint of self-interest.

Any history of urban commercial life must of necessity take stock of the meanings invested in retail destinations. More than simply the setting for a concentration of stores, Main Street by the early twentieth century symbolized and unified the new commercial forms emerging at that time. Although not every town had a skyscraper or an opera house, they all had a Main Street. In the late nineteenth century, American cities were fundamentally reshaped by the growing middle class, corporations, and mass production and consumption.[10] Driven by urban masses and cultivated by corporate brokers, a new commercial culture flourished in department stores, chain stores, hotels, movie palaces, amusement parks, and skyscrapers. During the opening decades of the twentieth century, such places came to define the landscape of the modern commercial city. Downtowns in America held out many possibilities, bringing people together and separating them in new ways. Since then, a vigorous debate has ensued: was this the beginning of a democratic heyday, uniting a divided society in the crush of urban crowds? Or was this the suffocating triumph of corporate and bourgeois consumer values? [11] Either way, this period placed a newly valued cosmopolitan commercial experience at the core of modern American life.

By contrast with the early decades of the twentieth century, the post–World War II decades brought a radical divergence between the fate of America's cities and the nation's robust commercial life.[12] While the nation's capitalist consumer ethos accelerated and spread on a global scale, cities stumbled. Dramatic and sometimes violent postwar developments — rapid suburbanization, racial integration, urban renewal, riots, and the rise of a new feminism — rattled city centers, and their implications for urban commercial life remained unclear. Was urban renewal good or bad for cities? If Americans accepted integration, could this revolution in race relations provide the boost needed by downtown business? When middle-class women reached beyond their roles as housewives and entered the workforce in growing numbers, who would do the family shopping, where would they do it, and what would this mean for urban commerce? Would the riots of the 1960s ultimately galvanize black capitalism? Would corporations or government be compelled to pump investment into ailing cities to address legitimate grievances and the frightening destruction of urban commerce? These questions, arising in the midst of the upheavals of the 1960s, challenged investors and shoppers to debate and envision the downtown's reinvention and the rise of new commercial values. In the postwar era of apparent decline (as commercial vitality seemed to depart from urban life), downtown stores continued to serve as sites for these renegotiations, just as they did during earlier decades of presumed centrality and growth.

The history of the downtown in the twentieth century, then, can be seen as one of gradual decline — and certainly that concept has dominated social commentary and scholarship for the past fifty years.[13] However, as an interpretive framework, decline obscures as much as it reveals. The evidence suggests that Main Street, as an economic and cultural artifact, has been constantly remade — by enterprising planners, investors, activists, and consumers. And decline itself has multiple meanings, depending on one's perspective. The history of downtown, instead of being determined by inevitable organic or economic laws, has been defined by uncertainties, sudden reversals, absurdities, and efforts throughout to create and sustain a market of profitable values. The "hulking" vacant stores of the 1990s symbolized not death and decline but another stage in the ongoing struggle to define urban commercial values amid proclamations of decline.

This is not a study of Hartford, Connecticut; St. Louis, Missouri; or Leesburg, Virginia, but of downtowns throughout America, and this national scope derives from the nature of Main Street investment. Downtown interest groups in cities of all sizes have constantly negotiated between the politics and resources of their local circumstances and the ever-changing array of improvement strategies popularized nationally — from the late-nineteenth-century municipal housekeeping campaigns to the late-twentieth-century historic preservation movement. Real estate consultants, professional associations, chain organizations, and federal programs have played especially important roles in the circulation of information, tools, ideas, advice, and values, thereby helping connect the story of each downtown to national trends. The interaction between national forces and local realities has been multifaceted. City planners and zoning specialists assisted with development guidelines for small and large cities across the country; retailers, appraisers, real estate agents, and developers shared beliefs about where stores should be located and about techniques for tracking shopper behavior, through journals and conferences; and academics in the fields of marketing and retailing geography published widely and often took in-house positions with companies in order to influence who purchased what on Main Street. In the 1960s other national influences emerged. Grassroots consumer-led protests such as the Civil Rights movement (and even the riots and looting) brought to light controversies over racially based exploitation in urban commerce and reconfigured commercial life in city after city, largely as a result of the combined impact of national media coverage and local economic disruptions. It is through this changing constellation of national actors that America's downtowns have been transformed.[14]

Over the course of the twentieth century, the scale of investment decision making became more national and centralized — encouraged by the proliferation of federal programs such as urban renewal; the concentration of downtown properties in the hands of insurance companies, banks, holding companies, and chains; and the maturation of a national real estate market. But what is really striking is the degree to which *early*-twentieth-century commercial investment converged on national models as well — a convergence hinted at by the millions of standardized Main Street postcards produced for cities across America in those decades. With this in mind, one must rethink the cliché that downtowns became more alike in the late twentieth century — a time of seemingly formulaic solutions, when even nostalgic strategies like historic preservation and the construction of historically themed urban festival marketplaces appeared to rival the mind-numbing similarities of suburban shopping malls.[15] Whether one considers the range of participants in downtown life or the variety of strategies, models, and ideas these investors can now draw upon, Main Streets are in many ways more, not less, heterogeneous than they were one hundred years ago.

In any given period of the twentieth century, there was an array of downtown improvement ideas that most places would have been likely to consider as they looked to the future (even if they ultimately rejected those plans), and this book follows those popular strategies. Beginning in the 1890s, the municipal housekeeping movement swept through the tiniest villages as well as the largest cities. Relatively few cities actually commissioned city plans by the 1910s, but many more brought in well-traveled planners like John Nolen and Charles Mulford Robinson as public speakers. Planners and other civic improvement consultants used these innumerable venues to promote the goals of dignifying and unifying Main Street. At least one village hired a city planner during these years in order to avoid the current improvement trends and maintain its "old-fashioned and quaint appearance." In the 1920s chain store executives established new models of national expertise. Headquartered in cities like New York, they prided themselves on being able to pick good Main Street properties anywhere in the country without leaving their offices, basing their authority upon the growing availability of scientific investment formulas and national real estate atlases. The Great Depression spawned a small but influential crop of confidential national newsletters that offered advice to anxious real estate investors. The drastic clearance policies of urban renewal, carried out on a large scale in big cities like St. Louis and Pittsburgh during the 1950s and 1960s, had spread by the early 1970s to increasingly smaller towns. Also by the 1970s, racial violence had modified the practices of urban commerce in all parts of the nation. And even more recently, historic preservation, although it was frequently discarded as an option in the 1960s and 1970s, has spread to affect "both the main drag of small towns and the older streets of large cities, attesting to a commonality of aim and effort," as an excited Ada Louise Huxtable observed.[16]

The sharing of ideas, investment formulas, conceptual frameworks, and personnel presumed that American Main Streets should and actually did resemble one another. A 1939 feature in *Architectural Forum* entitled "Main Street, U.S.A." typified that viewpoint, as the editors proclaimed: "Whether Fifth Avenue New York or High Avenue Oskaloosa, every U.S. Main Street has one common denominator . . . People." The editors elaborated upon this philosophy, insisting that "the shopping centers of most towns — large and small — have a good many common features." "They are more alike than different, as critics of the American Scene are fond of pointing out. 'Breakfast Number Three' is likely to consist of the same orange-juice, toast, and coffee in New York, N. Y. and New Albany, Ind., and the drug store in which it is served is sure to be as nearly like its big-city prototype as the proprietor can make it. Main Street in a big town is simply a small-town Main Street with added attractions." The editors in this instance chose to investigate the downtown of Bridgeport, Connecticut, as the prototypical "Main Street, U.S.A." because they claimed "that the business-man, realtor, builder, and architect should have no difficulty in comparing its features with those in his own home town." [17] This comparability was the essence of Main Street's apparent universality, and the striving for comparability was an important force shaping local investment decisions. [18]

In recovering the downtown's history, this book focuses not only on the important points of transformation — the emergence of an inspiring new Main Street ideal during the Progressive era, the challenges posed by 1920s metropolitan growth, the collapse of real estate values during the depression, the melodrama of urban renewal, civil rights demonstrations, riots, and the tantalizing breakthrough potential of nostalgic developments like festival marketplaces or Main Street preservation by the 1980s. It also explores the tools, ideas, and information investors relied upon in making fateful decisions about how the downtown should appear and be experienced, who should be there, and who should not. This approach has entailed poring over the files saved by downtown consultants to follow the articles they read and wrote, studying the confidential real estate reports that circulated in company offices, and looking through appraisers' camera lenses or out planners' office windows in order to understand how they saw the downtown. [19] The wide range of materials that have informed investment choices also confirm the intermingled economic and cultural meanings of Main Street's transformations. These sources include real estate appraisals, marketing studies, store location analyses, conference transcripts, professional journals and association records, confidential investment newsletters, city plans, Main Street postcards, trade newspapers (from *Women's Wear Daily* to *Traffic Quarterly*), chain store real estate records, federal program guidelines, and the office files of developers and consulting firms. I have sought out the broad cultural assumptions underpinning real estate decisions (and documents like appraisals of Woolworth stores), but I have also uncovered how economic development plans were enacted in cultural artifacts like Main Street postcards. Real estate history remains a remarkably understudied field, perhaps because of the perception that it involves only economic formulas and building permits. Yet its seemingly dry, narrow sources yield rich and vivid perspectives on a topic of great popular interest and broad cultural relevance.[20]

Although downtown real estate is economically valuable and symbolically potent, it is also composed of the mundane — artistic lampposts, garbage cans, storefronts, parking lots, lunch counters, plywood, broken glass, and red brick. For those involved in downtown investment, whether municipal housekeepers, civil rights protestors, real estate appraisers, shoppers, or preservationists, conflict over these "things" stirred intense disagreement, since (in their eyes) these things seemed to exemplify the very future and character of urban commerce. Throughout the twentieth century, decisions about Main Street's mundane material conditions revealed broader cultural and economic values — values that over time have said a great deal about people and the circumstances of their participation in urban commercial life. Together, these values have shaped the contours, meaning, and experience of many journeys downtown.

1

CITY BEAUTIFUL OR BEAUTIFUL MESS?
THE GENDERED ORIGINS OF A CIVIC IDEAL

In 1962 Walker Evans poignantly captured the memory of a vanished downtown "heyday": "'Downtown' was a beautiful mess," he wrote in an essay for *Fortune* magazine. "This was the time when commercial America was solidifying into what it is today. There are many central streets . . . that are lined with fifty-year-old buildings, in neighborhoods that still exude the atmosphere of 1911." Evans, one of the most influential photographers of the American scene, celebrated the "extraordinarily unbeautiful buildings," the "tangle of telephone poles and wires," and the "horse smells." He relished the stimulating disorder, the colorful brick buildings, and the congestion of the pre–World War I years. Yet he knew that these were the very qualities that were out of favor in the early 1960s, when urban renewal devalued and demolished Evans's "beautiful mess" of commerce to realize a new vision of commercial order. Amid the upheavals of "renewal," Evans hoped to retrieve for public consideration the evolving questions of what defined a "beautiful" downtown, what the downtown should look like, who should be there, and what activities were appropriate.[1]

Evans denied that he was driven by nostalgia — "that blurred vision which destroys the actuality of the past."[2] But was he right about the "actuality" of Main Street in 1911? Was it a "beautiful mess"? What did it look like at the turn of the century? What commercial visions of beauty, what cultural values and preferences, shaped how various interest groups saw, invested in, and experienced the downtown? Who had the authority to determine the appearance of Main Street? To answer these questions is to begin to understand how the commercial corridor known as Main Street came to be elevated during the Progressive era to the exalted status of a special American public space, uniting business interests and the public good.[3]

On several counts Walker Evans was exactly right. Overwhelmingly, the Main Street improvement agenda from the 1890s through the 1910s revolved around the mundane objects he described — wires, poles, paving, and waste. The modest yet transformative downtown investment strategies of this era remained remarkably influential right down to the drastic solutions of 1950s–60s urban renewal, and they continue to serve as a reference point in the early twenty-first century. Despite the constancy and prosaic nature of Progressive era goals, there was tension and controversy over how to build consensus behind them, who would monitor downtown standards, and whose interests would be served as Main Street was "improved." Against this backdrop, simple street objects such as lampposts assumed emotionally laden meanings for contemporaries as they negotiated jurisdiction over commercial aesthetics and the legitimacy of new professions — particularly city planning — devoted to civic design.

Evans was also correct to single out beauty as a key concept for turn-of-the-century downtown life, although celebrating the "beautiful mess" would have placed him in a distinct minority in 1900. The currents of change were sweeping in another direction at that time, toward the orderly visions of the City Beautiful movement. Whereas Evans relished the "tangle" of utility wires and poles, urban designers of 1910 called them eyesores and campaigned heatedly to replace them with underground conduits. City Beautiful played an important role in mediating the commercial aesthetics of the era — its directives at first admired as inspiring dignity and monumentality and later ridiculed as superficial and extravagant. The grandiose visions of the movement, exemplified by its sweeping watercolor renderings of civic center designs, have often distracted attention from the more ubiquitous projects of downtown transformation such as burying wires and removing sidewalk obstacles — crucial aspects of city "beautification" (see fig. 1.1).[4]

We shall also see in this chapter that the *Beautiful* in City Beautiful proved to be a gender-contested term. In particular, when we shift the focus from monumental plans to local beautification battles, we learn how gendered debates over standards of downtown beauty (and the influence of women in setting those standards) marked the birth of the modern city planning profession. By 1910 voluntary civic groups, mainly women's organizations, had carved themselves a housekeeping domain in downtown aesthetics. Women's clubs cleaned up the business streets and established new practices of downtown management, using the commercial streetscape to teach moral lessons about responsibility for public property. Their activism in urban design, including their sponsorship of early city plans, City Beautiful lectures, and inspirational civic rallies, introduced professional planners such as John Nolen

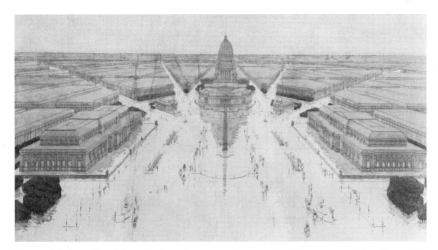

Figure 1.1 Jules Guerin's renderings have come to symbolize the monumental and unrealistic goals of the City Beautiful movement. This Guerin view of "The Proposed Civic Center Plaza and Buildings," commissioned by the Commercial Club of Chicago, shows all of the buildings in downtown Chicago at the same height. Such renderings implied a complete reconstruction of the city. This monumental view contrasted with the more modest and practical improvements highlighted in ordinary Main Street postcards of the same period — a transformation and beautification also promoted by downtown housekeepers and city planners. (Daniel H. Burnham and Edward H. Bennett, *Plan of Chicago* [Chicago: Commercial Club of Chicago, 1909], plate 132. Reproduced courtesy of the Art Institute of Chicago, gift of Patrick Shaw, 1991.1381.)

and Charles Mulford Robinson to skeptical local communities — and, most critically, legitimated these experts during the insecure early years of the planning profession.[5]

At the same time, women's downtown initiatives paved the way for men's commercial organizations to take up the cause of Main Street beautification too — by carefully defining such work as civic and public, rather than political. At the turn of the century, businessmen, like women in general, were expected to stay aloof from politics. When they embraced city beautification, business groups were able to follow the lead of downtown housekeepers and exploit the fluid, mixed public and private character of commercial space. The civic and public realm of downtown improvement, as delineated by the housekeepers, emerged at the turn of the century as an alternative base of authority contrasted with the political terrain that was off-limits to them. Blurring the lines between public and private, civic and commercial, women activists exercised impressive influence in transforming business districts across

America; it was not until the 1920s that women's role as consumers would come to the forefront in shaping downtown development. In their rhetoric, men and women of the late nineteenth century drew sharp distinctions between commerce and culture, especially fearing the supposedly corrupting force of commerce. Yet their actions demonstrated that commercial and cultural values overlapped.

In the 1910s, the mostly male planners and business groups and their allies adopted the women's clubs' strategies for transforming downtown's "beautiful mess" but distanced themselves from these municipal housekeeping origins.[6] Women quietly resigned their leadership roles in upgrading commercial aesthetics, pleased that they had succeeded in convincing others to take up their cause. Nonetheless, public squabbles over whether planners were trying to feminize the business district indicated both the potency of the female vision and the fact that some resented its implementation. Defensive and often pained debates over the values of downtown beauty in these years marked the transition from women's activism in commercial design to the professional leadership of city planners and business and city executives. And as these professionals assumed responsibility, we shall see how they redefined Main Street improvement to promote their own dreams of economic values. Truly, then, as Walker Evans noted, the question of beauty was a central issue defining Main Street at the turn of the century. Yet the feminizing influence of downtown beautification — which sought not only to clean up and transform Main Street but also to instill civic responsibility for the commercial environment — suggests that downtown's beauty was more complicated and contentious than Evans realized.

Women: "Natural Leaders" for the City Beautiful

By the time Mary Beard published *Woman's Work in Municipalities* in 1915, women had gained national recognition for their initiatives in beautifying the Main Streets of villages and cities across America. Amid the explosion of civic work at the turn of the century, women established the field of *municipal housekeeping* — a domain in which they attacked and struggled to reform the shabby conditions of America's business streets.[7] "There is no doubt," Beard wrote, "that women are the natural leaders for the realization of the city beautiful." In recognition of this fact, the editors of *American City* magazine assembled an entire Women's Number for the June 1912 issue, even though less than 10 percent of their subscribers were female. "The Old Order Changeth," proclaimed the editors, as they gave their stamp of approval to women's civic activities and chastised skeptics: "How needless was the widespread fear that woman's attempt to spell the task would work havoc to the social structure!" In the 1910s women enjoyed enthusiastic but also begrudging recognition for their civic initiatives.[8]

Nevertheless, a certain resentment shadowed these housekeeping women in their efforts to have the downtown sidewalks scrubbed. One Philadelphia "city father" was heard loudly damning the women's City Club, while kicking "all around the block" a rubbish can the club had installed downtown to encourage cleanliness. He was picked up by the police. Such ridicule became especially pointed when women's involvement crossed from voluntary club activity into paid employment. In Cleveland, Mildred Chadsey was appointed chief of sanitary police, supervising the city's garbage enforcement. A cartoonist depicted her "in a policeman's uniform with a lace flounce around the policeman's badge and a bow of ribbon on the billy as the only remnant of femininity." Although Chadsey was at first stung by the caricature, she felt reassured by a policeman's comment that his own wife, a "nifty housekeeper," would also qualify for the job. She decided to embrace the caricature, concluding that "if one of these men had at so early a stage grasped the idea that there was not such a chasm between housekeeping and municipal housekeeping, why need I fear that every citizen of Cleveland would not soon come to see the same thing?" Others did not respond as well to derision. One club woman from Reading, Pennsylvania, complained despondently to a city planner about her unrecognized efforts: "We earn the money by rummage sales and concerts, beg lumber, hardware etc. from merchants and money from individuals. We have been laughed at as 'queer old maids.'"[9]

As for the Philadelphia councilman who damned the local women's club, Mary Beard would have fully understood why he took out his frustrations on a mere garbage can. The enthusiasm for city planning and civic activism in this era reveled in the importance of such details — in fact, Beard noted that it had all started with a lamppost. The ambitious social ideals of city planning, she believed, could be traced to such modest origins — garbage cans, paved streets, and cleared sidewalks. Since well-lighted streets helped fight crime, "out of interest in the lamppost comes an interest in the causes of crime; proper housing, wholesome amusement, and employment may thus be intimately connected with an artistic street lamp."[10] Though critics might dismiss ornamental lampposts as frivolous, Beard and many others contended that such objects possessed deeper moral implications. Garbage cans and lampposts had opened the floodgates of women's municipal activism (see fig. 1.2).

Figure 1.2 Municipal housekeepers focused on the improvement of ordinary downtown street objects such as lampposts and trash cans in order to instruct the public about civic responsibility and respect for the public property of the business district. Their campaigns involved the revision of business practices, municipal ordinances, city public works agendas, and most important, people's ideas about what constituted an appealing downtown. (The artistic street lamps were in Denver, Colorado; photo courtesy of the Frances Loeb Library, Graduate School of Design, Harvard University; Charles Mulford Robinson Collection. The trash can photo appeared over the caption "A Minneapolis Street Trash Can," in *American City,* September 1913, 228.)

Espousing such views in the decades around the turn of the century, female urban designers threw themselves into improvement work as individuals and club women, as volunteers and paid professionals, and as newsworthy officials and anonymous dust-sweepers. An individual like Miss Mira Lloyd Dock of Harrisburg, Pennsylvania, was praised as "the original woman who kept prodding," who single-handedly championed civic improvement during "seemingly fruitless years."[11] But it was the organized club women who achieved particular prominence, because of their concentrated leverage and promotional skills.[12] The formation of a national association — the General Federation of Women's Clubs — in 1890 accelerated women's interest in downtown beautification. Thereafter, local clubs, as well as the national and state federations, reported on their progression from self-improvement and the study of literature to civic involvement. These club women were primarily white, native-born, and middle-class; and they were often related by marriage or birth to the businessmen and government men of their communities.[13] African American women also plunged into club organizing at the turn of the century. But their agendas infrequently addressed commercial beautification, for they marshaled their energies to fight neighborhood battles against poverty and racial discrimination.[14]

In small town and big city, the beautification movement swept through women's clubs. Originating in the 1850s in Stockbridge, Massachusetts, village improvement societies demonstrated the potential of community beautification to the women who dominated their ranks and to citizens generally.[15] Small towns that lacked businessmen's clubs often had well-organized women's clubs lobbying for local upgrades. By 1910 most large cities had a full spectrum of all types of clubs. Civic Improvement Leagues, the majority of which were composed of women, emerged during this period as a club form dedicated exclusively to urban improvement.[16] These variations in villages, towns, and cities advocated for very similar types of commercial beautification.[17]

As the movement gained force, women did not (and could not) exclude men, who were, after all, both the "city fathers" and business proprietors on Main Street. One hallmark of the downtown housekeepers was their focus on cooperative, reciprocal relationships. The women of Yankton, South Dakota, believed that their own diplomacy helped to overcome the initial disfavor of city officials, who viewed the very existence of their club "as a standing criticism of their administration." The clubs advertised their collaborative efforts by highlighting the invitations they received from mayors, businessmen's leagues, and city councils to join forces. The women's civic improvement society of Knoxville, Tennessee, declared on the front page of its bylaws that it functioned "in co-operation with the municipal government."[18] Some groups, such as the Wichita, Kansas, Improvement Association, began as clubs restricted to women but agreed to add men because "obviously the concerns of any town-development organization are the concerns of everybody in that town."[19] Flattery and manipulation helped women negotiate the boundaries of cooperation. One Mississippi club woman advised her sisters to avoid appearing in person before a city board unless invited. In lobbying for downtown improvement ordinances, she noted, "it is better to elect an advisory and cooperative board of men, who . . . will be so flattered at the term 'advisory' that it will warmly advocate your plans and fight an opposing mayor and board on their own ground."[20] Remaining in the background, to this author, was a key to the housekeepers' success.

In the minds of these women, cooperation was not merely a euphemism for deference. In Macon, Missouri, Edgar White recounted how a women's improvement league strategically inserted itself into the management of Macon's physical (and moral) landscape in 1903. "Hitherto," he wrote, "the men had wrought things out in their way, and had built streets, sidewalks, sewers, viaducts across the railroad, modern store buildings, and installed an electric 'white way' to take the place of the old street lamps. The women said they had done well, and immediately proceeded to show how to do still better." Once they had raised funds, "the women of the League began doing things the men had never even thought of."[21]

Not all municipal housekeepers were so tactful in their dealings with the male power structures. Mary Beard proclaimed bluntly that in the world of civic clubs, men were loafers and women were doers, for "thousands of men may loaf around clubs without ever showing the slightest concern about the great battle for decent living conditions that is now going on in our cities; but it is a rare women's club that long remains indifferent to such momentous matters." As another reporter put it, men were not lazy; they simply did not see the problem. Women applied themselves to civic challenges "that men have been quite blind to in their zeal for political prestige or for what they considered the 'big' things." And once housekeeping campaigns had gained steam, men were accused of indifference if they did not offer support. Some reformers were not shy about drawing attention to men's civic neglect. At times men seemed to block the path of reform: "Frequently," one consultant noted, "the chief obstacles in the way of civic progress have been those very groups which can best promote it; the clergy, the newspaper men and the business men."[22]

Once women had staked out responsibility in the realm of commercial aesthetics, few improvement tasks were beyond their reach. In matters related to downtown improvement, women gained a broad authority to intervene, and in each local environment they negotiated the specifics of their involvement. They avoided a firmly gendered division of labor.[23] In one city, street cleaning might be accomplished by municipal employees, while in another the merchants' club might hire the women's club to undertake the work. Either men or women could lead a campaign to pave sidewalks or raise money to conduct a window box contest. The overlapping of duties was debated in *American City:* "Are not men, then, equal to handling these problems? Is it not their work rather than women's? There is no logical reason why it should be their work rather than women's; there is every reason why it should be the work of *both.*" To be sure, most assumed that men and women had different perspectives, talents, and motivations: "CIVIC," the *American City* editors suggested, "could be spelled from either end."[24] Women and men, despite their distinct points of view, each had an investment in the City Beautiful as a public and private place.

At the turn of the century, through these arguments and in these venues, women seized moral authority over downtown aesthetics — an authority that they and their allies argued was their natural domain. After all, they observed, "beauty" fell under female jurisdiction. Beard insisted that "women have always set the moral and esthetic standard in the community in which they lived, and when they once get into this new field of making our cities more beautiful — a field which is really closest to their natural bent, they ought to accomplish wonders." Men, she suggested, "too often cannot see the moral issues at stake" in the physical environment, partly because (as another female reformer observed) they tended to reduce everything to economic values.[25] The 1910s, then, framed a cooperative tension between women as "natural" leaders and men as economic leaders. The female housekeepers, as urban designers, believed their unique talents allowed them to see and modify the moral properties inherent in the physical landscape. In their approach to downtown improvements, they raised issues of community responsibility and democratic citizenship. Their work was designed not only to upgrade the appearance of Main Street and make it safer and more prosperous, but also to set higher standards of citizen participation.

A Cartoon Which Helped a Clean-up Campaign

Figure 1.3 The cleanup campaign often marked the entry of women's clubs into urban beautification. Women tackled the accumulated debris of the business district, sometimes scrubbing the downtown sidewalks themselves. They also tried to get other citizens involved. This 1913 cartoon helped citizens envision some of the tasks encompassed in "Mothering a Municipality." (*American City,* June 1913, 599.)

"Mothering a Municipality"

What did "Mothering a Municipality" involve?[26] In one 1913 newspaper cartoon used to spur on a successful cleanup week, Chicago was depicted as the "mother" of four dirty sons — named "streets," "alleys," "back yards," and "vacant lots" — all rounded up in the wash basin for a good annual scrubbing (fig. 1.3). The cleanup day or week became a formulaic way for energetic women's clubs to get their start in civic improvement. In these campaigns, the business districts merited special consideration, for they had accumulated an astonishing mass of garbage, ash, dust, junk, and grime. In Tampa, the women's civic association "scoured and scrubbed the sidewalks and bricks" and gave blue ribbon awards for the most spotless premises in the business district. On occasion women appealed in vain for assistance from their city council or watched city officials fail in their own cleanup day, before stepping in, sometimes with their children in tow, to do the job themselves. One civic club "'made the dirt fly' in a phenomenal, almost spectacular, movement for municipal and civic betterment."[27]

Presenting themselves as whirlwinds of reform, women initiated or endorsed countless projects to beautify and regulate commercial districts, from repairing street paving to sponsoring comprehensive city plans. They pushed for the removal of street poles and wires wherever possible and lobbied to install ornamental streetlights. On hiding "unsightly housekeeping things" such as poles and pipes, one male author noted that "a woman would know how to plan that, just as a woman first thought of broom closets and fold-in ironing boards." Women promoted the cleaning and landscaping of trash-filled alleys and vacant lots to make them functional instead of sites for accumulating garbage. Particularly impressive was how one Ohio club set an example by transforming the rear yard of a dry-goods store from a junk-filled eyesore into an appealing garden (fig. 1.4).[28]

The clubs made unpaved or poorly groomed business streets another top priority, demanding proper paving or oil treatments to settle the dust. When local men refused to oil the streets, the women's club of Kinmundy, Illinois, asked their Chicago sisters for help. The Chicago club's president researched the proper formula and reported that "the women expect to get out with the brushes and cans and do the work." On the East Coast, the Women's Town Improvement Association of Westport, Connecticut (and one in Massachusetts), laid and repaired sidewalks. And in Arkansas, the Woman's Book Club of Osceola filled the mudholes in their streets themselves, departing significantly from literary pursuits.[29]

Street paving and cleaning out business yards affected commerce indirectly, but women also regulated the explicitly commercial aspects of Main Street life. They encouraged restrictions on billboards and business signs, since advertising not only scarred the landscape but also broadcast text and images that projected "flabby morals" and offended the city's civic guardians. To reform business practices that threatened public health, the clubs inspected the display of foods for sale on Main Street — ever on the alert for sacks of perishables left on the sidewalk or unscreened edibles in open sidewalk cases. Women also plunged into policing the sites of commercial recreation in the downtown — "those places of amusement where the young gather — dance halls, skating rinks, picture shows, penny arcades, amusement parks, etc." Such places came "naturally under the domain of the woman officer." Thus in many areas of downtown commercial life, women (paid and unpaid) cast themselves as inspectors and moral guardians. There was always the potential for conflict with businesses fearing that the women's actions bordered on boycott and censorship, so most downtown housekeepers endeavored to be "kind, tactful, firm and resourceful."[30]

Although downtown cleanup was in many ways becoming identified as

Figure 1.4 The women of an Ohio civic club were proud of their role in converting the back lot of this dry-goods store from an eyesore (*top*) into a landscaped, attractive site (*bottom*). Downtown housekeepers worked directly with business owners to persuade them to clear out rear lots and alleys, change their signs, and contain their sidewalk clutter in sanitary displays. (*American City,* December 1913, 542.)

women's work, since businessmen and city officials could hardly avoid encountering beautification initiatives, they took note of the housekeepers' goals
and accomplishments, even when they bristled at the interference. And
emerging urban design professionals, such as city planners, had their own reasons for following the women's campaigns closely.

Downtown Housekeepers and the Legitimation of City Planning

In the 1890s and the first years of the new century, public lectures and civic
revivals were favored ways for housekeepers to awaken among citizens "a
feeling of civic responsibility" for improving business districts.[31] Sponsoring
these inspirational lectures by visiting civic planning experts, and leading
their own cleanups, club women began a grassroots process that helped, over
time, to legitimate the early city planners who lacked solid professional standing. From 1900 to 1920, most Americans were unfamiliar with the emerging
field of city planning; they were as skeptical of the role of outside consultants
as they were familiar with the civic work of women's clubs. The women's moral
commitment to beautification resonated deeply with the planners' professional commitment to urban aesthetics, and these clubs were often the first to
insist on the need for national experts. Occasionally, especially in the earliest
years, they hired planners themselves.[32] Far more often, they brought in
steady streams of speakers on municipal improvement and city planning to
address public gatherings, hoping to jolt residents into seeing their communities in new ways. Women in turn often dominated the audiences.[33] They also
raised money, formed committees, and pushed their city administrators and
commercial clubs to hire consultants.

Elaborate week-long civic revivals ignited community awareness of the
moral stakes in downtown beautification.[34] Successful revivals usually built
upon the joint sponsorship of women's clubs, commercial clubs, and city government offices. Some civic revivalists hoped for a follow-up consulting job,
but more gave inspirational, educational lectures.[35] Charles Zueblin, trained
as a minister and a sociologist, was an exceptionally popular inspirational
speaker. His substantial credentials included founding Northwestern University Settlement in 1892, joining the new University of Chicago Sociology Department in 1894, and being elected president of the American League for
Civic Improvement in 1901. Between 1908 and 1910, Zueblin listed forty-five
engagements for civic lectures and revivals as a partial count of his speaking
activities, with most bookings involving multiple lectures. His ministerial
training enhanced his moral authority over civic life, yet he combined this

with fact-filled, practical talks appreciated by a range of citizens. Outside of his admiring circles, however, he had to confront skepticism, as revealed in an editorial from Albany, New York: "Mr. Zueblin does not speak like an inhabitant of Mars or an impractical celestial idiot."[36]

Fort Wayne, Indiana, hosted one such revival in early June 1909, which featured powerful lectures by Zueblin and solidified public support for city planning. Each day Zueblin spoke at 2:30 and 8:00 P.M. at the Majestic Theater downtown, with the evening talk preceded by a musical program. Thousands attended his lectures, and hundreds were turned away. His topics included "The Training of the Citizen" and "Harrisburg, a Typical Small City." As a result of the ferment, "the mayor declared himself heartily in accord with the revival and announced himself a thorough convert to the creed of cvic [sic] beauty."[37] The strategic use of slides was critical to the success of these revivals. Zueblin concluded "The Making of the City" with a slide of the street leading up to the theater. Viewers could plainly see that large, unsightly holes in the pavement were transformed by a downpour into mirrorlike pools that reflected plainly the banners advertising the revival. "Need of improvement could hardly have been more forcefully impressed," noted one reporter, "and the audience demonstrated that it saw the point by a storm of laughter and merriment." Through the catalyst of inspirational lectures and revivals, politicians and public alike were "converted" to the beautification movement — even the mundane challenge of street paving. On such fertile ground, consultant Charles Mulford Robinson clinched a contract that week to provide Fort Wayne with a city plan.[38]

Even as women's clubs and other groups opened the doors of their cities to the planners, the planners' tenuous professional identity as outside experts could become a heated topic of local debate. John Nolen's 1923 appearance in Lynn, Massachusetts, sparked the newspaper headline "Councillors Criticize Planning Board for Paying 'Expert' to Lecture." One councillor ridiculed the slide lecture technique so effective in the Fort Wayne revival: "I heard the lecture and I wouldn't give three cents to hear another like it.... When he started that illustrated lecture and the council chamber was darkened, one third of the audience took a nap." Another city father "expressed the opinion that the board 'should perform its own work without calling in professional men.'" Even a city with a planning board — thus having established sympathy for planning — could not agree upon the necessity of the professional, "expert" consultant.[39]

By the 1910s, some big-city officials had become familiar with the planning consultants and their writings, but the majority of local leaders had not met and were not even aware of the planners.[40] When Bridgeport, Connecticut, city leaders began a "lively" debate on John Nolen's 1915 plan, for example, the arguing participants suddenly agreed that they actually knew little about Nolen. "This whole dispute seems to be based on Nolen's report," one person observed. "We ought to have some information as to who Nolen is. I do not intend to speak disparagingly of him for I don't know anything in his favor or against him." John Nolen, by the time of his death in 1937, became the most influential city planner of his era, known around the country in his own right. But in the 1910s, it was often up to the women's club, the local civic league, or one small clique of businesspeople or city officials to introduce him. The plans commissioned by these groups' initiatives set the agenda for public discussion, while others did not necessarily understand either the nature of city planning or these outside "experts" who claimed to know so much about their city. Even in 1924, the city manager of Columbus, Georgia, would explain to a disappointed Nolen that his contract had not been approved because there was no "popular demand for city planning," and "comparatively few of us saw the necessity of it." The reaction against Nolen's contract was "due wholly to a lack of understanding of the people of your work."[41] In such local climates, the skills and track records of individual civic groups had significant impact on receptiveness to planning consultants and their improvement recommendations.

In many cases when women drove the sponsorship of a city plan, they either chose to withdraw from the limelight or were written out of the official history. In the small town of Lock Haven, Pennsylvania, the female Civic Club raised $1,590 "to acquire a city plan for the Board of Trade." From the start of their civic improvement campaign, one reporter indicated, the women "enjoyed the cooperation and support of a progressive, courteous city government and of a wide-awake Board of Trade." When John Nolen was hired in 1911 to produce the plan, he immediately confronted the ambiguity: was the men's commercial club in charge of the plan, or the women's civic club? He posed this question in a letter to Dora Merrill, president of the Civic Club. Merrill replied, "The Board of Trade stands sponsor for the city plan although the Civic Club is equally interested in the development of the town." Merrill assured Nolen that she would follow every step of his work "and shall do all that I can personally and as president of the Civic Club to carry out your suggestions." She acknowledged that not all members of both organizations backed him but reasoned that "morally" both stood behind him.[42] Here was an example of how women's clubs cooperated with men's clubs, but as the commercial aesthetics movement became absorbed into professional city planning and citywide planning commissions, the women's groups adopted behind-the-scenes roles.

As events unfolded in Lock Haven, the support of the Civic Club proved to be far more solid than that of the Board of Trade. When a new president took charge of the Board of Trade, it was Merrill who paid him a visit to make sure that he was behind city planning. She reassured Nolen that the Civic Club would follow her lead in keeping their concerns before the board's president. Telling Nolen to "cheer up," Merrill explained, "I am not 'big' . . . but I am a good fighter." Nolen acknowledged in his reply that he had "relied" upon the women's club but was still "not so sure of the Board of Trade." Ultimately he issued his report to both organizations.[43] Nolen saw clearly that Merrill and the club women, while publicly deferring to the Board of Trade, were morally devoted to city planning.

This crusading spirit so evident among female civic improvers was useful to the early city planners, and it was so effective that women achieved leadership positions that from some angles were interchangeable with male leadership. When a district official of the General Federation of Women's Clubs (GFWC) spoke in Lock Haven, she congratulated the audience on the fact that women had taken part in the city beautification movement. In her city, by contrast, "the get-together meeting was composed of all masculines, who went off and enjoyed a banquet, leaving the women at home." Nolen knew that "one man[,] red-hot on a subject, can save a city. It is equally true of one woman."[44] Yet the limits to that leadership were also evident: women's groups in the first dozen or so years of the century engaged often in unrecognized work in politics and public work in the streets. The GFWC official felt compelled to tell her audience in her municipal housekeeping speech that she was not a suffragette. The lines between "political" and "civic" were defined in the course of improvement campaigns and set the terms for "mothering a municipality."

Even though professional planners often depended upon the women's groups, their own official record sometimes erased the role of women's clubs who championed city planning. Indeed, planners sometimes saw ignoring these groups as essential to achieving their goals. When in 1912 Colorado Springs published Charles Mulford Robinson's *General Plan for the Improvement of Colorado Springs,* the city's women's clubs received no special acknowledgment in the published plan, which became the official history. The

Woman's Civic League claimed credit through other channels, however, for initiating and doggedly pursuing city planning in Colorado Springs, in the face of the city fathers' indifference. Mary Beard's version in *Woman's Work in Municipalities* recounted how the city's Civic League and Woman's Club obtained city funding for a comprehensive city plan and how "at their further instigation" Robinson was actually hired. After the report's publication, the women had to relentlessly urge upon inattentive city fathers "the wisdom of adherence to the plan." *American City* lauded the women's initiative in securing money and their influence in City Hall.[45]

Moreover, the Civic League's quarterly *Bulletin* recalled that, since the group's inception in 1909, a comprehensive city plan had been its first priority. With help from the Chamber of Commerce, the Civic League had hosted speakers like John Nolen and Charles Zueblin. They found that "the subject we have brought up arouses more discussion and heated argument than anything that has heretofore interested the city," and they succeeded in pushing the mayor and city council to pass a resolution to employ an expert landscape architect. In March of 1911, the *Bulletin's* editorial went out on a limb, criticizing the politicians' and businessmen's inactivity, and in October, despite the claim of the commissioner of public works that "he believes in city planning," the resolution to hire an expert still languished.[46]

But the Civic League pressed on in 1912, framing an argument that would stay at the forefront of battles over downtown reform — that the city fathers could not rise above entrenched self-interest to see the common good as women did. To avoid carrying out a comprehensive plan, they claimed, was a "selfish" act undermining the city's prospects. The women believed that a plan would not simply provide a framework for improving the physical city but would serve the further purpose of "drawing us all together in a close bond of common purpose." A plan, they explained, would lead to "welding the various interests of the community into a whole." The city fathers needed to see that the consensual work of city planning was worth the potential sacrifice of self-interest. The Civic Center that the women agitated for symbolized the inclusive coming together facilitated by planning. Once Robinson submitted his plan, the Civic League continued to prod the city fathers, urging publication of the plan and proposing the permanent city planning commission. With representation on the city's new commission secured, the Civic League chose to disband its own City Planning Committee because it believed it had finally convinced others to take up its city beautification agenda.[47]

Citizenship and the Civic Value of Commercial Space

Despite this kind of official obscurity in the pre- and postsuffrage years, women asserted moral authority over Main Street aesthetics and used the downtown landscape to teach lessons in citizenship. Certainly, well-organized and polished agitation against the "selfish" interests of the city fathers could command considerable attention. A new Woman's Club in Leesburg, Virginia, used a less sophisticated pantomime show in 1912 to launch a clean-streets campaign and civic rally. The details, as described for *American City*, educated the audience about the moral character of civic work and the downtown landscape:

> The first [scene] showed a village street — the pavement and gutters lit-tered with papers, orange peel and peanut shells — boxes and barrels on the sidewalk, and old pieces of dirty meat hanging in front of the butcher shop. A big basket marked "For Waste Paper and Trash" stood at the street corner. Along this street loitered a score of people representing the village population: the business man, the butcher boy, the nursemaid, two colored boys, two colored girls, the old farmer in town for the day, and a group of school children; and all of them as they sauntered along threw more waste into the street. The school children scattered banana skins and orange peel, and everyone threw down bits of paper, utterly disregarding the public waste basket.

This realistic depiction, wrote one spectator, met with howls of delight from the audience.

> A big poster proclaimed the scene as: "Before the Town Improvement League and the League of Good Citizenship came to our town."
>
> The "After" scene showed the same street perfectly clean, the same people walked along, but carefully threw all their waste into the public re-ceptacle. After the program, the audience dispersed, enthusiastic over the possibility of clean streets in Leesburg.

The message was clear: all citizens, not just voting citizens, not just men and city officials, but everyone from "colored" boys and girls to the businessman, had responsibilities if the community expected to achieve a "perfectly clean" street.[48] The middle-class women who staged the event were themselves ab-sent from the pantomime; they were (as in politics) behind the scenes writing the script, thereby setting the new aesthetic and moral standards that they, presumably, did not need to learn. However, they were now positioned to teach the entire town about these values.

Through such demonstrations, as well as through the penalties and prizes described earlier, women believed "the slovenly citizen would be taught the error of his ways" and the downtown would be redeemed. The historical record is full of cases in which men claimed that they had learned the moral lessons of urban beautification. J. Horace McFarland, president of the American Civic Association, for example, was often credited with being "the man who made over Harrisburg, Pennsylvania." He declined that honor, pointing out that "it was the women of Harrisburg who dinned and dinned into our ears until at last we men got ashamed of our laziness and selfishness as citizens."[49] Men's selfishness, especially businessmen's selfishness and self-promotion, contrasted with the women's club view that "by civics, we mean all work that benefits the city as a whole, and that helps every person in the city, high and low, rich and poor, fortunate and unfortunate."[50] Mrs. T. J. Bowlker of the Women's Municipal League of Boston made the contrast explicit: "The interests of men are divergent; property interests, and the interests of personal success drive the different classes of men far asunder, but the interests of women are convergent, and bring all classes close together." Civic improvement, to these women, represented a particular democratic ideal based upon the principle of bringing together divergent private interests into a common bond and agenda. Where men stood divided by respect for *private* property, women (as demonstrated in Leesburg) wished to instill respect for *public* property.[51]

Given such goals of enhancing citizenship, it is a revealing irony that most of the characters in Leesburg's 1912 pantomime, as well as the sponsors — the children, African Americans, and women — could not vote.[52] Lurking behind this kind of women's civic activism was the question of how it related to suffrage. Was this training in citizenship a preparation for responsible suffrage, or a substitution for it? Speakers on municipal housekeeping, aware of how their agitation for reform might be read, were often quick to distinguish their civic improvement campaigns from their position for or against women's rights or suffrage. Zona Gale (then chair of GFWC's Civic Department) viewed with cynicism the cooperative relationship that voluntary women's clubs cultivated with city officials precisely because of women's nonvoting status. Women and city officials, she wrote, could always accomplish "remedial, palliative things" or begin "big things" cooperatively. But ultimately, "there is only one direct means of cooperation between women's clubs and city officials — the franchise for women." Gale found that when women turned over their initiatives to the management of city government, which was often their goal, they watched helplessly as their project "became immediately one more prize in the spoils politics of the city." A 1914 display constructed for educational exhibitions echoed Gale's point in a more blunt fashion: on the left a model showed city streets overflowing with garbage. On the right, under the heading "When Women Have Votes," the garbage disappeared.[53]

Most downtown housekeepers, however, carefully declared that civic involvement was not the same as politics, and they believed that the difference was what made them powerful. In a sense, it is also what made their work transitional. The Civic League of Terre Haute, Indiana, stated that its aim was the improvement of the city, which it would accomplish "without in any way entering into politics." The General Federation of Women's Clubs came late to support suffrage, not endorsing it until its 1914 convention after enthusiasm had grown among local organizations.[54] These women's clubs proposed and lobbied for legislation, fought for the enforcement of local ordinances, and got voters to the polls for their favored causes, all the while excusing themselves from "politics."

Women's depoliticization of their own campaigns ironically enabled men's groups to more easily take up the task of civic improvement, often after ordinances were passed, demonstration projects were under way, city officials at least had their eyes opened, and the new standards had been brought to the public's attention. Commercial organizations such as boards of trade and chambers of commerce were supposed to stay out of politics too, for fear of appearing to meddle as special interest groups. Like the civic leagues, some commercial groups put these prohibitions in their constitutions or bylaws. One commercial executive announced in 1914, "The general interpretation that civic affairs are public affairs, not politics, means emancipation from the old idea that commercial bodies should keep out of anything that smacked of politics." Women's urban activism had defined civics as "public affairs, not politics" — paving the way for business interests to take on the civic cause of the "public good."[55]

Despite the rhetoric of democratic citizenship promoted by women's groups, their efforts to upgrade and regulate Main Street revealed other lessons of limited citizenship (besides their own lack of full suffrage). Launching a cleanup campaign in Salisbury, North Carolina, for example, the white-only Women's Civic Club "recognized that its success extended only to the boundaries of the negro quarter." The club became sensitized to the racial boundaries of cleanup and resolved the matter by organizing a Colored Women's Civic League for the African American community.[56]

Nor did beautification strategies apply to all Main Street businesses equally. In deciding whom to target, downtown housekeepers revealed their own moral judgments about what did and did not constitute an eyesore or an unacceptable practice. The disputes over illuminated projecting signs, for example, made certain types of business less welcome than others. As one proponent of sign regulation put it, "the class of business which uses these signs as an advertising medium is not a class of business which conduces to general commercial prosperity. . . . they are chiefly used by establishments open at night; in other words, cafes, cigar-stores, theaters, nickelodeons, dance-halls, saloons, pool rooms, bowling alleys, photograph booths and the like." The campaigns against merchants who obstructed the sidewalks also constrained certain businesses more harshly than others. In Lincoln, Nebraska, when an ordinance passed that banned the fruit vendors and shoe shiners who leased sidewalk space from abutting owners, it was fought by "those foreign-born citizens and others whom it affected the most." They insisted that earlier generations of Lincoln businesses had enjoyed a tradition of using sidewalks to display their goods, but Nebraska's Supreme Court ruled against them. Just because previous merchants had used the sidewalks, the court found, it did not follow that the city intended to lease the public sidewalk space "to undesirable persons who used the walks to cry out their business or vociferously offer their services." Loud, undignified, "undesirable persons" — most of whom were foreign-born — were targeted in this campaign to protect the "public's" claim to the sidewalk and "improve" the Main Street landscape.[57]

Ordinances to regulate municipal aesthetics not only differentiated among classes of business and merchants but sometimes singled out particular downtown populations for exclusion or inclusion as well. At its 1899 meeting, Denver's female City Improvement Society was especially proud of its downtown progress, including an antispitting crusade, in which it placed placards in stores, on public buildings, on telegraph poles, and in every streetcar. Their "unceasing agitation" resulted in the passage of an ordinance against spitting. But one casualty of the women's campaign for a decorative iron fence around the post office was a group of men who had congregated at that location. The society's secretary admired "the beauty of the fence in contrast to the row of men who daily sat on the coping and who incessantly smoked, chewed and spit to the disgust of every right-minded passer-by." In the name of beautification and cleanliness, such undesirable types were moved away from public downtown places.[58]

Thus might a democratic rhetoric of inclusive citizenship, beautification, and the public interest also hide real practices of exclusion. Such exclusions confirmed the perception held by many that downtowns in the 1910s, despite the inclusive rhetoric, were inherently middle-class and wealthy places. In this light, the new commercial aesthetics were seen as fundamentally bourgeois, carrying on the traditions of nineteenth-century urban public spaces such as parks, where the middle classes hoped to bring together a broad range of citizens, mostly to mold and educate them in proper middle-class behavior.[59]

Municipal housekeepers were fully aware that their vision of responsible citizenship also enriched the economic potential of the City Beautiful movement. Mary Beard explained that "city planning moreover has an economic value even when it is confined to beauty." Those "artistic" street lamps not only looked better and reduced crime, but they also attracted retail trade to Main Street at night. Women also gained experience in urban real estate during these years, by renting, owning, and managing their club quarters, women's lunchrooms, comfort stations for rural women and travelers, libraries, and settlement houses. Women obviously knew that a clean and beautiful downtown drew tourists and investors. Yet, the housekeepers *chose* not to foreground economic value, because it was precisely the obstacle of private self-interest they felt they had to overcome.[60] Instead of boosting investment, as mayors and businessmen were wont to do, they boosted citizenship.

When commercial housekeepers of the turn of the century moved into the background of downtown beautification efforts, it proved that they had won their campaign — at least in one important way. They had tried to get their fellow citizens not only to take their efforts seriously but also to share responsibility for enhancing civic life and public property. Many improvement clubs from the start had worked toward their own dissolution, intending that city government and other associations would take over their programs. Businesspeople, city officials, and the new city planning profession adopted the housekeepers' downtown beautification agenda — streetlights, eliminating the pole and wire "evil," cleaning and paving, and comprehensive planning. All were incorporated into the standard strategies of Main Street investors during the 1910s. "Beauty," a *Saturday Evening Post* reporter announced, "is described as the new business tool."[61]

As men's commercial organizations declared their newfound commitment to civic work during these years, they accepted the criticism that they had neglected such duties in the past, even wearing this confession like a badge of honor. The former president of the Pittsburgh Chamber of Commerce claimed that "increasing numbers of people in America are coming to believe that chambers of commerce and business bodies generally have a very great obligation toward, and duty in connection with, civic problems." In his 1915 history of American chambers of commerce, Kenneth Sturges traced the institution's evolution "from a business organization to a civic agency." Importantly, he noted that the phrase "civic interests" had recently been added to the "financial, commercial, and industrial interests" named in the national organization's bylaws. The American Civic Association in 1915 encouraged local commercial organizations in their trend toward "seeing and assuming" their "large responsibility for initiating and carrying out important civic improvement undertakings." [62]

When mayors and businessmen "converted" to the civic righteousness of improved paving and lighting and commercial aesthetics, they did so on their own terms. The City Beautiful proved to be something quite different in the hands of politicians, businessmen, and planners from what it was in the hands of Main Street housekeepers. With a nod to civic pride and the democratic ideals of civic centers, city leaders and planners seized on the promised increase in downtown property values. As one observer explained, the mayor of Birmingham, Alabama, "believes in the 'city beautiful,' not as a fad, nor a sentiment even, but as a business proposition. He believes it will enhance the property values of the city and that the work will prove to be a paying investment." [63] The 1915 history of chambers of commerce concluded that "the full value of the economic arguments in favor of civic improvement is thus apparent." Not surprisingly, business organizations expected to achieve public service through "selfish" motivations as well as "true civic loyalty." One headline called this conversion "The 'Commercializing' of Civic Movements." [64]

But the key to understanding women's activism as urban designers at the turn of the century is to recognize their initiative in defining a realm for themselves in setting commercial standards, cooperating with defensive city officials and businessmen, and then relinquishing that initiative once their civic values appeared to have caught on. Women achieved recognition for their leadership in the early 1910s, just as their agenda found other sponsors and their activism became less pressing. Women did not disappear suddenly from urban design, of course, but their participation changed. Increasingly in the 1920s they secured paid work as inspectors, planning librarians, secretaries for city planning commissions, and staff in the burgeoning consulting profes-sions.[65] Women's voluntary groups continued to monitor downtown beauti-fication, but in more supportive and secondary roles. In 1931 the League of Women Voters of West Hartford, Connecticut, passed a resolution approving of the creation of an architectural jury, "whose duty it would be to pass upon the exterior design and appearance of buildings erected in the business area." Professionalization provided educated women with some opportunities in city planning, as well as in related municipal reform fields such as social work and government. Hester Jaeger continued her position as executive secretary of the San Diego Civic Association after her marriage in 1929, despite the fact, as she wrote John Nolen, that her husband "wanted me to give up working and stay at home and be a nice little housewife."[66] In planning and urban de-sign, though, by the 1920s, women no longer received credit for originating the city beautification agenda and taking the lead through their clubs.

The accomplishments of downtown housekeepers would not only secure the successes of professional planners and open the doors of civic work to businessmen in the early twentieth century. In pushing forward the transfor-mation of the downtown based on standards of beauty and women's work, the women's groups also created enduring problems for the men who carried on their efforts.

"Pink Ribbons on Lampposts":
Feminine Frills and the Commercial Landscape

In 1914 a Bridgeport, Connecticut, newspaper headline announced the arrival of planner John Nolen but insisted, "Nolen's Assistants Not Going to 'Tie Pink Baby Ribbon' on Every Telegraph Pole."[67] As city planners assumed greater professional responsibility for downtown improvement in the 1910s, in partnership with their business and government sponsors, they loudly and self-consciously sought to distance themselves from the women housekeepers who in so many instances had validated planners' first efforts. Even though women activists deliberately relinquished their leadership roles in commercial beautification, the transition to male professionals was nonetheless marked in this decade by a public squabble about whether planners were trying to fem-inize the business district.

Most vociferously, planners ridiculed the threat of a feminized commercial landscape. During these insecure years of their profession, as planning con-sultants fought for legitimacy, they distinguished their own recommendations from those ideas' roots in municipal housekeeping and downplayed their

FRILLS, FRILLS, FRILLS.   —By De Mar

Figure 1.5 Because women had assumed leadership roles in setting new standards for commercial districts, the city planners, business leaders, and other allies who took over the women's campaigns had to defend themselves against accusations that they were feminizing the downtown landscape (by symbolically tying pink ribbons on the lampposts). This cartoon, a gendered critique of the City Beautiful, appeared on the front page of the *Philadelphia Record* on April 8, 1908, in response to the mayor's surprise call for civic improvements. (Courtesy of Jon Farnham.)

debt to women's clubs for opening doors to them. These roots proved to be a liability, because critics could too easily defeat reforms by challenging the masculinity of the civic designers and their downtown improvement goals (see fig. 1.5).[68]

The contest for the masculine legitimacy of the urban planning field, then, did not occur between male professionals and female club women. Rather, the tension emerged between men's organizations. On one side stood the professional consultants and their allies, and on the other side those unsympathetic businessmen and city officials who saw planning as a usurpation of individual initiative and property rights, as well as inappropriate outside interference with policymaking. Such critics cried "Confiscation!" of rights and property when asked to bury utility wires. After years of such struggles, Nolen lamented to fellow planners that the most "indispensable" participants, "the so-called business interests and the men who control city governments, are either antagonistic to the beautiful in cities or at best don't care about it."[69]

Critics indeed found the *Beautiful* in City Beautiful to be a vulnerable pressure point. They attacked early city planning as not just grandiose and impractical in its vision but as effeminate — preoccupied with "cosmetic" and superficial changes. In 1928 one writer recalled that only a decade earlier, "the words 'city beautiful' gave rise to gibes. The movement was regarded as impracticable, useless, unnecessary and extravagant. People thought of geranium boxes in front yards and pink ribbons on lamp-posts. Practical men distrusted the love of beauty as being mere sentiment. Besides the movement seemed to consist of putting a pleasing front on what was otherwise mean and monotonous — a sort of municipal cosmetic. The idea was to scatter about a few imposing public buildings, fountains and statues."[70] The attacks singled out both City Beautiful's grandiose and mundane street-level characteristics, with the mundane condemned as feminine sentiment and adornment. As late as 1921, the secretary of the Johnstown, Pennsylvania, City Planning Commission felt compelled to explain that the city's plan "does not mean 'tying pink ribbons on lamp posts.'"[71] The women's clubs had created the basis for these perceptions, which planners simultaneously built upon and repudiated.

The "gibes" aimed to discredit reforms by questioning the planners' masculinity (and, subtly, their heterosexual credentials) as well as their development agenda. One city planner recalled taking his proposal for a new bridge before a community leader of a western town. The "substantial citizen" responded by saying, "Oh you fellows make me tired. . . . Let us build our bridge, and then if you want to come along and put a few rosettes and Cupids on it, go to it — I don't care."[72]

On the defensive, planners rallied to deny links with what skeptics colorfully described as a feminizing adornment agenda for Main Street, hoping instead to redefine beautification in more palatable business terms, such as enhanced land values and advertising appeal. Nolen "confessed" that "many of those interested in city planning are afraid of the discussion of 'the beautiful' in connection with the city plan." He estimated that in the first fourteen meetings of the National Conference on City Planning, the organization had "never ventured to put upon its program any topic bearing directly upon the beauty of the city as a whole."[73] Planners seized on the image of tying pink ribbons on lampposts precisely to illustrate the absurdity of the accusations.[74] Instead of pink ribbons, they countered, beautification meant efficiency and utility and, especially, improved property values. In 1911 a St. Paul, Minnesota, paper quoted another defender of planning: "the idea of beautifying the city proposed by the city plan does not contemplate tying pink ribbons to the lamp posts and petitioning the park board to plant a few flowers in Rice Park. It means rather the enhancing of real estate values and making the city attractive to the traveler."[75] Land values, not pretty ribbons, were at stake.

By the late 1920s, the pioneering role of women activists in urban beautification was largely forgotten. Indeed, it became easier to acknowledge and take stock of the previous generation's defensiveness over the feminine roots of beautification.[76] One 1928 observer remembered that "the term [City Beautiful] was not altogether a success, for in red-blooded he-man America, the word beautiful still had the connotation of femininity. I think, however, we are outgrowing that rather crude stage of masculinism. We are being educated up to the point where we can feel that it is not a disgrace for masculine citizens to believe in beauty." A 1920s public relations bulletin for Dallas's Kessler plan revealed that "some of our civic leaders have been afraid to speak of 'beauty' for fear someone would make fun of them or think them weak and effeminate. Even some of our city planners had an idea that you must not speak the words, 'civic beauty,' or 'civic attractiveness' when talking with big, brawny Texans."[77] Since city planning had achieved security as a design profession, the pink-ribbon critique had lost its potency.

This story of how downtown beautification became "commercialized" illuminates how the commercial space of Main Street became invested with civic values of the public good in the first place and why by the 1920s it was not housekeepers but businessmen and their consultants who were the guardians of that value. In that decade, men could safely mention beauty partly because "slowly but surely the country is awakening to its economic value."[78] The new vision of commerce, found in the dignified, managed, Main Street retail corridor, was no longer rooted primarily in the moral and civic values promoted by the women's clubs but in the economic and advertising values of downtown businessmen and the other brokers of what historian William Leach has called this "land of desire." Some have bemoaned Main Street's twentieth-century history as the commercialization of a once public realm. Yet it is really the public and civic nature of downtown that requires explanation, as undertaken in this chapter and the next, not its commercial nature.

As the downtown housekeepers demonstrated, it was the hybrid public-private nature of urban commercial life — the evident intermingling of cultural and commercial — that so often provided the space for mobilizing competing visions of the future and for contesting values such as civic responsibility and citizenship. This was true of Main Street during the Progressive era, and it remained true throughout the twentieth century. The characteristics of lampposts, lunch counters, storefronts, garbage cans, and parking lots were thus politicized in ways that embodied some of the most heated and controversial value choices confronting Americans in the twentieth century, whether those choices involved gender roles, racial segregation and integration, or the threat to capitalism posed by the 1930s depression.

Turning to consider how local businessmen and their consultants adapted the housekeepers' vision and promoted a new kind of Main Street investment, the next chapter (like this one) follows not only the key players, such as planners Charles Mulford Robinson and John Nolen, but also a range of participants who may not have previously been recognized as urban designers. In chapter 2 the contributions of the anonymous commercial artists who "fixed" up Main Street in postcards are examined alongside the downtown improvement strategies put forward by famous planners.

2

FIXING AN IMAGE OF COMMERCIAL DIGNITY
POSTCARDS AND THE BUSINESS OF PLANNING MAIN STREET

If the panoramic watercolor renderings of City Beautiful reports captured the grandiose schemes of that movement, then ordinary Main Street postcards embodied the beautification approach promoted first by the municipal housekeepers and then by the planners and businessmen who carried the women's designs well into the twentieth century. Behind the grand and alluring renderings, City Beautiful era planning reports themselves proposed mundane downtown improvements very similar to those enacted in postcards when artists altered and "beautified" Main Street photographs. Together, the postcards and city plans of the early twentieth century articulated a new commercial vision — a dense streetscape of entrepreneurs presiding over a managed, simplified, and beautified retail corridor. As businessmen and planners popularized downtown beautification and broadened the support for its implementation, they commercialized the civic values held by the women's clubs. This newly dignified though modest commercial order (based as it was on the transformations of usually uninspiring objects like street curbs and utility poles) proved to be a surprisingly powerful and long-lasting force in downtown investment. The Progressive era's Main Street ideal dominated urban commerce, though of course it was modified according to the challenges of coming decades (unpredictable growth in the 1920s, collapsed land values in the 1930s, and ongoing suburbanization), until a new generation of investors tossed it all out for a different commercial order — a new kind of monumentality and destruction known in the 1950s as urban renewal. In the colorized, mass-produced Main Street postcard, downtown improvers had found an incomparably compelling statement of the commercial beautification agenda.

Walker Evans, the photographer who admired downtown's "beautiful mess," had a passion for collecting Main Street postcards. Writing in 1948, Evans found the postcards of his day to be decidedly inferior to turn-of-the-century cards. The old cards offered accurate insight into the true character of Main Street, or so he believed: "For postcards are now in an aesthetic slump from which they may never recover. . . . Gone is all feeling for actual appearance of street, of lived architecture, or of human mien. In the early-century days color photography was of course in its infancy. Cards were usually made from black-and-white photographs subsequently tinted by hand lithography. Withal, the best ones achieved a fidelity and restraint that most current color-photography printers have yet to match — notably in flesh tints and the rendering of patina and the soft tones of town buildings and streets." He acclaimed the old postcards as "honest, direct little pictures," their surfaces containing "some of the truest visual records ever made of any period." But how could hand-tinted lithographs achieve more "fidelity" or "feeling for actual appearances" than 1940s color photographs? Evans, who understood the subjectivity of the images on which postcards were based, was not so naive as to think that postcards literally replicated past urban landscapes. The shooting angle, the framing, and the cropping all contributed to the fiction of photography. Yet he insisted that the postcards offered "a well-nigh perfect record of place."[1]

In the early decades of the twentieth century, creating a new, beautified vision of the American downtown through postcards and civic plans became an obsession of Main Street businesses, city leaders, and investors. Thus the "place" mentioned by Evans and illuminated in the postcards was not a brick-and-mortar location but rather a territory within Americans' imaginations, a hopeful vision of urban commerce transformed. Based on photographic negatives, the postcard images were altered by artists and hand colored to present the desired view. The creation of the cards enacted the very same Main Street enhancement schemes that urban designers and city leaders had started to dream about, and they documented Americans' ideals of how their beautified central business districts should appear in a new commercial order.

As Evans understood, postcards did not replicate the city but "fixed the images" of the business district's physical landscape — the brick buildings, trolley cars, and pavement.[2] Hundreds of millions of these softly colored cards changed hands in the early twentieth century and shaped ("fixed") popular conceptions of Main Street USA. In one postcard after another, meticulous alterations were made to achieve the Main Street ideal. With tiny paint brushes, artists touched up photographs to repair broken-down sidewalks, to remove offending utility poles or signs, and to pave streets — improving the streets' physical realities. In these ways, the postcard artists labored in the field of municipal housekeeping. Through commercial means, they brought to an unprecedented national audience the beautification strategies of the women's civic improvement campaigns.[3]

The postcards and city plans were themselves artifacts of the Progressive era.[4] They reflected the commitment of business groups, city leaders, and design professionals to remake and promote the downtown as an ordered, regulated, dignified civic destination. It was a vision that downplayed the individual self-interest criticized by the housekeepers yet simultaneously sold the retail corridor. Optimistic and forward-looking, the postcards and plans described a commercial "place" improved according to these new downtown standards. Both laid out strategies for upgrading current conditions and lent credibility to the potential for a transformed urban commercial order. Both relied heavily on visual strategies to set these standards and establish a new Main Street ideal for America. Combining advertising, business, art, and a modest improvement agenda, they promoted complementary ways of perceiving and investing in the downtown, during the years when advertising was a novel, cutting-edge retailing strategy. The literally down-to-earth cleanup approach tackled by the postcards and plans was an elaboration of the Main Street investment agenda established by the housekeepers. It was in the postcards that the link between downtown improvements and advertising reached its fullest fruition — in the purposeful manufacture and dissemination of the image of a streetscape of entrepreneurs presiding over a beautified commercial corridor.

The potential for postcards to concretely demonstrate the effects of proposed urban improvements was recognized by urban designers. Planner Charles Mulford Robinson described the mutually reinforcing qualities of postcards and plans in his 1913 report for Raleigh, North Carolina. After condemning the familiar "curse of poles and wires," Robinson observed, "It is interestingly significant that among the colored postal cards showing views of Raleigh, the card illustrating Fayetteville Street, shows it with wires and poles removed." For Robinson, the postcard legitimated his planning recommendation, and because the card was provided to him by the Chamber of Commerce, it implied that the city's business leadership already approved of that beautification.[5] In local politics, advocates of even modest Main Street improvement programs usually met with some resistance, as the women's clubs' endeavors did. But in a postcard, one could implement the same changes without encountering objection, in order to demonstrate the power of a new model of urban commerce.

As the city fathers and their consultants adopted the housekeepers' beautification agenda, they redefined civic improvement by amplifying the economic and advertising values of cleaning up and reordering the downtown.
The result was a national investment strategy motivated by the vision of a new
Main Street — a dignified and simplified retail corridor, as opposed to the existing chaotic hodgepodge of individualistic storefronts, their conflicting and
intrusive promotional strategies, and their inattention to the deplorable condition of the business district environment. Businesspeople reformulated the
housekeeping agenda to promote modest yet transformative downtown improvements with long-term impact. Both the postcard enhancements and the
planning recommendations promoted Main Street as a unified, harmonious
retail destination, one managed by businesses able to reach beyond their
selfish differences and grasp their shared economic (and civic) interests.

Local Businessmen and Outside "Experts" Remake Main Street

The harmonious vision of cooperative enterprise, applicable as it was to
virtually all American communities, found a remarkable resonance that helps
explain why even today we recognize the appeal of such a Main Street concept. Yet this powerful national ideal gained character and finer definition as
it was tossed about in local politics, as well as between national consultants
and local business leaders. The new American Main Street took shape as the
groups that claimed responsibility for commercial aesthetics — particularly
the planners and designers, businesspeople, and city officials — negotiated
their differences and working relationships. As they debated the details of
sidewalk obstacles and projecting signs, they wrestled over the nature of urban commerce, namely, the tensions between individual entrepreneurial aspirations and the newly prominent cooperative ethos. The complementary
investment strategies promoted by Main Street postcards and city plans were
achieved in the context of not only the more convergent interests of national-
level planning and postcard consultants, but also amid shifting local alliances
and conflicts. Before turning to elaborate upon the specific improvements
that constituted the Main Street ideal, let's consider how the plans and postcards came to express such similar visions of urban commerce, as well as the
controversies over these visions among downtown interest groups.

The postcards and plans shared many characteristics of production and
sponsorship that contributed to their mutually reinforcing, national agendas
of commercial improvement. Both were produced by national consultant-
experts based in major cities in conjunction with local sponsors. In the case of

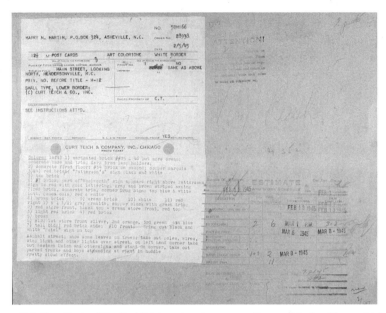

Figure 2.1 The clients of the Curt Teich postcard company often sent instructions, which became part of the company's client files. These folders also recorded information about the postcard sponsor, the quantity and type of card ordered, and a log of the hours the card spent in various stages of production. The sponsor for this 1945 postcard of Hendersonville, North Carolina, requested that the Main Street photograph be altered in detailed ways relating to the color of buildings and street objects, the legibility of store signs, and the removal of street poles and wires, overhanging lights, parked trucks, and the "boys standing at right in huddle." Working with or without such detailed instructions, the artists employed an array of Main Street improvements that remained standard practice into the 1950s. (Courtesy of Lake County [Ill.] Discovery Museum, Curt Teich Postcard Archives, card no. 5BH166.)

postcards, clients sent photographs to postcard companies, where artists designed the final product. Alternatively, company salespeople traveled from city to city, taking photographs and persuading local merchants to order and sell the view cards.[6] The Detroit Publishing Company, a business renowned for its quality products, provided its salespeople with a specially outfitted railroad car. Either the field salespeople or the clients conveyed their instructions (which varied greatly in the level of detail) to the company artists (see fig. 2.1). The Curt Teich Printing Company was one of the nation's largest and longest-operating postcard manufacturers. In its first decades, beginning around 1910, Curt Teich had 20 full-time artists employed to paint at its plant in Chicago. This number climbed as high as 150 during the 1930s and 1940s, Teich's peak

CENTER AVENUE, LOOKING EAST, MOORHEAD, MINN.

Plate 1 The artists' reinforcement of the curb, streetcar, and building lines unified the Main Street corridor. In addition, the colorizing process harmonized, beautified, and animated Main Street postcards in ways that planners and municipal housekeepers could only dream of. The result was a cleaned-up and visually enticing urban scene. Compare with the original and altered photographs in figs. 2.2 and 2.3. (Courtesy of Lake County [Ill.] Discovery Museum, Curt Teich Postcard Archives.)

Main Street at Night, Burlington, N. C.

Plate 2 When artists converted daytime street scenes into moonlit postcards, they illuminated store windows, sidewalks, streetlights, and stars to draw together and simplify the unruly reality of the commercial street. Compare with the original photograph in figure 2.6. (Courtesy of Lake County [Ill.] Discovery Museum, Curt Teich Postcard Archives.)

Looking up Western Avenue, Muskegon, Michigan

1B-H2329

Plate 3 Most businesses chose to advertise in postcards by portraying themselves as part of a dense streetscape of entrepreneurs. The local Woolworth sponsored this Muskegon card, yet the store (located four buildings down on the left) is invisible. Compare with the original and altered photographs in figures 2.7 and 2.8. (Courtesy of Lake County [Ill.] Discovery Museum, Curt Teich Postcard Archives.)

Dexter Avenue, Looking East, Showing State Capitol, Montgomery, Ala.

7A-H3251

Plate 4 The finished Montgomery postcard is strangely somnolent and empty when compared with the original photograph (see figs. 2.13 and 2.14). The decisions to eliminate people, signs, and vehicular traffic from Main Street photographs illustrated the dignified packaging that municipal housekeepers, planners, and postcards proposed for commerce. Business streets, these reformers and their allies argued, did not have to look "ugly" or "cheap." (Courtesy of Lake County [Ill.] Discovery Museum, Curt Teich Postcard Archives.)

production years. These employees were art-school trained, but they have not received the professional recognition enjoyed by other commercial artists for the style and innovation they brought to their alterations. Curt Teich printed more local view and advertising postcards than any other firm in the country, exemplifying the significant role of the postcard industry in commercial beautification and the larger dynamic of Main Street investment.[7] Many of the company's client files have survived, documenting correspondence with clients alongside the artistic transformation of photographs into postcards.[8]

Two national-level urban designers — John Nolen (1869–1937) and Charles Mulford Robinson (1869–1917) — dominated the planning consultant business in the early decades of the century, producing their reports in cooperation with local sponsors to shape commercial goals for cities around the country. These planners drew heavily on the fields of landscape architecture, architecture, and engineering.[9] Robinson is regarded as the most articulate publicist of the City Beautiful. He held thirty-five consulting jobs and published 25 reports, 3 books, and 100 articles. Before embarking in 1899 on a nearly twenty-year career in city improvement, Robinson worked in journalism (although he later trained in landscape architecture).[10] From the mid-1910s to the late 1920s, John Nolen directed one of the largest consulting practices in his field. He completed 450 contracts, including 62 comprehensive plans, 20 regional studies, and 33 new towns. Like Robinson, he published many influential articles and several books on almost every dimension of improving cities. Nolen is often remembered as a "practical" planner, albeit one influenced by the City Beautiful's visionary spirit. Nolen traveled constantly and energetically for his work, usually on extended, multicity journeys away from his Cambridge, Massachusetts, base. This extensive travel around the United States, together with his voluminous correspondence with his local contacts and hosts and his widely available publications, defined Nolen's role in both disseminating national planning goals and exchanging ideas with local leaders.[11]

The early plans and the postcards were heavily sponsored by local business executives interested in boosting their city's fortunes. In most places, business leaders came from the ranks of newspaper editors, retailers, and the manufacturing elite. Through their commercial clubs, businessmen hired planning consultants and led the opposition as well.[12] The postcard companies relied upon local store executives and news agencies for most of their Main Street orders. The retailers and news agencies in fact shared the same advertising interests; an influential 1920s study described "the close relationship between newspaper circulation of a city and the retail influence of that city's leading stores." *Printer's Ink* observed, "Nobody is in a better position to gather facts about local stores than the newspaper publisher," since his ad solicitors worked among the retailers. Thus plan and postcard sponsorship overlapped in the business community represented by retailers, newspapermen, and the commercial clubs.[13] In the case of the postcards, the news agencies (often regional in scope) and the burgeoning chain store clients also contributed to the national reach of the Main Street ideal.

For planners like Nolen and Robinson, the improvement of commercial aesthetics was a professional commitment. Once welcomed by a supportive faction, often their first challenge was to demonstrate to businesspeople and public officials the value of upgrading the downtown. Despite historians' emphasis on the rifts between City Beautiful and City Practical planners, basic agreement prevailed among professional planners where Main Street was concerned. Those trained in landscape architecture, architecture, and (increasingly) engineering jostled within the planning field for authority and jobs, and indeed conflicts broke out. But Robinson and Nolen, who together bridged the City Beautiful–City Practical gap, agreed upon the Main Street ideal's modest improvement strategies. Planners argued about labels and used different language to talk about the same challenges, but their field demonstrated unity behind the vision of a dignified Main Street.[14]

Businesspeople, city officials, and planners may have promoted a cohesive Main Street ideal, but they did not always do so harmoniously. These groups usually approached beautification from different starting points, which brought them into conflict with one another, as Nolen and Robinson well knew. Most important, since businessmen and city officials lacked the design professionals' near-righteous faith in the importance of upgrading and reordering the downtown environment, the door was opened to a much greater range of disagreement. While some local leaders announced themselves as "converted" to the new commercial standards, others became mired in factions when confronted with planning reports. In Reading, Pennsylvania, for example, in 1910 businessmen were decidedly unenthusiastic over a Nolen plan. In the opinion of the local *Herald* editors, the Board of Trade endorsement came "so tardily and so half-heartedly and so indifferently as to mean but little." In 1917 a supportive Bridgeport, Connecticut, Chamber of Commerce official confessed to Nolen his ongoing difficulties trying "to commit a group of men to action" regarding the "highly controversial" downtown section of Nolen's plan. A few months later the official proclaimed it an "impossible" task and abandoned the effort.[15]

The potential for conflict between the commercial men and the professional planners was rooted in more than businessmen's periodic obstructionism and disinterest. City boosters maintained a fundamental skepticism about whether consultants like Nolen were marketing a legitimate civic vision and had the city's interests in mind or whether they were more akin to hucksters and snake oil salesmen. After hosting a lecture by Nolen in 1919, the Association of Commerce of Marion, Indiana, refused to pay Nolen's traveling expenses, on the grounds that "business concerns do not pay expenses of traveling men who come into the city for the purpose of selling their products."[16] This characterization of his work touched a nerve for Nolen. He responded immediately, writing on Christmas Eve that had he not known the men of the committee, he would have taken their letter as "an insult to me personally and to the profession which I represent." He had come to Marion at the invitation of the committee, Nolen explained, in order to do Marion a favor. "I did not ask for an opportunity to come to 'sell' anything." Don't call planners "traveling men," he admonished. He and his peers were in fact the "opposite" of commercial travelers, and he drew the association's attention to the "uncommercial character of professional work." In a follow-up letter three weeks later, Nolen asserted that men such as himself promoted "new ideals" and had "no financial interest" in their lectures.[17] Such a claim again aligned planners more with the women's clubs than with the commercial men.

To Nolen, planners and commercial men were definitely standing in different places. A critical challenge in his work was the task of fixing an acceptable image of himself, his profession, and his ideals in the minds of local officials. Looking beyond the vehemence of Nolen's response, however, we see that the distinctions he clung to were not as vivid as he insisted, particularly since consultants lectured in locations, including Marion, where they hoped to gain a contract. Despite Nolen's efforts to distinguish between the commercial work of businessmen and the professional ideals of planners, and despite the very real tensions between these two groups, in practice they shared more commercial interests than the planners might willingly admit.[18]

Municipal officials faced a different set of issues in their work with planners and businesspeople. City administrators might lose their elected or appointed positions in the middle of improvement projects. In some places it was even difficult to determine which city administrative unit would handle business district recommendations. For any number of reasons, city officials might stand in the way of planning. A Nolen ally in Elkhart, Indiana, complained that he had been "hampered by an unfavorable city administration for some time" — a regime that was "lukewarm, or opposed, to everything in connection with the city plan." The potential for factionalism was expressed in this Reading, Pennsylvania, newspaper headline: "Study John Nolen's Plan before You Condemn It." Although some touted the blurring of lines between commercial men and city administrators on the cause of civic improvement, frustrating divisions did occur. Nolen's secretary described how "political complications disturbed the course of city planning" in La Crosse, Wisconsin, in 1919. The La Crosse mayor possessed a "hostile" attitude, "mainly because of his personal feeling toward the Chamber of Commerce, and there was opposition to the appointment of an official city planning commission." [19]

Despite the conflicts affecting the professional and commercial alliances behind downtown improvement, a consensus emerged in the early decades of the twentieth century concerning the needs of the business district. The Main Street problems identified by the municipal housekeepers as virtually universal — a dirty, cluttered, disorganized environment fostered by selfish business practices that hurt the community — had caught the attention of city leaders. Despite their reservations, many city leaders approved of the new vision for a more ordered, "beautified" commercial life, and they promoted this Main Street ideal to enhance their city's appeal. If America's downtown could become only a fraction as appealing, warmly glowing, clean, and organized as illuminated in the postcards and designed in the city plans, Main Street businesses could enjoy profitable and approving trade. Out of the tensions among and within the numerous downtown interest groups, a new Main Street ideal was agreed upon. Three key concepts — a clean and pleasing urban character, a united streetscape of entrepreneurs, and a dignified commercial corridor — together made up the guiding principles of downtown investment as they emerged in the Progressive era. [20]

A Clean and Pleasing Urban Character — Moorhead, Minnesota

When the Curt Teich postcard company received a photograph of Moorhead, Minnesota, in 1928 from a local client, the only explicit instructions were to "take out snow & large poles" and to colorize the image according to the company's "American Art" style (see figs. 2.2, 2.3, pl. 1). [21] In contemplating the somewhat gloomy vista of muddy Center Avenue, the postcard artists would have perceived the same challenges understood by downtown house-

Figure 2.2 The original 1928 photograph on which the Moorhead, Minnesota, postcard was based showed the uneven assets of most early-twentieth-century Main Streets, ranging from muddy, rutted roads to decorative streetlights. (Courtesy of Lake County [Ill.] Discovery Museum, Curt Teich Postcard Archives.)

keepers and city planners. The ragged conditions of a rutted street, ramshackle carts, and unsightly wires coexisted with promising brick buildings, uniform streetlamps, and other signs of the town's "wide-awake" hopes — parked automobiles lining the street, a trolley, and two dentists competing for trade. In short, Moorhead's photograph presented the uneven assets of so many American towns and cities. The artists beautified Moorhead, in the same way they enhanced thousands of other photographs, to portray a cleaned-up, unified Main Street. That they did this in Moorhead with so little instruction is testimony to how standardized the improvements had become by the late 1920s.

The key to transformation, as the city planners and women's clubs before them recognized, was in the details. From clean curb lines to uncluttered sidewalks, the details could convey the sense of an ordered and appealing destination. Robinson, writing for the Civic Society of Waterloo, Iowa, focused on

Figure 2.3 Postcard artists cleaned up the Moorhead photograph according to the new standards of downtown housekeeping and city planning. They paved the roads, fixed curb lines, and eliminated unsightly utility poles and wires. Here one sees the alterations under way. (Courtesy of Lake County [Ill.] Discovery Museum, Curt Teich Postcard Archives.)

"those little things, not difficult to correct, and making, by the frequency of their recurrence, a deal of difference in the aspect of the city." For Binghamton, New York, most downtown improvements fell into the category of "elementary needs" — amenities so basic that "these things hardly belong to city planning, for city planning presupposes their provision."[22] Yet the planners, as well as the postcard artists, had to confront repeatedly the fact that cities had not successfully addressed those "little" though transformative "things."

Figure 2.4 Of the common business district problems identified by city planners, the utility pole and wire "evil" was the most widely condemned. Only a few years before these criticisms took hold, however, poles and wires had indicated a progressive, up-to-date city. The contrast underscored that a new understanding of Main Street was emerging. (Charles Mulford Robinson, *A City Plan for Raleigh* [Raleigh, NC: Woman's Club of Raleigh, 1913], 22.)

The thing that received the most consistent and impatient attention was what the planners called the "pole and wire evil" — the street utility poles and overhanging wires that filled the urban skies (fig. 2.4).[23] Other descriptive terms for these objects were "hideous," "ugly," and "dangerous." A German-born city planner observed, "A beautiful thing you see in nearly all American cities . . . is the line of telegraph and telephone poles along either side of the streets. You look down the street and they look like a row of gallows." Not only did poles and wires "mar every view," but they obstructed firefighters and caused trees to be disfigured by trimming. Nolen cautioned audiences that ugly poles and wires also destroyed real estate values.[24] Consultants advised placing the wires in underground conduits and removing the poles whenever possible. Others marveled at how quickly opinions were changing about the preferred business environment of Main Street. An executive of the American Civic Association pointed out in 1907 that only fifteen years earlier the wires and poles had been "taken simply as a sign, ugly but necessary, of an important business thoroughfare."[25]

Through the elimination of wires and poles, and through the paving of streets, the postcard artists achieved their most wide-reaching Main Street cleanup. As in the Moorhead card, together the sky and street occupied the majority of a postcard's surface area. Moorhead's painted photograph (fig. 2.3) shows the utility poles hovering over the street, in the process of disappearing. "Taking out" the poles and wires was the most common client request, down to the 1950s.[26] But even in the budget postcard series, and in countless cards lacking client documentation, the artists painted over the "objectionable poles & wires" when they did little else.[27] The fact that some cities strung bare electric bulbs over Main Street was particularly offensive given the new streetlamps so popular during these decades. One postcard client thought it best to "block out the strand of electric lights as shown in photo," and the lighting received the same treatment as the utility wires. Similarly, Robinson advised Raleigh that "the strung bulbs must go. . . . They would not do credit to a country circus on a one-night stand."[28]

As for the streets, many cities were just struggling out of what Walker Evans called "the mud-rut period." This era is well illustrated in the Moorhead photograph. The artists customarily painted over poorly paved and unpaved postcard roadways with the fine-lined brushes of their trade, giving the streets a smooth, inviting expanse, even in the no-frills budget cards. For Moorhead, using gray for the street and white for the sidewalk, they reconstructed the surface to completely transform the vista. Of course not every client chose the street cleanup, but smooth paving was an easily implemented improvement, and most towns desired its transformative effects. One postcard client requested, "Make street smooth dark paving."[29] Planners strongly recommended paving the business section streets and alleys or complimented cities on their already "excellent" road surfaces and sidewalks.[30] Viewing Moorhead's Center Avenue, that women's book club in Arkansas comes to mind — the one that took on the project of filling in the muddy holes of their town's streets.[31] Within the growing national planning profession and the postcard industry, the place to start tackling improvements was at the level of the street — as in the women's clubs' beautification efforts.

For the postcards, the invention of the corridor perspective began in the hands of the photographers, in the framing and composition decisions that determined every card. Regardless of the true shape of the business district, it was primarily framed by the photographers as a linear corridor. The greatest exception to this rule were the large, complex cities such as New York, Chicago, Philadelphia, Detroit, and Boston, which favored aerial shots that obscured the street pattern. Even the bird's-eye views, shot from atop tall downtown structures, usually retained a linear perspective on the business street.[32] The Main Street view and the very concept of a downtown shopping corridor amounted to a managed interpretation of what was, in actuality, a complicated and diverse business district.

The treatment of Moorhead's street and sidewalk tells of the importance of street and building lines in creating a corridor effect — another preoccupation shared by planners and postcard artists. In the original Moorhead photograph, the streetcar tracks and curb lines virtually disappear in the muck. Artists used black to repaint crisp tracks and curb lines, constantly repairing the broken curbs and leveling irregular sidewalks to enhance the corridor perspective. Planners were similarly preoccupied with the corridor line. For Fayetteville, Robinson advised that "the streets will be surprisingly improved in appearance, and the whole town given a neater and more prosperous aspect, by the uniform street alignment which curbs alone can give." In evaluating the lines and proportions that established the business corridor of Oakland, California, Robinson argued that "absolute uniformity in material and line, permanence and neatness, are the ends desired." Accordingly, that city would have to replace its wooden curbs with stone or concrete.[33] The planning consultants bemoaned "patchwork" building lines, misplaced skyscrapers, and the dismally steep "canyon effect" of streets in large cities — not just because they all interfered with the "harmonious" corridor "vista," but because skyscrapers invited congestion and skewed land values. Tall buildings inflated real estate values in the immediate vicinity, supposedly causing injury to property owners farther away. Most of the early planners favored uniform height limits. For their part, the postcard artists did not lop off the tops of buildings but repainted in order to bring out the horizontal building lines, as can be seen in the views of Moorhead, to draw the eye down Main Street (fig. 2.5).[34]

In addition to cleaning up the sky and the street and employing street, curb, building, and trolley lines to unify Main Street, the postcards used colorizing to achieve a degree of beautification and harmonizing unavailable to planners or municipal housekeepers. The results could be spectacular. With the "American Art" sky treatment, for example, Moorhead's client chose a blue sky with puffy white clouds, fading to peach and yellow at the horizon (pl. 1). The artist made the road a uniform sand color. The row of once disparate buildings, treated in red brick, buff, and gray, were harmonized to the

An example of creditable
and unified architecture
spoiled by signs.

Unregulated signs on walks
give the city a ragged appearance and in the end do
not help the merchant as
one sign screens another.

The awning type of flimsy
canopies of uneven height
and unregulated design
should not be allowed. The
canopies are on city property and can be controlled.

Figure 2.5 Planners, like the postcard clients, favored unifying Main Street. Here consultants advised Houston residents (in the two lower captions) to smooth over Main Street's "ragged appearance" and straighten out irregularities such as awnings "of uneven height." In the top photograph the consultants indicated "an example of creditable and unified architecture spoiled by signs." (Hare & Hare, *Report of the City Planning Commission, Houston, Texas* [Houston: Forum of Civics, 1929], 59.)

Figure 2.6 The transformation of street scenes like the one in this 1940 photograph of Burlington, North Carolina, into moonlit postcards (see pl. 2) showcased the artistry involved in creating a cohesive, magnetic, even glowing commercial destination. (Courtesy of Lake County [Ill.] Discovery Museum, Curt Teich Postcard Archives.)

same tone and the uniform appearance of masonry. For night views, the artists used lighting to tie together the streetscape, adding an inviting glow to store and office windows, illuminating the streetlight globes, and bathing the entire scene in moonlight (fig. 2.6, pl. 2).[35] The tiny dots of color lithography added a unifying texture.

Although planners and downtown beautifiers could not control color as in the postcards, they too recognized how it transformed and integrated the image of Main Street. One newspaper article on beautification in Springfield, Massachusetts, proposed, "Color is the weak point of most American cities, and an ugly spotty red brick is too common." "Rich color" could potentially provide the "common quality dominating the street."[36] Since color fell within the realm of private choice, however, most beautifiers could only dream about achieving the same kind of unifying effect that postcard artists accomplished. Planners expressed their color ideals in the presentation renderings intended to inspire their clients and the public.

But where planners' watercolor renderings evoked a dreamed-of transformation sought through complete artistic freedom, postcard clients varied greatly in whether they demanded color accuracy. Some clients specified colors down to the smallest detail; one even sent a piece of roof slate to demonstrate the correct tint. The Woolworth in Quincy, Illinois, described precisely the building material and color to be used for each structure: "white tile, light tan brick, white and dark tan granite front," and so forth.[37] Others corrected the artists' proofs: for example, "street is black asphalt, not green and yellow moss-color as you have it." One client asked the artists to follow an old postcard as a guide, "except for brown which should be a trifle lighter."[38] But most were content to put their Main Street entirely in the hands of the artists, relying on these outside experts to create an overall effect rather than accurate details. The sponsor of a card for Johnson City, New York, requested that the artists "use own judgement for colors."[39] Accuracy was merely a matter of individual preference, since colorization provided the ultimate beautification whether or not the postcard image was true to the original. Colorization enhanced the pleasing urban character of cities like Moorhead and harmonized the Main Street retail corridor.

A Unified Streetscape of Entrepreneurs — Muskegon, Michigan

In 1941, when the local Woolworth in Muskegon, Michigan, commissioned a new Main Street postcard from Curt Teich, the challenges were perhaps not as glaring as the mucky, rutted roadway of Moorhead, but they nonetheless represented significant issues of order and vision to the postcard artists and planning consultants alike (see figs. 2.7, 2.8, pl. 3). Muskegon's improvements demonstrated strategies for handling increased pedestrian congestion and commercial growth and encouraged downtown businesses to cooperate in developing and selling Main Street as a dense yet magnetic retail destination.[40]

In the Muskegon photograph (fig. 2.7), the sidewalks would have first caught the trained eyes of city planners at the time. These consultants objected to excessive clutter — "sidewalk obstacles" — because they impeded Main Street trade and pedestrian movement and ruined or blocked the view with undignified objects. As cities faced mounting congestion, planners usually suggested the expensive solution of widening streets and sidewalks. Most communities, though, could not afford to do that. Clearing the sidewalks and

Figure 2.7 Like the downtown housekeepers before them, the postcard artists labored to clear cluttered sidewalks of obstacles and repair streets. This is the original photograph of Western Avenue, Muskegon, Michigan, that client F. W. Woolworth sent to the Curt Teich postcard company in 1941. (Courtesy of Lake County [Ill.] Discovery Museum, Curt Teich Postcard Archives.)

streets of obstacles could also enhance traffic flow — effectively widening the path of commerce when circumstances precluded actual street widening. Robinson explained to Fort Wayne, Indiana, citizens, "It is better for a merchant to have a sidewalk full of people than to have a portion of it so cluttered with the signs, counters, bicycle racks or show cases of his rivals that when practicable pedestrians take another street. Yet every merchant who counte-

Figure 2.8 The artistic cleanup of Western Avenue achieved in this altered photograph would have pleased city planners, who occasionally used postcards to demonstrate what they thought Main Street should look like. This image reveals especially well the artists' perspective. (Courtesy of Lake County [Ill.] Discovery Museum, Curt Teich Postcard Archives.)

nances sidewalk obstructions chooses a walk of things instead of a walk of people" (see fig. 2.9). Ideally, the sidewalk served as a pathway for shoppers. In his files, Robinson jotted some notes on the back of a 1913 Chicago photo: "sidewalk encroachments that compel people to walk at a distance from the show windows." On another photo he added, "The result of this is surely bad for trade."[41] The consultants, in the name of improved trade, judged as failures certain aggressive commercial practices that cluttered the sidewalk with things.

On their trips downtown, armed with cameras, Nolen and Robinson chronicled a long roster of offending sidewalk obstacles. They saved their most sarcastic and biting comments for such objects, in part because they felt that this aspect of the downtown streetscape could be easily controlled by municipal ordinance. In the Waterloo, Iowa, plan, a Robinson photograph of a pole adorned with assorted boxes and signs bore the caption: "Civic art on Fourth street." Little escaped the consultants' notice. Like the downtown housekeepers, they criticized promotional signboards on the sidewalk and the practice of displaying food in exposed outdoor cases. A preliminary planning study of Elkhart, Indiana, for Nolen's office documented how merchant side-

Figure 2.9 In a 1909 plan, Charles Mulford Robinson advised the citizens of Fort Wayne, Indiana, to clear the streets and sidewalks of advertising in order to provide more room for commerce. Without obstacles like advertisements, he noted in this photo's caption, the sidewalk would "accommodate a great many persons." (Charles Mulford Robinson, *The Improvement of Fort Wayne, Indiana* [Fort Wayne, IN: Press of Fort Wayne Printing Co., 1909], 17.)

walk cases meant that "the full pedestrian space is not utilized" — particularly troubling for the street intersections with the highest land values and rents. In San Jose, California, hitching posts crowded the streets, and store awnings were "so low that an average sized man has continually to duck his head." Battered, unpainted waste cans were "utterly unworthy" of these aspiring cities. Unwieldy "watering tanks" served as drinking fountains in Waterloo. Horse troughs took up space in Elkhart (where they were still desired by visiting farmers). Even the lowly barber pole was subject to the planners' complaints. Cumulatively, eliminating such obstacles would render the business street "spacious, clean and orderly."[42] The consultants hoped to sensitize citizens and businesses alike to see the downtown in new ways, so that familiar sidewalk objects would no longer appear acceptable.

Postcards helped promote the possibilities of open, uncluttered sidewalks. Painting over sidewalk obstacles became a standard task in the cleanup of

Main Street photographs for postcard production and did not require specific instructions. For their Muskegon client, the artists removed two sidewalk signs on the right, several pedestrians, and the "no parking" notice painted on the street. A drooping awning was repaired. On the left side of the street, the artists took out a trash can. When compared with the original photograph, the postcard presents clear, unobstructed sidewalks — a vista that Robinson and Nolen would have admired. The artists did this, and more, without directions. They eliminated poles and wires, evened the curb, paved over the street's large misshapen patches, and repainted the parking lines.[43] In other cases, the sidewalk and street cleanup proceeded according to explicit client wishes. Kaufmann's asked Curt Teich to "clean up sidewalk in front of" its Grand Island, Nebraska, store, and a Buffalo, New York, client requested a "clean street." Others singled out specific items for removal or repair, such as the Arkansas order pointing out that "the awnings are so floppy, it would probably be best to remove them" or the customer who asked the artists to "take out poles & wires & traffic light. Take out shadows."[44] When a Lawrence, Massachusetts, client demanded that a bus in the foreground be taken out, the artists substituted a clear sidewalk expanse, also eliminating a fire hydrant in the process.[45]

The average retailer who chose to advertise in Main Street postcards had already decided to subordinate his or her particular business interests in order to project a different kind of image — a streetscape of entrepreneurs. Although the local Woolworth sponsored the Muskegon postcard, the store is practically invisible, down the left-hand side of the street, partly blocked by a projecting sign. Indeed, Woolworth's competitor, S. S. Kresge, has a far more prominent location in the postcard. This situation — the invisibility or near-invisibility of the local retail sponsor — was very common in the postcards, especially for chain store clients.[46] It was unusual for a chain to commission a postcard from Curt Teich of its store standing alone (in most cases this effect required that the artists remove the adjacent shops) (figs. 2.10, 2.11). A Curt Teich employee in 1936 disclosed one reason why Montgomery Ward had asked the postcard artists to actually paint in the as-yet-unbuilt stores next to a new branch: the client "says put in next Bldg. so it wont appear as tho M.-W is out in the sticks."[47] The fact that, in contrast, office buildings and hotels (especially in larger cities) preferred to sponsor postcards of their lone buildings further reinforces the point that the synchronized Main Street corridor was primarily a retailing concept.

Figure 2.10 S. H. Kress & Company, which tended to erect more architecturally distinctive retail buildings, occasionally sponsored cards featuring a single store. This alteration sequence demonstrates how the single-store postcard made Kress stand out from its neighbors (compare this altered photograph of Congress Avenue, Austin, Texas, in 1940 with fig. 2.11). (Courtesy of Lake County [Ill.] Discovery Museum, Curt Teich Postcard Archives.)

The chains especially had a stake in promoting the ordered, cooperative Main Street landscape. The variety store managers knew that they drew patronage from existing pedestrian traffic, based on convenience shopping. Their strength, these businesspeople believed, lay in their numbers and in their collective appeal. Some store managers did insist that their sign alone should be highlighted in the postcards, as in the case of one Woolworth manager in Brunswick, Maine, who specified to Curt Teich, "& if possible only bring out Woolworth lettering." But the chains, which appeared downtown in increasing densities in the 1920s and 1930s, invariably shared the street view with their competitors and were usually happy to share the promotion. By choosing the unified street front, retailers helped create the Main Street ideal

Figure 2.11 The finished postcard has removed Kress's neighboring dime store competitors. Other retailers — including independent family shops and influential corner drugstores — also had single-store postcards made. But these were the exceptions. The dominant formula for postcards, as well as for planning, was a communal streetscape of entrepreneurs. (Courtesy of Lake County [Ill.] Discovery Museum, Curt Teich Postcard Archives.)

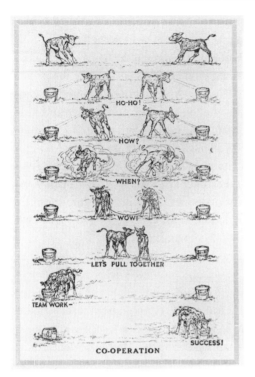

Figure 2.12 Merchants promoted values of cooperation, as in this postcard published by the Durham, North Carolina, Chamber of Commerce in 1911. The encouragement to "pull together" also underscored the geographical density desired in downtown districts. (Courtesy of the Division of Rare and Manuscript Collections, Cornell University Library; John Nolen Papers, 1890–1938, 1954–1960, collection no. 2903, box 24.)

as an advertising concept — a row of stores offering a convenient variety of goods and services. Through the postcards, individual interests were bound up in the interests of Main Street as a place.[48]

The Main Street postcards' cooperative values contrasted with the destructive individualism and selfishness deplored by the municipal housekeepers. A 1911 postcard sponsored by the Durham, North Carolina, Chamber of Commerce portrayed business interests as calves tied to one another, straining to reach separate milk pails, to convey the benefits of cooperation over competition. Their struggles resulted only in paralysis until they coordinated efforts to reach each pail together (fig. 2.12). This cooperation also evoked the economic value of a concentrated retail corridor in which merchants located close to one another. One appraiser admired Marshall Field's initiative in encouraging such density in downtown Los Angeles; that city "would have greater land values, more successful merchants and more profitable office buildings if there had been more concentration — more of a 'pull together' spirit on the part of the developers." The "'pull together' spirit" described merchants' cooperative efforts in advertising and beautification as well as their geographic concentration.[49]

Although women's clubs had chosen not to emphasize the communal advertising value of civic improvements, local businessmen seized the opportunity. Beginning around 1913, the Chicago Association of Commerce campaigned to place flower boxes in the windows of downtown office and hotel buildings. What some labeled mere feminine beautification the Chicago merchants called advertising: "While originally used only through a feeling of civic pride, the utilization of the plants and bay trees was found to be excellent advertising and often taken as an indication of the character of the firm using them."[50] In making use of the window boxes' advertising value, the men's commercial club altered the women's domain of civic value, and at the same time they fulfilled the women's push for cooperation.

Local newspapers and regional news companies had overwhelming reasons for promoting the cooperative urban commercial vision, a fact demonstrated in the news companies' frequent sponsorship of Main Street postcards. Because of their dependence on advertising, news organizations represented the retail interests of an entire community, while downtown businesses, in turn, relied on newspaper advertising. This coalescence of interests discouraged favoritism in how the news companies commissioned, altered, and distributed postcards. After all, the news companies sold their postcards through the competing retail outlets on Main Street. So, in sponsoring a postcard of Miami's Flagler Street, the Dade County Newsdealers specified, "Be careful to show Kresge, Woolworth and McCrory store signs." The Portland News Company had similar requirements: "Be sure to make Hay's drug store, Walgreen Drugs, and State Drug Company prominent." The postcard company representatives encouraged this coordinated advertising when, using their own photos, they peddled proposed cards up and down Main Street to all the local chain stores. One Curt Teich salesman suggested proceeding with production of a Wilmington, North Carolina, card, "whether or not you receive all the confirmations from the 10 c Stores in this town."[51]

Woolworth enjoyed elevated status at the postcard company because its stores commissioned so many cards, and the Woolworth case best illustrates the limitations to Main Street cooperation. Because of Woolworth's special leverage, a Curt Teich internal memo reminded its artists, "These Woolworth signs are important always, because Woolworth stores are one of our best customers, and should be shown correctly."[52] This special treatment of Woolworth signs was standard operating procedure. Clients had to make a pointed request when they did not want the Woolworth sign highlighted, as in the case of Jamestown, New York: "Do not bring out Woolworth sign to prominent [*sic*]," or that of Gardner, Massachusetts: "Be sure & do not bring out Woolworth sign because Newberry gets some of edition."[53] Curt Teich even developed a "red impression" technique for producing a crystal-clear Woolworth sign, whereby the artists cut the actual sign out of the photograph and substituted a uniquely precise, minute sign of their making. Another technique for manipulating the advertising visibility of stores was to make a sign illegible, as directed by notes on the back of a Lawrence, Massachusetts, photo: "Make Newberry sign NOT readable."[54] The harmonious Main Street ideal clearly had underlying competitive dimensions.

In these many ways, the Main Street improvement agenda expressed in the postcards and city plans represented a collective approach. Businesspeople, city officials, and planners worked toward accomplishing an unobstructed, sweeping corridor view. Local chain store leadership in particular appreciated Main Street's advertising value as a shopping destination, best demonstrated by the choice to sponsor Main Street postcards in which their own branch was not even visible. The downtown housekeepers would have approved of this unified street of entrepreneurs. Yet it was almost as difficult to discern the civic value of the new commercial ideal as it was to find the sponsoring business in so many of the Main Street cards, even using a magnifying glass to study the "things" of the downtown streetscape.

A Dignified Commercial Corridor — Montgomery, Alabama

In its handling of business growth, congestion, and commercial flow, the 1937 postcard improvement of Dexter Avenue in Montgomery, Alabama, is dramatic and puzzling, but typical. The original photograph shows a lively business street connecting the state capitol to a traffic circle with a large fountain at its center (fig. 2.13). Lined with parked cars, Dexter Avenue appeared to permit a steady stream of vehicles without choking congestion. The sidewalks bristled with people, and assorted signs and billboards promoted establishments and products. Why, then, did the client prefer the final postcard and its near-desolate streetscape? (fig. 2.14, pl. 4). In producing the postcard, artists erased most of the cars and pedestrians and all of the signs. A surprising number of postcard clients promoted their downtowns in this somnolent, apparently decommercialized state, and planners specified these "improvements" as well. Given the current preoccupation with the jostling, democratic potential of busy, early-twentieth-century streets, we must ask why so many clients

Figure 2.13 The transformation, especially the simplification, of this original 1937 photograph of the busy and bustling business district of Dexter Avenue, Montgomery, Alabama, dramatically enacted the newly dignified commercial ideals. (Courtesy of Lake County [Ill.] Discovery Museum, Curt Teich Postcard Archives.)

preferred to have the postcard stripped of most indications of bustling commercial life.[55]

As enacted in the Montgomery postcard, city planners and many postcard clients tried their best to portray a dignified commercial corridor in contrast to the "unobtrusive shabbiness" and "crazy dilapidation" that too often characterized Main Street in their eyes.[56] The improvers hoped to educate others to envision a different commercial standard — the restrained, dignified retail corridor of the city plans and postcards. The effort to redefine commercial aesthetics, building on the campaigns of municipal housekeepers, thus came down to a stark choice between two kinds of commercial life — ugly, shabby,

Figure 2.14 In this altered photograph of Dexter Avenue, the heavy hand of the artists in painting over the familiar if disorderly indicators of active commerce is evident. (Courtesy of Lake County [Ill.] Discovery Museum, Curt Teich Postcard Archives.)

and cheap, or beautiful and dignified. Contrary to the public impression, one proponent of the new ideal complained, "shabbiness in appearance and commercial activity are not inseparably associated."[57] A street like Dexter Avenue, the main approach to a state capitol, carried the extra burden that Charles Mulford Robinson demanded of the approach to North Carolina's capitol — "Much more than an ordinary business street," that thoroughfare required "restraint and dignity becoming its State importance."[58] To planning consultants such as Robinson and Nolen, restraint and dignity seemed in short supply in America's business districts. One pamphlet wondered whether the country had become "America the Cheap — America the Commercial — America the Ugly." The same pamphlet advised that "in America too Business should be taught to respect Beauty."[59] What is hidden in the postcards, but stated in the plans, is the way improvers attempted to dislodge one image of competitive, individualistic commercial life, even as they attempted to fix another — an image of a clear commercial vista in which the eye could travel, like a consumer, uninterrupted by the bodies of other shoppers and by the constant bother of hawkers and "cheap" sidewalk sales tactics.

Accordingly, for many postcard clients, improving and beautifying their Main Streets meant reducing or even eliminating cars and pedestrians. Instead of aspiring to capture the crowded popularity of their business district, clients gravitated toward the peaceful and more restrained portrait of the Montgomery postcard. One Curt Teich client phrased it bluntly: "Eliminate the automobiles and people." For the artists, systematic elimination became the accepted practice, as indicated by these instructions from the Austin News Agency: "It will be O.K. to leave the cars and the pedestrians in the post card."[60]

The planning consultants and postcard sponsors came to share a particular antagonism toward what everyone called congestion. By 1910 cities as varied as Roanoke, Virginia, and New Haven, Connecticut, complained about traffic. Horses, carts, streetcars, bicyclists, farmers, pedestrians, and increasingly automobiles clogged thoroughfares and competed with one another for space. In 1915 the narrow streets and industrial boom in Bridgeport, Connecticut, made relieving downtown congestion an absolute priority.[61] For one client after another, consultants diagnosed their problems as street irregularity and narrowness. They noted that most cities lacked thoroughfares tying their various sections together, and many roads dead-ended or had jogs. By the 1910s business streets, originally built for far less traffic and fewer parked vehicles, were under threat of being "choked." In 1920, under the watchful eye of other cities, Los Angeles experimented with a ban on downtown parking.[62] The planning practices of these decades strove to minimize the potential for jostling and bustle.

Postcard sponsors, envisioning an efficient business corridor with unimpeded flow, echoed the planners' language in their instructions to Curt Teich. Directions from Kinston, North Carolina, asked the artists to "relieve congestion of cars on street." Reflecting the merchants' interest in adequate parking, the artists often removed parked cars, as shown in the Montgomery postcard. Clients especially demanded that parked cars be eliminated from the foreground blocks: "Take out 4 autos marked X in foreground."[63] This permitted the artists to create an open, unobstructed view of the storefronts and sidewalk for pedestrian appeal. (See the effect in fig. 2.6 and pl. 2.) The notion of what looked right was tied to the traffic-flow goals advocated by planners, and it reinforced the dignified commercial aesthetics of the Main Street corridor ideal. The artists accomplished in hours what businessmen, consultants, and city officials fought over for decades.

The concern to appear up-to-date and urban also shaped the policy of removing or altering the vehicles in postcards. Curt Teich's client files from the 1930s and early 1940s were filled with requests such as "Streamline autos and make up-to-date" or "Take out . . . all old cars in 2nd block."[64] Artists regularly painted over the older, squared models to give them the rounded appearance consistent with the new cars coming off the production lines. One client asked, "Subdue cars so that the models are not very noticeable cars already out of date (modernize a bit)."[65] The form of transportation visible in a postcard said a great deal not just about how people traveled but also where the community was going. Trucks and farmers' carts were eliminated because they did not reinforce the urban, retail character of the street. Smaller towns, especially in the early years of the automobile, asked the postcard artists to either paint a car onto their Main Street scene or paste in a photographic image of a car from elsewhere.[66] In the 1910s and 1920s, a streetcar or tracks suggested the presence of nearby extended residential districts (which would be good for business), so artists habitually redrew the tracks once they had "repaved" the streets, as in Moorhead. But by the 1930s, the trolleys themselves began to reflect an older transit era. Just as cities began to rip out or pave over the streetcar tracks, postcard clients increasingly asked the artists to "take out tracks & make street smooth" and alter streetcars into buses.[67]

During the opening decades of the twentieth century, postcard treatment of pedestrians became increasingly heavy-handed — highlighting ongoing interventions to control the flow of pedestrians and thus define an appealing image of respectable commerce. In the earliest years (until abut 1920), cameras caught people walking, standing, socializing, and sitting in the street, and the artists left them there. Many postcards captured lone individuals standing at the side of the street or in the street, facing the roadway. Although these people appeared to be loitering, they were in fact waiting for trolleys. At first, artists also left in recognizable individuals frozen in the foreground of photographs. Yet even in these earlier cards, many clients selected photographs intentionally devoid of people.[68] By the 1920s, the artists assumed a more interventionist role in the matter of pedestrians. Pedestrians in the street were redefined as "jay-walkers," as one Curt Teich file called them, and removed.[69] "Blurred" people were painted over; so were individuals caught in the foreground, because not only were they recognizable, but as large objects they obstructed the street view. Since the earliest cards, artists had repainted features of the human body, but by the 1920s this practice became more pronounced. Using tiny dots, the artists also obscured the face of almost every pedestrian. And as the Montgomery card vividly demonstrated, it became common to thin out the sidewalk pedestrians as well as eliminate those in the street. A client from Rock Hill, South Carolina, demonstrated this attention to pedestrian location when he asked, "Take out wires and take people out of street — but not from sidewalk — leave policeman in street."[70] The artist interference evident in the Montgomery card did have detractors, who felt compelled to specify, "No artificial retouching," for example, or "Use photo as is. Take out nothing."[71] The increasingly substantial alterations strove for the simplified and less populated commercial corridor embodied in the Montgomery card and became the default practice.

Key to the new vision was the belief that the cacophony of individual interests, each shouting for attention, repelled trade and reduced the advertising value of the street as a unified destination. For the new professionals monitoring commercial aesthetics, projecting signs and cheap advertising had contributed more than their share to the "uglification" of the business district (fig. 2.15). They saw the "*Dignity of business signs* as an essential point in the creation of a beautiful city" and set the goal of "getting rid of undignified signs — the fire-sale sign, the roof sign, the projecting sign."[72] Consultants mustered arguments against the projecting signs in particular, few of them based on the kinds of moral issues raised by municipal housekeepers. In his Raleigh plan, Robinson claimed, "They shut off street views, they are usually ugly in themselves — especially by day — and they disfigure the architectural aspect of the buildings from which they protrude as excrescences." Nolen's report for Little Rock, Arkansas, observed that "the maze of signs in most cases becomes so difficult to decipher that there is little or no advertising value, and it constitutes a hazard to the public safety." One cartoon made these arguments quite literally: a defiant merchant admires his projecting sign, only to watch horrified moments later as the sign falls and kills his best customer (fig. 2.16).[73] Ironically, projecting signs were the creation of the corridor view, since that perspective rendered flush signs invisible.

The Montgomery postcard offered a stark illustration to the public of what their commercial district would look like without projecting signs and other obstructions such as poles, wastebaskets, and sidewalk advertisements. As with traffic congestion, the postcard artists received instructions about the management of signs which at times resembled the planners' language: "Re-

Figure 2.15 Critics like planner Charles Mulford Robinson targeted projecting signs because they believed that the cacophony of individual interests, each shouting for attention, repelled trade and reduced the advertising value of the street as a whole. (Charles Mulford Robinson, *The Improvement of Fort Wayne, Indiana* [Fort Wayne, IN: Press of Fort Wayne Printing Co., 1909], 29.)

move all other signs which are obstructing or objectionable," demanded a Louisville, Kentucky, client. In Newburgh, New York, this meant the removal of "big signs from roof tops," and on Front Street in Wilmington, North Carolina, a huge shoemaker sign was erased.[74] Of course, other postcard clients not only sought to preserve the cacophony of competing signs but also wished to amplify that effect by highlighting the signs. Some customers asked the artists to convert their photographs into night scenes in order to maximize the impact of illuminated projecting signs. One client expected the final card to "show neon signs and lots of lights."[75] Such variation illustrates that in the postcards, as in the planner debates, the dignified commercial ideal competed with the chaotic, bright, minimally regulated Main Streets the planners condemned as cheap, ugly, and shabby.

Since so many of the consultants' recommendations for restraint ran counter to prevailing aggressive commercial practices, critics accused the planners of being anticommercial. Robinson emphatically rejected this possibility. He acknowledged that "in the business street there is inevitably much that is bizarre, blatant, and distracting" and that it was "the very purpose of

Figure 2.16 This cartoon lampooned the selfishness and even the dangers posed when individual merchants insisted upon using projecting signs despite the condemnation by Main Street reformers. (Courtesy of the Archives and Rare Books Department, University of Cincinnati; Alfred Bettman papers, US-69-1.)

the business house to attract attention." Robinson insisted that the new ideal "would not destroy the commercial aspect of the streets, it would not have them shorn of the marks of enterprise and competition." Instead, he worked to redefine an appropriate aesthetic for business activities. The new vision "would not crush out of its ideal the whirr and hum of traffic, the exhilarating evidences of nervous energy, enterprise, vigour, and endeavor. It loves the straining, striving, competing, as the most marked of urban characteristics, and when it advocates broad streets conveniently arranged, it does this not to silence the bustle of commerce, but to make the efforts more surely and quickly efficient." [76]

Reformer Charles Mulford Robinson enthusiastically supported the business district's competitive dynamism, but he proposed a different packaging for "the bustle of commerce" — a more restrained business landscape with different physical signs and signals. Although Americans had become accustomed to their "ugly" streets, the design consultants believed that a more dignified but equally enterprising commercial district would attract shoppers downtown. The less-than-monumental recommendations about sidewalk obstacles and utility wires added up to a dramatically new business corridor — as the Montgomery postcard illustrated — and offered a promising formula for urban commerce.

Main Streets, Past and Future

In their beautification campaigns, the women's clubs intended that their transformations of the downtown streetscape would teach civic values, community responsibility for public property, and citizenship. Main Street business interests then made apparent something the municipal housekeepers chose to downplay. Approving of the beautification standards set by the housekeepers, acting in a cooperative manner that the women would have approved of, and prodded by consultants, businesspeople forged a new commercial ideal to advertise and invest in a dignified, managed, simplified retail corridor. Yet the businessmen's and professional planners' participation also altered the civic values and public interest inscribed on Main Street by the housekeepers. Planner Charles Mulford Robinson pointed out that "the business section is the one part of town to which all the residents themselves resort and in which all have a common interest." [77] But investors had more "interest" in the business district than other citizens. Most businesspeople accepted the civic and public values of downtown beautification but advanced their shared economic and property interests at the same time.

Although it has become popular to declare that during the 1910s the City Beautiful lost out to the City Practical in the minds of investors and urban designers, the short-term triumph and the longevity of Main Street beautification ideals demand that city beautification be declared a victor too. The haunting but impractical City Beautiful watercolors may have been dismissed within a few years as extravagant, but Main Street postcards endured. The dignified, cooperative retail corridor envisioned during the Progressive era persisted as a guiding investment concept, modified of course, until urban renewal of the post–World War II era popularized a drastically different solution for a shabby downtown. Americans had turned to demolition as a favored downtown "improvement" technique by the 1950s, and during that same decade the artistically cleaned up Main Street postcard gave way to unforgiving color photography. Even so, the modest, beautified Main Street corridor ideal would return at later points during the century, to animate such programs as Main Street preservation and business improvement districts. The downtown's heyday is more notable for the creation of a compelling and inspirational commercial vision, and for the values and interest groups that created that ideal, than it is for the actual achievement of that beautified streetscape.

As documented in the housekeeping campaigns, postcard transformations, and city plans, most American communities during the downtown's supposed heyday lay somewhere between "beautiful mess" and City Beautiful. On the one hand, commercial standards shifted to judge the existing business district as shabby, ugly, and symbolic of a deeper moral failure of community and citizenship. Through this lens, promoted especially by women's groups, downtown was a mess. On the other hand, beautification offered the potential for reinvigorated civic life and for enhanced economic and property values. As business interests came to prevail in the beautification cause, it is true that civic values were mobilized to advance the economic concerns of downtown investors. Yet their seductive and often successful promotions did not mean that business interests controlled the civic meanings of the commercial district. During the course of the twentieth century, later reformers (such as civil rights demonstrators) were able to manipulate the civic importance of commercial life to negotiate with entrenched business investors and bring people together downtown in ways not dictated by those in power. Protestors in the 1960s used the business district and urban commerce to demand civic improvements of their choosing, teaching lessons of citizenship with the objects of Main Street (such as lunch counters) just as the municipal housekeepers had done.[78]

The gendered nature of Main Street beautification did not disappear when women's activism receded. It was instead transformed, along with the very meaning of the term *City Beautiful.* The 1920s definition of commercial beautification, in which "beauty is described as the new business tool," emphasized a different relationship — indeed a business relationship — between women and Main Street. After the pink-ribbons debates of the 1910s marked the retreat of women as urban designers and beautifiers, women's primary role in Main Street development shifted to that of consumer. Women's consumer activities came to underpin the high value of downtown real estate.

3 "MRS. CONSUMER," "MRS. BROWN AMERICA," AND "MR. CHAIN STORE MAN" ECONOMIC WOMAN AND THE LAWS OF RETAIL

Describing "the Financial Power and Moral Responsibility" of the female financial head of the New York City schools, a 1912 article explained that she "did about twelve million dollars' worth of shopping." Her spending role made this important public official "a kind of magnified housewife." The shopping metaphor cast her economic and political power in a benign light, just as municipal housekeepers had built on nonthreatening female domestic responsibilities. By the 1920s, women controlled national consumer spending. Widely circulated Department of Commerce statistics announced that women spent 85 percent of America's income and helped men spend another 10 percent. One analyst concluded that "the hand that rocks the cradle is the hand that signs the check." This was the hand that determined the fortunes of urban commerce.[1]

This early-twentieth-century description of women shoppers as responsible, powerful, rational, and professional demands closer examination, since a very different public profile of women — as emotional, irrational, even hysterical consumers — prevailed during these years. In 1909 the *New York Times* carried the story "Women Madly Riot at Bargain Sales." One subtitle read, "Hysterical Women Knock Over Counters, Trample Merchandise, and Beat Each Other." The catalyst was a pair of sales at F. W. Woolworth and Adler department stores in Williamsburg, Brooklyn. The crowd, numbering about two thousand and consisting "almost entirely of women," pressed against the stores, lining the street and blocking traffic. Inside, merchandise induced a "destructive scramble among the maddened bargain hunters." Salespeople were "pushed aside like so many puppets." The police intervened. The manager of the Adler store said, "It was the angriest crowd I ever saw."[2]

All female consumers — hysterical bargain hunters as well as rational middle-class matrons — were indeed "magnified" in the eyes of downtown investors in the 1920s. During that decade of accelerating urban growth and multiplying commercial options, consumer decisions about where to shop played an instrumental role in dictating retail geography and the shape of metropolitan areas. Commercial real estate investors — especially the trend-setting chain store executives — became preoccupied with women shoppers because they recognized that women's behavior underpinned not only peak downtown real estate values but also alarming developments such as the apparent decline of small-town Main Streets and the unpredictable scattering of stores throughout city outskirts and residential neighborhoods.

Some women counted more than others to downtown investors. The responsible middle-class housewife, shopping for her entire family, spent more money than either the bargain hunter or the single downtown worker. Increasingly drawn from the suburbs and small towns into larger cities, housewives had more shopping options and were thus not a captive audience for downtown retailers. The housewife seemed to make rational consumer decisions that could be isolated, analyzed, and ultimately, the hope was, anticipated and guided by the use of scientific retail policies. Women from smaller cities and towns, as well as rural districts, figured prominently in these investor calculations, since their consumer choices had such dramatic impact on their home communities during the 1920s. At the same time, these mobile women were contributing to the economic health of larger cities, which accordingly were less a topic of concern.

Although the racial categorization of consumers had more invidious implications than divisions based on marital status or class, racial segregation on Main Street was also part of the larger effort to reorder commercial life amid unsettling changes; it too was an investment practice responding to and directing consumer habits. Under the sway of derogatory racial stereotypes, marketers showed little interest in the decisions of African American consumers, and investors' desire to channel shopping activity crossed over to the coercive and racist practices of segregation. Just as the desires motivating segregation most vividly revealed the 1920s strategies of controlling the consumer, the actions of African American women most vividly illuminated the limits to that control. Organized black women, for example, leveraged their shopping strength to achieve political goals. According to the Detroit Housewives' League, "It is our duty as women controlling 85% of the family budget to unlock through concentrated spending closed doors that Negro youth may have the opportunity to develop and establish businesses in the fields closest to them." The housewives based their shopping decisions on the hiring practices of manufacturers and retailers, hoping to pry open employment opportunities. This was not exactly the use of spending power that chain store executives had in mind when they marveled over women's economic role.[3]

In their efforts to anticipate and orchestrate the trends of urban commerce, investors often confronted consumers' own efforts to define the issues at stake on Main Street — initiatives that sometimes directly contradicted the proclamations of business leadership. This was especially true for the chain stores, which during this decade were striving to cement a central place for themselves simultaneously in retail practices, downtown real estate, and consumer habits. Shopping behavior and the experiences of urban commercial life were always more complex than chain store executives, zoning advocates, or segregationists desired.

Retail Geography Transformed

A number of factors in addition to female spending power converged in the 1920s to focus investor interest on the behavior of women shoppers. During this era of dynamic growth, the retail geography of the city was transformed. Speculators poured money into the purchase and development of land, and loose investments based on inflated expectations were the norm. Enabled by the automobile, families sped up their exodus to the suburbs, while retail and industry staked out new territory at the outskirts as well. Downtown land prices escalated well beyond previous limits. Modern skyscrapers sprouted, and chain store executives snapped up desirable Main Street sites across the nation. By the late 1920s, investors as well as the general public firmly expected (as in the case of Flint, Michigan) that "sites now devoted to business use in the downtown district will be developed with taller buildings." The migration of African Americans from the rural South into southern and northern cities (one-half million moving north between 1916 and 1919, and nearly 1 million more in the 1920s) reconfigured the boundaries and racial composition of many urban neighborhoods and brought new pressures to bear on commercial exchange. The decade's rapid property transactions, together with unpredictable business and residential expansion upward and outward, created demand for investment approaches oriented toward measuring and guiding metropolitan growth.[4]

All of these changes introduced new ambiguities and options into retailers' and shoppers' decisions regarding the future development of downtowns. The automobile and the bus increased shoppers' mobility, which prompted fears about the demise of small-town Main Streets. As chain stores expanded, their efficient, centralized organization threatened independent merchants' security and reconfigured the local dynamics of commerce. Black business districts in African American neighborhoods and downtowns opened up some new possibilities for consumers and entrepreneurs, while segregation limited other choices. Residential suburbanization strengthened the profit potential of neighborhood store centers. At the same time, shop owners in larger cities complained that downtown automobile congestion reduced the center city's appeal. Even as cities drained their surrounding regions of consumer dollars, a few pioneers such as Sears initiated automobile-oriented shopping outside the downtown core.[5]

The growing sophistication of consumers amplified investors' anxieties. Experts observed that a greater style-consciousness had altered the demands of the average American housewife, especially in smaller cities. Women whose lives did not normally lead them into metropolitan circles could now follow the current trends in consumer goods, thanks to the wide reach of movies, advertising, and magazines. If shoppers judged their local selection critically, it had now become easier for them to go elsewhere. Rural women, too, traveled to town regularly to shop on Saturdays, no longer staying at home while men made the excursions. As marketers and retailers adjusted to the newly perceived style sensitivity of white housewives, experts also used style as a marker to relegate African American women to the irrelevant margins of consumption. The stereotypes of black women — wearing second-hand, garish, mismatched, or inexpensive clothing — inherently assumed that they lacked style. Such stereotypes, falsely presuming knowledge of certain shoppers, served as an excuse for failing to see and weigh the real choices black consumers faced.

In recognition of the new consumer initiative and mobility, 1920s commercial real estate investors devised and assembled an array of tools to understand, anticipate, and sometimes control the consumer. Merchants turned to experts in marketing, city planning, economics, and real estate to put retailing decisions on a reassuringly "scientific" basis. Using improved approaches to deciphering shopper behavior, downtown investors could, in theory, make sound decisions and protect their property values.[6] The real estate concept of the *100% district* gained favor as part of the effort to bring security to downtown investment. It referred to the district of peak land values — that investment hot spot stamped with the best guarantee (see fig. 3.1). Commercial real estate atlases began to map 100% districts, which identified the

Figure 3.1 This city planning exhibit in Pasadena presented a three-dimensional map of property values in 1916. The towering pegs marking the "100% district," as well as the reasons for the variations in values, were of great interest to exhibit visitors. During the 1920s these topics also captivated investors, who increasingly recognized the overlap between cities' highest property values and their densest concentrations of female shoppers. (*American City,* October 1916, 374, no. 6827 Pasadena 2, John Nolen Pamphlet Collection, collection no. 6337, Division of Rare and Manuscript Collections, Cornell University Library.)

densest areas of female shopper traffic. The scholarly field of retail geography, particularly Reilly's Law of Retail Gravitation, explained puzzling consumer behavior in terms of rigid economic laws. Investors with more money to spend, such as the chain stores, turned to national consulting firms for market surveys and their customized assessment of consumer decision making.[7]

Whereas the 100% district, Reilly's law, and market surveys were adopted on a purely voluntary basis to measure, conceptualize, and forecast shopper activity, two other popular policies were involuntary and, in the case of segregation, coercive. Land-use zoning sought to anchor existing business districts and control new commercial growth, by designating areas on the city map exclusively for business development. Business zoning, whether for centers or strips, diminished the unpredictable scattering of stores and enforced the higher concentration of retailers found in a streetscape of entrepreneurs. Racial segregation and the consolidation of black business districts also used municipal laws to restrict consumer and merchant decisions in the name of, among other things, investor security and property values. By pushing the outer limits of control, segregation made that campaign for control evident. Despite a few efforts to analyze the "Negro market," stereotypes of the African American consumer were so entrenched that investors saw little need to ascertain the preferences and decisions of black shoppers.

At the core of the geographic transformation of urban commercial life and the efforts to control that transformation lurked the questions of who shopped where and how one could lure the most economically desirable consumer. This chapter explores the unexpected ways in which women's shopping behavior entered into the calculations of commercial real estate values. Beginning in the 1920s, largely owing to chain store leadership, the overlapping marketing, real estate, and retail fields determined that the highest concentrations of women shoppers underpinned peak downtown land values (which themselves were the highest values anywhere). Investors' notions of land value also hinged on how they categorized consumers by race, class, and marital status. Housewives shopping for their entire family promised higher property values than the presence of "flapper" office workers buying only for themselves, and African American consumers were presumed to reduce values.[8]

It has long appeared that only the low economic value placed on the housewife's time made shopping (especially the comparison shopping encouraged downtown) a viable use of her hours. One economist suggested in 1926 that downtown stores remained competitive only because the suburban woman's "time is not worth $100 per hour."[9] Yet from the 1920s through the 1960s, the housewife's unpaid work *was* valued and indeed captured by downtown investors in the form of high real estate prices that depended upon retail success (and thus women shoppers). Her economic importance was evident in the era's magnification of her and her consumer activities.

The old cliché of retail geography — "location, location, location" — was the primary concern of investors as the nation's commercial maps were redrawn during the 1920s. The investment approaches popularized then attempted to anticipate and channel shopper and retailer decisions about the location of commerce. Amid unpredictable metropolitan growth, it was gradually revealed that a central location no longer guaranteed proximity to shoppers. In 1920s urban commercial life, real estate locations increasingly assumed value and significance based more on their relationship to pedestrian traffic than on their geographic centrality. Retail geography mapped the consumer first.[10]

"Feet! Women's Feet!":
The Allure of Pedestrianism and the 100% Location

A key concept for those investing in downtown real estate was "pedestrianism" — identifying the lucrative areas of dense female shopping traffic within the city.[11] On September 11, 1929, counters employed by the Albert Wenzlick Real Estate Company clocked 38,881 women and 8,860 men at a fixed location in downtown St. Louis. Of the pedestrian traffic that day, 81 percent was female. In business districts where a men's and a women's side of the street had evolved, real estate expert Frank Slosson found "a very marked distinction in values, the women's side invariably having a much greater value than the men's side and the establishment[s] catering to women greatly outnumbering those catering to men." Ira Lurie, manager of the chain store department of a prominent real estate company, calculated that properties on the women's side commanded 10 percent higher rentals. "Women's feet," as the writer of real estate atlases put it, would lead the way to profitable retail locations (see fig. 3.2).[12]

The chain store executives and their consultants believed that some general "laws" of human behavior could at least partially explain these variations in urban property values. According to Lurie, retailers knew "that women do not like to cross a thoroughfare thick with traffic." Most also agreed with Mark Levy, a national expert on chain store leasing, who claimed that "of course, the lines catering to women prefer to locate on the shady side of the street. Women like to shop leisurely, or look into the store windows as they pass." Men, "not so particular," preferred shopping "away from the female traffic." Merchants would also be smart to locate on the side of the street where streetcars inbound from wealthy residential areas stopped, since a woman's "instinct" directed her to the closest sidewalk.[13]

Chain stores had a particular affinity for downtown hot spots, often choosing to pay the highest rents or owning properties at these choice locations. From the 1920s through the 1940s, the chains were perceived as trend-setters in efficient, lucrative retailing, and real estate brokers and downtown investors appreciated the boost chains had given to property values. Henry Wolfson, vice president of real estate for F. & W. Grand 5–10–25 Cent Stores, shared trade secrets with the readers of the *National Real Estate Journal*. In

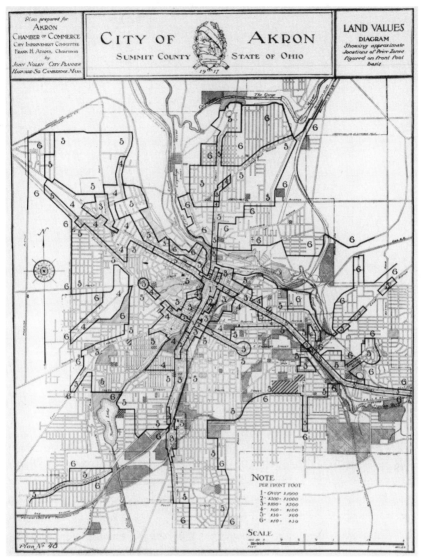

Figure 3.2 Peak downtown land values and rents also appeared clearly on two-dimensional planning maps such as this one of Akron, Ohio. The city's core retail corridor (and thus the presence of women pedestrians) was indicated by the highest rank of 1. Most of Akron's land was assessed at between $10 and $60 per front foot (categories 5 and 6), which explains why the business district values of over $1,000 per front foot were so intriguing to hopeful property owners. (John Nolen, *City Plan for Akron* [Akron: Chamber of Commerce, 1919], 22.)

P-51   Roll Call of Nation's Chain Stores on Washington Street, Phoenix, Arizona

Figure 3.3 By the 1920s chain stores were regarded by real estate and retail experts as the leaders in using the latest scientific techniques to find profitable Main Street locations. The presence of chain stores certified a vital downtown, as in this 1943 postcard. Yet, many consumers and other skeptics feared that the chains had a negative impact on independent stores and drained resources from the local economy. (Courtesy of Lake County [Ill.] Discovery Museum, Curt Teich Postcard Archives.)

a 1929 article, he proposed that "every discussion on chain store real estate must of necessity start with that all-inclusive, somewhat-elusive, much-talked-about, often-guessed-about '100 per cent location.'" Because chain stores analyzed business districts for their 100% locations and lesser spots, other investors in this period looked for the cluster of chain stores to identify the "best" downtown shopping district. The concept of a guaranteed 100% district captured the efforts of investors to find certainty in an unusually volatile real estate market (see figs. 3.3, 3.4).[14]

Beginning in the 1920s, most chains and the real estate agents who served them sought out sites with a "heavy flow of women traffic" and had pedestrians counted to analyze prospective store locations accordingly.[15] Chains "are interested only in women shoppers," proclaimed the author of the article "How to Submit Locations to Chain Store Companies." The nebulous 100% location encompassed the zones of highest pedestrian traffic, rent, profit, and

Figure 3.4 During the 1949 Christmas parade in Lowell, Massachusetts, the downtown streets brimmed over with exceptionally large crowds. The photograph captures how chain variety stores like F. W. Woolworth and S. S. Kresge dominated and defined the "100% location" for most cities. (Courtesy of Lowell National Historical Park; Lowe 5086.)

property value. But even those who quarreled about the definition of the 100% district agreed that the presence of women boosted property values. Mark Levy summarized a few of the definitions of the 100% district. First, he proposed "a definitely circumscribed area in a community where the women do most of the shopping." Second, he defined it as "the business section of a community where the greatest amount of retail trade is transacted." And third, Levy selected "that spot in a community where a merchant can render the greatest service and reap the greatest profit." In concluding, he returned to the central role of women, noting that "all of these definitions are related to one another, and also to the fact that women spend or influence approximately 85% of the family retail trade." Levy argued that "women and retail

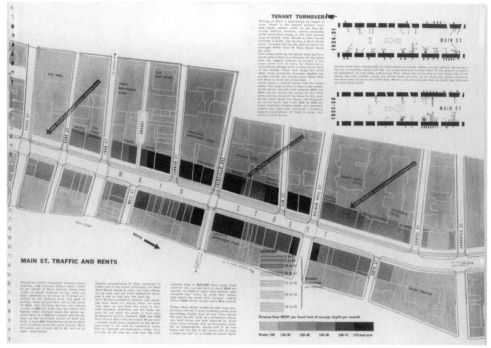

Figure 3.5 This 1939 study of Bridgeport, Connecticut, linked women shoppers with Main Street property values, a relationship that usually remained hidden in discussions of planning, investment, and urban design even as it was widely acknowledged among retail experts and marketing geographers. The Bridgeport article stated that "pedestrian traffic (especially women) means business, and business means higher rents." The thin lines drawn along the sides of Main Street represented the number of "women pedestrians per minute." Counting women downtown was part of the era's preoccupation with understanding shopper behavior and formulating laws in order to predict and control it. ("Main Street, U.S.A.," *Architectural Forum,* February 1939, 79.)

trade are inseparable, and retail trade is the basis upon which one hundred per cent districts are built" (fig. 3.5).[16]

From the late 1920s on, progressive stores scrutinized the character of pedestrian traffic. Different retail specialties seemed to have different peak locations, with some stores depending on certain subsets of women or on men. In the 1920s, for example, United Cigar Stores requested that a consultant count male pedestrians (of all classes). Delbert W. Wenzlick's company was acclaimed for its "most scientific" methods of store location analysis, including the ability to break down with precision the pedestrian stream. Although his firm had initially counted simply men and women, Wenzlick had recently discovered the value of dividing women traffic into two groups: "flapper" and "family shopper." His company's counters had tried tracking four categories: women — family shoppers; women — individual shoppers; men; and African American men and women. But by 1930 they had "abandoned the practice of counting colored people and instead are placing men in two classes." Wenzlick distinguished between executive or professional men on the one hand and clerks, mechanics, and everyone else on the other. When necessary, consultants turned to even more detailed class divisions.[17]

The distinction between the "flapper" and the "family shopper" illuminates how the family shopper — the housewife — usually had priority in the eyes of investors. In the first place, experts argued that the flapper shopped only for herself, whereas the housewife purchased for the entire family. But more important, the presence of downtown employees was largely taken for granted. Wenzlick said of the downtown workers: "We call this traffic 'structural'; it exists by virtue of the physical structures and office buildings in the vicinity. This traffic would exist regardless of retail stores or other ground floor use. It is the same day after day." Because the downtown worker was a captive audience, she did not need to be enticed. Investors valued the flapper's dollar but saw no need to further assess or influence her "structural" behavior. The housewife, in contrast, *chose* whether to shop downtown. Since the housewife's behavior affected retail policy and could in turn be influenced by retail policy, studying her decisions and the accompanying variables took up the bulk of investors' energies.[18]

Although they were serious about their scientific precision, the experts could also have a sense of humor about the pitfalls of pedestrian counting. Lurie described a hapless, exhausted counter, stationed at a New York City intersection at noon, who felt "as if he were standing at the bustling center of the world's population." Only later did he discover that "he had been counting the enormous crowds of foreigners who work in the women's wear factories in that district, and who spend the midday rest hour in parading up and down the street!" On the opposite end of the spectrum, a counter clocked few passersby at what had been regarded as a promising site, only to learn that he was working during a Jewish fast day. According to one "trade yarn," an individual in front of a store in Erie, Pennsylvania, recorded more passersby than the entire city population. It turned out "that he had a nervous disorder, and every time he twitched he registered a customer." Lurie described an applicant at his office who claimed he could keep counts simultaneously in more than ten categories: "men, women, boys, girls, automobiles, street cars, white people, colored people, and foreigners; how many folks looked in the shop windows, how many entered the stores," and so forth. His previous employment — as trap drummer in an orchestra — had required speedy fingers.[19]

Customers, through their daily shopping choices, held the balance of power in determining the downtown's profit center. Lurie cautioned that "even a powerful group of merchants are often unable to change the 100 per cent business district of a city." He pointed out that "anyone in my line of business has to be more than an expert in real-estate values. He has to be a continuously operating laboratory of human nature." "After all," another analyst noted, "value and value changes are products of human behavior." As women's shopping behavior came under particular scrutiny during the 1920s, investors wanted to know who the women were, where they were, and why they were "there" in the first place. Lurie recommended finding out whether women downtown were "strolling for pleasure, hurrying to catch a train, on their way to the theatre, or out on a shopping tour." The president of the People's Drug Store chain disclosed an important tip to the readers of *Printers' Ink:* "The Purpose of Passers-by is More Important Than Mere Numbers in Determining a Site's Potential Value."[20]

National consultants such as Lurie, Levy, Wolfson, and Wenzlick prided themselves on being able to sit in a New York City office and "tell almost instantly" the number of men and women passing a specific street corner in Fort Wayne, Minneapolis, or New Orleans. According to Lurie, "There are about 350 cities in the United States with more than 25,000 inhabitants. No two are exactly alike. Each city, each street, and often each block on the chief business streets is different in some particular. Yet all have the same general characteristics and follow the same laws." Paradoxically, Lurie asserted that national chain store executives "are likely to know the value of locations better than the local merchants." In order to bolster their somewhat self-serving claim of superior expertise, the men in the "business of country-wide store-renting" depended upon what they hoped were universal principles — such as the 100% district or general laws of human behavior.[21] Such laws both reinforced the authority of national consultants and promised security to investors.

Yet many investors needed immediate, detailed information about the peculiarities of blocks, properties, and pedestrian density in distant cities without going through the expense or trouble of hiring consultants. During the 1920s Nirenstein's National Realty Map Company met that demand, beginning to publish a series of atlases mapping the "Preferred Business Real Estate

Locations of the Principal Cities of the United States and Canada." The atlases guided investors to certified "one hundred percent preferred real estate locations," where values were projected based on (largely female) pedestrian traffic. Nirenstein's maps confirmed that location in relation to "crowds" was emerging to be the critical factor in determining commercial real estate values — not "mere expanse" of property or geographic centrality. "As the charts of cartographers through the ages have guided men of imagination, adventure and enterprise to the source of riches in distant lands, so are the Nirenstein Real Estate Atlases designed to point the way for their latter-day counterparts — the merchants and the investors — to the treasures which lie within the golden boundaries of Main Street, U.S.A." The analogy of treasure-hunting in remote lands, though appealing to investors' romantic imagination, probably did not assuage their practical anxieties.[22]

Reilly's Law and the Rational Economic Woman

In 1929 a university-based marketing specialist, William Reilly, offered chain store executives and other retailers a scientific law to explain a disturbing trend: women, it seems, were increasingly shopping out of town, a development that threatened the survival of many small-town Main Streets (even as it boosted the economic health and magnetism of bigger cities). For a half century Reilly's "Law of Retail Gravitation" remained the starting point for marketing geographers, who assumed positions in chain store research departments and advertising firms, as well as in academia.[23] Reilly's work both described the transformed investment climate that retailers wished to understand and laid out solutions. He tapped into the investor desire for security by claiming to base his law of shopping behavior on that most reliable and familiar of scientific principles — the law of gravity.[24]

Reilly observed that "not long ago the retailer was able to conduct a successful business without much knowledge about the consumer." Conventional retail wisdom, according to Reilly, was that "the housewife bought almost all of her merchandise in the city or town in which she lived." She "had less definite ideas about what she wanted" and purchased whatever her hometown merchant offered. He discovered that recently, however, the housewife had developed a new sensitivity to style, as movies, magazines, newspapers, and radio exposed her to the latest fashions. Increased leisure and improved standards of living gave her more time and money to devote to consumption. Simultaneously, the automobile — together with good roads — enabled her to trade farther afield. By the late 1920s, Reilly believed, only the poorest residents did all of their purchasing locally. Because the housewife's behavior had unsettled retailing, she became a subject of scientific study. "Most of the changes which have affected retailing in the last few years," Reilly wrote, "have happened *outside* the four walls of the retail store — in the mind of the consumer."[25]

Reilly based his theorem on a study of hundreds of Texas businesses and consumers, generalizing from this case to explain why women shopped where they did. He interpreted two dimensions of the nation's retail geography. First, he identified the territorial draw of "primary market" cities — those with populations over one hundred thousand that dominated the sale of both style and standardized goods. To do this, Reilly and his assistants obtained the charge account ledgers of leading area stores, produced a composite list of regional customers, and then checked this information against newspaper circulation records. Reilly's second goal was to understand the retail relationships among different-sized cities. His team evaluated merchandise in each community and conducted house-to-house interviews with housewives to measure what percentage of various classes of women shopped out of town.

A key contribution of Reilly's theorem was quantifying the pull that larger cities exerted on small-town shoppers. Reilly posited that people traveled to the most easily accessible, largest retail center. Retail, he explained, gravitated "from smaller to larger cities with striking consistency, in accordance with a definite law of retail gravitation." His simplest nonmathematical expression of the law was that "under normal conditions two cities draw retail trade from a smaller intermediate city or town in direct proportion to some power of the population of these two larger cities and in an inverse proportion to some power of the distance of each of the cities from the smaller intermediate city." The numerical exponents depended upon "the particular combination of retail circumstances" in each case. Reilly included the theorem's mathematical formulas in a short appendix.[26]

Reilly's pathbreaking focus on out-of-town trade and the magnetism of large cities reveals that in the 1920s it was small-town and rural women, rather than big-city dwellers, who were the determining factors in investor assessments of urban commerce. In highlighting this shopping trend, the law validated popular concerns about the threatened demise of the small town. Reilly's Texas sample confirmed that small-town Americans increasingly wanted to partake of metropolitan style, which was generally unavailable in their own communities. Reilly gave the example of Mrs. Jones, who "may be willing to motor 100 miles or more if she thinks she can find a hat that she likes — a hat that her friends at the bridge party have never seen and will admire because it came from a distant and larger city."[27] Many rural women, too, now that their isolation was diminished, were drawn into urban commerce for the first time.[28] This increased participation of rural and small-city women reshaped markets and caused investors to reassess their options.

These assumptions about consumer behavior, summarized in a law, presupposed that consumers followed rational, even quantifiable, economic motives. Shoppers appeared to "gravitate" in reliable patterns toward larger metropolitan areas. The concept embedded here, a bedrock notion for economists, marketing geographers, and others, is "the rational economic man."[29] In Reilly's law, the rational economic man was actually a woman. In fact, as was evident in Reilly's opening paragraph, the rational economic man was a housewife. Given the tendency to see the female consumer as emotional and in fact irrational, Reilly's assumption of women's rational, economic motives is distinctive and revealing. As investors in the 1920s endeavored to understand and guide the female consumer, and as they calculated her behavior in scientific formulas, they were compelled to set aside condescending stereotypes of women's emotional and hysterical behavior.

Although Reilly's research reinforced fears about small-town decline, his law also offered reassurance. Deciphering an underlying economic and geographic logic behind shopper actions made responding to their potential impact on Main Street less formidable. Using Reilly's formula, a merchant could calculate each town's place in the hierarchy of retail centers and could situate his business accordingly. Small towns were not dying, Reilly concluded, although their function was changing. He asserted that "the case of the small-town retailer is by no means a hopeless one if he will adapt his business to the place which he naturally occupies in the distribution system." Reilly singled out chain stores for their successful matching of merchandise selection and city size. In Reilly's authority we see the continued dependence upon out-of-town experts and national laws to explain what was happening on local Main Streets.[30]

Like the 100% districts and the pedestrian counts on which they were based, Reilly's landmark law helped investors make locational decisions by assessing where the housewife wanted to shop. However, Reilly's geographic orientation was different from the 100% district's concentration on a single city: he emphasized the regional retailing tensions between big-city magnet and struggling small town. Notably, Reilly's research did *not* focus on the rivalry between city and suburb, a competition that would not be fully recog-

nized until after World War II. He acknowledged that downtown congestion repelled customers, but it was not significant enough to factor into
his mathematical equation. Later marketing geographers seized upon Reilly's
foresight in mentioning poor downtown conditions at all.[31]

Market Surveys Meet the Consumer Mind

Reilly's law offered investors a quick, universal, and inexpensive way to
estimate shopper behavior, assess potential store locations, and decide where
to place their dollars, but investors with more money might commission a
customized market survey designed to understand the consumer's mind more
precisely. Against the sweeping certainty of 100% districts and Reilly's law,
market surveys opened up tantalizing, personalized views of who shopped
where and why. Market surveys revealed additional complexities of the
consumer mind not only because they were tailored to particular clients, but
more important, they often included excerpts from shopper comments. Surveys confirmed some core investor claims, contradicted others, and raised
consumer issues too messy to be included in neat economic laws.

Rudimentary market research had emerged around the turn of the century, accompanying the increased recognition of advertising's power. By 1905
advertising experts had begun to recommend using questionnaires and collecting statistical information, but only the most sophisticated companies actually undertook market studies. Beginning in the 1910s, advertising agencies
established their own research divisions to carry out surveys and other market investigations, as industry leader J. Walter Thompson Company (JWT
Company) did in 1915. Soon afterward, many chain organizations also opened
research and real estate divisions and generated in-house studies. As industry
experts well understood, those who researched and defined markets often had
the power to create them. By early-twenty-first-century standards, the 1920s
surveys seem crude and inaccurate. A notable 1920s practice, for example, was
to interview friends, relatives, and colleagues rather than to strive for broad
sampling. Nevertheless, these consultants conducted extensive surveys at retail locations, residences, and via mail-in coupons. It is the effort to evaluate
consumer attitudes that is significant here.[32]

In 1926 JWT Company launched an effort to redraw the retail industry's
maps of urban and rural markets when it published the reference volume *Retail Shopping Areas*.[33] The prevailing but illogical practice of collecting marketing statistics by state and county political boundaries had brought the
country's sales force to the point of rebellion, since their sales quotas bore

little relation to actual circumstances. People did not shop according to the limits of their voting districts. Consistent with the observations codified in Reilly's 1929 law, JWT Company reconceptualized markets as having urban centers and tributary areas. The agency's experts divided the United States into 683 "principal shopping centers" and 642 subcenters, effectively creating population clusters around sizable cities. At the core of these markets stood the large department stores; in fact, a city's significance in this hierarchy was determined by the presence of department stores having the widest radius of trade. Goods sold in these cities, *Retail Shopping Areas* recognized, "flowed freely into the suburbs and surrounding country." Small-town markets, in turn, needed to be defined in "relation to their rural, dependent population." This approach emphasized "people as markets rather than as political groups" and, like Reilly, highlighted the increased importance of shoppers from smaller cities and rural areas.[34]

In prioritizing out-of-town trade, JWT Company based its analysis on the practice of comparison shopping — an activity seen during these years as inherently female (partly because of the time required to pursue it). For the items described as shopping goods — such as musical instruments, rugs, furniture, heavy hardware, household equipment, and expensive clothing — retailers expected consumers to visit several stores in order to compare quality and price. One retail expert described in 1924 how "the average woman shops in *three* stores before purchasing. She is therefore attracted to the shopping districts where there is a group of stores to visit."[35] JWT Company's focus on comparison shopping and Reilly's emphasis on housewives' increased sensitivity to style were two mutually reinforcing but distinct concepts that put women at the center of efforts to redefine urban markets in the 1920s.

While the real estate, retail, and marketing industries produced these reassuring but abstract concepts to guide commercial investment, customer surveys allowed 1920s shoppers to explain their views of retail change in the most concrete terms — their mundane purchases, their neighbors, their local businesses, and their cities. In 1927 J. C. Penney hired the JWT Company to conduct customer investigations, and the records of this survey provide insight into a wide array of downtown consumer issues, especially for the smaller cities Americans of that decade eyed with concern.[36]

Consistent with Reilly's conclusions, the J. C. Penney survey subjects were indeed preoccupied with style appeal, out-of-town trade, and the general pressures exerted upon small-city shopping patterns by big-city and chain store competition. But the market surveys also indicate that consumers and corporate retailers made decisions based on other social values in addition to the rational economic values that Reilly outlined in his theorem. Local reactions to the impact of chain stores document that the complex geographies of shopping behavior were not only messier than investor laws proclaimed but also challenged the investors' scientific certainties. We shall see that although chain store men touted how their businesses boosted property values, shoppers responded more critically to the chains' projected impact on Main Street. For consumers, the chain presence seemed to fragment and differentiate the shopping patterns of various social classes in ways that threatened local businesses and signaled overall economic decline.

The July 1928 J. C. Penney study polled more than 1,600 people in four towns ranging in population from 12,000 to 35,000. The investigators selected Auburn, Little Falls, and Rome in New York state and Ashtabula, Ohio. They considered the stores in Ashtabula and Auburn to be successful operations and the other two to be "not so successful." They evaluated five marketing points: the class breakdown of customers, the relative importance of townspeople and farmers among shoppers, the most popular J. C. Penney goods, and the main reasons people were attracted to or resisted the stores. Besides pointed questions to generate answers for those lines of inquiry, the questionnaire provided a blank space for comments.[37]

In the somewhat dry language of survey analysis (especially compared to the customer comments), the investigators summarized their most significant findings. Having divided shoppers into four class categories based on residential areas, the researchers concluded that the two less affluent classes formed the greater part of Penney's trade, but about half of the respondents from tonier neighborhoods sometimes purchased goods there, too. Farmers proved to be more likely than townspeople to be Penney regulars. The most popular lines were piece goods, notions, hosiery, and working clothes. Interviewees who dismissed Penney's primarily cited its narrow selection of mostly inexpensive goods and competitor attractiveness. Other local problems included poor store location and appearance, weak business conditions, the pull of big cities on wealthier customers, and men's reluctance to buy clothing where women could watch. Satisfied shoppers credited low prices, value and quality for money paid, and the courtesy of clerks as the main attractions. The survey indicated that although women were the primary consumers, men in these towns did significant purchasing.[38]

The simplifying nature of survey analysis glossed over the subtleties of consumer opinions, but in their excerpted comments, shoppers revealed how they experienced and attached meaning to the retail changes of the 1920s — particularly chain store competition, style appeal, and small-town decline. Shopping behavior followed preferences guided by local social and economic customs, including family relations, prejudice, and class identification. According to these factors, individual shoppers judged who would go to a particular store and why and assessed where they themselves would feel comfortable. As they disclosed their decision making to investigators, it became clear that their reasoning, though certainly logical, entailed considerations that were difficult to quantify. That logic also incorporated vehement antichain sentiment that the JWT Company analysis, and certainly the chain executives, downplayed or ignored.[39]

Interviewees were especially concerned about the draining of local financial resources outside the community. Chain stores, which expanded dramatically in the 1920s, symbolized this threat.[40] Residents believed that chains cut into the business of locally owned stores. According to a Little Falls bus driver, women had once gotten off his bus at Lurie's, a popular local store, and then the Metropolitan 5 and 10, but in recent years J. C. Penney patronage had begun to interfere with these patterns. Many people expressed outright opposition to the chains. One said of them: "It puts local men out of business," and another observed, "They take money away from town." One woman, impressed by the influx of chain stores, wondered "if every store won't be chain soon." A standard motif was expressed when a person commented that these outside entrepreneurs were "taking money away from town and hurting the Rome business people." To some, the chains were "driving out old merchants," who were their relatives, friends, and neighbors. Perhaps most bitterly, one respondent insisted that "they never do anything for Rome — chain stores get the money in Rome and take it out of Rome." The new pattern of commerce ushered in a popular, grassroots understanding of how outside forces shaped local investment. The consumer suspicion of chain stores voiced in these three New York towns is striking given the virtual absence of antichain organizations in that state.[41]

Small-town Main Streets were in fact caught in a double bind: the dollars of frugal consumers leaked out through the chains, while out-of-town shopping siphoned off the dollars of the affluent. Those interviewees who took their trade to cities such as Utica, Rochester, and New York usually agreed on the inadequacy of fashions offered locally. One problem was that "everyone has seen the clothes if you buy here," indicating an elevated awareness of fashion trends and product distinctiveness. "I'm attracted out of town by style factor," said one interviewee; another went "out of town for range of selection and style." Chain variety stores bore the brunt of these criticisms of poor local selection, because "chain stores do not supply you with exclusive styles." The chains were "so standardized — styles copied, and get no originality." Outside purchasing had snob appeal, confirmed by the woman who wanted the "style and social prestige of out-of-town goods."[42]

Critical neighbors linked their city's decline with both chains and out-of-town purchasing: "Wouldn't buy stuff at a chain. That's the trouble with this town, everybody with money spends it outside." Residents commonly identified the town's retail circumstances with its overall present and future prospects. Interviewed customers made comments such as "It's all this town can afford — a low class store." "This town is dead." "Going to get out of this city — it's going to the dogs." "A city like Rome should have better stores." "Rome is afflicted with cheap stores." Interviewees freely discussed their concerns that chain stores were "cheap," which was often extrapolated to disparage the town's broader character. One noted: "Got the impression of cheapness because a chain store."[43]

Some respondents, of course, preferred chains. At least six interviewees appreciated their Penney manager's decision to buy shoes, sweaters, and rubber goods from local mills. Another enthusiast thought that the chain stores would brighten the town's economic future: "Chain stores like Penney will make Ashtabula more prosperous than all the words of the Chamber of Commerce." Others applauded the advantage of "cheapness" for poorer citizens — "Just the store for working people who get the most for their money there." One called Penney "splendid for poor people," and another commented that it was "cheaper and quite reasonable." Many Penney branches were known as the "workingman's" store (although that did not keep wealthier shoppers from patronizing them). Respondents observed that "most of the men working down at the railroad buy their things at Penney's," especially the popular overalls. Members of the managerial classes made comments such as "our hired men buy furnishings there" and "is a popular store with the hands in father's mill."[44]

Consumer attitudes suggested that the intensified chain store presence, by both repelling wealthier consumers and taking thrifty customers from local businesses, had contributed to small-town decline. Wealthier shoppers, with the means to visit larger cities, blamed the chains for diminishing local selection. Those with more limited resources appreciated the chains' greater array of less expensive goods. The link between social prestige, where one shopped, and the product itself was reconfigured to accommodate increasing mobility of the better off and the offerings of chains. Even as class-based patterns of consumption became more distinctive in consumers' minds (and were inscribed upon larger regions), both richer and poorer were guilty in the court of public opinion for drawing money away from local businesses.[45]

Other evidence confirmed this consumer perception that chains had exacerbated class differences in shopping behavior. In an effort to build local contacts in Birmingham, Alabama, New York City broker Dwight Hoopingarner wrote in 1927 to the prominent Birmingham real estate executive Robert Jemison Jr. Hoping that Jemison did not already have his own chain store contacts, Hoopingarner wanted the opportunity to serve as middleman, funneling promising sites from Birmingham to chains like W. T. Grant and McCrory. He assumed that Jemison knew the general requirements of "such people as Grants," but as a courtesy he appended a checklist of what chain stores looked for. Prospective sites, the broker advised, "should be similar as a rule to location of Woolworths and so forth on main street and on womens' [sic] side of street (i.e., dominance of pedestrian traffic composed of women who belong to workingmens' [sic] families and others who do not buy largely from ultra-stylish stores)." The checklist highlighted women's class affiliation and their identity as family shoppers more than their employment status. Perhaps most interesting is the description of chain shoppers as women whose purchasing decisions were *not* driven by style considerations (since they did not shop primarily in "ultra-stylish stores"). The explosive growth of a new kind of store together with improved shopper mobility helped rewrite the class geographies of consumption.[46]

Even as chains and out-of-town trade seemed to hurt local stores, the JWT Company investigators observed an increased flow of customers *into* towns from the surrounding countryside. Particularly dramatic was the case of Little Falls. Many there believed that dairy farmers from the region had kept the local stores alive. In town, factory workers were laid off when the Phoenix Knitting Mills moved south. A taxi driver, a newspaper executive, and immigrant workers described local "depression" conditions to interviewers. Yet the dairy farmers (primarily concerned with cheese production) had prospered. The Penney branch claimed that these farmers "and people from outlying towns have saved the day for their store," providing about 60 percent of the store's sales volume. Bus drivers noted the popularity of their Saturday routes for rural shoppers heading downtown, with one supporter insisting that "everybody goes down Saturday P.M. to Little Falls." The Saturday shopping routine for prosperous rural patrons reinforced the existence of distinct circles traveled by different classes of consumers — circles that nonetheless overlapped.[47]

Women of the professional and business class found that personal friendships and their husbands' professional ties determined their own shopping decisions. Such women either felt pressured to spread business around town to avoid the appearance of favoritism or, alternatively, patronized their husband's clients. They also at times rigidly steered clear of national chains in order to support their peers' businesses, rather than out of (or perhaps in addition to) snobbery toward chain store styles. A sea captain's wife counted as a neighbor and family friend the owner of a local store. She had tried to be loyal, but finding the clerks in his store too "saucy," she began shopping at J. C. Penney. Another woman "trades only with husband's patient who owns other stores." In the same town, a woman whose husband worked in a bank was "supposed to shop" at a specific local store; another woman married to a lawyer traded with his clients. Women married to insurance men claimed similar limitations.[48]

Attitudes toward a store's clerks influenced shopping choices because of the significant role clerks played in making customers "feel at home." One respondent captured this sentiment when she remarked that "clerks are 3/4 of the store." Ashtabula's clerks in particular drew rave reviews for their courtesy; one resident volunteered that her "mother comes in two miles to Penney for the clerks." Some stores, chains or independent, had extended special, remembered favors — obtaining a large size for a boy difficult to fit, for example. An Auburn interviewee revealed that salespeople were not judged purely on courtesy; she found J. C. Penney to be a "wonderful store because of the Protestant clerks." Shops run by Catholics, she added, lacked the "Protestant service." A Penney competitor in Rome had "clerks for each nationality." When the itinerant retail team of Nathan & Goldstein peddled goods in the rural areas of Little Falls, many residents contentedly used their services, but one bitterly stated that "them damn jews come around but I'll be damned if they get none of my business." Apparently the ethnic and religious identity of salespeople repelled some potential consumers as much as it attracted others.[49]

When researchers stopped and spoke with the pedestrians flowing by the traffic counters, the consumer mind proved to be more complicated than Reilly's law and the 100% district allowed — and its implications for investment, profits, and land values were unsettling. While national retailers and real estate experts loudly congratulated each other with the truism that chain stores created peak land values, local consumers expressed other views — that the stores were "cheap," that they contributed to economic decline by drain-ing out financial resources to national corporations, and that they put inde-pendents out of business. In the eyes of many local consumers, the presence of national chains even seemed to diminish local quality and selection, instead of elevating the appeal of Main Street, as chain store promoters insisted and as was evident in the investor concept of the 100% district. The profit value of the chains was clear to investors, but the social and economic value of the chain store to each local community engaged shoppers in heartfelt debate. Nothing highlights the chains' false security better than contrasting the grass-roots debates among shoppers with the words of a chain store real estate vice president: "No one can deny the salutary influence that the chain has had on local real estate. It has established values, it has brought more customers, it has improved property, and has created a healthy competition." An array of factors — few of them purely economic — informed customers' purchasing decisions, as retail was caught in a web of personal and symbolic community relationships.[50]

Zoning against the "Promiscuous Scattering" of Stores

Not all responses to the unsettling developments of 1920s retail geography were so solicitous of the views of consumers, or even of retailers. Land-use zoning, carrying the weight of municipal ordinance, mandated the separation of commercial, residential, and industrial activities and explicitly indicated where each could take place. In the context of retail location decisions, busi-ness zones aided efforts to impose order on an increasingly unmanageable situation. The underlying focus was to enforce the desired density and con-centration of stores, whether this meant tackling downtown congestion, the growth of outlying business centers, the migration of retail outward along streetcar routes, or the scattering of stores into residential neighborhoods. Zoning thus offered hope for both sorting out the problems of older business districts ("Most Shopping Centers Move but It's Different in Detroit") and effectively controlling the shape and growth of new retail development. By anchoring new and future retail centers — literally drawing them on the city map — zoning could take some of the anxiety out of commercial investment, but at the expense of regulating private business location decisions.[51]

The 1920s marked a decade of "phenomenal" growth for zoning. Although planning experts intended that zoning should accompany the broad strategiz-ing of a city plan, zoning quickly attracted independent popular support.[52] Until 1908 city planning reports made no mention of land regulation. By the late 1910s, private homeowners as well as business associations had begun to petition for small protective zones, without any reference to comprehensive plans. Ten years later, in 1927, leading consultant John Nolen observed that zoning had dramatically outstripped planning; three times the number of cities that possessed plans had passed zoning ordinances.[53]

Zoning specialists sought to correct urban disorder, believing that scientific organization was possible with encouragement from land regulations. To them, land utilization appeared "to be without rhyme or reason, a confused and baffling welter of anomalies and paradoxes." In New York City, for example, poor people lived in slums on high-priced land convenient to the business district. Nearly a half million workers labored in factories at the heart of commercial Manhattan. And "on patrician Fifth Avenue, Tiffany and Woolworth, cheek by jowl, offer jewels and jimcracks from substantially identical sites." Overall, "the assignment of the land to the various uses seems to the superficial observer to have been made by the Mad Hatter at Alice's tea party." To such zoning advocates, New York's land use "outrages one's sense of order. Everything seems misplaced. One yearns to rearrange the hodgepodge and to put things where they belong."[54]

Zoning had the potential "to bring order out of chaos in city development." As another expert put it, "zoning means the substitution of an economic, scientific, efficient community program of city building for wasteful inefficient haphazard growth."[55] This sensibility of order relied upon segregation to readjust the relationship between people and places, not only consolidating like uses of land (such as for business) but where possible separating the sites selling jewels from the sites selling jimcracks. As we shall see, some communities used zoning to create racially and ethnically homogeneous districts, too.[56] Advocates legally justified all land-use segregation on the basis of the state's police power to protect public health, safety, and welfare, but they also pledged that zoning would contribute to the prosperity and convenience of the citizenry, protect land values, and infuse city-building with "common sense and fairness."[57]

Zoning advocates shared a pressing desire to rearrange a city as one would rearrange a living room. In fact, domestic analogies helped rationalize zoning to the public. "A Zoning Primer" prepared for Secretary of Commerce Herbert Hoover implored, "We know what to think of a household in which an undisciplined daughter makes fudge in the parlor, in which her sister leaves soiled clothes soaking in the bathtub, while father throws his muddy shoes on the stairs, and little Johnny makes beautiful mud pies on the front steps." Zoning would eventually correct "this stupid, wasteful jumble." The executive secretary of the Zoning Committee of New York City asked, "What would we think of a housewife who insisted on keeping her gas range in the parlor and her piano in the kitchen?"[58]

The separation of land uses based on models of good housekeeping was one among several of zoning's gendered appeals. As described by Edward M. Bassett, keeping "stores on business streets and residences on residence streets" made both street types more attractive and preserved rental values. Streets with "solid business" had greater chances of success because "women prefer to do their marketing on a street having many stores." Furthermore, when stores clustered together, women only had to walk a few minutes from their home to the nearest business street.[59] Zoning upheld the density of the Main Street ideal by encouraging the "solid business" street and underpinned it with assumptions about women's shopping preferences.

Using deliberate decentralization, zoning experts hoped to control and focus a process already under way, in order to enhance the natural dominance of retailers in the downtown core. According to economist Robert Haig, in the competition for popular downtown space, retailers had a strong claim on the high rents and easy accessibility and had demonstrated less inclination to leave than, say, manufacturers. Even though suburban stores offered competition, Haig remained confident that the downtown department store, depending on moderate- and low-income female shoppers, had an unbeatable assortment of goods and thrived on congestion.[60]

An influential minority was less sanguine about the vulnerability of downtown retailers in the 1920s. Developer J. C. Nichols believed that congestion would in fact soon weaken downtown property values, despite efforts to widen streets, create new arteries, and provide parking garages.[61] Nichols also had reason to understand the threat that outlying retail posed to downtowns. In the early 1920s, he built one of the nation's first planned suburban shopping centers — Country Club Plaza — four miles south of downtown Kansas City, Missouri. Sears, Roebuck, and Company also pioneered systematic retail investment outside of central business districts.[62] Constructing its first retail outlets, Sears chose locations one mile from city centers. Like Nichols, Sears president Robert E. Wood had evaluated big-city automobile congestion and shopper inconvenience and predicted the declining centrality of the downtown. According to Wood, Sears' freestanding stores with parking lots were "a source of great amusement and wonderment to the department store world" in the 1920s.[63]

Although systematic investment in outlying retail as practiced by Sears and J. C. Nichols generated some concern, it was the *unplanned,* so-called promiscuous scattering of retail stores that most provoked zoning advocates (see fig. 3.6). The haphazard arrival of stores in residential neighborhoods left property owners guessing whether businesses would soon run rampant and ruin the existing character of the street. Would homeowners cash in on the higher values of business property? Random business brought the problems of "wagon deliveries, noise, litter and increased fire risk." To contain this type of unpredictable commercial growth, by the late 1910s planners promoted the designation of decentralized neighborhood store centers and zoned many miles of streetcar thoroughfares for business. Through these strategies, business zoning enforced new retailing patterns — outlying strips and enlarged neighborhood centers. The belief that it was "the natural law of city growth" for retail to seek "locations on main thoroughfares, especially at or near their intersection" further reassured investors.[64]

Given the irregular concentrations of most business development, the evenly spaced locations projected for 1920s neighborhood business centers were indeed planner dreams unfolding on a map (see fig. 3.7). For Flint, Michigan, in 1920 planner John Nolen explained that as the city's population (and auto industry) had expanded, stores were scattering along major avenues and clustering near factories. Nolen's zoning map proposed a network of widely distributed, neatly contained business districts serving neighborhoods. The fact that the new business centers would grow around strategic street intersections as well as emerging store clusters indicated how planners expected to channel naturally evolving land uses. For Lancaster, Pennsylvania, in 1929 Nolen chose "logical places" for the five new business zones he located at even intervals from one-half mile to two miles from the congested heart of the city. The business centers at issue contained up to about twenty stores catering to the nearby residents' daily needs. They did not offer the "style" goods found in downtown stores, nor did their appearance yet break with the street-oriented commercial blocks popularized on Main Street.[65]

Zoning for business along major streets ("strips") was enormously popular for much of the 1920s but lost supporters as it became clear that the technique often depressed rather than boosted land values. Bartholomew's 1920 plan for Hamilton, Ohio, stressed the goal of directing "future growth along scientific and orderly lines," and indeed nearly all of his proposed commercial

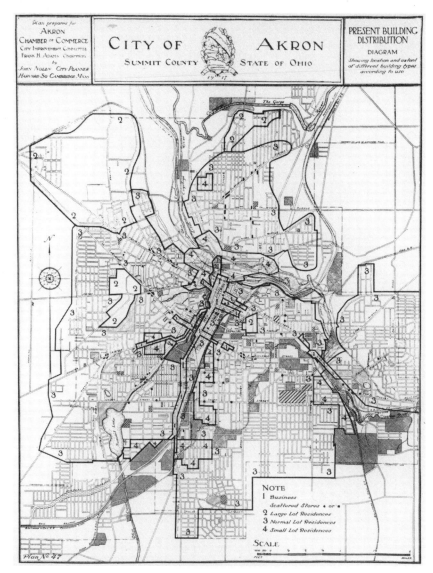

Figure 3.6 Stores were popping up unpredictably (some said "promiscuously") outside of primary business districts, provoking city officials and planners to use zoning to control commercial development. Scattered stores were indicated on this Akron map by small dots and squares. (John Nolen, *City Plan for Akron* [Akron: Chamber of Commerce, 1919], 20.)

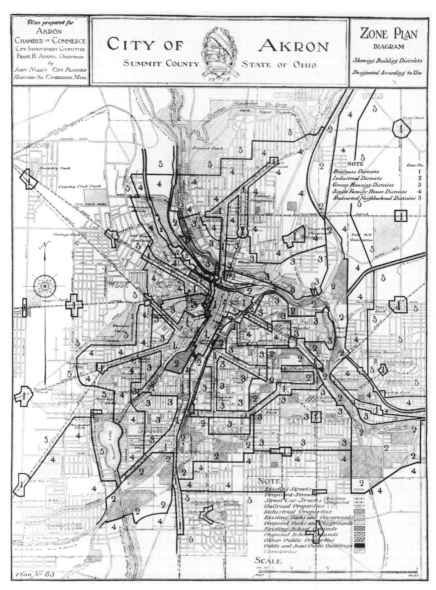

Figure 3.7 In order to contain retail location and prevent stores' random proliferation, John Nolen's zoning plan for Akron proposed an orderly pattern of new neighborhood business centers spread at even intervals. Nolen's hope for evenly spaced business centers is especially evident at the periphery of the plan, where his proposed commercial districts (designated by a 1) are often set in undeveloped or lightly settled areas (compare with fig. 3.6). (John Nolen, *City Plan for Akron* [Akron: Chamber of Commerce, 1919], 56.)

zones for Hamiliton were literally linear strips (fig. 3.8). In 1931 Harland Bartholomew explained his turn away from the practice: "It has become increasingly evident that not all frontage on all main thoroughfares, even though
zoned as business, could fully develop as good business property." In 1930, instead of strips, Bartholomew proposed for Knoxville a series of small business
districts arranged at half-mile intervals, extending the neighborhood centers
into undeveloped land.[66]

Invented in order to dictate retail location, enhance land values, and provide investment security, business zoning enjoyed such popularity that overzoning became a problem. Critics complained about speculators who made
quick profits by selling land newly zoned for business because the designation
itself inflated values.[67] The city engineer of Flint, Michigan, raised the issue
with John Nolen. In 1925 the engineer observed that it was "freely" discussed
that "business districts are usually given too much area." Accordingly, "these
so-called business frontages have only been developed to 10% or 25% of their
possibilities and this has resulted in less value at this time than would have
been the case had the property been reasonably restricted [i.e., zoned] to perhaps an apartment house district."[68]

In the 1920s, business zoning stepped in to control store location decisions
and shopper choices, since not all investors voluntarily "pulled together" to
achieve the managed downtown corridor of entrepreneurs made so enticing
in Main Street postcards. Zoning enforced a dense concentration of stores
at a time when businesses were scattering and popping up in places judged to
be detrimental to property values and the health of existing commercial districts. The efforts to prescribe the locations of specific consumers and businesses were based heavily on the belief that like uses created value in property,
whereas the mingling of different types of people and the integration of different activities such as shopping, work, and residence destroyed values. The
preference for separating land uses and people that was built into 1920s investment strategies contradicted democratic rhetoric about the open nature of
urban commercial life.[69] The era's most extreme attempt at controlling the pa-
rameters of urban commerce by dividing and dictating to shoppers and entrepreneurs was racial segregation.

Segregation and the Racial Boundaries of Urban Commerce

The unregulated movement of African Americans particularly troubled
many white city leaders and investors during the 1920s, a decade marked by
the "Great Migration" of blacks from the rural South into southern cities and

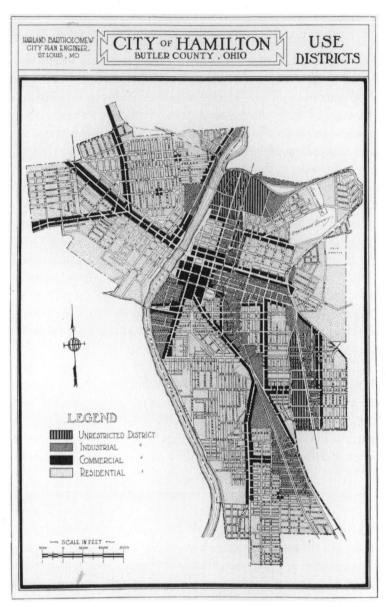

Figure 3.8 Harland Bartholomew, in his 1920 plan for Hamilton, Ohio, relied upon business strip zoning (depicted by solid black) to control the scattering of stores. Later in the decade he and others turned away from this strategy because mounting evidence suggested that its overuse failed to concentrate business and that strip zoning undermined rather than supported property values. As a technique for guiding business development, zoning constrained investors, not only consumer choices. (Harland Bartholomew, *City Plan of Hamilton Ohio* [Hamilton, OH: Chamber of Commerce, 1920], 48.)

from the southern regions into northern cities. The mobility of African American consumers, together with perceptions of their style sensibilities, took on distinctive connotations at a time when their decisions were setting into motion uniquely threatening and "undesirable" types of urban growth. Responding to these changes, a 1929 plan for Little Rock, Arkansas, recommended "the gradual establishment of [racial] districts which will be permanent in character, and which will protect both the white and negro populations in their development, and stop haphazard and undesirable growth throughout the city." The links people made between black consumer activity and the achievement of *upward* mobility and higher social status meant that the increasing mobility of African Americans was met and constrained by the boundaries of segregation.[70]

The search for securely "permanent" racial boundaries prompted numerous cities to employ the "legal compulsion" of zoning to create and enforce race-restricted districts. That practice, called racial zoning, was declared unconstitutional by the Supreme Court in 1917, but this ruling did not keep stubborn, mostly southern communities from continuing to enact the ordinances.[71] Although racial zoning represented the most dramatic effort to contain African American movement, far more pervasive in the nation were the less overt practices of segregation embedded in other municipal ordinances and daily traditions. A 1929 planning report for Houston, Texas, suggested that since "segregation by zoning has been proven unconstitutional, therefore the best method is by mutual agreement." In commercial life, "mutual agreement" meant the creation and consolidation of black business districts, as well as the segregation of Main Street shopping. These lines drawn by so-called mutual agreement were created to explicitly protect, among other things, property values.[72]

As a business practice, segregation pushed the outer limits of controlling the participants in urban commerce, but still it illuminates how the interactions among investors and consumers shaped urban form and commercial experiences. Whereas the average white downtown shopper had no idea that chain store investors tracked her activities so closely, the average African American was forced to make consumer choices every day which were obviously constrained by racial considerations. The pressing questions driving market surveys and Reilly's law also informed segregation — where to locate stores, where to shop and what meaning was attached to that decision, and what impact these choices had on land values — all under circumstances of unpredictable growth. Yet these questions, along with the key investment concepts of consumer mobility and style, were infused with additional social and economic meanings because of segregation's racial basis.[73]

In the 1920s and 1930s, the majority of real estate interests (from builders and real estate agents to academics and appraisers) firmly believed that the presence of African Americans and any kind of racial mixing depreciated property values. During these years, writers focused on the danger of what they called "infiltration" and "invasion," as well as the significance of race-based behavioral differences that supposedly influenced the ways land was used and valued. Only in the 1940s did a few professionals begin to challenge in print the prevailing "sweeping and unqualified predictions" that racial change inevitably brought values down. Looking back at the 1930s, then, one Federal Housing Administration appraiser stated bluntly that "it was commonly believed by all that the presence of Negroes or other minorities in a neighborhood was a serious value-destroying influence."[74] In investment thinking, whereas white housewife-shoppers drove peak values up, African Americans depressed values.

In commercial life, segregation potentially offered sufficient control over consumer behavior to reassure investors. Influential real estate consultant Frederick Babcock insisted that property value decline "can be partially avoided by segregation and this device has always been in common usage in the South where white and negro populations have been separated." Probably the majority of white Americans would have agreed with the conclusion of a 1932 presidential commission that "the most direct and usually the most effective argument in support of segregation is that Negroes depreciate property values." The very concept of an enforced black business district implied a new permanence for black businesses, which often had a migratory history of temporary locations.[75] The economic rationale for segregation underscored that Main Street value was not determined by some abstract economic calculus. Rather, value was defined by controlling the whereabouts of consumers and entrepreneurs. Figures 3.9 and 3.10 illustrate such efforts made by the city of Houston, Texas.

Segregation and the rise of black business districts fundamentally reshaped the shopping choices of African Americans and the location decisions of black-owned businesses and any enterprise catering to African Americans. Some familiar commercial practices ceased to be viable, while other new opportunities opened up. At first glance, the sharply drawn color lines implied that whites patronized the white shopping district and blacks established businesses and shopped in the Negro business district (or on white Main

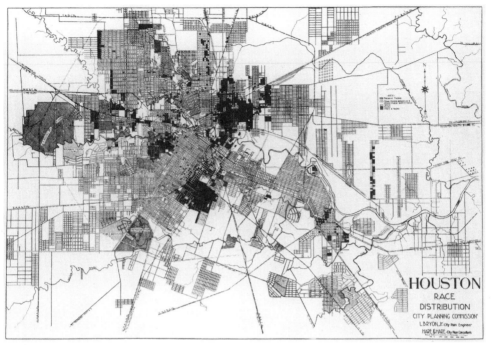

Figure 3.9 The mobility and growth of urban African American populations generated anxieties for businesspeople, planners, and city officials and resulted in extreme measures such as racial zoning for controlling urban commercial life and preserving property values. Although zoning by racial groups was declared unconstitutional by the Supreme Court in 1917, planners experimented with other ways to enforce racial districts. This 1929 "Race Distribution" map of Houston shows that the city had racially mixed areas (indicated as "white & negro" in the key) as well as concentrations of black residences. The city's three densest "negro colonies" surrounded the downtown. (Hare & Hare, *Report of the City Planning Commission, Houston, Texas* [Houston: Forum of Civics, 1929], 26.)

Street under restricted circumstances). Indeed, clear-cut racial separation was often the declared intent of segregationists, but in practice the racial geographies of urban commercial life were ambiguous and laden with various meanings and values. Partly this complexity was evident in the often integrated character of urban shopping, as historian Grace Hale has eloquently argued. But other factors influenced racial retail geographies: the politics of patronizing black or white businesses, violence as a force guiding business decisions, and the fact that the rate of business ownership by blacks on "Negro Main Street" varied greatly. There was also the tension the emergent black business

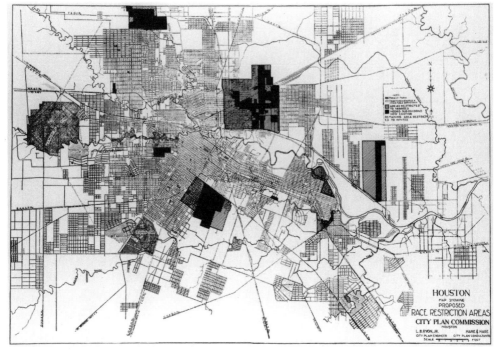

Figure 3.10 In "Proposed Race Restriction Areas," Houston's consultants drew sharp boundaries around black neighborhoods, cleared black residents from the areas west of the downtown, and eliminated mixed neighborhoods. Outside of the tightly bounded "areas restricted to negroes," Houston would be "restricted to whites." In practice, however, the lines in commercial life could not be sharp like those drawn on planning maps. (Hare & Hare, *Report of the City Planning Commission, Houston, Texas* [Houston: Forum of Civics, 1929], 27.)

districts faced between their potential for uniting blacks in commercial success and the ease with which the districts were marginalized and dismissed as places of illegitimate consumption.[76] The sharp lines drawn by segregationists shared some of the illusions of control over urban form and commercial practices employed by the postcard artists as they carried out their own "improvement" designs.

Negotiating Racial Values between the Lines

In the 1920s, according to sociologist Wilmoth Carter, "Negro main street had become a fixed institution in the city." This was true in Raleigh, North Carolina, where Carter's study was based, but she also argued that the Negro

Main Street was "generic, universal, and typical in American culture."[77] Of course, regional distinctions affected contemporaries powerfully. Traveling south to investigate the color line after the deadly 1906 Atlanta race riots, northerner Ray Stannard Baker was taken aback when he spotted a black-owned shoe store: he "did not know there was such a thing in the country." Consumer experiences varied by region as well; in the North black women had more freedom in the 1920s to try on goods in downtown shops, while in small southern towns, blacks were often compelled to keep low profiles as consumers, dressing simply and making themselves part of "the background."[78] But others saw the trends toward a national urban black business culture. The Great Migration caused black neighborhoods of the North to "fairly breathe of the [urban] South," according to economist Paul Edwards, especially in consumption patterns. At the annual meetings of newly formed national associations (such as the National Negro Business League and the National Association of Colored Women's Clubs), individuals found inspirational examples and cautionary tales and made useful contacts as national networks grew.[79]

The decisions shaping the location, formation, and clientele of black-owned businesses were framed differently from the parallel choices made by other retailers and investors. In fact, because of extreme legal and illegal compulsions, it is somewhat misleading to discuss the location decisions of black businesses as choices. At the end of the nineteenth century, black-owned businesses were well integrated into downtown areas across the nation, although they often occupied lower-rent basement or upstairs sites. The so-called Negro Main Streets emerged when stores were pushed from their central downtown spots to fringe locations or to sites near black residential areas or institutions like colleges. The burgeoning districts were bolstered by the addition of many brand new businesses, as this era witnessed the proliferation of black enterprise.[80] This clustering was not entirely voluntary. Using wills, deeds, and real estate practices, white building owners avoided leasing downtown properties to blacks.

Even more important in forcing black businesses to move from the downtown was the role of violence against blacks in general and against black businesses in particular. One scholar labeled the 1906 Atlanta riot a "daring commercial crime" because it was fundamentally a resentful white rampage against black-owned businesses and economically successful or influential African Americans. As it discouraged black investment downtown, the violence that held the boundaries of segregation was thus a brutal method for transforming urban retail geography. Fearing for their property and their lives, black proprietors looked elsewhere, and in the case of Atlanta this shift led to the creation of Auburn Avenue as a flourishing black business district during the 1920s. In the context of riots and other daily violence, black business-people and consumers sought a different kind of security from that offered by 100% districts.[81]

The impact of this geographic and economic marginalization for the racial makeup of black business clientele was mixed. For stores, the move away from the downtown core could mean the loss of white customers. The Raleigh study found that prior to World War I, blacks held a near-monopoly in the barbering and restaurant businesses, catering to whites at centrally located downtown sites. By the 1920s, however, the volume of white trade at black-owned downtown enterprises had shrunk significantly while white entrepreneurs had stepped into the vacuum. Also as one might expect, black-owned businesses in a black district near a black residential area might well have a virtually 100 percent black clientele. But black Main Streets located in the central business district could benefit from white pedestrian traffic. Whites walked through Raleigh's black Main Street (East Hargett Street) in the mornings and evenings on their way to and from work. In Atlanta a black-owned bank drew business from the black business street's white proprietors and from whites interested in keeping their financial dealings quiet. And when the bank emerged as one of the few in town to do well during the depression, it attracted even more white customers.[82]

Some locally prominent black businesses tenaciously persisted in the white downtown for decades and retained white customers, despite the pressures of segregation. In the 1950s, Atlanta's remaining downtown black businesses mostly dated to the 1920s. Participants in the National Negro Business League (NNBL) meetings celebrated such achievements, without lessening their pride in black Main Streets. One Florida man declared at the 1915 NNBL convention, "My tailoring business is in the very center of the business district on Main Street." The audience applauded these testimonials heartily.[83]

The pressures exerted against black businesses meant that the choices of African American consumers to patronize white- or black-owned businesses or to shop downtown or in a black business district were weighed as political statements, whether the customer intended that or not. The relationship between black business and black customers was a symbiotic one because of segregation, enriched as well as threatened by fear and hope of mutual dependency. The decision making of black consumers was evaluated according to calculations that differed from those applied to other shoppers. White market researchers essentially ignored black consumers, whereas for black investors the patronage of black-owned businesses affirmed racial pride. Because one's enterprise assumed political and moral value, racial solidarity involved a kind of "pulling together" that crystallized geographically in these new commercial districts. In 1906 Ray Stannard Baker was surprised by this growing "race consciousness" and the tendency for the "new Negro" to urge friends to patronize black professionals and retailers. At the same time, the assertion that African Americans had a moral obligation to support black business was contested and sparked resentments all around.[84] Complaints mounted that black businesses did little to compete for trade, out of the assumption that segregation compelled black consumers, morally and practically, to patronize them.[85]

Although African American businesses banked on the concept of racial solidarity, statistics indicated that African Americans spent only 10, 20, or 30 percent of their shopping dollars at black companies. These disappointing estimates motivated organized black business to systematically study the black consumer and black business practices in the late 1920s.[86] The NNBL in 1931 enlisted the help of the National Association of Colored Women to send questionnaires to fifteen thousand housewives across the country (though the project was aborted because of the depression). The formation of the national Colored Merchants Association (CMA) in 1929 supported retailers' renewed efforts to woo black shoppers and fight chain competition, through practical assistance with store remodeling and pooled purchasing. Promotional efforts were also directed at women; the Harlem CMA's first newsletter was subtitled "OF SPECIAL INTEREST TO HOUSEWIVES." In fact, even though black women played an active role in the National Negro Business League, the general trend in the black business community was to address women as consumers.[87]

If black shoppers suspected that at times black investors took them for granted, they knew beyond question that (for entirely different reasons) white retailers and marketers neglected them as well. Stereotypes and misconceptions clouded most white retailers' abilities to understand and appeal to black shoppers. Beginning in the mid-1920s, economist Paul Edwards launched several studies of the African American market and endeavored to replace stereotypes with consumer profiles based on fact. Ignorant merchants, Edwards observed, assumed that African Americans simply sought out "cheap" goods, emphasizing "price almost to the exclusion of other selling appeals." Manufacturers, retailers, and advertising agencies considered most blacks "unworthy of any serious consideration on their part." The automatic practice was to assign blacks to the lowest marketing brackets. Downtown executives' lack of knowledge about their own customers struck Edwards as particularly egregious. He found that the higher an executive was in a company hierarchy, the less he knew about "the amount of Negro trade and qualities purchased."[88] Operating with these assumptions, retailers dismissed the preferences of African American consumers as so basic, so obvious, and so cheap that they did not require attention.

Other prevalent stereotypes of black consumers led retailers to believe that African Americans were immune to the style factors revolutionizing retail according to industry standards like Reilly's Law of Retail Gravitation. To Edwards, the executives most likely to peddle stereotypes were those "who claim to know all about the Negro." One prevalent caricature depicted Negroes as miserably poor, "wearing old, misfit, thread-bare garments, with shoes out at the toe or running over at the heel, or as one dressed in extreme and comic pattern with pearl buttons flashing." Poverty would relegate anyone to the margins of marketers' imagination, but it was the presumed ignorance of style, essential to this common racial stereotype, that fully counted black shoppers out of consideration. Furthermore, according to the marketing executives, black women wore hand-me-downs given to them by white benefactors, and if they shopped at all they patronized "Ten Cent Row" at the fringe of downtown, or perhaps the marginal Jewish and black retailers in black business districts.[89] Such establishments were not the ones driving the real estate market or sponsoring expensive marketing surveys.

If anything, the consumption experience of African Americans was more complex than the white customer's — not simpler — because of racial segregation and discrimination. Using one stereotype to dispel another, Edwards claimed that "Negro women, like all women, enjoy shopping." He documented what only a few high-end stores seemed to know: black women, working-class included, spent more time and money at the better downtown stores than white retailers and marketers suspected. Inspecting the credit files of major downtown stores in three southern cities, Edwards found that whereas there were virtually no accounts held by white common laborer families, black families of the same class had opened significant accounts. He confirmed this with thousands of interviews with women and men.[90]

Edwards argued that working-class African American families had greater

sensitivity to style (and purchased higher-end goods) than their white counterparts: "Being great 'window shoppers,' urban Negro women, even of the
common and semi-skilled labor level, keep fairly well abreast of styles and
style changes." Since black women clustered in the dressmaking and seam-
stress trades, it was also logical that they had an elevated and experienced
sense of fashion. The homes of the black business and professional classes
possessed "taste" surprising to white visitors. An analysis of food consumption revealed that laborers' families did not simply buy the cheapest meats but
used "considerable discrimination in . . . meat selections." Edwards claimed
that blacks preferred brand names and standardized chain stores because they
hoped to avoid being cheated by unscrupulous merchants. Buying by brand
implied discriminating taste.[91]

Edwards turned up other details that would potentially interest manufacturers, marketers, and chain stores in black women. Marketers, Edwards
noted, had overlooked the fact that in their employment as domestic workers
and cooks, black women often controlled the food budget in white households as well as their own, and for that reason alone their desires required
consideration. That so many held paying jobs also distinguished them as consumers since they contributed one-quarter of the African Americans' purchasing power and often shopped at night because of their work schedules.
Husbands helped procure food by stopping at stores on their way home from
their own jobs, and children were often called upon to run errands to neighborhood shops.[92]

Within the confines of segregation, Edwards argued, what one bought and
where one shopped were statements of status and respectability. Transacting
business downtown could grant blacks psychological and practical rewards
unavailable elsewhere in white society, especially in the South. For an African
American, "establishing his desirability as a customer of the better stores
of the retail shopping district is another bid for respect. In many instances
he gains great satisfaction merely from the act of buying such an article as
an expensive hat in an exclusive store, regardless of the wisdom of making the
expenditure." A trip downtown could bring respectability and perhaps erode
stereotypes.[93]

Yet black consumers also risked distinctive hazards when they spent money
at white Main Street establishments. Whereas clerks determined whether
shoppers felt at home, according to the J. C. Penney surveys, for black clientele the clerk's reception loomed even larger. Sometimes it was just a matter of

being mocked by a salesperson. One young housewife in Raleigh described how a black woman from the country was waited upon in a white-owned downtown store:

> [The country women] blab, and grin, and twist, and the whites make fun of them and they don't know it. . . . Just last week I was in Dianne Shop and there was a colored woman in there trying on a sack dress. She looked awful in it, but those old white clerks kept telling her how nice she looked, and she kept saying, "At last I've found me a sack I can wear." She really made a fool of herself there and the clerks snickered and laughed to each other but kept on telling her how nice she looked. I just stood there and looked. Colored will let whites put anything off on them.

This middle-class black housewife was simultaneously disgusted with the clerks and embarrassed by the shopper's gullibility and lack of sophistication. The latent hostility harbored by superficially tolerant white salespeople was evident in the comments of a shoe department manager in a large southern store: "I'd rather have Negro than white customers, they are so much easier satisfied. But if one of them ever gets fresh with me, I'll crack him over the head with a chair." Edwards pointed out that the presumed agreeability of black customers was directly related to the fact that they did not "feel altogether at liberty to protest or to return merchandise."[94]

Middle-class status did not protect black consumers from encountering the wrong white clerk at the wrong time. John Dollard recounted an informant's story about a black physician from the North who moved to practice in a southern town. In transacting business at the local drugstore, the doctor forgot local custom and said only "yes" and "no" to the white clerk, who "flew into a rage and bellowed at him, 'Say, nigger, can't you say "Yes, sir"?'" That evening the doctor was kidnapped from his home by "a group of young white men" and beaten severely. He decided to leave town. The circulation of such stories contributed to the black business district's popularity.[95]

The dominant approach to the African American market continued to be neglect, but the preliminary efforts in the 1920s to collect facts about black spending suggested that black consumers defied both the assumptions of white marketing executives and the expectations of black business owners.[96] On the one hand, white investors wrongly worked from stereotypes that cast African Americans as consumers possessing the simplest, cheapest, most purely economic taste. Black businesses, on the other hand, could not count solely on the moral compulsions of segregation to draw black customers in their doors. Although this was evident in the aforementioned patterns of daily consumption, it was even more obvious when black women explicitly politicized their consumer choices. In major cities like New York and Detroit, they organized Housewives' Leagues to pressure companies into hiring young African Americans and helping them get started in business. The leagues demonstrated that moral responsibility indeed informed women's shopping decisions, but not as a blind loyalty to black-owned businesses. Rather, women exerted leverage by collectively withdrawing their patronage from targeted white companies, in order to change racially biased labor practices. It was, according to one conference program, the duty of all black women "to lecture, preach and hammer the doctrine of buying power solidarity into the minds of every Housewife."[97]

Black business districts, then, benefited from the political and moral imperatives of racial solidarity yet also struggled with the handicaps unique to this racial consolidation in urban commerce. The districts possessed what sociologist Wilmoth Carter called the "connective" power to bring together the black community — an enforced cross-class sociability. Often what this meant was that wealthier African Americans, who under nonsegregated circumstances would have numerous shopping and investment options, had their interests largely contained in the black business district. Looking back to the 1920s from the late 1950s, blacks in Raleigh noted the mixed-class nature of East Hargett Street, underscoring the presence of professionals, college students, and the middle classes in general. In the early 1920s, a group of men loitering on the street were likely to be doctors on their lunch break, according to an African American mail carrier. To be sure, not everyone mingled at the same places. In Raleigh, wealthier folks gravitated toward the hotel dining room, while the less well off felt at home in the pool hall. Tensions erupted between city people and the rural patrons who flocked to the city on Saturdays. One maintenance worker — a former "country boy" himself — observed, "You can hardly walk on the street on Saturday afternoon for the country people, and those who drink get all tanked up and knock you and if you say anything to them they want to fight."[98]

Black Main Streets succeeded partly because their investors offered services that black women could not always find on white Main Streets. African American women could never be sure that they were welcome in downtown restrooms and lounges. The black developer of key buildings on Raleigh's East

Hargett Street took extra steps to cater to the needs of rural and urban women, who rewarded him with their patronage:

> I used to notice how hard it was on women when they came to town and had no place to go to a rest room, so I said if ever I built I was going to remedy this. When I built the Lightner Building I had in mind making a nice place for women to go, so I put a rest room in there for them and everybody knew it was there. It didn't hurt my business any, it really made my building quite popular. . . . I really built the Arcade because my wife got tired of me bringing so many of my friends to the house to stay, but there was no place in town for them to stay.[99]

In Raleigh and other cities, women "bent on forays into the general shopping district and elsewhere" met at buildings like the Lightner, where they could also stow packages. All the activity — night and day — at the Lightner building's businesses helped make East Hargett Street a bustling destination.[100]

Although Raleigh's Negro Main Street was considered to be clean and respectable and a safe and convenient harbor for women, most black business districts had to battle with unsavory reputations for illegitimate carousing. The concentration of businesses catering to blacks had the impact of intensifying racial stereotypes and locating them on the map. Whites perceived a distinctiveness to the buildings, merchandise, dress, and demeanor of people in the black business district — and it was not the dignified, magnetic aura of the sought-after Main Street ideal. Instead, the prevalent belief was that the appearance and location of black business signaled lower-quality consumers and lower moral and economic values. The places where blacks shopped, whether on their own Main Streets or on the downtown fringe, were described as more congested and less attractive, with "grotesque sidewalk displays" of "cheap, unbranded merchandise." Dollard believed that blacks, because they presumably inherited "castoff" belongings and "social customs" from whites, were "marked off by a general sort of secondhandedness." Edwards mentioned "the general run-down appearance of everything" in black districts.[101] These comments went beyond municipal housekeeping critiques to conflate the stereotypes of blacks as poor consumers of mostly used goods with the appearances of their places of business.[102]

Black business districts benefited from their concentration of enterprises, but they evoked for white investors a very different concept of centrality from the chain stores' 100% district (itself based on proximity to housewife-pedestrian-shoppers). In contrast, economist Edwards pointed out that the center of black commercial life was "invariably to be found at a thickly popu-lated, fairly central point, frequently fringing upon the least desirable mixed areas of questionable city life." Instead of getting a helpful boost from their density, black business districts faced the opposite challenge of overcom-ing the negative, "questionable" values and associations placed upon their consolidation.[103]

As entrepreneurial opportunities opened up in the emerging business clus-ters catering to African Americans, the investors who stood to gain or lose by the fortunes of black business districts were themselves often white. The per-centage of black ownership on Negro Main Street varied widely by city but was usually low. Even the highest rates of black ownership meant that one out of every two or three businesses was white-owned. Wilmoth Carter traced ownership on East Hargett Street as the balance shifted over time from ma-jority white to majority black: 9 businesses owned by Negroes and 25 by whites in 1900; 8 by Negroes and 22 by whites in 1910; 30 by Negroes and 32 by whites in 1920; and 46 by Negroes and 26 by whites in 1930.[104] Further weak-ening their investment position was the fact that black businesses clustered in low-capital, small-scale enterprises such as groceries, general merchandise, and barbering.[105] And just as black consumers slipped below the radar of most marketing and retail executives because of prevailing stereotypes, black busi-nesses were subject to undercounting both because they were primarily small enterprises and because of a racially biased desire to disregard them. An ex-ample of this blindness is found in a 1927 "Economic Survey" of Lakeland, Florida, undertaken by the Chamber of Commerce. The report surveyed 205 retail establishments, noting that "while there are 101 negro business houses and professional offices these are not included in the list because of the dif-ficulty of securing accurate records."[106]

In the 1920s, the marginalization of black businesses and consumers was a dismissal that reflected, ironically, the centrality of racial geography to the val-ues of urban commerce. Black businesses were squeezed and forced out of downtown, and separate Negro Main Streets came into their own. For those African Americans who continued to shop downtown, Main Street offered prestige rewards but also held potential embarrassment and even danger, because of discriminatory retail practices and segregation codes. Sometimes claiming a street in the central business district, or sometimes sticking close to a black residential area, black commercial districts offered an alternative shopping venue. Though black Main Streets extended possibilities for uniting black communities, they had to battle unsavory reputations, they could not depend upon black patronage, and they contained many white-owned enterprises. African American shoppers, while facing these complicated choices, existed only as a stereotype for most white marketers and Main Street retailers. By the decade's end, a few researchers began to recognize that black shoppers did have "discriminating taste" and money to spend and did patronize downtown establishments — and these experts argued that since black consumers made such complicated choices, they were worthy of open-minded study too. But the prevailing expectation that segregation could control the racial geographies of commercial life and thus maintain property values persisted nonetheless.[107]

Location, Location, Location?

In the twenties, expansive commercial growth upward and outward occurred amid unsettling movements of people. Rural, southern African Americans sought better opportunities in cities, small-town residents felt the pull of urban culture, and a wave of suburbanization brought more middle-class mobility. Laws of human behavior, the guarantee of the 100% district, and Reilly's Law of Retail Gravitation — these all satisfied investors' desires for comforting, rational formulas offering an elusive security. They also all placed women at the center of worrisome changes such as small-town decline and the unpredictable scattering of stores, as well as at the promising peaks of downtown land values. As the links between women's activities and commercial property values became evident (and were highlighted by the cutting-edge chain stores and their consultants), channeling women shoppers and confining commerce became top priorities for investors. These investment approaches (along with customer surveys) varied in the degree to which they investigated or presumed to know the female mind. Yet they were all based on the belief that beneath consumers' apparent fickleness, women were rational economic actors whose reasoning could be tapped in order to anticipate future trends. The compulsions behind zoning and racial segregation were different: they took fewer chances with the independent decision making of consumers. Zoning tried to establish, with varying success, the exact locations and shape of future commercial districts. Segregationists tried to dictate the character of commercial exchange. Segregation's supporters may have failed to enforce zoning laws delineating racial boundaries, but they used other techniques (including violence) that encouraged geographic concentrations of businesses catering to African Americans.

Control of the consumer, like the security of the 100% district, would of course prove to be an illusion. All of the upbeat proclamations of the chain stores could not prevent customers from speculating that the chains were having a negative impact on local businesses. Consumers made their decisions based on many considerations that were difficult for investors to describe, let alone control. The phenomenon of racial solidarity under segregation, though very different from the solidarity of the Main Street ideal, provided a base of political, economic, and moral strength for black businesses and consumers. That was true despite the tendency of even allies to characterize black business districts as places of illegitimate carousing, despite the prevalence of white investment in black business districts, and despite the stereotyping and dismissal of black consumers by mainstream white marketers and retailers. And the limits to control would only become more obvious over time. The Civil Rights movement of the 1950s and 1960s perhaps most explicitly defied boundaries within urban commerce, but in those same decades white suburban housewives would again disturb downtown investors — this time by patronizing outlying shopping centers and, even more ominously, shirking their roles as full-time homemakers and consumers. By the 1970s, the residual appeals by downtown developers to rebuild the urban retail economy based on drawing in suburban housewives sounded unrealistic, outdated, and even desperate.

In the short term, the crisis of the Great Depression unfortunately proved that the 1920s anxieties about stability, predictability, and permanence in land values had been justified. Yet it appeared that the enormous energy expended for the purpose of understanding, anticipating, segregating, and ultimately controlling the consumer (and thereby urban form and commercial investment) was misplaced. Those investors who were primarily concerned in the 1920s about the unpredictable nature of women's independent decision making and the mobility of African Americans should instead have worried about the volatility of the stock market and the overall U.S. economy. When downtown property values collapsed in the 1930s, the cause had little to do with retail geography (although the crisis would have geographic implications). In the 1920s more people might also have questioned the stability of investment strategies like segregation that sought security and defended property values based on the logic of racial discrimination. Values such as these were not worth preserving.

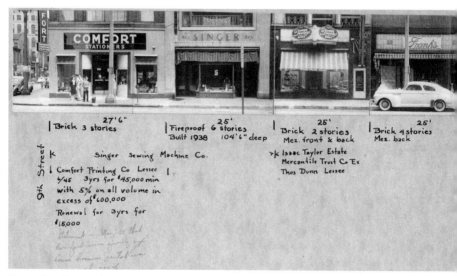

Figure 4.1 Just as these 1940s appraisal photographs took a hard and unforgiving look at downtown St. Louis, investors during the Great Depression reexamined their existing property holdings with new commitment. Recycling and reuse dominated downtown real estate, with demolitions leading to the construction of parking lots and one-story taxpayers and storefront modernization finding widespread support. Instead of the freewheeling horizontal and vertical expansion of the 1920s, investors explored Main Street's interior frontiers. (Courtesy of the Western Historical Manuscript Collection, University of Missouri, St. Louis; Roy Wenzlick Papers, 1882–1981, sl 574, box 5, file 144.)

In August 1932, as America plunged further into economic crisis, an Indianapolis physician wrote to her aunt in Memphis: "You spoke of so many buildings being empty in Memphis. Well, Indianapolis is surely the worst yet. The stores downtown look so empty unless it is for a big month-end sale, and I wonder how some of the little places make it go at all. Every few days another empty store room looms up and more folks are thrown out of work. A man told me yesterday that things were looking better, but I labeled him an op-

timist."[1] With the onset of the Great Depression, contemporaries could not avoid noticing transformations in the familiar downtown streetscape. This woman fixated on the sad aura of "empty" stores and buildings, observing that even those stores that were open for business had an understocked look to them. Other observers worried about the proliferation of vacant land and parking lots. Whereas in the 1920s investors mapped concentrations of women pedestrians and chain stores in order to understand and channel unsettling urban growth, the signature concern of the depression was the accumulation of empty property at the downtown core (see fig. 4.1).[2]

The crash and its aftermath underscored America's transformation from a speculative, dynamic society into a stagnant, contracting society. From the vantage point of later decades, the depression is usually portrayed as a hiatus, an interruption to the otherwise expansive long-term trends of twentieth-century metropolitan growth. Retailers and developers lamented that "neglect had overtaken our cities," with scant growth and few new, significant buildings.[3] According to this view, rents dried up as tenants went bankrupt, and property improvement practically ceased. Memories of the 1920s speculation-driven boom only accentuated the perception that little had happened in Main Street investment during the depression. Important planning ideas — from downtown public buildings and waterfront projects to suburban shopping centers — were incubated but not acted upon.[4]

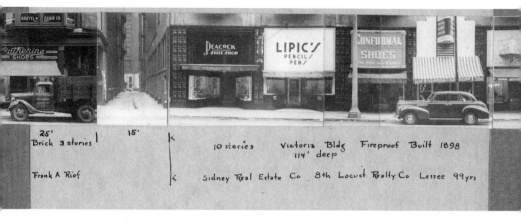

The wartime economy of the 1940s also appeared to have hindered urban development. As in the 1930s, retailers, other downtown executives, and city officials could plan but could not build — this time because wartime mobilization caused shortages of construction material and labor. Government regulations and administrative boards dictated which builders could undertake new construction and which could not. Investors purchased property with an eye toward the possibilities of postwar development, but of necessity, they postponed their plans. It appeared to many forecasters that the withdrawal of military spending would likely weaken the economy, as had happened on the heels of World War I. The question on people's minds was not whether there would be another postwar depression, but how long it would last.[5] The unusual ebb and flow of consumer activity also suggested that "normal" patterns were suspended during depression and war. The depression enforced frugality and disciplined, strategic consumption. During wartime, purchasing increased with elevated incomes, but it was rigidly limited by shortages of consumer goods and the disruptions in family life caused by massive military enlistment. By war's end, Americans chafed under pent-up consumer demand.[6]

Yet, in this apparently noninvesting era, not only was there plenty of investment activity, but also the culture of downtown investment was transformed and reoriented in significant ways. In the 1930s, Main Street improvement shifted to emphasize the reuse and upgrading of urban property — Main Street's "interior frontier" — rather than vertical and horizontal expansion. The crash prompted soul-searching among real estate professionals over the meaning of land value, and it turned a harsh, critical spotlight on the

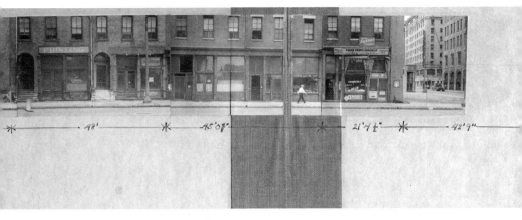

usually behind-the-scene appraisal industry and its methods of assigning value. At the same time, retail analysts were forced to acknowledge the worthlessness of most 1920s investment strategies. Main Street development took a curious turn: many owners demolished structures to put up parking lots or one-story "taxpayers," and storefront modernization was relentlessly hawked as a depression solution. As foreclosed downtown properties rapidly concentrated in the inexperienced hands of banks and insurance companies, and as a wide range of people faced loss and insecurity, a new generation of national real estate consultants emerged, armed with reassuring advice for handling the volatile ups and downs of investment. These depression trends represented not a hiatus but an innovative redefinition of wise investment practices.[7]

Not only did the crippled economy provoke a reorientation of investment philosophy toward the recycling and reuse of downtown land, but demolition and store modernization visibly altered the downtown landscape. Such efforts, undertaken to prevent loss or marginally improve income, seem modest when compared to the speculative outpouring of the 1920s. Nevertheless, they were resourceful strategies with long-term implications for postwar urban reconstruction policies. Given the severity of the situation for people invested in Main Street, and the blame and discredit leveled at real estate professionals, it would have been difficult for these interest groups to sit and wait passively for the crises to pass. Their economic livelihood and professional legitimacy depended upon their aggressive response.

The enormity of the challenge to professionals, together with the energy of the investor reaction, were both captured in this 1933 newspaper headline: "Must Revalue Practically the Entire World: Real Estate Appraisers Have a

Tremendous Task ahead of Them."[8] The headline put a dramatic spin on the day-to-day efforts of the ordinary participants in downtown investment (like appraisers) to "revalue" their approaches. Their work, easily overlooked in the vast dimensions of a volatile crisis, needed a bit of drama to catch people's attention, then as now. This melodramatic presentation was emblematic of depression solutions; it is reminiscent of the modernizers who turned to the luminous colors of structural glass veneers in order to liven up what seemed to be unremarkable and worn storefronts of brick and stone.

Appraisal Undermined: "Must Revalue Practically the Entire World"

The depression's across-the-board slump in land values devastated and confused investors and undermined existing forecasting techniques. Even recently built skyscrapers were demolished for parking lots, and merchants were grateful for any shoppers at all. Average citizens and real estate professionals alike began to ask what created and guaranteed land value in the first place, if it was not the crowd of consumers in the 100% district, tall buildings, zoning, and segregation. The crisis produced a rare moment in which the dominant twentieth-century business values of growth were widely challenged. On the defensive, and sometimes fighting for the survival of their fields, real estate professionals openly acknowledged their mistakes and sought solid ground on which to build their reputations anew. Appraisers were one group among many who faced the battles of their careers during the depression, reluctantly entering the fray as their work supporting the system of investment decisions came to light. Inasmuch as their calculations legitimated the peak values of the 1920s and then suffered the 1930s consequences, the re-

sponse of appraisers to the depression offers a unique window into the reori-entation of real estate culture during crisis. Their transformation is an index of how informed investors came to think about what was valuable and what was worthless in the downtown.[9]

In 1930, in the face of the stock market's initial collapse, those holding significant assets in real estate gloated a little, for theirs seemed to be a wiser investment. Unfortunately, land values took the same nosedive over the next few years. A survey of Chicago's business districts uncovered decreases ranging from 43 percent to 78.5 percent between 1930 and 1935, while a New York City study concluded that assessed values in 1939 had fallen even below those of 1889. Of all property types, downtown business properties endured some of the worst drops. Real estate appraisers glumly reported that "store tenants were in serious difficulty," as at one commercial property on South Halsted Street in Chicago. Rental payments at that building were "hopelessly in de-fault," with gross annual revenue plummeting from $74,400 to $40,500 and then down to $37,500. Everywhere, property managers and landlords lowered rents to the point where they just collected whatever they could. Leases were simply "not holding."[10]

Given the collapse of property values and the breaking of contractual agreements, 1930s investors had little faith in and less need for the supposedly systematic investment concepts and strategies that had been so popular in the 1920s. The appraiser of the Halsted property, for example, was unable to cal-culate an assessment based on rental income. Disappearing rents had under-mined the "income approach" to real estate appraisal, whereby the assessor used the income stream guaranteed by leases to calculate commercial property value. Retail expert Paul Nystrom explained: "Following the crash of 1929 many of the devices and methods that had been introduced into department-store practice during the 1920s were discarded. Indeed, it seemed for a time that most of the technical devices of retailing might, under the difficulties of the economic storm, be thrown overboard." Real estate professionals were forced to closely scrutinize existing methods, particularly those of real estate valuation.[11]

It was not only the isolated fact of collapse that undermined the real estate industry, but also the market's remarkable volatility over three decades, from the 1920s to the 1940s. As a leading figure in the appraisal business explained in 1964, "the prototype situation that may plague or frighten a lender is the tobogganing downhill slump from the boom conditions of 1927–28 to the depressed condition in 1932–34." The twenties boom had been heady, even if later it seemed confusing and irresponsible. Marcel Villanueva described how, in the 1920s, typically one extraordinary Main Street property sale could induce a city assessor to revise the tax base of an entire business district upward. Then came the crash. The era's volatility was a defining experience for the appraisal industry — the worst case scenario that would shape the reconstruction of the business for decades.[12]

As they tried to take lessons from the debacle of 1920s speculation, critics concluded that the false security of that era's zoning policies had helped nourish a fantasy world for investors. Business zoning, one writer explained, was based on expectations for growth and profit "that have no meaning in a world of reality." In practice, business zoning had thrown "great residential areas into the greedy maw of speculation." For the most part, though, blame for destructive speculation fell on the relatively unfettered nature of private decision making rather than on failed policies. The editor of the *American City* detailed what he called the "wild orgies" stimulated by decades of weak land use regulations: "Speculation enticing exploitation; overcrowding embracing underdevelopment; beauty consorting with blight; boom breeding bankruptcy."[13] In the permissive atmosphere created by flimsy government controls, self-interest had carried the real estate market into bed with perverse, multiple partners. Rather than allowing land to be used as "a commodity for exchange, exploitation and speculation," experts in the 1930s struggled to define a responsible investment approach, whereby land was "an essential element in building a decent, livable city."[14]

In order to survive the depression and address the revealed deficiencies of their work, the appraisal field reinvented itself. With a certain amount of hand-wringing and philosophizing, leading appraisers struggled to define key terms such as *land value* or at least recognize where confusion over these terms had tripped them up. They differentiated between subjective and objective analysis, as part of their stated effort to encourage long-term investment instead of speculation. To reassure themselves, their clients, and the public, appraisers began to demand of one another a detailed documentation of city character and projected development — incorporating what might be called a city planning approach into their reports. Values could thus be rooted more firmly in the undisputed facts of urban life rather than the unregulated opinions of individual appraisers. Finally, appraisers overhauled and tightened the profession's required credentials and organized two professional societies as well as a journal. Although real estate appraising had emerged as a distinct career around 1900, it was only in the early thirties that these trappings of professionalism were added. Through professionalization and the restructuring of its practices, appraisers hoped to offer the public "real accomplishments" in real estate stability.[15]

Existing appraisal techniques were revealed to rest on the shaky foundations of guesswork. In 1932 valuation expert Frederick M. Babcock admitted that competent appraising would have lessened the depression's severity and moderated the "speculative orgy" of city development.[16] The early years of the *Appraisal Journal* were filled with often emotion-tinged confessions of various inadequacies. Ivan Thorson wrote in 1936 about "the mental fog surrounding real estate" and the "confused thought regarding real estate values." Blind adherence to tables, charts, and false authorities generally had "resulted in many ridiculous situations, and . . . caused great embarrassment to many good appraisers." The *Appraisal Institute*'s president discussed the "disorganized conditions in appraisal procedure and the many serious errors, and in some cases abuses, that exist and have existed to so large an extent in real estate work." According to Frederick Babcock, the depression had taught "that the ordinary opinion valuation is utterly inadequate as a basis for sound realty promotion and as a guarantee of economic strength"; after all, it was based on mere opinion plus skimpy sales data. He had also observed that appraisers clung inexplicably to the expectation that all land would increase in value. Finally, it did not help that the profession contained "exceedingly few highly trained and competent appraisers."[17]

Babcock increasingly came to believe that the real estate industry's vague concept of value lay at the root of the problem. "We are all familiar," he wrote, "with the semantic morasses which surround definitions of the word 'value.'"

The term suffered both from having too many definitions and from being left undefined. Too often, upon examination, real estate terminology "appears to lack all real meaning." Even the very handbooks designed to clarify appraisal concepts failed. "It is not a help to clear thinking," wrote one authority, "when terms defined in the Terminology Manual run contrary to customary usage and are not subject to a single interpretation."[18] Babcock condemned as "hocus pocus" the standard technique of reconciling the numbers generated by the "three approaches" to value — income stream, replacement costs, and comparable sales. Appraisers had failed to win public confidence, he said, partly because they did not even appear to objectively weigh relevant factors, but instead presented "a biased and prejudiced conclusion." They were often called in at the end point of a real estate deal, where they merely calculated "a preconceived estimate" to facilitate the transaction. According to Babcock, professionals could never "know the 'real' level of values of real estate" but still needed to work out consistent practices for generating values by admittedly arbitrary means. In fact, appraisers should just admit that their "main job is to work hand-in-glove with the lending fraternity in providing a better and more reliable basis for the safe investment of funds."[19]

Babcock declared that new appraisal techniques were needed to accompany the contraction and reorientation of the urban land economy: "We appear to be passing from an era of expansion, during which valuation could not be more than careful guessing, into a period of stabilization and intense reconstruction, during which every device of forecasting and pertinent analysis will be introduced." He implied that appraisers might be forgiven their guessing in the past, since "expansion onto new land" in urban fringe areas had a freewheeling quality. But rearranging existing urban land uses (which properties and districts were devoted to which activities) in hard times required more sophisticated tools. America in the 1930s "may look forward to a long period during which we will consolidate, and redistribute the uses of the land which we have absorbed."[20]

In the aftermath of the 1929 crash, badges of professionalism, as well as detailed mastery of the factors shaping urban development, became essential trappings in revamping appraising to seem more objective. Restructuring professional qualifications had an immediate and obvious impact. About 120 leading appraisers formed the American Institute of Real Estate Appraisers, with the stated objective to "develop an agreement, which does not now exist, as to sound, proper, and reasonably uniform procedure for each of the varied appraisal problems."[21] Appraisers created an elite corps of professionals, who would be certified at different levels depending upon their training, accomplishments, and performance on written and oral exams. The initials MAI after an appraiser's name, standing for "Member American Institute," would indicate the highest certification. In theory, each firm would have a number of MAIs to set the standards for their office colleagues. Ultimately the best of the rank and file would aspire to membership, while all would benefit from the skills and responsibilities shouldered by the elite. This kind of initiative improved morale and provided sorely needed leadership for the real estate field.

In a move designed to remedy the field's deficiencies, professionally trained appraisers accepted the directive to master a vast quantity of facts relevant to the cities where their properties lay. In its new incarnation, appraising turned to the research of more established, usually more scholarly or scientific fields — such as economics, city planning, engineering, architecture, history, and statistics. Historical knowledge, for example, became a confidence-building tool, offering reassuring patterns and statistics. The *Real Estate Analyst* (hereafter referred to as *Analyst*), an investment newsletter created in the depths of the depression, built its reputation by charting the real estate cycles of U.S. history and predicting the exact circumstances of future recovery (see fig. 4.2). Downright inspirational was this January 1934 exhortation: "Become saturated with these facts and you will be surprised at your new enthusiasm and power." After a decade of preoccupation with legitimacy through facts, in 1943 the *Analyst* could at least claim that "perhaps no other profession requires such a broad background of knowledge as that of appraising." Lest one forget the weighty burden carried by the postcrash approach, there was the editor's favorite slogan emblazoned across some *Analyst* publications: "No man has any moral right to substitute opinion for facts."[22]

The new investment approach to appraising required knowledge of what contemporaries called principles of urban growth, a demand that mirrored the elevation of a city planning outlook within real estate generally. City planners' broad urban studies expertise — combining sociological, demographic, political, and economic analysis — seemed the right mix for legitimating claims of objective property estimates.[23] Writing in 1939, one expert needed three long, dense paragraphs to describe what an ordinary appraiser should know to do his job effectively. He began:

It is essential that he know how the city grew; what kinds of people live there; what their racial characteristics are; what their economic status is;

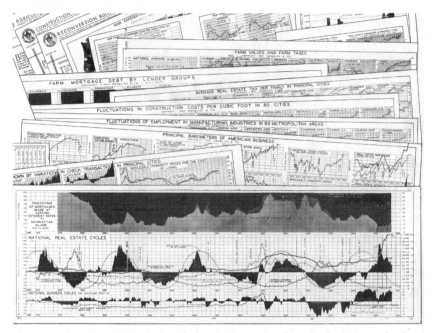

Figure 4.2 The collapse in land values during the depression discredited existing professional practices and techniques relating to real estate. New national consulting firms emerged to guide investors during difficult times. Consultant Roy Wenzlick won fame by using historical charts to predict the timing and circumstances of economic recovery. Wenzlick traced real estate cycles back to 1868, as in this chart, and offered limitless graphs and statistics to substantiate his investment advice to clients and subscribers to his company's newsletter. (Roy Wenzlick & Company brochure, circa 1948. Courtesy of Jim Appel.)

how they earn a living; what the natural geographic advantages of the city are; what railroad and water facilities and other means of transportation are available; into what districts the city is divided (business, residential, industrial, suburbs); what the commercial and industrial enterprises in the city are; what caused the large industries to locate in this territory; what the employment opportunities are; what the financial status of the city government is; what banking facilities are available; how the financial institutions survived the recent crisis; what the trend of taxation is; and what the social pattern is with respect to schools, recreational centers, and other cultural outlets.[24]

The urban studies approach, while requiring an impossible thoroughness, acknowledged that valuation was rooted in and needed to account for broader societal trends.

Depression embarrassments motivated appraisers to distance themselves from their own opinions about land values, encouraging them instead to muster an intimidating and supposedly objective list of facts. Yet opinion was actually the talent appraisers brought to each property. In 1948 Babcock argued that it was time to give up the obsession with gathering statistics. The lender "will boast that he wants 'facts' as opposed to 'opinions,'" but wouldn't it be better to ask the appraiser's professional opinion, Babcock asked. Indeed, by the 1940s close observers had begun to wonder whether all the strenuous professionalization had succeeded in improving appraising. In 1943 clients were asking "whether modern theoretical techniques have been able to produce more consistent results than pre-depression practices," and the answer was usually no.[25]

Despite depression-era pressures for fact-based assessments, the "investment" approach toward real estate still rested upon a consultant's informed *opinion* about human behavior and the future of urban commerce. Five or ten years hence, who did the appraiser think might be frequenting a certain part of town, and with what purpose? What kind of enterprise could succeed on a particular corner? Investors ultimately came back to the understanding that "real estate values depend on the movement and choices of people." The appraisal field, indeed all of property investment, was fundamentally a speculative social enterprise, based on human behavior and projections into the future.[26]

Putting up Parking Lots: The Paradox of Unbuilding Main Street

From the vantage point of their office on the seventeenth floor of the Water Board Building in downtown Detroit, staff members of the City Plan Commission could look out in 1936 and survey the impact of recent building demolitions (fig. 4.3). Holes had opened up in previously dense blocks, and parking lot entrepreneurs had taken over many of these spaces. The nine-story Temple Theater on Monroe Avenue was one landmark the planners had watched crumble. That building, once home to Detroit's most successful vaudeville theater, came down just a little over thirty years after its construction in 1901. The assessed value of the building and its land dropped from $1.097 million to $557,000 between 1927 and 1934. The nearby presence on

Figure 4.3 In 1936, these five downtown views presented a virtual panorama of parking lots when seen from the office windows of Detroit's city planning office. Instead of empty land at the suburban fringe beckoning, the vacant parcels and parking lots clustering at the downtown core were attracting the attention of investors during the depression. The parking lot in the upper left photograph marks the former site of the Temple Theater. (*The Planners' Journal,* September–October 1936, 117. Reprinted with permission from *The Planners' Journal,* copyright 1936 by the American Planning Association.)

Monroe of one of the city's largest department stores had not saved the theater or other once-bustling commercial destinations from the wrecking ball. In downtown Detroit, demolition for parking lots peaked in 1930 by number of buildings destroyed (68), but in 1931 32 buildings of much higher total value came down. Although these statistics made an impression, it was the view from the Water Board Building and the map of downtown parking lots (fig. 4.4) that most shockingly revealed the city's transformation. The picture was similar in cities across the nation. In Bridgeport, Connecticut, by 1939 one could "now park his car where once stood a theater, an ice cream plant, a Turkish bath house, a livery stable, a hotel, the telephone building and a couple of churches."[27] In 1936 there were actually fewer buildings in most cities than in 1929.[28]

While theoretically inclined appraisers and other concerned real estate leaders reexamined their practices and concepts of value, property owners, urban planners, and city officials moved to "attack the problem of preserving and restoring real estate values" on a daily basis. Tearing down buildings was one thing they did to protect or maximize their investment. Investors experimented with and popularized two concrete techniques in particular — demolition for the creation of parking lots and taxpayers (low-rise buildings whose income covered property expenses), and storefront modernization. Such strategies, favoring the reuse and reconstruction of urban land and buildings, were certainly not depression inventions. For decades, developers had aggressively replaced existing buildings with skyscrapers, erected stores on the sites of older commercial or residential structures, and rebuilt in the wake of devastating fires and other catastrophes. Stores had long upgraded their premises (see fig. 4.5).[29] In the 1930s, however, demolition and modernization became the dominant motifs of downtown development. And instead of the ever-taller structures Americans had come to expect, depression demolition produced one-story buildings and parking lots on Main Street.

In 1935 appraiser Walter A. Kuehnle marveled at the "strange phenomenon" downtown-watchers had noted of low-density (even no-density) land uses replacing taller structures, a development he admitted had bizarre implications for land values in the central business district. Yet despite the tendency of his colleagues to describe the growth of parking lots as "chaotic" and "alarming," he argued that "this reversal of the orthodox cycle of development" was deliberate investment policy, not just the random and desperate outcome of economic crisis. The demolitions and one-story replacements were logical, rational depression-era investment strategies based on calculations that could be explained.[30]

"It is indeed rather difficult, at first glance," Kuehnle wrote, "to see the soundness of wrecking a tall building to make way for a two-story building or parking lot." But his close examination of two recent cases unraveled this "Central Business District Paradox" and indeed found sound reasoning of

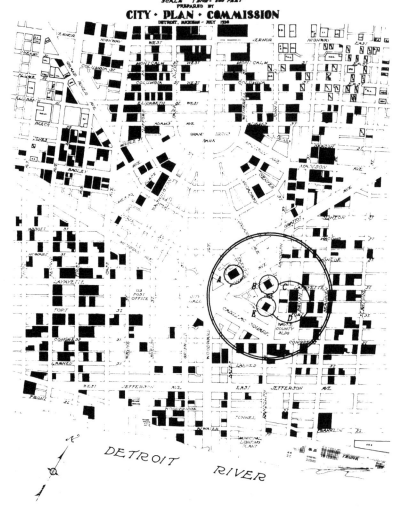

Figure 4.4 A map of Detroit's downtown parking lots revealed the true extent of demolition practices and confirmed that vacant land at the city's core would become a key development issue in the next decades. There is some truth to the view that this empty land, where prominent buildings recently stood, represented stagnation in real estate. However, at the time, the demolitions and parking lots indicated a significant, strategic, and resourceful reorientation of investment logic toward recycling and rebuilding. (*The Planners' Journal*, September–October 1936, 116. Reprinted with permission from *The Planners' Journal*, copyright 1936 by the American Planning Association.)

Figure 4.5 There was, in fact, some new commercial construction downtown during the 1930s besides one-story taxpayers and parking lots. Chain stores in particular took advantage of the decade's inexpensive land and labor costs. In 1938 S. H. Kress & Co. was preparing to erect a much larger store building across the street from its existing Alexandria, Louisiana, location. (Courtesy of the National Building Museum, gift of Genesco, Inc., 1989.13.1.3701.)

which he approved. One owner replaced a six-story store and office building with a two-story walk-up store and loft; another took down a four-story store in favor of a parking lot. It was popular to simply blame high property taxes as the major incentive behind such demolitions, but Kuehnle focused instead on the steady fall in rental income and building occupancy as the depression progressed. Between 1929 and 1933, both structures' effective gross income dropped in half, while occupancy slipped from 91 percent to 76 percent and from 92 percent to 60 percent. In an oversupplied market with "more modern buildings," the buildings had become "economically useless" because they lacked the magnetism to attract tenants and income. An epidemic of economic obsolescence, exacerbated by the depression circumstances, had silently undercut commercial buildings. Demolition, then, was a "stop loss" solution to slow or reverse financial drain. Where a parking lot replaced the four-story store and office building, the owner moved from a net loss of $10,110 to an annual profit of $200. Substituting the two-story store and loft building for the six-story store and office building increased the net income from $5,127 to $27,892 per year.[31]

The demolitions, parking lots, and taxpayers were, above all, practical depression solutions that required setting aside at least temporarily the reigning theories about downtown density and peak values. For example, the investment concept of determining the "highest and best use" for land had come into vogue among appraisers. Interested parties wrestled with how the highest and best use for supposedly prime downtown parcels might be a parking lot. Although the term *highest* did not mean tallest, one could see why even appraisers thought the phrase implied that taller structures would always generate higher values, especially given the recent history of the 1920s. Eventually appraisal practice and theory would have to find a way to accommodate such depression irregularities; guiding concepts would have to be revised in the future once the immediate crisis in urban real estate had passed.[32] In the meantime, investors would just have to keep on believing in the high value of their downtown properties as vacant land and empty stores accumulated around them and the usually comforting, generally accepted laws of appraising and investment were "abruptly" suspended.[33]

By the late 1930s, the real estate industry had accepted the one-story building as the baseline of new downtown construction (see fig. 4.6). Valuator Morris Goldfarb reasoned that in each construction decision his colleagues would have to determine whether the "highest and best use" was a one-story building, or "should it have more than one story?" Goldfarb chose a vivid example from "the very center of the 100 percent shopping area" to understand how an owner after responsible analysis could replace a ten-year-old modern bank building with a one-story-plus-basement retail building. Goldfarb's detailed investigation of the region, city, block, and property convinced him that a retail use should move into this key corner site surrounded by women's specialty shops, but at the same time he was deeply concerned about the problems of extensive vacant upper stories. The building could be refitted to accommodate a store below and offices above, but the appraiser concluded that this would be "economically disastrous" because of heavy competition for office tenants and because of an excessive building tax. Also, the hall stair

Figure 4.6 During the depression, taxpayers even appeared on Park Avenue and Fortieth Street in New York City. Their one- or two-story profiles in dense downtowns emphasized the hopes investors placed in ground-floor retail (and female customers), as well as the problems of renting upper floors. (*Architectural Forum*, July 1933, 86.)

leading to the upper stories occupied critical ground-floor frontage, reducing the chances of attracting a first-class retail tenant.[34]

The 1930s arguments favoring low-profile commercial buildings placed a premium on first-floor retail and thus on the role of women shoppers in protecting or reinvigorating downtown property values. First-floor store leases during these years generally determined an office building's success. Appraiser Cuthbert Reeves highlighted this basic, qualitative distinction between the first floor and all other floors: "Every office building depends upon renting the ground floor store rooms at a sufficient rental to capitalize the land investment and the building up to the second floor. The remaining floors do little more than amortize their cost and pay for service and management." One 1934 appraisal deemed it "uneconomic" to build a retail structure taller than one story, since "generally speaking, the upper stories in that type of improvement do not pay an adequate return on the extra building investment required."[35] Since ground-floor retail generated the main income of a building, and since offices were going empty, why even bother building upper stories?

Concerns about vacant upper stories in commercial buildings were not new, but in the 1930s that information was deployed differently in investment thinking to encourage the demolition of even recently constructed downtown buildings. Although the 1930s faith in low, horizontal structures downtown contrasted sharply with the vertical aspirations of 1920s skyscrapers, it had much in common with another form of 1920s real estate — the business strip developments. Similar arguments about vacant upper floors had fueled that 1920s "vision of a solid line of stores extending down every main thorough-fare or streetcar line," not to mention the development of early shopping centers.[36]

Frederick Babcock chose his words advisedly when in 1932 he wrote that there was "much vacant land (or rather 'ripe' land) in practically all down-town areas." The unsettling proliferation of parking lots, empty stores, and taxpayers in the downtown core signaled ripe opportunity to some investors. The editors at *Architectural Forum* characterized taxpayers as "the cocoons from which tall buildings spring." This analogy underscores the notion that investors engaged in productive, creative work during the depression, while perhaps appearing inactive. The same article cited another observer's hearty approval of the new low buildings "in the heart of New York." This writer wel-comed taxpayers as "the first symptom of returning sense." In them he saw evidence that some investors had faced "the fact that we are not going any-where to prosperity, but must start and build it over again. With two-story buildings, perhaps, at the beginning."[37] This type of deliberate demolition and low-rise construction would likely fertilize new opportunities.

But ripe or *rotten* was the pressing question applied to Main Street prop-erty. "Every American city of 6,000,000 or 6,000 population," *Business Week* announced in 1940, "shows symptoms of identical dry rot at its core." A "cav-ity" seemed to have opened up at the city's "heart." *Nation's Business* an-nounced that "economically speaking, our big cities are rotting at the core." The "depression-induced collapse" revealed, but had not created, the exis-tence of so-called business slums. Deflated property values drew attention to other downtown real estate problems, such as surprisingly high vacancies even in "normal" times, which were characterized as "dry rot." One could hardly rely upon physical appearance alone to identify business slums, one analyst argued, since they usually lacked the obvious poverty, dirt, and fear-some overcrowding of their residential counterparts.[38]

In the growing concentration of vacant land, parking lots, and low-rise buildings in the downtown, then, investors might see either decay or ripe opportunity.[39] Despite the belief held by some that tall buildings would eventually spring forth from the taxpayer "cocoons," many of the nation's foremost land value experts were not so sure. They suspected that after 1920s metropolitan growth, Americans might never again need to construct large numbers of new skyscrapers and subdivisions. Depression circumstances meant that "owners have no idea as to the future use of the property" (as noted in the Detroit parking lot study), in contrast with the brazen 1920s assumptions that anticipated ever-taller buildings at the urban core. This fundamental ambiguity made it especially difficult to rally around a singular, concrete, and compelling vision of future urban commerce.[40]

Modernizing Main Street

During the 1930s, building trade magazines carried alluring illustrations of the colorful glass panels one could use to transform a store's drab brick front. The depression added urgency to the ordinary pressures to upgrade store attractiveness, since in the supercompetitive real estate environment, a modest modernization might keep a business in the black. A popular option involved resurfacing the first-floor facade using a thin sheet of structural glass and redesigning the display windows and signs. Other owners shaved off projecting architectural elements such as bay windows and added smooth facing material like marble to entire buildings, as in the case of one "old" and "outmoded" building in downtown Cleveland.[41] Just as artistic lampposts and trash cans carried moral meaning at the turn of the century, the depression-era modernization campaigns transformed the mundane act of improving a storefront.

Given its focus on storefronts, the modernization movement (like taxpayer construction) underscored the contributions of women shoppers to rebuilding first-floor retail values. Harping on eye appeal and design taste, modernizers capitalized upon the previous decade's preoccupation with women's desires and buyer psychology. Modernization also highlighted the role of architectural style in determining real estate values. In contrast with the cooperative needs of the streetscape of entrepreneurs emphasized at the turn of the century, the competitive depression circumstances in which modernization flourished encouraged attention-getting individual storefront designs.

If you had money, the depression was in fact an excellent time to modernize, since material and labor costs were low. Compared to the plunge in other building construction, store modernization remained relatively steady through both the 1920s boom and the depression lows. Although this upgrading work did follow the contours of the general building cycle, its swings were not so dramatic. To begin with, modernization was far more pervasive than new construction, with the Main Street of Bridgeport, Connecticut, reporting only four new buildings between 1924 and 1938, while virtually all of the shops in the same period claimed to have modernized. During the 1930s the pace of storefront upgrading picked up: *Architectural Forum* identified 1936–38 as the biggest downtown modernization years in Bridgeport's history. Investments as modest as $50 were recorded in Bridgeport, though some had the resources for $10,000 storefront upgrades or comprehensive interior-exterior renovations that cost close to $100,000.[42]

Such consensus prevailed in the various branches of real estate business behind storefront modernization that it was difficult to distinguish between advertisements selling storefront materials and articles in professional journals (see fig. 4.7). Architectural publications, appraisers, government programs, chambers of commerce, and manufacturers all vigorously pushed modernization. The *National Real Estate Journal* featured before-and-after articles with titles such as "Modernizing Increases Rent $267.50 per Month" and "Transforming the Old Store into a Modern Rent Producer." An identical message appeared in advertising copy for structural glass: "From 39% Occupancy to 72% with the Help of Vitrolite." Harland Bartholomew's 1930 plan for Knoxville advised: "The appearance of Gay Street is marred by the prevalence of antiquated and unattractive store fronts. This is a condition that is gradually being rectified, for owners of retail business property are beginning to realize that unattractive store fronts impair the value of property and if they are to be able to meet competition the owners must bring their buildings up to date." For their part, appraisers argued that the failure to modernize might end a structure's economic life, since tenants had so many affordable buildings to choose from. The various promotions appealed to the competitive survival strategies of individual store owners.[43]

The modernizers' preoccupations with shopper psychology, architectural style, and retail competition intersected in a 1935 design contest to "Modernize Main Street," which was sponsored by glass manufacturer Libbey-Owens-Ford (LOF) and conducted by *Architectural Record* magazine. LOF published the winning designs and honorable mentions in *52 Designs to Modernize Main Street with Glass*, hoping to "stimulate the interest and imagination of hundreds of thousands of store owners throughout the country." The chairman

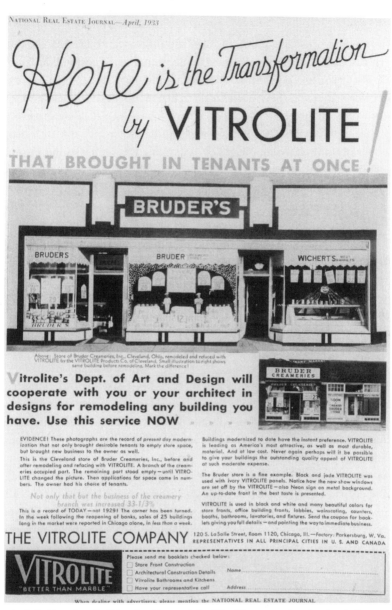

Figure 4.7 According to this advertisement for Vitrolite, a popular structural glass, modernization enabled the owner of a Cleveland building to attract one tenant to fill a vacancy, while the creamery increased its trade by one-third. The text informed readers that these developments were happening in the midst of depression: "This is a record of TODAY — not 1929!" Storefront modernization was small-scale investment compared to the skyscrapers of the 1920s, but under the circumstances it became a cutting-edge improvement strategy for business survival. (*National Real Estate Journal,* April 1933, inside back cover.)

of the jury predicted that modernization expenditures would boost the building trades, though there was no need to mention that the competition's sponsor LOF — which produced Vitrolite structural glass, plate glass, and other storefront materials — obviously stood to benefit disproportionately.[44] Of the allied trades, architecture had taken a hard hit because it was a dispensable luxury in tough times. In 1932 architectural employment sank to less than one-seventh of its 1928 volume. As a result, designers sought modest projects like store modernization, which in robust years they would have disregarded. Three thousand architects and designers submitted entries to the Modernize Main Street competition, and prominent architects were attracted to sit on the competition's jury.[45]

The competition asked designers to apply their skills to the "universal" challenge of upgrading small retail outlets: "The 'Main Street' in every city, town, village or community usually has at least these four stores: the food store, the drug store, the apparel shop and the automotive sales-and-service station." All but the automotive station fit on a typical narrow and long city lot of 25 by 75 feet. The problem stores could hardly have been made to look more unkempt and unappealing (see fig. 4.8). All of the storefronts appeared to be run-down, two of the photographs were crooked, all seemed out of focus, and all had been touched up in a most rudimentary manner. The slights were certainly intentional, since these photographs were reproduced in a premier design magazine. The final publication so marginalized the supposedly antiquated existing storefronts that their photographs appeared to be slipping off the edge of the page.[46]

In contrast, the successful competition submissions would need to satisfy the modern consumer by deploying 1920s consumer research — "all that has been learned in recent years about merchandise display and the buying psychology of the customer." The ordinary Main Street stores should "attract the public, display goods to the best advantage, and provide space, convenience, and light so that purchasing is a pleasure." Driving the belief in the redemptive power of modernization (and the condemnation of old-fashioned store facades) was the confidence that "psychologists have proven that the buyer's resistance is lowered when she is surrounded by an atmosphere which subtly whets that craving for the beautiful."[47] The formulas for attracting women shoppers had of necessity changed in the 1930s, focusing more on drawing in the scarce consumer than on locating the crowds.

The depression indeed forced a reconsideration of what made commercial

Figure 4.8 By manipulating the "before" photographs of older storefronts to make them appear more unattractive, modernization campaigns contributed to the gnawing concern among investors that Main Street was becoming obsolete. This "before" photograph of the Uptown Pharmacist was included in the 1935 Modernize Main Street competition. The fact that the weak image appeared in the design magazine *Architectural Record* confirms that the slights to existing Main Street storefronts were intentional. The participation of architects like Albert Kahn on the competition's jury indicated that during the depression Main Street store upgrades, ordinarily considered to be mundane and unworthy of professional designers, attracted the creative energies of even prominent architects. (*52 Designs to Modernize Main Street with Glass* [Toledo, OH: Libbey-Owens-Ford Glass Co., 1935], 23. Used by permission of Pilkington North America, Inc., and the Ward M. Canaday Center of the University of Toledo Libraries.)

Figure 4.9 Modernization was indeed an individualistic (the municipal housekeepers might have said "selfish") solution to downtown's problems. Little consideration was given to the relationship of a modernized storefront to the building's upper stories, neighboring buildings, and the retail streetscape generally. Structural glass came in a gorgeous array of colors, which entrants in the Modernize Main Street competition used liberally. Lined up on a real Main Street, the competition winners would have looked bizarre next to each other. Ajax Drugs, executed in pink, teal, grey, orange, and beige, earned honorable mention, while Ghaat, which won third prize in the food store category, appeared in pale blue and rust. (*52 Designs to Modernize Main Street with Glass* [Toledo, OH: Libbey-Owens-Ford Glass Co., 1935], 10, 29. Used by permission of Pilkington North America, Inc., and the Ward M. Canaday Center of the University of Toledo Libraries.)

destinations appealing and "beautiful." In praising the streamlined "simplicity" and "dignity" of the winning store designs, the LOF jury emphasized the competitive edge a distinctive modernization might achieve for an individual owner, rather than Main Street's overall effect (fig. 4.9).[48] The jury also admired the architects' unusual and stimulating color selections, as when "the Tropical green Vitrolite suggests the freshness so inviting to the shopper in search of provision." "Striking" designs helped merchants compete and indicated their clever, creative ability to "attract a great deal of attention on any avenue" but "without being bizarre." The city plans of the Progressive era had ignored storefront design, regarding it as a private architectural choice, and the postcards downplayed the advertising message of individual merchants.

Modernizers of the 1930s appreciated harmonizing qualities within each storefront design, not how stores harmonized with the downtown streetscape as a collective and magnetic destination.[49]

As these standards of beauty suggest, modernization as a depression-era investment concept meant the modernization of individual stores, not of Main Street or even of entire buildings. LOF's Modernize Main Street competition, despite its title, ignored the storefront's relationship to the upper stories of its own building, the adjacent businesses, and the Main Street corridor generally. The winning renderings appeared (impossibly) to be of freestanding stores, and the photographs of the original design challenge — the unappealing storefronts — lacked any clues to the commercial context. Neither did competition publications address how Main Street might look with one-story, bright, different-colored glass fronts scattered down the block — pink, next to green and white, next to an older brick structure, and so forth. The individually "simple" and "modern" storefronts transformed the collective Main Street environment into a clashing and complex streetscape. In 1939 *Architectural Forum* critiqued Main Street as a design "problem which has produced many brilliant individual solutions but which put together too often spell[s] chaos."[50] Like the 1930s demolition practices that left gaping holes between buildings, modernization disregarded streetscape unity in the name of economic survival.

Although material deterioration increased throughout downtowns during the depression, it was not the driving force behind the modernization movement, or behind demolition for that matter.[51] Since outdated style translated into weak market appeal, as investment authorities cautioned, even "a modern store building" could stand to be modernized.[52] Rather than purely addressing shabbiness, modernization campaigns encouraged changing preferences in architectural styles — a pressure that was intensified by the competition among downtown businesses to survive and by investor sensitivity to discriminating consumer taste.

The arguments behind depression modernization, like the logic of demolitions, illuminate how the older red brick store buildings so recently showcased in Main Street postcards were devalued during the depression. Koch's bakery in St. Louis had "sparkling, clean" windows and an appetizing display of goods. "But the exterior of the building was old, so old that it suggested the past instead of up-to-dateness." If a store exterior conveyed a "past" sensibility — "an obsolete appearance" — it might spell the building's economic death. "Old style" buildings, modernizers argued, could not compete for "desirable" tenants and buyers with stores that had pleasing, "present-day," modern exteriors.[53]

The popularization of streamlined architectural motifs and modern materials like structural glass crystallized the difference between old and new and enabled the labeling of earlier styles as antiquated. It was, and still is, easy to dismiss modernization as superficial. The act of resurfacing a building or storefront invited this description (*face-lifting* was one term used by contemporaries to describe modernization's effects). But the dramatic transformation of the Masonic Temple building in Oakland, California, demonstrated that the changing sensibilities were not merely a matter of taste; they were firmly tied to property values. Before modernization, the Masonic Temple building (fig. 4.10) "had an almost unbelievable amount of gingerbread and antiquated doo-dads. It is scarcely recognizable as the handsome structure at the right, which is now enhancing rather than depressing the values of commercial property in the older sections of the city."[54] The emerging preference for clean, sleek, flat, planes over the ornamented, gingerbread Victorian profile had enormous implications for Main Street, since most downtown commercial structures sported "antiquated" styles. The average Main Street building in Bridgeport, for example, was fifty years old in 1939.[55] In the modernization campaigns, we see the economic power of obsolescence to motivate the redesign of Main Street real estate.

Appraisers had to scramble to educate themselves about the new building materials and construction techniques (especially advances in heating and

Figure 4.10 Competitive depression circumstances placed additional pressures on investors to consider the impact of architectural style upon property values. The modernization of Oakland's Masonic Temple building removed the "gingerbread" and "antiquated doo-dads" from the original structure (*left*) and boosted the property's value. Modernization in the 1930s was a powerful tool with its own logic for transforming the downtown streetscape. (*National Real Estate Journal,* March 1936, 51.)

cooling and prefabrication). The value distinctions created by older materials such as brick, wood, or marble were well known, but recent innovations in glass, metals, and plastic had injected unknown factors into appraisal calculations. When Roy Wenzlick, editor of the *Real Estate Analyst,* addressed audiences around the country in 1935, he listened to concerns that the pace of obsolescence had accelerated. Experts like Wenzlick tried to reassure property owners that the public was much slower to embrace new materials and architecture than many assumed, yet the sense of quickened obsolescence persisted.[56]

Storefront remodeling put the ordinary retailer at the cutting edge of commercial aesthetics and modernity and linked his needs with those of renowned architects. Colorful structural glass, whether Vitrolite or Carrara Glass, helped define the very notion of modern in the 1930s — the decade of the glass's greatest popularity.[57] Modernization and the glass itself were equally at home, materially and philosophically, on New York's Fifth Avenue and in "smaller cities all over the land." LOF promised that Vitrolite would be "new today, modern tomorrow, beautiful always."[58] Indeed structural glass would be "modern tomorrow," in the sense that in future decades it would be associated with 1930s modern. Modernization would quickly move on to other materials and concepts, leaving colorful structural glass on Main Street storefronts to tell of the aspirations and values of the depression.

A cornerstone of 1930s commercial investment, storefront upgrades empowered owners to take action against further drops in property values and provided critical visual evidence that dollars still flowed to the central business districts. One promotional article claimed of modernization: "Stagnation in building is likewise giving way to activity through the example Realtors set owners in this work." With "little expense," outdated and even vacant store buildings "can be made to stand out from the others and be brought back into the paying class." The flurry around downtown modernization, as around building demolition, permitted real estate interests to discuss "activity" rather than "stagnation." [59]

In 1939 Libbey-Owens-Ford called the new downtown investment priorities "'The Interior Frontier' — the development of American city and town markets through the rejuvenation of old buildings." Less evocative and freewheeling than the suburban frontier or the heights scaled by ever-taller buildings, "The Interior Frontier" nonetheless mapped out new terrain. Suburban growth and skyscrapers had in their favor the fact that "the glamour of new things is irresistible," Harland Bartholomew wrote sympathetically. But given the economic collapse, he, like so many others, reasoned that it would be better to introduce new buildings "into the *older* districts and displace the *older* structures. There is less romance but certainly much more sound sense [in rebuilding]." [60] Most people agreed that parking lots, taxpayers, and storefront veneers lacked "romance" — despite the best efforts of artists in rendering bright, luminous glass facades. But in a decade of severe limitations, modernization and demolition embodied a fundamental shift from speculative metropolitan expansion to the recycling of downtown land and the close examination of opportunities for Main Street reinvestment.

"What Should I Do with Property Now Considered Worthless?": Canny Consultants Give Investment Advice

It is no coincidence that the nation's first two confidential real estate investment newsletters originated during the depression. Most commercial property owners hesitated over the choices at hand, such as wrecking buildings if income dropped or pouring money into modernizing possibly doomed stores. The *Real Estate Analyst,* the creation of Roy Wenzlick and his St. Louis–based consulting firm, began publication in March 1932. A major competitor did not appear until July 1937, when property management expert James Downs Jr. first produced the *Chicago Market Letter,* a monthly investment letter generated initially for the Chicago Real Estate Board. The real estate investor imagined and courted by these newsletters was defined in opposition to the speculator demonized by the crash. Whereas the speculator hoped for quick profit, the investor had a longer time frame and was "interested primarily in value." The concept of the investor legitimated the hope for reliable (even "permanent") values envisioned amid the failures and losses of 1930s real estate.[61]

The emergence of the newsletters underscored several defining characteristics of investment during the depression: a national real estate market unified by disaster, the demand for expert advice especially on that larger scale, and the more responsible identity sought by those involved in real estate. Over time, the newsletters themselves, as well as Wenzlick, Downs, and the firms they created, proved to have staying power. Wenzlick's newsletter, his bestselling 1936 book, and his endless national speaking tours all capitalized on the hunger for information about real estate, and through these venues he delivered advice with optimism and a flair for historical research and statistics. Wenzlick's father, Albert, ran a large and respected St. Louis realty company. After a stint in advertising and research for the *St. Louis Post-Dispatch,* Roy organized a research department for his father's business in 1928. Roy eventually went out on his own, after this research department spun off to become Real Estate Analysts, Inc., in February 1932, and a month later he began publishing the newsletter. One of the first MAIs in the country (though he never did much appraising himself, instead hiring others), Roy also received a Ph.D. in economics in 1942. On his speaking tours, he chatted with "older real estate men" wherever he went — which was one way he kept his finger on the pulse of real estate throughout his career. The newsletter, in its first decade or so, gave residential investment its greatest attention but slowly broadened by the late 1940s to include more commentary on commercial real estate. Publication continued until 1973. Wenzlick claimed that his was the first private organization in the world to accumulate and analyze research on urban real estate and that he was the "first man in the United States engaged exclusively in real estate counseling on a fee basis." In 1936 *Architectural Forum* credited the *Analyst* with being "real estate's leading dope sheet." Although he had a pioneering role in shaping real estate investment as a national field and a consulting profession, it was really his 1936 best-seller *The Coming Boom in Real Estate* that cemented Wenzlick's reputation.[62]

Founded in 1931 as Downs, Mohl, and Company, Jim Downs's firm specialized in property management for insurance companies and banks. Depression foreclosures concentrated property ownership in the hands of these large investors, who needed quick, expert help. Just as Wenzlick was one of the nation's first MAIs and professional real estate consultants, Jim Downs was the first Certified Property Manager, reflecting his early support of that field's professionalization, which was parallel to the developments in appraising. By the early 1940s the company had become Real Estate Research Corporation (RERC), the name it retains today. Whereas Wenzlick's operation depended heavily on appraisal clients, RERC diversified its services to eventually become a larger, more truly national company.[63] By the 1960s RERC had offices in more than ten cities and employed about 22 MAIs and 100 people overall — claiming to have more MAIs than any similar institution. This compared to Wenzlick's staff of 8–10 MAIs. Downs himself published a long-lived text in property management and held high-level public positions in Chicago's redevelopment programs and on federal rent-control boards during World War II. Like the *Analyst*, RERC's *Market Letter* was devoted to encouraging well-grounded real estate investing. The *Market Letter*, however, went beyond general forecasting to recommend buying, selling, or holding specific kinds of property. From its earliest issues, it gave roughly equal coverage to commercial and residential real estate. It never tried to imitate the remarkable statistical and historical depth of Wenzlick's publication.[64]

Although there were differences between the two newsletters, the firms, and their founders, it is the similarities that stand out: the underlying demand for well-researched, synthesized, national real estate investment information, as well as the distinctive confidential newsletter format each founder chose for disseminating advice. The people who knew the two firms best — long-term employees — recognized the essential overlap, which was exemplified by a major exodus from Wenzlick's company to RERC in the early 1960s. RERC's hiring raid attracted Wenzlick's two division heads, Jim Appel and Bill Randall. When Appel joined Wenzlick's firm in 1950, he had worked five years for St. Louis–based city planner Harland Bartholomew. It was a career transition that reinforced the close connection between planning and appraising through shared familiarity with land-use economics and zoning. Wenzlick's other division head, Randall, had been with him since 1937. In 1972 Appel stepped up to become president of RERC ten years after leaving Wenzlick.[65]

When one delves more deeply into these newsletters' audiences, how they were used by clients, and their analysis of downtown prospects, their innovations emerge even more distinctly. Tellingly, both the *Analyst* and the *Market Letter* began as local publications and then evolved to speak to a national market. The *Analyst* took "Saint Louis Edition" off its masthead in August 1934, whereas the *Chicago Market Letter* became the *National Market Letter* in 1946. During the years in which it made the transition, the *Analyst* doggedly raised the question of whether real estate cycles were primarily local or national. Because of its fixed nature, real estate as a commodity seemed chained to local forces. One city, the *Analyst* observed, could not ship surplus buildings to another place facing a shortage. When in his research Wenzlick discovered a 1904 boom in St. Louis real estate, he assumed that it was due to the World's Fair hosted by the city that year. But statistics Wenzlick compiled for other regions indicated a more general upswing, and he revised his logic. As the company accumulated figures on principal U.S. cities, it continued to rethink its views and ultimately concluded that the "basic cycles of real estate" were national. On topics from housing construction to retail sales and marriage rates, the *Analyst* published pages of charts for individual cities, revealing undeniable patterns as well as provocative variations. Without diminishing the importance of local factors, this suggested that the successful investor would have an eye on national trends. By the end of the war, both newsletters had staked their forecasting reputation on interpreting a national market for real estate investors. A geographic analysis done of *Analyst* subscribers in the late 1940s shows that it had achieved national scope in readership, with 860 cities and towns represented overall.[66]

The newsletters' heavyweight clients were those large institutions whose new real estate holdings made them a thirsty market for consultant information. By 1936 the *Analyst* could claim as subscribers "virtually all large banks, mortgage institutions, and insurance companies."[67] The Equitable Life Assurance Society's predicament was typical. During the 1930s, that insurance company acquired 14,500 city properties and 8,000 farms. A history of the firm relates that because of this inundation, "the personnel who had previously been concerned with lending mortgage money were confronted with the formidable task of administering a widespread holding of real estate, a task for which they were totally unprepared." In 1934 Equitable took the step of establishing its own real estate department (including twenty-five field offices) to manage the urban properties. When the *Analyst* examined the history of the life insurance industry's involvement in real estate, it found that the value of real estate owned by insurance companies climbed from $2.2 billion in the mid-1920s to $8.5 billion by 1936. The *Analyst* ran articles on real estate ownership by banks as well, finding, for example, that national banks liquidated depression holdings rapidly, whereas other banks retained these properties longer, hoping for better conditions. Besides banks and insurance companies, other subscribers involved in financing, building, selling, and appraising real estate included "lumber and building material dealers, real estate companies, manufacturers, retailers, security dealers, libraries, government offices and service associations."[68]

Although the initial $180 annual fee set a high bar for *Analyst* subscribers during the depression, Wenzlick could legitimately claim to have advised hundreds of thousands of ordinary people facing urgent decisions about real estate. For one dollar or a trip to the library, an individual investor could consult Wenzlick's 1936 book *The Coming Boom in Real Estate — And What to Do about It,* which carried the basic message of the newsletter (stripped of the complicated charts) and tackled real estate as an *"immediate practical problem."* The first day it was available, 10,000 copies sold out by 3 P.M. The book, which went on to sell 187,000 copies, was condensed for the July 1936 issue of Reader's Digest and garnered great publicity for Wenzlick. Wenzlick's excruciating research, historical view, and monthly tracking of important indicators allowed him to reassure Americans that a boom was around the corner and provide them with specific advice. Some of the thirty-three sample questions he promised to answer: "What Should I Do with Property Now Considered Worthless? What Should I Do If I Now Rent a Store? . . . If I Own a Store in a Good Location? In a Poor Location?" Later, Wenzlick observed that the book's popularity "proved that the public at the time was quite anxious to get any information they could on the real estate situation." Subscriptions to the *Analyst* tripled in the year following *The Coming Boom*'s publication.[69]

While *The Coming Boom in Real Estate* gave Wenzlick a broad audience of individual investors, the newsletters capitalized on confidentiality. Confidentiality, in-depth research, synthesized details from multiple sources, and up-to-date information were some of the qualities distinguishing the newsletters from other investment advice. Beneath the *Market Letter*'s masthead, the first lines announced: "Warning! The value of this letter lies in its being confidential advice as to the actual conditions prevailing in real estate at its date of issue." A private readership could act upon privileged information ahead of the masses. For several years the *Analyst* had advised subscribers to buy real estate because historical cycles indicated recovery in 1936. By the time the average investor read the same advice in *The Coming Boom,* building activity and prices were already rising precipitously. With the book Wenzlick did his part to make the *Analyst*'s predictions come true; this warming-up of Americans' attitudes toward real estate benefited the subscribers who had already jumped back into the market. The newsletter's confidentiality warning contrasted with the tradition within urban development professions of sharing useful information. For example, *American City* magazine from these years included this invitation to circulate its contents: "This Magazine is not copyrighted. Editors and Chamber of Commerce secretaries will find much material worth quoting in their publications."[70] As the usually low-profile appraisers faced glaring scrutiny because of collapsed land values, it is noteworthy that the newsletters as a new advising genre chose a confidential format to situate themselves even further behind the scenes.

No individual could possibly process the avalanche of facts available on real estate or stay on top of a frequently shifting investment climate — so the newsletters' synthesis was a unique service. They integrated information from dozens of professional journals and other sources that analyzed investment practices, as well as raw data generated by government publications. By the 1940s, Real Estate Analysts, Inc., claimed to have in its library "the most complete private collection of material on real estate and construction in America" (fig. 4.11). Furthermore, many journals addressed only the concerns of a specialized audience — appraisers, real estate brokers, city officials, builders, property owners, and so on — even though they all touched on decision making that was pertinent to real estate. In contrast, the newsletters helped create and define a new audience — the real estate investor. The newsletters filtered out narrow or extraneous professional debates, in order to focus on investment decision making. And whereas other journals mostly contemplated last year's statistics, the newsletters emphasized up-to-date coverage. In addition to the newsletters' monthly format, the *Analyst* published twenty or so specialized bulletins each year. Under its masthead in the mid-1930s, the *Analyst* described itself as "constantly measuring and reporting the basic economic factors responsible for changes in trends and values."[71]

The long, analytical articles of specialized professional journals, often presenting many sides of issues, translated poorly into concrete investment decisions. The *Market Letter* and the *Analyst*, in contrast, formulated advice by clearly stating the relevance to investment of the research it presented, using pithy summaries and an authoritative tone. Above all, Wenzlick insisted, "This service is intended to be practical. It should make you money." One reader wrote to Wenzlick to praise the blunt opinions his subscribers appreciated: "You are one of the few I know who has the courage to tell a cross-section of the industry and your customers what the truth is." Both publications boldly predicted the future, but the *Market Letter* more presumptively and aggressively told investors what to do with that information.

...OUR LIBRARY

For two decades we have been collecting material of all kinds ...facts, figures, reports, books, magazines, pamphlets ... everything we could lay our hands on which pertained to or affected real estate.

From these data we can find out almost anything we want to know about any city in the United States ... its downtown district, retail movement, population developments, residential trends, industrial pattern, and so on. We not only have this information for the present but, in some cases, we have data as far back as 1795.

From the world of material contained in the library, we are able to measure real estate and business cycles of the past in order to better forecast the future. It is here that the process of preparing your reports begins. The librarian assembles and classifies the data as received in the "raw" form before submitting them to the statistical department for further processing.

This library is the most complete private collection of material on real estate and construction in America.

In addition to its use in preparing our regular bulletins, the material contained in the stacks and files of our library is also used in providing special data for our clients focused on their own particular real estate and economic problems through the medium of . . .

Figure 4.11 Real Estate Analysts, Inc., claimed that its library held "the most complete private collection of material on real estate and construction in America." The new real estate investment newsletters and consultants emerging during the 1930s analyzed and synthesized this intimidating volume of information, trying to reassure clients and subscribers about the responsible, fact-based nature of postdepression real estate investment. (Roy Wenzlick & Company brochure, circa 1948. Courtesy of Jim Appel.)

Such bravado had to occasionally recognize the folly of forecasting, and it was the *Analyst* that most effectively mocked itself. Wenzlick said of his own book eight years after its publication that you could reread it "without laughing." Proud of correctly predicting the month and year of explosive real estate recovery, he still noted his good fortune: "This was pure luck, as no forecaster can call his shots that accurately without having a horseshoe in each pocket and one around his neck." Other times he used terms like "bunkum" to describe business forecasting and "best guesser" to describe the forecaster, and he wrote about crystal globes, whirling mist, parting clouds, and tea leaves.[72]

Given the dearth of useful, legitimate research (for the large institution and the small investor alike), the fearful depression context, and the national reach of these consulting firms, the creators of the *Analyst* and the *Market Letter* seized the opportunity to shape the discussion and assignment of real estate values in an era when *value* was a problematic term. Clients provided some feedback about their use of these investment tools. Wenzlick recounted the impact of the *Analyst*'s first year of projections: "So bleak were our forecasts that an executive of one large corporation told me that he kept our reports under lock and key. He feared that someone else in his organization might read them, [and] become infected with the pessimism in every line." A real estate agent wrote in to say that he had used a table from the July 1933 issue of the *Analyst* to win a commission from a bank to list four of its properties. He wished to relate that "those in charge of the real estate department said it was the first time that anyone had given them tangible support for his recommendations."[73] The newsletters promoted the concept of responsible, fact-based investing — whether educating the unprepared personnel in banks and insurance companies, helping the broker guide clients with confidence, or assisting city officials who managed properties obtained through tax defaults.

When investors accused Wenzlick's more pessimistic forecasts of actually bringing down market prices, it was evidence of how psychologically based contemporaries understood the market to be and also of the role the newsletters had in setting that psychological framework. One Cleveland man called Wenzlick personally and insisted that he had caused him to lose five thousand dollars because the effect of a talk he had given "was to demoralize the market so completely." Wenzlick doubted that he had such influence, but even in his disclaimers he seemed to take pleasure in the accusations, as hinted in the essay title "Am I a Menace to Real Estate?" His investor colleagues appreciated how Wenzlick's optimism could boost them and the market as well. The publisher of Wenzlick's *Coming Boom in Real Estate* sent around a bright banner emblazoned with the book's title. The president of a savings bank in New York City told Wenzlick that "it was so hard for him to convince himself that there was any possibility of real estate getting better that he tacked the streamer up on his wall to keep up his courage."[74]

Forecasters like Roy Wenzlick and Jim Downs knew the tools that insurance company presidents as well as ordinary store owners had at their disposal when making their investment decisions, and the consultants worked to get their advice publications ranked as indispensable resources. They found a role in predicting what the public would do and in actively shaping those trends. Inasmuch as people during the depression confronted unusually complicated questions and unfamiliar choices (for example, tearing down a recently constructed building), they could turn to the thoroughly researched recommendations of a new generation of national real estate experts. The consultants' deep and often historical investigations can be seen as another dimension of Main Street's interior frontier, like the soul-searching of appraisers, the modernization of storefronts, and the accumulation of empty land in the heart of the downtown. Like the St. Louis appraisal photographs that opened this chapter, Main Street interests took a hard, head-on look at the signs of opportunity and the indicators of decay and made their decisions accordingly. The demand for investment advice was one indicator of the activity and reorientation, not stagnation, that characterized urban real estate during the 1930s.

"Things Are Topsy-Turvy": Wartime Recentralization

When it seemed that the real estate roller coaster could not endure another violent twist, World War II hit the U.S. economy. Appraiser William Mac-Rossie tried to describe the overwhelming experience of disjuncture for his colleagues. Forecasting, he advised, "cannot be done by persons who went to sleep in 1925, 1930, or 1939 and are still asleep. It was during that period that tremendous economic forces turned this old world upside down and inside out, upsetting the traditions, social habits, and ideals upon which appraisers have long relied in their forecasts." The twenties boom, the depression, and then world war — such events had turned the world "topsy-turvy." To Homer Hoyt, William MacRossie, and countless other real estate experts, these "sudden reversals" meant that "accurate predictions as to the future course of real estate values were never more difficult to make than they are today." Swept up in the whirlwind of war news, the *Analyst* announced in 1939 that it would try to use weekly instead of monthly statistics whenever possible.[75]

As in the depression, world events penetrated to the core of the real estate business, revealing and challenging bedrock assumptions. Robert Armstrong told his fellow appraisers that the "apocalypse of violence and fear" precipitated by fascism threatened to sweep away the fundamentals of private property, capitalism, and democracy. He feared that the American "way of life" was flawed. "We are blinded too often by generalities that glitter," he wrote, and so had ignored deep problems such as poverty and unemployment. The nation needed "security without slavery, freedom without poverty, and progress without violence." The critical lesson was, "The time has come for us to reappraise not only the cities and the towns and the farms of this nation, but ourselves as well." The war, on the heels of the depression, demanded reevaluation of America's interdependent political, social, and commercial values.[76]

Wartime upheaval partly explains the contradictory projections made for downtown vitality during these years. In the final months of 1940, the Real Estate Research Corporation's *Market Letter* gloomily predicted continued decentralization and falling land values "over the next few years," since a "panacea for the ills of Central Business Districts" had not been found. The newsletter was wrong. In fact, wartime mobilization sparked recentralization and a downtown boom. Shortages and rationing enhanced the convenience of central-city living and the desirability of downtown office space, while the 1942 federal order freezing nonessential construction disadvantaged the growing suburban fringe. One month after America's entry into World War II, the *Market Letter* revised its pessimistic assessment, pronouncing that "commercial decentralization will be temporarily stopped." The federal government's wartime bureaucracy snapped up vacant downtown offices, at its peak in the fall of 1944 occupying nearly 12 percent of the nation's supply.[77]

However, it was the wartime constraints affecting the automobile that gave downtown real estate its biggest boost. Businesses reliant upon "mobile consumers" — mostly suburban stores and outlying business centers, but ironically including downtown parking lots — would be forced to fold. The consumer's limited mobility during the war penetrated to the core of the 1920s commercial investment formulas described in the previous chapter and, like so many of the depression crises, undercut the wisdom of those 1920s policies based on assumptions of constant growth. The *Market Letter* equated the impact of wartime auto restrictions with "the creation of the automobile itself." The gasoline shortage, the ban on new tires, and the prohibition against manufacturing new cars together dramatically curtailed auto use, a development forecasters believed "could suddenly precipitate a revolution in real estate." It followed that "all traditional shopping locations will benefit comparatively. Downtown sections will become more dominant in the general retail sales structure."[78]

Working people with some money to spend soon infused life into downtown streets and businesses. With men flooding into the armed forces, women comprised 83 percent of the newly employed stateside ranks and thus contributed disproportionately to the reinvigoration of downtown. In May 1943, the *Market Letter* observed of Chicago that "since the outbreak of World War II, the working population in the downtown area has increased sharply. Commercial establishments, eating places and amusement spots have definitely felt the influence of this increased population." Federal agencies took an additional 3.8 million feet of commercial space. A few months later, the newsletter confirmed that "the shopping population of the downtown has increased materially as a result of gas rationing and the closing of outlying stores."[79]

Even though some downtown enterprises benefited from this surge, the war economy still caused a contraction of retail tenants and crippled businesses dealing in "hardware, girdles, gadgets," and other vulnerable areas. Particularly hard hit in Chicago were grocery stores, meat markets, delicatessens, restaurants, and retail liquor stores, which together lost 2,054 outlets in 1942, while gas stations dropped 324 outlets. A December 1942 survey found a vacancy average of 14.1 percent, compared to 12.3 percent eight months earlier; the *Market Letter* predicted "a sharp increase" in vacancy over the next year. Overall, said the newsletter, "the store market situation *is now serious, will get worse.*" Throughout 1942, the *Analyst* similarly predicted that store vacancies would increase, perhaps 25 percent over two years. Wenzlick blamed inventory shortages and government price controls. The impact of vacancy on commercial rents varied from city to city but was generally worrisome, with 4 percent of cities in March 1943 reporting higher downtown rents than the previous year, 42 percent seeing a drop, and 54 percent holding firm. During the war, stores hit "an all-time high in percentage of total units vacant."[80]

Despite the signs of recentralization, the *Market Letter* remained convinced that downtowns would falter once the war's temporary salutary effects receded. In May 1943 it forecast "a major post-war problem for property owners in Chicago's central business district." The newsletter expected a "sharp shrinkage" in the downtown working population once the federal government pulled out its war-related offices. Only careful planning could avoid serious downtown conditions, since "presumably, the forces of decentralization will again be liberated." It struck a similar note in February 1946, explaining that "decentralization — dormant during the war [—] is again an active force in the reshaping of our cities and communities." The *Market Letter*'s pessimism was amplified by the "dire fear" haunting the immediate postwar economy that a severe depression would take hold. Wenzlick's more upbeat projections anticipated that although all downtowns would experience decentralization, "the best portion of the district will become better and land and building values in these areas will increase."[81]

As the nation reverted to a peace economy, the *Analyst*'s cautious optimism seemed to have more accurately anticipated the situation on Main Street, at least initially. This left the *Market Letter* puzzling over the downtown's surprising robustness. As early as 1944, downtown store vacancies and rents began to improve dramatically despite merchandise shortages (except in cities over five hundred thousand population). Resourceful property owners found alternative uses for empty retail space — storage, offices, and light manufacturing. During the second half of 1944, the number of cities reporting oversupply of retail space shrank in half from 54 percent to 21 percent, and those reporting a shortage jumped from 3 percent to 26 percent. The September 1945 *Market Letter* conceded that "government contraction is slower than expected and will finally be less than anticipated." A year later the newsletter reported, "In spite of decentralization, downtown pedestrian traffic is up." The increase in the number of men downtown reflected their return from military service. In July 1948 the forecasters struggled to explain yet another unexpected upturn: "Strangely enough the volume of business done downtown during the past year hit an all-time peak in dollar volume. Yet as we look to the pattern of space use over the next 30 years we foresee a change even more radical than that of the past three decades."[82] The downtown's surprising resilience challenged forecasters to keep an open mind, even if they maintained their pessimistic assumptions.

In fact, toward the end of the war, many investors still saw outstanding potential in downtown areas. Department stores, after faring poorly during the depression, experienced a wartime sales boom. In the mid-1940s, it seemed that most major stores were announcing expansion plans for their downtown operations: Dayton's in St. Paul, Thalhimer's in Richmond, and Marshall Field's in Chicago were just a few. Many had acquired adjacent properties in anticipation of postwar construction. Merchandise became available once again, automobile-related shortages ceased, and neighborhood stores revived. In 1946 Helen Canoyer marveled over the overwhelming interest among returning servicemen in opening businesses: "Probably at no time in the history of the United States have so many men and women been interested in starting a store as at the present time." Presumably the downtown would share in the boom.[83]

"An Age That Melts with Unperceived Decay"

Hoping to reconcile the contradictory evidence that otherwise confused Main Street analysts, many experts argued that the downtown's apparent vitality at the end of the war was a superficial economic health that masked underlying, long-term deterioration. Roy Wenzlick proposed to his newsletter subscribers that unless actual measurements were made by specialists, "much appears as it [once] was in our downtown districts." One might think, for example, that the numbers of pedestrians had not changed significantly. However, Wenzlick's statistics showed that over the previous twenty-five years the pedestrian crowds in downtown St. Louis had diminished by 44 percent. Urban land values remained slumped at depression lows, an important indicator not easily seen in the stores on Main Street. A 1957 plan for a pedestrian mall in Springfield, Oregon, described the postwar era as "An Age That Melts with Unperceived Decay."[84] In the late 1940s, it was indeed unclear what exactly was concentrating in the downtown core — parking lots, taxpayers, and vacant stores, as vividly underscored by the depression, or renewed, restocked crowds, the legacy of a surprising wartime recentralization.

By the late 1940s, the concept of Main Street — the unified, managed, dignified retail corridor so vigorously promoted by businesspeople and planners beginning in the Progressive era — had fallen on hard times. No longer the presumed center of commercial life, downtown had become "volatile and complex," in the words of *Architectural Forum* editors. Investors had begun to relinquish the belief that a unitary Main Street might satisfy the commercial needs of the American public. In addition, the volatile trajectories of investment during the 1920s–40s period had discredited the notion — prevailing in the 1920s — that the future contours of urban commerce could be projected with confidence. Depression and war left a legacy of cautious decision making based on the accumulation of weighty data.[85]

Even as the expanding suburban fringe again beckoned at the war's end, many investors retained the 1930s orientation toward the recycling and reuse of urban property. The May 1945 *Market Letter* anticipated that remodeling "will be one of the important factors in the whole post-war market." The newsletter cautioned that "in spite of much talk to the contrary, most obsolescence in buildings is economic and social, rather than physical." Thus "by the expenditure of relatively small amounts of money," an older structure could remain as appealing as any built in 1948. Another expert argued in 1945 that "the abandonment of Main Street for newer parts of town does the municipality little good. It would be far preferable to rejuvenate the old center with fewer but better stores even if it means tearing down and rebuilding." Not everyone rushed to resume 1920s suburban expansion. Many others planned to apply techniques of "remodeling" as well as "tearing down and rebuilding."[86]

Modernization and demolition in the 1930s, and the recycling they advanced, gave direction to post–World War II investors as much as 1920s expansion laid the groundwork for a suburban boom. We shall see in the next chapter how the depression distinctions drawn between "old" and "new," the identification of business "slums," and popularizing demolition as a cure for economic troubles established, together, key concepts and tools for urban renewal. Rather than simply suspending the dynamic growth of the 1920s, the depression reoriented commercial investment to tackle the problem of reconstruction. In 1947 Nathan Nirenstein pointed out that even though American cities had been spared wartime bombings, there were "everywhere extensive downtown areas upon which no buildings are standing." Downtown real estate, he argued, "is a prize beyond measure. It is a prize, however, that must be cherished, lest it be lost and its luster dimmed."[87] The vacant lots and taxpayers from strategic depression demolitions awaited reinterpretation and new investment choices.

5 "THE DEMOLITION OF OUR OUTWORN PAST"

In the midst of a lively urban renewal session at the 1955 International Downtown Executives Association conference, a prominent speaker seemed to digress from his topic of why two-income families could easily afford downtown luxury apartments. He delivered a "moral sermon" on the subversive threat of working, married women to family life in America. Let's take, he suggested, a boy who worked in his own office as an example. That boy married a stenographer, and their combined income was six hundred dollars a month. A second boy chose a "traditional family" and married a girl he would support.

> He is poor. When they come to an office party, the boy that comes with his working wife, arrive[s] in a nice new Chevrolet convertible and she is all dressed up. The poor boy who is raising a family, shows up in a 1940 Chevrolet and his wife is wearing a cheap $3.58 dress. This guy is the real citizen.
>
> In other words, we are debasing family life in America. You look at TV and a woman gets on the quiz show and they say, what do you do? She says, "I am a housewife." She says it as if she is ashamed of it. She isn't glamorous. She has no career. She has no money, probably.

In fact, the speaker's glorification of housewives and deprecation of working wives were not digressions from the topic of urban renewal. Women's activities — especially their shopping behavior — were central to both the downtown's growing problems and the justifications for redevelopment programs. As gender roles shifted and strained during the postwar decades, anxieties about wives working and "debasing family life" fueled concerns over downtown retail decline.[1]

With the war's end, public awareness of urban problems spread and deepened. A sense of impending downtown crisis crystallized around declining property values, empty lots, traffic congestion, waning retail sales, and shabby buildings. Urban renewal—the era's most drastic and influential solution for cities—sought to make America's downtowns appealing to white, suburban, middle-class women. Other consumers were closer at hand, particularly African Americans and ethnic minority populations living near the city center. Black consumers, marginalized and ignored by so many businesses in previous decades, had increased their downtown presence by the 1950s and had proved to be loyal customers (partly because of their more limited housing, transportation, and shopping options). Most downtown executives and public officials, however, spurned the opportunity to build on the existing African American shopping presence and turned their sights instead on the elusive white middle class. Redevelopers persistently argued that the residents of "slums" adjacent to the downtown threatened to "cheapen" and ultimately destroy the vitality of urban commercial life.

This chapter examines the role of gender, race, and obsolescence in shaping the emergent downtown crisis and subsequent rebuilding decisions. Postwar commercial aesthetics, sharpened in competition with new suburban shopping centers, were determined by concerns over who would be the ideal consumer—who would reinvigorate downtown property values and profits or breathe life into the malls. Whereas Progressive era planners defensively ridiculed the prospect of a feminized Main Street, downtown investors during the 1950s would have gladly tied pink ribbons on the lampposts if they thought it would attract suburban housewives. But instead of the modest Main Street beautification agenda of the Progressive era or the piecemeal and individualistic competitive strategies of depression-era demolition and storefront modernization, the postwar years brought comprehensive, large-scale redesigns—experimental new formulas for restoring the magnetism of commercial centers that often entailed destroying the "old" downtown in order to save it.

Analyzing the assumptions behind the urgent choices of urban renewal brings to the forefront tensions in executive boardrooms and suburban bedrooms over women's behavior, the disdain and indifference toward the increasingly visible nonwhite shoppers, and the ambiguities of judging even the physical condition of downtown and its supposed deterioration. In this we shall see the cultural underpinnings of downtown's economic crisis and the nation's commitment to urban renewal. The logic of 1950s redevelopment—a dramatic, even melodramatic, investment policy with enormous consequences for Main Street—deserves close investigation.

"'Downtown' Is Worried"

From the vantage point of the early twenty-first century, America's under-standing of its cities is inextricably bound up with the problems of poverty, crime, abandonment, and above all, racial tension. Yet this view belongs to the post-1960s era, reflecting the fact that 1960s violence remade the terms of urban life and urban policy. Racial conflict rushed to the foreground in the sixties, quickly becoming the overriding framework for interpreting the innu-merable, disparate, and disorganized facts of city life. It is somewhat surpris-ing, then, to realize that as the downtown crisis took shape in the 1950s, race was only one of many influential factors. In the years following World War II, the downtown crisis was multidimensional and complex, even elusive. Quite a few experts disagreed on whether a problem existed in the first place.

The downtown fears of the 1930s and 1940s had mostly circulated in the trade journals of city planners, administrators, and other urban specialists. But in the 1950s Americans were "inundated with stories about downtown's collapse," as one fed-up urban booster observed in 1962. Eisenhower's Hous-ing and Home Finance Agency chief noted in 1957 that "the attention which urban problems are receiving in the press and in national magazines suggests a widespread and growing public concern with this question." At a 1959 re-tailers' conference, one speaker poked fun at the entrenched gloom of mer-chants who had caved in to the "philosophy that 'Downtown is Doomed'" (and always had been). Middle-class daily life appeared to be changing; the opinion that "nobody goes downtown any more" became a new cliché.[2]

The 1950s witnessed a proliferation of organizations, committees, and pub-lications that singled out the problem of downtown survival. Most chamber-of-commerce-type civic associations formed prior to the 1950s addressed broad metropolitan issues. After the war, local associations emerged to spe-cifically tackle downtown decline. National organizations quickly followed, such as the International Downtown Executives Association in 1954, while existing groups created central business district committees. The Urban Land Institute's new Central Business District Council began panel studies of America's central cities in 1949. Between September 1961 and September 1963, one planning library received more than one hundred focused studies of cen-tral business districts. Of the new publications circulating advice for down-town interests, the *Downtown Idea Exchange* became the best known.[3]

For contemporaries, the nature of the downtown's decline was far from clear. The sheer volume of commentary attested to the fact that the crisis was not self-explanatory. One analyst wrote in 1964, "For a decade Downtown has been the subject of anxious attention, as if it were a patient with a serious, but undiagnosed disease." Business writers, retail analysts, scholars, and the popular press used a confusing variety of measurements for downtown decline, such as retail sales, store vacancies, lower "quality" clientele, run-down buildings, loss of manufacturing, and congestion (which after all could be a positive thing). It was difficult to determine the urgency of specific changes, since many (decentralization, for example) had long roots and were already familiar. In the late 1950s, retailers wondered whether the downtown in ten years would be "A Beehive or a Morgue." A *U.S. News and World Report* headline captured the gnawing but vague anxiety: "Shopping Spreads Out: 'Downtown' Is Worried."[4]

Disagreement over the severity of the downtown's condition prevailed, with numerous experts expressing faith in the downtown's continued viability. *Business Week* in 1951 reassured investors with the headline "There Are Lots of People Downtown," and a line from the story insisted that "State St. is no dead duck." In its publications the Urban Land Institute (ULI) — a nonprofit research corporation created by the National Association of Real Estate Boards — downplayed the competition between suburban and downtown retail. This perspective was informed by the fact that many ULI contributors were major developers who held investments in both places. One ULI technical bulletin argued, typically, that suburban retail growth fed upon population explosion, not the draining of the central city.[5] Architect Victor Gruen agreed that downtown and suburb fought a "phoney war." A retail executive testified to his colleagues that "our concept up to this point is that our branch stores should reflect the dominance of the main store," since, as another noted, they were "only as good and successful as the parent stores from which they draw their life blood." Outlying branch or "twig" stores ordinarily had less scope and assortment. "Blood" relations between downtown and suburban stores indicated cooperation and mutual concern as much as harmful competition.[6]

Fortune magazine in 1957 and 1958 ran a series of influential articles that also challenged the prevailing negative images, though from a different perspective. Americans had gone too far in condemning the downtown, urbanist Jane Jacobs explained in her essay. Trying not to minimize the downtown's problems, Jacobs found that Americans had overlooked the magnetism, the diversity, and the people who made downtown a vital, central place. "Bedraggled and abused," Jacobs insisted, "downtown does work." Overall, "we are becoming too solemn about downtown."[7]

Savvy businesspeople began to realize that their own morbid debates only worsened public attitudes toward the central business district. Stridently optimistic predictions reappeared in executives' conferences and publications in the late 1950s and early 1960s. One real estate investor–entrepreneur found a worshipful audience of downtown executives in 1962 when he laid his opinions and his money on the line. "To the theorist who says downtowns are on their way out, I say poppycock and balderdash. . . . As an investment area, downtown has a stability and a future far beyond anything I can foresee for suburban areas."[8] Investors used upbeat but defensive rhetoric to bolster the psychological framework that kept money flowing downtown.

But the optimism also reflected the fact that massive urban renewal projects were under way. "For one thing," a retail executive explained, "the cities are doing something about the downtown problem." The National Retail Dry Goods Association surveyed its members, a group that included major department stores, about their views on downtown decline. The survey showed "not only that there is an intense interest in the problem throughout the country, but also that much activity has been generated by it." Across the nation retailers had begun to participate in novel redevelopment campaigns.[9]

The Mantras of Urban Renewal

Since disagreement existed over the severity and the nature of Main Street's troubles, it is noteworthy that the same problems were listed so consistently to justify urban renewal that the list became a kind of incantation. The public's perception of urban renewal goals in 1954 were summarized by Eisenhower's Housing and Home Finance Agency (HHFA) chief, Albert Cole. From his own experience, Cole described the answers you would receive if "you went about the country asking various people what urban renewal is all about." Cole proposed, "You would be told that urban renewal is intended to save downtown business, or to clear up traffic congestion, or to restore worn-out areas to the tax rolls, or to create the City Beautiful, or to get rid of unsightly slum buildings."[10] Here were the main reasons as the public understood them: saving businesses (with a heavy emphasis on retail), resolving traffic and parking congestion, rebuilding property values (with implications for the city's tax base), and replacing shabby, worn-out structures. The consistency of this mantra can be measured in the similar beat of a 1965 plan for Erie, Pennsylvania: "The economic strength of virtually every downtown area in America is being dissipated by poor traffic circulation, insufficient parking, inharmonious usage, obsolete buildings, buildings in disrepair, declining property values, deficiency of shopper conveniences, general unattractiveness."[11]

Just as the 1950s arguments in favor of redevelopment settled into familiar justifications, historical explanations have converged to focus on locally committed business executives, "glamor-boy" mayors, the tragedy of "Negro removal," and the hopes and failures of architectural solutions.[12] As the story has been told, after the close of World War II, downtown business leaders and cooperative municipal governments spearheaded major urban improvement efforts.[13] Postwar projects replaced inadequate sewer and water systems and imposed air pollution controls. Highway legislation, radial freeways, and municipal parking alleviated traffic congestion and circulation problems. City agencies took over failing mass transit and attempted to upgrade transportation, partly by replacing streetcars with buses. Slum clearance captured planners' imaginations and embodied their hopes for cities. Several states passed enabling legislation for clearance projects, and then Title I of the 1949 Housing Act spurred further clearance and housing projects. Housing conservation and rehabilitation also found wide sponsorship in the early 1950s, though with disappointing results. Federal involvement initially remained limited in all of these urban improvement efforts. The inspiring downtown redevelopment projects of late 1940s and early 1950s — Pittsburgh's Golden Triangle, Baltimore, and Rochester — were primarily private initiatives.[14]

As momentum gathered behind redevelopment, the alliance of business executives and concerned public officials became especially skilled at bending the broad designations attached to federal urban renewal money so that it could be used for downtown redevelopment. Through congressional testimony, behind-the-scenes legislative bargaining, and a sympathetic press, the business-mayoral coalitions maneuvered the 1954 Housing Act and the 1956 Highway Act to further central city reconstruction.[15] The federal government became more directly involved in removing existing businesses and their old buildings and attracting new ventures to new complexes. This federal role was explicit in highway and freeway construction and in the 1954 Housing Act, which allocated up to 10 percent of federal capital grant funds for renewing nonresidential areas. As urban renewal shifted from private and municipal projects to federal funding, the transition did not mean a transfer to federal control. Local administrators proposed renewal districts and the specific remedies, and they implemented the programs. Designers of federal legislation drew upon state and local experiences. These multilevel initiatives added up to a "national decision to rebuild our cities."[16]

The consistency behind the 1950s justifications for urban renewal (and the later histories explaining it) can partly be attributed to a far-reaching publicity campaign launched in 1954. That year a cross-section of influential Americans founded an organization to stimulate public interest in urban renewal. The American Council to Improve Our Neighborhoods (ACTION) drew its members from the leadership of such associations as the Mortgage Bankers Association of America, the Chamber of Commerce of the United States, the National Association of Home Builders, the Congress of Industrial Organizations, the National Urban League, and the U.S. Savings and Loan League. ACTION's agenda called for the rehabilitation of sound housing, together with the removal of slums. It sought to end public apathy and inspire individuals and citizens' groups to take personal responsibility in tackling urban problems. Albert Cole told ACTION leaders at their inaugural meeting, "We want to sound the alarm throughout the country that will bring people running to the defense of their cities."[17]

Through member associations and an Advertising Council publicity blitz, ACTION hoped "to create a national climate of opinion" supporting housing improvement and urban renewal.[18] The Ad Council campaign, begun in September 1955, dramatically amplified ACTION's reach. Popular magazines like *Family Circle, Life,* and *Better Homes and Gardens* and newspaper magazine inserts like *Parade* and *This Week* carried stories inspired by ACTION press releases. Inquiries increased from 50 to 500 a week. The wording of articles about ACTION shows that they often sprang from the same press releases.[19] The barrage of press releases, synchronized with federal policies, must be seen as a factor in homogenizing and organizing the arguments in support of urban renewal into the mantra they became.

Diverse groups criticized urban renewal policies, of course, questioning the effectiveness of federal programs engaged in clearing slums and constructing public housing, downtown towers, and highways. Urban renewal inspired complaints about its implementation, fears about the federal power it evoked, and condemnation of what seemed like a monolithic vision of the rebuilt city. Many deplored the implicit racial agenda of slum clearance and dubbed that agenda "Negro removal."[20] Not surprisingly, some business associations objected to the public financing of redevelopment. The "most recalcitrant" National Association of Manufacturers wanted the federal program shut down as soon as possible.[21] Others vacillated. The president of the Mortgage Bankers Association of America publicly switched to support federal renewal, telling his membership that they had "to wake up to certain facts of life." Urban problems, he had come to believe, would not disappear on their own. Organizations with major downtown interests, such as the National Retail Merchants Association, had a predictable affinity for urban renewal, whereas other national associations saw renewal less favorably than their own local chapters did. Local business leaders, who observed firsthand the obstacles to revitalization, not only approved of federal intervention but demanded it. For example, the U.S. Chamber of Commerce stated that the federal government should get out of redevelopment aid, but local chambers often spearheaded renewal proposals.[22] Dissenters from the business world, however, usually debated over who would carry out urban renewal and how — not whether the drastic remedy was needed in the first place.

By the mid-1960s, federally supported urban renewal had touched large and small cities, and its impact would continue to ripple nationwide even as the critiques gained force. More than thirteen hundred redevelopment projects were under way, thirty-four square miles of land had been acquired, and demolition crews had taken down 129,000 structures. Of the approximately 650 participating cities, more than two-thirds had fewer than 50,000 residents, and 20 percent had fewer than 10,000. Measured in dollars, an estimated $3.014 million in federal grants had been spent by the end of 1962.[23] The history of this devastatingly influential investment policy remains firmly rooted in the long-standing explanations described here, many dating to the 1950s, and is ripe for reinterpretation.

The Downtown Crisis as Retail Crisis

Women are virtually absent from historical accounts of the downtown crisis and urban renewal.[24] What makes this remarkable is that in the 1950s retail seemed to hold the key to revitalizing the central business district, and women were the lifeblood of retail. Contemporaries framed most downtown troubles — such as traffic congestion, falling public transit ridership, and aging buildings — as liabilities in the retail struggle with the suburbs. The decline of Main Street retail held a special poignancy for Americans and served as a spur to redevelopment. Shopping represented a clearly human dimension of the economic crisis; as downtown executives and city officials mobilized to save the downtown retail core, they addressed the issue of who should or should not be in the downtown. They wished to reverse the declining "quality" or class of shoppers, a complaint that usually had racial overtones. And they intended to make the downtown attractive and safe for white, middle-class, suburban women. Redevelopers had precise ideas about who should support the revitalized downtown property values.

The 1950s urban renewal campaigns represented the peak of the twentieth century's faith in the promise of retail for invigorating America's urban commercial life. During this era, retailers and their businesses were seen as the glue binding the downtown economy together. Business analyst Frank Cox argued that the "retail district is the nucleus which holds together such services as professional offices, banks, personal services, industrial and financial offices, company headquarters, and all the components of a complex urban economy." Retail generated crucial tax revenues and pedestrian traffic, which supported other enterprises. According to a chamber of commerce representative, "retailers are the predominant factor in central business districts and are the backbone of downtown." At least one observer found nothing new in the postwar emphasis on downtown retail, writing that "the public has never, in relation to Downtown, conceived of itself as anything but a body of consumers." [25]

The supporters of downtown renewal drew more attention to the suburbanization of retail than to the residential and industrial decentralization that were also reshaping regional economies.[26] The publication of the 1954 business census fueled anxieties about retail decentralization, and those census figures were the most widely cited evidence of downtown retail weakness. The 1954 census showed that since 1948, during a time of prosperity and increased consumption, the downtown's proportion of metropolitan sales had slipped relative to suburban stores' sales. In forty-five metropolitan areas, total retail sales increased 32.3 percent, while sales in the central districts crept up only 1.6 percent. Although many downtowns had not suffered an absolute sales decline, the suburbs' relative gain appeared to be a dismal sign for Main Street. A new genre of shopping studies appeared, attempting to "discover attitudes and other motivating factors which either repel or attract persons to downtown or to suburban shopping centers." Suburban housewives had precipitated a so-called retail revolution, leading businesses away from downtowns to outlying locations. Those retailers who supported local urban renewal were pleased to claim downtown redevelopment as a retailing strategy in the battle against the suburbs.[27]

Department stores played instrumental roles, symbolic and otherwise, in redevelopment plans. More than most other institutions, department stores

had cultivated the belief that they underpinned and embodied the city's prosperity, and developers pointed to the vacant ones to galvanize support for
the drastic action of rebuilding downtowns.[28] In Baltimore, O'Neill's Department Store "became the symbol of downtown decay when it closed its doors
in 1954," according to an Urban Land Institute analysis. Announcement of
O'Neill's closing prompted some executives to investigate "what's going to be
done about the downtown situation." This led to one of the decade's first
downtown renewal projects — Charles Center.[29] Most communities could
not help but believe store closings reflected local decline, even though in these
decades family-owned department stores were increasingly snapped up by
distant institutions: retail holding company giants such as Allied Department
Stores, Federated Department Stores, and May Company; insurance companies; and universities. Some of the national conglomerates shut down stores
with great insensitivity to local circumstances. In Oklahoma City, Federated
closed Halliburton's — one of the city's oldest stores — during a special promotional event, "Saturday Downtown Value Day."[30]

Although discussions of women were rarely explicit in 1950s urban policymaking and investing, the role of the retail revolution alone in precipitating
the Main Street crisis and justifying downtown rebuilding calls attention to
the critical part white suburban housewives played in the urban redevelopment drama. The expectation that these women could be the potential saviors
of the downtown lay quietly in the technical pages of *Traffic Quarterly*, in the
blueprints of transportation engineers, in the meeting rooms of downtown
executives, and in the reports of planners and architects.

"Her Desires and Whims": Courtship by Design

The downtown had not merely deteriorated — it had failed by middle-
class women's standards. In the key elements of the crisis (traffic planning,
commercial design, and property values), suburban housewives were the focus of postwar downtown experts. The explicitly woman-centered commercial aesthetics appearing in suburban shopping centers captured the imagination of downtown investors too, who in the 1950s pinned their future survival
on a disappearing white, middle-class customer base. So for downtowns as
well as suburbs, the goal of attracting affluent suburban shoppers guided
decisions about parking, accessibility, building appearance, and the general
commercial "atmosphere." Main Street battled with malls not only for generic
business dollars, but also for customers of a particular gender and race.
Whereas in the Main Street contests of the 1930s, retail neighbors competed

against each other for scarce patrons, out of the postwar downtown–suburban center contests there emerged a new vision of what it took to become the magnetic retail hot spot for the white, middle-class shopper crowds.

For starters, retail analysts framed downtown's shabbiness as a "housekeeping" crisis. Just as the depression had accelerated the distinction between modern and obsolete, the brand new shopping malls made Main Street look outdated, despite (or sometimes because of) two decades of Main Street modernization. The current condition of downtown, according to renowned commercial designer Victor Gruen, "repulses shoppers." Housewives would prefer the clean, modern facilities of the shopping centers. "Attractive appearance and a sense of orderliness will pay its dividends," recommended another journal article. For the downtown "to gain some of the charm and attractiveness of the new center, a 'face-lifting' operation will be required." Downtown businesses stepped up improvements in order to compete with the women-pleasing shopping centers. As another analyst explained, the "central districts, when planning a complete modernization and rehabilitation, try to emulate the principles and elements that have been successful in the better regional centers."[31]

By casting physical deterioration in gendered terms, the experts implied that if only men judged the downtown's appearance, then the downtown crisis might not be as pressing. The South Bend, Indiana, Association of Commerce explained that "the majority of shoppers are housewives who are critical of poor housekeeping wherever they see it, including in retail stores." The *Downtown Idea Exchange* proclaimed that when improving downtown mass transit, planners should heed the fact that the woman shopper "expects the bus to be spick and span." Women, who supposedly cared more about external appearances because of their household standards, should even be allowed to pick the bus colors. *Traffic Quarterly* warned that only a foolish mall developer would slash the budget for building materials or landscaping. The shopper "has a garden of her own and feels happier, more relaxed, and more in a buying mood if she is surrounded during her shopping excursion with flowers, trees and grass of a handsomely landscaped mall."[32] Investors resurrected some of the same arguments invented by female municipal housekeepers in the 1890s to justify women's participation in civic affairs and urban design. In the 1950s, however, mostly male downtown interests invoked women's housekeeping standards in the name of mostly female consumers.

Renewal efforts indeed pursued "suburban homemakers" and "housewives," rather than working women or women of color living downtown, as their primary targets. As in the 1920s, downtown office workers were largely taken for granted. Not that investors did not occasionally survey with relief and gratitude the "thousands of working girls" employed downtown or see that "the higher the buildings, the greater the number of noonday customers. High office buildings mean women customers." But investors were also skeptical of working women's loyalty to the central business district. Roy Wenzlick claimed that suburban malls were blossoming in residential areas with large concentrations of downtown office workers. His real estate newsletter described the skyscrapers where many women worked as "sometimes detrimental to shopping districts" because they tended to "destroy harmonious shopping sections." When counting downtown pedestrians, his firm's researchers could supposedly distinguish between the working single woman and the housewife-shopper in an instant, and they were often directed to simply exclude the office worker, or "women individual shoppers."[33]

Downtown executives emulated what they called the "atmosphere" of the suburban malls — an enveloping, soothing environment intended to trigger a "buying mood."[34] Key concepts that developers intoned included a pleasant atmosphere, relaxation, comfort, and beauty. One booklet effused about the suburbs, compared to the downtown: "Look at the beautiful malls — with fountains and green trees — and soft, sweet music where women can shop in a relaxed and pleasant atmosphere." Victor Gruen highlighted the need for, "above all, the creation of a 'shopping atmosphere' which offers customers beauty, comfort and relaxation." Women supposedly spent more money amid plantings, sculpture, and piped-in music.[35]

In their book *Shopping Towns USA,* Gruen and real estate economist Larry Smith described how one shopping center outside Detroit used a two-hundred-thousand-dollar art budget to ascertain and create the right environment for women. Northland Center's art program "stressed the fact that the shopping center would be a place for activities connected with shopping, walking, and relaxation, that it would be visited by families — but to the largest degree by women and children." Accordingly, the mall's developers themed the numerous sculptures for "humor, color, movement, lighteartedness" to accommodate the supposed aesthetic and philosophical inclinations of women and children. Men's interests — "drama, heroism, or tragedy" — had no place in the predominantly female atmosphere.[36]

The apparently dry, narrow, technological problems of inadequate parking, traffic congestion, expressways, and mass transit stood at the heart of the downtown crisis, motivating extensive redesign. Yet *Traffic Quarterly* in the

1950s shows that from parking angle to building configuration, concerns about women shoppers permeated traffic engineering decisions. Downtowns had difficulty competing with the suburbs in various arenas of accessibility, an important 1950s commercial design concept. Access routes to the retail district, whether by car or public transit, demanded analysis, as did the relationship of parking to the stores. Since, as Richard Ratcliff put it, "the little woman who comes to shop" partook of the greatest number of downtown services, accessibility and convenience carried gendered meanings.[37]

The first challenge was delivering the shopper to the retail district. One real estate executive cautioned that "unless you make it convenient for a woman to go downtown, she won't go." The president of chain variety store TG&Y expressed skepticism about the viability of downtown locations because of accessibility and parking concerns: "We do not think the housewives (who are our main customers) will drive miles and miles to get downtown when they can obtain the same merchandise in better facilities in the suburbs" (see fig. 5.1). Yet shopping centers had to clear some of the same hurdles: "if it is not easy for the housewife to find her way into any center, she will give up and go away." She might find it "too hard to find her way through the complicated maze needed to maintain proper traffic speed." Highway engineers called the local highways that connected expressways and shopping centers "women's roads" because, as Homer Hoyt observed, "they are free from heavy congestions and minimize driving difficulties for women shoppers."[38]

Once she arrived by car, the shopper needed to park. A large suburban store discovered the consequences of not catering to female parking peculiarities. Its garage ramps "were so narrow they discouraged women drivers." Furthermore, planners had originally designed parking that permitted three cars between pillars, based on attendant parking. However, the center found that only two cars fit in the spaces designed for three, because "women shoppers, being timid, declined to get close enough to another car to run the risk of a scratched fender." Another analyst concluded that in park-and-shop design, "the parking should all be in front of the stores, with rear parking reserved for employees. Most people, particularly women, hesitate to drive 'around in back,' particularly with no assurance that they will find a parking space there." The layout needed to accommodate women's fear of "difficult 'maneuvering.'" Debating the choice between angled and straight parking, one planner explained in *Traffic Quarterly* that "the idea of using a simple angle is based on the turning radius of cars, presence of women drivers, and the desire to make parking virtually trouble-free." The *Downtown Idea*

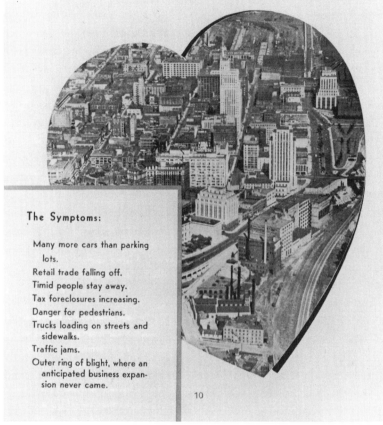

Downtown Saint Paul
Overstrained Heart of the City

The Symptoms:

Many more cars than parking
    lots.
Retail trade falling off.
Timid people stay away.
Tax foreclosures increasing.
Danger for pedestrians.
Trucks loading on streets and
    sidewalks.
Traffic jams.
Outer ring of blight, where an
    anticipated business expan-
    sion never came.

10

Figure 5.1 Among downtown decision makers during the 1950s, concerns about bringing women shoppers downtown were often expressed in coded language. Women were understood to be tentative drivers; thus, in this list of St. Paul's problems, "Timid people stay away" referred to women and their presumably weak driving skills. Other items, related to issues of downtown access and retail trade, also indirectly addressed the supposed perspective of women shoppers. "Ring of blight" stands out in this list as a coded reference for additional reasons. The phrase was used in the 1950s to describe the perceived "ring" of nonwhite neighborhoods that encroached upon the downtown, supposedly making Main Street less appealing to white suburban shoppers. (City Planning Board of St. Paul, *Planning St. Paul for Better Living,* ca. 1946, 10. Courtesy of the Division of Rare and Manuscript Collections, Cornell University Library; Russell Van Nest Black Papers, collection no. 3018, box 35, file 5.)

Exchange relished one advantage it thought the public transit–oriented downtown had over the suburban mall: "Women do not shine as 'experts' in parking a car." [39]

The definition and details of convenient parking plagued retail developers — how far the shopper was willing to walk to a store, and how she would get her packages back to the car. After all, why should the downtown shopper "struggle through traffic trying to find a parking place, end up by parking her car at a distance from the stores, lug a growing pile of bundles from store to store, and finally back to her car, only to find she has parked over the time limit, and has a ticket?" The *Real Estate Analyst* found that "four blocks is too far for the woman shopper to walk with convenience." One block was about right. A system that minimized the struggle with packages was essential to "free the shopper from the mental and physical burden of lugging her purchases from one store to another." A cartoon (fig. 5.2) depicted a fashionable but scowling young woman maneuvering to get to her car. She was weighed down with packages and trying to cope with a difficult child and a disruptive dog. Two happier alternatives were also portrayed: errand boys assisting her, and her arrival by car at a central pick-up point to collect her purchases delivered by conveyor belt. [40]

Trimming the distance between the store and parking had vital implications for new commercial construction, as well as for redevelopment. One Stop-and-Shop manager described how "the U-shaped shopping center laid out with wide parking aisles and generous parking stalls makes shopping pleasant for the female customer. Since she is so dominant in the mix of customers, the shopping center must appeal to her and cater to her desires and whims." Architects had presumably generated the popular U-shaped layout as a design solution accounting for women's parking needs. At the 1954 International Downtown Executive Association (IDEA) meeting, one participant had circumvented the inconveniences posed by 1870s buildings by tearing them down. This permitted construction of a five-hundred-car garage, with escalators "so that the individual can go up and get her own car, etc." *Architectural Record* in 1960 reported on how the downtown of Peekskill, New York, was remaking itself "in order to attract shoppers." A survey concluded that "the private motor car" held the key to retail. "The city must provide facilities adequate for the shopper who uses her car or take steps to minimize the need for its use." Because of the shoppers, then, the city needed to improve parking facilities, public transit, and even traffic lighting. [41]

Women's desire for convenience and beauty emerged as the motivating

CUSTOMER CARRIES THEM

CARRY-OUT SERVICE

CENTRAL PICKUP POINT

Figure 5.2 The delivery of the customer to her car with all of her packages was a central design issue for retailers in the 1950s. In this cartoon from a 1951 issue of the *Real Estate Analyst,* a woman scowls as she juggles her purchases while shepherding a disruptive child and a dog. The cartoon proposes two alternatives that could make shopping more "convenient" and "attractive," in the commercial development terminology of that time. Note the poor parking job — assumptions about women's driving skills also guided parking lot design and management. (Courtesy of the Western Historical Manuscript Collection, University of Missouri, St. Louis.)

theme for commercial design, in an all-encompassing planning approach. One expert indicated that "only recently has the suburban homemaker been given prime consideration in the designing of suburban shopping centers. By a logical evolutionary process, we are arriving at a design concept for the suburban center that she prefers as a shopping environment. It combines maximum convenience in all important elements — ease of access, minimum walking distance from car to store, store to store, and location of merchandise lines. It further combines all-weather shopping, built-in beauty, a community focal point, and other desirable elements." Another *Traffic Quarterly* contributor captured the shopping center's almost smothering design focus: "The emphasis must always be on the customer — her comfort, her convenience, her psychological reaction to attractive buildings, exciting show windows, and colorful flowers and trees."[42] Developers turned the decades-old preoccupation with women's retail choices into what sounded like a single-minded obsession.

Suburban developers tended to be the most explicit (and obsequious) about their desire to design for women and manage the entire spending experience. As with parking, shopping centers had an edge in creating female-centered space. Because of centralized management, one expert intoned, "every road, every walk, every shop location and store aisle is planned to expose the shopper to the greatest possible amount of merchandise and to influence her to spend her shopping dollars. At last, with an empty purse she heads homeward, tired (and we hope happy) taking with her everything she needs, and (as the developers hope) with little money left to spend elsewhere on other things." Downtown investors, lacking the same control over their environment, reinterpreted the centers' standards of "beauty" and "convenience" for central business districts.[43]

Downtown businesses worried that too many women and too much emphasis on their needs would scare away the male consumers who worked nearby. Thus in the 1950s, downtown department stores began creating and promoting special men-only facilities such as the soup bar in Thalhimer's. With this addition to the store, "a man can shop in the men's departments, have lunch, and never come within sight of the women's department."[44] Rich's Department Store opened a separate men's store based on the same premise: "to provide a real man's world, set apart from the teaming [*sic*] aggregate of women's business."[45]

Lest it seem that Main Street suffered an inevitable disadvantage in creating modern, feminized commercial environments, retail location expert Richard Nelson pointed out that downtowns had one thing — "emotional ties" — that the new shopping centers lacked. In fact the suburban mall's convenience and pleasant surroundings were "designed to overcome" the "emotions" many shoppers felt for the old downtown. Whereas the downtown held "memories," the shopping mall supplied glamour through "bright new store fronts and facilities, fountains, art, statuary, planting, and (not the least important) an undertone of music piped throughout the entire center."[46] Here was the recognition — rare in the 1950s — that history, in the form of people's fond memories, might enrich the value of Main Street rather than, in the form of aging and obsolete buildings, induce its destruction. It was not until the 1970s that downtown investors began to appeal with any success to those emotional ties.

Just as shoppers had created peak downtown land values in the 1920s, investors hoped that white suburban housewives could reinvigorate urban commerce in the postwar years. One 1956 study anticipated that "the shopping and working habits of the woman may be of increasing significance not only in terms of income to business but also in terms of the generation of sound retail land values in the central business district."[47] The belief that suburban women could save the downtown gained urgency from warnings like this one from *Business Week*: "If something isn't done about the problems of the city, downtown merchants stand to lose not only a lot of customers but also a considerable real estate investment. And the situation is becoming critical." In the 1940s, when outlying areas began to register property values that approached the downtown's, few were surprised that these new peaks emerged in suburban shopping centers.[48]

The Vanishing Homemaker:
"My Wife, Your Wife, and Your Neighbor's Wife"

Designs to build all-encompassing, desirable shopping environments for white middle-class women derived their motivation from reasons extending beyond these women's contributions to property values. In an intimate twist, redevelopers in the 1950s often had their own wives in mind when they schemed to bring the all-day family shoppers back. The downtown crisis had an element of domestic crisis, as male executives began to suspect that housewives were not finding the promised fulfillment in their societal roles as consumers and family managers. The postwar revolution in shopping behavior and its implications for downtowns can only be understood through the overlap of that revolution with the broader, emerging feminist revolution — a transformation in gender roles which itself would be led partly by suburban wives such as Betty Friedan.

Executives Roy Wenzlick, Jim Downs, and others felt the rumblings of change in the 1950s; after all, it was their job to anticipate societal trends that would affect real estate investment — everything from marriage and home ownership rates to how often people ate in restaurants.[49] Following World

War II, tensions grew between the overwhelming propaganda supporting female domestic bliss and the fact that women were entering the workforce in
unprecedented numbers. Working women confronted pervasive attitudes
that their place was in the home or in low-paying part-time employment. *The
Lonely Crowd* in the early 1950s described "the current attempts to re-privatize
women by redefining their role in some comfortably domestic and traditional
way." Postwar America glorified women's dependency upon their husbands.
Yet the frantic quality of such prescriptive literature hints at women's underlying discontent and uncertainty over gender roles. In the impending societal
crisis, middle-class women in the 1960s would acknowledge and voice their
dissatisfaction and would revolutionize the choice between suburban home-
making and other careers.[50]

In the meantime, during the 1950s, the executives preoccupied with the
downtown's survival were especially concerned with how housewives spent
their entire day, not just their shopping hours, and they regularly fell into the
habit of talking about their own wives. Jim Downs informed the IDEA urban
renewal audience in 1955 that their goal was to make it "desirable for my wife,
your wife and your neighbor's wife to go downtown and shop." Delbert Wenzlick personalized the domesticated economic power held by homemakers:
"Our wives have long had the reputation of spending the bulk of the family
budget." Describing how shopping occupied a central portion of the homemaker's day, he explained that "the family shopper goes downtown, or uptown, as the case may be, after she has washed the breakfast dishes and done
more or less work around the house; spends our money and goes home when
its all gone, or nearly gone, to get the evening meal."[51] Could *any* shopping
environment induce most middle-class women to want to spend all day shopping and homemaking? While executives made investment decisions to influence whether housewives shopped in the city or suburbia, the underlying
question was whether middle-class women would choose to shop during the
day at all. As their own wives considered their options, downtown executives
had reasons to worry that all-day shopping might be losing its luster.

Retail executives and others with downtown interests fondly described
for each other a lost golden age when shopping had provided personal fulfillment and excitement to middle-class women. A professor of retailing explained that given the "greater informality" of suburban living, "shopping became a casual excursion, or even something of a chore, rather than an exciting
event." A 1954 *Harvard Business Review* article confirmed that "downtown
shopping is no longer the 'national sport' of women shoppers, but rather an

intermittent chore." Shopping's exciting era, however, was elusive; one 1930 article also lamented shopping's decline as a rewarding all-day activity: "Ten years ago a woman would go shopping just to make a day of it. The trolley trip was refreshing. The woman moved from store to store, looking at this, pricing that, comparing values, and when she came to a crowd she bored her way to the middle of it. She came home late, thoroughly tired but happy, and probably had bought nothing at all. The day was an adventure itself before automobiles became common." Now women no longer had the desire to even compare merchandise.[52]

In a nutshell, "the old thrill of shopping is gone." The automobile (no matter how poorly driven) had supposedly opened up women's horizons and increased their options. "But with the car the woman leads a wholly different life. The car takes her outdoors every day, increases her contacts with people, makes life more interesting, and she does not waste any more hours in shopping than are necessary. Life has become too interesting in other directions."[53] Housewives found it wasteful to spend unnecessary hours shopping, and convenient outlying retail centers stepped into this transformed market. The anxiety, even resentment, that executives expressed about suburbanites' "interesting" motoring activities helps explain the pervasive belittling of the woman driver during these decades.

Suburban and downtown retailers competed to restore the fulfillment they believed women had once found in shopping. An architect described his conviction that designers should construct the shopping center as a *workplace* for women.

> Looked at in broader terms, Shopping is a Social Ritual. The wife and homemaker charged with the wise spending of the family income must be given the sense that she has *worked* at seeking out and discovering a uniquely right article at a justifiable price.
>
> It is not enough to have important purchases merely available. They must be as available as possible but in an atmosphere that suggests the culmination of a quest.

Designers built these assumptions of work fulfillment into their malls. Surveys had confirmed that the family shopper spent most of her day downtown, from ten in the morning to four in the afternoon, and investors hoped she would return home satisfied, with that "empty purse" (fig. 5.3).[54]

In their downtown revitalization plans, then, executives burdened the downtown shopping trip with unrealistic but urgent hopes for women's fulfill-

Figure 5.3 Downtown redevelopers aggressively targeted wealthy suburban housewives, like the one portrayed here, who were available to shop all day long. The photo's original caption asserted, "Shopping can be a pleasure. And it can be pleasant for the business man, too, if the future of his investment has been assured." Investors pinned their hopes for economic success, including sustaining high property values, on suburban housewives. At the same time, downtown investors disregarded or took for granted other ready consumer populations closer at hand, such as people of color and downtown office workers, and resisted the trend of married women turning to paid employment and professional careers. (Victor Gruen, "Planned Shopping Centers," *Dun's Review,* May 1953, 37.)

ment. Special salesmanship, one authority believed, could attract the housewife: "the kind of selling which makes a person want to buy what she really ought to have; something better, something more durable, something more satisfying, something that will build her ego and give a feeling of belonging, something that will make life more satisfying and beautiful." Creative marketing and merchandising could still nourish the "drama, glamour, excitement and stimulating atmosphere" that had made the downtown department stores successful in years past. The intent to build a woman's ego through her consumer experience of urban commerce spoke to men's concerns about housewives' satisfaction.[55]

Before the feminist movement of the 1960s gathered momentum, downtown decline provided an opportunity to indirectly discuss the independent economic decision making of suburban housewives, as well as their changing needs. If housewives did not find contentment in homemaking, the unsettling possibility arose that they might seek ego rewards elsewhere. Men's and women's fears about the implications of working wives were channeled into other, related arenas, such as the suburban retail revolution and the downtown crisis. In 1963 Betty Friedan's best-selling book *The Feminine Mystique* directly addressed suburban housewives' dissatisfaction and launched an explicit national debate about female fulfillment.[56]

This brings us back to James C. Downs Jr.'s apparent digression during the urban renewal session of the 1955 IDEA conference. Working women, he believed, were "debasing family life in America." Housewives felt "ashamed" of their status — their unglamorous, careerless lives. Downs argued that the man whose wife stayed at home was "the real citizen." Consumption patterns framed Downs's perceptions: the new Chevrolet convertible versus the 1940 model; the "dressed up" working wife versus the homemaker's "cheap $3.58 dress." Working wives made possible much of the postwar affluence and spending.[57] Downs's concerns — stay-at-home wives and the morality of shopping behavior — indeed animated the urban renewal debate over downtown retailing. Behind the downtown crisis lay a shopping crisis, and behind the crisis of women-as-shoppers lay unresolved tensions over women-as-workers and women-as-wives. Anxiety about where women shopped reflected anxiety about where women spent all of their time, as the post–World War II downtown crisis lurched ahead because of women's increasingly independent decisions about their own careers.

The overwhelming response to *The Feminine Mystique* confirmed that Betty Friedan had a resonant way of describing the gender issues faced by the white suburban middle class. She did not believe that there was "an economic conspiracy directed against women," but for dramatic effect she played out that scenario:

> I am sure the heads of General Foods, and General Electric, and General Motors, and Macy's and Gimbel's and the assorted directors of all the companies that make detergents and electric mixers, and red stoves with rounded corners, and synthetic furs, and waxes, and hair coloring, and patterns for home sewing and home carpentry, and lotions for detergent hands, and bleaches to keep the towels pure white, never sat down around a mahogany conference table in a board room on Madison Avenue or Wall Street and voted on a motion: "Gentlemen, I move, in the interests of all, that we begin a concerted fifty-billion dollar campaign to stop this dangerous movement of American women out of the home."

The final line of this executive conspiracy-that-never-happened was, "We've got to keep them housewives, and let's not forget it."[58] The 1950s downtown redevelopment efforts to woo the suburban housewife had their place in this nonconspiracy.

"Downtown May Well Be Abandoned, or Else Be a Negro Shopping District"

The retailer preoccupation with attracting white middle-class housewives in the 1950s reflected not only the exodus of these women to suburban stores (and paid employment) but also the fears of a downtown awash in a tide of lower-income and ethnic consumers. Redevelopers were worse than ambivalent about the prospect of boosting downtown vitality with the available but usually poorer and nonwhite customers from adjacent residential neighborhoods. Jim Downs, in his opening comments to the 1955 IDEA conference, noted that "the purpose of the downtown association is to raise the number and quality of the people that are downtown." Poor neighborhoods constituted "a ring of low purchasing power." According to Downs, "your real interest in redevelopment is, in replacing the population immediately adjacent to the downtown area, so as to develop a better market for downtown facilities." Executives supported residential redevelopment with an eye toward the downtown's retail health and appropriate consumer populations. Redevelopers described a downtown under siege — threatened by a surrounding "ring" of blight associated with the much-discussed migration into cities of poor African Americans, Puerto Ricans, Native Americans, and Appalachian whites.[59]

Retailers adjusted slowly to what one marketing professor called "the 'new' downtown customer." Pleas for appreciating and working with the new customer addressed an alarmed and sometimes narrow-minded community of businesspeople who saw decline in class and race terms, not just numbers. An East Coast executive confided his predictions to a *Fortune* reporter. "I know what's going to happen, but I don't know that I want to see it in print. The type of customer is going to be lower and lower as the years go on; and in twenty years — though I'm not sure of the timing — the downtown store will become a basement-and-budget type of operation only." The suburbs were seen as drawing off the "upper-crust" customer. Cheap goods and cheap people went hand in hand, but downtown investors would not witness this "decline" without a fight.[60]

Concerns about declining downtown customers and goods were deeply tied to fears that the encircling slums would overrun the central business district. A 1958 *Fortune* magazine article explained that slums "are eating away at the heart of the cities, especially their downtown areas. The slums would, in fact, be much easier for the cities to endure if they were off in fringe areas. But in . . . almost every major metropolitan city — the slums envelop and squeeze the core of the city like a Spanish boot."[61] *Life* magazine vividly illustrated this threat in an article entitled "An Encroaching Menace." It began this way: "The slums of Chicago each year have pushed closer to the heart of the city. Some of the worst came only six blocks from the glittering skyscrapers. There a newly-aroused and desperate city stopped them. But elsewhere in the metropolis, every month, new slums are being born." An aerial photograph depicted twenty-three square miles of "hopelessly blighted" slums as "a solid red ring around the heart of downtown" (fig. 5.4). Redevelopment could save the "glittering skyscrapers" from being extinguished by encroaching blight.[62]

The vaguely "spreading," "crawling," and "burrowing" slums posed a more specific threat: that the downtown would become a local shopping destination for nearby residents and cease to draw from entire regions. One retailing textbook prompted its students, "If the lower-income class still lives in downtown areas approaching the slums and if these people do not demand broad and choice assortments, why should the downtown store stock broad assortments?" Investors assumed that "slums are poor customers."[63]

Of course, racial and ethnic tensions permeated the ring-of-slums concept in the 1950s. Although the urban renewal approach of forced relocations meant that each participating city had to negotiate its unique ethnic divisions, it was black-white differences that received the widest national attention.[64] One critic complained that the press manipulated racial tensions by painting a "'horror picture' of the liberal but naive northern city, throttled and trampled upon by the 'uneducated, criminal Negro Frankenstein.'" *Scientific American* in 1957 attributed the declining "character" and "cheapness" of the central shopping district to racial incursion: "The downtown stores, with non-white and low-income customers more and more predominant in their clientele, tend to concentrate on cheap merchandise. . . . But in most cities — Chicago, Boston, Los Angeles are good examples — the main streets become infested with 'sucker joints' for tourists; all-night jewelry auctions, bargain linens and cheap neckties, hamburger stands, and bars with jazz bands. The slums, in other words, are spreading to the central business district." The city's attraction of poor and nonwhite customers induced this "honky-tonk transformation of the downtown business areas." The racialized fears that downtowns might become "lower-class ethnic islands" of commerce added urgency to the calls for urban renewal and articulated a preference for who should be downtown.[65]

To many downtown investors, the prospect of serving poor, nonwhite shoppers was a "nightmare," not a vision, of future urban commercial life.

Figure 5.4 Fears for the downtown's future included the anxiety that it might become an African American shopping district, a scenario that some investors found more threatening than abandonment. In 1955 *Life* magazine featured this image in an article entitled "An Encroaching Menace." The caption read, "Two slum buildings, soon to be razed and replaced by a vast housing project, bracket the Palmolive building a few blocks east in Chicago." Supporters of redevelopment argued that the urban renewal programs of the 1950s and 1960s would save downtown skyscrapers and department stores from the adjacent poor, largely nonwhite neighborhoods. (*Life*, April 11, 1955, 125. Reproduced with permission of Fritz Goro/ Time Life Pictures/Getty Images.)

One university study projected what would happen to the typical medium-sized American city — "Case City, U.S.A." — by 1980. Without intervention, Case City (in reality, Trenton, New Jersey) would become a "nightmarish, ethnic and low-income ghetto. Downtown may well be abandoned, or else be a Negro shopping district." Downtown could turn into a "commercial slum," and "big slum areas, like these Negro-occupied tenements close by a railroad, could easily engulf the city." For these city planners, complete abandonment and domination by black shoppers were equally appalling future scenarios for the downtown.[66]

Supporters of postwar urban renewal policies found dramatic appeal in the encroachment threat and the presumed decline of downtown retail. Victor Gruen, a famous commercial designer, and Larry Smith, a real estate economist, argued that downtown decline would continue "as long as the ring of blighted and slum areas which surrounds so many of our downtown districts is not broken. . . . The slum clearance and rehabilitation sections of the Housing Act of 1949 might very well open the way to eliminate the slums which choke the downtown areas."[67] Even before legislators modified the Housing Act of 1949 in 1954 to permit aid to nonresidential projects, redevelopers viewed housing policy in relation to the downtown. The proposed rebuilding of poor neighborhoods to enhance the downtown had long precedent in master plans. But in the 1950s the actual occurrence of massive demolition and rebuilding had gained momentum.

The indirectness of these justifications (constricting slums and cheapening retail) for renewal derived impact from the fact that in the early 1950s, most policymakers and investors avoided discussing racial issues publicly. Jim Downs, while describing "the race problem" of redevelopment relocation, pointed out that "sometimes public speakers do not make a direct allusion to this fact." This silence was slowly set aside as the Civil Rights movement made discussions of race and urban problems "less inhibited." HHFA director Cole, in "shirt-sleeve" conferences with citizens around the country in 1955, "was surprised to learn how many people talk about minority housing, Negro housing, bankers and others." In response, he "brought to Washington people on all sides of this problem. Never before had they sat there and discussed this problem frankly and honestly. It can be done."[68]

It also became increasingly common to unmask and challenge the race-based motivations behind redevelopment. Community outrage erupted over a 1952 Atlanta plan that condemned Auburn Avenue, a core African American business and residential district, as a slum area choking the downtown. Responding to protests, city officials redrew their maps. They retracted the plans to shift "the colored center of gravity" and generally "beautify" the black business district by replacing the small, jumbled shops with a monumental civic center. Learning from such episodes, redevelopers played down the use of the offensive word *slum*. At one urban renewal clinic, the "expert who moderated these sessions warned against the promiscuous use of the word 'slum,' since it reflects adversely on the people themselves living in these areas. To be successful, the program must enlist the support of such people and gain their cooperation. This cannot be done by calling them crime-ridden, disease-ridden, and personally unwholesome." [69]

Although an array of factors explained and fueled changes in urban life, in the 1960s racialized interpretations began to drown out the others. At the decade's beginning, there was an eager rush among journalists to discuss race and urban development. By attributing all urban problems to the "Negro in-migrant," one expert regretted, "writers for the weekly periodicals of national circulation are having a field day. A real understanding of the urban complex either requires too much of their time, or is too great a challenge for their intellects. Or, perhaps, it is not sensational enough to sell the magazines." Said *Fortune* magazine in 1962, "the Negro problem is what city planners and officials are really talking about when they refer to The City Problem." The city's only hope was to face up to this fact. The lumping together of African Americans with "a long list of city problems," here presented to sensitize readers to difficulties faced by blacks, foreshadowed the even greater reliance upon racial factors to explain all urban problems that would follow the riots of the mid-1960s.[70]

The Wrecking Ball of Obsolescence

In 1954 and 1955, the head of the U.S. government's Housing and Home Finance Agency, Albert Cole, was in high demand as a speaker around the country. Congress had just passed the Housing Act of 1954, making Cole one of the Eisenhower administration's lead promoters of urban renewal. Cole and his colleagues had a lot to explain. Why should Americans support government-sponsored demolition of portions of the downtown — the very buildings they had cherished? Urban renewal was a drastic, large-scale solution, especially when compared to the modest improvement strategies of the Progressive era, but also in relation to the spotty demolition and modernization of the depression. In the postwar period, Americans still had to be weaned from the Main Street ideal, which previously had been so central to concepts of commercial health. The key to effecting this break was the manner in which Cole and other redevelopers successfully promoted the belief that an era in the downtown's history had closed. They labeled the "old" downtown and its modest aspirations "obsolete," moving the vital downtown into the realm of outmoded memories and out of the living present.

In an era when the primary fears for the future of urban commercial life (namely, racial changes and the fading role of suburban housewife-shoppers) were usually expressed indirectly, it was the concept of obsolescence that re-developers wielded as a weapon to remake downtowns. Obsolescence rendered certain districts powerless and eligible for destruction. It was literally the label used in federal, state, and local redevelopment documents to certify buildings for demolition. The word *obsolete* appeared in speeches, conferences, articles, investment newsletters, government reports, and real estate appraisals; two scholars found that it was the "operative term" in urban renewal. A typical condemnation read like this assessment of Pittsburgh: "When World War II ended, Pittsburgh's downtown area was a smog-blanketed huddle of grimy old buildings. Exhausted by the war effort, the City had drifted into obsolescence."[71] This relegation of Main Street to the past set the terms for moving forward to the improvement agenda of urban renewal.

On August 9, 1954, Albert Cole addressed an audience in Kansas City after attending a demolition ceremony at a redevelopment site. He proposed that the demolition ceremony was "new and unique in our American community customs. Normally in the past, our civic ceremonies have had to do with the laying of a cornerstone, the opening of a new building or bridge or other monument to our steady growth. This time we meet to initiate a tearing down — the elimination and demolition of our outworn past. That, I think, is significant. It is symbolic of a new maturity. . . . We must not only build, but we must tear down and rebuild again." In the 1950s, rebuilding indeed became the cornerstone of downtown investment strategies.[72]

Not cavalier about "the elimination and demolition of our outworn past," Cole was sensitive to the fond attachments his audiences might have to the downtown. He explained that "much of our approach to the problem of slum and blight depends on how we look at it. . . . We look at our towns and cities through two pairs of eyes. We sometimes see them through the eyes of our younger days — the way they were in years past." Cole asserted that nostalgic views were legitimate: "Usually this is a pleasant recollection. We see behind the growth and grime of years to the streets, the shops, and homes and trees as we like to remember them." At the same time, through what Cole called "the more mature eyes of the present," we could see the necessity of tearing down the old. We experience shock at seeing "once vital sections of the city . . . now down-at-the-heels and disreputable, decaying and skidding toward a slow but certain death." Only radical surgery, as urban renewal was often called, could save the patient. Cole invoked the comforting inevitability of organic decline to reassure Americans of the need to rebuild.[73]

Cole recommended a third pair of eyes for viewing cities, sketching out a new, motivating urban vision, albeit one that required a willingness to "eliminate" the worn-out past. "We need to see them not as they once were, not solely as they are today — but to envision them as they should be and can be in the future." Cole sought to bring his audience to this third point of view, saying, "This ceremony today denotes your decision to rebuild a part of your past to serve your future. . . . You have begun the task of clearing a large and potentially valuable downtown section that had become a financial burden and a social liability to the whole city."[74]

Suburban shopping centers, as shown earlier in this chapter, had raised, transformed, and further feminized the obsolescence standards of commercial aesthetics. One expert described the downtown retailer's challenge: you looked at "your old and out-dated building and tried to think of how you could make your store, a building probably twenty-five, fifty or one hundred years old, look like some of the modern stores in our shopping centers." Describing Main Street as "seedy," "gone-to-pot," and "dowdy," the *Downtown Idea Exchange* asserted in the 1950s that "in scores of cities the downtown area hasn't had a face-lifting — not to mention a mere face-washing — in decades." In that decade, the radical solutions of urban renewal ultimately took center stage. Architect Victor Gruen concluded that "the cure of obsolescence . . . is not periodic remodeling of interiors and storefronts, a few street widenings, and other makeshift devices." The *Downtown Idea Exchange* proposed that "the *antiquated building* poses a thorny problem. Downtown could be modernized tremendously if some of these were knocked down and replaced with more up-to-date efficient structures." In Cole's words, the worn-out past must be "eliminated," not remodeled.[75]

As they determined that the diverse streetscape aesthetic of small, older, independent storefronts was obsolete, redevelopers labeled the small retailers' merchandising techniques obsolete, too. Critics chastised merchants for allowing the business district's appearance to deteriorate and condemned their depression-era storefront modernizations as inadequate and counterproductive. According to this accusation, Main Street had brought on its own troubles by turning to "panicky, piecemeal" solutions "consisting largely of tricks, gimmicks, and promotion ideas plus a few parking garages and one-way streets." *Gimmicks* was a word frequently used to trivialize existing efforts at retail survival. Downtown merchants, because of their monopoly, ineffectually endured a "Horse-and-Buggy-Age traffic design." One critic expressed his view that "downtown merchants have been incompetent capitalists with a captive audience for a long time." Sitting "on their fannies too long" with their old buildings, small merchants were already pursuing a path of "self-destruction."[76] Actual destruction would be the logical next step.

The proprietors of these smaller businesses were usually kept out of urban renewal planning by the large chains and department stores. Prominent re-tailers cultivated connections with local politicians and had a special claim on city morale, and the national chains had broad-based resources that made them desirable tenants. Such assets gave both access to the redevelopment process. Furthermore, the frustrated and overwhelmed small retailers were often of a different ethnicity than the executives spearheading redevelopment. Such was the case in New Haven, Connecticut. Most of the several hundred businesses relocated by the Church Street redevelopment were Jewish-owned. Excluded from the planning process, they first heard of the renewal proposal in the newspapers. Smaller operations, according to one Illinois survey, were "introverted" and presented a "dampened spirit." City officials sponsoring downtown plans were often unable to get these merchants on board.[77]

Thus the retailers out of step with urban renewal were stigmatized as stuck in the past and obsolete themselves, and they failed to mount an effective defense against these accusations. The Illinois investigator concluded, "The small businessman's beliefs are strongly tinged with a romantic yearning for the past, of a longing for a return to an older individualism, hoping somehow to reconstruct that 'Golden Age' in the American past when everyone was downtown; when the selling was an easy, friendly, and personal thing; and when profits came without any of the growing worries associated with present baffling changes." Resistant small merchants understood that an era of urban commerce was closing but were unable, according to redevelopers, to move forward to a bright new future because of their fundamental passivity and "romantic yearning."[78]

By the late 1950s, as more Main Street buildings fell to renewal, a counter-movement invigorated by urbanist Jane Jacobs asserted that old, diverse, small stores had economic and aesthetic value. Some began to argue that buildings actually improved with age. In 1960 *Architectural Forum* ran a gal-lery of photographs that celebrated "these odd old store fronts" (fig. 5.5). Where Cole and others found grimy buildings, *Architectural Forum* admired the storefronts as having "human richness" and "the kind of rich raw color which improves with age, acquiring heart with layers of city grit." The writer

Figure 5.5 By the late 1950s a polite countermovement had arisen to challenge the destructive power of urban renewal and the accompanying view that downtown was obsolete. Its proponents celebrated the jumbled, irregular vernacular of small stores, along with individualistic commercial artifacts like barber poles, pickle barrels, and hand-painted business signs. The caption appearing with this admiring photo gallery informed the reader that

They look hale and hearty, but since being photographed three of these eight old storefronts have perished before progress.

"three of these eight old storefronts have perished before progress." The article showcased "well-worn" storefronts and "Main Street's Vanishing Patina"— exactly the qualities that redevelopers condemned. The unstandardized layout of the photographs underscored the irregular vernacular at stake. (*Architectural Forum,* January 1960, 110–11.)

marked the passing of both the physical streetscape and the accompanying retail organization of independent storekeepers: "Casualties . . . of today's mass
building, the city's colorful old storefronts are poignant reminders of what has
been lost." Main Street demolition "may be something to be uneasy about."[79]
Certainly this was a polite protest, but it made the point that obsolete or worn
out was only one way of describing older downtown businesses and buildings.

It is an important irony of post–World War II downtown redevelopment
that many dimensions of the "old" Main Street ideal that had been discarded
as inadequate for downtown were implemented in the new suburban shopping centers. In the 1950s and 1960s, it seemed that suburban centers had
achieved the simplified, managed commercial environment so elusive to the
downtown for a half century. The *Downtown Idea Exchange* could only urge
businesses to cooperate with each other to create a "sparkling, unified look,"
whereas shopping centers were able to enforce these Progressive era principles. One typical 1952 shopping center lease shaped "the total visual effect"
of the center by demanding that stores both "maintain individual expression"
and "relate harmoniously to the general character of the center and to their
immediate neighbors." The lease regulated the projection, placement, and
size of signs and forbade "individual awnings." Echoing postcard colorization
techniques, the shopping center management required that "colors must har-
monize with the color scheme" of the surrounding stores. Individual expression was desired within a range of conformity.[80]

The term *obsolete* succeeded as a way of describing Main Street in the 1950s
because the public accepted that description. The rapid abandonment of older
neighborhoods and architectural styles was legitimated as a national character trait. One design consultant pointed out that "it is, perhaps, among our
chief characteristics as a nation to reach for something new and better and to
discard what is no longer wanted. Real estate is no exception to the rule." A
real estate professional concluded that, unlike Europeans, who preserve their
heritage, "Americans are fanatics for everything that's new. We dwell upon
modernity — we must keep up with the Joneses, and will not be outmoded."
Redevelopers, particularly the retail executives who spearheaded or cooper-
ated with urban renewal, possessed intimate familiarity with the power of obsolescence. As purveyors of consumer culture, their profits depended upon
convincing customers (often with sophisticated advertising techniques) that
their current belongings were obsolete. Proponents of urban renewal promoted a view of the downtown consistent with their selling expertise, and

Americans ratified the concept partly because of their broader acceptance of obsolescence in their consumption-oriented society.[81]

Using the investment concept of obsolescence, urban renewers broke amicably with previous, relatively modest and stable visions of the future downtown. This break was not so much an outright rejection of the past, as many scholars of modernism contend. Rather, downtown renewal's supporters *and* opponents embellished a collective memory of a vibrant downtown heyday, effectively moving the vital downtown from the living present to the realm of history. They described a downtown golden age, vaguely located in the pre–World War I years and eroding since then. The title of Walker Evans's 1956 article "'Downtown': A Last Look Backward" illustrates the power of nostalgia to clear the path for urban renewal even among those who lavishly admired Main Street. For both sides, brick became "old" brick; the downtown became the "old" downtown.[82]

It is tempting to say that the downtown had become run-down by the 1950s and simply needed to be torn down and rebuilt. But even the terminology handbook used by appraisers said that obsolescence, that key concept of urban renewal, was "not the result of mere age or wear (physical deterioration)."[83] Confronting a messy, chaotic Main Street environment in the early twentieth century, municipal housekeepers and other Progressive era investors aspired to make modest but transformative improvements required to achieve a dignified, unified Main Street corridor. A half century later, downtown investors surveyed their own Main Street disorder, as well as the trends they deemed to be disturbing, and chose to tear it all down and start anew.

Rebuilding the Downtown for Whom?

Amid the many melodramatic proclamations about creeping slums uttered in support of urban renewal, it was easy to overlook the quieter assertion that downtown's uniquely heterogeneous population offered it economic advantages. In the 1950s, there were reasons to question the prevailing wisdom of relying exclusively upon middle-class customers. In contrast to the suburban malls, "designed and located to appeal to a homogeneous market," the downtown was distinctive for drawing "its business from the whole urban area and from all ethnic groups and classes of people." Redevelopers, fearing that the mix would tilt toward domination by poor, nonwhite consumers, turned their back on this diversity. But other urban boosters believed that "the real fruits of civilization can probably only grow in a downtown atmosphere with its mixture of people from many different backgrounds." [84] This was indeed a potent defense of downtown commercial life against suburban replacement.

The case of bargain-basement retailing in the 1950s provides one example of diverse shoppers enhancing (rather than eroding) the downtown's competitive position. When bargain basements gained popularity in the early twentieth century, department store executives reluctantly admitted that the basements aimed to draw low-income consumers — "the shawl trade, the industrial worker, that segment of the city not too frequently seen in the aisles of the main store." The controversial issue at the time was whether the stores were intentionally segregating customers, separating "the masses from the classes — the basket from the automobile trade." One Lord & Taylor buyer in 1901 tried to pierce the democratic rhetoric: "Carriage custom will no more mix with 'basket' trade than will oil with water. Prate about equality as we may, the fact remains that class distinctions exist here as abroad, though not as numerous or sharply drawn." While welcoming more classes under one roof and maximizing profit from previously marginal space, the basement offered a device for separating consumers as well.[85] By the 1950s, downtown department stores primarily used their basements to compete with chain stores and discounters, carrying unbranded first-quality merchandise and seconds.

The new suburban centers were built without bargain basements — a decision that suggested disinterest in the budget-conscious customer. Almost immediately industry analysts speculated that this design choice would have disastrous economic consequences. One 1956 article pointed out that there were "plenty of price-conscious suburbanites," as well as "low and middle cost housing areas in the suburbs." In 1961 *Women's Wear Daily* made the argument more forcefully: "The conventional retailer committed a sin of omission when he did not locate bargain basements in his post-war suburban shopping centers." Perhaps homogeneous commercial life was bad for business.[86]

Back downtown, bargain basements made critical contributions to the retail economy, belying the derogatory stereotypes of "cheap" goods and "cheap" customers. "Despite the tendency for management to treat basements as 'step children,'" one article reminded investors that in catering productively to "lower income customers," these departments drew heavy traffic. The predominantly working-class Basement Store of J. L. Hudson achieved noteworthy success, especially in men's work clothing. The *Daily News Record* claimed that the store "resolutely helps the downtown remain Detroit's biggest shopping section, despite the increase in neighborhood store business." The Basement Store was air-conditioned, carpeted, and lighted in a "modern manner" and provided the same services as the upstairs store. Working-class customers, including a mix of men and women, repaid J. L. Hudson's and helped keep downtown Detroit competitive.[87] In Newark, "one of the country's most depressed downtown areas," Bamberger's Department Store had "met the reality of a high percentage of low-income, non-white customers by modernizing its basement operation." Although the 1960s civil rights demonstrations would reveal that Main Street stores had not truly "met the reality" of nonwhite customers, retailers had found ways to profit from the different markets that coexisted downtown.[88]

On the eve of the 1960s civil disorders, the downtown's status as the city's heterogeneous commercial district was in particular flux. For those who desired it, downtown's diversity held a symbolic resonance that went beyond its economic potential to investors, as it embodied hopes for the supposed liberal openness of America's democratic ideals. An appraiser described the complex crowds: "Once in the central area, peoples of all classes and nationalities merge in a common melting pot. They form a heterogenous mass from which it is impossible to segregate and characterize individual pedestrians."[89]

Yet it *was* in fact possible "to segregate and characterize individual pedestrians," as real estate consultants had done for decades. In the years after World War II, Americans rebuilt their downtowns in order to attract white, middle-class housewives to support the business district's property values. Redevelopers and retailers expressed much ambivalence over nonwhite shoppers and nearby "slum-dwellers," and most appraisers continued to believe that the "co-mingling of all groups regardless of race, nationality and economic status" was "a basic cause of loss of real estate values and blight."[90] Only the accelerated civil rights protests beginning in 1960 forced a true reconsideration of the value of African American shoppers (see chapter 6) — a reevaluation that was unfortunately marked by unprecedented suspense and violence.

In his late-1950s speaking tours, Albert Cole tried to inspire his audiences with the potential of drastic downtown redevelopment: "We are impatient to start living in these bright refurbished towns and cities that urban renewal promises." The urban renewal vision may have been "bright," but it lacked the compelling glow of the Main Street ideal that it displaced. As Cole's choice of words suggests, downtown renewal's picture of future urban commercial life was also hazy on the specifics. For such a self-consciously modern investment concept, it is striking that urban renewal was more effective in condemning the old, vital downtown to the past than it was at imagining a new guiding vision. At the same time, the negative, "nightmarish" alternatives to redevelopment evoked by alarmists were more potent motivating forces than any positive, magnetic ideal.

Finally, although the justifications for large-scale downtown redevelopment attacked Main Street's shabby features, the renewal plans failed to provide significant new street-level objects and thus gave little guidance for storefronts, lampposts, trash cans, sidewalks, and their implications. Besides the preoccupation with creating attractive and fulfilling shopping environments (think of landscaping, sculpture, and piped-in music) and convenient parking for the white middle class, there were a lot of retailing details left for others to worry about. And indeed it was around the details — lunch counters, plywood storefronts, vacant lots, old brick, and new "historic" gaslights — that the meanings given to downtown commercial life would continue to swirl.[91]

6

THE HOLLOW PRIZE?
BLACK BUYERS, RACIAL VIOLENCE,
AND THE RIOT RENAISSANCE

In November 1968, Winton Blount, president of the U.S. Chamber of Commerce, was concerned about the impact of racial violence on the fate of American cities. When he addressed the annual meeting of Alabama's state Chamber of Commerce that month, Blount spoke as an insider who saw troubling national trends. After starting out in Tuskegee on the heels of World War II, he had built up his construction business in Montgomery. It used to be, he said, that a community might be judged by the number of smokestacks, "But today, smokestacks are not enough." Instead, "the general condition of the people, and how they get along with each other is all important." Violent urban unrest was threatening to strangle commerce. In the eyes of the world, noted Blount, "you can best be known for your riots, or your lack of riots." Alabama — home to some of the era's most infamous racial violence — knew firsthand the experience of "unfavorable nationwide publicity," and audience members must have nodded in sympathy when he said, "Other areas throughout the nation have since had similar difficulties."[1]

By the end of the decade, American business executives in cities of all sizes and in all regions could indeed commiserate over the threat racial violence posed to their economic vitality. As Blount observed, it did not matter whether "you are in a metropolitan center or not." When protests over civil rights and voting rights abated in the South in 1964 and 1965, the turmoil picked up elsewhere — in places like Cleveland, New York City, Rochester, Jersey City, and Los Angeles. The "urgent demands" of the disadvantaged were forces "at work to some extent in every community." For those interested in downtown commerce, the omnipresence of violence (and the fear of it) established new standards for evaluating urban commercial life in the 1960s. Cities without violence and racial tensions saw their reputations and business prospects — their air of peacefulness and homogeneity — enhanced because of that absence. And cities enduring unrest were compelled to confront and interpret these shattering experiences and rethink their attitudes toward the future of downtown commerce accordingly.[2]

As violence became a defining force in commercial investment during the 1960s, it arrived in many forms. Urban renewal and highway construction destroyed familiar shopping streets and neighborhoods and severed access from other districts to the downtown. Vietnam war protestors, student and "hippie" demonstrations, civil rights conflicts, riots, and rising crime — all of this blended together into "THE WAVE OF VIOLENCE WHICH IS SWEEPING MUCH OF URBAN AMERICA."[3] But it was the decade's persistent and explosive racial conflicts that seemed most threatening to urban economies and demanded the most immediate response. Since civil rights battles and riots deeply affected stores and other commercial destinations, the fear of violence haunted business owners, other investors, and shoppers engaged in the most ordinary Main Street activities.

One photograph (and the story behind it) captures some of the ways 1960s violence transformed the downtown (fig. 6.1). Appearing in March 1969 in the *Journal of the American Institute of Planners,* the photograph shows people crowding the sidewalk in front of a Thom McAn shoe store. They appear to be shoppers, striding purposefully amid the bustle of a sizable city. Two men in the foreground, however, stand out — partly because of their concerned expressions, and partly because they are walking in the middle of the street. One looks up at the sky; the other wears an armband. The title of the accompanying article, "Black Control of Central Cities: The Hollow Prize," draws attention to the fact that just about everyone in the photograph appears to be African American (except the helmeted police officer); the title ominously suggests some kind of power struggle. Closer examination reveals that these people, marching in the same direction, are protestors.[4]

The photograph — taken on Main Street in Durham, North Carolina, on Friday morning, April 5, 1968, the day after Martin Luther King Jr.'s assassination in Memphis — highlighted not only the tense threat of violence that circumscribed the downtown but also raised a number of other questions. What was the role of African Americans on Main Street? Were they protestors, rioters, or shoppers? What would their impact be on the downtown? The description of the city as a "hollow prize" pushed these questions further, implying that the fight was for control of a place that was increasingly empty of value.

Whether bloodshed reigned or nonviolent protest won the day, the atmo-

Figure 6.1 This photograph depicts a silent march in Durham, North Carolina, on April 5, 1968. The photo, and the story behind it as described in the text, captures some of the ways racial conflict in the 1960s transformed the downtown and raised new questions for the future of urban commerce. The image accompanied a 1969 article entitled "Black Control of Central Cities: The Hollow Prize," which appeared in the *Journal of the American Institute of Planners*. (Reproduced with permission of Billy E. Barnes, photographer.)

sphere of racial conflict moved from the periphery to the center of American commercial life in the 1960s. Between 1960 and 1964, sit-ins and mass demonstrations introduced vivid images of downtown conflict to all Americans as integrationists and resisters fought battles in broad daylight with television cameras whirring. After 1964 national attention shifted to so-called ghettos, to ghetto merchants, and to allegations of exploitative retail practices. Widespread looting and arson would plague urban commerce into the early 1970s, reaching beyond the well-known examples of Watts, Detroit, and Newark to touch smaller cities throughout the nation.[5]

Amid this turmoil — and the weekend of nationwide violence following King's murder — the photograph of Durham's silent protest march seemed to capture a moment of calm. But violence lurked all around. The man looking at the sky, local activist Howard Fuller, later explained that he had spotted figures with rifles on the downtown rooftops and could not tell whether they were Ku Klux Klan snipers or policemen. The man with an armband, a member of the local black college's football team, had been enlisted with his teammates by Fuller as a security force. That day, Fuller was credited with "almost single handedly" keeping peace in the city the previous night, turning back an angry crowd before it reached downtown. The prickly peace of the march proved to be illusory, or at least not sustainable. The following night firebombs exploded at eleven locations in Durham.[6]

In their respective regions, the riots and boycotts were deeply implicated in the lore of downtown decline, speeding (it was said) white flight to suburbia and shopping malls and sapping the vitality of both Main Street and black business districts. Business leaders such as Blount saw little difference between the violence of civil rights conflicts and that of riots, for both challenged the vitality and existing order of downtown commerce, and both loomed large in the popular imagination. Yet investors faced too many questions and issues arising from the turmoil to draw a simple causal link between the unrest and urban disinvestment, even though this was tempting. Inasmuch as the civil rights demonstrations and the riots constituted strategies for "improving" Main Street, the violence revealed shockingly profound disagreement over Main Street's present and future.

To be sure, violence gave drama and legitimacy to the post–World War II preoccupation with downtown decline, but violence also challenged investors and shoppers to debate and create new commercial practices and values. The racial conflicts drew attention to the increasing dependence of downtown businesses on African American and other nonwhite consumers and required that investors and merchants, no matter how reluctant, respond decisively and publicly to that reality. Facing demands for desegregation, retailers at first could not decide whether integration would ruin them, save them, or have no impact at all. In later years, the riots brought despair while also raising the hope that corporate America would rebuild, thereby remedying past racial injustices. Could heretofore underappreciated black consumers and black businesses in fact resuscitate urban commercial life? Would blacks take over urban businesses, leading to a resurgence of black entrepreneurship? Or would the violence itself, while revealing crippling Main Street flaws, undermine any chance of rebuilding a more democratic, inclusive commercial life? In these chaotic years of presumed decline, downtown stores — both the hollow and the prized — would serve as sites for the negotiation of new urban values.

Black Buyers: Downtown's Overlooked Salvation?

The 1960–64 civil rights era of mass demonstrations marked, among other things, a prolonged and violent struggle over the place of African American consumers on Main Street. The protests brought to national attention what the retail industry had increasingly recognized in the 1950s — the likelihood that downtown businesses in the South and the urban North needed black customers in order to survive. Yet hostilities ignited when African Americans attempted to share equally with whites the places of urban commerce. The question plaguing downtown investors was which American consumers would underpin those high but wavering commercial property values — whites, nonwhites, or a peaceful mix. Even as the short-term economic impact of civil unrest came into unfortunate focus, the long-term impact of integration on downtown values was unclear to shoppers and merchants alike.

Before the 1960s, only the rare white investor or consultant challenged the prevailing dogma that the presence of African Americans or race mixing on Main Street brought property values down. Black consumers were ignored, marginalized, and even feared by white Main Street investors, a practice codified in the South as segregation. Many supporters of urban renewal in the 1950s hoped to reverse the trend of nonwhite shoppers downtown with the demolition of close-in black neighborhoods, new highway construction, and drastic downtown rebuilding (fig. 6.2). These actions were taken in the name of business district improvement and the attempt to bring back the white suburban shopper.

Yet it was also in the 1950s that mainstream retail trade journals such as *Women's Wear Daily* (*WWD*) began to take a more positive interest in the increasingly urban-oriented African American consumer market. This was occurring, as one 1962 report stated, because "the Negro population in major urban centers could be the salvation of downtown stores." Others more modestly raised the question of whether retailers were missing an opportunity by ignoring nonwhite shoppers. When in 1954 *WWD* investigated how merchants were responding to the "Shifting Strata of Population" in San Francisco, one chain executive argued that "Downtown Oakland merchants are becoming more and more dependent on the Negro customer." This, he believed, was a positive trend, and he thought retailers had a duty to protect and enhance the improved economic position gained by nonwhites since the war.[7] Thus downtown businesses had begun to openly discuss the notion of black shoppers as an overlooked resource even before mass civil rights demonstra-

Figure 6.2 New highways and various urban renewal projects cut off many residential neighborhoods from the downtown in the 1950s and 1960s. In Winston-Salem, North Carolina, on a May morning in 1965, this man stood at the end of a fenced-off street that previously led into the commercial district. Often the nonwhite and poorer residents of these close-in neighborhoods were deemed to be less desirable consumers by many downtown retailers. (Reproduced with permission of Billy E. Barnes, photographer.)

tions appeared on the scene. A debate finally emerged, to replace the decades-old investment cliché that segregation preserved property values and ensured business prosperity.

Another sign of the growing recognition of nonwhite customers was the disagreements that sprang up over the potential pitfalls of focused marketing to African Americans. Retailers pondered, for example, the impact (positive and negative) of the "conspicuous absence of colored mannequins" in Harlem. Although customers had increasingly requested more diverse mannequins, white merchants regarded this innovation as "tricky" and "risky," for they feared offending customers. The director of Greater New York's Urban League favored the marketing move but "cautioned against the use of stereotypes" in developing the models. When asked about the idea, the owner of a dress shop that had been on 125th Street for thirty-five years cautioned, "We want to please our customers without racial distinction but they might think such a move would be over-solicitous."[8] Merchants resisted changing the outward signals — the racial identity of models in television and print advertising, the mannequins — that broadcast publicly whether black shoppers should feel welcome.[9]

Black urbanization and white suburbanization had made African Americans "more and more the central city customer" in the South and the North, yet retailers were reluctant to acknowledge and cater to black consumers. Critics (including marketers) asserted "that retailers and manufacturers are overlooking, ignoring, or even chasing away, unknowingly, the Negro buyer," proving that the vast majority of businesses were "willing to gamble on the loss" of the African American market. As in the case of the mannequins, most merchants had thought about the changing demographics but had done nothing. And while businesspeople wrung their hands about using black mannequins (afraid of appearing "over-solicitous"), during the same years retailers fell over themselves attempting to attract the elusive white suburban shopper, carefully designing a consumer environment they thought would draw her back. In a particularly prophetic choice of words, one 1959 article investigated the charge that "merchandisers are napping and neglecting the $18–19 billion Negro market, while much of it marches right by the downtown store." In a few months, black customers would indeed be "marching" by the stores as protestors, and merchants would no longer be able to ignore their impact.[10]

"Don't Drift Downtown": The Weapon of Economic Aggression

One goal of the civil rights demonstrators was improving Main Street according to their own vision of an integrated commercial life, and the marches, placards, rallies, demonstrations, boycotts, and various sit-ins, lie-ins, and kneel-ins brought a new kind of black presence (or absence) downtown. In the early 1960s, as the nonviolent protestors took to the stores and the streets in large numbers, southern white resistance quickly made the downtown air thick with tension, resentment, and fear. Between the 1960 lunch-counter sit-ins at stores like Woolworth and the 1963 riots, bloodshed, and bombings in Birmingham, the intensity of physical violence mounted steadily. The year 1963 witnessed unprecedented, widely televised mass demonstrations, with peaceful protestors taunted and pried from their seats at lunch counters and marchers beaten. The Civil Rights movement finally forced downtown businesses to acknowledge their dependence on black consumers. But the economic aggression used by the protestors to reform Main Street was transformed by white resistance into a stigmatizing violence that came to figure prominently in the explanations of downtown decline in the South. The atmosphere of violence drove away patrons, black and white. By decade's end it was unclear whether integrated urban commerce could sustain the downtown economy or whether the violence had ruined any chance for improvement.[11]

In the first months of the sit-ins, merchants became concerned not only about protests but also about the violent response that might engulf their businesses. Bomb threats became a familiar aggravation for variety stores and their customers. In Greensboro, North Carolina, "the pressure of white hecklers had threatened to make the situation explosive" and forced Woolworth and Kress to close early one Saturday to avoid catastrophe, as countless stores would do during the decade. As sympathy picketing and new demonstrations spread across the Carolinas; Virginia; Washington, D.C.; New York; and Florida, anxiety took firm hold of retailers. "Merchants aren't saying much about this," reported one source in Washington, "but they're scared to death, because they are afraid they will lose business either way."[12]

Interactions that in other contexts might be seen as part of the normal bustle and jostling contact of downtown life became the sparks that ignited racial violence. In Portsmouth, Virginia, one hundred African Americans packed into Rose's lunch counter, since all the other counters had heeded police advice to shut down. A waitress reported that "some Negro boys had leaned against the backs of customers." Witnesses claimed that a young black man "banged a white boy's head against the counter." The ensuing "scuffle" shifted to the street and "broke into a chain-swinging street fight today between white and Negro teen-agers." This kind of density did not bode well for city cash registers. In High Point, North Carolina, a fistfight erupted after whites taunted protestors leaving the local Woolworth. In Chattanooga, fire hoses were turned against a mixed "mob" of several thousand. Police escorted sit-in participants from a drugstore in South Carolina, after an angry crowd of whites "hurled" a bottle of ammonia into the store. In the same disturbance, a black demonstrator was knocked off a stool, and another was pelted with egg. Heckling, making sexual threats, elbowing, shoving, and tossing itching powder were other resistance tactics that greeted the efforts of African Americans to be treated as normal downtown customers.[13] Within a few weeks of the first 1960 sit-ins, widespread patterns of "lesser" violence were established on Main Street. As more dramatic disturbances took center stage,

Figure 6.3 Because of civil rights protests and white resistance to integration, tension and fear became a daily part of Main Street commerce. In this May 1963 demonstration in Raleigh, North Carolina, women walked on the inside for greater protection against possible attack. The threat of severe violence (as seen in other cities on the local news) also remained on people's minds. These protestors asked, "Will Raleigh Become Another Birmingham?" (Reprinted by permission of the *News & Observer* of Raleigh, North Carolina. Print courtesy of the Department of Cultural Resources, State of North Carolina.)

the chronic minor conflicts ceased to get the same attention from reporters, yet they set the tone for daily downtown interactions.

The escalating violence increasingly portrayed downtown as a place where one might encounter confrontations and physical injury, even on a mere shopping excursion. "As a Negro woman student left a store in Raleigh, N.C.," one reporter observed, "a white man raked a cigar across the back of her sweater. 'Did you burn it?' she asked in a quiet voice. He turned away smiling and folded his arms." His live ash, however, had fallen from her sweater onto his coat sleeve and smoldered there. The burning ash likely symbolized for the reporter the simmering segregationist hostility setting the pace of conflict.[14] During marches, women often walked on the more protected side, away from the street, while men took the outside. One woman recalled, "The marchers on the outside were the ones who were willing to risk their lives to protect the others, that they were to throw their bodies forcefully on us to take us to the ground, to protect us from any kind of danger" (fig. 6.3).[15]

The scale and frequency of violence around the sit-ins and boycotts rose to match people's fears, and the reporters' language became less restrained. A "near-riot" developed in Tallahassee. Beatings, mass arrests, and firebombings rocked Jacksonville. A Woolworth sit-in in Jackson, Mississippi, witnessed "racial violence burst into full scale." In Nashville hundreds of integrationist demonstrators occupied the downtown and rallied nightly in the Sears parking lot.[16]

Cities were regularly catapulted back into the news, since they often resolved one race issue only to see a different one arise. Savannah endured disturbances in 1960 around integration, but in 1963 there again was "a pall hanging over the downtown business sector." That year the problem was black employment. The "several-times-daily mass assemblies, the alarming display of determined force, the omnipresent city and county police and riot equipment ever on the ready, and the constant reports of incidents of violence have kept the streets, squares and stores almost deserted." Also in 1963, a year after desegregation in Mobile, Alabama, pickets suddenly resumed in front of Woolworth. Only this time the White Citizens Council carried the signs, which read "Help Integration. Trade at Woolworth" (fig. 6.4). Southern cities saw the 1968 marches sparked by Martin Luther King Jr.'s assassination as yet another convulsion of periodic protest. In any given community, the levels of outright conflict ebbed and flowed, but as a national composite, the "nonviolent" violence stretched across the decade, with boycotts and marches continuing long after the riots began.[17]

Of course, Birmingham in 1963 came to embody the worst civil rights–related violence, but peaceful protests also rocked that city's commercial and civic order. On May 7, 1963, *Birmingham News* reported, "Swarms of Negro school students flooded the downtown section this afternoon, sweeping shoppers and passersby before them, causing traffic jams and turning a large section into 45 minutes of confusion" (fig. 6.5). Over the previous weeks, police had crafted a geographic defense of the downtown shopping district, whereby African American protestors were held back by a police line near the black district bordering on downtown. More than a thousand students — shouting, singing, praying, and clapping — circulated through the major department stores and obstructed key shopping intersections. "For a minute or two there was near pandemonium with sirens screaming, Negroes singing and chanting and horns of impatient drivers blowing." One hundred students paraded through the premier local department store, Loveman's; many of them lay down in protest. The most serious accusation against the young people was

Integration Spur to Sales InSouth;NewThreatsLoom

Figure 6.4 Chain stores, department stores, and the adjacent sidewalks were the focus of confrontations over the place of African Americans on Main Street during the early 1960s. Protestors on all sides of civil rights issues picketed stores. The pattern resulted in sporadic disruptions of commercial activity, sometimes spanning many years. Here, members of the White Citizens Council in Mobile, Alabama, protest desegregation in 1963, even though that city's lunch counters and other facilities had been integrated for a year. Their ironic motto "Help Integration: Trade at Woolworth" also raised a crucial new question for retailers — whether integrated consumer crowds would hurt or actually save the struggling Main Street businesses. (*Women's Wear Daily,* September 23, 1963, 21.)

Figure 6.5 This photograph appeared in the *Birmingham News* on May 7, 1963, above the headline "Swarm over Downtown Area." A thousand young demonstrators broke through the police lines isolating the downtown shopping district and circulated peacefully through the stores and streets. This created apparent chaos for motorists and shoppers, however. For city leaders who were already fearful of integration, the image of African Americans overtaking the city's key retail intersection and "swarming" stores could be more symbolic of disorder than actual violence like the tear gas bombing pictured in figure 6.6. (Photo by the *Birmingham News*, copyright 2001. All rights reserved. Reprinted with permission.)

that the sprinting students "shoved" white women shoppers aside in their press to reach the stores. For city leaders who harbored racial fears and dreaded the prospect of integration, the specter of African Americans overrunning the city's key shopping intersection and "swarming" stores could be more symbolic of disorder than any actual violence. In essence, the dense 100% district had become "integration corner." [18]

Three months later actual violence came to downtown Birmingham businesses in the form of a tear gas bomb that exploded on Loveman's main floor during lunch hour (fig. 6.6). Within minutes, "the sidewalks outside the store were crowded with shoppers, coughing, gagging and vomiting." Unconscious

Figure 6.6 When a tear gas bomb exploded in Loveman's Department Store in Birmingham in August 1963, most people immediately concluded that it was the work of segregationists. Photographs of unconscious shoppers being carried to ambulances did not enhance the "relaxing," "attractive" atmosphere cultivated by downtown investors hoping to bring back suburban housewives. Events such as this further stigmatized the downtown as a violent and dangerous place. (Birmingham, Ala., Police Department Surveillance Files, no. 1125.7.20. Courtesy of the Department of Archives and Manuscripts, Birmingham Public Library.)

women "sprawled" on the sidewalk and in the alley. One reporter pointed out that most of the fleeing women wore high heels. Ambulances rushed six victims to the hospital, eighteen sought treatment at the hospital on their own, and countless others turned to private physicians. Luckily, once the initial discomfort from the fumes had passed, none of the sufferers endured long-term harm.[19]

The Loveman's bomb, the downtown "swarm," the firehosing of children — this was not the relaxing, pleasant shopping atmosphere that downtown investors hoped to create in response to suburban competition. Numerous witnesses testified that a white man wearing a blue business suit dropped the bomb and fled out a side door, and city officials were certain that the perpetrators opposed Loveman's recent integration of its lunch counter. For nearly a month, members of the National States Rights Party, wearing "Nazi-type uniforms," had passed out leaflets in front of Birmingham's major department stores. Carrying anti-Semitic placards and Confederate flags, they blamed Jews for "all the integration problems." A downtown boycott lasting more than a year had cut the city's business by about 30 percent. Few blacks were seen shopping downtown, and there were more empty storefronts than during the depression. The boycott's effectiveness prompted one downtown worker to propose that the "swarming" protestors should indeed have been welcomed like a rush of customers during a dry spell: "When those Negroes ran into Loveman's the sales people should have said 'hooray!'"[20] Humor hinted at the critical question of who was welcome downtown, especially given the difficult economic circumstances and threatening forecast facing the business district.

Most merchants hoped that the impact of the violent events would be temporary and recovery would soon follow, but the situation in Birmingham deteriorated. A month after the department store bomb, four children were killed by an explosion in their downtown church. This was an unspeakable personal tragedy. It was also a downtown tragedy. The retail industry incorporated such atrocities into their regular accounting of sales figures, and the results were bizarre. *Women's Wear Daily* said of Birmingham: "Hard hit last Monday and Tuesday by a weekend explosion of racial violence and death, downtown department and specialty stores had made a rapid recovery by mid-week." Six months later, another headline read, "Race Riots Upset Jacksonville Sales," when demonstrations and mass arrests sent shoppers flocking to the malls.[21]

Birmingham's violence fanned fears that the turmoil "may spread to other cities" (see fig. 6.3). One 1963 investigation for the hardware industry used Birmingham as a case study of how civil rights battles were affecting business. That report concluded (even after the church bombing) that "in spite of regional, social and economic differences, Birmingham has much in common with cities around the country." There was little point in pitying Birmingham for its horrifying headlines, since the problems it exemplified could be found in Peoria. The anxieties easily reached outside the segregated South, especially as issues like discriminatory hiring practices sparked demonstrations. There were also sympathy pickets in other cities. When a nationwide Christmas boycott was proposed by African Americans to protest the Birmingham bombings, *WWD* predicted that "particularly hard hit would be merchants in large northern cities with a heavy proportion of Negro populations." At the same time, by unnerving businesspeople around the country, Birmingham's example provoked greater cooperation with the goals of desegregation elsewhere.[22]

To retailers, the "powerful weapons" of boycotts and pickets were often more damaging than rock-throwing demonstrators. At times it seemed that all sides in the conflict expected to make their points by cutting off Main Street trade. In Birmingham, as the spring 1963 boycott heated up, the Reverend Martin Luther King Jr. asked African Americans to return their store credit cards and stop shopping in the city center. He told an audience that "downtown Birmingham will not be left alone until our freedom is won." Five weeks later, twelve miles outside of the city, Klan members were advised by their leadership to do the exact same thing. Police Chief Bull Connor also chimed in with his own demand that citizens stop patronizing downtown businesses that desegregated. In complicated civil rights battles, stores were sometimes boycotted simultaneously by segregationists and integrationists.[23]

Segregationists increased the scope and visibility of their pickets and boycotts during the early 1960s. In Little Rock, Arkansas, the Capitol Citizens Council mailed thirty thousand postcards to whites in the region's cities, asking the recipients to withhold their business from stores serving African Americans. In fact, rumors of a nationwide "counterboycott" circulated periodically. In Bogalusa, Louisiana, segregationist counterpickets walked next to young African American demonstrators on Main Street. The segregationists carried signs reading "White Man, Give This Merchandise Your Business" and "Support This Business Place. Fight Communism." One shoe shop's radio commercial encouraged citizens to "defeat the agitators by going to town to shop." City police, state troopers, and FBI agents "lined the sidewalks."[24] It was difficult to sort out the meaning of such a complicated spectacle for Bogalusa business, other than its significance in lost dollars.[25]

The economic aggression was successful enough at damaging downtown businesses that retailers were rightfully frightened. They (and the reporters that dogged them) turned to metaphors of murder to describe the protestors' nonviolent strategies. Black customers "are now using the boycott technique to cut at the merchant's economic vitals," noted one article. A banker in Chester, Pennsylvania, described the demonstration strategies there as strangulation: "They've got Chester business by the throat and they're choking it to death." Blame for economic fatalities was not exclusively placed on the integrationists — merchants who sympathized with the civil rights cause faulted white resistance for the prolonged conflict.[26] Other retailers, fearful of appearing weak, publicly denied feeling any economic impact, claiming (as did one South Carolina source) that "Negro customers streamed past the pickets" and sales had remained steady.[27] But it was hard to continue with such denials in the face of obvious turmoil. During Atlanta's peak Christmas buying season in 1960, retail sources estimated that department stores lost virtually 100 percent of the African American trade. Reporters relentlessly tried to pin down the exact sales losses. "Most merchants are reluctant to comment openly," observed one reporter, speaking of Raleigh, "but they admit the sit-downs have hurt business." Sales receipts for the women's shoe section of a Jacksonville department store tallied $800 one day during the 1964 Easter boycott, compared to $2,200 the previous year. Business in some Natchez, Mississippi, stores dropped by 50 percent during a particularly impressive 1965 boycott, and city leadership caved in to all of the protestors' demands.[28]

Although the scale of economic damage further dramatized and publicized the high numbers of black customers, merchants still had a tendency to "almost universally deny having any idea of how much they depend on Negro patronage," according to *Ebony*'s publisher. Birmingham's boycott brought out the facts that Pizitz's Department Store customarily had 50 percent black trade and that Atlantic Mills Thrift Center relied upon a customer base that was 75 percent black. *WWD* in 1962 reported that 20 percent of all downtown consumers were black, but the individual store numbers released by *Ebony* were often significantly higher. In Knoxville, merchants turned the boycotts into an opportunity to declare publicly how little they cared about their African American clients, no matter how numerous. Rumors flew that the city's department stores were going to initiate a counterboycott in which they would refuse to serve African Americans in any department. Some stores permanently closed their lunch counters, and one retailer said of black consumers: "They need us more than we need them."[29] Many southerners resented having their economic dependence upon African American shoppers emphasized; one Birmingham segregationist ridiculed and belittled black spending power when he argued defensively "that a Negro boycott is like throwing spitballs at a bull."[30]

Variety chain stores like Woolworth and Kress — so closely identified with urban commercial life since the 1920s — were particularly hard hit by the demonstrations. Their vulnerability came partly from their southern downtown locations and the fact that "their Northern outlets are often almost equally dependent on Negro buying."[31] Yet it was also true that the same attributes that made chains and key department stores valuable real estate made them magnets for protest. The stores offered connections to both the national business scene and local leadership and embodied the practical and symbolic qualities of the 100% district. When shut out of one lunch counter or store, protestors easily and conveniently moved to another nearby business, just as comparison shoppers and appraisers appreciated.[32] Dense pedestrian traffic, together with peak land values, guaranteed that protestors would have audiences and get the attention of authorities, in the relative safety of the public eye. The qualities of urban commercial life that attracted the protestors underscored the ambiguous mixing of public and private found in the stores and their retail districts. Public visibility coexisted with private business domains, an advertising rhetoric of inclusivity with exclusionary practices, and allegiance to profit with devotion to civic good. Legal and social ambiguities created a fruitful space for conflict.[33] During the boycotts, protestors effectively manipulated this ambiguous public-private identity to achieve their goals.[34]

Besides stigmatizing the downtown as a dangerous place, an area to avoid, the civil rights conflicts undercut the prevailing "bring-the-shopper-back" strategies in other ways. The experience of fear downtown stood in direct contrast to, and gave a new depth of meaning to, contemporary efforts to create a relaxing and pleasant atmosphere downtown for suburban women shoppers. Even when they did not take a firm position on boycott principles, whites and blacks avoided downtown because of the "tense atmosphere." In Chester, Pennsylvania, a reporter found that "the singing and marching and the turmoil create a climate of fear." One furniture and appliance retailer there said that customers "phone to tell us they're afraid to come downtown. Just the threat of a demonstration and the streets are empty." Outright violence or mass arrests deterred even the most devoted shoppers, and retailers were especially attentive since most of their customers were women. In Nashville, New Orleans, and countless other places, "shoppers are staying away from the downtown area as long as the threat of violence and lawlessness remains."[35]

Downtown retailers had no doubt that all the turmoil meant that white women consumers were escaping to the calm of the new outlying shopping centers. In Chester, Pennsylvania, merchants agreed that "shoppers have not been molested" and that no one had been pushed around, but nevertheless the demonstrations were "enough to scare a woman." The reporter wondered, along with Chester's merchants, whether Main Street would ever "woo them back." In Greenville, South Carolina, a bomb threat at Kress, street violence, and lunch-counter demonstrations "sent many housewives to shopping centers which have not been hit by demonstrations." Birmingham found that "white women shoppers, fearful of potential violence, did not come downtown either. Instead they turned to the nearest shopping centers and suburban branches for their needs." On a long-term basis, "this could accelerate decentralization of shopping facilities in Birmingham." In 1963 the twenty-one shopping centers in the county surrounding Savannah were "enjoying a bonanza in catering to those shunning the downtown area" because of demonstrations.[36]

There was less agreement over where African Americans shopped during boycotts. From suburban Atlanta shopping centers came reports of "sizable Negro customer traffic" during an effective December 1960 protest. The success of boycotts was linked to the presence of black business districts offering acceptable alternatives in cities like Birmingham, Atlanta, or Tuskegee, yet the extent to which the surge of patronage sparked new African American business endeavors varied greatly. Whereas a "shiny new drugstore for Negroes" opened in downtown Atlanta, "little attempt was made by Negroes to open stores of their own" in Birmingham.[37] Unfortunately for the boycotters, the stores in black neighborhoods were often owned by whites and were sometimes unappealing for other reasons as well. Even though nearly half the population of Winston-Salem was black, downtown store managers expected a weak boycott because they knew, according to a reporter, that "there are virtually no stores in the Negro areas of Winston-Salem which offer the merchandise carried in downtown white-operated stores." White-owned stores in black neighborhoods also generated complaints about poor-quality goods, price gouging, and rude service. One such store in Winston-Salem attracted pickets for, among other things, selling rotten meat and calling customers "Niggers" (see fig. 6.7). African Americans may have increased their use of mail-order catalogs and door-to-door sales. When necessary, they did without new things. One participant said, "Our freedom is more important to us than new household appliances."[38]

Main Street merchants' advertising strategies, including the "gimmicks" dismissed by the supporters of urban renewal, withered in racially tense climates. In places like Jacksonville and Savannah, city and county officials periodically arranged for regular broadcasts on radio and television to advise shoppers to avoid the downtown area. Officials in Jackson, Mississippi, canceled the Christmas parade, afraid of "large gatherings or street crowds" that

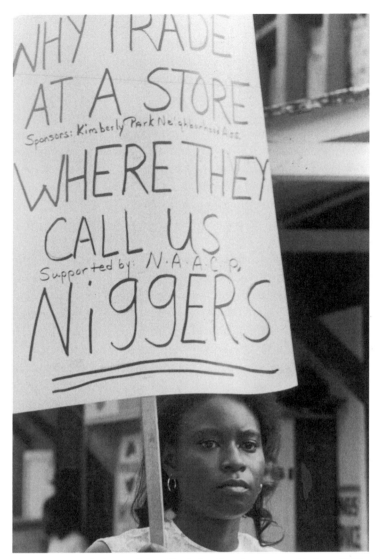

Figure 6.7 Residents of Winston-Salem, North Carolina, demonstrated in June 1966 against the discriminatory practices of a neighborhood store. White shoppers avoided downtown protests and violence by shopping in suburban malls and neighborhood stores, but African American consumers were more constrained in their options since they often had grievances with neighborhood businesses. Downtown investors found themselves at a difficult crossroads. It might be tough to woo back even their most loyal Main Street customers once these customers had become accustomed to suburban shopping. At the same time, African Americans might lose interest in Main Street after encountering prolonged and violent resistance to their full participation in urban commercial life. (Reproduced with permission of Billy E. Barnes, photographer.)

might spark demonstrations, although large downtown crowds were the very essence of the holiday's economic success. Birmingham launched a downtown promotion, including store beautification and the creation of "malls and beauty spots," in early 1963, to attract the shoppers, "white and non-white, who once thronged its stores." Birmingham's promotion, because it occurred in the midst of the devastating boycotts and violence, was not quite identical to those of other struggling Main Streets — it included, for example, an appeal to nonwhite consumers. During weeks of spring sit-ins and arrests, the city unveiled sixty "flowerama" boxes, as well as the "beautification" of vacant store windows. CORE launched a boycott in St. Louis with stickers reading, "Don't Buy Downtown for Freedom" in the midst of downtown promotions and sale days.[39]

The demonstrations also directly interfered with the early 1960s emphasis on improving transportation, mass transit, and parking in order to enhance the shopper's access to the downtown and deliver her to the store. In Jacksonville, "several leading arteries into town were sealed off for several hours," and not surprisingly, business jumped up in the outlying shopping centers. A New Orleans executive, observing a drop in downtown pedestrian traffic, feared that "many customers, reading of racial violence in Jacksonville, are avoiding travel on New Orleans integrated buses to the business section as a result." Shopper anxieties about recently integrated buses shed a different light on the urban renewal era's preoccupation with transit and delivering the customer downtown. The New Orleans case also suggests how closely retailers and shoppers kept their eyes on events in other cities and shaped their behavior accordingly. In an effort to overcome such transportation obstacles, Birmingham's Downtown Action Committee offered free bus rides home from downtown for those who made purchases at member firms.[40] Moreover, the pickets, prayer circles, and angry white crowds created a new kind of congestion concern, because they blocked sidewalks and entrances, often prompting arrests or citations on that basis.[41] Law officers also did their part to crowd the sidewalks. In one telling account, a reporter noted that "retailers generally felt that the arrival of Federal troops in the Birmingham vicinity has not restored shopper confidence."[42]

The social unrest did foster a greater sense of unity among downtown competitors, who saw the necessity of a united front in negotiations. Protestors usually identified the entire downtown as their target, rather than individual stores, and this also induced diverse interests to cooperate. Boycott mottos included "Don't Drift Downtown" (Birmingham), "don't shop downtown"

(Chicago Loop), and "Stay Off Main Street" (Memphis). In various cities black leaders declared "an economic withdrawal, stay-away-from-downtown-movement," or they called downtown "off limits."[43] One variety store manager revealed that he had forged "a closer association with managers of competitive variety stores than ever before." In Birmingham, a *WWD* reporter observed that downtown spokesmen had unanimously converted their attitude from glum to optimistic as they forged ahead with improvement programs despite ongoing violence. Clearly retailers had agreed to cooperate, despite their differences. The reporter called the optimism remarkable, but every merchant contacted by the news service stuck to the same line.[44]

"To put it crudely, civil unrest is bad for business," noted the director of Birmingham's Chamber of Commerce, as he attributed the city's economic slowdown to racial unrest. The *Hardware Merchandiser* reported fear among civic leaders that the "violence may discourage some companies contemplating relocation from investigating what the city has to offer." The day that Birmingham's April 1963 sit-ins began, Sears officials were in town to assess the feasibility of locating two or three additional stores there. Southern business-people pored over statistics documenting the outside investment lost by Little Rock since the desegregation crisis there. A store manager elsewhere expected that the disruptions "not only will hurt expansions of existing variety stores, but might mean that some will stay out of communities" until the seemingly endless conflict ceased. After "outbreaks of violence followed by mass arrests," a spokesman for the Woolworth in Tallahassee believed that "unilateral integration, in the face of local hostility, would close down the store."[45]

S. H. Kress & Company was ready to blame its troubles on demonstrations even though its economic circumstances belied such a clear-cut explanation. In the 1950s, Kress chose to remain downtown while its competitors benefited from the suburban boom. By 1958 the company faced a crisis of declining profitability, and an internal management coup attempted to reverse the trend. Kress's downtown presence and its regional concentration in the South made it especially vulnerable to the civil rights disruptions. Unrest in the 1960s, then, proved to be a handy scapegoat for the company's multifaceted economic woes. The 1960 Kress Annual Report explained, "Since February, 1960, our company has been subjected in varying degrees to picketing, sit-in demonstrations and boycotts because of segregated lunch counters in certain southern stores. This pressure has not been confined to the south alone, but has also occurred in regions where our stores have always been fully integrated. In certain cities, racial tension has caused shoppers to avoid downtown areas where our shops are located." Kress claimed that it had not attempted to force integration on unwilling communities because it "would inevitably lead to the closing of the affected stores."[46]

Occasionally, company spokespersons conveyed a more complicated and subtle picture of their investment choices, denying that there was any kind of inevitable trajectory leading from integration agitation to businesses shutting down. A few days after mass demonstrations paralyzed Birmingham's shopping district, the Belk Department Store chain announced that it would close its unit there. Belk's president rejected the speculation that the closing was a response to local protests, saying "that the decision to close is a business one based on general conditions and the store's own experience over a period of years, and that it should not be credited to racial troubles in that city." He added that the store "simply couldn't make a living there." Although this comment did not reassure Birmingham leaders, it points to the broader metropolitan economic trends in which 1960s racial unrest occurred.[47]

In the 1960s, civil rights protestors forced key downtown retailers such as Belk, Kress, and Woolworth to make public statements about the place of African Americans in past, present, and future urban commerce. Such merchants, under the intense gaze of the nation and the world, faced very explicitly their own part in making decisions that shaped downtown business values. The civil rights conflicts infused urban commerce simultaneously with demoralizing tension, regret at losing a familiar way of business, and hope for something better.

Patrons Gained, Patrons Lost: Integration and Main Street Values

When the boycotts began, many retailers assumed that under integration they would lose their white patrons. The implication — encouraged by white supremacists — was that stores could have either black or white customers, but they could not have both. One reporter wrote that the southern merchant was "caught in a racial dilemma between status-quo white customers on the one hand, and Negro customers on the other." Employing black workers in downtown retail posed similar risks. An attorney in 1965 described merchants as "caught between two firing lines," where the employment of African Americans in sales or "other exposed areas could spell business disaster and white boycotts." Could integration actually boost business? Few had convincing answers. In Winston-Salem, four months after lunch-counter integration, "Just how many Negro patrons have been gained and how many white patrons lost is something no one can say exactly." Those "whites who gave up their seats for good" had done so "quietly and without incident." Anxieties were fanned by announcements like the one by McCrory in 1964 that it had closed stores because they had become unprofitable in the wake of integration.[48]

The retail managers themselves were another unknown factor in calculating the long-term impact of integration. Unquestionably, white discomfort with African Americans in urban commercial life shaped disinvestment choices. Most of the career employees who had come up under the old system of race relations remained in their jobs in the 1960s and became decision makers in a new era. In May 1952, for example, a white Kress manager inspecting one of the Los Angeles stores commented, "General maintenance standard low. . . . Colored help attitude not cooperative. Two slovenly colored boys sitting on top of stockroom table eating lunch amidst accumulation of cartons and what appeared to be general litter. . . . Did not want to stay here long." The executive's assessment of the store's present condition and future potential, inseparable from his racial viewpoint, induced him to recommend selling the property. In the 1960s, some managers and proprietors would quit their jobs or close their stores rather than oversee integration.[49]

Ironically, the implementation of integration was often uneventful. " 'I wouldn't have believed it,' said one woman with many years' experience at a food counter. 'There's not been one word said between a white customer and a Negro in my hearing. Not one!' " Another manager, whose business suffered during four months of boycotts, said, "If I'd known it could have been done this easily, I'd have been for it right from the start." Local media in cities like Houston, Dallas, Atlanta, Nashville, and New Orleans contributed to the calm by agreeing not to publicize integration agreements and the desegregation process.[50]

During the earliest 1960 boycotts, liberal observers had already begun to make the case that integration boosted business. A mid-1960 Southern Regional Council study insisted that "no store in the South which has opened its lunch counters to Negroes has reported a loss of business. Managers have reported business as usual or noted an increase." Whites, it seemed, had responded calmly to integration — "without a break in their shopping routine." Other evidence indicated that not only had southern retailers (with the exception of Birmingham) rebounded once the violence passed, but many stores appeared to do better after integration prevailed. The *National Market Letter* proposed that if these trends continued, retailers could access "the untapped sales potential of the Negro population."[51] In the minds of these observers, a rejuvenated, downtown-oriented black middle class, together with whites who accepted the new order, promised to restore vibrancy to downtown property values.[52]

National media descriptions of the demonstrators helped build the case for the rise of black consumers as a considerable force by emphasizing the middle-class dress and demeanor of protestors, especially when contrasted with the trouble-making hecklers. A *New York Times* article covering the first 1960s sit-ins mentioned the "well-dressed" African American college students, and another used the phrase "well-groomed." A reporter elsewhere called protestors "neatly-dressed, quiet-spoken, articulate and determined" (fig. 6.8). This journalistic practice continued further into the decade. When four hundred St. Augustine College students marched at lunchtime in downtown Raleigh after King's assassination, the local paper reported, "The marching group was mixed, with many women students, many dressed in party fashions." Yet these reassuring assertions of middle-class respectability (along with the fact that the students were singing "We Shall Overcome") only reached the public eye because of protest and provocation on Main Street. The marchers' fashionable dress was also accompanied by the ominous warning of a male student: "There is going to be complete anarchy."[53]

Case by case, store managers and owners facing demonstrations and violence scrambled to assess sales volume and property values in whatever way would preserve their financial stake. In estimating the sales performance of the Memphis Kress in 1968, the manager insisted on excluding the impact of racial conflict from his calculations, since he did not want his store to be devalued by the company. He asked that 1968 figures not be used, because of "the boycott, the King incident, and renovation." In Birmingham, a prominent realty executive complained to the city's Board of Equalization that a proposed increase in the J. J. Newberry property assessment was unwarranted. It was true, he admitted, that the store had undertaken improvements, but sales volume had not increased, "particularly as Newberry is one of the principal sufferers from the negro boycott against downtown merchants." A year later, as he passed the daily protests and sit-ins near his office, the same broker requested that the Board of Equalization defer reappraising the 100% district until the period of "change in down-town retailing" had passed. Lost income induced property owners to hope that appraisers would lower downtown values or at least postpone any increases, so that taxes would not rise. Furthermore, they argued, the impact of prolonged disruptions to trade remained to be seen, and they should not be penalized in the meantime.[54]

Figure 6.8 In February 1964 the *Baltimore Afro-American* publicized the news that over the previous six months "top Department Stores and Food Chains" had at last become "regular advertisers" in the black press. The mass demonstrations and boycotts on Main Street in the early 1960s had drawn national attention to what the press described as "well-dressed" African Americans, who were by implication demanding consumers. For "Mister Retailer," as merchants were addressed in this advertisement, the boycotts and demonstrations were an introduction to the "Negro Market." By late 1963 mainstream advertisers and merchants finally had been induced to take an interest in black consumers. A handwritten note attributes this ad to the February 24, 1964, *New York Times*. (Courtesy of Baker Library, Harvard Business School, Resseguie Collection, box 10, Negro Retailers and Race Relations file.)

Of course, the very purpose of boycotts was to change people's shopping habits. Even those who hoped African Americans could "save" downtown were uncertain whether blacks would be enthusiastic about Main Street after facing such violent resistance. Following Atlanta boycotts in the early 1960s, many people did not resume downtown trade. One 1963 study found that black shoppers "felt 'cold' towards the picketed stores. They indicated that they did not want to spend their hard-earned dollars in stores that wanted their business but 'were ashamed to be caught with Negroes.'" The contrast with the downtown stores' customary efforts to please customers was not lost on black shoppers. The study concluded that "it will take a long time to undo the harm done. Some of the damages inflicted might be of a permanent nature."[55]

By the mid-1960s, the new patterns of increased nonwhite shoppers downtown (and increased white patronage of suburban malls) were evident to anyone who followed retail trends. What remained unclear was whether investors judged this to be the rise of enlarged, integrated crowds of urban consumers that promised business vitality or the "nightmarish" domination feared in Trenton ten years earlier. The answer had significant implications for commercial values. However, in the mid-1960s there were new reasons to be pessimistic about the future of urban commerce.

In July of 1964, rioting erupted in Harlem and Bedford-Stuyvesant in New York City. Afterward, a young civil rights worker wondered aloud whether Mississippi had "finally come" to New York. That same week, young black demonstrators in Memphis shouted "Harlem" as they threw bricks at police cars and damaged other property. Over the next years, one might have wondered whether it was the other way around — had New York come to Mississippi?[56] The six black men shot in the back by police during 1970 riots in Augusta, Georgia, were shocking even by northern standards of urban violence.[57] West Point, Mississippi, illustrated some of the changes afoot. In 1967 blacks rioted and looted for two days in that city of ten thousand after a policeman was accused of beating a young African American. A white businessman took matters into his own hands. He sent truckloads of soda, hot dogs, and watermelons to the black community, along with two popular black bands, and the violence evolved into a street party. The next riot in West Point followed the assassination of Martin Luther King Jr. Every white-owned business in the black part of town was burned. White-owned businesses that reopened were burned repeatedly, so that two years later there were no white proprietors in the black neighborhoods of West Point. The explosions in Harlem and West

Point marked frightening new trends that would plague urban commerce into the 1970s.[58]

The nation's attention shifted mid-decade from southern civil rights battle-grounds like Birmingham to the riot scenes of Los Angeles, Newark, and Detroit. These cities, along with places like West Point, Durham, and Cleveland, tell of a complex mix of boycotts, marches, and riots that brought violence to the core of urban commercial life throughout the nation. The new patterns of looting and arson added extensive physical devastation to the woes of urban business — a level of destruction that oddly enough would be compared to the accomplishments of urban renewal.

The Riots — Merchants, the Poor, and Urban Rubble

The evening before the peaceful, if tense, Durham march, in the nation's capital the proprietor of a Seventh Street shoe store tried to close his shop as a menacing crowd collected around him on the sidewalk. Abraham Gritz managed to put up the iron bars that protected his store windows, but before he could lock the door, the crowd moved in on him. They swore at him and roughed him up. After taking his keys, wallet, and watch, individuals from the crowd entered Gritz's store to steal the shoes he had stocked at peak levels in anticipation of the Easter rush. Gritz fled on foot. A block away he was able to catch a ride home to Silver Spring from an African American. A few doors down from Gritz, the owner of Log Cabin Liquors and two family members crouched at the door of their store until a break in the crowd offered them the chance to sprint to their car. The African American manager of a High's milk and ice cream outlet escaped in a milk truck that had just completed its delivery. The proprietor of Zevin's Hardware stood his ground at the door of the business he had operated for fifty years until his son nervously convinced him to go home. While other black-owned businesses on the block posted "Soul Brother" signs, James Briscoe did not do this for his secondhand radio and TV shop, because he "didn't really care to identify with that bunch." Above the liquor store, a sixty-seven-year-old African American physician locked his safe, yelled "I'm gone!" to his secretary, and rushed down the stairs to save his brand new blue Mercedes Benz parked outside. His secretary caught a taxi home. By the next morning, April 5, the buildings housing these businesses (and the apartments above them) were smoldering rubble (fig. 6.9).[59]

It was not difficult to pinpoint the sparks that ignited riots in the 1960s. Angry crowds responded with terrifying destruction not only to King's murder but also to the injury of previously unknown African Americans at the hands

Figure 6.9 By the middle and late 1960s, a different kind of racial confrontation had begun to transform urban commerce. In the riots following the murder of Martin Luther King Jr., this stretch of H Street in Washington, D.C. (between Twelfth and Thirteenth Streets), was firebombed much like the Seventh Street block where Abraham Gritz's shoe store had stood. The ubiquitous aerial photographs of gutted buildings and blocks tended to obscure the individual stories of proprietors and residents. Widespread looting and arson seemed to target particular businesses, which suggested to social scientists and policymakers that merchants' exploitation of poor consumers was one of the factors shaping the pattern of rioting. (Courtesy of AP/Wide World Photos, no. 5256175.)

of police or others. Groups of demonstrators gathered in city streets, smashing windows and sometimes stealing goods. The worst property losses were incurred when Molotov cocktails tossed into stores or on top of one-story commercial buildings resulted in charred ruins. Frightened and angry police and national guardsmen sometimes shot protestors and looters; sniper fire, stray bullets, and accidents took many lives as well. Hundreds of cities saw this unfold on their own streets. In some cities it happened every summer, in some

two or three times in the decade, and in others only once. In many places —
Detroit was a particularly illustrative example — residents at first thought
they could avoid the riots but then came to fear them chronically.

By the early 1970s, press observers noted that riots had lost their power to
shock and even major unrest rarely made it into the national news anymore.
As the nation's biggest cities simmered down, riots came to smaller cities
and suburbs where the police usually lacked special training. New Bedford,
Massachusetts; Lawrence, Kansas; Homer, Louisiana; Hagerstown, Maryland;
Peoria, Illinois; Albuquerque; Chattanooga; Houston; Miami; Hartford; and
Asbury Park were just a handful of the cities experiencing riots in 1969, 1970,
and 1971. The reduced news coverage after 1968 partly explains why historians
and others have overlooked both the continued violence and its spread to
smaller places around the nation.[60]

Police brutality and inadequate employment, housing, and education were
all cited as key underlying conditions for the violence, but widespread commercial destruction (like that of Seventh Street in Washington) raised the possibility that the riots were "really consumer revolts."[61] Interviews with merchants, observers, and riot participants encouraged the belief that much of the
looting and firebombing was organized and had targeted primarily white-
owned businesses — especially those with a reputation for cheating customers. Debates swirled on the street corner and in academic and policy circles
over whether the character and structure of urban retailing had become so
poisoned that it had brought this disaster. Of course many objected to this
dire characterization of urban commerce, and others saw the rioting as criminal opportunism deserving of law-and-order retaliation, not soul-searching
analysis. But like it or not, the rioters pushed so-called ghetto retailers into the
glaring spotlight of 1960s urban policy and investment analysis. Two key
questions dominated these debates. First, what role had the relationship between black consumers and urban merchants played in generating the riots?
Second, was the violence an attempt to force white business owners out of urban retailing, in order to pave the way for a new generation of African American investors?

Anecdotal evidence built up to suggest that the violence was rational and
had targeted specific stores. In Cleveland, an elderly black man watching firefighters douse the ruins of several food stores muttered: "'The goddam white
devils were selling that rotten meat. . . . But they got to that devil,' he said smiling, 'and they put a barbequing on his goddam rotten meat.'" Nearby, a disabled black veteran said, "I want to see whitey burned out of this area and

black people going into business here." In Washington, the owner of Log Cabin Liquors, Irving Abraham, described seeing people direct the crowds to specific stores. In Harlem after the April 1968 riot there, a reporter delved into the "get back at whitey" theme. He observed that as one woman packed a box with looted food, she called to her neighbor "This man's been stealing from us for years." A Washington consumer affairs lawyer claimed that many of the stores vandalized during the April 1968 riots "were the ones we've always been having trouble with."[62]

With the support of prominent scholars and politicians, the suspicions about the reasons for the violence solidified into a full-blown exploitation theory of urban commercial life. The exploitation theory, well represented by sociologist David Caplovitz's influential 1963 book *The Poor Pay More*, proposed that urban merchants, mostly white absentee investors, had preyed upon poor city residents who lacked shopping options. Caplovitz's theory had taken shape in the context of a growing consumer protection movement and was later credited (along with *The Other America*, by Michael Harrington) as a spur for Lyndon Johnson's war on poverty. Once applied to the riots, the exploitation theory alleged that the looting and burning were at least partly retribution for inflated prices, inferior goods, expensive credit, and rip-off schemes. According to a *New York Times* reporter, Caplovitz told Congress that the violence "was motivated by anger at merchants who bilk the poor." Historian Robert Fogelson, author of a key report on the rioters for the National Crime Commission, agreed with the diagnosis that the rioters were selective in their rage; he found the violence to be, in his words, "an articulate expression of very specific grievances." In the *Harvard Business Review*, marketing professor Frederick D. Sturdivant argued that unscrupulous retailers had perverted the potential for positive human contact across class and race lines inherent in the shopping experience. Instead, urban dwellers confronted a "degrading shopping environment," and the resulting "frustrations . . . produced the spectacle of looted and burned stores throughout the nation." Sturdivant used "moms and pops" derogatorily to describe an "inefficient" and "backward" small business system. He favored instead the introduction of large-scale retailers into poor neighborhoods. He also condemned "unethical" and "parasitic" businesspeople who preyed on disadvantaged consumers.[63]

The inclination to blame the urban shopping experience for the riots was further validated by Lyndon Johnson's top consumer adviser, Betty Furness. Furness pulled no punches after the nationwide violence that followed King's death. She warned "ghetto based retailers" that "they had better stop 'swindling' slum dwellers or face more pillaging and burning in the months ahead." In a prepared address before the American Society of Newspaper Editors, Furness said the recent violence showed that "the poor are being swindled, or feel they're being swindled" by local merchants. Although many fumed at Furness's offhand distinction between being swindled and feeling swindled, there was an important lesson in her wording. The exploitation theory's popularity proved that at the very least "ghetto" businesses had failed in public relations, especially if the rioters *believed* that they were being bilked. The belief became a force of its own within commercial life, undoing and obscuring constructive relationships that did exist between merchant and consumer.[64]

When the Kerner Commission added its weight behind the exploitation theory, it further discredited the "riffraff" thesis, which was the prevailing alternative explanation. The riffraff thesis described a series of rioter stereotypes and placed responsibility for the violence on individuals rather than economic and social discrimination. The stereotypes included the "outside agitator," the "wholly uneducated fool," and the "yokel fresh from a Southern farm who is unable to cope with the intricacies of urban life." Accordingly, the "mindless" and "irrational" looting undertaken by "riffraff" was condemned as pure criminal materialism — an illegal shortcut to desired possessions that was devoid of political commentary. The view of rioters as rational, righteous, aggrieved consumers stood in stark contrast with the view that they were mindless thieves.[65]

The few humorous reflections on the riots virtually all directed attention to the consumerist overtones of looting. The African American physician on Seventh Street could not keep himself from laughing at a looter who emerged from the supermarket across the street with "so many hams in her arms that she kept dropping them." Comedian Flip Wilson tried out some riot jokes in the summer of 1968. The *New York Times* reviewer thought that "even a slum haberdasher would laugh" when Wilson called his suit "'my riot outfit. Got it in Cleveland last year out of the window,' he says. 'I saw some other things I wanna get. I'm waiting till August[.] Do my shoppin' in the *summer*?'"[66]

Especially after King's murder, any lightheartedness detected amid the looters implicitly challenged whether their actions were at all politically motivated. In Washington, several reporters emphasized "a carefree, hit-and-run mood," a "holiday mood," and laughter, as furled umbrellas shattered plate glass and goods were snatched downtown and in other neighborhoods. Most looters seemed not "angry or mournful" but rather "appeared to be having a

Figure 6.10 Not all rioting matched the stereotype of angry mob action. In Washington, D.C., looters calmly removed merchandise from the Paul Bennett Co., Ltd., the Cambridge Shop, in front of passers-by. The photograph's caption in *Women's Wear Daily* indicated that the looters were "seemingly out for a weekend stroll." The consumerist overtones of looting sparked some of the strongest reactions to the riots, including the exploitation theory that viewed rioters as justified by their anger at unethical merchants; the ire of conservatives over what they judged to be unpunished criminal acts of theft; and even the humor that comedians, witnesses, and others expressed in the midst of the anxious circumstances. (*Women's Wear Daily,* April 8, 1968, 34. Reprinted with permission of Guy de Lort /*Women's Wear Daily.*)

good time." Some even paused to try on clothing they had stolen. Much of this happened in broad daylight before the eyes of office workers waiting for buses home. "There was no violence, no gunplay," emphasized a reporter. In Baltimore on Fremont Avenue, looters and bystanders alike "appeared to be peaceful and cheerful at the time." Four looters arrested in a downtown Dayton shoe store were described as "giggling youths." [67] Just as boycotts had sparked chronic violence, the riots had their share of eerily peaceful looting (fig. 6.10).

Although portraying looting as a shopping spree could fuel conservative critiques, the consumer overtones of the violence were terribly disturbing and provocative. One reporter speculated that "the pictures of looters staggering under loads of booty past policemen" had done more "to enrage and confuse the public" than anything else. Yet the option of using deadly force to stop looting was worse. A Washington police officer said after the King riots, "I'm not going to shoot a kid over a pair of shoes." Harlan Johnson "was killed by the police as a looter" in Trenton that week, shot in the back after allegedly stealing a shirt from a downtown store. Johnson turned out to be a college sophomore, a divinity student, whom witnesses claim was trying to stop the violence. One man was shot in Newark while running across the street with a case of liquor. The only two deaths in a May 28, 1968, riot in Louisville, Kentucky, were two alleged looters shot by police.[68] Attorney General Ramsey Clark had to remind citizens that looters should not be shot, since property crimes did not warrant death or excessive force. He compared it to shooting accused bank embezzlers or drunk drivers. "What terrible fear or hatred would cause us to shoot looters?" Clark asked. Yet the public's confusion might be excused when the same week the mayor of Chicago, Richard J. Daley, ordered city police on April 15, 1968, "to shoot arsonists and looters in the future."[69] Proprietors who shot at looters and looters who attacked merchants offered the most extreme illustrations of "tensions" in urban commercial life.[70]

The idea that the rioters had targeted white-owned businesses was as popular as the exploitation theory. Many sources fueled this belief. The national press kept close tabs on whether African American stores were attacked or bypassed, and black separatist rhetoric exhorted African Americans to eliminate vestiges of "white colonialism," which often meant white companies that traded mostly with blacks. One Washington, D.C., high school student expressed her opinion that the riots were directed at white stores, irrespective of their retail practices. She gave the example of a store on her block run by "this Jew white man and he was very nice." He had always treated a particular single mother well, giving her milk for her children. Yet when riots struck, the student "saw her right in there pulling out everything she could."[71]

Other evidence challenged the simplicity of assuming that the rioters expected to drive out white business. For one thing, the possibility that Jewish and "Uncle Tom" businesses were also targets complicated the issue. To militant young blacks, the figure of the comfortable black physician rushing to save his Mercedes might have fanned their anger toward the selfish bourgeoisie. On the west side of Washington's Seventh Street between R and S, four of the ten stores looted and burned were owned by blacks, while six other black-owned stores remained untouched. The thirteen residents on the block who lost their homes and virtually all their belongings were African American, and many of them were elderly or children.[72] Anti-Jewish sentiment raised additional questions. Previously Jewish neighborhoods had become African American, partly explaining the significant presence of Jewish merchants. Because Jews had so actively supported the Civil Rights movement, militant separatism apparently aimed at eliminating Jewish businesses came with a special dose of confusion and betrayal. Although presumptions prevailed that "white" investors were being intentionally driven out, little statistical evidence had been amassed.[73]

It was also unclear what role white provocation and vandalism played in the destruction. In Rochester, New York, some reports claimed that the presence of a brawling "band of drunken white youths" early in the riot was "a significant factor in bringing the mood of the crowd to its kindling point." One African American man identified the tormenters as Italian Americans and claimed that they should share blame for the hysteria and riots. A white linotype operator in New Brunswick, New Jersey, reported seeing three white youths firebomb a plumbing supply store in a black neighborhood. In 1966, as Troy, New York, tried to confront discrimination in housing and employment, white youths drove through "the predominantly Negro downtown area" at night shouting, "Riot, you niggers," and racist graffiti appeared on black churches. People interviewed in a predominantly Italian neighborhood in Newark witnessed "white youths stoning Negroes," while reporters saw "men sitting in doorways with rifles cradled in their laps." Yet Newark police indicated that not one white person was arrested relating to the violence (see fig. 6.11).[74]

Naturally, merchants resented the allegation that they had done anything to deserve violent attack. At the height of their own fear and desperation, proprietors had to contend with the accusation that they had exploited poor customers. The owner of an auto accessories store on Seventh Street was especially bitter at Furness: "'I want to get back at Betty Furness,' Nathanson said heatedly. 'We have never handled any shoddy merchandise. We have never charged one person one price and another person another price. We weren't sought out. We were just in the line of fire. Why, we don't do 5 per cent of our business with the people who live in the neighborhood.'" At times it seemed that the rioters received more sympathy, from the government at least, than

Figure 6.11 The role of white provocation in sparking riot violence outside of the South has not been studied. Numerous reports of white instigation appeared in newspapers during the 1960s. Here, men hoisting racist banners and confederate flags drive through the riot areas of Chicago's Southwest Side on August 5, 1966. (Courtesy of AP/Wide World Photos, no. 542130.)

did the victimized businesses.[75] As the police and the national guard intermittently refrained from confronting and arresting looters, hoping to reduce bloodshed and retaliation, commercial investors argued that their livelihoods were being sacrificed. Now they were being undeservedly blamed for inciting the violence in the first place.

Although businesspeople usually had the upper hand over the urban poor in political deal-making as well as daily retail exchange, the rioters' initiative and the popularity of the exploitation theory unquestionably put urban retailers and other investors on the defensive. In 1967, when Roy Wenzlick published a hard-line editorial against the rioters at the end of an unnerving summer of upheaval, the spontaneous response by the real estate investment community revealed something of the temper of that group. The excited flurry that circulated Wenzlick's editorial far and wide suggests that in 1967 conservative real estate people felt they lacked effective national spokesmen defending business, attacking the rioters, and critiquing the government response. The article, which appeared in Wenzlick's investment newsletter, stimulated more than 150 readers to write letters ordering reprints and offering praise and appreciation. Real estate professionals, bank presidents, academics, Rotarians, insurance company executives, newspapers, and title insurance companies asked for hundreds of copies. A senior executive of Woodmen Accident and Life Company based in Lincoln, Nebraska, bought one thousand reprints to distribute to the company's entire staff, as well as to "people whom we regard as being centers of influence." Others sent the editorial to political representatives (including President Lyndon B. Johnson) and newspapers, distributed them at professional gatherings, and borrowed excerpts for speeches.[76]

Wenzlick said the harsh, intolerant things many conservative (and racist) Americans wished the government would say about the reasons for the destruction. He claimed that "we have encouraged the uncultured, the disadvantaged, and the unskilled to believe that they could achieve more than is humanly possible in a short time, and from their disillusionment has come resentment and revolt." People were not poor because they lacked money, Wenzlick argued. "People are poor because they either have little ability, or have not worked hard enough to develop the abilities which they have." Wenzlick quoted Abraham Lincoln: "Let not him who is houseless pull down the house of another, but let him work diligently and build one for himself, thus by example assuring that his own shall be safe from violence when built." Hearing the words of Betty Furness and the Kerner Commission, many businesspeople fumed over their belief that government leaders were apologetic to the rioters, anxious to make excuses for their behavior, and too quick to throw financial resources at poverty programs. While all Americans struggled to understand the meaning of the violence, real estate investors had a particular interest because it was their buildings that were being pulled down.[77]

The riots of the 1960s directed national attention to "ghetto" retailers, the exploitation theory, and the question of whether black investors could possibly lay the foundations for a newly vibrant urban commercial life. To a greater degree than is generally recognized, the violence and its consequences directly affected downtown business districts, not only the commercial areas of black neighborhoods. For good reason, the more complete commercial destruction in black neighborhoods attracted investigators anxious to understand and prevent racial violence. The blocks of ruins and empty lots where once-thriving business corridors had hummed — such as Springfield Avenue in Newark, Twelfth Street in Detroit, or Central Avenue in Los Angeles — these were the magnets drawing reporters and social scientists.

Figure 6.12 Curfews following on the heels of violence further sapped the vitality of urban commerce. This was evident to children as well as adults, as shown in this drawing of the desolate streets of downtown Washington, D.C., by a junior high school student. (Sunday Magazine, *New York Times*, June 2, 1968, 73.)

The immediate but mostly indirect effects of center city violence on downtowns seemed evident — certainly people were less likely to make shopping excursions with riot threats hanging in the air. Business slowed down or ground to a halt throughout affected cities regardless of where the looting occurred. Curfews gained popularity as they proved their effectiveness; retailers appreciated that curfews calmed violence but still groused about the repercussions for trade (see fig. 6.12). And inasmuch as the riots sped up the longer-term middle-class "flight" from cities, downtown retail suffered further. There were also more direct forays into the downtown by rioters. Most commonly, what the papers usually described as "roving groups of Negro youths" broke plate glass and sometimes grabbed store window merchandise. There was also the "spread" or "spilling over" of looting and arson from close-in neighborhoods. Such was the case in Miami in August 1968 and in Natchez, Mississippi, in June 1968.[78]

But at times downtown stores figured more centrally in the violence. In the "fashionable downtown shopping district" of Washington, D.C., after King's murder, an unusually high number of nationally known chain stores and well-known retailers (such as Woolworth, G. C. Murphy, Kresge, Florsheim, Sears, Lerner, and Paul Stewart) were firebombed or looted. Stores in downtown Newark on Broad Street were burned down during the July 1967 riots in that city. Downtown Memphis limped through 1968, plagued by the garbage strike, boycotts, a "short" riot on March 28, and King's assassination. (See figs. 6.13, 6.14.) Although Washington police in 1968 were caught by surprise and had to be diverted to the downtown area from assignments a mile to the north, in many cases officials acted quickly at the first sign of unrest to protect downtowns. The night of King's murder, Boston police "sealed off" the downtown "section which contains the city's largest stores." A few days later police blockaded downtown Cincinnati after an apparently racially motivated stabbing there and rioting in a northern suburb.[79]

Regardless of location, race, religion, resources, or moralities, most individuals with a stake in urban retail during the 1960s experienced anxiety because of the riots, from national business leaders to corner store managers and shoppers. In his 1968 speeches, the president of the U.S. Chamber of Commerce tried to cultivate an ethos of calm confidence and stability among the rank and file. But his own choice of supposedly reassuring words hinted at the prevailing mood: "These are not the problems of a nation coming apart at the seams or on the brink of national disaster." That same year a Detroit police inspector described some of the fears local business owners brought to him. One man called because of a shattered window. "'He was practically hysterical. I asked him when had a window broken last, or any other trouble, and he said nine years ago. No trouble, not even a broken window, for nine years. But to him it's a crime wave. He was ready to pull out,' said the 44-year-old inspector." In one two-week period during the summer of 1967, the Washington, D.C., Retail Bureau received 150 false reports of "planned civil disturbances." On July 28 that same summer, unfounded rumors of impending violence flew up and down the eastern seaboard. "Everybody's got the heebie-jeebies," commented a policeman at Manhattan headquarters.[80]

Uncertainty in the shadow of the 1960s riots had a different tenor from most other kinds of investor insecurity. The collapse in urban land values during the depression and the corrosion sped by suburbanization were slow and comfortable challenges when compared to the possibility of one's business going up in flames. Most businesspeople did not know how to prepare for

Figure 6.13 On Broad Street in Newark, New Jersey (the city's main commercial thoroughfare), firemen soaked a burning building containing Hartley's Luggage and Gifts, Jordan Jewelers, Rite Aid, and the New Jersey Beauty Culture Academy. The downtown looting and arson occurred during the first days of Newark's deadly July 1967 riots. In many cities, window-smashing, looting, and other disturbances threatened the downtown streets as well as the business districts of black neighborhoods. (Courtesy of AP/Wide World Photos, no. 2152364.)

Figure 6.14 Riots persisted in all sections of the nation through the early 1970s, occurring in smaller cities and suburbs like New Bedford, Massachusetts; Lawrence, Kansas; Homer, Louisiana; and Peoria, Illinois. Southern cities — not often associated with riots like those in Newark and Detroit — experienced their share of unrest. In Memphis, Tennessee, looting broke out downtown following a march led by Martin Luther King Jr. in support of striking garbage workers on March 28, 1968. In the confusion that ensued on South Main Street, young demonstrators still holding their placards from the march had to dodge the police officer's club intended for alleged looters. During the entire decade of the 1960s, Main Street continued to earn its unfortunate reputation as an unpredictably dangerous place for pro-testors, shoppers, and merchants alike. (Courtesy of AP/Wide World Photos, no. 3277908.)

such a threat. To accompany an article entitled "If Riots Erupt Again . . . ," *Nation's Business* published a drawing of a lone man staring out of his discount furniture store into the street as shadowy figures run by his shop (fig. 6.15). Self-help booklets distributed by various commercial and other organizations gave fearful and jittery businesspeople concrete techniques for weathering riots. Guides like "Store Planning for Riot Survival" advised how to organize employees, acquire emergency equipment, protect customers, and defend the store premises. Tips included using a camera "to photograph threatening looters" and flooding the roof to minimize damage from firebombs when

Figure 6.15 With this artist's sketch, *Nation's Business* suggested in March 1968 that each urban proprietor faced the threat of riot-related violence alone. This man, presumably the furniture store owner, stands paralyzed and vulnerable, surrounded by plate glass, as shadowy figures race by in the street and smoke begins to fill the air. In the wake of violence, or even just anticipating violence, individual investors also faced their own decisions about their stake in urban commerce — whether to stay or leave, depending upon their unique considerations. (Drawing by Paul Hoffmaster.)

violence moved into the immediate area. Naturally, though, advice differed depending on the authority. Whereas "Store Planning for Riot Survival" scoffed at the value of a disaster guide locked in the safe and advocated for inclusive employee training, the Metropolitan Washington Board of Trade's twenty-three-page *Confidential Disaster Control Guide* sternly advised masking all preparations for violence as ordinary routines. Expensive items, for example, should be moved nightly to the back of the store and covered over, but employees should have "the impression that this is the best way to keep merchandise clean." The *Guide* underscored the merchants' weighty burden of secret preparations: "IF YOU *VIOLATE* THIS RULE YOU COULD CAUSE A RUMOR OR EVEN A RIOT."[81]

The interdependence of retailers was stressed in the negative: "DON'T YOU LET THE RETAILING COMMUNITY DOWN!" Washington's Retail Board established an elaborate communications system, at the center of which moved the board's manager, carrying a radio for contact at all times. A network of chain stores agreed to convey reliable information about disturbances in any D.C. business district to the manager, who would then contact registered member stores in the vicinity of actual rioting. The *Guide* warned that this communication system might break down, that the board's manager would not have time to answer questions when he called to report an emergency, and that stores might be cut off from law enforcement authorities, without phone, electricity, or water. Ultimately, "When the time comes, each store faces the riot problem alone."[82]

When people's worst fears came true, and their businesses were destroyed, it might be months or even years before the debris was bulldozed and hauled away. Weed-filled lots marked spots that had once embodied the aspirations of all kinds of investors. Some vacant sites became destinations for the unemployed and elderly, places for children to play, or shelter for yet another entrepreneurial crowd — traffickers in illicit drugs and prostitution. Other lots filled quickly with new buildings and new businesses. Over time, the empty parcels became community gardens, playgrounds, or housing and were incorporated into larger redevelopment plans. After decades passed, a few of these retail corridors finally moved beyond their violent 1960s history. Some were reinvigorated by new immigrant groups, others showcased the accomplishments of black entrepreneurship or perhaps a corporate benefactor, while still others found new vibrancy assisted by federal legislation such as the Community Reinvestment Act of 1977. But that jumps ahead, because in the short term, individual investors had decisions to make.

"Build, Baby, Build" — Jesse Jackson, August 1969

If glossy structural glass storefronts spoke of Main Street's hopes during the depression, then plywood and cinder block proclaimed the mood in the 1960s.

The "new style of architecture" was sarcastically dubbed Riot Renaissance. Vacant buildings needed the protection of boarded-up windows, but stores still in operation opted for the new style too. It took perseverance and financial resources to maintain glass windows — one tire dealership in Hartford had its windows smashed twenty-eight times. Plate glass gave way to walls of brick and plywood — the latter a popular "decorating item" that aged slowly to grayer tones. New construction also experimented with variations on Riot Renaissance. In Watts, a White Front discount store rebuilt using a "fortress-like" design after the riots — with slit windows "too small for a Molotov cocktail to penetrate."[83] At first, boarded-up windows and missing displays were panic signs indicating that the proprietors expected imminent violence. But over time plywood and rubble took on a look of permanence. One reporter suggested that "the weather-beaten plywood board is replacing the gleaming steel and glass skyscraper as a symbol of the American city."[84]

The question on many people's minds was how the violence could lead to anything but disinvestment. Given the physical devastation and the difficulty of responding constructively in a panicky climate, the default expectation was that the riots would depress sales, drag down real estate, and worsen urban prospects generally.[85] The rioters had asserted that bitterness, exploitation, and violence had their place in urban commercial life, and the physical scars kept that message alive. Many businesses did not or could not reopen, while others left cities immediately or over the next few years. Yet unresolved questions made it reasonable to hope that the destruction had revealed legitimate flaws in urban commercial investment and might inspire new directions for rebuilding. The most pressing issues were whether black investors would step in to fill the vacuum, what role existing businesses could play in reestablishing urban vitality, and whether well-financed corporations and chain stores could pump additional resources into cities.

It is easy to focus on the flight of businesses from cities in the aftermath of the violence, because "white flight" has become such a familiar theme in urban lore. Even though so many retailers did ultimately leave, it is significant that every business district maintained its own balance among somewhat predictable responses. The situation on Central Avenue in 1968, three years after the Watts riots, as one real estate appraiser described it, was illustrative of the balancing act. Not surprisingly, those who sold their properties expressed "a desire to leave the area." Other owners were content to wait and see what happened. A third core group "indicated an interest in rebuilding the district."

One investor had rebuilt a drugstore, while another was "anxious" to put in a small shopping center. Sell and leave, wait and see, or stay and rebuild. In the simplest terms, these were the choices.[86]

For those deciding whether to leave, the path out of urban investment was not easy. Most could not simply turn away from their businesses. The circumstances made selling one's building or business difficult, even at a loss. The market was glutted. As one Harlem merchant said, "Your store isn't worth a dollar to sell. So we stay here."[87] Some had operated businesses for decades and had trouble letting go. Others had recently plunged into new ventures. Many had done well based on positive relationships with customers, employees, and neighboring businesses, and they were reluctant to leave their existing networks. Some were limited in their choices by the dictates of insurance policies; others had even fewer choices because they lacked insurance entirely. For the most part, insurance premiums and other costs of doing business in cities only went up after the riots. Some businesses were eligible for loans and other assistance from various organizations; others were not. And it was not just "white" flight; investors of all racial backgrounds had to weigh their options. Urban proprietors varied in their ability to tolerate anxiety or threats in their daily lives.[88]

Numerous merchants, whatever their preferences, could not wait out the drop in customers caused by the violence or the longer-term damage to the popularity of urban shopping. In 1970 Detroit's former mayor marveled: "People think there is a no-man's-land" downtown — that "you get your head shot off" in the business district at noon. One Hartford tire dealer summed up the "lingering effect" of riots. He estimated that during the extended summer violence of 1967, "his business dropped 40 per cent and that even today many people simply won't come into the neighborhood to shop. They have a deeply uneasy feeling that outbursts could occur again." In the late 1960s you did not have to look far to find a downbeat story about the prospects for urban commerce.[89]

Just as the civil rights demonstrations earlier in the decade had hinted at the potential boost African American shoppers could bring to the downtown economy, the aftermath of rioting drew attention to the promises of black capitalism. The riots had sent the message that blacks wanted more control over their communities. Surveying the rubble, some anticipated what one headline proclaimed a "shift in values." A positive (even "exhilarating") refrain was that the riots had created a constructive, mobilizing sense of community for African Americans as they pulled the pieces of cities back together.[90] Investment was one way blacks could increase their stake in urban life and provide insurance against further rioting. Programs sprang up to help African American entrepreneurs. In Washington, next to a row of burned-out national chain stores, a bright new black-owned men's clothing store (Mr. Man) opened shop with assistance from the Small Business Administration. A black-owned bank labored to open in Dayton, Ohio, boosted by Urban League campaigns. In Pittsburgh, the United Black Front was raising capital to buy a variety store, a fish market, a pharmacy, and a cleaning shop. The Famous Hot Dog Stand passed into black ownership and reopened as The Hot Dog Hut after refurbishing. In Philadelphia a successful shopping center, Progress Plaza, brought seventeen stores and offices to a former riot area, thanks to backers like Reverend Leon Sullivan.[91]

Many observers questioned whether blacks had the financial backing and experience to make their vision of black capitalism materialize. Despite all the talk, complaints abounded that it was nearly impossible for African Americans to get bank loans. Failure rates for all new business ventures were high, and there were reasons to worry about what would happen next if too many fledgling experiments in black capitalism folded. And even if African American entrepreneurs succeeded in setting up viable businesses, would it be enough to reinvigorate urban commerce? Blacks were traveling to shopping malls too, as any visitor to Northland Mall outside Detroit could tell you in 1971. Detroit's auto manufacturers had committed nearly $10 million to establish black proprietors in inner-city dealerships formerly owned by whites. After only a few years, however, the companies "decided that even blacks can't do much business there." One African American car dealer in Chicago described what "a big thing" it was for black families to shop in the suburbs: "That's were half my business goes." Looming in people's minds was the question of whether "black control of central cities" — a scenario including investment as well as political power — was indeed "the hollow prize."[92]

From the first antiwhite slogans it was clear that another key issue would be what role existing commercial investors would play in the post-riot years. Would corporate America and the small companies forget the antagonism and stay, hoping to spur greater, more determined commitments and a resurgence? As smoke slowly cleared, so did some of the "get-whitey" rhetoric. In many cities the enormity of the challenge — rebuilding amid terribly deteriorated conditions — was overwhelming enough to bring together disparate groups in the emergency. For a brief while, the news seemed full of pledges from corporate America to help rebuild. Boosters celebrated every decision to

Figure 6.16 In the late 1960s and early 1970s, ordinary street scenes such as this one contained hopeful as well as discouraging signs of the prospects for urban commerce. When in 1970 Woolworth reopened this Washington, D.C., branch that had been burned out two years earlier, *Nation's Business* showcased the company's use of black construction workers and employees and drew positive attention to the decision to remain in the city. However, plywood fronts like those boarding up the chain store on the left were plentiful, and the wood veneer became symbolic of the style ironically dubbed "riot renaissance." (By permission of Fred Ward / Black Star.)

build a new store, remodel, or simply stay. When Woolworth replaced a Washington, D.C., branch that had been burned out in 1968 rioting, *Nation's Business* announced, "Woolworth Helps Give Downtown Its Ups" and showcased the company's use of black construction workers and employees (fig. 6.16). In the ten years after the Newark riots, Prudential Insurance Company more than quadrupled its downtown real estate investments, while Blue Cross–Blue Shield and Western Electric put up skyscrapers.[93] Though looters and snipers caused $250,000 worth of damage to one furniture and appliance store in Newark, the manager (an African American) and the owner took this as a wake-up call to make their store "a better neighbor." The manager explained that they had never really expected a riot in Newark, and certainly not at their store. Eighty percent of the company's employees were African American, it contributed to local black charities, and most of the clientele were black as well. Since the riots the manager had set up a "Community Room" in the store, which was available at no charge for meetings. This store pushed itself to put out an even larger welcome mat for its black customers.[94] Such decisions suggested it was reasonable to hope that the destruction could inspire new approaches that addressed the shortcomings of urban commerce.[95]

And then there was the confusing matter of property values in the damaged districts. For their part, real estate appraisers were poorly prepared, in the words of one consultant, to "judge the effects of riots or civil disobedience." The assumption was that values had dropped, but appraisers lacked techniques for incorporating violence and destruction into their calculations and hesitated to create narrow guidelines.[96] Some businesses watched their trade rise because their competitors had been reduced to rubble. One appraiser found this to be true for the S. H. Kress store on Central Avenue in Los Angeles. The store, relatively intact, now stood amid a host of newly vacant lots. Real estate sales indicated a likely decline of 20 percent, but the county assessor insisted that property values had not fallen. The appraiser, Robert Steele, discovered that "in support of the assessor, the manager of the variety store on the subject property said that retail sales actually had increased following the riots."[97] Nearby, a reopened drugstore experienced a similar increase in sales over pre-riot conditions. Despite the devastation, neighborhood purchasing power and demand remained steady. In Pittsburgh, Hill Pharmacy did a bustling business after four major drugstores nearby had burned down.[98] One standard technique for estimating commercial real estate values utilized the property's income stream (in these cases, sales figures). Thus their improved income indeed implied that these properties had gone up in value.

In the case of the Kress building, the appraiser compromised by determining that business property was depressed but that the condition was only temporary because "an enthusiastic community spirit" and energetic local organizations impressed him. The fact that "the citizens expect their area to have a future!" induced Steele to upgrade his projections, because the visualization of future urban commerce was so critical to appraising. An accompanying photograph entitled "Business as usual" depicted one man shining another's shoes against a backdrop of rubble — an image intended to convey the determination and resourcefulness of local entrepreneurs (fig. 6.17). It captured the balance between hope and despair and the fact that, as one reporter declared of Newark ten years after the riots, "the seeds of rebirth and promise coexist with decay and deprivation." Yet the selection of a shoe-shine enterprise had a probably unintended second meaning. Shoe shining was exactly the kind of employment the younger generation hoped to escape. One Harlem man described the rioters as "heroes of a sort" for not putting on "the green jacket"

Figure 6.17 This photograph, appearing in a 1968 issue of an appraisal journal, sat above a caption reading "Business As Usual." The image was intended to represent the perseverance and entrepreneurial determination of Los Angeles residents after the 1965 riots. Yet shoe shining was exactly the kind of employment the younger generation hoped to escape. (© Bettmann/CORBIS; used with permission.)

and going "down to the nearest shoe-shine parlor." This was not the kind of "business as usual" most blacks had in mind when they worked toward increased black investment in cities.[99]

It is no accident that the 1960s riots provoked searches for the most ironclad investment security attempted during the century. The optimistic promise of the 100% district, a sufficient guarantee a few decades earlier, had failed.

Urban commercial life had come to embody inflammatory racial tension, so that it now seemed to require an extraordinarily stigmatizing investment guarantee. A revealing proposal came from Frederick Sturdivant, the marketing professor who condemned mom-and-pops and hoped to entice more large-scale retailers to cities. He argued that plenty of urban businesses, particularly supermarkets, yielded respectable profits. Sears and J. C. Penney, according to Sturdivant, had survived transformed urban conditions and had done well. He proposed an "investment guarantee" plan to protect companies against the "abnormal risks" of urban commerce. The contract would cover physical damage from civil disorder and would compensate stores for operating losses during periods of unrest. Sturdivant's proposal could not guarantee profit, of course, but instead it offered a way to restructure urban investment so that participants could imagine profits while accommodating risks of violence.[100]

Most Main Street investment strategies of the twentieth century rallied around powerfully motivating positive visions, beginning with the Main Street postcards and cleanup campaigns of Progressive era beautification. In the postwar era of presumed decline, the Civil Rights movement and urban renewal offered the promise of remedying Main Street's troubles, even if the paths proved to be violent and the results were ambiguous. All of these visions incorporated critiques of existing circumstances to justify the new goals. The riots presented a different challenge. The riots offered a negative vision of immolation, a fiery alternative intentionally sought by protestors who seemed to say that all the other remedies (such as civil rights progress and urban renewal) were inadequate and it would be better if cities just burned down. Like the photograph of men going about "business as usual" amid the ruins, those who tried to move forward from the riots had to unearth the unlikely positive and constructive messages from the rubble. The horrifying news images of the riots in the 1960s would be difficult for urban investors to overcome, unlike the photographs criticizing the "pole and wire evil" fifty years earlier.

The "Build, baby, build" slogan was typical of efforts (such as black capitalism and corporate responsibility) to rally around positive inspiration for the future. In the summer of 1969, Jesse Jackson, then the director of economic programs for the Southern Christian Leadership Conference, was leading the picketing of Chicago construction sites in order to win jobs for African Americans. He claimed that although despair two years earlier had led to rioting and the infamous motto "Burn, baby, burn," plumbers' jobs at fifteen thousand dollars a year had inspired a new slogan — "Build, baby, build."[101]

The Promise of Resurrection

It is disturbing that federal officials surveying riot damage in the spring of 1969 were sometimes unable to distinguish riot destruction from "the normal decay that occurs in the slums and the abandonment of buildings under urban renewal programs." From the perspective of urban commerce and the urban landscape, the racial violence of the 1960s had more in common with postwar urban renewal than might at first meet the eye. Although the riots appeared to be spontaneous eruptions of commercial destruction, many wondered whether the looting was actually a calculated (and justified) response to the exploitation of urban consumers. Urban renewal dignified the demolition of stores as government policy. Yet urban renewal — the downtown investment policy with the most rationalized and repeated supporting arguments — was also irrational, as embodied in the idea of tearing down Main Streets in order to save them. Urban renewal destroyed black business districts in the name of highway development and leveled viable Main Street businesses in order to construct retail complexes. Some city residents saw the similarities between the effects of riots and those of urban renewal. A black member of Boston's City Council insisted that "far more physical destruction and far more lives have been bent, twisted and wrecked in Boston by urban renewal than by rioting." Together, the painful conflicts surrounding civil rights protests, the riots, and the wrecking ball of urban renewal did their part to put race, violence, and more vacant lots at the core of urban commercial life.[102]

Despite their stated or imputed goals, the outcome of the civil rights battles, urban riots, and urban renewal for downtown business remained unclear. We have seen how difficult the integration agenda was to carry out on Main Street, how the ensuing violence eroded economic strength, and how downtown businesses remained ambivalent about the prospect of relying on African American consumers. The contradictions of urban renewal quickly became evident, too. Publicly, of course, businesses and government supporters proclaimed that redevelopment "must inevitably help." But on-the-ground experiences challenged that mantra. Downtown New Haven, by 1962, had already lost all but one of its department stores. A massive redevelopment program razed much of the main shopping street (while luring a new Macy's). Many older small businesses did not survive relocation, and four square blocks of retail were converted into "practically a ghost town." Renewal, in other words, seemed to be destroying what was left of downtown retail. One characterization of redevelopment described it as "the urban equivalent to 'death and resurrection,'" a description that might, in its mingled despair and optimism, equally apply to the riots.[103]

By the 1970s, the fear of decline was itself a force to be reckoned with. Main Street interests had recognized for decades that the rhetoric of decline posed a threat to downtown land values. "Downtrodden Downtown Downgraded in Downright Downpour of Down-Talk," mocked a 1954 *Women's Wear Daily* headline. The *National Market Letter* cautioned its readers in 1972 that "there is a great danger in the urban analysis business of creating self-fulfilling prophecies that aggravate already serious problems. For example, any 'authority' who forecasts continued deterioration of a specific downtown may contribute to the decision of a large firm located there to move to the suburbs."[104]

To many, the riots represented the most treacherous turn of events for postwar urban America. Those who hoped that the violence might spark an era of increased downtown investment might reasonably be dismissed as pollyannas. Yet the riots did force a reconsideration of investor responsibilities, and they generated opportunities and arguments for reinvestment. The door had opened wider for African American investors, though at a tragic price.[105] Even as pessimism reached new highs in the 1970s, a new generation of experiments — festival marketplaces, pedestrian malls, downtown shopping malls, the National Trust's Main Street program, and historic preservation — took root with varying success. Although predictions of inevitable decline may have generated both anxiety and a certain comfort, participants in downtown commercial life in fact faced many decisions that would shape the future.

From Central Avenue in Watts, the skyline of downtown Los Angeles is visible eight miles north through the smog. In 1992 the daughter of a black community builder in Watts articulated what was on many minds then (after riots followed the Rodney King verdict) as she surveyed the downtown skyline: " 'Less than 30 years ago the tallest building you could see was City Hall which is 27 stories,' she said. 'Now look at it. They built the whole downtown. And what does Watts have? A shopping center and a few houses.' "[106] For the most part, the investment innovations of the 1970s and 1980s — historic preservation, festival marketplaces, and so on — had more impact on downtowns than on neighborhood commercial districts. On riot anniversaries, reporters returned periodically to the sites of the worst 1960s neighborhood violence in cities like Newark and Detroit, often finding that too little had changed. When measured against the goal of addressing the needs of poor city residents, the money and attention lavished on downtown commercial districts seems

misdirected. Here was another zero-sum equation that has plagued investment debates since the 1960s — investment is described as helping either urban neighborhoods *or* downtowns.

But the success stories of urban commercial investment after the 1960s
must indeed be partly attributed to the riots. The racial violence of the 1960s
did threaten to undermine the foundations of downtown as well as neighborhood commerce. Most importantly, the riots and civil rights demonstrations
highlighted in their respective ways that urban commerce was a critical place
where the different people of America came together. If business sites and
transactions could spark such conflict, then urban commercial sites were also
places where race relations might be repaired. In the last decades of the twentieth century, there was a resurgence of interest in the democratic potential of
Main Street exchange, a belief that found influential adherents besides writers
and urbanists like Mike Davis and Michael Sorkin.[107]

James Rouse, one of America's most prominent commercial real estate developers during the 1960s, 1970s, and 1980s, saw urban commercial life that
way. He became known for promoting the belief that urban commerce, above
all, constructively brings people together. Rouse, whose company developed
Boston's Faneuil Hall and Baltimore's Inner Harbor, was the nation's "festival
marketplace" guru. The surprising success of Faneuil Hall, opened in 1976,
sparked imitations across the country. Although Rouse has often been singled
out as downtown's "savior," before turning to festival marketplaces he had
poured his energies into suburban shopping mall development.[108] The key
point here is what "converted" Rouse to urban revitalization. In a 1981 interview, Rouse explained that his inspiration, his conversion, followed "the city
riots of the 1960s."[109] Perhaps the beleaguered optimists of the late 1960s
would find encouragement in these new directions.

Even as downtown buildings fell to urban renewal in the postwar decades, entrepreneurs carted off the rubble to recycle it in historically evocative new ventures. The developers of Salt Lake City's Trolley Square, an old car barn site refurbished into a shopping and entertainment center, paved its walkways with tons of bricks from downtown demolitions in the 1960s. Wood, marble, iron, and glass were salvaged from St. Louis slum clearance and used to enhance the old-fashioned patina of Gaslight Square, another historically themed commercial district. By the late 1970s, cities like St. Louis and Chicago supplied a national market with used brick, though demand was greatest in the South.[1] Old materials were being used to create a historic atmosphere and give urban commerce new life. After decades of strenuously forward-looking modernization strategies, downtown investors began to mine the past for inspiration.

In the 1970s, continued abandonment coexisted with hopeful experimentation, and tear-down approaches persisted while historically themed development and preservation gained credibility. In commercial districts like Gaslight Square and Trolley Square, private investors transformed old, distinctive buildings or neighborhoods into magnetic entertainment destinations. James Rouse's festival marketplace formula built upon these precedents but also created a new model through the national scope of his company, public financing and subsidies, special events, and his own philosophies of public space. Prior to the 1976 opening of Rouse's Faneuil Hall, downtown retail investors across America had labored for forty years without a splashy success story.[2] In the mid-1970s, the National Trust for Historic Preservation launched its Main Street Pilot Project, applying principles of historic preservation to commercial revitalization in small cities. The large scale of urban renewal's destruction gave urgency to the new goal of preserving districts in addition to individual landmarks.[3] In another strategy — especially favored by small- and medium-sized cities — pedestrian mall development involved entirely or partially closing a city's main retail thoroughfare to traffic and introducing landscaping and other design amenities found in suburban shopping centers.[4]

Other innovations of the 1970s employed the tear-down-and-rebuild techniques of urban renewal. In large cities, investor pioneers worked closely with local government to bring enclosed shopping malls and mixed-use office-retail-civic developments to the downtown. A big-city office-building boom enhanced the potential for attracting downtown workers into shops. Ever-smaller cities endured decentralization and turned to the hope offered by demolition and urban renewal. In their 1989 study, downtown scholars Bernard J. Frieden and Lynne B. Sagalyn identified the 1970s as an underappreciated "golden age" of retail investment and experimentation. Underscoring the thirst for new ideas, hundreds and sometimes thousands of inquiries poured in to the pioneers of innovations like the pedestrian mall, Main Street preservation, and festival marketplaces. To Faneuil Hall's architects, it seemed that "every city in America" called to attract the developer's interest.[5]

Most signs in the 1970s indicated continued decentralization. As one business reporter recalled, "those were the days when downtowns were collapsing into themselves."[6] Countless cities remained untouched by festival markets, historic preservation, or other innovations. Yet a shift was under way — one that architectural critic Ada Louise Huxtable called at the time a "radical change" and "a genuine breakthrough" affecting both small town and big city.[7] The possibility emerged that run-down and abandoned Main Street structures had preservation value, that developers might recycle old buildings to simultaneously evoke history and stimulate consumers. These movements to market the past indicated a fundamental shift in approaches to downtown investment.[8]

When the lens pulls back to include the 1980s and 1990s, the trend toward using nostalgia in commercial development becomes even clearer. The New Urbanism movement, creating walking neighborhoods with their own retail centers, has also been nourished by nostalgia for design-enhanced, denser, sociable communities like those that supposedly existed in the past.[9] And New Urbanism was not just a strategy for improving suburban subdivisions. In the 1990s, Smyrna, Georgia, built an entirely new downtown one block away from its old one because the old one, beloved as it was, had been left with little to preserve in the aftermath of a destructive road widening. The postmodern trend in architecture borrowed design elements liberally from the past, to

Figure 7.1 In the final decades of the twentieth century, commercial developers began to mine the past for inspiration — a trend seen in formulas like historic preservation, festival marketplaces, and the New Urbanism. This August 8, 1999, cartoon satirized the idea that "cutting-edge" suburban shopping mall developers had discovered an "incredible retailing concept": Main Street. In 2002 when a new outlying mall — the Shops at Southpoint and Main Street — opened in Durham, North Carolina, it included replicas of key downtown Durham commercial buildings and even duplicated a signature smokestack. Southpoint's promotional materials asserted that consumers would enjoy the old-fashioned atmosphere evoked by lampposts and brick paving. (Reproduced with permission of Bill Griffith.)

comment upon, reinterpret, honor, or simply evoke past environments without trying to recreate history. In what many viewed as an ultimate irony, cutting-edge suburban shopping mall development in the year 2000 meticulously replicated the old Main Street environment in its entirety (see fig 7.1).[10] And by the end of the twentieth century, historic preservation had grown from its inauspicious first encounters on Main Street to become the most popular downtown revitalization strategy for smaller American cities.[11]

In these ways and others, nostalgia became a potent force shaping downtown development and ultimately a controversial force in setting Main Street values. Consumers responded by opening up their wallets as investors had hoped. Baltimore's Inner Harbor development, because it involved demolition of so much of the existing historical fabric, is a good example of how, even in the absence of precise historical contexts and direct connections to consumers' memories, visitors appreciated environments inspired by nostalgia. The all-new shopping and entertainment pavilions of Harborplace, developed by the Rouse Company, opened in 1980. Historian Jon Teaford has pointed out that in Harborplace's case, visitors were drawn in and charmed by the "romance of Baltimore's bygone seafaring tradition." Measured by the crowds, this clean-slate approach to infusing downtown commerce with historical themes worked, and the dearth of actual structures from the harbor's past did not seem to matter. A reporter's review of the district a year and a half after it opened enthusiastically found that, "best of all, it is a link to history"

Figure 7.2 The successful opening of Baltimore's Harborplace in 1980, one of the Rouse Company's first festival marketplaces, demonstrated that even in the absence of precise historical contexts, consumers appreciated environments bathed in nostalgia. This 1976 aerial photograph of what would become the site of the Harborplace pavilions reveals Baltimore's clean-slate approach to historically evocative commercial development. In Baltimore it was the "romance" of the city's vanished maritime traditions that provided an appealing "link to history." (Courtesy of Columbia Association Archives; JWR Photographs and Prints, no. I.XI.0078.)

(figs. 7.2, 7.3).[12] Critic Huxtable was thrilled to see "a public subscribing to an increasingly sophisticated set of urban values" — a public newly "responsive" to the appeal of what she called "old-fashioned" commercial environments.[13]

In sharp contrast to the consuming public, however, intellectuals have advanced more negative assessments of nostalgia's place in downtown development. Christine Boyer, who writes of the "stench" of nostalgia, is typical of these deeply skeptical critics. Boyer believes real estate interests have per-

Figure 7.3 The visitor's eye-level experience of Baltimore's historic harbor was dominated by the boxy lines of contemporary architecture and by modern furnishings such as the streetlights along the water's edge. In this rendering, the restored tall ship, the *Constellation*, stands out as a rare historical artifact. (Courtesy of Columbia Association Archives; JWR Photographs and Prints, no. I.XI.0081.)

verted historical sensibilities and historic preservation to serve their financial interests. Nostalgia, in the hands of developers, has become a vehicle to consumption, she argues, and has been harnessed to orchestrate Main Streets as phony "historicized stage sets." The result is not just bad history, insists Boyer, but the crass commercialization of a public realm that was previously shaped by diverse values and interests. She describes festival marketplaces like South Street Seaport Museum in New York as "holes in the heart of our cities and gaps in our present concept of history."[14] Boyer, Max Page, and others have debunked the assumption that historic preservation was intrinsically pitted *against* development. Some preservationists have argued that they resisted development by protecting buildings from market forces. But according to these recent studies, preservation is no longer seen as an alternative to market-driven development; in fact it now appears to be the enabler of, even the catalyst for, developer profit.[15]

Contrary to the view of academic critics that developers fully controlled the marketing of the past, there was no omniscient path in the 1960s and 1970s leading investors to manipulate the public's interest in history. Few would dispute that developers have exploited nostalgia over the past thirty years to make profits at downtown destinations. Yet in the 1970s not only did real estate interests have to confront widespread pessimism about the future of Main Street, but there was every reason to think that nostalgia would appeal only minimally and marginally to the consuming public. The dwindling and failing chain stores like Woolworth sold nostalgia too — but they did so to a mostly aged, geographically constrained, and low-income customer base. Retail analysts pointed out that nostalgia might possess magnetism (especially whenever variety chains announced store closings), but it had not kept the dime stores in business. This line of thinking led one reporter to conclude that "nostalgia is a poor customer." [16]

The strategy of using the past as a commercial motif did not emerge clearly or suddenly in the minds of developers during the 1970s. Overemphasizing the revelatory impact of Faneuil Hall and the country's bicentennial celebration overlooks the rocky route investors navigated to adopt historical sensibilities, as well as the resistance and detours encountered in that reorientation. Most participants in Main Street investment during the 1960s and 1970s ignored arguments for historic preservation and were unaware of what it could offer economic development. During the same years several heralded festival marketplace precursors failed: previously thriving historically themed commercial districts were left to revert to vacant storefronts or worse. Even James Rouse, otherwise so articulate in expressing his development principles and motivations, was casting around in uncharted territory of downtown revitalization when he found surprising success with the old buildings of Faneuil Hall.[17]

Just as developers had no monolithic understanding about how to exploit the value of the past, consumers were not pawns in the hands of investors. Consumers had their own agendas, and they too manipulated, debated, and experienced nostalgia's place in urban commercial life. Behind even the easily ridiculed longings for "simpler" times lay potentially subversive sentiments. Affection for the modest, affordable consumer era symbolized by variety stores like Woolworth in many ways represented a rejection of the planned and accelerated obsolescence of late-twentieth-century consumption. To shop at Woolworth was to seek out not just an inexpensive item but exactly the same item that had been available ten or even thirty years earlier. That very undertaking spurned the planned obsolescence of products in most stores, where styles were purposefully discontinued quickly in order to stimulate interest in the new rather than the old.

Nor could retail developers dictate how consumers would respond to historically themed environments, since shoppers had their own experiences and made decisions independent of developer intent.[18] Planners did try to promote certain messages (no matter how vague), as was evident in this claim for the South Street Seaport Museum by its executive vice president: "We have to tell people that they have real roots here . . . that this place is significant . . . because their very existence is tied to this place: They are what they are partly because of what went on here." Yet visitors possessed different "roots"—a word that carried racial connotations in the 1970s because of Alex Haley's book by that name and the television miniseries based upon it.[19] Filtered through specific family stories or concrete personal experiences, the public's nostalgia for past commercial environments was not necessarily vague. On Main Street those experiences and stories ranged from childhood adventures downtown to being denied service at lunch counters. We have already seen how in the 1960s retailers woke up to the effects of consumer initiatives such as selective buying, undeclared boycotts, and outright protest. Not surprisingly, in the 1970s, 1980s, and 1990s consumers were far more likely to raise, face, and debate difficult issues unearthed by nostalgia than were developers — most of whom shied away from controversial topics of downtown history. In the process, Americans have constructed their own alternative histories of urban commerce, judging for themselves what has constituted improvement and what has constituted decline.

The Variety Store's Last Stand

By the 1970s, the very buildings that seventy years earlier had brought people together in new ways and brokered a vibrant commercial culture had become "white elephants."[20] The streets of cities large and small were pockmarked by the vacated properties of familiar chains and local businesses. What did the vacant and closing stores mean? What would now define urban commercial culture, if not the crowds? The chain variety stores, so instrumental during the early twentieth century in creating Main Street and its high property values, were also at the center of 1970s efforts to redefine urban commercial life amid proclamations of decline.

Alone in the 1970s among the chain variety stores, Woolworth kept and intensified its primary stake in downtown locations. Kresge had quietly closed its "old-style" Main Street stores and then changed its name to Kmart in 1977 to recognize the company's new discounter identity.[21] As the fastest growing retailer of the mid-1970s, Kmart's arrival on the local scene, usually a few miles outside the city center, brought apprehension to existing merchants.[22] J. C. Penney was reinvented in a different way, transforming itself into a shopping mall anchor.[23] These two chains took on new commercial and geographic identities, while Woolworth retained its urban variety store format. Other once-significant players dropped out of the competitive ranks. Kress, after staying downtown "too long," frantically overexpanded into the suburbs and then limped into the seventies under Genesco ownership.[24] W. T. Grant filed for bankruptcy in 1975 and was liquidated a year later. So by 1978 it was already "Woolworth: The Last Stand of the Variety Store" — making the company a key institution for understanding downtown investment in the closing decades of the twentieth century.[25]

By the 1970s Woolworth had settled into its competitive niches, both in inner-city areas untouched by Kmart and on Main Street. Like other variety chains, Woolworth closed Main Street locations and entered the discount business with Woolco. But Woolco lagged far behind Kmart, and the business press concluded that Woolworth's heart remained in the variety store business.[26] During the 1960s, the company opened large stores in downtown areas, making explicit statements about its faith in Main Street's future. In 1970 Woolworth located its biggest store in a struggling part of Boston, and twenty years later the company singled out its variety stores for "demonstrating particular strength in major urban centers, especially inner cities, where they serve as a valued neighborhood resource." To one real estate consultant, the Woolworth in Willimantic, Connecticut ("the largest and the dominant retail store in the CBD"), had become "deeply associated" with the downtown.[27] As the New York *Daily News* pointed out, "whether it was Mayberry or 125th Street, Woolworth was downtown."[28]

From the early 1960s to the mid-1970s, economic prosperity boosted retail sales, but the downtown's proportion of overall sales slipped, and store vacancy was "unconscionably high." Typical of the boom, Woolworth saw its sales nearly double between 1964 and 1974. But profits had not kept up, and the corporation was struggling even before the mid-1970s recession — the worst retailing slump since the Great Depression. The chains closed hundreds of small Main Street units in the name of greater efficiency and located most of their replacements in the suburbs. In ten years Woolworth alone closed 734 smaller stores, opening 172 larger ones with the same total selling space.

Topeka, Kansas, illustrates these trends, with the number of stores dropping from 291 in 1958 to 168 in 1972. In those years, while county sales figures escalated by 135.5 percent, sales downtown dipped 10.4 percent and downtown's share of county sales declined dramatically from 39.1 to 14.9 percent. Sears and J. C. Penney left Topeka in the mid-1960s for a nearby shopping center, and by 1977 Kresge, McClellan, and Grant were gone. Woolworth was preparing to close as well.[29]

While retailers and consumers speculated among themselves about the future of Main Street, the formal job of predicting value fell to real estate appraisers. In 1976 and 1977 Woolworth hired the Real Estate Research Corporation (RERC) of Chicago to undertake reuse appraisals of store properties the variety store had decided to close. Projecting property values was intertwined with the act of imagining future uses for vacated commercial space. Appraisals — often detailed twenty- or thirty-page reports — offer a window on how investors envisioned and evaluated the potential character of downtown commercial life. Such real estate documents were rarely simple numerical statements; rather, they told stories about commercial values in specific communities, regions, and the nation. Reviewing local history, current commercial strength, and regional trends, investigators typically spoke with bank officials, store managers, real estate brokers, planners, city officials, and Chamber of Commerce representatives.[30]

The confidential real estate files of the S. H. Kress chain add to our understanding of 1970s chain store struggles to define a future for Main Street. Unlike Woolworth, Kress had invested in elaborate, architecturally distinctive Main Street properties. These landmark downtown buildings continued to dominate Kress's image, even as the company scrambled to establish a hold in shopping centers. Employee morale fluctuated wildly throughout changes in corporate ownership and management philosophy.[31] During these years, Kress personnel expended tremendous energy just keeping the remaining Main Street stores afloat or, alternatively, shutting down stores and redistributing resources. The real estate department's records tell us about such endeavors, illuminating as well the dynamic between local managers and corporate headquarters. Internal documents, never intended for public eyes, show how investors defined the vacancy market and tried to make the most of it.

Soulless Shells? The Multiple Meanings of Vacant Stores

It was easy, in the 1970s, to focus on the depressing and discouraging implications of store closings and find in them confirmation of long-term decline. Woolworth's consultants, as they sought out the next likely uses of the retail buildings, disclosed that the Main Street initiatives under review in the mid-1970s were familiar from the previous two decades — modernization, urban renewal, various marketing efforts by aggressive merchants and city officials, and an occasional pedestrian mall. There did not appear, in these reports, to be any exciting new revitalization solutions for the struggling chain stores. When a store closed, the merchandise usually disappeared in a week, leaving for inspectors "lint, cobwebs, and trash." Investors certainly recognized the negative impact that closings and vacancies could have on the shopping and business communities. The authors of one revitalization report, *Shoppers' Paradise*, described how empty buildings were "symptoms of physical deterioration," which challenged merchant confidence and eroded "the shopping environment." Since the news of Woolworth's closing would itself negatively affect the local real estate market, the company's consultants tried to work anonymously.[32]

Yet to investors, there was no such thing as simply a vacant store with universal meaning or symbolism. Turnover in commercial real estate had been high for as long as anyone could document. The RERC consultants found this recycling to be especially dynamic in small cities, noting that "properties, regardless of age and condition, tend to be utilized over and over by merely rehabilitating the existing structure." When Woolworth accelerated its closings in the early 1990s, the corporation in its public statements downplayed the local distress provoked by that policy and instead emphasized the constant recycling of buildings in commercial life and the opening of new opportunities. This perspective extended to the company's lore about its earliest days. According to one official history, F. W. Woolworth's casualness in opening and closing stores "indicates that he regarded physical locations as simply soulless shells to house merchandise and offer it for sale."[33]

As a real estate concept, vacancy had some promising connotations because it suggested that a property remained actively in the market. Vacancy meant potential for sale and reuse, no matter how unlikely. RERC's *National Market Letter*, for example, distinguished between "vacant" and "charged out of the market picture" entirely. Once "abandoned," a property could no longer be counted as vacant. Although the real estate industry was certainly vulnerable to pessimism (especially in times of economic crisis such as the 1930s depression or the 1960s racial violence), in the 1970s many investors hoped that commercial vacancy would invite creativity to envision new uses and improve values. The *National Market Letter* observed that "the application of imagination to vacant store spaces can frequently pay off well."[34]

Location helped determine the prospects of vacant stores just as it broadcast the status of occupied ones. Every real estate professional, the *National Market Letter* expected, "should know the difference between quantity and quality in local vacancy." Distinguishing among vacant properties served the chain stores' interests because in past decades they had selected and defined the best urban sites. Woolworth's 1970s appraisals continued to refer to the "traditional" 100% corner, even though that concept's implied guarantee had expired. In Greenville, South Carolina, where Woolworth sat at the peak intersection, the consultants found an "abundance of well-located vacant retail space." Investigators in Port Richmond, Staten Island, counted thirteen vacancies out of thirty-six storefronts. Even the "best-quality retail store" had closed, and lower "quality" vacancies were indicated by boarded-up windows and doors. The constellation of empty stores affected the value of any given property, because they were evaluated in relation to one another. In the vacancy market, some were better positioned than others.[35]

The distinction between vacant first-floor and upper-story space also spoke volumes to Main Street experts about a site's potential. For decades, unoccupied upper floors had become so common, even in thriving commercial districts, that they were taken for granted. One-story downtown taxpayer buildings had proliferated forty and fifty years earlier to avoid this very problem, and low-profile suburban construction also bowed to the upper-floor challenge. In Biddeford, Maine, the second story of Woolworth had remained empty for ten or fifteen years, and the consultants judged that it was not worth the effort to try to fill it. An occasional property had upper-story tenants, which attested to a dense commercial life. The Woolworth in Maynard, Massachusetts, had a recording studio upstairs, and many of the buildings on the street had second-story offices and apartments. The Oneida property had managed to lease renovated upper-story space to two attorneys. But Maynard, Oneida, and also Rutland, Vermont, were the exceptions. Second-story vacancies carried lower expectations.[36]

Probably nothing said as much about the vision of a community's future commercial life than the scenarios sketched out by consultants and others of possible new uses for closing or vacant stores. The "remodeling possibilities" were "presented as serious alternatives to prospective purchasers." Actual or potential buyers and tenants made a consultant's work easy, as in Oneida, where an adjacent bank wished to expand into the Woolworth building.[37] A lucky few among the Woolworth cohort could hope to sustain a reasonably similar market value. Because Woolworth was the only general merchandiser in Lawrence, Massachusetts, the consultants believed its "replacement should be exactly the same."[38] However, many Main Streets in the 1970s experienced a change in what the appraisers called retailing "character" or "climate." Usually this meant a transition to "marginal" or "secondary" retail uses, which previously stood at the edge of commercial districts — used furniture, used clothing, and arts and crafts shops. Most of the Woolworth properties in the 1970s required creativity to imagine their prospects.[39]

For investors, a hierarchy of possible reuses indicated each building's future value, with the most significant distinction demarcating retail from nonretail. Retail continued to command higher rents and purchase prices, whereas conversion to nonretail use (although often an imaginative undertaking) was itself an indicator of diminished vitality, according to professionals. So recommending conversion for storage or housing a charitable organization, as in the case of Port Richmond, communicated the expectation that the commercial nature of the city would continue to recede, replaced by something unknown but definitely less attractive. In St. Paul some of Woolworth's former retail neighbors had been replaced by the American Indian Center and Lutheran Social Services of Minnesota. A more promising nonretail prospect was the goal of attracting IBM offices in Endicott, New York. In Topeka, city acquisition for urban renewal offered the "best hope"; otherwise, Woolworth might have to try selling the property for storage. Importantly, the appraisers could admit defeat, indicating that the vacancy market was not founded on bottomless, unrealistic optimism. Ultimately, Port Richmond disappointed the consultants: "Market conditions indicate that there is no realistic array of likely reuses. There is simply no significant demand for vacant space."[40]

The absence of vacant stores in the 1970s, like their presence, did not tell an obvious story. The three vacancies in Fond du Lac, Wisconsin, suggested an intact and vibrant downtown. Yet the consultants warned that "the relatively small amount of vacant space is not, however, a good indication of the future retail character of the downtown." The appraiser had information not available to the general public about the intentions of other stores to move or close, so that soon the city's entire prime block might be empty. Such inside information, including unfounded rumors, further complicated the market.[41]

The irony of vacant stores occupying the 100% district eventually induced investors to reconsider the definition of prime retail property to describe 1960s–70s conditions. The notion of a 100% district had spread in the 1920s through the leadership of chain stores, and it offered a technique for predicting (and creating) retail success and high values based on locating the densest concentrations of women pedestrians. By the 1960s, vacancy and eroding downtown property values, in tandem with a decline in pedestrian shopping and the changing consumption preferences of suburban housewives, rendered the 100% district a largely outdated concept. The Real Estate Research Corporation gradually adjusted to this change. Its *Market Letter,* since 1947, had recommended "buy," "hold," or "sell" for different types of property. Initially, "prime" retail embodied the 100% district, and "secondary" included everything else, but in 1953 suburban stores were added to the prime category. RERC favored investment in prime location stores but advised selling all secondary properties. In 1959 RERC added qualifiers for "superior" downtown locations, to suggest buying "the *best* of downtown locations in towns or cities which are experiencing growth in their employed labor force and where adequate steps have been taken to effectively offset the forces of retail decentralization." It helped if the property had "prime tenants of demonstrated stability," which often meant national chains. A 1962 newsletter acknowledged that "our definition of 'prime' as it applies here has been tightened considerably." By the mid-1960s, the prime retail investment category accompanied an aerial photograph of a suburban shopping mall. The factors underpinning "prime" location and profitable commerce had been deliberately redefined.[42]

Although the appraisers worked within regional and national assumptions of Main Street decline, they believed that merchant skills and city leadership had the capacity to either overcome or accelerate downward economic trends. The unusually "aggressive reaction" of Allentown, Pennsylvania, to suburban competition impressed the consultants; the city "acted before the anchor department stores left downtown." With new public buildings and a downtown mall, store vacancies dropped dramatically and a refreshing "spirit of pride and cooperation" infused Allentown's actions. In Fond du Lac, "a strong promotion-oriented merchant" might succeed in the Woolworth space where another would fail, while in Topeka a "select group of individual merchants . . . experienced substantial increase" despite twenty years of sharp decline. The case of Oneida illustrated how passive retailers, by losing sales to outlying shopping plazas, could let a city down. The *National Market Letter* advised clients to base commercial investment decisions largely on the aggression of merchants and city officials. When in 1970 the *NML* backed away from its recommendation to buy prime retail property, it did so after seeing a reduction in "entrepreneurial people willing to work long hours for low profits." [43]

RERC's investigation of these Woolworth sites underscored the unpredictable impact of the era's most aggressive downtown improvement strategy — urban renewal. The outcome of Willimantic's 35.5 acre redevelopment, begun only a few years earlier in 1973, was "unclear." The displacement of sixty-five businesses at least temporarily had the effect of "reducing the retail consumer attraction of the CBD." Topeka's "somewhat successful" renewal had started in 1960 and had "indirectly" stemmed decline by inspiring others to renovate. For St. Paul, redevelopment would "somewhat bolster the marketability of the property," but overall the efforts would not reverse "decay." The major plans of Lawrence, Massachusetts, were expected to have little impact. "Because of the predicted decline," RERC advised, the Lawrence property should be sold "as soon as possible." The phased rehabilitation of the central business district undertaken in Taunton, Massachusetts, had hurt Main Street because the new downtown mall provided more competition than sales boost. Urban renewal efforts spanning from 1960 initiatives to current 1977 blueprints had ambivalent results. Depending upon the specific scenario, they had positively, negatively, or indeterminately affected downtown property.[44]

As redevelopment reconfigured urban racial geographies, it clarified the fact that many white investors balanced the threat of vacancy against the threat of racial incursion. White shoppers sometimes found minority presence to be more troubling than empty buildings. Appraisers saw evidence of this during Willimantic's redevelopment: "Some of the minorities living in this low-income residential area have relocated to the previously vacant upper floors on Main Street. Reportedly, this relocation has created some customer concern." [45] Trenton's future, as seen in previous chapters, was posed as either abandonment or a "nightmarish" Negro shopping district. Downtown stability in the minds of investors seemed to seesaw between these two unsettling trends.

The reports' confidential nature freed them from boosterish compulsions, but they also stand in revealing contrast to the brazen certainty (and optimism) of confidential appraisals from other eras, such as the 1920s. The Woolworth consultants chose their descriptive terms from a narrow range of cautious qualifiers: Maynard, Massachusetts "appears relatively healthy," and the outlook for Lebanon, New Hampshire, was "moderately positive." Others were deemed "viable" or "stable," as in the cases of Endicott, New York; Allentown, Pennsylvania; and Topeka. The most conservative comment was reserved for Greenville, Texas: "The business district will continue to house a number of stores." For Taunton, Massachusetts, "no significant value appreciation trends" were foreseen, while St. Paul's prospects were "marginal" and the trends for Rutland did "not appear favorable."[46]

In the 1970s, there were many reasons to believe that vacant downtown stores, emptied of the crowds that had given them significance, symbolized decline. One could easily see the "hollow shells" of Woolworth buildings as "fossils," as one reporter described them. Yet private real estate sources like the Woolworth appraisals, stripped of public grandstanding and posturing, capture cautious, ongoing efforts to invent new values and profit by them. Negotiating the complexities of vacancy, reuse, racial transitions, and prime location compelled investors to confront their fears of decline on a daily basis. Stakeholders in downtown real estate faced the prevailing pessimism and the apparent dearth of new ideas, to try to restore commercial vitality to Main Street. Far from a sense of absolute frustration with closings and vacancies, these investors worked with the ambiguous meanings of the changed and changing downtown landscape to create new opportunities. From this point of view, the empty retail spaces were "niches" for future enterprise. At their most optimistic, investors understood vacancy not as decline but as a necessary part of progress. "Economic progress," the *National Market Letter* explained, "requires . . . decay and death."[47]

"Now the Animals Will Come"

By the early 1970s, an honest downtown executive had to admit that the efforts of the previous twenty years to lure suburban homemakers back downtown had largely failed. Tellingly, the 1976–77 appraisal reports for Woolworth did not even mention housewives. Investors of the 1970s turned increasingly to working women, single women, people of color, families, men, tourists, and teenagers to keep up income. The housewife would not be ignored, but other previously taken-for-granted or unrecognized groups would be actively courted for their economic role in downtown commercial life.[48]

Critiques of the 1950s–60s woman-centered aesthetic strategies emerged, fueled by the impact of feminism on both the design professions and consumers. The work of architects, traffic engineers, and store planners to cater to the convenience, accessibility issues, and desires of housewives sounded somewhat naive and outdated by the mid-1970s and, at least in the downtown, had missed the mark. One *New York Times* article tersely concluded, "Trees and birds are perfectly nice, but no one really goes shopping to see them." The design embellishments of America's downtown pedestrian malls — landscaping, Muzak, fountains, benches, ornamental structures — came under attack and in some places were dug up by the early 1980s. The clutter and "gizmos," according to one Washington, D.C., planner, could make a pedestrian mall look "like a miniature golf course." Shoppers worried that "muggers" would take refuge behind the leafy trees, and sometimes it seemed that loiterers and "winos" were the groups best served by the comfortable benches.[49] While the pedestrian mall concept succeeded in some cities, like Denver, Colorado, or Burlington, Vermont, designing-for-women approaches largely backfired in many others.

As more women entered the design professions, feminists challenged the gender assumptions underpinning retail design. In 1973 *Chain Store Age* featured an interview with store planner Thelma Cupino entitled "You're Not Designing Stores for Women Shoppers." For Cupino, "designing a store for women doesn't mean tacking on unnecessary frills." She saw a fundamental paradox in having men design for women shoppers: "Design work is after all, an expression of an individual's personality and most men would not want their work to be considered 'feminine.' Yet they are trying to appeal to feminine personalities — or at least should be." She charged that few male store planners actually shopped in the places they designed, further limiting their effectiveness.[50]

The housewives of the 1950s had become the office workers of the 1970s, 1980s, and 1990s. The women's movement mobilized by Betty Friedan encouraged suburban women to push for employment outside the home and to admit that shopping was not as personally fulfilling as retailers and marketers presumed it to be. "Today only about 40% of American women are full-time housewives," the *National Market Letter* reminded readers in 1972. Looking ahead twenty-five years to the millennium, *NML* saw fewer differences between men and women. The trend toward two-income households (and the big-city skyscraper boom of the late twentieth century) placed more working women downtown. Yet stores would have to actively cultivate office workers, since "the fact that these white-collar employees come into the business district every day does not seem to make them strong customers of downtown retail establishments."[51]

When businesses floundered after trying hard to appeal to women, retailer relationships with female consumers could sour quickly. Under such circumstances, middle-class women became yet another destructive force in the eyes of investors. We find an example of this resentment inside a dimly lit W. T.

Grant store in 1975. Grant, once Woolworth's next biggest variety store rival, collapsed that year in a manner described in newspapers as "humiliating" and "staggering." At the time it was the second largest failure in the history of American business, behind Penn Central Railroad, and the largest in retailing history. In a last-ditch effort to save the chain, Grant put fashion first and appealed to its 80 percent female shopper base. When this tactic failed, the store's suppliers forced the chain, in bankruptcy court, to liquidate. In Westerly, Rhode Island, a *Fortune* reporter described how store manager Albert Duclos paced the locked store with another employee: "Most of the lights were out, and they wandered among the counters, thinking about how beautiful it looked and how the customers at the liquidation sale would ravage it. The floor seemed to gleam brighter than ever. All the merchandise sat in neat rows. The store was immaculate. 'Now the animals will come,' Duclos blurted out angrily." His colleague replied, "They'll tear the place up. . . . You'll never recognize it by the first night." To these retailers, not only had women failed to save the store, but they were now going to rip it apart. Just as 1920s investors had celebrated the female shopper's creation of peak downtown values, in the 1970s investors blamed female consumer habits for causing commercial decline.[52]

When downtown interests finally found a promising new formula for bringing white suburbanites back — the festival marketplaces popularized by developer James Rouse — they pulled in the whole family, not just housewives. Because it transformed a cluster of mostly vacant market buildings into a wildly successful downtown shopping district, Boston's Faneuil Hall redevelopment was held up as a national model. Baltimore's Harborplace and Milwaukee's Grand Avenue were other early Rouse successes, inspiring dozens of imitators. Ironically, after decades of anguished failures by retailers to attract suburbanites to urban markets, intellectuals and urban designers expressed ambivalence about suburbanites' return. Critics accused Rouse-style marketplaces of suburbanizing the downtown.[53]

For James Rouse, the success of Faneuil Hall in attracting suburbanites and tourists was less notable than the accomplishments of Philadelphia's Gallery at Market East. The Gallery's site, Rouse pointed out, had been stigmatized as a deteriorated downtown retail district with inexpensive shops and half-empty department stores serving mostly black clientele. In his opinion it was easier to draw suburban shoppers to a largely vacant, unknown wholesale district like Quincy Market than it was to rejuvenate an area that had gained the reputation of a black shopping district. The Gallery opened in 1977, shortly after Faneuil Hall Marketplace. A four-level, glass-enclosed mall, it linked two department stores. In sum, Philadelphia's Market Street — an existing retail district that had declined and seen a change in the racial composition of customers — was more typical of the challenges facing American downtowns. When the anticipated suburban crowds did not materialize, the developers successfully retenanted the mall for its city customers, 80 percent of whom arrived by mass transit.[54] Although it never enjoyed the publicity boost experienced by Faneuil Hall or Harborplace, the Gallery at Market East proved that downtown retail could revive even without suburbanites, with the help of nonwhite consumers. Here was evidence that an integrated clientele could in fact reinvigorate urban commerce — that test question of the 1960s.

Gaslights and the Dark Side:
Nostalgic Market Formulas before Faneuil Hall

Since festival marketplaces became the hottest fad of 1980s downtown retail, and historic preservation would become the single most influential Main Street investment approach of the late twentieth century, it is perhaps surprising to realize that their initial spread during the 1960s and 1970s was slow, halting, and interrupted by troubling failures. Retailers and developers, as well as their consultants and financiers, looked skeptically upon the idea that old downtown buildings could be renovated into profitable retail destinations. Scott Gerloff, an advocate during the "early years" of Main Street preservation (the 1970s), described how he "was able to drum up enthusiasm for residential historic districts, but when I got downtown, peoples' eyes glazed over and they began looking for exits when I started talking about preservation." Places like Gerloff's hometown of Sioux Falls, South Dakota (and the Main Streets in the Woolworth reports), were still experimenting with urban renewal, parking lots, and pedestrian malls — everything except preservation. Believing preservation was antidevelopment and antiquarian, most businesspeople were not, as Gerloff described, even interested in listening.[55]

The potential value of history to commercial development was not yet recognized by the vast majority of U.S. developers and real estate consultants. Entirely absent from the 1976–77 Woolworth assessments, for example, was any sense that the historic features of old buildings on Main Street could add value to downtown properties — and these reports were produced by a sophisticated national consulting firm dedicated to ferreting out all strategies for enhancing urban commercial life. The blurry, illegible photographs accompanying the Woolworth appraisals symbolize the consultants' inattention to the stores' physical presence. The descriptions of pressed tin ceilings, wood or linoleum floors, and brick color were only included to convey the structure's condition, materials, code compliance, and degree of renovation.[56]

The hesitant, uneven proliferation of historically themed commercial development before the landmark success of Faneuil Hall indicates some of the limits to selling "historicity" in downtown development during the 1960s and 1970s. Most instructive were the spectacular and haunting failures. Just a few months before Faneuil Hall opened in the summer of 1976, *New York Times* architectural critic Ada Louise Huxtable described in her column the "sinister and unreal" turn that one of the earliest 1960s nostalgic commercial developments had taken. The decline of Gaslight Square in St. Louis, Huxtable marveled, was one of "the most curious and frightening episodes in the recent, clouded history of urban change." Fifteen years earlier the refurbished Gaslight district had flourished in a blend of Gay Nineties and Roaring Twenties entertainment. By the mid-1970s it had become a derelict, high-crime "no man's land." It was enough, wrote another reporter, "to make a lover of cities cry" (figs. 7.4, 7.5).[57]

Gaslight Square's unexpected rise and anguished collapse reveal some of the uncertainties and obstacles that confronted those who experimented with old buildings and historical themes in downtown revitalization. When it first took shape in the late 1950s, Gaslight Square emerged from conditions that were almost universally suspect in commercial real estate development. The square sat in one of those mixed urban zones judged by most contemporaries to be unsavory and deteriorating. Once a fashionable business street anchored by important cultural institutions, by the postwar years it was known for its antique shops ("old ladies selling impossible things") but also for its prostitution and gay bars. The street marked the racial dividing line between the mostly black northern half and mostly white southern half of the city. Gaslight Square drew creative energy and much of its early financing from two destructive forces: St. Louis's massive urban renewal clearance generated the avalanche of building parts that furnished the district's emerging historical ambience, and a 1959 tornado flooded the budding destination with insurance money and curiosity-seekers. Within a year of the tornado, Gaslight had rebounded to become the city's premier entertainment destination and was claimed by St. Louis leaders as a key component of that city's hopes for revi-

Figure 7.4 The successes of festival marketplaces (and what many have dubbed the nostalgia industry), together with the nearly universal popularity of Main Street preservation in the 1980s and 1990s, obscure the fact that during the 1960s and 1970s there was great skepticism among downtown investors about the benefits of historically themed commercial development. The volatile history of Gaslight Square in St. Louis, an early precursor to the festival marketplaces, is especially illuminating. In its prime during the early 1960s, Gaslight quickly became a magnetic destination for St. Louisans, suburbanites, and conventioneers. In the foreground of this 1963 photograph, outdoor seating adds to the welcoming ambience of the wide sidewalk (originally for the carriage trade) that served the district as a public promenade. Atmospheric gaslights helped set the mood, as did this restaurant's five columns salvaged from a nearby mansion. (Courtesy of the Western Historical Manuscript Collection, University of Missouri, St. Louis. Photograph by George McCue.)

talization. It became a magnet for tourists and conventioneers, for well-heeled middle-aged suburbanites and beatniks. It was in every regard an unlikely success story.[58]

Really a T-shaped intersection with some broad sidewalks that once accommodated carriage trade, Gaslight Square was not especially distinctive architecturally. Its key landmark was the Musical Arts Building, which was completed in 1904 and served as the training ground for famous musicians and creative talents such as Helen Traubel, Tennessee Williams, and Betty Grable (fig. 7.6). But besides this building, which itself was terribly damaged by the 1959 tornado and a devastating fire in January 1962, the district was a

Figure 7.5 By the late 1960s, the derelict ruins of Gaslight Square stood as a somber warning about the risks of urban commercial revitalization, especially to those investors weighing the value of nostalgic motifs. This 1973 photograph depicts the same establishment shown in figure 7.4. (Courtesy of the Western Historical Manuscript Collection, University of Missouri, St. Louis. Photograph by George McCue.)

hodgepodge of unremarkable commercial and residential buildings that had been adapted ad hoc to the business of bars, restaurants, coffee shops, and clubs. Many of the new enterprises rehabilitated previously vacant, derelict structures.[59]

The nostalgic themes and design inspiration arose not from the existing architecture but from the original investors, who sought in various ways to create entertainment environments according to ornate, approximately Victorian or Gay Nineties aesthetics that were out of favor. Yet this was not an effort to preserve the historic interiors or exteriors of St. Louis by saving and relocating them. Rather this was assemblage and collage with salvaged fragments. At times, the eye-popping nostalgic designs themselves evoked the enormous scale of local destruction. The Crystal Palace, put on the national map by Jay Landesman for outstanding alternative theater and music, had so much salvaged art glass that comedian Lenny Bruce called it "a church gone bad." The Three Fountains Restaurant recycled wood paneling and chandeliers from lost townhouses and a 1904 World's Fair Christopher Wren replica, burled

Figure 7.6 Completed in 1904, the Musical Arts Building was one of Gaslight Square's few architecturally and historically distinctive structures. In the late 1950s, it was instrumental in attracting the first entrepreneurs who launched the area's rise. Later, the owners cut the building down to two stories after this devastating January 1962 fire, leaving the area with an even less distinguished architectural profile. Gaslight's nostalgic appeal was based on several overlapping historical themes — the Gay Nineties, later blended with the Roaring Twenties, as well as creative interior designs that recycled salvaged architectural fragments from St. Louis's massive urban renewal projects. (Reproduced with permission of Thelma Blumberg, photographer. Print courtesy of the Western Historical Manuscript Collection, University of Missouri, St. Louis.)

mahogany office doors with ebony trim from the riverfront Mercantile Exchange building, a railing from the demolished Grand Avenue suspension bridge, and countless other wood, metal, and stone elements. The earliest proprietors, sharing an affection for these objects, often knew exactly where each one had originated. Fighting the tide of "chrome and plastic" bars, these early

Figure 7.7 In the early 1960s, the first Gaslight Square enthusiasts believed that they had stumbled upon a formula that could reinvigorate other struggling downtown areas. Known widely as an antiques district, these shops were essential to Gaslight's offbeat aura and its reputation for salvaging and inventively reusing the city's cast-off artifacts. But like so many of the antique stores, Hirschfeld's (seen here in the late 1950s) was forced out when rents and property values rose. This turn of events by the mid-1960s prompted many insiders to wonder whether commercialism had ruined the district. (Reproduced with permission of Thelma Blumberg, photographer. Print courtesy of the Western Historical Manuscript Collection, University of Missouri, St. Louis.)

entrepreneurs cultivated what they called a saloon atmosphere without pretending that they were resurrecting a lost era. Their originality was assured, for example, when "environmental engineer" Jimmy Massucci used hundreds of telephone booth doors to design the interior of his club, Vanity Fair. These investors unabashedly created something new, building on the neighborhood's intriguing artistic yet edgy heritage and the warm associations they personally had with the cast-off historical artifacts from local demolitions (figs. 7.7, 7.8).[60]

Gaslight Square's initial appeal to people from outside the neighborhood arose from the area's bohemian and beatnik character. While Jimmy Massucci, Dick Mutrux, and Fred Landesman applied their talents to creating historically evocative interior designs for their businesses, Jay Landesman

Figure 7.8 The Vanity Fair, photographed circa 1960, was one of the original Gay Nineties saloons. Well-heeled patrons flocked to the bohemian atmosphere, the range of musical entertainment, and the avant-garde theater, remaking the scruffy intersection into St. Louis's hottest nightspot. (Reproduced with permission of Thelma Blumberg, photographer. Print courtesy of the Western Historical Manuscript Collection, University of Missouri, St. Louis.)

brought Beatnik credentials from years spent in Greenwich Village. He attracted significant new talents to the Crystal Palace, from Phyllis Diller, Dick Gregory, and George Carlin to Barbra Streisand, Kenneth Rexroth, Mike Nichols, and Elaine May. In addition to his theater, there were folksingers, jazz, long-haired poets selling their wares by the sheet, espresso bars, erudite bartenders who read Nietzsche aloud during slow times, a drugstore with an art gallery, and lots of intellectual company. The modern, nonconformist theme was evident in the names of the early businesses — Laughing Buddha, Insomniac, and The Dark Side. Dick Mutrux was in the real estate and property management field, and the others also presumably made a decent living, but still the district thrived on its oddball, offbeat reputation and was occasionally even described as anticapitalist and radical. A European theme was evident through the district's early years — the numerous outdoor sidewalk cafés, a Parisian-type kiosk, the almost inexplicably dense strolling crowds and people-watching, St. Louis's only French restaurant (The Three Fountains), and exotic Italian espresso machines (fig. 7.9). Mutrux himself had

Figure 7.9 This kiosk outside the Musical Arts Building in Gaslight Square advertised the promising, eclectic entertainment mix circa 1960: classical and flamenco guitar, Dixieland and jazz, coffeehouses and saloons. The juxtaposition of Victorian and modern is evident in establishment names like the Crystal Palace and The Dark Side. Inspiration for the Parisian-style kiosk, the wide sidewalks, the French restaurant, and the espresso machines came from European cities. The weak American case for experimenting with historical themes and old buildings in commercial development meant that in the 1960s and 1970s most of the pioneers in this field cited European models. (Reproduced with permission of Thelma Blumberg, photographer. Print courtesy of the Western Historical Manuscript Collection, University of Missouri, St. Louis.)

spent part of his early years in Switzerland, where his father was born, and one of his brothers ran a restaurant in Paris. The Old World "flavor" seemed to blend with St. Louis's own history and French heritage. Otherwise the district was unified primarily by the individualistic atmosphere of each establishment. The design element lending coherence to the Square was the early-

Figure 7.10 With residences converted ad hoc to restaurants and various historical designs applied to nondescript architecture, Gay Nineties was indeed a loose characterization of Gaslight's patchwork appeal. In 1963, for example, the Natchez Queen (*left*) sat next to O'Connell's Pub. That same year the area businesses found a powerful unifying theme and "historical" motif when they installed gaslights on the sidewalks. (Courtesy of the Western Historical Manuscript Collection, University of Missouri, St. Louis. Photograph by George McCue.)

twentieth-century gas lamps rescued from a utility company warehouse and installed in May 1963. These streetlights, together with the ones on business and residential properties, cast "a continuous soft glow of warmth and nostalgia," as admired by the newspapers (fig. 7.10).[61]

The first wave of Gaslight Square entrepreneurs and their observers knew that the creative mix fermenting at the antique crossroads of Olive and Boyle in 1959 was far more than a nostalgic entertainment formula. The imaginative recycling of discarded artifacts was, as Jimmy Massucci put it, "the way to rebuild St. Louis."[62] In Gaslight Square, beatnik culture and its rejection of sterile, homogeneous suburban life was harnessed as a force in urban commercial revitalization.[63] A *picker,* the term Massucci's friends used to describe him, was someone who would buy "things that people consider to be junk . . . and they laughingly put it in their truck and drive away because they know that they have found something that is incredibly valuable."[64] This was interesting, "artzie," clever, and profitable, but it was also dubbed "one-man urban renewal." For a preservationist audience in 1963, the arts editor of the St. Louis

Post-Dispatch, George McCue, described what was happening at Gaslight Square as "Private Renewal without Federal Aid."[65] Rehabilitation caught on in the surrounding neighborhood. The early investors took pride in the fact that suburbanites were not only abandoning their televisions and spending nights out in Gaslight, but they were renovating old houses and returning to live in the city. To encourage this influx and provide "the advantages of suburban life in the middle of the city," Dick Mutrux planned a bath and tennis club nearby. Massucci had anticipated in the late 1950s what no one could really believe — that buses would be dropping off conventioneers and tourists. From a scruffy intersection, Gaslight grew in a few years to become a major St. Louis attraction. In 1965, as the district showed obvious signs of faltering, the mayor explained what everyone already knew — that he depended upon Gaslight to draw business and conventions to the city.[66]

As new investors flocked to Gaslight during the early 1960s, ironically it became a cliché that "the creeping paralysis of commercialism" was a key contributor to the district's eventual decline.[67] The new entrepreneurs employed gimmicky historical themes but abandoned the beatnik, antique-district heritage and the recycling of urban artifacts. In the Roaring '20s club, there were nightly prohibition raids, complete with jail quarters for the rounded-up patrons. Landesman and Massucci moved on to other ventures in other places, and as real estate prices and rents skyrocketed, the antique businesses began to leave as well. The loose coherence that had enveloped the first Gay Nineties assemblages and the modern beatnik-jazz-folk scene began to fray. By 1965, go-go bars had set up shop. So-called teenyboppers and bikers clogged the streets but did not spend much money. The new proprietors failed to perpetuate the district's original creative spark, although for a few years the crowds continued to grow. At its peak more than thirty-five nightspots, ten restaurants, and other coffee bars, art galleries, and bookstores jammed into the two-block area. One club owner and artist — Jorge Martinez — recalled that on weekend nights thirty or forty thousand patrons took over Gaslight.[68]

But by 1965 it was becoming apparent that the unlikely mix of black and white, rich and poor, beat and establishment, tourist and resident had lost its stability. A murder shifted news coverage of the Square to dwell on crime, and suburbanites began to stay away. A scientist from Santa Monica touched off a storm when he made "A Plea for Gaslight Square" in a letter to the St. Louis *Post-Dispatch* that year. "This unique spot carved out from the slums is being reclaimed by them," he wrote in a heartfelt appeal. A jewelry store, according to its proprietor's handwritten sign in 1965, "closed due to business collapse in

Figure 7.11 By 1969 Gaslight Square had moved through the go-go bars and the teeny-bopper clientele, and the businesses were mostly abandoned. The truncated Musical Arts Building is at the left, and broken gaslights, installed only six years earlier, appear in the foreground. The developers of other nostalgic commercial revitalization projects in the 1960s and 1970s — Underground Atlanta, Larimer Square in Denver, Trolley Square in Salt Lake City, Ghirardelli Square in San Francisco, and Boston's Faneuil Hall— pondered the lessons of Gaslight and other failures. Commercializing nostalgia and history was not a guaranteed formula either for urban revitalization or for profit. (Courtesy of the Western Historical Manuscript Collection, University of Missouri, St. Louis. Photograph by George McCue.)

area." The district that only a few years earlier had been compared with New Orleans's French Quarter and New York City's Times Square rapidly lost businesses and customers, and in 1967 the gaslights were turned off. In these waning years, a new crop of downtown commercial developments with historical themes were now mentioned in the same sentence with Gaslight — Denver's Larimer Square, San Francisco's Ghirardelli Square and Cannery Row, and Underground Atlanta. But by then the results of the St. Louis Gaslight experiment were desperately discouraging (fig. 7.11).[69]

In 1960 investors and patrons salvaged discarded and devalued bits and pieces of the city of St. Louis and reassembled them to create a surprising new history, high real estate values, and a promising nostalgic formula for downtown redevelopment. Victoriana became a creative tool of urban renewal — a cast-off era given a new look in an edgy, racially mixed district also known for

prostitution, gay bars, and women antique dealers — in the hands of beatnik and nonconformist entrepreneurs rebelling against the monolithic homogeneity of both suburbia and slum clearance. Eventually, though, some of
the same forces that brought Gaslight Square into being also left it in sham-
bles. By 1968 the urban violence that had seized so many cities had a final,
chilling effect on Gaslight Square. Everyone reasoned that if the riots came to
St. Louis, they would occur in Gaslight — "Because what else could you burn
down in St. Louis to get any publicity," recalled Richard Mutrux. On different
evenings the rumors would circulate among proprietors that "they're going to
come tonight, and they're going to burn us out." The violence never came, but
these rumors seemed to end any hopes for the district's success. In the early
1970s the boarded-up storefronts, empty clubs, and broken gas lamps constituted what one reporter called "the world's most modern and up-to-date urban ruins." These crumbling ruins granted the area "instant antiquity" — but
not the kind any of its developers had sought.[70]

The investors and developers who pioneered historically themed commercial districts in the 1960s and 1970s kept a close eye on one another's fortunes and noted several other failures in this period (though none were as
dramatic and widely known as Gaslight's). After a promising start in 1973,
Kansas City's River Quay slid toward abandonment and decrepitude by 1977.
The original developer, bucking local skepticism, had begun to restore the
downtown commercial neighborhood with artists' studios, shops, and restaurants. A range of musical entertainment flourished, from jazz and rock and
roll to country and barbershop quartets. But patronage plummeted a few
years later under a second developer, when bombings, murders, robberies,
kidnapping, and arson ruined the cultivated entertainment ambience. The explanation seemed clear: the Italian underworld had moved in, bringing bars,
strip clubs, and porn shops. The ensuing turf battle destroyed the reviving district.[71] In the volatile equations that led to real estate investment, nostalgic formulas clearly provided no guarantees.

The most-cited success story of the 1960s was San Francisco's Ghirardelli
Square. Opened in 1964, twelve years before Faneuil Hall, Ghirardelli was a
festival marketplace triumph more than a decade before the phrase was coined
and popularized by James Rouse's company (see fig. 7.12). The conversion of
former factory buildings (used variously to produce woolens, boxes, and later,
syrups, liquors, coffee, and chocolate) received a merit award from the American Institute of Architects.[72] Framed in the shells of old buildings, the expensive specialty shops, restaurants, and offices rang up high sales figures; one

Figure 7.12 Until the reconstruction of Faneuil Hall, San Francisco's Ghirardelli Square, which opened in 1964, was the most widely cited success story in downtown commercial revitalization utilizing old buildings. But even those responsible for Ghirardelli's transformation into a modern urban entertainment complex had difficulty appreciating its historical appeal and the jumbled old red brick buildings. This project's origins, in contrast with that of Gaslight Square in St. Louis, mark the emerging influence of professional preservationists and larger-scale investors. When high-rise development threatened the Ghirardelli chocolate factory block in 1962, a preservationist interested a prominent San Francisco family in purchasing this nearly-three-acre waterfront property. Here Ghirardelli Square is seen from the bay, with high-rises in the background, in a photograph from about 1970. (Courtesy of the Bancroft Library, University of California, Berkeley; Scenes at Ghirardelli Square, San Francisco, ca. 1960–ca. 1979, Banc Pic 1982.105-PIC.)

brochure claimed that 1967 sales reached $132 per square foot, nearly double the $70 averaged by area shopping malls. The unique stores, waterfront-oriented public square, and "carnival-like lights" set the kind of mood Rouse festival markets would later emulate. Ghirardelli was located on a nearly three-acre site with a spectacular view of the bay, under one ownership. The project originated in 1962, when a preservationist interested members of a prominent

San Francisco family — William Matson Roth and his mother, Lurline P. Roth — in purchasing the property. The Ghirardelli chocolate company had announced plans to relocate its factory operations, and the immediate neighborhood was under the pressures of high-rise development. Roth formed an advisory board and began to solicit ideas and proposals from dozens of architects, designers, and experts in leasing and commercial property management.[73]

As Roth and his consultants hammered out a preservation-development plan for the Ghirardelli complex, they eschewed nostalgic approaches and ultimately agreed upon what one consultant called "a happy combination of old and the better modern."[74] In early 1963, when the development concepts were still up in the air, Roth insisted in a memo to the advisory board that the site's old structures "will be used as *buildings*— not as nostalgic reminders of the past. (No tie-in, for instance, with the gaslights of the Victorian Park)." Once it was settled that most of the buildings would be saved, the question of how a modern retail-entertainment center should incorporate historical elements was negotiated in the details of lighting, signs, benches, paving, and railings. Here, even the board's staunchest preservation advocate — Karl Kortum, director of the nearby Maritime Museum and likely the person who drew Roth to the buildings in the first place — agreed that they should not slavishly recreate an old-time atmosphere with gaslights. In April 1963, Kortum instructed Roth's Ghirardelli coordinator, Warren Lemmon, "There is an overtone of modernity that you will want to bring to the premises, of course, because you are marketing neither an old chocolate factory, per se, or a Disneyland street-of-yesterday."[75]

As it turned out, as the Ghirardelli concept evolved during 1962 and 1963, the development team seemed strangely unaware of the complex's unique historical assets. The fact that modernist architects and landscape designers were hired to carry out a preservation-oriented development agenda partly explains why the disagreements over Ghirardelli's design, management, and merchandising focused on whether the plans *concealed* the site's historical features. In 1963, upon viewing a preliminary set of landscape architect Lawrence Halprin's drawings, Karl Kortum fired off an alarmed letter to Roth about Halprin's insensitivity: "With determination, almost brutality, he has used the style of architecture which I call 'world's-fair-hasty' throughout. He has *forced* the site to accept it." Kortum denounced the plan's "rigid grid of squares and rectangles," the "thick, gauche, expensive and dangerous" hand railings that looked like "warmed-over Brasilia," and the ordinary paving. "Why should your rich, thematic, status-laden property be tricked out to look like every international airport on earth?" he asked. In contrast, Kortum had scoured San Francisco and recommended two indigenous types of paving that he believed conveyed warmth and human scale and had "a local historical quality." Kortum was certain Halprin would reject them on that basis, as he had rejected a "simple, slender" balustrade that Kortum found in a book titled *Colonial Ironwork in Old Philadelphia* (see fig. 7.13).[76]

Kortum's review of the first brochure draft (written by an advisory board member) led him to urgently lecture the board and Roth about both the marketability of history and the precise historical qualities of the factory block. The brochure, he believed, was "timid" and "bland," reflecting a "lack of faith in what you have." There was "little rejoicing," he observed, in the clock tower (patterned after Chateau Blois in France) or the quoined and crenellated buildings. Instead of admiration for "the thickset, evolutionary, Florentine jumble of your buildings" that gave the block its "charm," Kortum identified "an overtone of haste to clean up and systematize the landscape." The brochure ignored historical events relevant to Ghirardelli — San Francisco's first factory, the production of uniforms for Union troops in the Civil War, and links to the Gold Rush and famous San Franciscans. "History is marketable," he interjected, as was "distinctive architecture in a period of increasing blandness." The developers had not grasped these valuable historical assets and instead conveyed "a feeling of concealment — . . . an ambivalence in the background somewhere."[77] In the absence of a clearly developed preservation concept, Kortum had identified a troubling theme in the deliberations and designs thus far — an ambivalence toward, and even an obscuring of, how historical details made the site attractive and valuable.

Most participants in Ghirardelli's development process — Roth, the advisory board, and the consultants — had difficulty tackling the "jumble" of red brick buildings. They were more taken with the potential of the open spaces and the events that could occur there. In their deliberations, the developers tended to lump the brick buildings together as a problem whose treatment would fall into place later. Halprin observed in his first sketches, "It's quite clear that much of the old brick stuff should stay. But some should come out!!!!" After advisory board member Proctor Mellquist devoted pages to fleshing out a carnival theme and detailed possibilities for food stores and restaurants, he noted, "This leaves the big old red buildings in need of some compatible use, at least the upper floors of these buildings." Perhaps they would be suitable for "warehouse-style retailing," he speculated vaguely. Advice so-

Figure 7.13 Ghirardelli Square's developers explicitly eschewed nostalgic appeals (like gaslights) and settled on a blend of historic and contemporary, or as they described it, "old San Francisco" and "European." It was the public plaza and the open spaces that most held their attention, and the owner turned to prominent modernist architects and landscape architects to draft the designs. Envisioned as a commercial destination for men as well as women, Ghirardelli (like Gaslight) achieved this expanded audience by providing upscale food and drink, art, entertainment, and a unique environment. This photo of the plaza is circa 1970. (Courtesy of the Bancroft Library, University of California, Berkeley; Scenes at Ghirardelli Square, San Francisco, ca. 1960–ca. 1979, Banc Pic 1982.105-PIC.)

licited from other designers and investors reflected the same lack of interest in the "old brick stuff," with at least two experts proposing that the exteriors of the "basically unattractive" factory buildings be painted, perhaps yellow with white trim. Even though the development team quickly agreed that most of the factory buildings should be saved, that decision did not grow out of an appreciation for the old brick factory landscape.[78]

Figure 7.14 Many tourists today are surprised to learn that the enormous sign calling attention to Ghirardelli Square is original to the factory building, as shown in this circa 1920 photograph of the factory block. People often assume that the sign was a brilliant marketing ploy, added by the developers in the 1960s to generate excitement about the Square. In fact, Ghirardelli Square's attention to self-promotion, attractive plazas, and landscaping was inspired by the factory's own emphasis on these very issues throughout its early history. This focus did not arise out of the need to sanitize a messy manufacturing site or compete with the pleasing design elements of shopping malls in order to create what critics might call an artificial, commercialized historical theme park. When the factory was originally built, much effort went into making it attractive and clean-lined and promoting it to the general public. (Courtesy of the Bancroft Library, University of California, Berkeley; "D. Ghirardelli Co. Photograph Album of Chocolate Manufacturing Process," no. 51, Banc Pic 1992.036-ALB.)

Those with modernist sensibilities may have had difficulty accepting and working with the irregularities of old buildings, but the Ghirardelli complex was neat, ordered, and clean-lined — typical of the better early-twentieth-century factories (fig. 7.14). In many ways the factory buildings were much closer to modern retailing standards than one might first imagine. By the 1910s and 1920s many factories were designed and maintained with tourists and advertising potential in mind as well as manufacturing requirements. They contained observation platforms and walkways, as well as stained glass

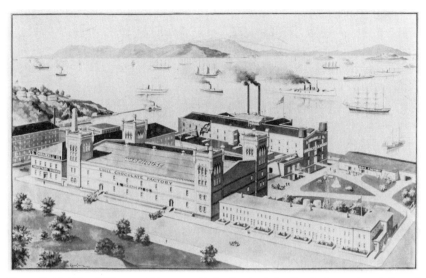

Figure 7.15 Ghirardelli's own history provided a firm basis for the design and marketing of key elements in Ghirardelli Square. This 1903 painting shows the factory's early commitment to landscaping. While some of the plantings were undoubtedly postcard-style embellishments, photographs confirm the presence of greenery, and even the embellishments speak to the decorative aspirations expressed for early-twentieth-century factories. The fountain in the 1960s plaza (fig. 7.13) stands at the approximate site of the fountain in this 1903 rendering, in the center of the triangular garden. (Courtesy of the Bancroft Library, University of California, Berkeley; 1857–1962 Ghirardelli Block Scrapbook, 4, MGS, Banc Mss 82/84c.)

and other architectural flourishes, and their external appearance was often a matter of civic pride (as in the case of the Ghirardelli clock tower).[79] The company's enormous sign was as well suited to promoting the redeveloped Ghirardelli Square in the 1960s as it was to broadcasting the chocolate company's name when it was placed atop the factory in the 1920s. Bill Roth specifically modeled Ghirardelli Square's landscaping on the factory's own historical traditions. Critiquing the excessive paving in Halprin's early plans, Roth directed: "In order to keep the old Ghirardelli feeling we want as much greenery, including trees, lawn, shrubs and espalier areas as possible."[80] A 1903 portrait of the complex reveals extensive landscaping and a fountain (in about the same location as at Ghirardelli Square) (fig. 7.15), and photographs confirm that this was not a fictitious representation. It might otherwise be tempting to assume that Ghirardelli Square's emphasis on landscaping and fountains was inspired by competition with the envied greenery of suburban shopping malls. In later festival marketplace complexes, such as South Street Seaport, critics might legitimately accuse developers of sanitizing historical sites into artificial stage sets, but in Ghirardelli Square, beautification gained inspiration from the site's own industrial past.

Roth and the advisory board paid far more attention to property management issues and concocting a successful tenant mix than to which of the site's historical features might draw crowds. The board seriously considered how a wax works with a historical theme and a museum of historic San Francisco would fit on the site. But the list of experts and sites Warren Lemmon actually visited, and the other models cited as examples for discussion, showed that the primary concerns lay in understanding shopping center management. Lemmon consulted with Al Waller, manager of Town and Country Shopping Centers at Palo Alto and San Jose, and in Scottsdale, Arizona, he toured the Fifth Avenue Shopping Center, as well as the American Heritage Wax Museum. He visited the Nut Tree in Vacaville, California (where he was advised by the owner that "the business promoter who in due course learns how to commercialize on the historical background of California and the West should have a successful venture and suggested that the Ghirardelli property might be given a unique appeal along these lines"). Stuart and Caree Rose, ultimately selected to develop Ghirardelli's commercial concept and management, had made their reputation by converting a 1924 Sausalito, California, parking garage into a shopping complex called Village Fair in 1956.[81] Proctor Mellquist and others also referred Lemmon to the Los Angeles Farmer's Market; Simpson's Garden Town (Pasadena); Disneyland; Knott's Berry Farm; Lloyd's Center (a Portland, Oregon, shopping mall); Tivoli; and the Food Circus at the Seattle World's Fair.[82]

Roth and his advisory board ultimately agreed upon the development theme that Stuart Rose and Karl Kortum had pushed them to pursue: "European is a great word for you," Kortum explained. "It is a new-old word. It can be given a very chic marketing. Now let's put the two halves together. Old San Francisco and the European tradition. You couldn't ask for more. Not if you laboriously (and expensively) hired copywriters, packaging specialists, designers, decorators and architects to create a theme for you." Roth and his team frequently cited the innovations of European department stores, but Kortum also kept the board apprised of the fact that local, nonretail examples were stirring up enthusiasm for reusing old buildings. He described the trend in the Ghirardelli neighborhood toward remodeling old warehouses and industrial space into offices. (Halprin himself had moved his practice into the Davis Hardwood Company planing mill; the Johnson & Joseph ship chandlery and the Haslett Warehouse were two other noteworthy conversions.) One investor learned the hard way that it was more profitable to enhance "the native qualities of the fine old building" than to create conventional office space by covering brick walls and squaring arched windows. These preservation ideas had spread from nearby Jackson Square, where, according to Kortum, investors had recognized the "commercial value in a stylish old building."[83]

Despite their preoccupation with shopping mall models, Ghirardelli Square's investors slowly settled upon a different concept — a specifically urban entertainment district not based entirely on shopping and female consumers; instead, they designed a place that they, as mostly male, city-oriented professionals, would frequent. Even in his first sketches, Larry Halprin felt the magnetism of the destination he helped create: "I think a *motel*—very good one would be marvellous here. urban. urbane. lots of things to do. shopping, restaurants, an off-beat theatre. avant garde painting & sculpture on the plaza. rotating exhibits — I'd come & stay for a weekend myself!" The developers still worried, as Roth did, about accommodating "the weary housewife who has done her morning shopping." Yet this offbeat and artistic destination would appeal to men, too; the plans were reminiscent of how the Gaslight Square proprietors had created saloons for their own enjoyment and that of their friends. Roth wanted the "Square to be a stage where things *happen:* outdoor music and plays; kite contests; art shows; political meetings (?); etc." He and others described night lighting, enticing smells, gourmet food, and "urban variety." Halprin imagined a "BEEHIVE OF EXCITEMENT."[84]

For those who reveled in the distinctiveness of Ghirardelli Square's unique historical context, such plans were "nervous, tricky, and had nothing to do with Ghirardelli," as Karl Kortum said of Halprin's sketches. The Tivoli "carnival" atmosphere, more than a decade later modified to Rouse's softer "festival" concept, was a universal plan that could (like international airport architecture) be imposed anywhere. The plans and the discussions behind them worked too hard at being exciting and offbeat, without revealing originality worthy of, or indigenous to, the site. Kortum believed that the plans missed the point: "I'll be damned if I can see any reason to pursue the insipid, trees-planted-in-big-tubs, let-us-work-at-being-gay theme," given the "dazzling" possibilities of this historic site. Excitement, consultant David Pesonen pointed out to Warren Lemmon, was historically specific and site specific — not the universal experience implied by Halprin's beehive idea.[85]

The proponents of a more historically rooted development theme for Ghirardelli, then, resisted the imposition of world's fair flags, carnival excitement, and international "hasty" architecture, as much as they rejected historical recreations or fantasies like Williamsburg and Disneyland. They believed the factory block had unique potential to blend the historical and the modern in a profit engine that could stem the destructive tide of bland high rises in San Francisco. The preservationist participants in this blending process (especially Kortum and Pesonen) had to continually keep before the developers' eyes the value of history and old buildings, and out of the frank conflicts and discussions emerged creative compromises and new visions of urban commerce. The square would not stand in direct competition with other retail entertainment; according to Pesonen, the people drawn to "the historical magnets which will shortly surround the Ghirardelli property" will be a different crowd. With the right approach, "if the Ghirardelli property is treated with this kind of love it can embrace a great, shy, rock-solid foundation of the Bay Area's population that no architectural phoenix rising in isolation would even comprehend." "Development of the Ghirardelli property is not simply a problem of architecture," Pesonen explained to Lemmon, "it is a problem in city planning." Working with an old building, particularly a landmark structure, was different from working with other shopping centers, in that "the roots of the Ghirardelli buildings go out in both time and space." For Pesonen, the distinctive fifteen-foot-high letters of the illuminated Ghirardelli sign, erected in the early twentieth century, exemplified this beaconlike reach and historical magnetism. The fact that the advisory board divided a few months later over whether to even retain the Ghirardelli sign confirms Pesonen and Kortum's suspicions that the developers, though creative in experimenting with new urban entertainment forms, still did not fully appreciate the distinctiveness of their historical site.[86]

The long gap between the opening of San Francisco's Ghirardelli Square in 1964 and Faneuil Hall's opening in 1976 was filled with a smattering of comparable experiments.[87] In 1965 private investors launched Larimer Square in Denver, a one-block area of upscale shops and galleries occupying cleaned-up buildings dating to the 1860s and 1870s. Eight Salt Lake City investors converted a large trolley barn to house movie theaters, shops, and restaurants, opening Trolley Square for business in 1972. After a group of cautious Atlanta executives had proof that others profited from renovated nostalgic districts, they undertook the development of Underground Atlanta. A few businesses opened there by 1969, but it would be several years before the previously

sealed-off underground street was fully operational as an 1890s-themed destination. After some initial success, Underground Atlanta struggled through
most of the 1970s (as fearful whites avoided the downtown) and declared
bankruptcy in 1982. St. Louis tried again after Gaslight with Laclede's Land-
ing in the mid-1970s.[88] These were all private renewal projects, mostly controlled by a single developer organization but sometimes generated by or
supported by a critical mass of small-scale individual entrepreneurs.[89] Ghirardelli Square's success did not translate quickly into a significant trend. One
retail analyst made an impassioned plea in 1974 for recycling older downtown buildings into new retail development; unfortunately, he knew "of only
a few cases where existing buildings were incorporated or used in any way
when a shopping center was constructed." Ghirardelli Square was in fact his
model. His audience, he assumed, would be familiar with Ghirardelli's accomplishments: "What we need is more of this sort of thing." Yet investors
were resistant to this exhortation and did not recognize and validate the potential profit offered by nostalgia and historical atmosphere until after Faneuil
Hall's success.[90]

The American case for recycling old buildings in the 1960s and 1970s
was inconclusive enough that the architects and developers who pioneered
this kind of redevelopment usually cited European cities as their inspiration.
Benjamin Thompson, architect for Faneuil Hall and South Street Seaport,
claimed to be creatively sparked by the street markets, gardens, and river
walks of Lausanne, Copenhagen, Paris, and Venice. The Manchurian-born
developer of Cannery Row, who bought his factory a year before Ghirardelli
Square opened, said his idea came to him from farmers' markets, Bruges, and
the laws of Italian towns that required renovation, not demolition. The short-
comings of the American precedent were also evident in unheralded renovations like the Old Market section of downtown Omaha, Nebraska. Originally
a warehouse district that outfitted westward-bound wagon trains, the Market
was developed in the early 1970s as an upscale commercial center with stores,
restaurants, and clubs. One family — the Mercers — had owned most of the
Market since its original warehouse days. At a time when bulldozers were still
the popular solution to vacancy and disuse, family members claimed that the
direct French example emboldened them to rehabilitate the district. According to one Mercer, "We thought the buildings were of architectural interest,
and because my father lived in Paris, we thought there was no reason 100-
year-old buildings couldn't make an attractive area."[91] As in the examples of
Gaslight and Ghirardelli Squares, direct European experiences provided the

Figure 7.16 The surprise popularity and financial success of Boston's Faneuil Hall Market-place finally validated the concept of historically evocative commercial redevelopment, but the road leading to the August 1976 opening day was a tortuous one. James Rouse labeled this photograph for his personal files: *"Signing the lease:* A beginning for Faneuil Hall after 2 year negotiation with City of Boston." The path was marked by the skepticism of bankers and the public, and sometimes by the doubts of Rouse himself. The public-private nature of festival marketplaces as downtown commercial ventures distinguished them from precursors like Ghirardelli Square. Here Rouse stands between Robert Kenney, head of Boston's Redevelopment Authority, and Mayor Kevin White, in front of an "open for business" sign. (Courtesy of Columbia Association Archives; FHM January 1975–June 1976 [1 of 2], box 422, James W. Rouse Papers.)

rationale for reusing old buildings, even when local creativity and experimentation clearly played a role.

Thus, by the time Faneuil Hall opened, there were many reasons to wonder whether the revitalized historic market would succeed. Besides debacles like those in St. Louis and Kansas City and the unimpressive records of Underground Atlanta and Chicago's Old Town, the American prototypes were few and far between. As the developer of Larimer Square, Mrs. Dana Crawford, found, lending institutions responded negatively to proposals for preservation-based redevelopment.[92] In Boston, the events leading to the revitalization of Quincy Market were frustrating and convoluted — including the decade of local skepticism, complicated negotiations with the city over

Figure 7.17 In the months after Faneuil Hall Marketplace opened, James Rouse and his colleagues relished their success but also scrambled to understand the site's unexpected magnetism. A largely abandoned set of very old market buildings had been converted into a modern marketplace that appeared to work for tourists, Bostonians, and suburbanites alike. Rouse shared others' excitement that Faneuil Hall was the most promising downtown retailing experiment in the nation, but he knew that its implications for the future of urban commerce were unclear. (Courtesy of The Rouse Company.)

the project's every dimension, and the fact that investment capital eventually came from New York because Boston financiers were too reluctant. Ada Louise Huxtable said of the Faneuil Hall development process: "It was agony all the way."[93] A few months before opening day, Rouse wrote to Mayor Kevin H. White, "The Markets are beginning to overcome doubt that has beset them" (see figs. 7.16, 7.17).[94]

Both the planning stages for Faneuil Hall and the surprise success of the complex induced James Rouse and his development staff to rethink key ingredients of downtown magnetism like tourist appeal, accessibility, and the contributions of old buildings. As Rouse educated himself for Faneuil Hall's conversion by visiting Ghirardelli Square, Larimer Square, and Pioneer Square, he was continually "amazed at how many of these shops exist and apparently survive in these places — many in basements, reached only through arcades and downstairs or at upper levels with similar access." Even more revealing was the extent to which the Rouse Company underestimated the crowds that would engulf Faneuil Hall upon its opening and the scrambling the company did to understand and somehow get ahead of this success. In a September 1976 memo to his employees, Rouse explained that the food and dining market potential had proved to be two or three times greater than their predictions and that they had been "so determined not to build 'a tourist trap'" that the company had failed to see the "huge potential" of tourism. Rouse asked his staff to ensure that the distinctive marketplace did not "slip into being a shopping center." As for the entertainment, "We don't know much about this yet, but it is certainly clear that the early crowds have been delighted with the opportunity to be entertained." He speculated about the positive urban image of cities that Faneuil Hall seemed to project. Although that "good city" drew "richness . . . from the heritage of the old buildings" and the intimacy of market exchange, Rouse also acknowledged the contributions of the site's flowers, trees, benches, and open spaces.[95]

Though unsure of what exactly they had helped build, Rouse and other participants saw its promise for the American downtown. Amid recent efforts at urban revitalization, Rouse wrote a few weeks after the market opened, "notably and critically lacking has been any significant new life in retailing. . . . In Faneuil Hall Marketplace we have raised the window on a bright new possibility for the city. . . . It may bring more life, vitality, personality, beauty and sense of community to Boston than anything that has happened in our times." Leo Molinaro pointed out the need to distill the spirit of Faneuil Hall for other cities without "packaging" or "peddling" it. "It's not just the national publicity that is getting to people but the very idea of Faneuil Hall seems to spread a glow over people interested in downtown that I haven't seen before." He did not believe that the spirit or success was "dependent on old buildings or on Boston's unique make up and location." Rouse asked for a shopper survey with questions "that evoke the deep reactions to help us know what are the cords [sic] that are being touched by Quincy Market to cause such enthusiastic reactions and large crowds." The marketplace's director, Roy Williams, placed a hold on new merchandising directions in October 1976, explaining, "There is much still unknown about what we have created at Quincy Market and what is going on there."[96] Although Faneuil Hall Marketplace's success could not have been predicted, once it had become a reality, the Rouse Company worked energetically to understand the magnetic and inspirational character of this relatively small preservation-development project and its relevance to other cities.

"People's Eyes Glazed Over":
Main Street Preservation in the 1960s and 1970s

In addition to sharing many of the difficulties faced by festival market-places and their precursors, the Main Street historic preservation movement did not have a flashy, inspirational example like Faneuil Hall. In fact, the three pilot cities in the National Trust for Historic Preservation's Main Street program struggled with various disappointments in the late 1970s and early 1980s. On the merits of their own accomplishments, Galesburg, Illinois; Hot Springs, South Dakota; and Madison, Indiana, did not stir up a national following. Yet in quiet, low-key ways, Main Street preservation would achieve a much broader reach than festival marketplaces. Preservation ultimately touched far more communities and continued to gain momentum into the early twenty-first century. The uneven results of the Main Street pilot program were part of a long-term experimentation process that built credibility slowly. During this rocky trial period, preservation efforts benefited from both the general boost festival marketplaces gave to downtown revitalization and the specific boost they gave to nostalgia.[97]

Whereas historically themed markets relied upon private developers or public agencies to assemble properties, in Main Street preservation each individual owner had to be convinced of the economic value of history. Accordingly, Main Street preservation encountered more grassroots resistance from local businesspeople than did festival marketplaces or their precursors. Engaging in preservation meant that merchants and property owners had to reverse their decades-long commitment to modernization. The reorientation from forward- to backward-looking improvement strategies did not occur easily or quickly during the proving years of the 1960s and 1970s. The chain organizations, less sensitive to local or grassroots initiatives, proved to be particular laggards in recognizing the potential of preservation, just as the Woolworth reports suggest.

For many Main Street proprietors and investors, it was often the cooperative ventures of the 1960s and 1970s — pedestrian malls, urban renewal, art commissions, bicentennial programs, and campaigns to preserve historic districts — that brought the historic values of commercial buildings to their attention. But even when introduced to the appeal of historic features, most merchants resisted preservation. To begin with, in the 1970s historic preservation was still trying to shed "any lingering image of socialites and antiquarians trying to put musty buildings into moth balls." The mothball analogy underscores the prevailing belief that preservationists actually removed historic structures from the real estate market, as they dove in to rescue buildings from redevelopment threats. In contrast, 1970s Main Street preservationists hoped to enhance these buildings' market value.[98]

As it was reconceptualized for use in late-twentieth-century economic development, preservation also had to overcome its associations with feminine emotions and socialites' causes in order to be taken seriously by downtown executives. Ada Louise Huxtable pointed out that the best preservation was "not the work of little old ladies playing house, but of unsentimental business interests." A reporter admired Ghirardelli Square soon after its opening as "a shining example of preservation without sentimentality." Historic preservation still had to break out of the mostly feminized domain of historic house museums and define a nostalgic sense appropriate to self-styled, hardheaded, mostly male investors.[99]

The resistance of small-scale investors to Main Street historic preservation during these years is well illustrated in the refusal of merchants on Pittsburgh's South Side to participate in a late-1960s campaign to restore nineteenth-century storefronts. Despite endorsement by the local Chamber of Commerce, the Community Council, the mayor, and the press; outreach in lectures and pamphlets; and free design assistance from local architects, the retailers turned their backs on the preservation proposal. The executive director of Pittsburgh's History and Landmarks Foundation, which had initiated the campaign, concluded that "the concept that a restored Victorian shopping district will be good for business remains too unusual, almost too simple, to be convincing to South side merchants. It baffles their notion of progress which to them has always meant discarding the past and modernizing." In breaking sharply with the modernization mantra of the last forty years, preservation too bluntly contradicted what merchants had worked so hard to obtain since the 1930s, from storefront upgrades to urban renewal. It became clear by the early 1970s that preservationists had built more effective bridges to government agencies than to the business community.[100]

At the time of the 1970s Woolworth closings, then, because of this divide between preservationists and retailers, a store's unrenovated condition was a terrible problem, not a profitable opportunity for restoration. *Forbes* estimated that half of the Woolworths in 1978 had "outdated facades and cluttered counters," making them "unattractive to modern shoppers."[101] Chain store headquarters only infrequently satisfied the renovation needs of their units, especially during times of financial or management turmoil — as in Kress's case in the 1960s and 1970s. Correspondence between Kress's real estate office and the branch stores is filled with unmet demands for new fixtures and store improvements. An especially pitiful letter arrived at the New York office in 1970 from a store manager in Valdosta, Georgia: "Our store mannequins are in bad shape. Most have broken fingers or arms and are chiped [sic] or broken in some fashion. Please help me. It is hard to display apperal [sic] with out mannequins and it looks bad to use broken mannequins."[102]

Communication about stores' physical conditions was often mangled in the gap between company headquarters and the far-flung branches. The manager of the Webb City, Missouri, Kress gave a rousingly optimistic evaluation of his store in 1966. But an outside inspection in 1968 found that the "store is in terrible physical condition." The inspector wrote, "Don't believe this store has ever been renovated since it opened many years ago"—and it had been constructed in 1916. It is possible that the manager judged his store's old-fashioned appearance to be perfectly acceptable. It is also possible that he did not want to draw attention to the store, knowing it would be closed if found run-down.[103]

Main Street investors who proudly held on to old buildings were usually condemned as backward and were certainly not hailed as pioneers of new trends. The buildings themselves were still more likely to be classified "obsolete" for urban renewal purposes than "historic" for preservation. Stores still favored modernizing their facades, as the New Orleans Kress did in 1963 when it covered its five-story, 1913 terracotta front with interlocking porcelain enamel panels. In fact, in the 1970s new techniques for covering over older buildings, including metal screens and siding, gained in popularity. A fad for covering upper floors with mansard roofs was nostalgically inspired but nonetheless obscured historic buildings. Sneering at certain Main Street retailers in Memphis, a 1966 *Women's Wear Daily* article marveled that "some merchants sporting hundred-year-old stores seem convinced that age and value are identical." Everyone else knew that "those old, rickety buildings were bad for business."[104]

Yet chain stores and other merchants were beginning, inadvertently, to encounter circumstances where "old" was in fact becoming highly valued. In the mid-1970s several Kress managers were surprised to discover that, because of the elaborate architectural qualities of many Kress buildings, local planning committees admired the old stores. In Memphis, for example, "age" did prove to be valuable ten years after the sneering *WWD* article. A 1978 clipping from the *Commercial Appeal*, featuring a large photo of the store, proclaimed it a "landmark" on the new downtown mall. "If you're into architecture," the reporter noted approvingly, "the Kress building is easily the most intriguing downtown. Its facade is in intricate multicolored terra cotta, dating from 1927. And, unlike several of the older buildings, you can still browse around in the dime store on the ground floor." In passing this article to distant Kress executives, the Memphis store manager reported that his building was "included in a number of old landmarks that the re-building of downtown will be patterned after." Reluctant to credit the cooperative mall and growing interest in historic structures (rather than his own initiatives) for improving business, the manager admitted that the increase in tourists "helps some." [105] The Kress property thus gained unanticipated value from an unlikely source — without the awareness or even the support of the chain store. [106]

Even when a chain store manager understood that local sentiment toward the building had warmed up, national headquarters could be slow or simply unable to respond with the resources to enhance this kind of nostalgic magnetism. From Montgomery, Alabama, a Kress store manager (J. C. Spike), with the support of his district manager (C. L. Thomas), waged an urgent campaign to get the attention of the New York office. In the early 1970s an ambitious urban renewal plan had begun to transform downtown Montgomery. This included the preservation of selected local landmarks and the revitalization of the "old" waterfront commercial district. Turn-of-the-century streetcar service was restored, and there were new and completely renovated downtown department stores, a hotel, a commerce building, a bank, and a parking garage. The Kress building sat in the midst of all this change, the company sullenly arguing with the landlord over who should pay for adherence to the urban renewal project's "Property Rehabilitation Standards." Spike and Thomas sent local newspaper coverage to New York, circling each improvement and noting the date of completion and insisting that the Kress building needed a major renovation. Finally losing patience, Thomas demanded a response: "This is *not 'Pie in the sky'* for 21st Century! Much *is complete* and *most will be complete* by end of '71. Lets investigate seriously leases, etc. + whether *and* when *we* should renovate!! ADVISE." Thomas and Spike must have been disappointed with the flat response that came a few days later. Yes, the "comments and newspaper publicity" had been received, and New York was "aware" of Montgomery's downtown plans. New York did not plan to upgrade the Montgomery Kress "in the near future" but wished to be kept informed and would tentatively schedule a renovation the following year. [107]

For smaller downtowns in the 1970s, scattered interest in applying preservation to commercial development coalesced when the National Trust for Historic Preservation launched its Main Street Pilot Project in late 1975. The trust cited Corning, New York, as a model and also reported that a groundswell of inquiries had pushed its own experiment into operation. Kept on track by the trust's on-site project managers and informed by detailed consultant reports, local merchants in the pilot cities built on and enhanced their street's historical qualities as a shopping destination.[108] Learning from these experiments, the trust established the National Main Street Center in 1980 and went on to sponsor hundreds of small-town and big-city commercial preservation initiatives; it inspired state-run and private programs as well. The trust gave Main Street preservation a national lobbying voice, helping to swing more federal financial support behind preservation as an economic development tool and simultaneously increasing skepticism toward urban renewal. As one close study of Seattle's journey from renewal to preservation concluded, federal intervention (spurred by the trust's activities) legitimated preservation during years when business elites and city officials did not yet grasp its economic value.[109]

The struggling variety chains never benefited from the growing Main Street preservation movement, the festival marketplaces, and the revaluing of old commercial buildings, despite their exposure to these new trends. Chains like Woolworth, McCrory, and Kress seemed unable to purposefully cater to their customers' nostalgia — a failure that applied to both their handling of the historical aspects of their buildings and the merchandising and marketing of the interior retail experience. In the 1990s Woolworth cut back the department with the highest nostalgia value, closing many lunch counters or converting them to coffee bars. At those counters often sat the company's most diehard fans, and the lunch-counter meal was a signature chain store memory (even for the civil rights era).[110] Later owners of the dime store buildings in the 1980s and 1990s sometimes capitalized on the public's fond memories for Woolworth or Kress by incorporating the building's shell into their enterprises, but by then the stores themselves were gone.[111] If the variety stores intended to exploit the public's nostalgia for past commercial environments or harness the growing interest in historic preservation as an economic development tool, it did not show.

Rouse's Rise, Woolworth's Demise

As the variety chains rode out their last rocky decades at the end of the twentieth century, there was a grassroots outpouring of customer nostalgia despite the chains' inability to intentionally evoke that sentiment. The typical variety store customers — older and frugal, low-income, taking public transit or walking — participated in urban commercial life in ways that defied the pronouncements of market analysts. Though it is not quite a "non-market" perspective on the market, the variety store customers of the 1980s and 1990s offer an alternative story of consumers infusing their own brands of nostalgia into urban commerce. Their actions tended to subvert market trends toward fast-paced obsolescence in consumer goods and environments, as well as the popularity of expensive products and gourmet foods.[112]

In the 1990s retail market analysts declared unanimously that the dime store concept had no appeal in the world of modern consumption. When Woolworth closed its remaining American variety stores in 1997, Kurt Barnard of Barnard's Retail Marketing Report observed that the company had "died many years ago, but it just wasn't buried." One marketing professor asked, "What did they sell that you couldn't buy somewhere else?" Others insisted that the chains had no niche left and were indistinguishable from convenience stores. These analysts paid little attention to the variety stores' customers, who by definition were not the high-spending consumers retailers preferred. After all, those loyal variety store regulars had apparently failed to keep the stores open. "Who on the planet would want to go" to variety stores, asked one national consultant. He declared: "The variety store industry in the United States is a cadaver. It's history."[113]

But reporters and a sentimental public lingered sadly over the variety store funerals, understanding something that the analysts missed. The stores may have failed as competitive modern merchandisers, but they unquestionably had a unique appeal. As one reporter put it, "some shoppers are loyal to the point of fanaticism." "We say they bleed McCrory blood," a spokesman from that store revealed. Most analysts had difficulty grasping this fierce devotion. They dismissed the loyalty as irrelevant since it appeared to be a weak market force.[114]

What lay behind such customer loyalty? For one thing, memories that stretched back decades, since the variety stores served an older population. Older people had not necessarily been favored clientele in better times, but now downtown retailers were more dependent upon these customers. Of course customers of all ages patronized variety stores, but the devotion of older clients stood out. Reporters interviewed the elderly shoppers who stopped by several times a week and the lunch gangs who met daily. When the stores closed, employees worried about where their elderly customers would go for companionship and an affordable meal. Less sympathetically, an analyst observed that "every time there's an obituary in the newspaper, they lose a customer." The 1977 Woolworth report for St. Charles, Missouri, described how the aging entrepreneur population matched their older customers, who — getting to the heart of the matter — were "beyond prime consuming years." The merchants of Oneida, New York, would have to get by with "below-average consumer spending." Ironically, the less dynamic 1970s, 1980s, and 1990s Main Street shopper was sometimes the same 1950s shopper, now older and poorer.[115]

Chain store customers defied prevailing investor assumptions and preferences in other ways. They clung to the old-fashioned "pedestrianism" and public transit that had popularized downtown shopping districts in the first place. Everyone in the retail industry knew that "the developer's first law of shopper behavior says that the American shopper will not willingly walk more than 600 feet." Yet octogenarian Thelma Wills, with her elegant silver beehive, walked four miles round trip every day to her favorite variety store lunch counter in downtown Bremerton, Washington. Residents from a senior citizen center who strolled to their downtown Woolworth once a week had to find transportation out to a mall when the store closed. Many urban and lower-income customers walked or took the bus because they had no other options; others did so because of convenience or because they enjoyed the experience.[116]

Against the tide of indulgent consumption and planned obsolescence that (according to critics and boosters) characterized American consumerism, Woolworth customers were frugal, and even more distinctly, they expected to see the same goods year after year. The profit-leading chain for Woolworth Corporation was Foot Locker, which prospered from the rapid obsolescence of its merchandise — new sneaker models. But variety store shoppers habitually sought out familiar, often old-fashioned merchandise that they claimed they could not find elsewhere: "thingamajigs" such as thirty-nine-cent diamond engagement rings, pant-stretchers, caps, and "plain, serviceable stationery with faint blue lines on it."[117] And while market analysts claimed that they could not detect the variety chains' unique appeal, reporters repeatedly captured the admiration that customers expressed for the odd juxtaposition of ordinary and inexpensive objects found in these stores. This was "the sort of place where one could buy a pet turtle and a hair net and then enjoy a grilled cheese sandwich and some cole slaw at the lunch counter." Such remembrances commonly opened with a phrase such as: "Where else do you get . . . ?" In contrast with the promotion of gourmet food prevalent at festival marketplaces, the dime store lunch counters offered simple, old-fashioned, low-priced fare. Indeed, comfortable thriftiness was the way, one reporter noted, "that Americans shopped for generations." The frugal era symbolized by the five-and-dime had been abandoned as part of the "total revolution in the American way of living and buying."[118]

Just as the festival marketplaces and historic preservation gained momentum in the 1980s, energized by the appeal of historically evocative commercial environments, the chain variety stores were flagging and stumbling despite their own nostalgic aura. Woolworth-brand nostalgia was a deeply felt, broad-based, grassroots phenomenon, even if it did not translate into the kind of financial windfall demanded in the late twentieth century.[119] In the five-and-dimes, many saw "a door into the past" or "a window to a way of life that had disappeared." This particular type of entertainment value actively sought by five-and-dime customers was not unlike the appeal festival marketplaces hoped to have. William Kreujinski visited the Woolworth in downtown Buffalo, New York, several times a week "'just to pass the time. This place is kind of like a museum. I'm going to miss coming in,' he said."[120] The case of the five-and-dimes shows that this commercial institution gained its historical meaning from consumer and employee nostalgia for a thrifty, pedestrian world of old-fashioned, simple food and merchandise — not from the proclamations and decisions of retailers, investors, and market analysts.

The Tyranny of Downtown Memories

In the 1980s and 1990s, as historically themed retailing caught on downtown, developers and retailers were understandably interested in evoking only the most pleasantly stimulating historical topics. The public, however, was more likely to raise and debate controversial issues relevant to the downtown's history. Indicative of festival marketplace goals, a Rouse prospectus for Albuquerque proposed creating a destination that would prompt "nostalgic recall of 'fond' memories of the old downtown." Nationally, investors hoped that almost everybody could find a "fond" memory to draw them downtown — in many cities the "great" era of maritime commerce was a popular theme. Many Americans agreed that stepping into a historically evocative retail environment — whether the scripted festival marketplaces or an old-fashioned Woolworth — was "like passing through a time tunnel and entering a cozy and dependable world."[121]

Yet opening a window onto the past, even a contrived one, implicitly raised the question of how contemporary urban commercial experiences compared with those of the past. Needless to say, retailers could not control people's memories or limit their interest to warm rather than hot topics—a lesson learned many times during the racial protests of the 1960s. In the late twentieth century, as history increasingly shaped investment strategies, consumers did not share a generic sense of nostalgia—and they tended to disagree over the characteristics of the past and future trajectories of urban commercial life.

In 1997–98 a museum exhibit celebrating dime store architecture stimulated conflict among visitors over the meaning of Main Street nostalgia. The National Building Museum in Washington, D.C., staged "Main Street Five-and-Dimes: The Architectural Heritage of S. H. Kress & Co." The show's visitor comment books overflowed with many of the familiar, innocuous personal stories that reporters had gathered when the variety stores closed: remembrances of childhood outings with a grandparent, the independence of a trip downtown, or a first job. A visitor noted concisely, "One word: nostalgia." "It was a rare nostalgic treat," wrote another. The visitors used an exhibit of commercial architecture to reflect upon their own lives and their personal experiences of urban commerce. There were many others who lamented the decline of architectural and business values—not a surprising reaction, given the show's focus on design, artifacts, and a specific company. These visitors characterized commercial design of the early twentieth century as representing pride, integrity, class, elegance, and artistic quality, while approving of Kress's apparent sense of corporate responsibility. Wal-Mart was usually cited to demonstrate how far American commerce had fallen in these respects.[122]

But it was integration—a topic not even raised in the exhibition's interpretive panels, only evident in the photographs—that prompted the most heated debate and quickly revealed nostalgia to be anything but a generic concept. One visitor wrote, "Memories of a happier, kinder world—a world that was safe." This was just the kind of fond sentiment the festival marketplace investors would have appreciated. In this case, someone responded in the margin: "Yes—before all the dangerous negroes ruined everything." On September 8, 1997, a person enthusiastically noted, "Reminded me of my childhood, when you could go into a 5 + 10 with 10¢, buy something, and come out with some change, too!" But the next writer savored something else: "I enjoyed the shots of 'whites only' drinking fountains—the way it should be." Others later added "Nazi pig" and "republican," with arrows pointing to the prosegregation remark. In yet another instance, a museum visitor volunteered that "segregation was good for the country. We should bring it back."[123] Both those warmly remembering innocent childhood experiences *and* those warmly remembering a segregated past evoked the theme of decline in urban commercial life.

Other visitors questioned outright whether America's past commercial life had in fact been better, based on their observation that the experiences of African American consumers (and most patrons) had only improved. Today's Wal-Mart might not be as "beautiful" as Kress, read one entry, "but at least they let everyone drink from the same water fountains and use the same restrooms." "The Birmingham store w/o blacks in it made me remember the unfair dual society I put up with in North Carolina," recalled a visitor. While some reminisced about a cherry Coke with grandmother, others also brought up sit-ins and segregated lunch counters — "A reminder of a not so honorable past." Another pointed out, probably to those overwhelmed by "warm fuzzy feeling," that "some change is good," especially the elimination of colored water fountains. The architectural beauty of the Kress stores featured in the exhibit held little positive value to these visitors if it symbolized a segregated, unfair society.[124]

One exchange in particular captured the debates occurring in the exhibition hall and the comment books and some of the dynamics that prompted guests to challenge oversimplified nostalgic narratives of decline. A visitor wrote: "I enjoyed looking back in time — interesting coincidence shed a bit of depth on it — another visitor commented that it took you back to a simpler time & as I began to agree in my head, I saw the photos of the shiny water fountains marked 'White' and 'Colored.' Simpler perhaps but was it better?" In this interaction one sees how easy it was to slip into vague reverie about the urban past but also how quickly a specific personal experience could induce one to challenge the certainty of decline. The fact that this individual's reassessment was triggered by encountering a historical photograph of what other people remembered from their own lives — segregated water fountains — is suggestive. Adding further "depth" in the margins, someone answered the writer's question: "Yes, it was better then before the Negroes messed everything up." Here again was racist nostalgia agreeing for hateful reasons with unfocused fondness for the past. Responding to a museum exhibit, itself resonant with the museum-like qualities of the dime stores and historically themed marketplaces, visitors welcomed the opportunity to engage with each other over the meaning of urban commerce. Another entry read, "I agree, however, with the person who wrote earlier that some comment or discussion of the very prominently featured segregated water fountains, counters, etc. should accompany those photos." And the issues raised could be debated even without the exhibition, as recognized by the guest who "skipped the exhibit, loved the comment book." [125]

Two visitors wrote still another declension narrative of twentieth-century urban commercial life — drawing undoubtedly unanticipated conclusions from the exhibit. One insisted, "Segregation killed these stores. People moved away to the suburbs. Caldor & K-Mart followed them. If there were black faces in the 1930's photo's, maybe Main St. USA could have been saved . . . The fault lies not in the stores. . . ." Another man claimed that God would not have allowed the Kress chain to survive because of its racist history. [126] According to this interpretation, entirely free of nostalgia, segregation had "killed" Main Street. From this perspective, the 1960s Civil Rights movement indeed remade Main Street too late to save it.

The disagreements over integration provoked by the 1997–98 Kress exhibit in fact confirm that the critical impact of 1960s upheavals on downtown commerce was still unfolding and being negotiated thirty years later. In the 1990s, black consumers weighed the belief that Woolworth supported urban retailing against news reports that blacks faced discrimination by store clerks who scrutinized their credit cards or wrote codes on their checks. Eddye Bexley, an African American, disclosed in 1997 that she had avoided Woolworth for thirty-seven years after participation in a 1960 Tampa protest poisoned her associations with the place. On the ground in a festival marketplace, one might be forgiven for not realizing that a core inspiration for Rouse was the 1960s riots and his belief that a new type of urban commerce could heal the nation's racial rifts. Yet his companies experimented with different ways to foster black entrepreneurship, management opportunities, and patronage. Rouse's Gallery at Market East offered one example of how a revitalized downtown retail economy could build successfully upon an integrated clientele. Rouse's optimistic and idealistic rhetoric was partly what earned his company's projects so much favorable attention. [127]

At the close of the twentieth century, Americans could draw upon and create multiple decline and improvement narratives to understand what was happening on Main Street. Amid the various memories sparked by names like F. W. Woolworth and S. H. Kress, the "warmest remembrances" of Main Street included not only first dates or childhood outings with grandparents but also fond longings for segregation. These alternative nostalgic versions, which challenged the simplistic view that urban commerce was somehow better in the past, suggest how the interested public could engage critically with the historical themes employed in late-twentieth-century downtown development. Like the thrifty chain store consumers dismissed by market analysts, these 1990s debates over history demonstrate how people turned nostalgia to their own purposes and invested urban commerce with their own meanings. Historic Main Streets and festival marketplaces (no matter how vague, contrived, or inaccurate) have helped keep alive visions of populated and democratic urban commercial life amid extensive abandonment and proclamations of decline.[128] Even that 1990s symbol of Main Street decay — the increasingly empty and irrelevant variety store — though unable to financially exploit the nostalgia trends, nonetheless stimulated public interest in how downtowns might be reinvented and what values should be central to a newly imagined urban commercial life. In the early twenty-first century, the balance between democratic and exclusionary ideals is still being negotiated.

Brick by Brick

Calvin Trillin admitted in 1977 that he enjoyed sampling the historically themed markets, but already he found the old-brick motif to be repetitive and more than a little mind-numbing: "The brick exposed in Ghirardelli Square in San Francisco tended to look like the brick exposed in Pioneer Square in Seattle, which had some similarity to the brick exposed in Old Town, Chicago, or Underground Atlanta or the River Quay in Kansas City or Larimer Square in Denver or Gaslight Square in St. Louis." This criticism — that cities were losing the unique characteristics that distinguished one from another — would only grow in volume over the next twenty-five years. To Trillin and many others it seemed that nostalgic redevelopment projects were homogenizing the urban commercial experience. Just as all suburban shopping malls looked alike, now cities had begun to look alike. The lament over the loss of a presumed diversity of urban environment and urban experience was another powerful assertion of decline.[129]

Yet one need only consider Trillin's list of places to see the general folly of assuming that similar design motifs (like red brick) indicated identical experiences. Gaslight Square, as we have seen, took a "sinister and unreal" turn toward abandonment in the mid-1960s, as did River Quay in the 1970s. Ghirardelli Square, in contrast, has unfailingly brought tourists to the San Francisco waterfront, while Seattle's Pioneer Square remains unusual in its ability to draw upscale customers and tourists without chasing away the down-and-out patrons of the city's public spaces. Although many cities have turned to similar nostalgic strategies since the 1970s, using the same bricks did not give them the same history or the same future.

Downtowns are in no more danger of homogenizing today than they were during the heyday of Main Street postcards, under national chain store leadership in the 1920s, or in the wake of urban renewal. Throughout the twentieth century, investors constantly pursued or rejected strategies with national reach. From some angles, the pressures toward conformity appear to have been stronger at the beginning of the twentieth century than at the end of that century. A few hundred or thousand Progressive era Main Street postcards can dull the senses more quickly than 1980s Rouse Company plans. In the details of how clients and artists intervened to create the postcards, one sees the shared downtown improvement ideals of activist club women, early city planners, and Main Street businesses. In creating and circulating so many cards, Americans affirmed that they valued the homogenizing formula as much as they valued each city's distinctive characteristics.

At the end of the twentieth century, downtown investors could draw on more — not fewer — approaches to remaking urban commercial life, from the modest improvements of the Main Street ideal to modernization, demolition and rebuilding, and nostalgic preservation hybrids. Developers and consumers could turn for inspiration or discouragement to a wide array of examples from the past, including 1890s club women (whose work is sometimes compared to that of 1980s–90s business improvement districts), resourceful depression-era appraisers, 1960s looters, or trend-setting business leaders like James Rouse. There were more architectural styles, notably modernism, to borrow from or spurn. Urban renewal, 1960s riots, and even depression-era demolitions have left large and small vacant parcels for new projects. And for all the concern about surveillance and security enforcement in the late twentieth century, the end of segregation provides one example of how downtown development now exerts less control over consumers and investors than it did eighty years ago.[130]

The frequent debates and uncertainty over the future of urban commerce suggest the coexistence of multiple downtown ideals and possibilities, replacing unitary notions that prevailed at different times during the twentieth century — such as presumed centrality and growth, segregation, or decline. The tremendous range of downtown conditions should provide some reassurance that American cities will not become indistinguishable. Some Main Streets languish, virtually abandoned. New immigrants have entirely reinvigorated others. Historic preservation has generated many success stories, while some places have maintained dominant department stores and still others thrive on discount retail. Some are defined by new construction. Big-city downtowns usually have a patchwork of all of the above.

A sampling of how several former Woolworth buildings and sites are used today (and proposals for their future uses) indicates the variety of downtown commercial experiences at the beginning of the twenty-first century. As Main Street in Keene, New Hampshire, rebounded from a 1992 low point (which included the loss of Woolworth), several businesses — Hannah Grimes Marketplace, TCBY, and Church and Main Advertising — moved into the renovated Woolworth structure. In Greenwich, Connecticut, an upscale Saks Fifth Avenue store opened in a Woolworth building, after a complete remodeling. Not too far away in Middletown, Connecticut, citizens debated whether a proposed "high-quality" Salvation Army thrift store would help or hurt downtown's prospects. More acceptable bargain retailers moved into downtown Woolworth sites in Seattle and Boston, including Ross Dress for Less, Marshalls, T. J. Maxx, and H & M. The owner of a vacant Woolworth building in Buffalo, New York, inspired by other success stories, hoped to attract a factory outlet mall. Nightclubs signed leases for portions of Woolworth buildings in San Diego and Ventura, California. The redeveloper of the Denver Woolworth building (once one of the world's largest) preferred purchasing a vacant structure (it had been empty for five years), because that made it easier to re-fit for the high-tech companies he intended to attract. Educational institutions have also redesigned former retail properties, as in Hartford, where the G. Fox & Company department store was renovated for use by a community college.[131]

Elsewhere, Woolworth buildings were demolished in order to build office towers (Omaha), and hotels (New Orleans). In Houston, numerous old commercial structures like the Kress building were converted for residential lofts during the 1990s, but the Woolworth building in that city was replaced by a twelve-story parking garage including forty thousand square feet of retail. At the other end of the spectrum, the former Woolworth building in Butler, Pennsylvania, collapsed in broad daylight after only four years of vacancy. Despite the obvious neglect that had weakened the structure, the site had an active owner who was trying to find a new tenant. In Camden, New Jersey, the former downtown Woolworth building sits empty and apparently forgotten — representative of all the other empty commercial sites that do not make it into the news.

In 2000 a provocative set of preservation issues swirled around the Greens-boro, North Carolina, Woolworth building, site of the February 1960 civil rights sit-ins that drew the national spotlight to the issue of Main Street inte-gration. The now "run-down vacant store" was at the center of yet another controversy — over whether the structure should become a civil rights mu-seum and, if so, who exactly should preserve and interpret that history. Vari-eties of nostalgia, like various interpretations of history, have been capable of opening up productive debates with many participants, viewpoints, and outcomes. In this sense, nostalgia is not a generic force imposing bland and monolithic narratives on the past, present, or future of urban commer-cial life.[132]

During the late twentieth century, downtown development strategies that retained, referenced, and reused the past emerged slowly but with great im-pact, signaling a major reorientation in how people engaged in and profited by urban commercial life. Such historical sensibilities, appearing in unex-pected places and used by a great variety of participants, overcame significant resistance to animate the key issues and debates of urban commerce. Down-town vacancy and the ebbing vibrancy of old commercial ways coexisted with experimental new approaches, many of them rooted in nostalgia for the "au-thentic" commercial experiences that were disappearing. Just as the old red bricks of downtown buildings were relaid in festival marketplaces, this dwin-dling and simultaneous resurgence were closely related. From organized and professional Main Street historic preservation programs to vacant variety stores, festival marketplaces, and the creative and unorthodox recombination of old building parts by bohemian entrepreneurs, nostalgia in many forms in-spired new directions for Main Street while almost always sparking disagree-ment and negotiation. During these decades, people experimented with the impact of historical themes upon the structures and nature of urban com-merce. In the context of redevelopment, then, nostalgia has proved to have multiple and often confusing meanings. Besides the invented nostalgia of fes-tival marketplaces and their precursors, for example, there was also a grass-roots public nostalgia for dime stores that defied the pronouncements of the retail market analysts. There was racist nostalgia for segregated downtowns. In recent decades, developer interest in exploiting the past has indeed become an important force in remaking urban commerce, but it is only a small part of the story.

As I write these last pages, the world's attention is riveted on the meaning and future of a vacant parcel of downtown real estate — the site once occupied by the World Trade Center.[1] When the sun goes down, towering stadium lights switch on to brilliantly illuminate the sixteen-acre hole (fig. C.1). If you didn't know lower Manhattan, from a few blocks away the lights might make you think you were approaching a sports arena — the kind of facility trying to draw crowds in so many cities these days. The hole itself looks like a construction site that has just been excavated and is awaiting the laying of foundations. But there are no plans yet for what will rise at this spot. With this in mind, the scene looks like a tabula rasa, as a friend has observed.

Because of the World Trade Center site, there has probably never been a time when it was more obvious to the general public that the investment choices shaping our cities are not on inevitable trajectories but are indeed choices shaped by many different participants and frameworks. The uncertainty over lower Manhattan's future is palpable, and competing interest groups and issues appear in the news every day. Some do hope — while others despair — that so-called market forces will return the same commercial uses and values that were established during the Twin Towers era. Yet so many other factors bear down upon the site besides the pocketbooks of those who have property and profit at stake. Memories play an enormous role here, with choices looming about how to honor both the heartbreaking loss of life and the achievements and altered symbolism of the World Trade Center. Survivors' organizations have registered their opinions. There are the legal constraints of leases, debts, contracts, zoning, and rights of way, not to mention discussion of reinstating the old grid system erased by the towers' construction in the 1970s. Architects, urban designers, planners, and other real estate consultants track the public debates but also bring in the agendas and

Figure C.1 This September 11, 2002, photograph shows the World Trade Center site illuminated at night. (Courtesy of AP/Wide World Photos/Louis Lanzano, no. 6427892.)

popular trends of their own professions. Public authorities from all of the relevant jurisdictions, from the local community board on up to the president of the United States, have their say. Other uninvited groups and voices step forward with input. What should the new development look like, and whom should it attract?

At its best, the decision-making process for the World Trade Center site is a search for inspiration, in which countless sources and people will be drawn upon to imagine and then build the future for downtown commerce. As such, it is an extraordinary case that illuminates the ordinary workings of downtown real estate in the twentieth century. The site is not truly a blank slate, because there are so many preexisting legal guidelines, inherited issues, and memories. It is more like an empty and brightly lit stage with lots of directors, scripts, auditions, designers, audiences, and reviewers. Various histories will be constant reference points, but ultimately something new will be produced.

That will be true even if, as some have suggested, they replicate exactly what was destroyed.

The concept of historic preservation might at first seem irrelevant to Ground Zero, since so much has been obliterated at the site, and there appears to be little to preserve. But preservation, the most widely supported downtown investment strategy of the late twentieth century, will shape rebuilding on the World Trade Center site mostly in conceptual and nostalgic ways. It is as a development approach, not as a literal preserver of buildings and bricks, that preservation provides insight into the ways in which history is central to the rebuilding challenge — especially the search for inspiration amid devastation.

Today, when Main Street preservationists work to win over local leaders and other citizens, they sometimes show slides of Main Street postcards from the early twentieth century. That effort is made not to promote the recapturing or recreation of a past heyday. Rather, preservationists today appreciate the same motivational qualities that businesspeople, artists, planners, and improvement clubs originally valued in the postcards, when nearly a hundred years ago they hoped the cards would help transform the practices of urban commerce. What stood out then and stands out now is the confidence exuded by the creators of the Main Street ideal when they crafted that orderly and popular vision. Today's decision makers confront a much more confusing array of options and uncertainties — the inheritance of the entire twentieth century.

It is easy to envy the sense of control presumed by these Progressive era participants — but it was control over an ideal, not over downtown's unruly reality. And it was an ideal hammered out after years of activism, agitation, and disagreement. Many hands, from unknown artists and club women to prominent business leaders and design professionals, contributed to the improved commercial landscapes embodied in the postcards. Main Street postcards were infused with glowing colors and light so that the scenes almost appeared to be organically illuminated from within. Yet this was no more the freeze-frame portrait of a "natural" historical moment than is the million-watt illumination of the World Trade Center site.

Given the art and artifice of the Progressive era strategies for Main Street, it is fascinating and disturbing that so many of the late-twentieth-century approaches emulating that era have been dismissed for producing fake urban environments. In Albuquerque, a local leader justified his opposition to a 1980s Rouse Enterprise proposal by claiming that "people want something a lot more urban and real." According to this critic, the festival marketplace concept threatened to Disnify the city: "Why someone would want to go downtown and watch someone make fudge is beyond me."[2] The complaints about increasingly artificial, homogeneous, and exclusionary cities have in fact been legitimated and made comprehensible by 1950s Disney models, as well as by the example of 1960s–80s suburban shopping malls. Michael Sorkin's plea "for a return to a more authentic urbanity, a city based on physical proximity and free movement" echoes these concerns and has solidified them for many contemporary intellectuals.[3]

But preoccupation with a lost urban authenticity, proximity, and freedom of interaction confuses the question of whether the downtown was once a "demi-paradise" of "democratic space" with whether that mixing place was and is still a powerful ideal. Downtown investors, retailers, planners, officials, and citizens have continually redefined and limited that ideal and have then been guided by their interpretations. For the success of current efforts to reinvigorate downtowns, as well as for historians, it is important to recognize that the democratic, melting-pot downtown has been an evolving ideal, not a past accomplished reality from which Americans have strayed. Throughout the twentieth century, that democratic ideal has teetered in balance with exclusionary ideals and investment practices that regarded the melting-pot concept as a dangerous and risky mistake.[4]

There is no authentic downtown past to contrast with a fake urban present, just as there is no lost democratic heyday. The experiences provided by historically themed marketplaces are as authentic as those found on a deserted Main Street or on the bustling sidewalks in front of a magnetic city department store. The problems facing urban commercial life are not the developer profit motive or the exploitation of the past or even the issue of decline.

The real challenge is the one revealed by the unforgiving lights at the World Trade Center site — the fact that what Americans choose to do with their downtowns is an authentic statement of the nation's values and its visions of the future. During the 1920s, women's increasingly independent decision making drove the unpredictable engines of urban growth, leading investors to create mechanisms of prediction and control (from market surveys to segregation) and newly gendering the basis of peak downtown land values. Depression-era investors reworked modernization, demolition, and the fundamentals of real estate appraising to find opportunities even while the prevailing expansion models had collapsed and capitalism itself was being reevaluated. Urban renewal hoped to lure white suburban homemakers downtown in order to rebuild the urban retail economy on their dollars. In this process, developers not only disregarded close-by African American consumers but also unsuccessfully resisted the trend for middle-class women to enter career employment. Protestors in the 1960s targeted sites of urban commerce, demanding the renegotiation of American race values. During the course of the twentieth century, Main Street has been a place to teach, debate, exclude, fantasize, argue, include, make new dreams, and revisit old ones.

As should be obvious from this book, one cannot simply read these values from lampposts, storefronts, real estate atlases, construction statistics, empty lots, or skyscrapers. It has been the people — their crusades, their financial stake, their ideals, and their changing priorities — that have given meaning, hopes, and limitations to the material condition of downtown and that ultimately have given Main Street its form. This interplay puts buildings up and takes them down.

Those who have shaped downtown's future have entered the spotlight of history in a variety of ways. It was in the Progressive era that reformers most self-consciously used Main Street like a stage. The Woman's Club of Leesburg, Virginia, scripted a pantomime show to bluntly instruct the public in the moral responsibility of cleaning up Main Street, while civic revivalists like Charles Zueblin lectured in theaters to similarly convert their audiences. Chain store executives pushed themselves to the center of investment trends in the 1920s and sought out scientific strategies that would enhance their lead position. The depression crisis suddenly exposed the usually behind-the-scenes appraisers to close scrutiny, and those participants remade their profession out of necessity. The designers and supporters of urban renewal attempted to create a vision as compelling and internally illuminated as the Main Street ideal it replaced. Civil rights protestors forced themselves onto the stage because their very presence there, as consumers, employees, and entrepreneurs, might change the traditions of urban commercial life. Those who rioted and looted in the 1960s destroyed the stage, some hoping that arsonists' fires would prove the existence of structural flaws. New investors, as well as long-time investors with new ideas, tried to imagine and build new stages in the wake of the riots. Nostalgic developers since the 1960s have labored self-consciously and heavy-handedly with historical themes and amphitheaters, but clearly they are not the first to understand the power of building a stage at the city's commercial center. Sometimes the creative artifice of twentieth-century urban commercial life has accomplished its objectives, and sometimes it has not, but the actor has always been human initiative of one kind or another, not a natural or organic condition.

No vacant lot in American history has received as much scrutiny as the World Trade Center site. The investment dynamics shaping its future, however, are like those that shaped most other downtown places in the twentieth century. It remains to be seen which constellation of values and participants will chart the course of downtown real estate and urban commerce in the twenty-first century.

LIST OF ARCHIVAL COLLECTIONS

Baker Library, Harvard Business School
— Historic Corporate Report Collection
— Resseguie Collection

Bancroft Library, University of California, Berkeley
— "D. Ghirardelli Co. Photograph Album of Chocolate Manufacturing Process,"
  no. 51, Banc Pic 1992.036-ALB
— Materials relating to Ghirardelli Square, ca. 1910–81, Banc Mss 82/84c
— Scenes at Ghirardelli Square, San Francisco, ca. 1960–ca. 1979, Banc Pic
  1982.105-PIC

Birmingham Public Library, Birmingham, Ala., Department of Archives
and Manuscripts
— Birmingham Area Chamber of Commerce Scrapbooks
— Birmingham Police Department Surveillance Files
— Jefferson County Board of Equalization Appraisal Files
— Robert Jemison Jr. Papers
— V. J. Elmore Stores, Inc., Construction Files

Columbia Association Archives, Columbia, Md.
— James W. Rouse Papers
— JWR Photographs and Prints

Cornell University Library, Division of Rare and Manuscript Collections
— Frederick Morrison Babcock Publications, collection 4087
— Henry Andrews Babcock Papers, collection 3022
— John Nolen Pamphlet Collection, collection 6337
— John Nolen Papers, collection 2903
— Russell Van Nest Black Papers, collection 3018

Duke University, Rare Book, Manuscript, and Special Collections Library
— J. C. Penney and F. W. Woolworth Research Reports, 16 mm Microfilm Collection,
    J. Walter Thompson Company Archives. Hartman Center for Sales,
    Advertising & Marketing History.
— Postcard Collections
— Rencher Nicholas Harris Papers, 1857–1965

Dwight D. Eisenhower Library, Abilene, Kans.
— White House Central Files

Frances Loeb Library, Graduate School of Design, Harvard University
— Charles Mulford Robinson Collection
— Vertical files

Hagley Museum and Library, Wilmington, Del.
— U.S. Chamber of Commerce Records, Accession 1960
— Trade catalogs

International Downtown Association, Washington, D.C.
— The organization's private collection of historical records

J. C. Penney Company Archives, Plano, Tex.

Lake County Discovery Museum, Wauconda, Ill.
— Curt Teich Postcard Archives

Missouri Historical Society, St. Louis
— Scrapbook Collection

National Building Museum, Washington, D.C.
— Kress Archive Collection
— "Main Street Five-and-Dimes: The Architectural Heritage of the S. H. Kress
     & Co. Stores," National Building Museum Visitor Comment Books,
     May 1997–March 1998

National Retail Federation, Washington, D.C.
— The association's private library

Philadelphia City Planning Commission Library, Philadelphia
— Vertical files

Real Estate Research Corporation, Chicago, Ill.
— The firm's private collection of reports, on microfiche
— National Market Letter

St. Louis Public Library, main branch, St. Louis
— Gaslight Square Clippings File, Local History Collection, History
     and Genealogy Department

Temple University Libraries, Urban Archives, Philadelphia
— Housing Association of the Delaware Valley Pamphlet Collection

Ward M. Canaday Center for Special Collections, University of Toledo Libraries
— Libbey-Owens-Ford Glass Company Records

Western Historical Manuscript Collection, University of Missouri, St. Louis
— Thelma Blumberg photographs
— Gaslight Square Collection
— George McCue photographs
— Real Estate Analyst
— sl 26, Albert Wenzlick Real Estate Company Records (1910–60)
— sl 574, Roy Wenzlick Papers (1882–1981)

NOTES

ABBREVIATIONS

BPL Birmingham Public Library, Birmingham, Ala.

CMRC Charles Mulford Robinson Collection, Frances Loeb Library, Graduate School of Design, Harvard University

FMBP Frederick Morrison Babcock Publications, collection 4087, Division of Rare and Manuscript Collections, Cornell University Library

GSC Gaslight Square Collection, Western Historical Manuscript Collection, University of Missouri, St. Louis

GSCF Gaslight Square Clippings File, Local History Collection, History and Genealogy Department, St. Louis Public Library, main branch

HABP Henry Andrews Babcock Papers, collection 3022, Division of Rare and Manuscript Collections, Cornell University Library

HADV Housing Association of the Delaware Valley Pamphlet Collection, Temple University Libraries, Urban Archives

JCPCA J.C. Penney Company Archives, Plano, Tex.

JNP John Nolen Papers, collection 2903, Division of Rare and Manuscript Collections, Cornell University Library

JNPC John Nolen Pamphlet Collection, collection 6337, Division of Rare and Manuscript Collections, Cornell University Library

JWRP James W. Rouse Papers, Columbia Association Archives, Columbia, Md.

JWTCA J. Walter Thompson Company Archives, Rare Book, Manuscript, and Special Collections Library, Duke University

KAC Kress Archive Collection, National Building Museum, Washington, D.C.

LOF Company Records
 Libbey-Owens-Ford Glass Company Records, Ward M. Canaday Center for Special Collections, University of Toledo Libraries

MGS Materials relating to Ghirardelli Square, ca. 1910–81, Banc Mss 82/84c, Bancroft Library, University of California, Berkeley

MHS Scrapbook Collection, Missouri Historical Society, St. Louis

NML *National Market Letter*

NRF National Retail Federation, Washington, D.C.

NRRR Negro Retailers and Race Relations file, Resseguie Collection, Baker Library, Harvard Business School

PCPCL Vertical files, Philadelphia City Planning Commission Library

RC Resseguie Collection, Baker Library, Harvard Business School

REA *Real Estate Analyst*

RERC Real Estate Research Corporation

RWP Roy Wenzlick Papers (1882–1981), sl 574, Western Historical Manuscript Collection, University of Missouri, St. Louis

USCCR U.S. Chamber of Commerce Records, Accession 1960, Hagley Museum and Library, Wilmington, Del.

WWD *Women's Wear Daily*

INTRODUCTION

1. Quotation in William Hathaway and Joanne Johnson, "Those Who Relied on G. Fox Wondering Where to Go Next," *Hartford (Conn.) Courant,* September 12, 1992, A9; Garret Condon, "Recalling the Store's Heydays," ibid., A1. On most Saturdays, Hartford residents were the only customers in the store.

2. Anita M. Seline, "Closing Plan Takes Officials by Surprise," *Hartford (Conn.) Courant,* September 12, 1992, A8; Gregory Seay, "Retail Chain Losing Name in Merger," ibid.

3. Ken Gepfert, "Newberry, S.C.: The Art of a Renaissance," *Wall Street Journal,* Southeast Journal News Roundup, September 25, 1996; Jennifer Steinhauer, "Woolworth Gives Up on the Five-and-Dime," *New York Times,* July 18, 1997, A1, D4; Bernard J. Frieden and Lynne B. Sagalyn, *Downtown, Inc.: How America Rebuilds Cities* (Cambridge, MA: MIT Press, 1989), 13. Tired of the funereal proclamations surrounding the announcement of Woolworth's final closings, the owner of Sonny's 5 & 10 Variety faxed the message "We're Not Dead!" to the *Milwaukee Journal Sentinel.* Amy Rabideau Silvers, "We're Not Dead!" *Milwaukee Journal Sentinel,* August 27, 1997, 1.

4. In the G. Fox story, evidence of messy human decision making, rather than inevitable forces, was abundant, belying any simple explanation of market forces. The owner of a downtown clothing store believed that "for the last three or four years [May] executives have been bleeding that store dry." Dave Drury, "With Latest Departure, Downtown's Future Becomes Bigger Gamble," *Hartford (Conn.) Courant,* September 12, 1992, A1.

5. Eli Lehrer, "Students Sad over Losing Major Downtown Retailing Draw," *Ithaca (N.Y.) Journal,* July 18, 1997, 7A.

6. Condon, "Recalling the Store's Heydays," A1; Grant Parsons, "Closing Time at the Five & Dime," *Raleigh News and Observer,* December 31, 1993, D1.

7. Discussing future policy, Carl Abbott highlights the symbolic and actual importance of the downtown in integrating American social groups. He proposes that "social inclusiveness" is the downtown's "one advantage," since the downtown might be "an effective setting for integrating old minorities, new minorities, and majority society. It remains the one part of the metropolis that most effectively generates new ideas by bringing together the greatest range of groups and individuals." Carl Abbott, "Five Downtown Strategies: Policy Discourse and Downtown Planning since 1945," *Journal of Policy History* 5, no. 1 (1993): 22. The urban history literature that foregrounds the fragmentation and divisions of cities in the twentieth century is massive. The notes accompanying a recent retrospective on Arnold Hirsch's *Making the Second Ghetto: Race and Housing in Chicago, 1940–1960* (New York: Cambridge University Press, 1983) are a good place to start. See essays in the *Journal of Urban History* 29, no. 3 (2003): 233–309.

8. Jon C. Teaford, *The Twentieth-Century American City,* 2d ed. (Baltimore: Johns Hopkins University Press, 1993), 8, 17.

9. Michael Sorkin, ed., *Variations on a Theme Park: The New American City and the End of Public Space* (New York: Hill and Wang, 1992), xv. Mike Davis, *City of Quartz: Excavating the Future in Los Angeles* (New York: Vintage Books, 1990), 226–28.

For Goldfield and Brownell, the department store was specifically a women's democracy: "In the increasingly segregated American city, the department store was a democratic institution where working-class women and the wives of banking and insurance executives mingled." David R. Goldfield and Blaine A. Brownell, *Urban America: A History,*

2d ed. (Boston: Houghton Mifflin, 1990), 113–18, 271. Studying the department store as a workplace, Susan Porter Benson found complicated, hierarchical relationships. Susan Porter Benson, *Counter Cultures: Saleswomen, Managers, and Customers in American Department Stores, 1890–1940* (Urbana: University of Illinois Press, 1986).

David Nasaw's research leads him to conclude, "We have lost not simply buildings and parks but also the sense of civic sociability they nourished and sustained." Gone are "the heterogeneous crowds." David Nasaw, *Going Out: The Rise and Fall of Public Amusements* (New York: Basic Books, 1993), 1. In her study of nineteenth-century New York and Boston, Mona Domosh locates the decline of public space before the twentieth century — not directly challenging the existence of a heyday, but pushing it further back in time. Mona Domosh, *Invented Cities: The Creation of Landscape in Nineteenth-Century New York and Boston* (New Haven, CT: Yale University Press, 1996), 157.

These beliefs in the downtown's democratic past must be contrasted with the focus in nineteenth-century historiography on the ideology of separate spheres — in which the business district stood as a homogeneous, male, white, bourgeois place. For an analysis of the downtown as "white man's" space, see Sharon Zukin, *Landscapes of Power: From Detroit to Disney World* (Berkeley: University of California Press, 1991), 180–81.

The most effective analysis I have read of the potential meanings of jostling proximity is in Mary Ryan, *Civic Wars: Democracy and Public Life in the American City during the Nineteenth Century* (Berkeley: University of California Press, 1997), 14–15. The downtown jostling metaphor of American democracy is made more complex when one asks how the ideal would be gendered in the early twentieth century, since women were specifically not supposed to rub shoulders with strangers. And in many cities African Americans would have faced dangerous consequences if they rubbed shoulders with whites.

10. The opening decades of this modern commercial era, with their new building forms and the accompanying social and economic relationships, have generated much scholarship. Some examples include William Leach, *Land of Desire: Merchants, Power, and the Rise of a New American Culture* (New York: Pantheon Books, 1993); Domosh, *Invented Cities;* Angel Kwolek-Folland, *Engendering Business: Men and Women in the Corporate Office, 1870–1930* (Baltimore: Johns Hopkins University Press, 1994); John Kasson, *Amusing the Million: Coney Island at the Turn of the Century* (New York: Hill and Wang, 1978); Carol Willis, *Form Follows Finance: Skyscrapers and Skylines in New York City and Chicago* (New York: Princeton Architectural Press, 1995); Paul Groth, *Living Downtown: The History of Residential Hotels in the United States* (Berkeley: University of California Press, 1994); Abigail Van Slyck, *Free to All: Carnegie Libraries and American Culture, 1890–1920* (Chicago: University of Chicago Press, 1995); and Elizabeth Collins Cromley, *Alone Together: A History of New York's Early Apartments* (Ithaca, NY: Cornell University Press, 1990).

11. David Nasaw captures the democratic heyday viewpoint, while William Leach describes the stultifying victory of consumer capitalism. Nasaw, *Going Out;* Leach, *Land of Desire.* The polarization of the contemporary debate — shopping as frivolous and superficial versus its potential to remake the urban economy and America's democratic potential — is revealing of retail's provocative symbolism. On the theories of the post–World War II decades that "conceived planned shopping centers as the means not just to sell merchandise but to improve social and civic life," see Howard Gillette Jr., "The Evolution of the Planned Shopping Center in Suburb and City," *Journal of the American Planning Association* 51 (autumn 1985), 449.

12. Not surprisingly, the era of the presumed decline of urban commercial life has found far fewer historians. See especially the essays in William R. Taylor, ed. *Inventing Times Square: Commerce and Culture at the Crossroads of the World* (Baltimore: Johns Hopkins University Press, 1991); and Richard Longstreth, *City Center to Regional Mall: Architecture, the Automobile, and Retailing in Los Angeles, 1920–1950* (Cambridge, MA: MIT Press, 1997), xvi. On postwar consumer culture, see Lizabeth Cohen, *A Consumer's Republic: The Politics of Mass Consumption in Postwar America* (New York: Knopf, 2003); and Andrew Hurley, *Diners, Bowling Alleys, and Trailer Parks: Chasing the American Dream in the Postwar Consumer Culture* (New York: Basic Books, 2001). Jackson Lears takes his history of American advertising into the post–World War II years when consumer culture lost its urban foundations in *Fables of Abundance: A Cultural History of Advertising in America* (New York: Basic Books, 1994). Thomas Sugrue challenges the inevitability models of urban deindustrialization in *The Origins of the Urban Crisis: Race and Inequality in Postwar Detroit* (Princeton, NJ: Princeton University Press, 1996), 11. See also John Cumbler, *A Social History of Economic Decline: Business, Politics, and Work in Trenton* (New Brunswick, NJ: Rutgers University Press, 1989), an informative book working within narratives of decline.

13. On the public discourse of decline, see Robert Beauregard, *Voices of Decline: The Postwar Fate of US Cities* (Cambridge, MA: Blackwell, 1993), and "Representing Urban Decline: Postwar Cities as Narrative Objects," *Urban Affairs Quarterly* 29, no. 2 (1993): 187–202.

Most recently, the enduring power of the rise-and-fall framework is evident in Robert M. Fogelson's important book *Downtown: Its Rise and Fall, 1880–1950* (New Haven, CT: Yale University Press, 2001). Fogelson focuses on the debates, divisions, and alliances among downtown experts over regulating and shaping key dimensions of the center city, especially rapid transit (subways and elevated trains), building height limits and skyscrapers, and the early formative years of urban renewal programs (the 1940s). He also synthesizes Americans' opinions of these (heavily big-city) innovations. In this volume, my examination of the cultural assumptions guiding development also uncovers the role of factors such as gender and race, both of which complicate a rise-and-fall narrative.

14. My focus on national-level downtown strategies builds upon recent interest among urban and planning historians in images, ideas, discourse, and especially culture. The intellectual history of city planning, for example, emphasizes the flow of planning principles across geographic boundaries. In a 1993 article, Carl Abbott treats the "'downtown' as a constructed concept," hoping to demonstrate "that public action about central business districts has been rooted in a partially autonomous realm of changing ideas." Robert Beauregard examines "public discourse," particularly as the "mechanism for conveying, through its representations of urban decline, pragmatic knowledge about how and where to live and invest and, more importantly, as a discursive device for centering that knowledge in a comprehensible and legitimate story." In her case study of post–World War II downtown Omaha, Janet Daly-Bednarek considers how local planners drew selectively from a body of nationally available planning advice, while negotiating with local constituents. Carl Abbott, "Five Downtown Strategies," 7; Beauregard, *Voices of Decline*, 7; Janet Daly-Bednarek, *The Changing Image of the City: Planning for Downtown Omaha, 1945–1973* (Lincoln: University of Nebraska Press, 1992), 3–4. Robert Fairbanks's study of Cincinnati and Dallas from 1940 to 1960 found that planners and developers shared a

"conception of the city" and participated in a national "changing discourse." Although the two seemed "to have little in common," Fairbanks concluded that "the rhetoric and actions of leaders in both cities with regard to metropolitan planning and downtown redevelopment remained quite similar." Fairbanks, "Metropolitan Planning and Downtown Redevelopment: The Cincinnati and Dallas Experiences," *Planning Perspectives* 2 (1993): 237–38, 250.

15. The perceived homogeneity of downtowns has long generated both criticism and admiration. During the 1920s novelist Sinclair Lewis satirized the dull, narrow-minded, booster perspective he saw encased in America's Main Street corridors. Real estate appraiser Joseph Laronge agreed with Lewis that "there is something purely American" about Main Street. But Laronge, writing in 1938, warmly approved: "I need not dwell long upon the importance of maintaining and preserving in all of its present splendor the truly American institution of downtown." Sinclair Lewis, *Babbitt* (New York: Signet Classic, 1922); Sinclair Lewis, *Main Street* (New York: Signet Classic, 1920). Joseph Laronge, "Traffic Counts," *Journal of the American Institute of Real Estate Appraisers,* April 1938, reprinted in *Selected Readings in Real Estate Appraisal* (Chicago: American Institute of Real Estate Appraisers, 1953), 732. Joseph Laronge, "Should We Get Excited about Retail Decentralization?" *National Real Estate Journal,* December 1938, 54.

16. John Nolen, *Report on the Town of Wayland* (Cambridge, MA: Published by the author, 1911), 1, 13. Ada Louise Huxtable, "The Fall and Rise of Main Street," *New York Times,* May 30, 1976, 146. Nolen tried to help Wayland "avoid doing anything with the direct intention of stimulating real estate values or increasing the population of the town."

17. "Main Street, U.S.A.," *Architectural Forum,* February 1939, 73–75. Other shared features, according to this article, included a sociable atmosphere, parking difficulties, emulation of "modern" standards in storefronts, ten-story skyscrapers, old mixed with remodeled buildings, large neon signs, and a mix of dignified and "non-conformist" businesses. Downtown problems were also generalized to apply to cities of all sizes. *Business Week,* for example, introduced a special report stating, "Every American city of 6,000,000 or 6,000 population shows symptoms of dry rot at its core." "Rebuilding the Cities," *Business Week,* July 6, 1940, 35.

18. Just as this study builds upon the assumption that Main Streets were "more alike than different," it emphasizes the interchangeability between the terms *downtown* and *Main Street.* Both terms captured the informal, vernacular concept of an urban commercial center.

19. A series of pamphlet collections and clippings files saved by prominent national consultants, investors, and organizations together served as a guide to the published materials (periodicals, articles, leaflets, newsletters, and speeches) that downtown interest groups relied upon. Included were the collections of planners Charles Mulford Robinson (1890s–1910s) and John Nolen (1900–1930s), the Philadelphia City Planning Commission Library vertical files (1930s–1970s), files of the Housing Association of the Delaware Valley (1950s), retail trade articles in the Resseguie Collection (1950–1960s); consulting firm Real Estate Analyst's files (1960s–1970s), and developer James W. Rouse's personal files (especially those from the 1950s–1970s). This approach gave focus to my reading of the vast published downtown-related literature of the twentieth century and grounded my research in the sources I knew investors consulted.

20. In seeking to understand the cultural framing of economic decision making, focus-

ing on real estate, city-building, and the built environment, I am indebted to many historians and others whose scholarship occupies the intersection of these fields. I would especially single out the publications of Elizabeth Blackmar, Christine Boyer, Lizabeth Cohen, Richard Francaviglia, Howard Gillette, Jonathan Goss, Thomas Hanchett, Greg Hise, Kenneth Jackson, Richard Longstreth, Max Page, Mary Ryan, David Schuyler, William Taylor, Lisa Tolbert, and Carol Willis.

CHAPTER 1

1. Walker Evans, "When 'Downtown' Was a Beautiful Mess," *Fortune,* January 1962, 101. One scholar claimed that Evans "invented the image of vernacular America." Lesley K. Baier, *Walker Evans at Fortune 1945–1965, Wellesley College Museum, Wellesley Massachusetts, 16 November, 1977 to 23 January, 1978* (Wellesley, MA: Museum, 1977), 19. For other discussions of 1900–1920 as a Main Street golden age, see Carole Rifkind, *Main Street: The Face of Urban America* (New York: Harper and Row, 1977), xii; and Richard V. Francaviglia, "Main Street U.S.A.: A Comparison/Contrast of Streetscapes in Disneyland and Walt Disney World," *Journal of Popular Culture* 15, no. 1 (1981): 143, 146.

2. Evans, "When 'Downtown' Was a Beautiful Mess," 101.

3. Historians identify the Progressive era as a watershed moment in how Americans perceived cities. Peter Hales has documented the connections between urban photography and promotional attitudes toward the city in the nineteenth century, including entrepreneurship, urban planning, and city boosting. Hales argues that in the "grand style" that dominated urban photography from about 1870 until the 1893 World's Columbian Exposition, photographers edited out the unpleasant aspects of urban life, showcasing instead buildings and monumental scenes. Although that did complement the grandiose aspirations of the City Beautiful movement, this chapter and the next trace the emergence of a different visual style appropriate instead to commercial beautification — one revealed in the more modest and mundane Main Street improvements advocated by city plans and Main Street postcards during the early twentieth century.

The second style identified by Hales is the "reform style" — exemplified by the shock techniques of Jacob Riis in the 1890s. Riis photographed New York City's destitute in dark, crowded spaces, intending to provoke the middle class into reform. Peter Hales, *Silver Cities: The Photography of American Urbanization, 1839–1915* (Philadelphia: Temple University Press, 1984), esp. 18, 53, 62, 71–72, 80, 109, 113, 127, 157–58, 175–76, 254, 266–67.

Another relevant development at the turn of the century was the emergence of what historian Alan Trachtenberg has called *urban tourism.* Residents and visitors had long enjoyed exploring cities, but in the 1890s written and pictorial representations began to emphasize this perspective. Such images (like postcards) celebrated ordinary and picturesque urban views. Trachtenberg points out that this genre often grew out of men's experiences and freedom, particularly their walks home from work. Alan Trachtenberg, *Reading American Photographs: Images as History, Matthew Brady to Walker Evans* (New York: Hill and Wang, 1989), 180–87. Middle-class women, despite proscriptions to the contrary, engaged in their own forms of urban tourism, as Sarah Deutsch describes in "Reconceiving the City: Women, Space, and Power in Boston, 1870–1910," *Gender and History* 6, no. 2 (August 1994): 202–23.

4. Stanley Schultz, for example, mentioned only the "grandiose" City Beautiful plans "at their silliest." Historians shifted their sights from monumentality to smaller-scale im-

provements and their proponents when Jon Peterson traced City Beautiful roots to late-nineteenth-century urban movements such as municipal art, civic improvement, and outdoor art. He stressed the upsurge from local, grassroots efforts, rather than the top-down influences of architects and the 1893 Chicago World's Fair. Daniel Bluestone scrutinized the familiar topic of monumentality from new angles — such as the competition between civic and commercial monumentality. William Wilson's overview surveys how the City Beautiful movement functioned within particular cities, shaped by relationships among businessmen, city officials, planners, and civic groups. Wilson argues that since the "practical" planners won out, they wrote a history dismissive of City Beautiful. Stanley K. Schultz, *Constructing Urban Culture: American Cities and City Planning, 1800–1920* (Philadelphia: Temple University Press, 1986), 211–12; Jon A. Peterson, "The City Beautiful Movement: Forgotten Origins and Lost Meanings," *Journal of Urban History* 2, no. 4 (August 1976): 415–34; Daniel Bluestone, "Detroit's City Beautiful and the Problem of Commerce," *Journal of the Society of Architectural Historians* 47 (September 1988): 245–62; William H. Wilson, *The City Beautiful Movement* (Baltimore: Johns Hopkins University Press, 1989).

5. The gendered dimensions of city planning have only recently been taken up by historians, and the Progressive era has provided the major entry point. Peter Hall sought out "founding mothers" in the field with little success. Eugenie Birch, Jon Peterson, William Wilson, and others looked beyond the lists of professional planners to consider the impact of female civic workers. Susan Wirka recently identified forgotten "founding mothers" from the first decade of the century who advocated a "strand" of planning that she calls the City Social, which lost out to both the City Beautiful and the City Practical, resulting in an exodus of women from the field by the 1910s. Daphne Spain believes that, as argued in this chapter, the role of municipal housekeepers in the City Beautiful movement is more central than has been recognized. Hall is cited in *Planning the Twentieth-Century American City*, ed. Mary Corbin Sies and Christopher Silver (Baltimore: Johns Hopkins University Press, 1996), 55; Eugenie Birch, "From Civic Worker to City Planner: Women and Planning, 1890–1980," in *The American Planner: Biographies and Recollections*, ed. Donald A. Krueckeberg, 2d ed. (New Brunswick, NJ: Center for Urban Policy Research, 1994), 469–506; Peterson, "The City Beautiful Movement," 415–34; Wilson, *The City Beautiful Movement*; Susan Marie Wirka, "The City Social Movement: Progressive Women Reformers and Early Social Planning," in Sies and Silver, *Planning the Twentieth-Century American City*, 55–75; Daphne Spain, *How Women Saved the City* (Minneapolis: University of Minnesota Press, 2001), 13, 249, 252–53. See also Bonj Szczygiel, "'City Beautiful' Revisited: An Analysis of Nineteenth-Century Civic Improvement Efforts," *Journal of Urban History* 29, no. 2 (January 2003): 107–32.

6. When discussing the Progressive era, I sometimes use the terms *commercial men* and *businessmen* even though women were also Main Street entrepreneurs during this time. Similarly, the term *club women* broadly recognizes the men who were involved in the women-dominated improvement leagues. My usage follows the practices of this era, when people gendered these phrases despite the underlying mixed-sex realities.

7. The term *municipal housekeeping* as used at the turn of the century, and as used by historians, has a broad scope to encompass the variety of women's urban reform activities. This chapter examines municipal housekeeping's role in commercial life and Main Street — hence the terms *downtown* and *Main Street housekeeping*.

8. Mary Ritter Beard, *Woman's Work in Municipalities* (New York: D. Appleton, 1915), 307; "Editorial Comment," *American City*, June 1912, 801. Enthusiastic credit was granted to women in Alan Bright, "How Women's Organizations May Improve Methods of Street Lighting," ibid., 893; and Zona Gale, "A Club That 'Studied America,'" ibid., June 1913, 624.

9. "Notes," *Civic League Bulletin* (Colorado Springs, CO), October 1911, 6. Mildred Chadsey, "A Woman Chief of Sanitary Police: Cleveland the First City to Discover This Logical Field for Women Specialists," *American City*, June 1912, 871–73. Blanche Zieber to John Nolen, ca. October 1909, box 32, Reading file 1, John Nolen Papers, collection no. 2903, Division of Rare and Manuscript Collections, Cornell University Library (hereafter cited as JNP). For another account of ridicule, see Beard, *Woman's Work in Municipalities*, 310. A pioneering woman judge, head of Chicago's Court for Delinquent Girls, actually tied a pink ribbon in a neat bow around her gavel. "America's Only Woman Judge Is Doing a Big Work," *New York Times*, May 25, 1913, SM4. During the same years, when New York City's first female commissioner took charge of the Department of Corrections, one of her employees joked about "the possibilities of pink ribbons and things to trim the chandeliers" but concluded that she was just a good new boss. "Miss Davis Takes Hold of Her Work," *New York Times*, January 3, 1914, 3.

10. Beard, *Woman's Work in Municipalities*, 293. The debates over the civic meaning of street objects such as trash cans indeed indicate the narrowing of the nineteenth-century's wide-ranging "civic wars" described by Mary Ryan — yet also suggest why the sentiments behind downtown housekeeping were so forceful. See Mary Ryan, *Civic Wars: Democracy and Public Life in the American City during the Nineteenth Century* (Berkeley: University of California Press, 1997).

11. "Need of Closer Civic Fraternity," clipping dated June 3, 1909, box 17, file Fort Wayne, Charles Mulford Robinson Collection, Frances Loeb Library, Graduate School of Design, Harvard University (hereafter cited as CMRC).

12. Anne Firor Scott has suggested that there is a "danger of being carried away by the women's own infectious enthusiasm for their work, to the possible detriment of balanced analysis." She questions the "reliability" of Beard's book, because of the absence of citations. Indeed, both the *American City* women's number and Beard's book have promotional qualities. Scott concludes that even if the accomplishments described are glossed over or exaggerated, the underlying work is still remarkable, though perhaps more complex than Beard and the club writers imply. Yet I also cite throughout this chapter many examples of conflict, resentment, indifference, and resistance within the club reports and Beard's accounts. Less common, but still present, are outright admissions of failure. Whenever the same story appeared in the *American City* and Beard, Beard's account is true to the magazine, even though she did not use footnotes. Anne Firor Scott, *Natural Allies: Women's Associations in American History* (Urbana: University of Illinois Press, 1991), 112, 150–51, 224 n. 33 (quotations on 112, 151).

13. Mary I. Wood, *The History of the General Federation of Women's Clubs* (Norwood, MA: Norwood Press, 1912), 71–73, 253. Helena Marie Dermitt, "The Value of Co-operation between Men and Women in Public Work," *American City*, June 1912, 846. For an overview of the uneven transition from self-culture to social justice among women's clubs, see Scott, *Natural Allies;* and Karen Blair, *The Clubwoman as Feminist: True Womanhood Redefined, 1868–1914* (New York: Holmes and Meier, 1980), 98–103. See also Robyn Muncy, *Creating a Female Dominion* (New York: Oxford University Press, 1991); Lori Ginzberg,

Women and the Work of Benevolence: Morality, Politics, and Class in the Nineteenth-Century United States (New Haven, CT: Yale University Press, 1990); Kathleen McCarthy, *Noblesse Oblige: Charity and Cultural Philanthropy in Chicago, 1849–1929* (Chicago: University of Chicago Press, 1982). On personal relationships between the club women and the city's male leaders, see Wilson, *The City Beautiful Movement*, 75.

14. Scanning the indexes to the records of the National Association of Colored Women's Clubs (NACW) reveals this difference in agenda with the General Federation of Women's Clubs. For a detailed analysis, see Dorothy Salem, *Black Women in Organized Reform, 1890–1920* (Brooklyn: Carlson Publishing, 1990); and Anne Knupfer, *Toward a Tenderer Humanity* (New York: New York University Press, 1996). Daphne Spain found that NACW increasingly turned toward municipal housekeeping. Sarah Deutsch draws distinctions between how white and black club women related to the reform geography of Boston. Spain, *How Women Saved the City*, 83; Deutsch, "Reconceiving the City."

15. At the same time, the story circulated that village improvement had been sparked by the demands of summer visitors from the city — illustrating how inspiration for investment strategies flowed among different-sized places. The suburbs also inspired village improvers. On the history of the Village Improvement Societies, see Wilson, *The City Beautiful Movement*, 42–45; and Mel Scott, *American City Planning since 1890* (Berkeley: University of California Press, 1969), 65–67. For a turn-of-the-century account of the first society, its woman founder, and the role of summer visitors, see Jessie M. Good, *Village Improvement*, box 20, file [Village Improvement], CMRC. Although many of the folders in the CMRC collection are not labeled, they are organized alphabetically. I have supplied the likely name of the file in brackets.

16. On big cities versus small towns, see Richard Watrous, "How to Organize for Civic Work," *American City*, January 1913, 38. On women composing "the great majority" of improvement clubs, see Clinton Rogers Woodruff, "Woman and Her Larger Home: Marvels of Improvement Wrought by Womankind in American Cities and Towns," *Good Housekeeping*, January 1909, 10, box 16, file [Civic Improvement], CMRC. In some towns women worked through the civic committee of the local men's commercial club. "Nation-Wide Work for Civic Betterment," *American City*, June 1912, 839.

17. Scott, *Natural Allies*, 142–45. One count found that improvement groups between 1903 and 1906 increased from 1,200 to 2,000. A 1909 estimate placed the number at over 3,000. Scott, *American City Planning since 1890*, 66; Woodruff, "Woman and Her Larger Home," 10.

18. For Yankton, SD, "Worked for a Permanent City Plan," *American City*, June 1912, 917; examples of invitations extended to women's clubs include Mrs. Ernest R. Kroeger, "Smoke Abatement in St. Louis," ibid., 907; "Nation-Wide Work for Civic Betterment," 834, 838; Beard, *Woman's Work in Municipalities*, 308–9. "By-Laws of Civic Improvement Societies of the City of Knoxville, Tenn.," *Knoxville, Tennessee: The City Beautiful* (1908), box 17, Civic Improvement Societies file, CMRC.

19. Beard, *Woman's Work in Municipalities*, 315–16. On drawing men in, see Scott, *Natural Allies*, 145. Some cities had male-dominated civic leagues with female members or committees. See Charles Mulford Robinson's files on Civic Improvement Societies in box 17, CMRC.

20. "Nation-Wide Work for Civic Betterment," 833.

21. Edgar White, "In the Little City of Maples," *American City*, October 1913, 329.

22. Beard, *Woman's Work in Municipalities*, 318; on men as blind, Maud van Buren, "Children and Town Improvement," *American City*, June 1914, 542; on men as obstacles, "Civic Revivals Conducted by Charles Zueblin, Publicist," n.d. [probably 1910], box 21, file Zueblin, Charles, CMRC. A "Southern Woman" complained: "Man's lack of interest in this effort is the greatest difficulty she has to contend with, and without his cooperation her hand is tied." Mary Walton Kent, "Letters to the Editor," *American City*, June 1912, 905.

23. My conclusions here differ from Eugenie Birch's point that "a clear division existed by mutual consent between men's and women's civic activities." Birch, "From Civic Worker to City Planner," 473. In comparing the men's City Club and the Women's City Club of Chicago, Maureen Flanagan found that although the men and the women took on similar issues, such as garbage removal, they had very different approaches. Men credited business motivations, whereas women measured the interests of all citizens. Maureen Flanagan, "Gender and Urban Political Reform: The City Club and the Women's City Club of Chicago in the Progressive Era," *American Historical Review* 95 (October 1990): 1032–50. In reading correspondence between the Carnegie Foundation and local groups, Van Slyck discovered that women valued libraries in moral terms, while men discussed economic development and tourism. Abigail Van Slyck, *Free to All: Carnegie Libraries and American Culture, 1890–1920* (Chicago: University of Chicago Press, 1995), 135–36.

24. "Editorial Comment," 801–3. The secretary of the American Civic Association advised, regarding civic leagues: "Perhaps it may be a woman who is best fitted for the presidency. If so, don't fail to make her president." This writer saw the civic league as the united effort of business and women's clubs. Watrous, "How to Organize for Civic Work," 40, 38.

25. Beard, *Woman's Work in Municipalities*, 306–7; "Letters to the Editor," *American City*, June 1912, 905.

26. Lecture title from Miss Mary A. McDowell, University of Chicago Settlement. Edward L. Burchard, *City Welfare: Aids and Opportunities*, Chicago School of Civics and Philanthropy Bulletin no. 13, October 1911, 42, box 17, Exhibitions file, CMRC.

27. For cartoon, *American City*, June 1913, 599; "What an Ohio Club Is Doing," ibid., December 1913, 541; Elizabeth Askew, "The Tampa Civic Association — Its Aims and Work," ibid., June 1913, 620; for examples of women stepping in after frustration, "Nation-Wide Work for Civic Betterment," 825, 835; "Some Brief Stories of Work Worth Doing," *American City*, June 1912, 919; on making dirt fly, Mrs. Ross W. Barrows, "A Women's Club Which Raised the Money for a City Plan," ibid., 861. Street cleaning was an evolving "science," modeled on George Waring's accomplishments in New York City. On the removal of dirt as women's work, see Nancy Tomes, *The Gospel of Germs: Men, Women, and the Microbe in American Life* (Cambridge, MA: Harvard University Press, 1998).

28. Bright, "How Women's Organizations May Improve Methods of Street Lighting," 893; on poles and wires, Beard, *Woman's Work in Municipalities*, 312; "unsightly housekeeping things" quote in Martha Candler, "A Town Made for Happiness," *Woman's Journal*, August 1928, 30, no. 6827 Mariemont 10, John Nolen Pamphlet Collection, collection no. 6337, Division of Rare and Manuscript Collections, Cornell University Library (hereafter cited as JNPC); "What an Ohio Club Is Doing," 542.

29. "Nation-Wide Work for Civic Betterment," 826, 827, 831; Beard, *Woman's Work in Municipalities*, 313–14. Women also campaigned to enact or enforce antispitting ordi-

nances. In Chicago, the women's club enlisted the help of school children to hand out thousands of cards, politely accosting violators of the antispitting ordinance on the spot. The organizer of the crusade had many "horrid" and "amusing" things said to her. "Nation-Wide Work for Civic Betterment," 827.

Another beautification strategy was the window box competition or, as in Minneapolis, the installation of "hanging gardens" on the lampposts. Ironically, the objection to the latter plan was that it might cause Minneapolis to be mistaken for a country town. Howard Strong, "The Street Beautiful in Minneapolis," *American City,* September 1913, 229.

30. On regulation of business signs, Woodruff, "Woman and Her Larger Home," 9; "flabby morals," Beard, *Woman's Work in Municipalities,* 303; on sidewalk food display, see issues of *Housewive's League Magazine* and "Nation-Wide Work for Civic Betterment," 833, 841; on women officers policing amusements, Mrs. Alice Stebbens Wells, "Women on the Police Force," *American City,* April 1913, 401. On being tactful, Katherine G. Leonard, "The Pure Food Victory Won by the Women of Grand Forks," ibid., June 1913, 603; see also White, "In the Little City of Maples," 330. For a case study of organized women regulating Main Street commercial life, Gregory A. Waller, *Main Street Amusements: Movies and Commercial Entertainment in a Southern City, 1896–1930* (Washington, DC: Smithsonian Institution Press, 1995), 21–22. Women's clubs argued that advertising should be limited to, and regulated in, commercial districts. General Federation of Women's Clubs, "Save the Beauty of America: The Landscape Is No Place for Advertising," no. 3880.1, JNPC.

31. Quote from "Nation-Wide Work for Civic Betterment," 840. Typical testimony came from Wyoming, where men learned "the efficiency of women in arousing public sentiment and securing cooperation" (844). See also Askew, "The Tampa Civic Association," 619.

32. A few of the earliest published planning reports were commissioned by women's clubs. The Woman's Civic Betterment Club of Roanoke, Virginia, sponsored John Nolen's 1907 plan *Remodeling Roanoke.* In 1913 the Woman's Club of Raleigh published Charles Mulford Robinson's *City Plan for Raleigh*—the fruit of five years of labor to bring in a landscape architect. The gender composition of other sponsoring clubs is more ambiguous. See Robinson, *Report on the Improvement of the City of Ogdensburg, New York* (Ogdensburg, NY: N.p., 1907); and Kelsey and Guild, *The Improvement of Columbia South Carolina: Report to The Civic League, Columbia South Carolina* (Harrisburg, PA: Mount Pleasant Press, 1905).

33. John Nolen's business correspondence is filled with lecture requests from women's clubs. See JNP. On the majority of women in the audience for planning-related talks as well as zoning hearings, see *Fort Wayne (Ind.) Journal-Gazette,* June 5, 1909, quoted in "Comments on Civic Revivals and Civic Lectures," box 21, file Zueblin, Charles, CMRC; "Council Takes No Action on City Zone Plan," *Elkhart (Ind.) Truth,* April 6, 1922, box 25, file Elkhart, Indiana, 1920–21, JNP; "'City Beautiful' Not First Need," *Bridgeport Standard,* October 18, 1913, box 22, file 15, JNP.

34. The application of evangelical techniques to city planning and the gendered implications of this fervor have not been studied. Little research has been done on audiences related to the promotion and reception of city planning.

35. The Reverend Caroline Crane, a renowned sanitary consultant and civic revivalist, popularized civic work in Minnesota with a lecture tour of seventeen cities. Crane got her

start by testing public health specialist George Waring's model on six blocks of Main Street in Kalamazoo, Michigan, in 1904. Between 1905 and 1917, Crane inspected sixty-two cities and fourteen states. She founded the Civic League of Kalamazoo in 1904, promoting the need to include men in the movement to clean cities up. "Nation-Wide Work for Civic Betterment," 832; Mrs. Caroline Bartlett Crane, "Some Factors of the Street Cleaning Problem," *American City*, June 1912, 895; Suellen Hoy, *Chasing Dirt: The American Pursuit of Cleanliness* (New York: Oxford University Press, 1995), 80–85; Suellen Hoy, "'Municipal Housekeeping': The Role of Women in Improving Urban Sanitation Practices, 1880–1917," in *Pollution and Reform in American Cities, 1870–1930*, ed. Martin Melosi (Austin: University of Texas Press, 1980); and "Cleaning Up American Cities," *Survey*, October 8, 1910, 83, box 16, file [Clean-up Campaigns], CMRC.

Other lecturers whose materials were collected by Charles Mulford Robinson included Lenora Austin Hamlin of the Chicago Women's Club; Howard Evarts Weed, a landscape architect of Portland, Oregon; Dana W. Barlett, author and "Superintendent of Bethlehem Institutions." Box 19, file [Lectures], CMRC.

36. The quote is from "Comments on Civic Revivals and Civic Lectures," 7. Zueblin was forced to resign from the University of Chicago faculty in 1908 for "speaking publicly against business interests." Joan Draper, "The Art and Science of Park Planning in the United States: Chicago's Small Parks, 1902 to 1905," in Sies and Silver, *Planning the Twentieth-Century American City*, 110–13. Charles Zueblin, "Democracy in Literature, Education, and Life," box 21, file Zueblin, Charles, CMRC; "Civic Revivals Conducted by Charles Zueblin, Publicist" (1910), ibid.; "Comments on Civic Revivals and Civic Lectures," 4.

37. "For the Children," *Fort Wayne (Ind.) Journal Gazette*, June 4, 1909; and "Fort Wayne Civic Revival," box 17, file Fort Wayne, CMRC. Zueblin credited "some of the city's progressive women" with starting Fort Wayne's civic revival movement and putting it in motion through a rabbi. He recognized the Commercial Club and the banker chairman of the revival for bringing about the movement's success. "Civic Revivals Conducted by Charles Zueblin, Publicist."

38. "Beauty an Asset in Business Way," *Fort Wayne (Ind.) Sentinel*, June 4, 1909, box 17, file Fort Wayne, CMRC; "The Doing of It," n.d. [June 1909], ibid. The express purpose of the revival in Grand Rapids, Michigan, was to secure city council appropriation for a plan. See John Ihlder, "Remaking Grand Rapids," *Survey*, December 25, 1909, 424–26, box 17, file Grand Rapids, MI, CMRC; "Civic Revivals Conducted by Charles Zueblin, Publicist"; "Comments on Civic Revivals and Civic Lectures," 1.

39. "Councillors Criticize Planning Board for Paying 'Expert' to Lecture," *Lynn (Mass.) Telegram-News*, December 19, 1923, box 77, file Lynn 1, JNP.

40. In 1905 the Detroit Board of Commerce's Committee on Civic Improvement introduced Robinson: "[He] is well known in connection with the propaganda for civic improvement, and [his] writings on that subject have wide circulation." But Detroit was not an average city. By 1920 it was the fourth-largest in the country, and it had hosted most of the nation's leading City Beautiful planners and architects. *Improvement of the City of Detroit: Reports Made by Professor Frederick Law Olmsted, Junior, and Mr. Charles Mulford Robinson to the Detroit Board of Commerce* (Detroit: Detroit Board of Commerce, 1915), 3; Bluestone, "Detroit's City Beautiful and the Problem of Commerce," 246.

41. "Lively Hearing on New Bridge Site," *Bridgeport (Conn.) Evening Post*, April 22,

1915, box 22, file 27, JNP. Walter Richards to John Nolen, October 23, 1924, box 24, file Columbus, JNP. Nolen gave a public address in Bridgeport during the summer of 1913, and in August a city plan commission was formed. Looking back to the 1916 controversies over Nolen's Bridgeport plan, his secretary believed that "the citizens in general were unacquainted with the advantages to be derived from city planning." Charlotte Parsons, "Bridgeport #141," *Summaries of Selected Projects* (1937–38), 6, box 1, JNP.

42. Barrows, "A Women's Club Which Raised the Money for a City Plan," 861; Nolen to Dora Merrill, May 29, 1911, box 28, file Lock Haven 1, JNP; Merrill to Nolen, June 5, 1911, ibid.

43. Merrill to Nolen, January 14, 1912, box 28, file Lock Haven 1, JNP; Nolen to Merrill, February 27, 1912, ibid. John Nolen, *A New Plan for Lock Haven* (Cambridge, MA: Published by the author, 1912).

44. "A Union of Forces for the City's Good," n.d. [probably February 1912], box 28, file Lock Haven 1, JNP; Nolen to Merrill, April 13, 1912, ibid.

45. Beard, *Woman's Work in Municipalities,* 314; Mrs. William C. Sturgis, "A Women's Club with a Desk in the City Hall," *American City,* June 1912, 891–92.

46. *Civic League Bulletin,* October 1911, 2; October 1910, 2–3; March 1911, 1; October 1911, 7. The *Civic League Bulletin* copies courtesy of Pikes Peak Library, Colorado Springs, Colo. Robinson also saved some issues in his files: box 17, file Colorado Springs, CMRC.

47. *Civic League Bulletin,* April 1912, 1; October 1911, 1, 8; March 1913, 5.

48. Mrs. Imogen B. Oakley, "The More Civic Work, the Less Need of Philanthropy," *American City,* June 1912, 809. On citizen responsibility, see also Crane, "Some Factors of the Street Cleaning Problem," 897.

49. As quoted in Beard, *Woman's Work in Municipalities,* 298.

50. Oakley, "The More Civic Work, the Less Need of Philanthropy," 805. "Civics," one Illinois clubwoman wrote, "really means municipal housekeeping." "Nation-Wide Work for Civic Betterment," 827.

51. Mrs. T. J. Bowlker, "Woman's Home-Making Function Applied to the Municipality," *American City,* June 1912, 869. Most of the eight pledges demanded of the GFWC Junior Civic League Members involved protecting public property. "Constitution and By-Laws," Junior Civic League of the Civic Department, GFWC, box 17, file Children — Study and Learning, CMRC. On using streets, parks, and the urban landscape generally to teach children (including juvenile offenders) the responsibilities of citizenship, see Mary T. Watts, "The Why and How of a Park in a Small Town," *American City,* June 1912, 869; Harlean James, "The Baltimore Flower Market," ibid., April 1913, 392; and the Children files, box 17, CMRC.

52. A Lexington, Kentucky, study discovered that the local Civic League targeted African Americans and school children for its City Beautiful lectures with films and stereopticon shows in downtown theaters. Waller, *Main Street Amusements,* 72.

53. Zona Gale, "How Women's Clubs Can Co-operate with the City Officials," *American City,* June 1914, 537; Educational Exhibition Company, *Educational Exhibitions* (Providence, RI: Remington Press, 1914), 34, box 17, file [Exhibitions], CMRC. Municipal housekeeping rhetoric about clean cities sometimes suggested "clean politics" as well. "Nation-Wide Work for Civic Betterment," 843. Even when club women disavowed politics, the suffrage issue gave their work an edge — the threat of the unknown impact of

women's political power. See Beard, *Woman's Work in Municipalities,* 318; and "Editorial Comment," 801.

54. "Civic League of Terre Haute, Ind.," box 17, file [Civic] Improvement Societies, CMRC; Blair, *The Clubwoman as Feminist,* 111–14.

55. John M. Guild, *Commercial Organizations and Civic Affairs* (Washington, DC: American Civic Association, 1915), 1, box 17, file Dayton, Ohio, CMRC; H. D. W. English, "The Function of Business Bodies in Improving Civic Conditions" (1908), 6, box 17, file [Commercial Organizations], CMRC. Women's activism in commercial design, and their definition of civic work, reveals a new side of female Progressive era politics — one that was potent though often nonfeminist, nontemperance, nonsuffrage, and nonlabor.

56. "Clean-up Campaign" in J. Harold Braddock, "Ideas for the Commercial Executive," *American City,* October 1913, 333.

57. *Special Bulletin on Pending Council Bill 245, Permitting the Extension of Over-Head Street Signs* (St. Louis, 1911), n.p., box 16, file Advertising, CMRC; "Obstruction of Sidewalks," *Municipal Journal,* November 17, 1909, box 19, file Sidewalks, CMRC.

58. "City Improvement Society," Denver, 1899, box 17, file [Civic] Improvement Societies, CMRC. The production boom of World War I drew crowds of young men to many cities, transforming, if only briefly, the moral issues of downtown streets. Zenas Potter, "War-Boom Towns: Bridgeport," *Survey,* December 4, 1915, 237–38, box 22, file 23, JNP; "Bridgeport as Our Own 'Essen.'" *Boston Evening Transcript,* October 23, 1915, box 22, envelope 35, JNP.

59. On the intent and reality behind the class dynamics of parks and amusement parks, see David Schuyler, *The New Urban Landscape* (Baltimore: Johns Hopkins University Press, 1986); and Kasson, *Amusing the Million.* William R. Taylor examines Grand Central Terminal to understand how class hierarchies were projected in urban commercial space. See "The Evolution of Public Space in New York City: The Commercial Showcase of America," in *Consuming Visions: Accumulation and Display of Goods in America, 1880–1920,* ed. Simon J. Bronner (New York: Norton, 1989), 287–309. On the wealthy bias of civic centers, see "Model for World Is Speaker's Hope for Washington," box 17, file [City Planning], CMRC.

60. Beard, *Woman's Work in Municipalities,* 295. On libraries as urban real estate, see Van Slyck, *Free to All,* 133. On clubhouses, lunchrooms, and the general phenomenon of white middle-class women building downtown, see Deutsch, "Reconceiving the City," 209, 215–16. On YWCAs, see Spain, *How Women Saved the City,* 44. For an unusual argument favoring downtown improvements because of women's self-interest — particularly their pervasive ownership of nearby properties, see Bright, "How Women's Organizations May Improve Methods of Street Lighting," 893. Deutsch discovered a "shockingly" high level of female property ownership in Boston's Back Bay. "Reconceiving the City," 207. Women's role as urban property owners is a rich topic deserving of systematic study.

61. On women's clubs working toward their own dissolution, Scott, *Natural Allies,* 152. Quote from Albert W. Atwood, "The Soul of a City," 2, reprinted from the *Saturday Evening Post,* 1928, no. 1235.3, JNPC.

62. English, "The Function of Business Bodies in Improving Civic Conditions," preface; Kenneth Sturges, *American Chambers of Commerce* (New York: Moffat, Bard, and Co.,

1915), xii, 64–65; J. Horace McFarland and Richard B. Watrous, introduction to Guild, "Commercial Organizations and Civic Affairs."

63. Woodruff, "Woman and Her Larger Home," 3. The allusions to "fad" and "sentiment" were likely veiled jabs at City Beautiful as practiced by women.

64. Sturges, *American Chambers of Commerce*, 234, 216; "The 'Commercializing' of Civic Movements," *American City*, April 1914, 321. Once they jumped into civic work, commercial groups claimed to do it better than anyone else. See such assertions in Clinton Rogers Woodruff, "How to Promote the Efficiency of Commercial Organizations," ibid., August 1914, 135; and George B. Ford, "Chambers of Commerce and City Planning," ibid., May 1914, 449.

65. On women's options in planning work in the 1920s, see Birch, "From Civic Worker to City Planner." A Miss Leonard worked for John Nolen in 1911, traveling to Lock Haven to collect data and making a good impression on the community. See April and May 1911 correspondence, box 28, file Lock Haven 1, JNP. A 1923–24 GFWC brochure stated that "in the past" women's clubs had seen city planning and housekeeping as "women's work" and that they should get back to that agenda. This captures the reduced agitation by women in these fields, even while their interest continued. "General Federation of Women's Clubs, 1923–4," box 69, file GFWC, JNP.

66. Francis Jones to Nolen, August 12, 1931, box 59, file Hartford and West Hartford, JNP; Hester Scott Jaeger to Nolen, May 4, 1929, box 35, file San Diego, JNP.

Eugenie Birch examines how the professionalization of planning reshaped the national organizations devoted to civic improvement. By 1917 the movement had two wings — one open to citizen participants (the American Civic Association and the National Conference on City Planning) and one open only to professionals (the American City Planning Institute, which had formed that year). Though effectively excluded from the latter, women continued to participate in the former. Birch, "From Civic Worker to City Planner," 479. For an account of the older improvement groups — the American League for Civic Improvement and the American Park and Outdoor Art Association — which merged in 1904 to create the American Civic Association, see Wilson, *The City Beautiful Movement*, 35–52.

67. "To Combine Beauty with Utility, Aim of City Planners," *Bridgeport (Conn.) Telegram*, May 30, 1914, box 22, file 15, JNP. On pink ribbon replacing blue or lavender as the popular lingerie trim, see "Pink a Popular Color," *New York Times*, July 23, 1911, X7.

68. Historians have identified the fears an entire generation felt about the feminization of American society during the Progressive era and the World War I years. See Arnaldo Testi, "The Gender of Reform Politics: Theodore Roosevelt and the Culture of Masculinity," *Journal of American History* 81 (March 1995): 1509–33. Testi considers how reform, which was seen as a women's activity, needed to be made acceptable for men. Paula Baker, in a pathbreaking article, argued that in the explosion of government programs during the Progressive era, the public sector assumed responsibility in realms considered to be women's work. Paula Baker, "The Domestication of Politics: Women and American Political Society, 1780–1920," *American Historical Review* 89, no. 3 (1984): 620–47.

69. "The Removal of Overhead Wires: They Are Dangerous and Unsightly," American Civic Association, Department of City Making, 1907, 15, no. 2922.1, JNPC. John Nolen, "The Place of the Beautiful in the City Plan: Some Everyday Examples," National Confer-

ence on City Planning, 1922, 6–7, no. 320.7, JNPC. Nolen argued here that so-called practical men showed in their daily spending choices that they cared about the "beautiful."

70. Atwood, "The Soul of a City." On cosmetics, gender, and business at the turn of the century, see Kathy Peiss, *Hope in a Jar: The Making of America's Beauty Culture* (New York: Henry Holt, 1998).

71. Leo J. Buettner, *Making the City Plan Effective*, no. 210, American City Pamphlets, from a paper read before the American Civic Association, November 14, 1921, JNPC.

72. Atwood, "The Soul of a City," 2. On rosettes, see Jonathan Farnham, "A Bridge Game: Constructing a Co-operative Commonwealth in Philadelphia, 1900–1926" (Ph.D. diss., Princeton University, 2000).

73. Nolen, "The Place of the Beautiful in the City Plan," 6, 13. In this speech Nolen also offered an extended defense against the "pink bows on lamp posts" critique, which he argued had nothing to do with the notion of the beautiful in city planning.

74. The pink-ribbons-and-bows phrases appeared in print many times. See also "A Union of Forces for the City's Good." In an excellent chapter on critics of the City Beautiful movement, William Wilson chose a pink-bows quote but did not relate its gendered context. Wilson, *The City Beautiful Movement*, 288.

75. "City Planners Are Encouraged," *St. Paul Pioneer Press*, April 11, 1911, box 34, file Saint Paul Clippings, JNP.

76. Roanoke, Virginia, provides a case study of the impact earlier women's club initiatives had on local planning, since the women's Civic Betterment Club sponsored a plan in 1907, and twenty years later the city commissioned another plan, both from John Nolen. See box 33, files Roanoke, JNP. See Kevan Frazier, "Taking Matters into Their Own Hands: The Woman's Civic Betterment Club and the Introduction of Professional City Planning to Roanoke, Virginia," paper presented at the Society for American City and Regional Planning History conference, Washington, DC, November 18–21, 1999.

77. H. A. Overstreet, "Arousing the Public Interest in City Planning," paper presented at the National Conference on City Planning, Dallas Texas, 6, box 35, file 5, Russell Van Nest Black Papers, collection no. 3018, Division of Rare and Manuscript Collections, Cornell University Library (also published in *American City*, June 1928). John E. Surratt, *Information Bulletin: For Success in City Building* (Dallas, Texas: n.d.), 34, no. 6827 Dallas 9, JNPC.

78. Atwood, "The Soul of a City," 2.

CHAPTER 2

1. Walker Evans, "Main Street Looking North from Courthouse Square: A Portfolio of American Picture Postcards from the Trolley-Car Period," *Fortune*, May 1948, 102. James C. Curtis, *Mind's Eye, Mind's Truth: FSA Photography Reconsidered* (Philadelphia: Temple University Press, 1989); and Alan Trachtenberg, *Reading American Photographs: Images as History, Matthew Brady to Walker Evans* (New York: Hill and Wang, 1989), 231–85, examine Evans's own art, as well as his views on others' "photographic editing of society" (Evans's phrase, quoted in Trachtenberg, *Reading American Photographs*, 287).

2. Evans, "Main Street Looking North from Courthouse Square," 102.

3. Scholars have begun to grant postcards legitimacy as historical documents, first becoming interested in the earliest, more "photographic" cards with fewer alterations. Skepticism about postcards arises partly from a preoccupation with their photographic hon-

esty (their less reliable photographic information). Typically, scholars have seen the cards as "part historic document, part artistic license" or more simply as fantasy. Kim Keister, "Wish You Were Here! The Curt Teich Postcard Archives Depict Americans As They Saw Themselves through the First Seven Decades of the Twentieth Century," *Historic Preservation* 44 (1992): 54. See also Hilary Renwick and Susan Cutter, "Map Postcards and Images of Place," *Landscape* 27, no. 1 (1983): 30.

Discarding the belief that postcards are inadequate photographic records, this chapter suggests ways of contextualizing the cards within the conventions of their own genre. The alterations are thus subject to analysis, instead of being seen as inaccuracies. Steven Dotterrer and Galen Cranz compare early postcards to other media of their day such as published photographs, stereo cards, and newspaper sketches. "The Picture Postcard: Its Development and Role in American Urbanization," *Journal of American Culture* 5, no. 1 (spring 1982): 46.

A rare analysis of postcard alterations is John W. Ripley, "The Art of Postcard Fakery," *Kansas Historical Quarterly* 38 (summer 1972): 129–31. The cut-and-paste tall-tale postcards of about 1910 — featuring imaginary animals, children eating six-foot watermelons, and other giant produce — have received attention. Cynthia Rubin, *Larger Than Life: The American Tall-Tale Postcard, 1905–1915* (New York: Abbeville Press, 1990); Hal Morgan, *Big Time: American Tall-Tale Postcards* (New York: St. Martin's Press, 1981).

4. Postcards remained popular throughout the twentieth century but achieved "fad" status between 1901 and 1915. For most of these years, almost 1 billion postcards were sold annually. The postcard entered the American mail system by the 1880s, but until the U.S. Postal Act of 1898 established a special one-cent rate, they remained an oddity. The first American commercial postcards were souvenirs from the Chicago World's Fair of 1893. German printing houses initially dominated the field, with American clients sending negatives abroad. World War I curtailed patronage of German plants, allowing American firms to compete. Brooke Baldwin, "On the Verso: Postcard Messages as a Key to Popular Prejudices," *Journal of Popular Culture* 22 (1988): 15; Kelly Henderson, "The Art of the View: Picture Postcards of Virginia, 1900–1925," *Virginia Cavalcade* 40 (1990): 66. On alleged lower quality after 1918 because of new manufacturing techniques, see John M. Kaduck, *Mail Memories: Pictorial Guide to Postcard Collecting* (Des Moines, IA: Wallace-Homestead, 1975), 6. See also George and Dorothy Miller, *Picture Postcards in the United States, 1893–1918* (New York: Clarkson N. Potter, 1976), 32, 149.

5. Charles Mulford Robinson, *A City Plan for Raleigh* (Raleigh, NC: Woman's Club of Raleigh, 1913), 25. Postcard located in box 19, file Raleigh, Charles Mulford Robinson Collection, Frances Loeb Library, Graduate School of Design, Harvard University (hereafter cited as CMRC).

6. Postcard companies also at times bought out the inventories of local photographers. Postcards facilitated the creation of "a network of nationally shared images," specifically "a national *urban* culture," according to Dotterrer and Cranz, "The Picture Postcard," 49.

7. Lithographer Curt Teich founded a general printing firm in 1898, three years after immigrating to the United States from Germany. He caught on to the postcard craze in 1905, getting his start with the local view cards. After the 1909 tariff act taxed German cards, Teich sold 150 million postcards a year for the next three years, rising to an estimated 250 million annually. The firm emphasized competitive images at lower prices, relying upon quantity production for its profit margin. In the 1930s and 1940s, Teich

produced a significant percentage of that period's linen-stock cards. The firm closed in the 1970s, possibly because it was slow to convert to chrome prints based on color negatives.

The local souvenir view cards — images of everyday cityscapes and vacation destinations — were the backbone of Curt Teich and the postcard industry. Teich calculated its pricing by building in a loss on the card's first run and making a profit on the reprints. The average local view went through eight printings, as compared to the average advertising card, which had only one or two. More than ten thousand towns and cities appeared in Curt Teich postcards. Of the company's 380,000 total production, about 6 percent are classified as street views. Henderson, "The Art of the View," 66–70; Miller, *Picture Postcards in the United States*, 164; Keister, "Wish You Were Here," 54, 57, 60. A 1941 "House Telegram" in one Curt Teich client file suggests that there was a Local View Sales Division, but it is not clear whether the company artists developed specialties, such as Main Streets. "Main Street in Buffalo" (Otto Ulbrich Co., Buffalo, NY, 1941), Curt Teich Postcard Archives, no. 1BH2143 (see note 8).

8. This extraordinary collection, the Curt Teich Postcard Archives, is held at the Lake County Discovery Museum in Wauconda, Illinois. The client files, which usually contain the original photographs and the specific requests guiding their artistic transformation into postcards, are available beginning in 1926. Details of the production process, such as how many hours were spent on retouching each photo, are recorded on the outside of the envelope. The smallest common order was 1,000 cards, whereas the biggest cities and distributors requested 25,000 copies, and there was a rare order for 50,000 (a Times Square scene, for example). In the 1930s and 1940s, a popular order size for a local Woolworth was 3,500 cards, while news agencies gravitated toward 12,500 orders. A rush request might be completed in a week, but a three-to-four-week turnaround was more typical.

Client directions were conveyed in several forms. Often they were typed up and included on the large file label. In these cases it appears that a Curt Teich employee processed the requests and paraphrased them based on verbal instructions given in the field to the Curt Teich salesman at the time the order was placed, or possibly they were written down during phone orders. Many clients included their own handwritten or typed instructions with their order. The client usually had the option of reviewing a proof and making suggestions at that point. To the best of my knowledge, the details of this production process, from order through artwork and printing, have not been examined for Curt Teich postcards or any other company. When quoting from client requests typed onto the file labels, I converted the often all-uppercase lettering into upper and lower case for ease of reading.

Curt Teich's geographic index, organized by state and then city, is also a useful source — it recorded who ordered how many copies of which views.

9. One 1927 publication listed 201 comprehensive plans made between 1905 and 1926, with 87 of those issued between 1920 and 1926. Norman Johnston, "Harland Bartholomew: His Comprehensive Plans and Science of Planning" (Ph.D. diss., University of Pennsylvania, 1964), 8.

10. William H. Wilson, *The City Beautiful Movement* (Baltimore: Johns Hopkins University Press, 1989), 4, 45, 74; Park Dixon Goist, *From Main Street to State Street: Town, City, and Community in America* (Port Washington, NY: Kennikat Press, 1977), 122–27; Jon A. Peterson, "The City Beautiful Movement: Forgotten Origins and Lost Meanings," *Journal of Urban History* 2, no. 4 (August 1976): 426–28. Sherry Piland, "Charles Mulford

Robinson: Theory and Practice in Early Twentieth-Century Urban Planning" (Ph.D. diss., Florida State University, 1997).

11. Nolen specialized in small and medium-sized cities — in the 50,000 to 100,000 population range. Johnston, "Harland Bartholomew," 56. On Nolen as a city practical planner, see Wilson, *The City Beautiful Movement,* 290. John L. Hancock, *John Nolen, Landscape Architect, Town, City, and Regional Planner: A Bibliographical Record of Achievement* (Ithaca, NY: Program in Urban and Regional Studies, Cornell University, 1976). Recent analyses of Nolen include Kevan Frazier, "Big Dreams, Small Cities: John Nolen, the New South, and the City Planning Movement in Asheville, Roanoke, and Johnson City, 1907–1937" (Ph.D. diss., University of Western Virginia, 2000); Thomas W. Hanchett, *Sorting Out the New South City: Race, Class, and Urban Development in Charlotte, 1875–1975* (Chapel Hill: University of North Carolina Press, 1998); R. Bruce Stephenson, *Visions of Eden: Environmentalism, Urban Planning, and City Building in St. Petersburg, Florida, 1900–1995* (Columbus: Ohio State University Press, 1997); Millard Rogers, *John Nolen and Mariemont: Building a New Town in Ohio* (Baltimore: Johns Hopkins University Press, 2001). Cornell University possesses Nolen's business records; less well known is the correspondence with his wife covering decades of extensive professional travel, held in the Nolen Family Papers, Schlesinger Library, Radcliffe College.

12. Wilson, *The City Beautiful Movement,* 75. For example, the majority of contributors to the city planning fund for Hamilton, Ohio, were merchants. Harland Bartholomew, *City Plan of Hamilton, Ohio* (Hamilton, OH: Chamber of Commerce, 1920), 65. For community studies investigating the role of businessmen in Progressive era urban improvement, see Donald Doyle, *New Men, New Cities, New South: Atlanta, Nashville, Charleston, Mobile, 1860–1910* (Chapel Hill: University of North Carolina Press, 1990); John Cumbler, *A Social History of Economic Decline: Business, Politics, and Work in Trenton* (New Brunswick, NJ: Rutgers University Press, 1989); David Hammack, *Power and Society: Greater New York at the Turn of the Century* (New York: Columbia University Press, 1982).

13. William J. Reilly, "Methods for the Study of Retail Relationships," *University of Texas Bulletin,* no. 2944, November 22, 1929, 16, 18. "Giving Commercial Service," *Printer's Ink,* August 29, 1906, 6. In 1915 former newspapermen dominated among chamber of commerce secretaries. Kenneth Sturges, *American Chambers of Commerce* (New York: Moffat, Bard, and Co., 1915), 131.

14. One example of conflict among professionals is Robert Anderson Pope's response to the Bridgeport City Plan Commission, which had solicited Pope's critique of Nolen's work. Pope "heartily opposed" the principles advocated by Nolen and Olmsted: "The fact of the matter is that Landscape Architects are not qualified to deal with City Planning because of their training in this profession." Pope questioned landscape architects' abilities to ascertain the "economic value of the social effort." Pope described himself as a "Landscape and Garden Architect." Pope to E. W. Schrewe, Esq., May 1, 1915, box 22, file 26, John Nolen Papers, collection no. 2903, Division of Rare and Manuscript Collections, Cornell University Library (hereafter cited as JNP).

15. "The Loan and Why," *Reading (Pa.) Herald,* November 11, 1910, box 89, file Reading Newspaper Clippings, JNP. George Gove to Nolen, March 8, 1917; August 17, 1917, box 22, file 22, JNP.

16. Marion Association of Commerce to Nolen, December 19, 1919, box 77, file Marion, Ind., no. 20, JNP.

17. Nolen to Marion Association of Commerce, December 24, 1919; Nolen to Dr. E. O. Harrold, January 15, 1920, box 77, file Marion, Ind., no. 20, JNP. Planners were cautioned not to have real estate interests in cities where they consulted, since it would invalidate their work. George Dudley Seymour, *Our City and Its Big Needs: A Series of Four Articles* (New Haven, CT: Chamber of Commerce, 1912), 5, no. 6827 New Haven 2, John Nolen Pamphlet Collection, collection no. 6337, Division of Rare and Manuscript Collections, Cornell University Library (hereafter cited as JNPC).

18. By July Nolen learned that the Marion job had been awarded to someone else. John Nolen to R. G. Brusch, July 23, 1920, box 77, file Marion, Ind., no. 20, JNP. For a discussion among planners about personal salesmanship versus promotion of planning, see correspondence forwarded between John Nolen, the Olmsted Brothers firm, and Flavel Shurtleff, April 12, 1930, box 71, file Binghamton, JNP.

19. On the negative impact of a new mayor on planning in Flint, Michigan, see Irving Root to Nolen, May 8, 1922, box 89, file Flint 4, JNP; on debate in Bridgeport, Connecticut, where the business district was a priority, see City Plan Commission to Nolen, March 3, 1915, box 22, file 26, JNP; Elkhart quotation in Carl Greanleaf to Nolen, November 3, 1924, box 25, file Elkhart, Ind., 1920–21, JNP; "Study John Nolen's Plan before You Condemn It: Give It a Careful Reading, Then Read It Again," *Reading (Pa.) Herald*, March 7, 1910, box 89, file Reading clippings, JNP; on the blurring of lines between commercial men and public officials, John M. Guild, *Commercial Organizations and Civic Affairs* (Washington, DC: American Civic Association, 1915), 2, box 17, file Dayton, Ohio, CMRC; Charlotte Parsons, "La Crosse, Wisconsin, January 1919–December 1919," in *Summaries of Selected Projects* (1937–38), 3, box 1, JNP.

20. The postcard examples cited in this chapter extend from the 1910s through the mid-1950s, because the basic approach of artistically improving the cards according to the Main Street beautification ideal persisted during these decades and was only abandoned in the 1950s (at the same time the Main Street ideal was set aside for urban renewal). The touch-up techniques evolved over time in ways noted in this chapter. The linen cards, produced 1930–59, mark the single greatest change in that they invited more dramatic alterations. Linen cards are identified by an *H* in the production code. Although there is much to analyze in the earliest cards, the existence of the client files beginning in 1926 added invaluable evidence. For a detailed analysis of postcards from the earlier decades, see Alison Isenberg, "Downtown Democracy" (Ph.D. diss., University of Pennsylvania, 1995), 112–208.

A rough analysis of computerized postcard records confirms that Main Street views were most popular among Curt Teich clients in the first three decades of the twentieth century. Although an annual breakdown was not possible, the average for 1900–1930 was about 440 Main Street orders yearly. This dropped in the early 1930s below 100, then settled between 100 and 170 until the late 1950s; after that it stayed below 100. Christine Pyle, "Street Scenes from the Curt Teich Postcard Archives"; and Christine Pyle to Alison Isenberg, May 28, 1996, both in author's possession.

21. "Center Avenue, Looking East, Moorhead, Minn." (1928), no. 119615. All postcard citations in this chapter refer to Curt Teich postcards. Additional information on each card was drawn from the geographic index located in the Curt Teich Postcard Archives and the client files (for most cards dated 1926 and after). Wherever possible, I have included in parentheses the year of production and the postcard sponsor. In the few cases

in which sponsor information from the geographic index, the client files, and the postcard differed, I included the multiple sponsors. The code found in each citation is the card's Curt Teich production number.

22. Charles Mulford Robinson, *The Wellbeing of Waterloo: A Report to the Civic Society of Waterloo, Iowa* (Waterloo, IA: Matt Parson and Sons Co., 1910), n.p.; see also John Nolen, *The City Plan of Flint, Michigan* (Flint, MI: City Planning Board, 1920), 7; Robinson, *A City Plan for Raleigh,* 32–33; and Charles Mulford Robinson, *Modern Civic Art; or, The City Made Beautiful,* 4th ed. (New York: Arno Press, 1970), 139. Charles Mulford Robinson, *Better Binghamton: A Report to the Mercantile-Press Club of Binghamton, N.Y.* (Cleveland: J. B. Savage Co., 1911), 33.

23. Robinson, *Better Binghamton,* 45; for illustrated examples, see John Nolen, *Greater Erie: Plans and Reports for the Extension and Improvement for the City* (Erie, PA: Press of Ashby Printing Co., 1913), 65; and Cass Gilbert and Frederick Law Olmsted, *Report of the New Haven Civic Improvement Commission* (New Haven, CT: New Haven Civic Improvement Commission, 1910), 19; Charles Mulford Robinson, *The Beautifying of San Jose: A Report to the Outdoor Art League* (San Jose, CA, 1909), 14; John Nolen, *Planning a City for the People: Report for the City of Schenectady (New York) to the Board of Parks and City Planning* (Cambridge, MA: Published by the author, 1913), 17; John Nolen, *Replanning Reading: An Industrial City of a Hundred Thousand* (Boston: George H. Ellis Co. Printers, 1910), 11; Charles Mulford Robinson, *Report of Sacramento, California* (Sacramento, CA: Sacramento Chamber of Commerce, 1908), 35; John Nolen, *A New Plan for Lock Haven: Report to the Board of Trade and the Civic Club* (Cambridge, MA: Published by the author, 1912), 8.

24. Charles Mulford Robinson, *Report on the Improvement of the City of Ogdensburg, New York* (Ogdensburg, NY: N.p., 1907), 4; "Will Hear No Song of Wires," *Rochester (N.Y.) Post Express,* March 21, 1908, box 21, file Wires, CMRC; Frederick L. Ford, *The Removal of Overhead Wires: They Are Dangerous and Unsightly* (N.p.: American Civic Association, Department of City Making, Leaflet no. 13, 1907), 5, no. 2922.1, JNPC. The German-born planner is E. E. Schrewe, quoted in "To Combine Beauty and Utility, Aim of City Planners," *Bridgeport (Conn.) Telegram,* May 30, 1914, box 22, file 15, JNP. On the destruction of real estate values, see "Parks and the City Plan," *Madison (Wis.) Democrat,* April 26, 1910, box 90, file Lecture Clippings, JNP.

25. Quotation from Ford, "The Removal of Overhead Wires," 3, 7. A Columbia, South Carolina, plan noted that recently "a maze of overhead wires" and "a forest of bare poles" were exciting signs of prosperity. Kelsey and Guild, *The Improvement of Columbia South Carolina: Report to the Civic League, Columbia South Carolina* (Harrisburg, PA: Mount Pleasant Press, 1905), 35.

It is significant that Charles Mulford Robinson's hometown of Rochester, New York, claimed to have pioneered the burying of wires in conduits beginning in 1892, using ferrets to run the wires. "Many Miles of Wire in Ground," *Rochester (N.Y.) Democrat,* January 13, 1910, box 21, file Wires, CMRC.

26. Sample requests in 1950s client files: "13th Street, Looking North, Lincoln, Nebraska" (Lincoln News Agency, Lincoln, Neb., 1952), no. 2CH1677; "Market Avenue Looking North, Canton, Ohio" (Ralph Young, Canton, Ohio, 1953), no. 3CH95.

27. "Tijuana, Mexico" (1954), no. 4CH712. Smaller towns in budget series: "Main Street, Looking North, Baxley, Ga." (Barnes Drug Store, Baxley, GA, 1929), no. 5522-29;

"Main Street, Abita Springs, La." (Carey's Drug Store, Abita Springs, LA, 1929), no. 5894-29; "Haywood Road, West Asheville, N.C." (Asheville Post Card Co., Asheville, NC, 1929), no. 5808-29. An examination of early Main Street cards often reveals wire traces against the buildings, where they were more difficult to remove, as well as trolley rods without connecting wires. Contemporary photographs were retouched with the same techniques. See illustrations in Cynthia Read-Miller, *Main Street, U.S.A. in Early Photographs: 113 Detroit Publishing Co. Views* (New York: Dover, 1988).

28. "Howard Street, Hibbing, Minn." (*Hibbing (Minn.) Daily Tribune*, 1937), no. 7AH3541. See also "Commercial Street, Astoria, Oregon, Junction Old Oregon Trail and Oregon Coast Highway" (1938), no. 8AH3212. Robinson, *A City Plan for Raleigh*, 35. See also Robinson, *Report on the Improvement of the City of Ogdensburg, New York*, 4.

29. Evans, "Main Street Looking North from Courthouse Square," 102; for smooth paving quote, see "View of Main Street [Lancaster, Ohio]," (Welsh News, 1942), no. 2BH1177. See also "Main Street Looking East at Night, Painesville, Ohio" (C. L. Carle, Ashtabula, OH, 1942), no. 4BH1421; "Third Street Looking West, Jamestown, N.Y." (Weakley-Olson, Jamestown, NY, 1939), no. 9AH1881; "Main Street Looking West, Norristown, Pa." (Lynn H. Boyer Jr., Wildwood, NJ, 1941), no. 1BH2221; "North Park Street Looking South, Warren, Ohio" (Mahoning Valley Dist. Agency, Youngstown, OH, 1941), no. 1BH1741.

30. *Improvement of the City of Detroit: Reports Made by Professor Frederick Law Olmsted, Junior, and Mr. Charles Mulford Robinson to the Detroit Board of Commerce* (Detroit: Detroit Board of Commerce, 1905), 63; *Fayetteville's Opportunities: Report of Charles Mulford Robinson to the Fayetteville Park Commission* (June 4, 1909), n.p., NAC 6827, Fay 1909, Frances Loeb Library, Graduate School of Design, Harvard University.

31. For a discussion of smooth streets by downtown housekeepers, see Susie Brochelle Wright, "Improvement of a Georgia Town," in *Village Improvement*, by Jessie M. Good, n.d., box 20, file [Village Improvement], CMRC. The rate at which cities chose smooth pavement, and their options at the turn of the century, are analyzed by Clay McShane, *Down the Asphalt Path* (New York: Columbia University Press, 1994), 59–62.

32. John Williams Reps, *Bird's Eye Views: Historic Lithographs of North American Cities* (New York: Princeton Architectural Press, 1998); Spiro Kostof, *The City Shaped: Urban Patterns and Meanings throughout History* (Boston: Little, Brown, 1991).

33. *Fayetteville's Opportunities*; Charles Mulford Robinson, *A Plan of Civic Improvement for the City of Oakland, California* (Oakland, CA: Oakland Enquirer Publishing Co., 1906), 19. See also Robinson, *The Beautifying of San Jose*, 14.

34. On the harmonious vista, see Robinson, *A City Plan for Raleigh*, 98; and Nolen, *A New Plan for Lock Haven*, 8. On uneven building line, Gilbert and Olmsted, *Report of the New Haven Civic Improvement Commission*, 26–27; on the relation of tall buildings to narrow streets and the canyon effect, Nolen, *Replanning Reading*, 11; Charles Mulford Robinson, *The Improvement of Fort Wayne, Indiana* (Fort Wayne, IN: Press of Fort Wayne Printing Co., 1909), 33–34; Robinson, *Modern Civic Art*, 124; on skyscrapers and height limits, Robinson, *A City Plan for Raleigh*, 35. For an 1890s example of a women's club's interest in harmonious vistas and the proportions of building height to street width, see "Prize Competition Instituted by the Woman's Union of Rochester, New York" (May 1896), box 16, file Buildings, CMRC.

35. "Main Street at Night, Burlington, N.C." (F. W. Woolworth, 1940), no. 0B209.

Instructions to the artists often specified the illumination of streetlights and windows —
a practice "left up to art department for a good effect" — as well as moonlight treatment.
Most night scenes were converted from daytime photographs. "Canal Street by Night,
New Orleans, La." (A. Hirschwitz, New Orleans, LA, 1941), no. 1BH1197; "Market Avenue
Shopping Center, at Night, Canton, Ohio," (Ralph Young Publishing Co., Canton, OH,
1941), no. 1BH1852; "East Broadway by Night, Ybor City, Fla." (Hillsboro News Co.,
Tampa, FL, 1939), no. 9AH119; "Main Street at Night, Greenville, S.C." (Asheville Post
Card Co., Asheville, NC, 1929), no. 5910-29; "Curtis Street at Night, Denver, Colo." (San-
born Souvenir Co., Denver, CO, 1929), no. A-5663-29.

36. "Dwellings and Business Blocks," in *Let Us Make a Beautiful City of Springfield,
Massachusetts: A Series of Sixteen Articles Reprinted from the Springfield Republican with Il-
lustrations* (Springfield, MA: Republican Co., 1901), 49, box 20, file [Springfield], CMRC.
Another contemporary recommended the "judicious use of color" to enliven business
streets. George Kriehn, "The City Beautiful," *Municipal Affairs* 3 (1899): 595, as quoted in
Peterson, "The City Beautiful Movement," 420.

37. For a slate sample mailed to Curt Teich, "United States Post Office, Saginaw, Mich."
(Reid Paper Co., Saginaw, MI, 1937), no. 7AH3132. "Maine Street, Quincy, Illinois" (1940),
no. 0B373-N. See also "Queen Street, Looking North, Kinston, N.C." (North Carolina
News Co., Durham, NC, 1940), no. 0B508.

38. "Looking East on Gurley Street, Prescott, Arizona" (Lollesgard Specialty Co., Tucson and Phoenix, AZ, 1942), no. 2BH1506; "Looking East from Union Depot, along 25th
Street, Ogden, Utah" (Deseret Book Co., Salt Lake City, UT, 1938), no. 8AH2734; "Main
Street, Salt Lake City, Utah" (Deseret Book Co., Salt Lake City, UT, 1938), no. 8AH2740;
and "Looking East on Congress Street, Tucson, Arizona" (Lollesgard Specialty Co., Tucson and Phoenix, AZ, 1951), no. 1CH1090. On referencing an old postcard, "Sears, Roebuck and Company's New Super Store, Baltimore, Maryland" (I. and M. Ottenheimer,
Baltimore, MD, 1941), no. 1BH1525. See also "Street Scene on Malvern Avenue, Showing
Pythian and Baptist Hospitals and Baths, Hot Springs National Park, Arkansas" (Wood-
cock Mfg. Co., Hot Springs National Park, AR, 1951), no. 1CH1366; "Canal Street, New
Orleans, La." (1941), no. 1BH1666. Sometimes the colors were described by a Curt Teich
salesman in the field rather than the client.

An excerpt from a five-paragraph color correction shows how precise clients could be:

The porte cochere beyond is a Richfield Oil station which is always YELLOW with blue
lettering. Beyond that you show a tan building. This should be GREY with brown trim.
The hotel MAGMA is red brick, not brown; and the building of same size beyond is all
cream color with a little red tile trim. You show the front of this brown same as hotel.
Make it cream.

Here the street pavement is *not asphalt* but is light concrete color; and the white
spot you have at far end of street is tan or dust, or gravel road starting up toward the
water tank. Use your reading glass and you will see you have painted over a little grey
house up the hillside; and just to left and below it under a tree is a rust-brown cottage.
"Main Street, Looking toward Apache Leap, Superior, Arizona" (Lollesgard Specialty
Co., Tucson and Phoenix, AZ, 1942), no. 2BH1500

39. "Main Street Looking West, Johnson City, N.Y." (Walter R. Miller Co., Bingham-

ton, NY, 1939), no. 9AH2289. See also "Times Square at Night, New York City" (Frank E. Cooper, New York, NY, 1938), no. 8AH2794.

40. "Looking up Western Avenue, Muskegon, Michigan" (F. W. Woolworth, 1941), no. 1BH2329.

41. Robinson, *The Improvement of Fort Wayne, Indiana*, 16. Nolen, *Replanning Reading*, offers an example where consultants thought it too expensive to widen the street and emphasized clearing the sidewalks instead. Other traffic remedies included widening parallel streets to relieve the main thoroughfare and cut-throughs to alter inconvenient traffic patterns. The 1913 Chicago photos are located in the file Sidewalks, box 19, CMRC.

42. Robinson, *Modern Civic Art*, 165; Robinson, *The Wellbeing of Waterloo*; Robinson, *A City Plan for Raleigh*, 26; Robinson, *The Improvement of Fort Wayne, Indiana*, 18; Chamber of Commerce, Elkhart, Indiana, "Planning Survey," October 1920, 17, box 25, Elkhart, IN, file 1920–21, JNP; Robinson, *The Beautifying of San Jose*, 16.

43. "Looking up Western Avenue, Muskegon, Michigan," no. 1BH2329. See also "Main Street at Night, Looking South, Sumter, S.C." (Asheville Postcard Co., Asheville, NC, 1938), no. 8AH3175.

44. "Third Street Looking East, [Grand Island, Nebraska]" (Kaufmann's, 1942), no. 2BH1139; "Main Street in Buffalo," no. 1BH2143; "Street Scene on Malvern Avenue, Showing Pythian and Baptist Hospitals and Baths, Hot Springs National Park, Arkansas," no. 1CH1366; "Main Street Looking West, Johnson City, N.Y.," no. 9AH2289. Other examples: "Sears, Roebuck and Company's New Super Store, Baltimore, Maryland," no. 1BH1525; and "Washington Street South from Market Street, Tiffin, Ohio" (F. W. Woolworth, 1933), no. 3A219.

45. "Essex Street, Main Business Section, Lawrence, Mass." (Louis Pearl, Lawrence, MA, 1945), no. 5BH955.

46. Other Woolworth examples: "Chestnut Street Looking North, Atlantic, Iowa" (F. W. Woolworth, 1931), no. 1A1922; "Main Street, Oneonta, N.Y." (F. W. Woolworth, 1952), no. 2CH1551; "Walnut Street, Looking East, Murphysboro, Illinois" (F. W. Woolworth, 1935), no. 5A222-N; "Ocoee Street, Looking South, Cleveland, Tenn." (F. W. Woolworth, 1936), no. 6AH2328; "Main Street Looking South, Rockland, Maine" (F. W. Woolworth, 1940), no. 0B670; "View of Fayetteville Street Looking toward Capitol, Raleigh, N.C." (F. W. Woolworth, 1914), no. A49455; "West Dominick Street from James Street, by Night, Rome, N.Y." (Wm Jubb Co., Syracuse, NY, and F. W. Woolworth, 1915), no. A55414; "Washington Avenue, El Dorado, Ark." (F. W. Woolworth, 1935), no. 5A172-N; "Bird's-Eye View, Columbus, Neb." (F. W. Woolworth, 1933), no. 3A302-N; "Main Street at Night, Burlington, N.C." (F. W. Woolworth, 1940), no. 0B209; "Box Butte Avenue, Alliance, Neb." (F. W. Woolworth, and Kent News Agency, Scottsbluff, NE, 1940), no. 0B349-N; "Main Street, Looking North, Miami, Okla." (F. W. Woolworth, 1940), no. 0B487-N.

Examples of other chains and independents sponsoring cards in which their branch is virtually invisible: "Central Avenue Looking West, Middletown, Ohio" (G. C. Murphy, 1935), no. 5A484-N; "Exchange Place, Waterbury, Conn." (F W Grand Stores and Harold Hahn Co., Inc., New Haven, CT, 1940), no. 0B830-N; "Main Street, Trenton, Missouri" (S. H. Kress and Co., 1941), no. 1B161; "Clinton Street Looking North, Defiance, Ohio" (Beatty Stationery Store, 1935), no. 5A391; "Garrison Avenue from 9th Street, Looking West, Fort Smith, Ark." (McCrory and S & S News, Fort Smith, AR, 1934), no. 4A652.

47. "Montgomery Ward & Co. Retail Store — Central Ave. — St. Petersburg, FLA."

(Montgomery Ward & Co., Saint Petersburg, FL, 1936), no. 6AH2538. Figs. 2.10 and 2.11: "S. H. Kress and Co. [Austin, TX]" (Austin News Agency, 1940), no. 0BH1029.

48. "Maine Street, Looking North, Brunswick, Maine" (F. W. Woolworth, 1940), no. 0B658. On the preference in this era for indirect advertising — selling an idea rather than a product, see William Leach, *Land of Desire: Merchants, Power, and the Rise of a New American Culture* (New York: Pantheon Books, 1993), 54.

49. "Co-operation" (Durham, NC, Chamber of Commerce, 1911), box 24, file Durham, NC, JNP; Cuthbert E. Reeves, *The Valuation of Business Lots in Downtown Los Angeles* (Los Angeles: Los Angeles Bureau of Municipal Research, 1931), 31.

50. "Window-Boxes in Business Section," *American City,* September 1914, 223.

51. "Main Shopping District, Miami, Fla." (Dade County Newsdealers Supply Co., 1941), no. 1BH888; "Congress Square, Portland, Maine" (Portland News Co., Portland, ME, 1941), no. 1BH2581; "Front Street, Looking North, Wilmington, N.C." (Service News Co., Wilmington, NC, 1941), no. 1BH1659.

52. "Looking East on Gurley Street, Prescott, Arizona," no. 2BH1506.

53. "Third Street Looking West, Jamestown, N.Y.," no. 9AH1881; "Parker Street Looking East, Gardner, Mass." (C. W. Hughes & Co., Inc., Mechanicville, NY, 1938), no. 8AH2410. Similar points are found in "Night View of Market Street, Harrisburg, Pa." (J. B. Hoffman, Harrisburg, PA, 1941), no. 1BH2490; "East Main Street, Galesburg, Ill." (Illinois Camera Shop, Galesburg, IL, 1940), no. 0BH765.

54. Examples of red impression technique include "Front Street, Looking North from F. W. Woolworth Co. Store, Wilmington, N.C." (1931), no. 1A1612; "Superior and Adams, Toledo, Ohio" (Buckeye News Co., Toledo, OH, 1938), no. 8AH2523. On making a sign illegible, "Essex Street, Main Business Section, Lawrence, Mass.," no. 5BH955. See also "Gay Street, Looking North, Knoxville, Tenn." (Standard News Agency, Knoxville, TN, 1939), no. 9AH2116.

55. "Dexter Avenue, Looking East, Showing State Capitol, Montgomery, Ala." (Ehler's News Co., Birmingham, AL, 1937), no. 7AH3251. The photograph was the client's property.

56. "The Social Settler," *Transcript,* May 8, 1907, no. 3880.11, JNPC.

57. "A Real Campaign of Civic Education," *Providence (R.I.) Journal,* December 9, 1906, box 19, file Providence, RI, CMRC.

58. Robinson, *A City Plan for Raleigh,* 32; *Improvement of the City of Detroit,* 45. The Montgomery card offers an example of how an avenue with a major traffic circle at one end was framed as a linear corridor.

59. National Committee for Restriction of Outdoor Advertising, *What Attracts the Tourist to Your Town?* n.p., no. 3880.2, JNPC; see also Robinson, *A Plan of Civic Improvement for the City of Oakland, California,* 20, for the ugly-beautiful choice.

60. "Huron Avenue Looking South, Port Huron, Mich." (Port Huron News Co., Port Huron, MI, 1941), no. 1BH1023; "S. H. Kress & Co. [Austin, TX]" (Austin News Agency, 1940), no. 0BH1029. See also "Central Avenue Looking South, Dunkirk, N.Y." (McClenathan Printery, Inc., Dunkirk, NY, 1940), no. 0BH935; "Saginaw Street Looking North, Flint, Michigan" (Lovegrove's Wholesale, Inc., 1953), no. 3CH1392; and "Street Scene on Malvern Avenue, Showing Pythian and Baptist Hospitals and Baths, Hot Springs National Park, Arkansas," no. 1CH1366.

61. John Nolen, *Remodeling Roanoke: Report to the Committee on Civic Improvement* (Roanoke, VA: Stone Printing and Manufacturing Co., 1907), 10; Gilbert and Olmsted,

Report of the New Haven Civic Improvement Commission, 21; box 22, Bridgeport files 15 and 20, JNP.

62. Nolen, *Replanning Reading,* 10; Robinson, *Better Binghamton,* 33, 52; Nolen, *San Diego,* 61–62; Robinson, *The Improvement of Fort Wayne, Indiana,* 33–34; Robinson, *Modern Civic Art,* 102, 118–19; Scott L. Bottles, *Los Angeles and the Automobile: The Making of the Modern City* (Berkeley: University of California Press, 1987), 52–91.

63. "Queen Street, Looking North, Kinston, N.C.," no. 0B508; "Ocoee Street, Looking South, Cleveland, Tenn.," no. 6AH2328. See also "Night View of Market Street, Harrisburg, Pa.," no. 1BH2490; "West Side of Public Square, Newark, Ohio" (Welsh News Agency, Mansfield, OH, 1940), no. 0B178; "Broad Street, Looking North, Selma, Ala." (Selma Stationery Co., Distributors, Selma, AL, 1940), no. 0B713; and "Main Street at Night, Burlington, N.C.," no. 0B209.

64. "Broad Street Looking West at Night, Elyria, Ohio" (Lorain Novelty Co., Lorain, OH, 1941), no. 1BH842; and "Queen Street, Looking North, Kinston, N.C.," no. 0B508.

65. "Night View of Jefferson Street, Roanoke, Va." (J. P. Bell Co., Inc., Lynchburg, VA, 1941), no. 1BH798.

66. The Moorhead card shows both the elimination of a truck and repainting of tracks after paving (figs. 2.2, 2.3, pl. 1). For a request to take trucks out, see "Front Street, Looking North, Wilmington, N.C.," no. 1BH1659; for a request to convert trucks into cars, see "Main Street, Looking North, Hendersonville, N.C." (Harry N. Martin, P.O. Box 324, Asheville, NC, 1945), no. 5BH166. For an example of painting in a car, see "Street Scene, Boyne City, Mich." (ca. 1906), no. A521; for a pasted example, see "Main Street Looking West, Mansfield, Ark." (Central Drug Co., Mansfield, AR, 1928), no. A119481.

67. "Third Street Looking West, Jamestown, N.Y.," no. 9AH1881; and "Main Street, Greenville, S.C." (Asheville Postcard Co., Asheville, NC, 1936), no. 6AH2666.

68. "Main Street Looking West, Uniontown, Pa." (I. Robbins & Son, Pittsburgh, PA, 1913), no. A44198; Isenberg, "Downtown Democracy," 158–59.

69. "Looking West on Federal Street, Youngstown, Ohio" (Youngstown News Agency, Youngstown, OH, 1951), no. 1CH1414. Clay McShane has traced the evolution of the street from a pedestrian zone into a traffic way during this era. By 1910 crosswalks had taken firm hold. *Down the Asphalt Path,* 57–80, 187–88. Peter Baldwin has an excellent and detailed analysis of how the uses of urban streets were transformed during these years. Peter Baldwin, *Domesticating the Street: The Reform of Public Space in Hartford, 1850–1930* (Columbus: Ohio State University Press, 1999).

70. "Main Street, Looking East, Rock Hill, S.C." (Rock Hill Newsstand, Rock Hill, SC, 1942), no. 4BH1473. A sample of other pedestrian-thin or -empty cards, some including requests to take out people: "West Side Square, Centerville, Iowa" (1941), no. 1B105; "Broad Street, Looking North, Selma, Ala.," no. 0B713; "Maine Street, Quincy, Illinois," no. 0B373-N; "Main Street, Salamanca, N.Y." (Sloans News Room, Salamanca, NY, 1939), no. 9A778-N; "Clinton Street Looking North, Defiance, Ohio," no. 5A391; "Superior and Adams, Toledo, Ohio," no. 8AH2523.

71. "Maxwell Street, Chicago" (Aero Distribution Co., Inc., Chicago, IL, 1941), no. 1BH1454; and "Main Street, Victoria, Texas" (Gulf Coast News, Victoria, TX, 1941), no. 1BH2002. See also "Fremont Street, Las Vegas, Nevada" (Boulder Dam Service Bureau, Boulder City, NV, 1938), no. 8AH3108; "Pikes Peak, Alt. 14,110 Ft., from Pikes Peak Avenue, Colorado Springs, Colorado" (Sanborn Souvenir Co., Denver, CO, 1952), no. 2CH1503.

72. "Eastern Editor Declares Santa Barbara Initiates New Trend in Civic Beauty and Architecture," reprint from *Santa Barbara Daily News*, no. 6827 SB11, JNPC. National Committee for Restriction of Outdoor Advertising, *What Attracts the Tourist to Your Town?*

73. Robinson, *A City Plan for Raleigh*, 31; John Nolen, *Little Rock Arkansas: Report to Accompany Preliminary Plans*, May 1929, box 39, JNP. See also Robinson, *A Plan of Civic Improvement for the City of Oakland, California*, 17. Another critique targeted "architectural anarchy — superposed signs askew at all sorts of angles, giant effigies of bottles and of bugs that suggest an advertising delirium." "The Social Settler." "Killed! My Best Customer" (ca. 1922–26), box 6, file 4, Alfred Bettman Papers, US-69-1, Archives and Rare Books Department, University of Cincinnati.

74. "Broadway Looking East, Louisville, Ky." (Readmore News Co., Louisville, KY, 1942), no. 2BH930; "Broadway, Newburgh, N.Y." (Ruben Publishing Co., Newburgh, NY, 1941), no. 1BH1669; "Front Street, Looking North, Wilmington, N.C.," no. 1BH1659. The files were filled with requests to eliminate individual signs — either out of competitive sentiments or because a sign obscured something of greater significance, announced a temporary promotion that would outdate the card, promoted a particular product rather than a place of business, or was deemed to be tasteless.

75. "Main Street, Ellsworth, Maine, 'The Friendly City'" (H. C. Stratton Co., 1941), no. 1BH1673.

76. Robinson, *Modern Civic Art*, 132, 157, 152.

77. Robinson, *Better Binghamton*, 33; see also Robinson, *The Improvement of Fort Wayne, Indiana*, 24; Robinson, *A City Plan for Raleigh*, 80; and Nolen, *The City Plan of Flint*, 54.

78. This longer-term view of Progressive era downtown reform suggests that although in the shorter term beautification might have been "co-opted" or "perverted" for economic gain and invoked for the efficient order of, for example, segregation in the 1920s, over the decades the record is more balanced. On the commandeering and perversion of urban environmental reforms, see Baldwin, *Domesticating the Street*, 7–8, 260.

CHAPTER 3

1. Frank Parker Stockbridge, "A Woman Who Spends Over Forty Million Dollars Each Year," *American City*, June 1912, 814–15; A. Lawren Brown, "How to Sell Real Estate to Women," *National Real Estate Journal (NREJ)*, December 22, 1930, 10–11.

"Mrs. Consumer," in the chapter title, is from Christine Frederick, *Selling Mrs. Consumer* (New York: Business Bourse, 1929); "Mrs. Brown America" from "The Negro Woman Goes to Market," *Brown American*, April 1936, 13; and "Mr. Chain Store Man" from George A. Young Jr., "What Chain Stores Want from Real Estate Brokers," *NREJ*, December 9, 1929, 38.

2. "Women Madly Riot at Bargain Sales," *New York Times*, April 25, 1909, 4. Kathleen Donohue argues of these decades that "those who wanted to establish the consumer as an active and pivotal player in the political sphere defined him as male. Those who wanted to establish the consumer as a passive and marginal political identity coded her female." Both sides "assumed that a consumer who was cerebral, rational, and scientific was male." Kathleen G. Donohue, "What Gender Is the Consumer? The Role of Gender Connotations in Defining the Political," *Journal of American Studies* 33 (1999): 20, 41.

3. As quoted in Darlene Clark Hine, ed., *Black Women in America: An Historical Ency-*

clopedia (Brooklyn, NY: Carlson, 1993), 1:584–85. The power of organized consumers was known to Americans in the 1920s. See, for example, Dana Frank, *Purchasing Power: Consumer Organizing, Gender, and the Seattle Labor Movement, 1919–1929* (Cambridge: Cambridge University Press, 1994). In Harlem more radicalized activists found the Housewives' League approach to be steeped in "bourgeois propriety." Winston Charles McDowell, "The Ideology of Black Entrepreneurship and Its Impact on the Development of Black Harlem" (Ph.D. diss., University of Minnesota, 1996), 107–17.

4. Wm. H. Babcock and Sons, "Report on Survey of the City of Flint, Michigan," April 5, 1929, 4, box 3, Henry Andrews Babcock Papers, collection no. 3022, Division of Rare and Manuscript Collections, Cornell University Library (hereafter cited as HABP). Growth-inspired 1920s appraisals have an eerie ring today because of the imminent depression. A 1927 report described Chicago's peak retail district: "We doubt if there is any section anywhere which has a more stabilized value. There is no evidence of which we are aware that would indicate there would be any slackening in retail business in this territory. In fact, the reverse is the case." Wm. H. Babcock and Sons, "Appraisal Report of the Carson Pirie Scott & Company's Men's Building," February 10, 1927, 9, box 4, HABP.

On 1920s growth, see M. Christine Boyer, *Dreaming the Rational City: The Myth of American City Planning* (Cambridge, MA: MIT Press, 1983), 137–99; and James R. Grossman, *Land of Hope: Chicago, Black Southerners, and the Great Migration* (Chicago: University of Chicago Press, 1989), 3–4. Historians have begun to argue that commercial development often led suburban growth or at least was essential to the planning of residential suburbs. Greg Hise, *Magnetic Los Angeles* (Baltimore: Johns Hopkins University Press, 1997); and Richard Longstreth, *The Drive-In, the Supermarket, and the Transformation of Commercial Space in Los Angeles, 1914–1941* (Cambridge, MA: MIT Press, 1999). On the decentralization of retail in the nineteenth century, before the arrival of electric streetcars, let alone automobiles, see Michael P. Conzen and Kathleen Neils Conzen, "Geographical Structure in Nineteenth-Century Urban Retailing: Milwaukee, 1836–90," *Journal of Historical Geography* 5, no. 1 (1979): 55–66. The authors suggest that existing retail dictated the location of mass transit lines, not necessarily the other way around.

5. Richard Longstreth's publications tell an intricate story of experimentation in retail form that makes the inevitable unfolding of shopping malls look like the cliché that it is. In addition to the works cited above, see "The Diffusion of the Community Shopping Center Concept during the Interwar Decades," *Journal of the Society of Architectural Historians* 56, no. 3 (September 1997): 268–93; "The Neighborhood Shopping Center in Washington, D.C., 1930–1941," *Journal of the Society of Architectural Historians* 51 (March 1992): 5–34; *City Center to Regional Mall: Architecture, the Automobile, and Retailing in Los Angeles, 1920–1950* (Cambridge, MA: MIT Press, 1997).

6. In the 1920s experts recast the salesmanship of previous decades as unscientific and intuitive, also describing pre-1920s Main Street investment as simple and certain. "Modern" chain stores promoted such oversimplifications to gain an edge over independent competitors. See J. Freeman Pyle, "The Determination of Location Standards for Retail Concerns," *Harvard Business Review* 4, no. 3 (April 1926): 303; James J. Doran, "Factors Influencing the Purchasing of a Retail Store," *Journal of Retailing*, October 1926, 9; Lew Hahn and Percival White, eds., *The Merchants' Manual* (New York: McGraw-Hill, 1924), vii; John Alford Stevenson, *Problems and Projects in Salesmanship* (New York: Harper and Brothers, 1923), xix.

7. Investors could read about all of these techniques in trade magazines such as the *Journal of Retailing, Printer's Ink,* the *National Real Estate Journal,* and *Women's Wear Daily.*

8. During the 1920s, land values assumed a more prominent role in investing as rising real estate prices affected mortgage lending. When evaluating loan security, lenders (and appraisers) came to rely "almost exclusively" on "the supposed value of the real estate itself." The relationship between projected income and expenses (especially debt service) was de-emphasized, on the assumption that if the loan went bad, the property's value would cover the loss. The presumption of a continued upward trend encouraged this dependency. Frederick M. Babcock, "Response of Mortgage Lender to Cycle," typed manuscript of a talk given to Georgetown University Savings and Loan Forum, December 4, 1964, 2, box 3, Frederick Morrison Babcock Publications, collection no. 4087, Division of Rare and Manuscript Collections, Cornell University Library. John Nolen found that the value gap between business and residential properties was "bridged by exceptionally high residential values and the more isolated lower cost store locations." Nolen, "Report on Civic Survey and Preliminary Plan for Akron Ohio," insert after p. 22 of typed manuscript, 1917, box 18, John Nolen Papers, collection no. 2903, Division of Rare and Manuscript Collections, Cornell University Library (hereafter cited as JNP).

In the late nineteenth century, Henry George propelled land values into public debate by challenging the existing land tax system, which let owners walk away untaxed from the value increases in their unimproved properties.

9. Robert Haig, "Toward an Understanding of the Metropolis," *Quarterly Journal of Economics* 40 (1926): 429.

10. See Wm. H. Babcock and Sons, "Valuation Report of Store Property Located at 6443 to 6457 Sheridan Road, Chicago, Illinois," January 29, 1931, 4, box 3, HABP.

11. Nathan Nirenstein, "There'll Always Be a Main Street," *Appraisal Journal,* January 1947, 105.

12. Delbert S. Wenzlick, "Pedestrian Traffic," *NREJ,* August 18, 1930, 20–21; Frank S. Slosson, "The Principles of Locating Chain Stores Successfully," *NREJ,* December 12, 1927, 52; Ira A. Lurie, "Who Has the Best Location in Your Town?" *American Magazine,* n.d. [probably late 1920s], 21, no. 3250.1, John Nolen Pamphlet Collection, collection no. 6337, Division of Rare and Manuscript Collections, Cornell University Library (hereafter cited as JNPC).

13. Lurie, "Who Has the Best Location in Your Town?" 20, 127; Mark Levy, *Chain Stores: Helpful and Practical Information for a Real Estate Broker* (Chicago: NAREB, 1940), 9. See also Helen Canoyer, *Selecting a Store Location* (Washington, DC: Bureau of Foreign and Domestic Commerce, 1946), 29. Delbert Wenzlick argued that some "accepted theories" (including women's preference for the street's shady side) were "absolutely without foundation." Wenzlick, "Pedestrian Traffic," 20.

14. See Young, "What Chain Stores Want from Real Estate Brokers," 35–36; Lurie, "Who Has the Best Location in Your Town?" 129; Henry Wolfson, "Traffic-Location-Trends as Considered by the Chain Store," *NREJ,* July 8, 1929, 39, 41; Henry Wolfson, "Factors Which Influence Chain Store Location," *NREJ,* March 31, 1930, 35; Slosson, "The Principles of Locating Chain Stores Successfully," 49. The possibility of having too many chains in a 100% district was also recognized. Henry Wolfson, "How to Make Leases with the Chain Stores," *NREJ,* June 1938, 43.

Chain stores transformed retailing amid significant backlash in the 1920s and 1930s. Legislation designed to tax the chains out of business proliferated. In 1930 *Business Week* counted 260 antichain organizations, concentrated most heavily in smaller cities of the South and the Midwest. Paul Gilmore attributes this hostility not only to the threatened livelihood of independent stores but also to a resentment of "unfair" big business techniques and a perceived lack of connection to local communities. Paul Gilmore, "Remodeling Markets: The Anti-Chain Store Movement and the Grocery Store," Research Seminar Paper 63, May 13, 1999, Center for the History of Business, Technology, and Society, Hagley Museum and Library, Wilmington, Del. See also F. J. Harper, "'A New Battle on Evolution': The Anti-Chain Store Trade-at-Home Agitation of 1929–1930," *American Studies* 16, no. 3 (fall 1982): 407–26; Terry Radtke, "Shopping in the Machine Age: Chain Stores, Consumerism, and the Politics of Business Reform, 1920–1939," in *The Quest for Social Justice II: The Morris Fromkin Memorial Lectures, 1981–1990,* ed. Alan D. Corré (Milwaukee: Golda Meir Library, 1992), 120–42; Carl G. Ryant, "The South and the Movement against Chain Stores," *Journal of Southern History* 39, no. 2 (May 1973): 207–22; and Godfrey M. Lebhar, *Chain Stores in America, 1859–1962* (New York: Chain Store Publishing Corp., 1963).

15. Wolfson, "Traffic-Location-Trends," 40. Chains pioneered the first pedestrian counts. W. H. Meserole, "The Qualitative Character of Pedestrian Traffic," *American Marketing Journal,* July 1935, 157.

Most chain stores had their own real estate departments, which dealt directly with a set of regional or nationwide brokers specializing in chain store clients. These brokers acted as middlemen between the chains and local brokers or property owners. Small-city brokers also inundated chain store executives with direct mailings about their properties, hoping to spark interest. Once the chain had identified prospects and had collected information from afar, it sent a representative to the city. Stanley K. Green, "How to Submit Your Location to the Chain Store: Suggestions to Brokers in the Smaller Cities," *NREJ,* November 25, 1929, 13–14; D. R. Davies, "How to Submit Locations to Chain Store Executives," *NREJ,* January 6, 1930, 23–25; J. Russell Thorne, "How to Build a Business of Chain Store Leasing," *NREJ,* November 1936, 30–33.

16. Davies, "How to Submit Locations to Chain Store Companies," 24; Wolfson, "Factors Which Influence Chain Store Location," 37–38; Richard U. Ratcliff, "Notes on the '100 Per Cent' Concept in Retail Location Analysis," *Journal of Land and Public Utility Economics,* August 1939, 350; and Mark Levy, *Chain Stores,* 8, 27. Levy, former president of the Chicago Real Estate Board and treasurer of the National Association of Real Estate Boards, created a nationwide list of 100% districts. Mark Levy, "One Hundred Per Cent Locations," *Journal of Real Estate Management,* February 1938, 291. He revised the list for *Chain Stores,* 13–22. See Wolfson, "How to Make Leases with the Chain Stores," 42. Another expert, Richard Ratcliff, thought Levy's definition of the 100% district was too broad, but he agreed that women's shopping created high property values and rents. Ratcliff, "Notes on the '100 Per Cent' Concept in Retail Location Analysis," 350–51.

17. Wenzlick, "Pedestrian Traffic," 19, 22. On admiration of the ability to break down the pedestrian stream, see Wolfson, "How to Make Leases with the Chain Stores," 42; Canoyer, *Selecting a Store Location,* 23.

18. Wenzlick, "Pedestrian Traffic," 22.

19. Lurie, "Who Has the Best Location in Your Town?" 127–28.

20. Ibid., 20, 129; H. Morton Bodfish, "Population and Peak Land Values in Business Districts," *Journal of Land and Public Utility Economics* 6 (August 1930): 271–72; M. G. Gibbs, "How a Prominent Chain Picks Store Locations," *Printer's Ink*, November 10, 1927. See also Wolfson, "Factors Which Influence Chain Store Location," 37–38.

21. All quotes from Lurie, "Who Has the Best Location in Your Town?" 20, 128–30. A host of "how to" articles appeared offering small-city real estate agents suggestions for doing business with chains. Most of them belittled the real estate knowledge of local merchants, property owners, lawyers, and brokers. Davies, "How to Submit Locations to Chain Store Companies," 25; and Thorne, "How to Build a Business of Chain Store Leasing," 30.

22. "Crowds" and "mere expanse" taken from Nathan Nirenstein, *Preferred Business Real Estate Locations of the Principal Cities of the United States and Canada* (Springfield, MA: Nirenstein's National Reality Map Co., 1929), frontispiece; long quote from Nathan Nirenstein, *Man — The Builder* (Springfield, MA: Nirenstein's National Realty Map Co., n.d.), 11.

23. At the time of the theorem's publication, Reilly was an associate professor of business. For evidence of the long life of Reilly's theorem, which was revised periodically, see Gordon H. Stedman, "The Rise of Shopping Centers," *Journal of Retailing* (spring 1955), reprinted in *Changing Patterns in Retailing: Readings on Current Trends,* ed. John Wingate and Arnold Corbin (Homewood, IL: Richard Irwin, 1956), 174–75; Eli Cox and Leo Erickson, *Retail Decentralization* (East Lansing, MI: Bureau of Business and Economic Research, Graduate School of Business Administration, Michigan State University, 1967), 1–3; Saul B. Cohen and William Applebaum, "Evaluating Store Sites and Determining Store Rents," in *Store Location and Development Studies,* by William Applebaum et al. (Worcester, MA: Clark University, 1961), 78; Harvey Casey Jr., "Forecasting Shopping Goods Sales in Proposed Suburban Centers," 3–4, vertical files FH34C, Philadelphia City Planning Commission Library, Philadelphia; Richard Nelson, *The Selection of Retail Locations* (New York: F. W. Dodge Corp., 1958), 148–51. Ken Jones, *Specialty Retailing in the Inner City: A Geographic Perspective,* Atkinson College Geographical Monographs, no. 15 (Downsview, Ont.: York University, Atkinson College, 1984), 2–5.

24. Reilly's law was "not a matter of theory or opinion but a law in the true sense of the word." William J. Reilly, *The Law of Retail Gravitation* (New York: Published by the author, 1931), 33.

25. All quotes from William J. Reilly, "Methods for the Study of Retail Relationships," *University of Texas Bulletin,* November 22, 1929, 7–8. See also Reilly, *The Law of Retail Gravitation,* 40–42.

26. Reilly, "Methods for the Study of Retail Relationships," preface, 9–12, 16 (all quotes from 16). Besides primary markets, he defined two other types. Secondary retail markets dominated the style and standardized goods of families with annual incomes of less than three thousand dollars. Tertiary markets (very small towns) provided the convenient distribution of standardized goods. Reilly claimed that prior to his own work in 1927, no one had systematically studied the phenomenon of out-of-town trade.

27. Reilly, "Methods for the Study of Retail Relationships," 8, 10 (quote from 10). In Reilly's law we see small cities and towns trying to compete with the magnetism of big-city department stores, the latter described in William Leach, *Land of Desire: Merchants, Power, and the Rise of a New American Culture* (New York: Pantheon Books, 1993). Two 1960s

analysts attributed the law's 1930s popularity to its explanation of small-town decline. Cox and Erickson, *Retail Decentralization*, 1–3.

28. In rural and small-town Mississippi, although store owners encouraged women to shop, men dominated the world of general stores, doing the family purchasing even into the 1920s. Wealthy rural women had long possessed the metropolitan connections extended to the less well off in the 1920s. Ted Ownby, *American Dreams in Mississippi: Consumers, Poverty, and Culture, 1830–1880* (Chapel Hill: University of North Carolina Press, 1999), 11, 82, 93.

29. See the essays in Marianne A. Ferber and Julie A. Nelson, eds., *Beyond Economic Man: Feminist Theory and Economics* (Chicago: University of Chicago Press, 1993). Rebecca M. Blank's contribution is useful for clarifying how feminist theory is only one of many critiques of economists' rational economic choice model. Blank, "What Should Mainstream Economists Learn from Feminist Theory," 133–43.

30. Reilly, "Methods for the Study of Retail Relationships," 8–9, 37, 46–48 (quote from 46).

31. Ibid., 35–36; Cox and Erickson, *Retail Decentralization*, 3.

32. On the limitations of 1920s surveys, see Roland Marchand, *Advertising the American Dream: Making Way for Modernity, 1920–1940* (Berkeley: University of California Press, 1985), 35, 74–76. Manufacturers, newspapers, salesmen, and academics also undertook their own surveys. On marketing techniques and creating markets, see Susan Strasser, *Satisfaction Guaranteed: The Making of the American Mass Market* (New York: Pantheon Books, 1989), 124–61.

33. The JWT Company grew in the years after World War I to become the largest advertising firm in New York City. In the two years after the war, it expanded its staff from 177 to 283. Marchand, *Advertising the American Dream*, 6. The JWT Company had begun publishing another U.S. reference overview, *Population and Its Distribution*, in 1912. The company's surviving records from the 1920s include verbatim staff meeting minutes, research reports performed for clients or its own archives, and external and internal bulletins. They are held in the J. Walter Thompson Company Archives, Hartman Center for Sales, Advertising and Marketing History, in the Rare Book, Manuscript, and Special Collections Library, Duke University (hereafter cited as JWTCA).

34. *Retail Shopping Areas* (New York: J. Walter Thompson Advertising Co., 1926), iii, 31–32.

35. J. Walter Thompson and Company, *Population and Its Distribution*, 4th ed. (New York: McGraw-Hill, 1926), iii; *Retail Shopping Areas*, 31–32; James H. Greene, *Principles and Methods of Retailing* (New York: McGraw-Hill, 1924), 51.

36. The JWT Company had J. C. Penney's account until 1935. Beginning in 1925, the firm bid unsuccessfully for F. W. Woolworth's business by performing sample surveys. See "Office Investigation of Woolworth Stores," August 21, 1925, reel 49; "Woolworth Stores," October 2, 1928, reel 49. Reports in 1936–37 for Woolworth were optimistically labeled "new business." See "F. W. Woolworth Company: Reports on Store Front Interviews and House-to-House Survey in Trenton, New Jersey," August 1937, reel 52; "Analysis of Customers of Two Woolworth Stores," January 1937, reel 51; "Market and Media Study for Woolworth," January 1936, reel 51; "Consumer Interviews on Twenty Selected Articles Purchased in Woolworth Stores," November 1937, reel 256. All reels referred to in this note are from the 16mm Microfilm Collection, JWTCA.

37. "J. C. Penney Co. Investigation among Consumers in Ashtabula, Ohio, Auburn, Little Falls, and Rome, New York," July 1928, reel 197, 16mm Microfilm Collection, JWTCA.

38. Of the 299 farmers interviewed, 119 (40%) said they traded regularly at Penney's, whereas only 325 of the 1,339 townspeople (24%) did so. "J. C. Penney Co. Investigation among Consumers," 2, 4–6, 12. On the JWT Company's policies of classifying consumers, see Marchand, *Advertising the American Dream*, 65.

39. The customer responses in the remainder of this section are from "J. C. Penney Co. Investigation among Consumers in Ashtabula, Ohio, Auburn, Little Falls, and Rome, New York." The customer comments are quoted, by city, from 23 pages entitled "J. C. Penney Consumer Investigation." The investigators selected and even rephrased the excerpts but did not weed out criticisms of Penney's.

40. In ten months of 1924–25, four chain stores opened in Muncie, Indiana, of *Middletown* fame. Robert S. Lynd and Helen Merrell Lynd, *Middletown* (New York: Harcourt Brace Jovanovich, 1929), 45. The percentage of total retail sales by chains of four stores or more increased from 4 percent in 1919 to 9 percent in 1926 and 25 percent in 1933. Gilmore, "Remodeling Markets," 5.

41. "J. C. Penney Consumer Investigation," Little Falls, 4, 6; Ashtabula, 4; Rome, 1, 3. *Business Week* found only one antichain organization in New York state in 1930. "In 35 States 260 Bodies Are Fighting Chain Stores," *Business Week*, April 9, 1930, 22, cited in Gilmore, "Remodeling Markets," 8.

42. "J. C. Penney Consumer Investigation," Little Falls, 1, 2; Rome, 1; Auburn, 5; Ashtabula, 2.

43. It does not appear that the interviewers fished for ideas about the town; these responses connecting store class and town class answered questions about where one bought overalls or dress shirts. Ibid., Ashtabula, 2; Little Falls, 2, 3; Rome, 1, 2, 3; Auburn, 5.

44. Ibid., Ashtabula, 2, 3, 4; Little Falls, 1, 5; Auburn, 2, 3, 6, 7; Rome, 4.

45. One study of 1930s Cleveland discovered a "hierarchy" of stores relating to physical and social geographies. Jeanne Catherine Lawrence, "Geographical Space, Social Space, and the Realm of the Department Store," *Urban History* 19, pt. 1 (April 1992): 64–83.

46. Dwight L. Hoopingarner to Robert Jemison Jr., February 7, 1927, file 6.1.25.29 "H," Robert Jemison Jr. Papers, Department of Archives and Manuscripts, Birmingham Public Library.

47. "J. C. Penney Co. Investigation among Consumers," 10–11; "J. C. Penney Consumer Investigation," Little Falls, 5, 6. Grace Hale argues convincingly that, especially compared to the traditions of general store shopping, urban commerce showed the potential for mixing different populations. Saturday afternoon, she claims, was the most integrated time of week in the South. Grace Hale, *Making Whiteness: The Culture of Segregation in the South, 1890–1940* (New York: Pantheon Books, 1998), 123, 182–85. See also Ownby, *American Dreams in Mississippi*, 97.

48. "J. C. Penney Consumer Investigation," Ashtabula, 1, 2, 4; Auburn, 1; Little Falls, 3, 4. Carol Kennicott, in Sinclair Lewis's *Main Street* (New York: Signet Classic, 1920), experienced these pressures as the wife of a physician.

49. "J. C. Penney Consumer Investigation," Little Falls, 2, 5; Ashtabula, 2, 4; Auburn, 4; Rome, 5. Ted Ownby points out that in small towns there had been women clerks only since about 1900. Ownby, *American Dreams in Mississippi*, 92–93.

50. Wolfson, "Traffic-Location-Trends," 41.

51. Back-page advertisement placed by a real estate firm, *NREJ*, March 1915. On downtown movement as an expression of vitality, see William H. Wilson, *The City Beautiful Movement* (Baltimore: Johns Hopkins University Press, 1989), 78. One study of department store relocations during the nineteenth century found that New York City's department stores leapfrogged north rapidly, while Boston's barely budged, with local elite culture explaining most of this contrast. Mona Domosh, "Shaping the Commercial City: Retail Districts in Nineteenth-Century New York and Boston," *Annals of the Association of American Geographers* 80 (1990): 268–84. See also Hahn and White, *The Merchants' Manual*, 13–15.

52. Coleman Woodbury, "The Size of Retail Business Districts in the Chicago Metropolitan Region," reprinted from *Journal of Land and Public Utility Economics*, February 1928, 85, no. 6827 Chicago 32, JNPC. American land-use zoning drew from both indigenous housing, fire, and health reforms, as well as from German precedents. Pre-1900 U.S. zoning focused on separating incompatible uses, such as Chinese laundries from residential neighborhoods. The German precedent addressed over-all residential deterioration and population congestion, by combining land-use and building-height zoning. The first U.S. zoning experts hoped to replicate the results demonstrated in cities such as Frankfurt. Mel Scott, *American City Planning since 1890* (Berkeley: University of California Press, 1969), 73–78; Peter Hall, *Cities of Tomorrow: An Intellectual History of Urban Planning and Design in the Twentieth Century* (Cambridge, MA: Basil Blackwell, 1988), 58–59.

53. Scott, *American City Planning since 1890*, 75, 152–55, 227.

54. Quotations from Haig, "Toward an Understanding of the Metropolis," 403; Developer J. C. Nichols proposed that a field of real estate science should be established — "realology." J. C. Nichols, *Responsibilities and Opportunities of a Real Estate Board* (Chicago: National Association of Real Estate Boards), 3, 7, no. 3014.1, JNPC.

55. Harland Bartholomew, *A Comprehensive City Plan for Knoxville, Tennessee* (Knoxville, TN: City Planning Commission, 1930), 106; Herbert S. Swan, untitled transcript of article in *American Architect,* ca. 1919, 2, no. 1600.18, JNPC.

56. "Separation, or exclusion in order to preserve or enhance value, is zoning's very essence, and racial and ethnic separation have been recurrent themes in its evolution, adoption, and implementation." Yale Rabin, "Expulsive Zoning: The Inequitable Legacy of *Euclid,*" in *Zoning and the American Dream,* ed. Charles M. Haar and Jerold S. Kayden (Chicago: Planners Press, American Planning Association, in association with the Lincoln Institute of Land Policy, 1989), 103. Arthur C. Comey, "The Value of Zoning to Business," *Current Affairs,* February 12, 1923, no. 1605.11, JNPC.

57. Theodora Kimball Hubbard and Henry Vincent Hubbard, *Our Cities of To-Day and To-Morrow* (Cambridge, MA: Harvard University Press, 1929), 164; Bartholomew, *A Comprehensive City Plan for Knoxville, Tennessee,* 105–6.

58. Advisory Committee on Zoning, *A Zoning Primer* (Washington, DC: Department of Commerce, 1926), 1; Swan, untitled transcript, 1.

59. Edward M. Bassett, "Stores in Residence Zones," release for Saturday noon, December 25, 1926, no. 1605.9, JNPC.

60. Haig, "Toward an Understanding of the Metropolis," 404, 406–7, 415–19, 423, 425. See also Pyle, "The Determination of Location Standards for Retail Concerns," 303.

61. J. C. Nichols, "The Planning and Control of Outlying Shopping Centers," *Journal of Land and Public Utility Economics*, January 1926, 17. Traffic counts in the late 1920s dramatized the impending crisis. In Houston, in 1914, out of an average hourly total of 173 vehicles, 133 were horse-drawn. Ten years later, a count at the same location averaged 950 vehicles hourly, of which only 1 was horse-drawn. Hare & Hare, *Report of the City Planning Commission, Houston, Texas* (Houston: Forum of Civics, [1929]), 33.

62. Around very large cities such as Chicago and Los Angeles, downtown department and specialty stores had spawned branches in suburbs like Pasadena, Hollywood, Evanston, and Oak Park. Reilly, "Methods for the Study of Retail Relationships," 36. Richard Longstreth has studied other interwar community shopping centers (including those outside Philadelphia, Dallas, Cleveland, and Los Angeles) besides the well-known Country Club Plaza. Longstreth, "The Diffusion of the Community Shopping Center Concept during the Interwar Decades." On retail leadership setting location strategies during these years, see William Worley, *J. C. Nichols and the Shaping of Kansas City: Innovation in Planned Residential Communities* (Columbia: University of Missouri Press, 1990). James Worthy, *Shaping an American Institution: Robert E. Wood and Sears, Roebuck* (Urbana: University of Illinois Press, 1984).

63. "Gen. Wood's Speech at Economic Club 2/5/1938," 3, courtesy of Vicki Cwiok, Sears Roebuck and Company Archives, Hoffman Estates, Ill.; Robert E. Wood, *Mail Order Retailing — Pioneered in Chicago* (New York: Newcomen Society of England, 1948), 10–11. As demonstrated by Country Club Plaza and his residential developments, Nichols believed in the powers of planning and zoning to aid property values. He regretted that real estate executives had been slow to recognize the importance of planning. Nichols, "The Planning and Control of Outlying Shopping Centers," 20–22; Nichols, *Responsibilities and Opportunities of a Real Estate Board*, 7.

64. "Janesville Wisconsin: A Report on the Civic Survey with Preliminary Plans for Improving Existing Conditions," 1919, box 18, JNP; Bassett, "Stores in Residence Zones," 1. The earliest twentieth-century city plans rarely referred to retail business outside the central business district. Outlying business growth and scattered stores became a problem in the 1920s primarily because they defied any predictable order and threatened residential real estate values — not because they threatened downtown business.

65. John Nolen, *The City Plan of Flint, Michigan* (Flint, MI: City Planning Board, 1920), 22–23, 62–63; John Nolen, *Lancaster, Pennsylvania: Comprehensive City Plan* (Lancaster, PA: City Planning Commission, 1929), 52–57. The appropriate spacing of business centers generated "much discussion" among planners. Lawrence V. Sheridan, "How Much Property Should Be Zoned for Business," in *Problems of Zoning* (addresses delivered February 6, 1930, at the Zoning Session of the Seventh Annual Meeting of the Chicago Regional Planning Association), 3, no. 1605.30, JNPC. See also John Nolen, *Comprehensive City Plan, Roanoke, Virginia, 1928* (Roanoke, VA: Stone Printing and Manufacturing Co., 1929), 25, 56. On the design of neighborhood business centers and their transition to more automobile-oriented layouts, see the work of Richard Longstreth, especially *The Drive-In*, 133–34, 154–57.

66. Harland Bartholomew, "Business Zoning," *Annals of the American Academy of Political and Social Science* 155, pt. 2 (May 1931): 101–4; Harland Bartholomew, *City Plan of Hamilton, Ohio* (Hamilton, OH: Chamber of Commerce, 1920), 2. In Bartholomew, *A*

Comprehensive City Plan for Knoxville, Tennessee, "promiscuous scattering" appears on pages 114 and 169. See also Hare & Hare, *Report of the City Planning Commission, Houston, Texas.*

67. Property owners petitioned their zoning commissions to designate specific properties for business, hoping to profit by this. The secretary of Roanoke, Virginia's City Planning Commission conveyed to John Nolen the pressure he had experienced from petitioners. Eugene Arnold to Nolen, September 11, 1928; Nolen to Arnold, September 13, 1928, box 33, Roanoke file 5, JNP.

68. Harry C. McClure to Nolen, September 24, 1925, box 89, Flint file 7, JNP. On unscrupulous profiteers, see Scott, *American City Planning since 1890,* 240–42; and Sheridan, "How Much Property Should Be Zoned for Business," 4. Some tried to scientifically calculate appropriate retail frontage. Woodbury, "The Size of Retail Business Districts in the Chicago Metropolitan Region," 85–91.

Provocative research by Yale Rabin suggests that the districts of commercial and industrial overzoning overlapped in the 1950s and 1960s urban renewal sites and were part of a long-term effort to convert black residential areas to commercial uses. Rabin coined the term *expulsive zoning* for this and related practices. Rabin, "Expulsive Zoning," 101–21.

69. Opponents disputed zoning because it limited the rights of property owners. On businesspeople and zoning, see Haig, "Toward an Understanding of the Metropolis," 433–34. For an example of property owners challenging zoning's constitutionality, see Sheridan, "How Much Property Should Be Zoned for Business," 2. On the fear that it would discourage construction, and on the public's misunderstanding of zoning, see "Planning Whys and Otherwise: From Papers and Discussions at the Annual Conference of the Association, Williamsport, Pennsylvania, February 22–23, 1929," *Bulletin of the Pennsylvania Association of Planning Commissioners,* bulletin CPC17, July 1929, 47, no. 6825 Pennsylvania 31, JNPC.

70. "Little Rock, Arkansas: Report to Accompany Preliminary Plans," May 1929, 32–33, box 39, JNP. For an excellent discussion of the symbolic importance of geographic mobility in the battles over segregating transportation, see Grace Hale, *Making Whiteness,* 126.

71. The 1917 case was *Buchanan v. Warley,* in which the Court found that the racial zoning ordinance of Louisville, Kentucky, violated the property rights of white owners. Baltimore enacted the first racial zoning ordinance in 1910, and other cities that followed (into the 1940s) included Richmond, Norfolk, Roanoke, Winston-Salem, Birmingham, Atlanta, St. Louis, Oklahoma City, New Orleans, Indianapolis, and Dallas. Rabin, "Expulsive Zoning," 106–7. Birmingham was reprimanded in 1949 for racial zoning. Norman Williams Jr., "Zoning and Planning Notes," *American City,* November 1950, 137. Especially useful is David Delaney, *Race, Place, and the Law, 1836–1948* (Austin: University of Texas Press, 1998), 93–147; and Christopher Silver, "Racial Origins of Zoning," *Planning Perspectives,* May 1991, 189–205. The term *legal compulsion* is from Haig, "Toward an Understanding of the Metropolis," 433–34.

72. Hare & Hare, *Report of the City Planning Commission, Houston, Texas,* 25–28. An identical sentiment is expressed in Harland Bartholomew, "Can Blighted Urban Areas Be Rehabilitated?" *NREJ,* September 1, 1930, 21. Grassroots interest in zoning's potential for racial segregation is seen in "Planning Whys and Otherwise," 50.

73. A fascinating example is found in a lengthy 1926 feasibility analysis of a proposed

commercial district for African Americans in St. Louis. The report discussed the prevalence of "distinct southern traditions, customs and prejudices," as distinguished from "'Jim Crow' laws": "This feeling upon the part of the white people of Saint Louis is so deep grained and well established that there does not appear to be any chance of a change in the present practice. For these reasons the colored people are required to establish or patronize their own amusement and recreation facilities." The proposed development's commercial success depended upon whether racial prejudice would continue to exclude blacks from districts patronized by whites. Albert Wenzlick Real Estate Company, "Studies and Analyses Covering a Proposed Colored Amusement and Building Project to Be Located in Saint Louis, MO," sl 26 Albert Wenzlick Real Estate Company (1910–60), Report 1926, Western Historical Manuscript Collection, University of Missouri, St. Louis.

74. This overview of evolving beliefs about race and property value was taken from Luigi Laurenti, *Property Values and Race: Studies in Seven Cities* (Berkeley: University of California Press, 1960), 8–24. On the "paramount importance" of racially based behavior differences in causing decline, see Frederick Babcock, *The Valuation of Real Estate* (New York: McGraw-Hill, 1932), 86, 90–91; Bartholomew, "Can Blighted Urban Areas Be Rehabilitated?" 21; and Bodfish, "Population and Peak Land Values," 275. Quotes from Belden Morgan, "Values in Transition Areas: Some New Concepts," *Review of the Society of Residential Appraisers*, March 1952, as quoted in Laurenti, *Property Values and Race*, 15. See also Charles S. Johnson, *Negro Housing: Report of the Committee on Negro Housing* (Washington, DC: President's Conference on Home Building and Home Ownership, 1932), 48. The revisionists pointed to other correlated factors — socioeconomic data, class differences, and building conditions — rather than race itself.

75. Babcock, *The Valuation of Real Estate*, 91; Johnson, *Negro Housing*, 44; Wilmoth Carter, *The Urban Negro in the South* (New York: Russell and Russell, 1973), 50–53. A leading textbook also advised that "frankly" northern cities should utilize the "rigid segregation" employed by southerners, "no matter how unpleasant or objectionable the thought may be to colored residents." Northern segregation would keep racial peace and protect property values. Stanley McMichael and Robert F. Bingham, *City Growth Essentials* (Cleveland: Stanley McMichael Publishing Organization, 1928), 343. For a concise overview of the factors encouraging and dictating segregation during these decades, see Joe Trotter Jr., *Black Milwaukee: The Making of an Industrial Proletariat, 1915–45* (Urbana: University of Illinois Press, 1985), 66–74.

76. For their part, appraisers were given advice that acknowledged how difficult it was to evaluate the impact of racial differences — this belied the simple dictum claiming that African Americans lowered property values. A leading appraisal manual offered a distinctly shaky, hocus-pocus technique for calculating land value in black neighborhoods and those potentially undergoing racial transitions. After all the information was collected, it "should be mulled over for twelve hours before the report is written. Another *twenty-four hours* should then be allowed to elapse before the report is reviewed." Only then should the report be issued, if the appraiser still had confidence in its conclusions. Stanley McMichael, *McMichael's Appraising Manual*, 3d ed. (Englewood Cliffs, NJ: Prentice-Hall, 1944), 56.

77. Wilmoth A. Carter, "Negro Main Street as a Symbol of Discrimination," *Phylon* 21 (fall 1960): 237; Carter, *The Urban Negro in the South*, 20. Carter's article is based on her

1959 University of Chicago sociology thesis, "The Negro Main Street of a Contemporary Urban Community." Her *Urban Negro in the South,* first published in 1962, is an excellent, overlooked study of Raleigh, North Carolina. She performed about four hundred interviews with shoppers and business owners in 1958. See also Franklin D. Wilson, "The Ecology of a Black Business District: Sociological and Historical Analysis" (M.A. thesis, University of Wisconsin, 1975), 11–12. Wilson examined Birmingham, Alabama, collecting most of his data, including twenty taped interviews, in 1965.

78. Ray Stannard Baker, "Following the Color Line," *American Magazine,* May 1907, 15. See also John H. Burrows, *The Necessity of Myth: A History of the National Negro Business League, 1900–1945* (Auburn, AL: Hickory Hill Press, 1988), 39. On keeping to "the background," Paul Kenneth Edwards, "Distinctive Characteristics of Urban Negro Consumption," (Ph.D. diss., Harvard University, 1936), 162.

79. Edwards, "Distinctive Characteristics of Urban Negro Consumption," 3, 26. In 1930, 5 million of the 12 million southern blacks were "urban." Edwards's dissertation built on the conclusions of his previous book on southern urban black consumers, in order to make a strong case for a national market. His research into the behavior of black consumers in the South uncovered significant variations among cities such as Nashville, Birmingham, Atlanta, and Richmond, emphasizing local conditions at the expense of North-South distinctions. Paul K. Edwards, *The Southern Urban Negro as a Consumer* (New York: Prentice-Hall, 1932). The National Negro Business League was organized in 1899, the National Association of Colored Women in 1896.

80. Carter, *The Urban Negro in the South,* 47–50, 230. An analysis of small-town antebellum Tennessee found preliminary evidence that "both black and white entrepreneurs operated businesses side by side on streets leading from the public square." Lisa Tolbert, *Constructing Townscapes: Space and Society in Antebellum Tennessee* (Chapel Hill: University of North Carolina Press, 1998), 229. On the increase and diversification in black business during the early twentieth century, especially after 1905, see Robert C. Kenzer, *Enterprising Southerners: Black Economic Success in North Carolina, 1865–1915* (Charlottesville: University Press of Virginia, 1997); Walter Weare, *Black Business in the New South: A Social History of the North Carolina Mutual Life Insurance Company* (Durham, NC: Duke University Press, 1993); Robert Weems, *Desegregating the Dollar: African American Consumerism in the Twentieth Century* (New York: New York University Press, 1998), 10.

81. Dwight Fennell, "A Demographic Study of Black Businesses, 1905–1908, with Respect to the Race Riot of 1906" (M.A. thesis, Atlanta University, 1977), 1–4, 19, 28, 37 (quote on 3). Fennell described the police targeting of Negro "dives." Saloons were also marginalized (though not demolished!) by middle-class blacks. The National Negro Business League did not allow tavern keepers to actively participate in its annual meetings. Burrows, *The Necessity of Myth,* 61–62. A study of Charlotte, North Carolina, documented city officials' threats to remove black businesses from the downtown in the early 1900s and the corresponding rise of a thriving black business district in the Brooklyn neighborhood. Thomas W. Hanchett, *Sorting Out the New South City: Race, Class, and Urban Development in Charlotte, 1875–1975* (Chapel Hill: University of North Carolina Press, 1998), 130–33.

82. Carter, *The Urban Negro in the South,* 50–53; Edwards, "Distinctive Characteristics of Urban Negro Consumption," 16. One East Hargett theater had no white customers because of the white management's policy, and a large white-owned property on East Har-

gett was off-limits to African Americans because of the will of a previous owner. Carter, *The Urban Negro in the South*, 152–54; Carter, "Negro Main Street as a Symbol of Discrimination," 239. An Atlanta study found that almost 20 percent (30 percent by value) of the accounts in a Negro bank were held by whites. Robert J. Alexander, "Negro Business in Atlanta," *Southern Economic Journal*, April 1951, 456, 457, 461.

83. National Negro Business League, *Annual Report of the Sixteenth Session and the Fifteenth Anniversary Convention Held at Boston, Massachusetts* (Nashville, TN: African M.E. Sunday School Union Print, 1915), 190, 153, 184–85 (quote on 190).

84. Baker, "Following the Color Line," 15; National Negro Business League, *Report of the Survey of Negro Business* (Tuskegee, AL: Tuskegee Institute Press, 1929), n.p.; the term *symbiosis* is used in McDowell, "The Ideology of Black Entrepreneurship," 62, 93. "The old-fashioned darkey," Baker wrote, "preferred to go to the white man for everything; he didn't trust his own people." Baker, "Following the Color Line," 15.

85. In the 1950s, Carter's consumer interviews showed that overwhelmingly the top two reasons given for trading on Negro Main Street were "To patronize Negroes," and "Feel it my duty to use them." Together these had 452 first and second rankings in importance, whereas the next categories—"Convenient location," "Satisfactory service," and "Courteous operators"—garnered 31, 17, and 15 votes respectively. Carter, *The Urban Negro in the South*, 140.

86. "How Negroes Spent Their Incomes, 1920–1945," *Sales Management*, June 15, 1945, 106, as cited in Weems, *Desegregating the Dollar*, 10; Albon L. Holsey, "Interracial Cooperation in Business," *Southern Workman*, September 1931, 380; Burrows, "The Necessity of Myth," 118.

87. Weems, *Desegregating the Dollar*, 17–20; Albon L. Holsey, "Negro Women and Business," *Southern Workman*, August 1927, 343. Women had participated in NNBL conventions from the earliest years. In his 1905 keynote address, John Wanamaker praised the gathering for the surprising presence of women—"your partners." In 1931 they comprised 31 percent of the NNBL membership. National Negro Business League, *Annual Report of the Sixth Annual Convention of the National Negro Business League Held in New York City, August 16, 17, 18 1905*, 174, in *Records of the National Negro Business League*, ed. John H. Bracey Jr. and August Meier (Bethesda, MD: University Publications of America, 1994), microform; McDowell, "The Ideology of Black Entrepreneurship," 142–48 (newsletter quote on 148).

88. Edwards, "Distinctive Characteristics of Urban Negro Consumption," 165; see also Edwards, *The Southern Urban Negro as a Consumer*, 95. Edwards studied the "Negro market" for eight years, living for three years in a black Nashville neighborhood near Fisk University, where he taught. He worked three years for national advertisers, honing their sales techniques for the Negro market. Edwards's research was the basis of a 1935 U.S. Department of Commerce report, "Purchasing Power of Negroes in the U.S. Estimated at Two Billion Dollars." Historian Weems marks this report as a turning point in black business strategies to appeal to the profit interests of white companies. It is worth noting that advertising executives generally looked down upon their audiences. Roland Marchand, *Advertising the American Dream*, 66–71; Weems, *Desegregating the Dollar*, 28–29.

89. Edwards, "Distinctive Characteristics of Urban Negro Consumption," 16, 107, 119, 128–29. Grace Hale has investigated the place of attire in stereotypes of African Americans, particularly as reflected in advertising. Hale, *Making Whiteness*, 153–58. She has also

analyzed the critical role that images of African Americans played in selling goods to whites; Ted Ownby finds that beliefs about blacks helped define the "bad" consumer, so that whites could be "good" consumers. In the South it was expected that blacks should look poor but at the same time be the true, weak-willed, "bad" consumers. Ownby includes a fascinating discussion of style and consumer choices under slavery. Ownby, *American Dreams in Mississippi*, 75–76.

90. Edwards, "Distinctive Characteristics of Urban Negro Consumption," 119–20.

91. Ibid., 130, 150, 81, 100–103 (quotes on 130, 150, 81). "She Buys by Brand!" exclaimed the article "The Negro Woman Goes to Market," 13.

92. Edwards, "Distinctive Characteristics of Urban Negro Consumption," 91, 100–103.

93. Ibid., 163, 110 (quote on 163). It was on downtown shopping trips that blacks, in their dress clothes, favorably impressed whites. At work, and walking or taking the bus home from work, African Americans usually wore work clothes that indicated their status.

94. Carter, *The Urban Negro in the South*, 196–97; Edwards, *The Southern Urban Negro as a Consumer*, 97.

95. John Dollard, *Caste and Class in a Southern Town*, 3d ed. (New York: Doubleday Anchor Books, 1957), 340. The most famous example of the perils of interactions with white clerks is from 1955 — Emmett Till. Till, a fourteen-year-old Chicago boy visiting relatives in Mississippi, was lynched for allegedly speaking to, whistling, or leering at, a white woman behind the sales counter of a small country store. On the deep impact Till's murder had on one activist, see Anne Moody, *Coming of Age in Mississippi* (New York: Dell, 1968), 121–38. For an analysis of racialized constructions of motherhood in the aftermath of Till's death, looking at the offended white woman and Till's mother, see Ruth Feldstein, *Motherhood in Black and White: Race and Sex in American Liberalism, 1930–1965* (Ithaca, NY: Cornell University Press, 2000), 86–110.

96. There were other indications besides Paul Edwards's work that mainstream marketers were taking note of the Negro market. The introduction to the NNBL's 1928 survey of black business was written by the director of research for the J. Walter Thompson Company. Black business leaders worked hard to funnel statistics about the black consumer market to white companies, though appeals like "Mrs. Brown America Is Important!" sometimes had a plaintive tone. Burrows, *The Necessity of Myth*, 140; "The Negro Woman Goes to Market," 13; Weems, *Desegregating the Dollar*, 48.

97. "Souvenir Program, Thirty-Fourth Convention National Negro Business League and the Third Convention, National Housewives League, August 23–24–25, 1933, Durham, N.C.," 31. Family Album, 99, box 33, 9-C, Rencher Nicholas Harris Papers, 1857–1965, Special Collections Library, Duke University. McDowell, "The Ideology of Black Entrepreneurship," 107; "The Negro Woman Goes to Market," 13.

98. Carter, *The Urban Negro in the South*, 115, 154–55, 161, 170–71, 177–78 (for Negro Main Street as "connective," see 155); Edwards, "Distinctive Characteristics of Urban Negro Consumption," 117. Carter noted the irony of people from country backgrounds turning their backs on rural visitors. Over the decades it became harder to distinguish the country from the city people. Carter, *The Urban Negro in the South*, 137–39, 159, 164, 172–74 ("country people" quote on 173).

99. Carter, *The Urban Negro in the South*, 121–22, 174–75, 178 (quote on 121).

100. Quote from Edwards, "Distinctive Characteristics of Urban Negro Consumption," 117. Ordinary citizens took pride in the fact that whistling and unwanted male at-

tention was kept to a minimum on East Hargett Street. Carter, *The Urban Negro in the South*, 132–33, 174.

101. On the appearance and respectability of East Hargett Street, see Carter, *The Urban Negro in the South*, 50, 154–55, 158–60, 164, 170–72; on "grotesque sidewalk displays," see Edwards, *The Southern Urban Negro as a Consumer*, 79; Dollard, *Caste and Class in a Southern Town*, 102–3; on "run-down appearance," see Edwards, "Distinctive Characteristics of Urban Negro Consumption," 108. On perceptions of illegitimate carousing, see Gregory Waller, *Main Street Amusements: Movies and Commercial Entertainment in a Southern City, 1896–1930* (Washington, DC: Smithsonian Institution Press, 1995), 29, 168–69; Wilson, "The Ecology of a Black Business District," 20–22.

102. African Americans also brought up the "open secret" that some blacks neglected their establishments. But when in 1915 Nannie Borroughs worried that "in many cases you can tell a colored man's place of business the moment you lay eyes upon it," she was judging business practices, not people's character. NNBL, *Annual Report of the Sixteenth Session*, 164–68.

103. Edwards, "Distinctive Characteristics of Urban Negro Consumption," 116. As examples of business centers bordering on undesirable, "mixed" areas, Edwards listed Beale Street, Memphis; Rampart Street, New Orleans; Cedar Street, Nashville; Milan and Prairie Streets, Houston; Druid Hill Avenue, Baltimore; South Street, Philadelphia; State Street, Chicago; and Lenox Avenue, New York City.

104. Carter, *The Urban Negro in the South*, 54–55. See also Edwards, "Distinctive Characteristics of Urban Negro Consumption," 116. Dollard, *Caste and Class in a Southern Town*, 4. In 1931 only 2 percent of the groceries in Harlem were owned by blacks. Edwin E. Hurd, "A New Cooperative Movement," *Southern Workman*, June 1931, 38. Of Harlem's speakeasies, 90 percent were white-owned in 1929. McDowell, "The Ideology of Black Entrepreneurship," 97.

105. McDowell, "The Ideology of Black Entrepreneurship," 32.

106. Lakeland Chamber of Commerce, Publicity Department, "Economic Survey of Lakeland, Florida" (1927), 32, no. 6827 Lakeland 1, JNPC. Lakeland's population was about 20 percent black.

107. The Great Depression's impact on the racial dimensions of urban trade varied. On Beale Street in Memphis, black business failures led to an increase in white ownership, whereas in Atlanta by the mid-1930s, a flurry of activity among blacks resulted in a wave of new businesses, and in Harlem the number of black enterprises rose as well. Some white merchants took a greater interest in attracting black trade. NNBL's initiatives of the late 1920s were hard hit by the disintegration of the Colored Merchants' Association. The Housewives Leagues accelerated their campaigns, and "Don't buy where you can't work" became a unifying slogan. For some, the depression seemed to mark a decline for the black business district — a time when it lost its firm hold on the middle class and its cross-class character began to slip. Radicalization of the black community encouraged movement beyond the bourgeois solutions promoted by the NNBL. McDowell, *The Ideology of Black Entrepreneurship*, 107, 171, 177–78; Robert W. O'Brien, "Beale Street: A Study in Ecological Succession," *Sociology and Social Research* 26 (May–June 1942): 436; Alexander, "Negro Business in Atlanta," 461; Carter, *The Urban Negro in the South*, 54, 226, 232. On the view that it no longer mattered much in the 1950s where black entrepreneurs located, see Carter, *The Urban Negro in the South*, 226.

CHAPTER 4

1. Edei to Aunt Camilla, August 6, 1932, 3, Annie Pope Van Dyke Family Papers, MS 257, The Mississippi Valley Collection, Memphis State University. Outlying business buildings built in the 1920s also had "tremendous vacancies" in the 1930s. "Report on Economic Survey of Los Angeles and Southern California," January 30, 1934, 31, box 3, Frederick Morrison Babcock Papers, collection no. 4087, Division of Rare and Manuscript Collections, Cornell University Library (hereafter cited as FMBP).

2. Vacant stores were not a phenomenon unique to the depression. They attracted attention in the 1920s as a retail problem, but after the depression and World War II, vacant stores were seen as a downtown problem. One researcher, studying Buffalo, New York, between 1918 and 1928, commented, "In traveling through the trading sections of many towns we are struck by the number of empty, lifeless store fronts." Edmund D. McGarry, *Mortality in Retail Trade* (Buffalo, NY: University of Buffalo, Bureau of Business and Social Research, 1930), xvii. Although in the 1930s it was tempting to blame the "long rows of empty stores" on "emergency depression conditions," the bad news was that "most of these studies [of retail vacancy] were made in the good old days of prosperity or so-called 'normalcy.'" Clarence S. Stein and Catherine Bauer, "Store Buildings and Neighborhood Shopping Centers," reprinted from *Architectural Record*, February 1934, 1, vertical file FH34S, Philadelphia City Planning Commission Library, Philadelphia (hereafter cited as PCPCL). See also Paul Converse, "Business Mortality of Illinois Retail Stores from 1925 to 1930," Bureau of Business Research, University of Illinois, Urbana, 1932, Bulletin no. 41, 30–31.

3. Untitled clipping, *Women's Wear Daily*, March 22, 1957, box 15, file Urban Renewal, Resseguie Collection, Baker Library, Harvard Business School. Victor Gruen, "Planned Shopping Centers," *Dun's Review*, May 1953, 37, vertical file FH34G, PCPCL. Richard Nelson counted only ten new major downtown department stores in the nation between 1929 and 1958. Richard Nelson, *The Selection of Retail Locations* (New York: F. W. Dodge Corp., 1958), 88. On the depression as a hiatus, see Joseph Laronge, "Should We Get Excited about Retail Decentralization?" *National Real Estate Journal (NREJ)*, December 1938, 22. On the depression preventing "long-planned improvements," see "Modernization Boosts Income of Four Realtor-Managed Properties," *NREJ*, January 1936, 45.

4. Kenneth Jackson, *Crabgrass Frontier: The Suburbanization of the United States* (New York: Oxford University Press, 1985), 259; and Janet Daly-Bednarek, *The Changing Image of the City: Planning for Downtown Omaha, 1945–1973* (Lincoln: University of Nebraska Press, 1992), 93.

City planning boomed during the 1930s and World War II, but with mixed outcomes. The New Deal elevated planning from a "struggling profession" to "national policy." M. Christine Boyer, *Dreaming the Rational City: The Myth of American City Planning* (Cambridge, MA: MIT Press, 1983), 203. In a study of Portland and Seattle during World War II, Carl Abbott found that despite enthusiasm for planning to guide war mobilization, "the very quantity and pressures of wartime planning hindered rather than helped in the establishment of city planning as a central function of local government." Carl Abbott, "Planning for the Home Front in Seattle and Portland, 1940–45," in *The Martial Metropolis: U.S. Cities in War and Peace*, ed. Roger W. Lotchin (New York: Praeger, 1984), 163–64.

5. Stateside defense installations often encouraged independent suburban enclaves of

military production, to the disadvantage of central cities. See essays in Lotchin, *The Martial Metropolis,* esp. 224–25.

6. Despite rationing and shortages, consumer spending increased nearly 50 percent between the war's beginning and 1944. William Chafe, *The Unfinished Journey,* 2d ed. (New York City: Oxford University Press, 1991), 9–10.

7. The image of depression inactivity was so powerful that in 1940 Homer Hoyt claimed that "for the last ten years our sky lines have been static," in the same paragraph where he stated that old buildings were being torn down. Homer Hoyt, "Urban Growth and Real Estate Values," *Appraisal Journal,* October 1940, 332–40, reprinted in *Appraisal Thought: A 50-Year Beginning* (Chicago: American Institute of Real Estate Appraisers, 1982), 73.

8. "Must Revalue Practically the Entire World," *Boston Evening Transcript,* June 10, 1933, pt. 3, 1, no. 1430.157, John Nolen Pamphlet Collection, collection no. 6337, Division of Rare and Manuscript Collections, Cornell University Library (hereafter cited as JNPC).

9. Frederick M. Babcock, *Real Estate Valuation,* Michigan Business Studies, vol. 4, no. 1 (Ann Arbor: University of Michigan, Bureau of Business Research, 1932), preface. On economists being ridiculed as "astrologers," see Richard T. Ely, "Real Estate in the Business Cycle," reprinted from *American Economic Review Supplement,* March 1932, 138, no. 3014.11, JNPC.

10. Roy Wenzlick, "The Stock Market Collapse," *As I See — Real Estate Analyst (REA),* September 25, 1946, 278; *Market Letter of the Chicago Real Estate Board,* June 24, 1938, 3; H. M. Propper, "Saving Our Blighted Downtown Areas," *Nation's Business,* May 1940, 22, 92; Marcel Villanueva, *Planning Neighborhood Shopping Centers* (New York: National Committee on Housing, 1945), 9, vertical file FH34V, PCPCL; Wm. H. Babcock & Sons, "Valuation of Property Known as 6426–6448 South Halsted Street, Chicago, Illinois," March 20, 1934, 4, 6, box 3, Henry Andrews Babcock Papers, collection no. 3022, Division of Rare and Manuscript Collections, Cornell University Library (hereafter cited as HABP); for leases "not holding," see Cuthbert E. Reeves, *The Valuation of Business Lots in Downtown Los Angeles* (Los Angeles: Los Angeles Board of Municipal Research, 1931), 14.

11. Wm. H. Babcock & Sons, "Valuation of Property Known as 6426–6448 South Halsted Street, Chicago, Illinois," 6; Paul H. Nystrom, "The Future of the Department Store," *Journal of Retailing* 8, no. 3 (October 1932): 68; Babcock, *Real Estate Valuation,* author's note.

12. Frederick M. Babcock, "Response of Mortgage Lender to Cycle," Georgetown University Savings and Loan Forum, December 4, 1964, box 3, FMBP. Villanueva, *Planning Neighborhood Shopping Centers,* 9. A 1925 appraisal of a Chicago property leased to Woolworth advised that though the first-floor rent was $4,300, it appeared that the owner could get $12,000. Wm. H. Babcock & Sons, "Valuation of Property Known as 1247–49 South Halsted Street," February 25, 1925, 1, box 3, HABP.

13. Frederick Ackerman, "Population Expectations, Zoning, Appraisals, and Debt," *American City,* October 1934, 49–50; and Harold S. Buttenheim, "Possible Modifications of Urban Land Policies in America," prepared for the meeting of the American City Planning Institute, St. Louis, October 21, 1934, 1, no. 1561.21, JNPC. One study concluded that since even the most stable-seeming downtown properties had fluctuated wildly in income between 1908 and 1933, investors had fooled themselves about the predictability of values

long before the depression. See Ivan A. Thorson, "Rationalizing Appraisal Practice," *Appraisal Journal,* July 1936, reprinted in *Appraisal Thought,* 37.

14. Jacob Crane and Coleman Woodbury, "Land Prepared for City Building," paper prepared for discussion at the Annual Meeting of the American City Planning Institute, Pittsburgh, PA, November 13, 1932, 1–3, no. 1563.22, JNPC. See also Propper, "Saving Our Blighted Downtown Areas," 94; and Reeve Conover, "Let's Quit Gambling in Land," *American City,* March 1935, 85.

Real estate slumped in the years 1893–1907, deflating a boom that had begun in the 1860s. Real estate agents professionalized in the wake of this slump, for example taking on the trade name Realtor, which referred to members of the newly formed National Association of Real Estate Boards. See Jeffrey M. Hornstein, "The Rise of the Realtor®: Professionalism, Gender, and Middle-Class Identity, 1908–1950," in *The Middling Sorts: Explorations in the History of the American Middle Class,* ed. Burton J. Bledstein and Robert D. Johnston (New York: Routledge, 2001), 217–33.

15. James H. Burton, *Evolution of the Income Approach* (Chicago: American Institute of Real Estate Appraisers, 1982), 36, 245; Philip Kniskern, "A Message from the President," *Appraisal Journal,* October 1932, reprinted in *Appraisal Thought,* 1–2. "Report on Economic Survey of Los Angeles and Southern California," 31.

The field's restructuring was not entirely voluntary. Kenneth Jackson has explained how the requirements of New Deal federal lending programs (particularly the Home Owners Loan Corporation beginning in 1933) helped create a uniform national appraisal system implemented by trained individuals. Jackson, *Crabgrass Frontier,* 196–97.

16. Babcock, *Real Estate Valuation,* author's note, 3.

Babcock's long career, from the 1920s to urban renewal, illustrates how appraisal work was finding its place at the heart of twentieth-century real estate investment. In 1920 he joined his father's Chicago real estate firm, becoming a partner and staying until 1931. During 1933–34 he worked in-house at Prudential Insurance Company, performing studies of regional real estate conditions in the United States and handling large foreclosure cases. From 1934 to 1940, Babcock worked as assistant administrator at the Federal Housing Administration. There he "organized and operated entire underwriting staff of the FHA, established techniques, merit system, and training program; was fully responsible for all case decisions." He "created the underwriting and appraisal system of the FHA" and was "principal author" of the agency's underwriting manual. The 1940s found him again in private industry, finally setting up his own consulting practice in 1944. Babcock published widely, including two books: *The Appraisal of Real Estate* in 1923 and *The Valuation of Real Estate* in 1932. See "Experience and Qualifications: Frederick M. Babcock" and the document beginning "Frederick M. Babcock counsels and appraises . . . ," both in box 3, FMBP. Frederick M. Babcock and his brother Henry Babcock (also an appraiser) left manuscript collections to Cornell University.

17. Thorson, "Rationalizing Appraisal Practice," 34, 35, 37, 46; Babcock, *Real Estate Valuation,* author's note, 3–6; Kniskern, "A Message from the President," 1. On "appearing ridiculous," see also Ayres Du Bois, "The Capitalization Process," *Appraisal Journal,* January 1935, reprinted in *Appraisal Thought,* 29.

18. Efforts by lawyers and in the courts to nail down such terms only made matters worse, as in the case of *fair market value.* Frederick M. Babcock, "Valuation of Mortgage Investments," paper delivered at the Appraisal Study Conference, School of Business, In-

diana University, Bloomington, March 30, 1948, box 3, Speeches file, FMBP; A. B. Kissack, "The Efficacy of Appraisal Procedure," *Appraisal Bulletin #17 — REA,* 1943, 86. The author of a widely used appraising handbook identified fifty-four kinds of value. Stanley L. McMichael, *McMichael's Appraising Manual,* 4th ed. (Englewood Cliffs, NJ: Prentice-Hall, 1951), 10–11. On the persistence of vague terminology into the 1970s, see Burton, *Evolution of the Income Approach,* 245.

19. On bias and preconceived estimate, see Babcock, *Real Estate Valuation,* author's note, 3–5; on "real" values and "hand-in-glove," see Babcock, "Valuation of Mortgage Investments," 7, 10; Frederick M. Babcock, "What Bonbright Does for the Real Estate Appraiser," ca. 1937–38, 1–2, box 3, Miscellaneous Papers file, FMBP.

20. Babcock, *Real Estate Valuation,* 1–2.

21. Kniskern, "A Message from the President," 1–5, esp. 2. The Society of Real Estate Appraisers, focusing on residential real estate, formed during the same years.

22. "The Shadows on the Moon," *REA,* January 1934, 228; Kissack, "The Efficacy of Appraisal Procedure," 86; for slogan, see *Investment Bulletin #4 — REA,* 1937, cover page; and "The Canny Mr. Wenzlick of St. Louis and His 'Coming Boom,'" *Architectural Forum,* June 1936, 512.

23. In the *American City* magazine's index during the 1930s, under "real estate" the editors advised readers to "see planning." See also Morris Ashton, "Highest-Best Use," *Appraisal Journal,* January 1939, reprinted in *Appraisal Thought,* 63. For predepression advocacy of applying "basic principles of city growth" to reduce the "errors in forecasting to a minimum," see Richard M. Hurd, *Principles of City Land Values,* 4th ed. (New York: Record and Guide, 1924), 159.

24. Morris Goldfarb, "The Appraisal of Retail Store Properties," *Journal of the American Institute of Real Estate Appraisers,* January 1939, reprinted in *Selected Readings in Real Estate Appraisal* (Chicago: American Institute of Real Estate Appraisers, 1953), 678–79. See also H. Morton Bodfish, "Population and Peak Land Values in Business Districts," *Journal of Land and Public Utility Economics* 6 (August 1930): 275–77; and Herbert S. Swan, "Land Values and City Growth," *Journal of Land and Public Utility Economics* 10 (May 1934): 201.

25. Babcock, "Valuation of Mortgage Investments," 11. Kissack, "The Efficacy of Appraisal Procedure," 85. For accusations of backsliding and continued weak professional recognition, see "Appraising by Many Is Becoming a Racket," *As I See It — REA,* May 28 1941, 128; "Highest and Best Use," *Appraisal Bulletin — REA,* January 31, 1950, 34–35. Distinguishing between "scientifically formed judgement" and "haphazard guess" was not easy. Kniskern, "A Message from the President," 1–2; Henry Wolfson, "Chain Stores Now Bidding for New Locations," *NREJ,* January 1936, 30.

26. Quote from Thorson, "Rationalizing Appraisal Practice," 34; Ashton, "Highest-Best Use," 68. See also A. B. Kissack, "Incompatible Environment," *Appraisal Bulletin #20 — REA,* 1944, 97.

27. A 1927 Detroit survey showed 110 privately owned lots holding 7,720 cars. By 1933 those numbers were 265 lots for 17,251 cars, and a 1936 study, which included garages as well as lots, showed spaces for 31,724 cars. Milwaukee followed the same trend. Walter H. Blucher, "The Economics of the Parking Lot," *Planners' Journal,* September–October 1936, 113–19. In St. Louis, the square footage devoted to parking lots went from 58,690 in 1931 to 361,591 in 1950 and 496,962 in 1956. Roy Wenzlick, "The Shift in Retail Uses in the Downtown District," *As I See — REA,* September 28, 1954, 422–23. In Bridgeport, "Sur-

rounding Main Street is an irregular patchwork of cleared land on which thrive 43 public parking lots," twenty-six of which had appeared since 1928. "Main Street, U.S.A.," *Architectural Forum,* February 1939, 81.

28. Roy Wenzlick, *The Coming Boom in Real Estate — And What to Do about It* (New York: Simon and Schuster, 1936), 7, 21. See also "Is the Boom Still Coming?" *Investment Bulletin — REA,* April 12, 1938, 937.

29. Joseph W. Catherine, "Replanning Our Cities and Curing Blight," *NREJ,* November 1938, 54. For a unique, in-depth study of demolition and rebuilding, see Max Page, *The Creative Destruction of Manhattan, 1900–1940* (Chicago: University of Chicago Press, 1999). The use of New Deal programs, at all levels of government, to undertake demolition work further legitimated the practice as policy.

30. Walter R. Kuehnle, "Central Business District Paradox," *Journal of the American Institute of Real Estate Appraisers,* January 1935, reprinted in *Selected Readings in Real Estate Appraisal,* 370–71. On chaotic and alarming growth, American Transit Association, "Tomorrow's Cities," ca. 1945, 24, box 36, Russell Van Nest Black Papers, collection no. 3018, Division of Rare and Manuscript Collections, Cornell University Library.

31. Kuehnle, "Central Business District Paradox," 370–71, 374–76. The building tax, Kuehnle pointed out, was a mere 10 percent of the tax bill.

32. This common point of confusion for appraisers was acknowledged in the field's manual, *Appraisal Terminology,* as discussed in Ashton, "Highest-Best Use," 62.

33. Kuehnle, "Central Business District Paradox," 371.

34. Goldfarb, "The Appraisal of Retail Store Properties," 678–79, 681–82. The disposal of closed bank buildings was a common problem during the 1930s. See E. E. Mountjoy, "A Use for Unused Bank Buildings," *American Bankers Association Journal,* March 1934, 64–65; and "New Use for Old Banks, Some Recent Transformations," *Architectural Forum,* January 1934, 82. One report to the liquidation committee for a downtown Chicago bank (just opened in 1929) explained that locally the industry had consolidated in twenty years from 27 banks to 10. Wm. H. Babcock & Sons to Liquidating Committee, Foreman-State National Bank, Chicago, Illinois, August 1, 1932, 16, box 1, HABP.

35. Reeves, "The Valuation of Business Lots in Downtown Los Angeles," 19. Wm. H. Babcock & Sons, "Valuation of Property Known as 6426–6448 South Halsted Street, Chicago, Illinois," 3. On the ground floor and higher stories as "the two distinct parts of the property," see James R. Appel, "Commercial Land Values," *Appraisal Bulletin — REA,* January 25, 1957, 27.

The practice of using the first floor for offices, which was found in a few American cities (e.g., St. Louis and New Orleans) did not favorably impress valuator Frederick Babcock, who thought they gave downtown a "wholesale district" look. Frederick Babcock, "Report on Economic Survey of St. Louis and the St. Louis Region," December 2, 1933, 19, box 3, FMBP.

36. On strip development, see Hoyt, "Urban Growth and Real Estate Values," 75.

37. Frederick M. Babcock, *The Valuation of Real Estate* (New York: McGraw-Hill, 1932), 68; "Tax Payers," *Architectural Forum,* July 1933, 86. One analyst noted a trend from constructing taxpayers to opening parking lots. Blucher, "The Economics of the Parking Lot," 114–15. Another depression opportunity was the possibility that the tax-abandonment of urban lands and subsequent municipal ownership could be a boon to city planners. Tracy B. Augur, "The Tax-Abandonment of Urban Lands: A Planning Opportunity. Paper

prepared for discussion at the annual meeting of the American City Planning Institute at Pittsburgh, PA," November 13, 1932, no. 1571.57, JNPC.

38. "Rebuilding the Cities," *Business Week,* July 6, 1940, 35; Propper, "Saving Our Blighted Downtowns," 20.

39. See the inconclusive, contradictory answers to the question "Is the Increase in Parking Lots a Healthy Sign?" in Blucher, "The Economics of the Parking Lot," 119.

40. Babcock, *Real Estate Valuation,* 1–2; Hoyt, "Urban Growth and Real Estate Values," 239; Goldfarb, "The Appraisal of Retail Store Properties," 678, 681–82; Blucher, "The Economics of the Parking Lot," 115.

41. "Modernizing Increases the Business of Store Tenants," *NREJ,* October 1933, 24.

42. "Alterations and Repairs," *REA,* October 31, 1949, 440. In Bridgeport, the storefront spending figures were $91,290 between 1924 and 1929, $131,440 between 1930 and 1935, and $224,255 between 1936 and 1938. "Main Street, U.S.A.," 82–85; "Property Management," *REA,* December 1933, 218. On the decline in nonresidential construction, see U.S. Tariff Commission, *Sheet (Window) Glass: War Changes in Industry Series,* Report no. 9, Washington, DC, February 1945, 6–7.

43. "From 39% Occupancy to 72% with the Help of Vitrolite," *NREJ,* January 1936, 57. See also *23rd Annual Report of the Libbey Owens Ford Glass Company* (Toledo, OH: Libbey-Owens-Ford Glass Co., 1939), 21, box 4, file 6, Libbey-Owens-Ford Glass Company Records, Ward M. Canaday Center for Special Collections, University of Toledo Libraries (hereafter cited as LOF Company Records); and Libbey-Owens-Ford Glass Company, Vitrolite Division (hereafter cited as LOF), "Vitrolite Colorful Structural Glass: A Libbey-Owens-Ford Product," 1930s, Trade Catalogue L6948 193-a, Hagley Museum and Library, Wilmington, Del. "Modernizing Increases Rent $267.50 per Month," *NREJ,* February 1933, 45; "Modernizing Establishes New Rental Values," *NREJ,* January 1933, 31; "Transforming the Old Store into a Modern Rent Producer," *NREJ,* September 1933, 27; "Modernization Boosts Income of Four Realtor-Managed Properties," 45. For other success stories, see "Remodeling Portfolio," *Architectural Forum,* February 1939, 89–108; "Seventeen Examples of Successful Modernization," *Architectural Forum,* January 1933, 45–68; and Chamber of Commerce of the United States, *Construction and City Development: Suggestions for Activities of Chambers of Commerce,* 1936, 3, no. 515.1, JNPC. Harland Bartholomew, *A Comprehensive City Plan for Knoxville, Tennessee* (Knoxville, TN: City Planning Commission, 1930), 169. One appraiser claimed that storefronts became obsolete every five to seven years, even though they were only remodeled every ten years. George L. Schmutz, "The Appraisal of Retail Store Property," *Appraisal Journal,* January 1940, reprinted in *Selected Readings in Real Estate Appraisal,* 1170.

44. Because LOF and the Pittsburgh Plate Glass Company dominated the flat glass market, LOF's stake in modernization went deeper than the obvious anticipated financial gain from sponsoring the competition. As substantiated in the "Flat Glass" antitrust case of 1948, LOF had conspired with another manufacturer (the Pittsburgh Plate Glass Company) to unfairly control plate glass production. Together, the two companies made virtually all of the structural glass in the United States. Select Committee on Small Business, U.S. Senate, Report 1015, *Studies of Dual Distribution: The Flat-Glass Industry* (Washington, DC: U.S. Government Printing Office, 1960), 26–33. *U.S. v. Libbey-Owens-Ford Glass Company et al.,* U.S.D.C., N.D. Ohio, Western Division, Civil Action No. 5239. In the 1940s Pittsburgh Plate Glass Company undertook its own promotional competition. Art

Brown, "You Won't Recognize Main St.," *Nation's Business*, September 1945, 113; *22nd Annual Report of the Libbey Owens Ford Glass Company* (Toledo, OH: LOF Glass Co., 1938), box 4, file 6, LOF Company Records.

45. *Architectural Record*, July 1933, cited in Talbot Faulkner Hamlin, "The Architect and the Depression," *Nation*, August 9, 1933, 152, no. 310.51, JNPC. About 10 percent of the overall economy was in the building trades. LOF claimed that its competition coordinated with the federal government's "extensive program to 'Modernize Main Street,'" including the insuring of modernization loans up to $50,000 by the FHA. FHA archivists have been unable to confirm the program's enactment. *52 Designs to Modernize Main Street with Glass* (Toledo, OH: LOF Glass Co., 1935), 2–7, 76.

46. *52 Designs to Modernize Main Street with Glass*, 4, 23; "Program, Modernize Main Street Competition," *Architectural Record*, July 1935, 1. William Leach discusses how the popularization of large plate glass store windows from the late 1890s to the 1920s broke with the traditions of open-air display. Vitrolite modernizations of the 1930s in turn drew attention to the building more than the displayed goods (which themselves were often showcased more selectively in smaller display windows). Similarly, the color innovations of the 1890s–1920s in window displays contrasted with the 1930s focus on the color of the storefront itself. Modernization techniques of the 1930s applied to the ordinary store as well as the large department stores discussed by Leach. See "Facades of Color, Glass, and Light," in *Land of Desire: Merchants, Power, and the Rise of a New American Culture*, by William Leach (New York: Pantheon Books, 1993), 39–70. On store windows during the 1930s, see "Main Street, U.S.A.," 86–87.

47. *52 Designs to Modernize Main Street with Glass*, 4, 23, 50.

48. Ibid., 8, 10, 11, 18, 21, 33.

49. Ibid., 7, 10–11, 21, 23, 24, 26, 50. On the virtues of "striking" stores, see also "A Modern Store Building Is Modernized," *NREJ*, January 1936, 60; "Modernizing Increases the Rental Value of Old Stores," *NREJ*, November 1933, 47. LOF had produced Vitrolite in white since 1907 and in a range of opaque colors since 1922. *24th Annual Report of the Libbey Owens Ford Glass Company* (Toledo, OH: LOF Glass Co., 1940), 20, box 4, file 7, LOF Company Records. From the valuation point of view, it was important to avoid extremes in architectural taste. Frederick Babcock, "Report on Economic Survey of San Francisco and Northern California," February 14, 1934, 35; and Babcock, "Report on Economic Survey of Los Angeles and Southern California," 15, 31, both in box 3, FMBP.

50. Modernized "first-floor" storefronts sometimes extended so high that they obscured second-story windows. "Main Street, U.S.A.," 75, 86. By the 1940s there was a trend toward modernizing entire business blocks — a direction encouraged by the Pittsburgh Plate Glass Company. Brown, "You Won't Recognize Main St.," 115; *23rd Annual Report of the Libbey Owens Ford Glass Company*, 21.

51. On "a general appearance of decay and dejection" downtown, see Harland Bartholomew, "Can Blighted Urban Areas Be Rehabilitated?" *NREJ*, September 1, 1930, 17. See also Propper, "Saving Our Blighted Downtown Areas," 20; and Goldfarb, "The Appraisal of Retail Store Properties," 681.

52. "A Modern Store Building Is Modernized," 60; "Modernizing Establishes New Rental Values," 31.

53. "Modernizing Increases the Rental Value of Old Stores," 47. Other adjectives used by modernizers to describe the problem storefronts included "dilapidated," "rundown,"

"old," and "obsolete." "From 39% Occupancy to 72% with the Help of Vitrolite" (advertisement), *NREJ*, November 1933, 57; "New Stores Revive Old Building," *NREJ*, May 1933, 34. "Modernizing Increases Rent $267.50 per Month," 45.

54. "Cooperative Modernization Campaign Rebuilds Values in Downtown Oakland," *NREJ*, March 1936, 51. See Bartholomew, "Can Blighted Urban Areas Be Rehabilitated?" 19; J. C. Knapp, "Obsolescence Insurance Involves an Architect, Not an Insurance Company," *Architectural Forum*, May 1933, 440; and Ernest M. Fisher, "How Architects Can Help to Stabilize Land Values," *American Architect*, November 1934, 22–24.

55. "Remodeling Portfolio," 96; "Main Street, U.S.A.," 82.

56. William MacRossie, "Appraising in a War Economy," *Appraisal Journal*, April 1943, reprinted in *Appraisal Thought*, 97; Bartholomew, "Can Blighted Urban Areas Be Rehabilitated?" 19; Roy Wenzlick, "Is the Rate of Obsolescence on Improved Real Estate Increasing?" *Factual Selling No. 368 — REA*, 1936, 1–2. The Bridgeport survey showed how quickly air conditioning caught on during the depression. "Main Street, U.S.A.," 82.

57. Marietta Manufacturing Company's Sani Onyx was the other major product. On the history of structural glass, see U.S. Department of the Interior, National Park Service, "The Preservation of Historic Pigmented Structural Glass (Vitrolite and Carrara Glass)," *Preservation Briefs*, February 1984, Pamphlet 89.193, Hagley Museum and Library. See also Douglas A. Yorke Jr., "Material Conservation for the Twentieth Century: The Case for Structural Glass," *Bulletin for the Association for Preservation Technology* 13 (1981). On the changing popularity of modernization after the 1930s, see Nelson, *The Selection of Retail Locations*, 47. Nelson later became president of the Real Estate Research Corporation discussed in this chapter.

58. LOF, "Vitrolite Store Fronts and Building Exteriors," 1930s, 2, Trade Catalogue L6948 193, Hagley Museum and Library; LOF, "Vitrolite Colorful Structural Glass." Small towns did experience the impact of storefront structural glass. See the examples of relatively isolated southern communities (Tuskegee, Alabama, is one case) in the construction files of V. J. Elmore Stores, Inc., Department of Archives and Manuscripts, Birmingham Public Library.

59. "Modernizing Increases Rent $267.50 per Month," 45.

60. *23rd Annual Report of the Libbey Owens Ford Glass Company*, 21; Bartholomew, "Can Blighted Urban Areas Be Rehabilitated?" 20.

61. *REA*, August 1932, 57; "Investment and Speculation in Real Estate," *Investment Bulletin No. 37-2 — REA*, 1937, 1. On permanent values, see Bartholomew, "Can Blighted Urban Areas Be Rehabilitated?" 21.

62. Roy's older brother Delbert was REA's first president, but Roy bought out his interest in 1935. "The Canny Mr. Wenzlick of St. Louis, and His 'Coming Boom,'" 510, 512. On chatting with older men, see Roy Wenzlick, "These Are the Principles That Determine the Rent of Retail Shops," *As I See It — REA*, January 26, 1942, 14. For claims about REA's pioneering roles, see Roy Wenzlick, "The Art of Forecasting," *As I See — REA*, March 24, 1949, 100. "First man" quote from "Economic Surveys and Comprehensive Planning . . . by Roy Wenzlick & Company," Roy Wenzlick & Co., St. Louis, ca. 1960, box 10, file 362, collection sl 574, Roy Wenzlick Papers, Western Historical Manuscript Collection, University of Missouri, St. Louis (hereafter cited as RWP).

The American Society of Real Estate Counselors appears to have formed in 1953 or 1954. A charter member, Wenzlick held certificate number 27. "Qualifications of Roy Wenzlick as a Public Speaker on Factors Affecting Real Estate and Construction," box 2, file 27, RWP. Many of REA's research files, as well as business correspondence, speeches, and sample reports, are in the RWP collection. Because Roy Wenzlick had the *Analyst* microfilmed for the convenience of subscribers, it is available outside of archival collections. Records from his father's firm are also in the Western Historical Manuscript Collection.

63. According to Jim Downs's son, Anthony Downs of the Brookings Institution, RERC did not significantly expand its consulting work until about 1950. Anthony Downs spent his early career writing for the *Market Letter*. Phone interview by author with Anthony Downs, November 29, 1999. Roy Wenzlick and Company also gradually diversified its services to include reassessment appraising (for tax purposes), municipal surveys, retail location studies, and urban renewal appraising. In 1970 Wenzlick's company was bought by First Union, Inc., but then fizzled out under its new ownership.

64. RERC published thousands of research reports, city plans, market studies, appraisals, and newsletters for the national investment audience and individual clients. Mark Lindley, "James C. Downs, Jr., CPM: A Tribute to the Pioneer of Property Management," *Journal of Property Management*, January–February 1982, 3–7. "James Downs Dies: Former Civic Leader," *Chicago Sun-Times*, October 30, 1981. Clippings courtesy of RERC.

65. Appel, after military service, started with Bartholomew because of his fond memories of a planning course Bartholomew taught at Appel's undergraduate institution, the University of Illinois. Appel left RERC in 1976 to open his own appraising firm in St. Louis, which partly filled the void left by the recent closing of Wenzlick's company. Phone interview by author with James Appel, MAI, February 18, 2000; second interview, St. Louis, March 31, 2000. Roy Wenzlick was polite in negotiating with an RERC executive vice president about abruptly transferring his key employees to their new jobs at RERC. "Transcript of telephone conversation," May 20, 1963, box 1, file 13, RWP.

66. "Are Real Estate Cycles National or Local?" *REA*, February 1935, 363; "Are Saint Louis Figures Typical of the United States?" *REA*, April 1934, 259–60; "Bifocals," *Investment Bulletin — REA*, February 20, 1939, 31; "Roy Wenzlick & Co." undated brochure, ca. 1948, courtesy of Jim Appel. Data broken down by individual cities, which were very expensive to collect, were usually more valuable to subscribers. George Massengale, "General Report on Publications," August 21, 1972, 22, box 10, file 352, RWP. On underestimating the significance of geographic differences in economic recovery, see "We Lose a Few Tail Feathers," *REA*, October 28, 1941, 274.

67. Wenzlick, *The Coming Boom*, 4. Insurance companies and savings banks, many of which signed on in the 1930s and 1940s, proved to be the most loyal long-term subscribers. Roy Wenzlick to Tony Ciarleglio, memo, July 27, 1972, 1, box 10, file 352, RWP.

68. R. Carlyle Buley, *The Equitable Life Assurance Society of the United States, 1859–1964* (New York: Appleton-Century-Crofts, 1967), 2:1011–13. Courtesy of John Coss, Equitable Archives, New York, NY. Real estate mortgages declined as a percentage of insurance company assets (from 43 percent in the mid-1920s to 20 percent in the mid-1930s, largely owing to intense caution and the dive in new construction). "Life Insurance Companies as Mortgagees," *REA*, June 1937, 748, 750; "Real Estate Owned by National Banks," *REA*, May 28, 1941, 138–39; "Real Estate Holdings of Banks," *REA*, August 27, 1941, 214; "Roy Wenzlick & Co." undated brochure, ca. 1948. The array of entities involved in real estate

investment is documented in the letters to Wenzlick from subscribers. See box 1, files 12–14, RWP.

69. The *Analyst's* subscription rate stepped down to $75 in 1940, and then climbed slowly to $120 in 1962. Roy Wenzlick to George Massengale, memo, August 22, 1972, 1, box 10, file 352, RWP. "We Crow," *REA*, October 28, 1941, 276; on public as anxious, *As I See in 1944 — REA*, March 1944, 95; on sample questions and practical problem, see Wenzlick, *The Coming Boom*, 5–6. *Analyst* subscribers peaked at 1,025 in 1948, then dropped to 800 by 1959 and 500 in 1972. Handwritten note appended to Massengale, "General Report on Publications." Over the years the *Analyst* honed abbreviated versions of their publication, offering a digest and a version called *Trends* for lower subscription rates.

70. *American City*, October 1938, 152.

71. "We Crow," 271; "Roy Wenzlick & Co." undated brochure, ca. 1948; *REA*, August 1936, 589. Wenzlick was widely admired for his excellent statistics. His firm spent a lot of money ($100,000 by 1936) gathering data. "The Canny Mr. Wenzlick and His 'Coming Boom,'" 510–13.

72. "To the Broker," *REA*, September 1933, 187. Melvin Lanphar to Wenzlick, November 3, 1958; see also Michal Sumichrast to Wenzlick, June 3, 1958, both in box 1, files 12–14, RWP. *As I See in 1944*, 96; "We Crow," 271–76. The self-mocking usually appeared at self-conscious forecasting moments such as the first issue of the year or in reviews of successes and failures. "Forecasts for 1937," *REA*, January 1937, 660; "Forecasts for 1936," *REA*, January 1936, 493; "The Smoke Clears," *REA*, December 26, 1941, 331; E. G. Johnson, "Mortgage Prospects under the 'Fair Deal,'" *Mortgage Bulletin — REA*, March 14, 1949, 89.

73. Wenzlick, *The Coming Boom*, 5; "To the Broker," 187. One 1959 letter from a person who had been a subscriber since 1937 explained the newsletter's usefulness over the years; another described "scurrying to my old binder" to compare a current issue with past advice. M. Penn Phillips to Roy Wenzlick & Co., August 26, 1959; and C. M. Paine to Roy Wenzlick & Co., October 8, 1958, both in box 1, files 12–14, RWP. Subscribers often requested copies of articles to send to associates, politicians, and employees.

74. Roy Wenzlick, "The Factors Which Will End the Boom," *As I See It — REA*, February 24 1949, 45; Roy Wenzlick, "Am I a Menace to Real Estate?" *As I See It — REA*, June 30, 1948, 254. The *Analyst* quoted an unnamed forecaster reflecting on the nature of the business: "Forecasting consists of making guesses concerning what guesses the public as a whole will make in the near future concerning the more distant future about which they have no evidence." Often, the public "will guess wrong regarding the future and will implement their guesses with their dollars." "21 Forecasts for 1944," *REA*, January 1944, 1.

75. MacRossie, "Appraising in a War Economy," 91, 97; Homer Hoyt, "War and Real Estate," *Appraisal Journal*, April 1942, reprinted in *Appraisal Thought*, 85; *REA*, October 25, 1939, 239. The *Analyst* claimed that 1943 was the most difficult year in ten years of forecasting. "Real Estate in 1943?" *REA*, January 27, 1943, 1.

76. Robert H. Armstrong, "Valuation Problems in an Unbalanced Economic World," *Appraisal Journal*, January 1941, reprinted in *Appraisal Thought*, 78–79, 83–84.

77. *Market Letter*, October 31, 1940, 3; December 30, 1940, 3; January 7, 1942, 2. See also Roy Wenzlick, "The Decentralization of Cities," *As I See — REA*, December 30, 1942, 405–6. Although they were grateful for government occupancy during the depression and the war, downtown investors afterward became anxious for government offices to shrink

faster, because of a shortage of office space. In early 1947, *REA* noted that federal occupancy was still 9 percent. "Urban Real Estate — Commercial," *REA*, January 24, 1947, 13.

Most new construction had wound down before the federal ban against it. The directive improved the access of some priority cities to construction resources. Exceptions to the ban included commercial structures costing less than five thousand dollars and essential maintenance or repair work. Roy Wenzlick, "The Freezing Order on Construction," *As I See — REA*, April 15, 1942, 103–6.

78. The ban on manufacturing new cars had less impact than restrictions affecting their operation. *Market Letter*, January 7, 1942, 1–3.

79. Ibid., May 12, 1943, 2; September 13, 1943, 3–4.

80. Ibid., May 12, 1943, 2; June 5, 1942, 2; January 11, 1943, 3. Outlying commercial rents fared worse than downtown's: outlying rents rose in 2 percent of cities, dropped in 59 percent, and held in 39 percent. *REA*, March 25, 1943, n.p.; *Market Letter*, September 13, 1943, 4.

The *Analyst* found that in nondefense cities, "stores appealing to the luxury trade are having the greatest mortality." Wenzlick alerted subscribers to the recent New York State court cases voiding some long-term leases because War Production Board restrictions had interfered with trade. "Six Months after Pearl Harbor," *As I See It — REA*, June 1942, 175–76; *REA*, September 1942, 306. Shrinking store occupancy mirrored the wartime emphasis on production over consumption. The newsletter compared the refitting of manufacturing plants to how "hundreds of thousands of our citizens are being 'converted' from salesmen to welders, from experts to expediters, from mothers to moulders." *Market Letter*, January 11, 1943, 3–4.

81. *Market Letter*, May 12, 1943, 2; February 13, 1946, 3; "dire fear" from *Mortgage Bulletin — REA*, December 9, 1949, 511; on "the best portion of the district," see Roy Wenzlick, "The Decentralization of Downtown Districts," *As I See — REA*, July 1945, 189–90; Roy Wenzlick, "The Outlook," *As I See — REA*, February 1944, 53.

82. *Market Letter*, July 12, 1944, 1–2; "Decreases in Various Real Estate Factors," *REA*, December 1944, 338; *Market Letter*, September 12, 1945, 2; August 16, 1946, 4; July 1948, 3. For other contradictory evidence of downtown economic vitality, see *Market Letter*, August 1947, 4; November 1947, 3. The slow pace of government office contraction also surprised *REA*.

83. Malcolm P. McNair, "Department Stores on Uneasy Street," in *Changing Patterns in Retailing: Readings on Current Trends,* ed. John Wingate and Arnold Corbin (Homewood, IL: Richard Irwin, Inc., 1956), 44. "Plan Expansion of $1,500,000 at Dayton Co.," *Women's Wear Daily (WWD)*, December 21, 1945, box 4, Dayton's file; "Thalhimer's Planning Big Expansion," *WWD*, May 4, 1944; and "Thalhimer's Changes in Excess of $3,000,000," *Richmond News Leader*, September 15, 1947, box 14, Thalhimer's file; *WWD*, January 18, 1945, box 7, Harvey's file; *WWD*, December 8, 1944, box 7, Hammel's file; *WWD*, July 5, 1944, box 7, A. Harris file; all in Resseguie Collection, Baker Library, Harvard Business School. *Market Letter*, July 12, 1944, 1–2; Helen Canoyer, *Selecting a Store Location* (Washington, DC: Bureau of Foreign and Domestic Commerce, 1946), iii. See also "Population Factors in Retail Locations," *Appraisal Bulletin — REA*, October 20, 1948, 395; and William Street, "Deep Downtown Dynamic," 44th Annual Meeting, Chamber of Commerce of the United States, vertical files VF NAC 1670S, 4, Frances Loeb Library, Graduate School of Design, Harvard University. On buying shopping center sites for post-

war expansion, see A. B. Kissack, "Locational Advantages," *Appraisal Bulletin #25 — REA,* 1945, 120.

84. Wenzlick, "The Shift in Retail Uses in the Downtown District," 421; Springfield Chamber of Commerce, *Shoppers' Paradise: An Experiment in Downtown Revitalization* (Springfield, OR: Springfield Chamber of Commerce, 1957). On the slump in land values, see *Market Letter,* May 15, 1945, 3 – 4.

85. Villanueva, *Planning Neighborhood Shopping Centers,* 7; "Main Street, U.S.A.," 88.

86. *Market Letter,* May 15, 1945, 4; Villanueva, *Planning Neighborhood Shopping Centers,* 8.

87. Nathan Nirenstein, "There'll Always Be a Main Street," *Appraisal Journal,* January 1947, 105.

CHAPTER 5

1. Urban Redevelopment session, *Proceedings of First Annual Meeting,* International Downtown Executives Association (cited hereafter as IDEA), October 1955, 12, courtesy of International Downtown Association, Washington, D.C., office. The speaker was James C. Downs Jr., described in chapter 4 above. At this time he was head of Chicago's Housing and Urban Renewal Authority and president of the Real Estate Research Corporation.

2. Laurence Alexander, quoted in "Downtown Revitalization," *Stores Magazine,* March 1962, 23; Albert M. Cole to Gabriel Hauge, June 27, 1957, OF 120-C, Slum Clearance (2), box 617, Official File, Eisenhower, Dwight D.: Records as President, White House Central Files, 1953 – 61, Dwight D. Eisenhower Library, Abilene, Kans.; J. Palmer Murphy, "Insuring a Successful Downtown Operation," in *The Successful Future of the Independent Retailer* (New York: National Retail Merchants Association, 1960), 23. Cliché from Alexander, "Downtown Revitalization," 23. There is a similar lament in "Improved Traffic Flow and Expressways" session, *Proceedings of First Annual Meeting,* IDEA, October 1955, 9. Although many predicted the downtown's demise, not everyone mourned its loss. See Everett G. Smith Jr., *Downtown Change in Three Middle-Sized Cities* (Urbana: Bureau of Economic and Business Research, University of Illinois, 1964), 57.

3. Leo Adde, *Nine Cities: The Anatomy of Downtown Renewal* (Washington, DC: Urban Land Institute, 1969), v; Laurence Alexander, *Downtown Associations: Their Origins, Development, and Administration* (New York: Downtown Idea Exchange, 1966); Smith, *Downtown Change,* 2. A city planning literature sprang up seeking to define and draw boundaries around the central business district. See Raymond E. Murphy, *The Central Business District* (Chicago: Aldine-Atherton, 1972); Raymond E. Murphy and J. E. Vance, "Delimiting the CBD," *Economic Geography* 30 (July 1954): 189 – 222. For a recent contribution to the debate, see Richard Brown, "Delimiting the Perceived Downtown: A Perceptual Approach" (Ph.D. diss., University of Pennsylvania, 1991).

4. Smith, *Downtown Change,* 2; Arthur Kaufman, "Central City: A Beehive or a Morgue by '68," *Women's Wear Daily* (*WWD*), May 28, 1958, box 15, file Urban Renewal, Resseguie Collection, Baker Library, Harvard Business School (hereafter cited as RC); "Shopping Spreads Out: 'Downtown' Is Worried," *U.S. News and World Report,* November 7, 1952, 58.

5. "There Are Lots of People Downtown," *Business Week,* October 6, 1951, 138, 142; J. Ross McKeever, *Shopping Centers,* ULI Technical Bulletin no. 20, July 1953, 7; Richard Lawrence Nelson and Frederick T. Aschman, *Conservation and Rehabilitation of Major*

Shopping Districts, ibid., no. 22, February 1954, 4–5; and Leo Grebler, *Europe's Reborn Cities,* ibid., no. 28, 1956, foreword. See also *Shopping Centers Restudied,* ibid., no. 30, February 1957; *Urban Land* newsletters; and Hal Burton, ed., *The City Fights Back* (New York: Citadel, 1954), 147–49.

6. Victor Gruen, "Dynamic Planning for Retail Areas," *Harvard Business Review* 32, no. 6 (November–December 1954): 53–54, vertical file FH34G, Philadelphia City Planning Commission Library, Philadelphia (hereafter cited as PCPCL). *Merchandising Problems in Planning the First Branch Store* (New York: Merchandising Division, National Retail Merchants Association, 1961), 17, proceedings of panel at 1961 National Retail Merchants Association convention, courtesy of the National Retail Federation, Washington, D.C. (hereafter cited as NRF); Harold B. Wess, "Department Stores Can Stay 'Tops,'" *Department Store Economist,* March 1953, reprinted in *Changing Patterns in Retailing: Readings on Current Trends,* ed. John Wingate and Arnold Corbin (Homewood, IL: Richard Irwin, Inc., 1956), 51; Edward Stanton, *Branch Stores* (New York: National Retail Dry Goods Association, 1955), 18. See also "Retailers' Problem: Reviving a Sick, Old 'Downtown,'" *Business Week,* January 15, 1955, as reprinted in Wingate and Corbin, *Changing Patterns in Retailing,* 197; and *Branch Store Operations* (New York: National Retail Dry Goods Association, 1954), 2, proceedings from 1954 National Retail Dry Goods Association convention, courtesy of NRF.

7. William H. Whyte Jr. was associate editor. Jane Jacobs, "Downtown Is for People," *Fortune,* April 1958, reprinted in *The Exploding Metropolis,* ed. William H. Whyte Jr. (Garden City, NY: Doubleday, 1958; reprint, Berkeley: University of California Press, 1993), 138. The Rockefeller Foundation contacted Jacobs based on this article; as a result, she expanded her ideas into *The Death and Life of Great American Cities* (New York: Random House, 1961).

8. Leo F. Corrigan, quoted in Alexander, "Downtown Revitalization," 21.

9. J. Gordon Dakins, "Management Perspective: The Expansive Retailers of the West," *Stores Magazine,* October 1962, 3; "Retailers' Problem," 193.

10. Albert Cole, 1958 speech, 3, transcript in box 416, file 3, Housing Association of the Delaware Valley Pamphlet Collection, Temple University Libraries, Urban Archives (hereafter cited as HADV Pamphlet Collection).

11. Erie (Pa.) Redevelopment Authority, *Downtown Erie Renewal* (Erie, PA: McCarty Printing, 1965), 5, vertical file 34.2E, PCPCL.

12. See Jon Teaford's *Rough Road to Renaissance: Urban Revitalization in America, 1940–1985* (Baltimore: Johns Hopkins University Press, 1990), a recent synthetic work on urban renewal. He uses the phrase "glamor-boy dynamos" to refer to "the bright young mayors of the 1960s" (200–201). The classic analyses of urban renewal include Martin Anderson, *The Federal Bulldozer: A Critical Analysis of Urban Renewal, 1949–1962* (Cambridge, MA: MIT Press, 1964); Scott Greer, *Urban Renewal and American Cities: The Dilemma of Democratic Intervention* (New York: Bobbs-Merrill, 1965); Jeanne R. Lowe, *Cities in a Race with Time: Progress and Poverty in America's Renewing Cities* (New York: Random House, 1967); and James Q. Wilson, ed., *Urban Renewal: The Record and the Controversy* (Cambridge, MA: MIT Press, 1966).

13. Robert Beauregard has taken a different approach to urban renewal, focusing entirely on the powerful discourse of urban decline. Robert A. Beauregard, *Voices of Decline:*

The Postwar Fate of US Cities (Cambridge, MA: Blackwell, 1993). See also Carl Abbott, "Five Downtown Strategies: Policy Discourse and Downtown Planning since 1945," *Journal of Policy History* 5, no. 1 (1993): 5–27. Three major case studies are Joel Schwartz, *The New York Approach: Robert Moses, Urban Liberals, and Redevelopment of the Inner City* (Columbus: Ohio State University Press, 1993); Thomas H. O'Connor, *Building a New Boston: Politics and Urban Renewal, 1950–1970* (Boston: Northeastern University Press, 1993); and David Schuyler, *A City Transformed: Redevelopment, Race, and Suburbanization in Lancaster, Pennsylvania, 1940–1980* (University Park: Pennsylvania State University Press, 2002).

14. Baltimore's Charles Center project began as a private-municipal venture but eventually tapped into federal funds. Teaford, *The Rough Road to Renaissance*, 81–121, esp. 107. For admiration of Pittsburgh, Baltimore, and Rochester for avoiding subsidy except for eminent domain, see Stephen G. Thompson, "Urban Renewal and the Ambivalent Businessman," *Architectural Forum*, June 1959, 148–49. On Pittsburgh and Baltimore inspiring others, see "ACTION's Rousing Mr. Rouse," *Architectural Forum*, May 1950, 230.

15. On the growing interest of the real estate and construction industries in downtown problems, see "Rebuilding the Cities," *Business Week*, July 6, 1940, 35. Historians have increasingly acknowledged private-sector leadership in initiating, planning, and shaping urban redevelopment policy. These works rarely argue that business leaders co-opted public officials or perverted the policy process; instead they emphasize the common goals and interests of business leaders and public officials. Bernard J. Frieden and Lynne B. Sagalyn, *Downtown, Inc.: How America Rebuilds Cities* (Cambridge, MA: MIT Press, 1989), 17–27; John Mollenkopf, *The Contested City* (Princeton, NJ: Princeton University Press, 1983); Teaford, *The Rough Road to Renaissance*; Christopher Silver, *Twentieth Century Richmond: Planning, Politics, and Race* (Knoxville: University of Tennessee Press, 1984); Marc Weiss, *The Rise of the Community Builders: The American Real Estate Industry and Urban Land Planning* (New York: Columbia University Press, 1987); Arnold Hirsch, *Making the Second Ghetto: Race and Housing in Chicago, 1940–1960* (New York: Cambridge University Press, 1983). Robert Fogelson points out that downtown business interests had established the rationale for close-in slum clearance (and ensuing benefits for the business district) by the early 1940s; their actions must be weighed in understanding the Housing Act of 1949, as much as later urban renewal legislation. Robert M. Fogelson, *Downtown: Its Rise and Fall, 1880–1950* (New Haven, CT: Yale University Press, 2001), 357.

16. Quote from Edmund N. Bacon, "The City Image," in *Man and the Modern City*, ed. Elizabeth Geen, Jeanne R. Lowe, and Kenneth Walker (Pittsburgh: University of Pittsburgh Press, 1963), 31. On the impact of local and state models upon federal legislation, see Hirsch, *Making a Second Ghetto*.

17. See "Program of 'Action' Is Aimed at Solving City Slum Problems," *Camden (N.J.) Courier-Post*, September 9, 1953; and August 1955 newspaper kit compiled by the Advertising Council, both in box 84, file 10, HADV Pamphlet Collection. Albert Cole, speech to ACTION meeting on November 15, 1954, reprinted in *Congressional Record*, November 16, 1954, ibid. A few years after leaving his HHFA post, Cole became the head of ACTION. President Eisenhower also spoke at ACTION's founding luncheon, stating that the organization "seems to represent, to me, much more emphatically than do most

groups almost the philosophy of government by which I try to live." Malcolm S. Forbes, "A Time for Action," *Forbes Magazine of Business,* October 1, 1955, box 84, file 10, HADV Pamphlet Collection.

18. Major General Irving, "Action for Better Living," *Magazine of Prefabrication,* August 1955, 28, box 84, file 10, HADV Pamphlet Collection. One cannot easily isolate and measure the impact of the Advertising Council propaganda or the resistance to its messages. Nonetheless, the council commanded extraordinary access to channels of "mass education and persuasion," as its founders proclaimed. The Advertising Council had its origins in advertising executives' attempt to counter depression-era suspicions of their industry and corporate business generally. World War II enabled these executives to prove themselves in public service campaigns and forge a profitable connection with the national government. The War Advertising Council then reorganized to form the Advertising Council. Robert Griffith, "The Selling of America: The Advertising Council and American Politics, 1942–1960," *Business History Review* 47 (autumn 1983): 388–94, 411–12.

19. For an example of similar wording, compare Roy W. Johnson, "Operation Face Lift," *Trusts and Estates Magazine,* 1957; and Robert Cowan, "Banking's Key Part in Urban Renewal," *Journal of the American Bankers Association,* May 1957, in box 84, files 10–11, HADV Pamphlet Collection. The campaign had access to 55 newsletters, 6,700 newspapers, 700 trade publications, 2,500 radio stations, and 500 television stations. On the impact of the campaign, see "First ACTION Annual Report," box 84, file 12, HADV Pamphlet Collection. Before the ad council campaign, ACTION articles appeared in such trade publications as *Savings and Loan News, Mellon Bank News,* and the *Magazine of Prefabrication.* See articles in boxes 84 and 85, HADV Pamphlet Collection. See also press kits, *ACTION Reporter* newsletter, pamphlets, and studies, in the same collection.

20. Urban Redevelopment session, *Proceedings of First Annual Meeting,* IDEA, October 1955, 2–3, 12–13. Whites as well as blacks protested "Negro removal." Conservative whites feared a "fiendish scheme," as displaced African Americans tried to move into white neighborhoods.

21. Thompson, "Urban Renewal and the Ambivalent Businessman," 147. Interestingly, Roy Wenzlick's *Real Estate Analyst,* which opposed so many forms of federal intervention, reluctantly advised subscribers to support urban renewal. Roy Wenzlick, "Urban Redevelopment," *As I See — REA,* November 18, 1955, 493–96.

22. Stephen G. Thompson, "Where Realty Leaders Stand on Urban Renewal," *Architectural Forum,* April 1959, 109; Thompson, "Urban Renewal and the Ambivalent Businessmen," 147–49. See also "The Businessman's Stake in Urban Renewal," *Architectural Forum,* November 1959, 146–47.

23. Of these 1,300 projects, 732 had overcome the major planning and approval hurdles. William L. Slayton, statement before the Subcommittee on Housing, Committee on Banking and Currency, U.S. House of Representatives, November 21, 1963, reprinted in *Urban Renewal: People, Politics and Planning,* ed. Jewel Bellush and Murray Hausknecht (Garden City, NY: Anchor Books, 1967), 380–82; U.S. Housing and Home Finance Administration, 16th Annual Report (Washington, DC: U.S. Government Printing Office, 1962), reprinted in Bellush and Hausknecht, *Urban Renewal,* 387.

24. This is also noted by Beauregard, *Voices of Decline,* 297–98. He proposes (in the spirit of provoking discussion) that the declining urban core symbolized the weakened

male role in society. He suggests that "commentators shy away from interpreting urban decline in gender terms, in part, to avoid this basic and bothersome discovery."

25. Frank Emery Cox, "Transportation and Parking Facilities in Downtown Rehabilitation," *Traffic Quarterly*, October 1957, 485; Murphy, "Insuring a Successful Downtown Operation," 26–27; on "body of consumers," see Smith, *Downtown Change*, 57. On the singular importance of retail to the downtown economy, see also Melvin R. Levin and David A. Grossman, "The Expressway Impact on a Secondary Central Business District," *Traffic Quarterly*, April 1961, 196; and Eli Cox and Leo Erickson, *Retail Decentralization* (East Lansing: Bureau of Business and Economic Research, Graduate School of Business Administration, Michigan State University, 1967), 1.

The belief that downtown property contributed disproportionately to the municipal tax base helped forge cooperation among disparate interests. One statistical study from 1953 challenged this assumption, finding that downtown payments contributed only 3.65 percent of total municipal revenue in 1951. Accordingly, the argument to fight decentralization based on "'preserving values in the downtown district' is a mistake." James Appel, "The City's Stake in Its Downtown District," *Appraisal Bulletin — REA*, December 31, 1953, 549–51. On the allegedly crippling tax burden, see Teaford, *The Rough Road to Renaissance*, 18–19, 22–24, 44–52.

26. Teaford, *The Rough Road to Renaissance*, 17–20. Contemporaries understood suburbanization to be both a "natural" and a government-induced process; either way, it lay beyond the control of ordinary merchants. See Kenneth Jackson, *Crabgrass Frontier: The Suburbanization of the United States* (New York: Oxford University Press, 1985).

27. "The Businessmen's Stake in Urban Renewal," 146; quote from C. T. Jonassen, *The Shopping Center versus Downtown* (Columbus: Bureau of Business Research, Ohio State University, 1955), 58. Other studies include Stuart Rich, *Shopping Behavior of Department Store Customers* (Cambridge, MA: Harvard Business School, 1963); and *Shopping Habits and Travel Patterns*, ULI Technical Bulletin no. 24, March 1955. On redevelopment as a retail strategy, see "Retailers' Problem," 193–95; James R. Lowry, *The Retailing Revolution Revisited*, Ball State Monograph no. 16 (Muncie, IN: Ball State University, Publications in Business, 1969), 19–20.

28. Department stores generated about 10 percent of the average city's retail business. "Fluctuations of Department Store Sales," *Business Analyst — REA*, November 10, 1948, 427. In 1996 Kenneth Jackson wrote, "Until recently, central cities were almost defined by the locally owned department stores, which dominated local life." Kenneth Jackson, "All the World's a Mall: Reflections on the Social and Economic Consequences of the American Shopping Center," *American Historical Review* 101, no. 4 (October 1996): 1117. *WWD* has countless examples of this phenomenon. In Hartford, "G. Fox is not a store, not a department store . . . it is, as Mrs. Auerbach calls it, 'The Center of Connecticut Living.'" "What Is Hartford?" *WWD*, October 10, 1964, box 6, G. Fox File, RC. Conversely, in Nashville, Tennessee, an upstart department store unsettled the city's self-image. *WWD*, November 6, 1951, box 7, Harvey's file, RC. See also Wess, "Department Stores Can Stay 'Tops,'" 55. Stephanie Dyer argues that in the 1930s and 1940s Philadelphia's major department stores were "divesting from downtown real estate" despite loud commitments to Center City. Stephanie Kay Dyer, "Markets in the Meadows: Department Stores and Shopping Centers in the Decentralization of Philadelphia, 1920–1980" (Ph.D. diss., University of Pennsylvania, 2000), 133.

29. Martin Millspaugh, ed., *Baltimore's Charles Center: A Case Study of Downtown Renewal*, ULI Technical Bulletin no. 51, 1964, 13.

30. *WWD*, January 23, 1961; and "Focus," *WWD*, February 15, 1966, 1, both in box 7, Halliburton's file, RC. See also Cox and Erickson, *Retail Decentralization*, 43. On insurance companies and universities purchasing department stores after the war, see box 12, Real Estate Sales by Department Stores file, RC. In Oklahoma City residents dated the city's decline to 1955 when the local Sears closed.

31. Victor Gruen, "Planned Shopping Centers," *Dun's Review*, May 1953, vertical file FH34G, PCPCL; Howard T. Fisher, "Can Main Street Compete?" *American City*, October 1950, 101; Kenneth C. Welch, "The Regional Center and Downtown," *Traffic Quarterly*, July 1958, 380.

32. Laurence Alexander, *27 Most Influential Articles from Downtown Idea Exchange* (New York: Downtown Idea Exchange, 1958), 12; *250 Best Ideas from Downtown Idea Exchange* (New York: Downtown Idea Exchange, 1958), 19; and Lathrop Douglass, "Shopping Center Design," *Traffic Quarterly*, July 1958, 421. Not everyone agreed on the importance of landscaping to downtown renewal. In Fort Worth, one bank president raised objections to plantings in a proposed pedestrian mall: "I don't want to do business in a botanical garden." Jeanne R. Lowe, "What's Happened in Fort Worth?" *Architectural Forum*, May 1959, 138.

33. Seymour Buckner, "The Independent Retailer — Downtown or Shopping Center," in *The Successful Future of the Independent Retailer* (New York: National Retail Merchants Association, 1960), 38, courtesy of NRF; John E. Mertes, "Creative Site Evaluation for the Small Retailer," Small Business Management Research Reports, University of Oklahoma, December 1962, 157; on outlying malls springing up near where white downtown workers live, see Roy Wenzlick, "The Future of Retail Store Properties," *As I See — REA*, August 15, 1947, 297; on skyscrapers interfering with the shopping district, A. B. Kissack, "Locational Advantages," *Appraisal Bulletin #25 — REA*, 1945, 118; on distinguishing shoppers, "Shopping Habits and Pedestrian Traffic," *Appraisal Bulletin — REA*, November 24, 1948, 453.

34. The *Downtown Idea Exchange* gave pointers on how to compete with suburban standards, such as providing better downtown lighting "especially for women." Another tip suggested, "The downtown *Courtesy Center* or *Freshen-Up Center* appeals to the ladies. Offer comfortable chairs for resting, phones, rest rooms, possibly make-up tables and as many other good services as possible." *250 Best Ideas from Downtown Idea Exchange*, 5, 8–9. Liz Cohen has detailed the services offered by regional shopping centers in their efforts to become true community centers. Lizabeth Cohen, "From Town Center to Shopping Center: The Reconfiguration of Community Marketplaces in Postwar America," *American Historical Review* 101, no. 4 (October 1996): 1056–59.

35. Buckner, "The Independent Retailer," 39; Gruen, "Planned Shopping Centers."

36. Victor Gruen and Larry Smith, *Shopping Towns USA: The Planning of Shopping Centers* (New York: Reinhold Publishing, 1960), 154.

37. Richard Ratcliff, *Proceedings of First Annual Seminar*, IDEA, September 1954, 160–61. Ratcliff belittled "the little woman," while indirectly recognizing her importance to the downtown economy. On convenience as the new watchword, see Malcolm P. McNair, "Department Stores on Uneasy Street," in Wingate and Corbin, *Changing Patterns in Retailing*, 45. On the value of accessibility, see Wenzlick, "The Future of Retail Store Properties," 295; and "Inaccessibility of Business," *Appraisal Bulletin — REA*, September 14, 1948,

358. Half of IDEA's first conference addressed transportation and parking. *Proceedings of First Annual Meeting*, IDEA, October 1955, 7.

38. Mason Case, "Outlying Business Districts," *National Real Estate Journal (NREJ)*, September 15, 1930, 30; "The Logistics behind T.G. & Y.'s Swift Growth," *Chain Store Age*, December 1966, E19; Douglass, "Shopping Center Design," 413; Homer Hoyt, "Suburban Shopping Center Effects on Highways and Parking," *Traffic Quarterly*, April 1956, 185, vertical file FH34H, PCPCL.

39. Burton, *The City Fights Back*, 151; Richard L. Nelson, *The Selection of Retail Locations* (New York: F. W. Dodge Corp., 1958), 237, 261. Welton Becket, "Shopping Center Traffic Problems," *Traffic Quarterly*, April 1955, 170; Alexander, *27 Most Influential Articles from Downtown Idea Exchange*, 31. See also Wenzlick, "The Future of Retail Store Properties," 297–98.

40. For women lugging bundles, see Fisher, "Can Main Street Compete?" 100; and "Inaccessibility of Business," 358. The cartoon is in "Planning Suburban Shopping Centers," *Appraisal Bulletin — REA*, February 28, 1951, 115. See also the editorial "The Future of the American Out-of-Town Shopping Center," *Ekistics* (Harvard Graduate School of Design, 7th Urban Design Conference, August 1965), 96, vertical file FH34R, PCPCL.

41. Bart J. Epstein, "Evaluation of an Established Planned Shopping Center," in *Store Location and Development Studies*, by William Applebaum et al. (Worcester, MA: Clark University, 1961), 21; *Proceedings of First Annual Seminar*, IDEA, September 1954, 187; "The Record Reports: Peekskill Polls Shoppers to Win Retail Trade," *Architectural Record*, August 1960, 62.

42. Welch, "The Regional Center and Downtown," 373; Douglass, "Shopping Center Design," 420. It was possible to overstate women's impact on design decisions and real estate. A. Lawren Brown argued that "there never would have been any real estate to buy or sell had it not been for women." Brown believed that women had led "the great exodus from the city to the suburbs" and that Americans had to rebuild the cities accordingly. A. Lawren Brown, "How to Sell Real Estate to Women," *NREJ*, December 22, 1930, 10. Richard Nelson attributed America's higher rate of retail decentralization to the higher numbers of women drivers. Nelson, *The Selection of Retail Locations*, 29.

43. Douglass, "Shopping Center Design," 410–11. The downtown pedestrian mall popularized in the late 1950s was another effort "to re-make downtown in the image of a suburban shopping center." Laurence Alexander, "Some Second Thoughts on Downtown Malls," *Stores Magazine*, October 1959, vertical file FH34A, PCPCL.

44. "Thalhimer's Opens with Larger Boys', Men's Selections," *Daily News Record*, September 17, 1947, box 14, Thalhimer's file, RC.

45. "Rich's Plans New Building to House Store for Men," *Daily News Record*, November 28, 1950, box 12, M. Rich & Bros. file, RC. Lizabeth Cohen has argued that the suburban shopping mall symbolized the feminization of public space. This research suggests another way of looking at the issue, proposing that the suburban mall created a new kind of female-dominated commercial space because (unlike Main Street) it effectively removed men from the retail district during the regular work week. Downtown commercial space had focused on attracting women since the 1920s. Cohen, "From Town Center to Shopping Center," 1053–55, 1072.

46. Nelson, *The Selection of Retail Locations*, 247.

47. Gerald Kirkbridge Taylor Jr., "A Study of the Relationships of Land Value and Land

Use in a Central Business District" (master's thesis, Georgia Institute of Technology, 1956), 59, cited in *The Central Business District in Transition: Methodological Approaches to CBD Analysis and Forecasting Future Space Requirements*, by Shirley F. Weiss (Chapel Hill: University of North Carolina, Research Paper no. 1, City and Regional Planning Studies, May 1957), 10–11, vertical file FH34W, PCPCL. Urban planner Shirley Weiss was bringing to her colleagues' attention the conclusions of Taylor's Atlanta study, highlighting the argument that between the 1920s and the 1950s the link between women shoppers and peak downtown land values had strengthened. Weiss was unusual in explicitly raising this topic; it is hard not to speculate that this was related to her own gender.

48. "Retailers' Problem," 192. See also Larry Fitzmaurice, "St. Paul to 'Redesign' Downtown Area to Halt Shoppers' Strike," *Sales Management*, January 1, 1945, 78. On suburban land value peaks, see Wenzlick, "The Future of Retail Store Properties," 297.

49. The entrance of women into the real estate profession during the 1930s and 1940s (focusing on residential property), but especially after World War II, also emphasized the masculinity of commercial realty and underscored the identity of male real estate agents as city-builders. See Jeffrey M. Hornstein, "The Rise of the Realtor®: Professionalism, Gender, and Middle-Class Identity, 1908–1950," in *The Middling Sorts: Explorations in the History of the American Middle Class*, ed. Burton J. Bledstein and Robert D. Johnston (New York: Routledge, 2001), 232.

50. David Riesman, *The Lonely Crowd: A Study of the Changing American Character* (Garden City, NY: Doubleday, 1953), 320. Elaine Tyler May has delineated a broader cultural anxiety in the 1950s about the "domestic containment" of women. Elaine Tyler May, *Homeward Bound: American Families in the Cold War Era* (New York: Basic Books, 1988). By 1960 twice as many women were employed as in 1940. Married workers increased between 1947 and 1952 from 7.5 million to 10.4 million, and working mothers increased from 1.5 million to 6.6 million. William Chafe, *The Unfinished Journey*, 2d ed. (New York: Oxford University Press, 1991), 84–85, 123–26.

William H. Whyte argued that corporate wives' adaptability, sociability, and self-sacrifice were crucial to their husbands' career success. Although, according to prescriptive literature, men achieved satisfaction at home, many women suspected their husbands' emotional fulfillment came from work and quietly resented their husbands' stimulating office life. William H. Whyte Jr., *Is Anybody Listening?* (New York: Simon and Schuster, 1952), 145–205, esp. 164–66. Whyte describes reactions to *Fortune* magazine's study of corporate wives in *The Organization Man* (New York: Doubleday, 1957), 175, 287–91, 401.

51. Urban Redevelopment session, *Proceedings of First Annual Meeting*, IDEA, October 1955, 4; Delbert S. Wenzlick, "Pedestrian Traffic," *NREJ*, August 18, 1930, 21. See also Brown, "How to Sell Real Estate to Women," 10–12. Married women's spending power only increased with the spread of credit cards. Cohen, "From Town Center to Shopping Center," 1075.

52. McNair, "Department Stores on Uneasy Street," 45; John P. Alevizos and Allen E. Beckwith, "Downtown Dilemma," *Harvard Business Review* 32, no. 1 (January–February 1954): 118; and Case, "Outlying Business Districts," 30. See also "Main Street — The Bulwark of Retailing," *Chain Store Age*, February 1957, administrator's edition, reprinted in *Retailing: Principles and Methods*, ed. Delbert Duncan and Charles Phillips, 5th ed. (Homewood, IL: R. D. Irwin, 1959), 85, 87.

53. Case, "Outlying Business Districts," 30.

54. Richard M. Bennett, "Random Observations on Shopping Centers and Planning for Pedestrians," *Architectural Record,* September 1957, 217; Kissack, "Locational Advantages," 118; and Douglass, "Shopping Center Design," 410–11. The centers did become true workplaces for many married suburban women who secured part-time employment there. Cohen, "From Town Center to Shopping Center," 1075.

55. Wess, "Department Stores Can Stay 'Tops,'" 53.

56. Betty Friedan, *The Feminine Mystique* (New York: Dell, 1963), 207.

57. Chafe, *The Unfinished Journey,* 127.

58. Friedan, *The Feminine Mystique,* 207.

59. James C. Downs Jr., Urban Redevelopment session, *Proceedings of First Annual Meeting,* IDEA, October 1955, 1–2. On the need for "quality shoppers" residing near downtown, see Herbert Gans, *People, Plans, and Policies: Essays on Poverty, Racism, and Other National Urban Problems* (New York: Columbia University Press, 1993), 199. In the late 1950s, the press paid increasing attention to the racial composition of northern cities. See "Population — Racial Groups" file, vertical file FC67, PCPCL.

60. Mertes, "Creative Site Evaluation for the Small Retailer," 203, 143–45; Dero Saunders, "Department Stores: Race for the Suburbs," *Fortune,* December 1951, 173. In the 1950s most plans intended the revitalized downtown to accommodate "elites" rather than "average people." Frieden and Sagalyn, *Downtown, Inc.,* 16–19.

61. Daniel Seligman, "The Enduring Slums," *Fortune,* December 1957, reprinted in *The Exploding Metropolis,* 119.

62. "An Encroaching Menace," *Life,* April 11, 1955, 125–27, box 84, file 10, HADV Pamphlet Collection. It is possible that the use of red to characterize the "encroaching menace" would have resonated with fears of Communism. See, too, the photo of new downtown skyscrapers in Pittsburgh framed by walls of partly demolished building, Burton, *The City Fights Back.*

63. For various ominous descriptions of slums, see ACTION pamphlets, box 84, file 10, HADV Pamphlet Collection; and Albert M. Cole, speech to ACTION meeting on November 15, 1954, reprinted in *Congressional Record,* November 16, 1954, box 84, file 10, HADV Pamphlet Collection. The retail text is Wingate and Corbin, *Changing Patterns in Retailing,* 197; slums as "poor customers" in "The Businessman's Stake in Urban Renewal," 146.

64. During the course of the first urban renewal project in Portland, Maine, in the 1950s, 50 percent of the uprooted families were "non-white" — they were Italian, many of them first-generation immigrants. *Urban Renewal in Selected Cities: Hearings before a Subcommittee of the Committee on Banking and Currency, United States Senate* (Washington, DC: U.S. Government Printing Office, 1957). In Boston's West End redevelopment, working-class Poles and Italians predominated. Gans, *People, Plans, and Policies,* 194–95.

Slums, practically by definition, were home to non-WASPS. One Chicago housing official asserted that Appalachian whites were "about the only sizeable group of white, Protestant, old-line Americans who are now living in city slums." Seligman, "The Enduring Slums," 114. See also Charles Silberman, "The City and the Negro," *Fortune,* March 1962, 90. Fragmentary evidence suggests that land values in Japanese and Chinese business districts were at times higher than in adjacent "Occidental" districts. Stanley L. McMichael, *McMichael's Appraising Manual,* 3d ed. (New York: Prentice-Hall, 1944), 50.

65. George Schermer, "The *Real* Story about the Big City," February 6, 1959, vertical

file FC67.2P, PCPCL. Schermer directed Philadelphia's Commission on Human Relations. Morton Grodzins, "Metropolitan Segregation," in *Scientific American,* October 1957, cited in *Urban Renewal in Selected Cities,* 19–20. Grodzins expressed similar views in his *Metropolitan Area as a Racial Problem* (Pittsburgh: University of Pittsburgh Press, 1958), 12–13, vertical file FC67G, PCPCL.

66. "Nightmare or Dream?" *House and Home,* October 1957, 140 E-H. This was an ACTION-sponsored study carried out by the faculty and students of the University of Pennsylvania's city planning program.

67. Gruen and Smith, "Shopping Centers," 67–68. Similar sentiments are expressed in "Retailers' Problem," 195; and *Proceedings of First Annual Seminar,* IDEA, September 1954, 162.

68. Urban Redevelopment Session, *Proceedings of First Annual Meeting,* IDEA, October 1955, 3; Schermer, "The *Real* Story about the Big City," 9; Albert Cole, address to Pittsburgh Housing Association at Gateway Plaza, May 11, 1955, 5, box 416, file 3, HADV Pamphlet Collection. On the novelty of publicly discussing racial issues, see "Population—Racial Groups" file, vertical file FC67, PCPCL. Although the 1950s are no longer seen by most historians as "a period of public innocence," the obsession with creeping slums behind urban renewal in the 1950s needs to be reconciled with the supposed discovery of poverty in the 1960s. The phrase is from Allan Talbot, *The Mayor's Game: Richard Lee of New Haven and the Politics of Change* (New York: Harper and Row, 1967), 166.

69. *Up Ahead: A Regional Land Use Plan for Metropolitan Atlanta* (Atlanta: Metropolitan Planning Commission, February 1958), 69, 71, 92. For community protest, see the pages inserted at the front of the plan in the copy at the Fine Arts library, University of Pennsylvania. "ACTION Urban Renewal Clinic," *American City,* February 1957, box 84, file 11, HADV Pamphlet Collection.

70. Schermer, "The *Real* Story about the Big City," 2; Silberman, "The City and the Negro," 89–90. Silberman gave the full list of problems: "When city officials talk about spreading slums, they are talking in the main about physical deterioration of the areas inhabited by Negroes. And when they talk about juvenile delinquency, or the burden of welfare payments, or any of a long list of city problems, officials are talking principally about the problems of Negro adjustment to city life" (89).

71. Frieden and Sagalyn, *Downtown, Inc.,* 15; and J. Stanley Purnell, "The Inner City: Human Resources and Human Conflicts," speech before the Mott Adult Education Program of the Flint Board of Education, Flint, MI, November 9, 1964, 2, transcript in box 85, file 3, HADV Pamphlet Collection. For a bibliography of pre-1935 articles on obsolescence, see Mary Ethel Jameson, compiler, "Obsolescence of Buildings," *Journal of the American Institute of Real Estate Appraisers,* January 1935, reprinted in *Selected Readings in Real Estate Appraisal* (Chicago: American Institute of Real Estate Appraisers, 1953), 602–7.

72. "Address by Albert M. Cole, Administrator of the Housing and Home Finance Agency at the Luncheon of the Redevelopment Authority of Kansas City, Following Demolition Ceremonies at the Northside Redevelopment Project, Hotel Muehlebach, 12:00 PM, Monday, August 9, 1954," 1, OF 25, Housing and Home Finance Agency, 1954 (2), box 201, Official File, Eisenhower, Dwight D.: Records as President, White House Central Files, 1953–61, Dwight D. Eisenhower Library.

73. Ibid., 2–3.

74. Ibid., 3–4. Elsewhere Cole described yet another relevant perspective that I would

call a rearview-mirror take on downtowns. Since many city executives had followed the trend to live in the suburbs, they and their families had a removed, commuting relationship to the city core. Cole asked an audience of urban renewal supporters: "Do we keep moving out farther from the center of the city because we like to travel? What is happening to that business area we left downtown — that shrinking island of congestion cut off from the rest of the city by slums and blight?" Albert Cole, speech to ACTION meeting on November 15, 1954, reprinted in *Congressional Record,* November 16, 1954. See also Victor Gruen and Larry Smith, "Shopping Centers: The New Building Type," *Progressive Architecture,* June 1952, 67, vertical file FH34G, PCPCL; and John Dyckman, "Bringing Back People Is Not the Point," *Challenge,* December 1961, box 52, file 33, HADV Pamphlet Collection.

75. Buckner, "The Independent Retailer," 34. Alexander, *27 Most Influential Articles from Downtown Idea Exchange,* 8, 11; Gruen, "Dynamic Planning for Retail Areas," 53; *250 Best Ideas from Downtown Idea Exchange,* 7–10.

76. For panicky solutions and gimmicks, James W. Rouse, "Will Downtown Face Up to Its Future?" *Urban Land,* February, 1957, 1; on horse-and-buggy age, Fisher, "Can Main Street Compete?" 100; on incompetent capitalists, Smith, *Downtown Change,* 60; Burton, *The City Fights Back,* 155; for fannies and self-destruction, see "Focus: Main Street's Rich Uncle — Uncle Sam," *WWD,* February 15, 1966, box 15, file Urban Renewal, RC.

77. Raymond E. Wolfinger, *The Politics of Progress* (Englewood Cliffs, NJ: Prentice-Hall, 1974), 298–356; Smith, *Downtown Change,* 58–60.

78. Quote from Smith, *Downtown Change,* 58–9. The Eisenhower administration's urban renewal files show that some groups did contest the obsolescence label. In 1954 the Small Business Administration disagreed with the HHFA over the Washington Square Southeast Project in New York City. Consultants took issue with the redevelopment report's definition of obsolescence: "The report states that 82 percent of the commercial buildings are obsolete, being more than 50 years old. . . . The report does not consider the fact that this obsolescence would be a reason for demolishing most of the industrial area of New York, not only this particular district." The proposal came close to saying that age itself justified demolition. Thomas McCaffrey Jr. and Alexander Summer, "Report on Washington Square Southeast Project," 4, attached to cover letter from Wendell B. Barnes, administrator, to J. W. Follin, director, Division of Slum Clearance and Urban Redevelopment, Housing and Home Finance Agency, dated May 5, 1954, OF 120-C, Slum Clearance (1), box 617, Official File, Eisenhower, Dwight D.: Records as President, White House Central Files, 1953–61, Dwight D. Eisenhower Library.

79. "Main Street's Vanishing Patina," *Architectural Forum,* January 1960, 108.

80. *250 Best Ideas from Downtown Idea Exchange,* 7–10; Gruen and Smith, "Shopping Centers," 98. Liz Cohen describes how the early regional malls "set out to perfect the concept of downtown, not to obliterate it." Here she refers specifically to the mall as a community center, as well as the physical layout of "stores lining both sides of an open-air pedestrian walkway that was landscaped and equipped with benches." Cohen, "From Town Center to Shopping Center," 1055–56.

Even as demolition transformed Main Streets, advisers continued to promote the relatively modest investment strategies established during the Progressive era. The 1950s *Downtown Idea Exchange* reads like a catalog of suggestions from 1910s city plans. Among its "250 best ideas," the newsletter proposed eliminating the "most garish and blatant overhanging signs," the "mess of *overhead wires*," and "*downtown clutter*" such as "posters, standards, signs, posts, etc." Merchants needed to emphasize the "good housekeeping of sidewalks." The newsletter even suggested "harmonizing" the look of the street by painting the floors above the second story the same color.

81. Marcel Villanueva, *Planning Neighborhood Shopping Centers* (New York: National Committee on Housing, Inc., 1945), 5, vertical file FH34V, PCPCL; Joseph Laronge, "Should We Get Excited about Retail Decentralization?" *NREJ,* December 1938, 22. On convincing customers of obsolescence of goods, see Mark Hutter, "The Downtown Department Store as a Social Force," *Social Science Journal* 24, no. 3 (June 1987): 244. See also Roland Marchand, *Advertising the American Dream: Making Way for Modernity, 1920–1940* (Berkeley: University of California Press, 1985); William Leach, *Land of Desire: Merchants, Power, and the Rise of a New American Culture* (New York: Pantheon Books, 1993).

82. Walker Evans, "'Downtown': A Last Look Backward," *Fortune,* October 1956, 157. In Hartford, Connecticut, the *New York Times* thought that "the nostalgic may feel a pang for the passing of the colorful 'Hill,' with its narrow, aging brick buildings undermined by time." "In History's Shadow, a Symbol of the Future," *New York Times,* November 24, 1963, sec. 11, p. 6. See Max Page, *The Creative Destruction of Manhattan, 1900–1940* (Chicago: University of Chicago Press, 1999), for a detailed analysis of the use of history to support urban demolition; and M. Christine Boyer, *The City of Collective Memory: Its Historical Imagery and Architectural Entertainments* (Cambridge, MA: MIT Press, 1994), on the role of memory in modernism.

83. Wenzlick, "Urban Redevelopment," 493.

84. Mertes, "Creative Site Evaluation for the Small Retailer," 152; Murphy, *The Central Business District,* 1. See also Helen Canoyer, *Selecting a Store Location* (Washington, DC: Bureau of Foreign and Domestic Commerce, 1946), 24–25. For "the real fruits," see "The Future of the American Out-of-Town Shopping Center," 101. The quote probably paraphrases a statement made by Ed Bacon.

85. "Store's Bargain Mart: A Later Development of Department Retailing," *Dry Goods Economist,* May 18, 1901, 21, box 2, Basements file, RC. On interactions among different classes in the stores, see Susan Porter Benson, *Counter Cultures: Saleswomen, Managers, and Customers in American Department Stores, 1890–1940* (Urbana: University of Illinois Press, 1986). The "shawl trade" comment was made by a Strawbridge & Clothier official in a 1950 letter, describing the expected appeal when their basement Budget Store opened in 1922. Edwin S. Severson to Charles Taylor, August 26, 1950, series V Real Estate Records, box 33, "S&C: Budget Store, Philadelphia, 1950" file, Strawbridge & Clothier Collection no. 2117, Hagley Museum and Library, Wilmington, Del.

86. "Basement Departments 'Left at Post' in Race of Dept. Stores to Suburbs," *Daily News Record,* April 4, 1956; "Stores in Centers Hit for Omitting Bargain Basements," *WWD,* November 29, 1961, both in box 2, Basements file, RC.

87. "Basement Departments 'Left at Post' in Race of Dept. Stores to Suburbs"; Stuart Hanger, "Hudson's 37-Year Old Basement Store Has Personality, Dignity of Its Own," *Daily News Record,* September 12, 1957, 18, box 2, Basements file, RC.

88. Ed Gold, "Bam's Units Due to Be Nearly Doubled to Fifteen by 1968," *WWD,* June 4, 1963; and Richard Rosenthal, "Focus . . . Frank Merriwell at Bam's," *WWD,* April 7, 1965, both in box 2, L. Bamberger & Co. file, RC. Only an unusual basement in the 1950s claimed to draw all classes. In Filene's Basement (Boston), "befurred Beacon Hill dowa-

gers bargain hunt side by side with working girls and 'upstate' new Englanders." Joan Clark, "Filene's Famous Basement Marks 50th Anniversary," *WWD*, August 27, 1958, box 2, Basements file, RC.

89. Joseph Laronge, "Traffic Counts," *Journal of the American Institute of Real Estate Appraisers*, April 1938, reprinted in *Selected Readings in Real Estate Appraisal*, 739.

90. A. B. Kissack, "Adverse Real Estate Trends and City Planning," *Appraisal Bulletin — REA*, March 25, 1943, 56.

91. Albert Cole, 1958 speech, 3, transcript in box 416, file 3, HADV Pamphlet Collection.

CHAPTER 6

1. Winton M. Blount, "Are We Doing Enough?" November 21, 1968, 10–11, series I, box 22, unmarked binder of Blount speeches, U.S. Chamber of Commerce Records, accession 1960, Hagley Museum and Library, Wilmington, Del. (hereafter cited as USCCR). The speech was made in Birmingham. If a community has social disorders such as racial violence, Blount said elsewhere, all the skyscrapers and cultural centers "will not be enough to prevent people from shunning such a place." Winton Blount, "Smokestacks Are Not Enough: The Changing Role of the Modern Chamber," Membership Luncheon, Denver Chamber of Commerce, October 25, 1968, 5, ibid.

2. Winton B. Blount, "Get Ready for a Bigger Job," speech before the American Chamber of Commerce Executives Management Conference, Portland, Oregon, October 9, 1968, 1–2, series I, box 22, unmarked binder of Blount speeches, USCCR. Market analysts speculated that all municipal bond offerings would be hurt by violence, not merely those of specific cities. John H. Allan, "Will the Riots Hurt Municipal Bond Sales?" *New York Times* (*NYT*), August 13, 1967, 115.

3. On "wave of violence," crime and property values, see Real Estate Research Corporation (RERC), *National Market Letter* (*NML*), July 1964, 3. For a blended discussion of crime, civil rights agitation, and recent riots in Rochester and Harlem, see RERC, *NML*, August 1964, 2. On antiwar violence, especially on campuses, see John Darnton, "Antiwar Protests Erupt across U.S.," *NYT*, May 10, 1972, 22. For a Main Street that did not recover after a violent August 1970 Vietnam war protest involving twenty thousand demonstrators (three people died), see Matea Gold, "It's Suffered a Riot and a Recession," July 25, 1999, *Los Angeles Times*, B1. Although fear of crime was a part of many anxieties related to personal security downtown (walking a long distance to a parked car, for example, or rumors of impending protests), it was usually subsumed in these other issues and very rarely drove investment debates itself.

4. H. Paul Friesma, "Black Control of Central Cities: The Hollow Prize," *Journal of the American Institute of Planners*, March 1969, 75.

5. Under segregation, a less visible form of violence had shaped daily Main Street life. Whites had a way of denying that conflict. See Robert J. Norrell, *Reaping the Whirlwind: The Civil Rights Movement in Tuskegee* (Chapel Hill: University of North Carolina Press, 1998), 107–8.

6. The quoted comment was by a spokesman for North Carolina College (now North Carolina Central University), where the angry crowd ended up the night of April 4 and where two thousand gathered the following morning to march two miles to City Hall. Ann Kruger, "2,000 Hold March and Hear Mayor," *Durham Sun*, April 5, 1968, 1–2; Stan Swofford and Ann Colarusso, "Fires Strike 11 Places in Durham," *Durham Morning Herald*,

April 7, 1968, 1. On the Durham march as peaceful, see Frances Lonnette Williams oral history, in "Let Us March On: Raleigh's Journey toward Civil Rights," exhibition catalog for exhibit of same name, presented by the Raleigh City Museum, opening on April 9, 2000, 31–33. Durhamites experienced unique regret since on the day that King was shot, he was originally scheduled to be in Durham.

Details of the Durham photograph were obtained from a September 13, 2000, interview by the author with the photographer, Billy Barnes, in Chapel Hill, North Carolina. Director of public relations for the North Carolina Fund in the 1960s, Barnes documented poverty, activism, and community social programs in the state. Fifteen hundred of his NCF photographs are available in Wilson Library, University of North Carolina, and the balance are in his possession. The editors of the *Journal of the American Institute of Planners* did not explain the photograph's content (but they did place it on the issue's cover as a powerful image). Until I spoke with Barnes, I did not realize that the photo depicted the Main Street of the city in which I currently lived.

7. Center for Research in Marketing, Inc., "The Dynamics of Purchase Behavior in the Negro Market," 1962, cited in "Study Shows Negroes Buy in Local Stores," *Home Furnishings Daily (HFD)*, October 31, 1962; "San Francisco Stores Gear for More Non-White Patrons," *Women's Wear Daily (WWD)*, September 22, 1954, 14, both in box 10, Negro Retailers and Race Relations file, Resseguie Collection, Baker Library, Harvard Business School (hereafter cited as NRRR, RC). Despite its title, this file had little on black business but rather focused on black consumers and the impact of civil rights demonstrations. Most stories were from retail trade papers, primarily *WWD*. The clippings did not generally include the page numbers.

8. Joseph Wolfe, "Absence of Negro Mannequins Raises Queries in Harlem," *WWD*, August 27, 1957, NRRR, RC. At the time, no so-called colored mannequins were available; the few in use were figures that had been "dipped" ("recolored but not newly sculptured").

9. In the 1950s, some of economist Paul Edwards's 1930s points about the African American market finally found wider acceptance — the facts that blacks were drawn to high-quality stores and goods, that they dressed well because they could not afford to look "shabby," and that they basically bought what other people did. Some retailers held on to the mistaken assumption that the black shopper was "strictly a budget buyer." Along with the new appreciation could come stereotypes, such as condescending suggestions for reaching black consumers through "billboards with little text and eye-catching illustrations," based on the belief that blacks did not "respond" to routine advertising. "Negro Preference Is Seen for Buying at Better Stores," *WWD*, September 29, 1954. "Treat Negro Customer As You Would White," *Daily News Record (DNR)*, August 21, 1959. Paul Edwards is discussed in chapter 3. Ralph W. Jones, "The Negro Market: Many Stores Fail to Push for Additional Business," *HFD*, August 19, 1959. *Ebony* publisher John H. Johnson described how African Americans had rescued the hat industry when other Americans lost interest in the product. Marshall M. Jacobson, "Whites Moving to Suburbs: Negroes Seen Filling Store Sales Gap," *DNR*, September 19, 1959. All articles in NRRR, RC. This had particular poignancy because under segregation blacks were often specifically forbidden to try on hats.

Robert Weems points out that Johnson had financial interests in encouraging white businesses to advertise to blacks. *Ebony*'s advertising income almost tripled between 1962 and 1969. Weems finds that the trend toward catering to white corporations came at the expense of black business. Robert Weems, *Desegregating the Dollar: African American Consumerism in the Twentieth Century* (New York: New York University Press, 1998), 74–76.

10. On "overlooking" black buyers who were increasingly downtown consumers, "The Negro Market: Potential Business Seen $18–19 Million," *HFD*, August 17, 1959; on stores as willing to gamble, "Negro Poll: 89% Favor Yule Boycott," *WWD*, September 26, 1963; on marching by the store, Jones, "The Negro Market: Many Stores Fail to Push," all in NRRR, RC.

11. On the numerous 1950s downtown protests and sit-ins besides the Montgomery bus boycott, see Harvard Sitkoff, *The Struggle for Black Equality* (New York: Hill and Wang, 1981), 69–96; 1957 and 1958 clippings in NRRR, RC. See also Norrell, *Reaping the Whirlwind;* Elizabeth Jacoway and David R. Colburn, eds., *Southern Businessmen and Desegregation* (Baton Rouge: Louisiana State University Press, 1982). Greensboro, North Carolina, marked the intensification of civil disobedience downtown. More than two hundred cities witnessed protests in 1960 alone. Steven F. Lawson, *Running for Freedom* (New York: McGraw-Hill, 1991), 72.

Most historians of the sit-ins focus on the crusades' impact upon the participants and the movement, of course, not on downtowns. Most analyses of 1960s urban race violence do not include the civil rights melees of the early 1960s. See Robert Beauregard, *Voices of Decline: The Postwar Fate of US Cities* (Cambridge, MA: Blackwell Publishers, 1993), 161–81, esp. 163–64. In analyzing the era's African American campaigns of economic retribution, Robert Weems argues that historians have overemphasized the role of liberal white altruism. Weems describes the "pragmatic conservatism" of American business. Weems, *Desegregating the Dollar,* 70.

12. On Greensboro, "Negroes' Sitdown Hits 2 More Cities," *NYT,* February 9, 1960; on merchants "scared to death," John T. Norman, "Negro Lunchroom Issue May Reach Supreme Court," *WWD,* February 25, 1960. See also "Virginia Acts to Strengthen Trespass Laws," *WWD,* February 26, 1960; "Retail Losses Cited in Negro Sitdowns; Spread Is Feared," *WWD,* February 25, 1960. All in NRRR, RC.

13. "Negroes' Protest Turns into Melee — Chains and Tire Tools Used in Brawl in Virginia — Raleigh Pickets March," *NYT,* February 17, 1960; "Negroes' Sitdown Ends in Fist Fight — Whites Taunt and Throw Snowballs at the Group in High Point, N.C.," *NYT,* February 16, 1960; "Retail Losses Cited in Negro Sitdowns"; Claude Sitton, "Negroes' Protest Spreads in South: Reaches to South Carolina Stores amid Violence," *NYT,* February 13, 1960; all in NRRR, RC.

14. Claude Sitton, "Negro Sitdowns Stir Fear of Wider Unrest in South," *NYT,* February 15, 1960, NRRR, RC.

15. Frances Lonnette Williams, in "Let Us March On," 33–34. The same woman explained that the fear of snipers was particularly strong on Fayetteville Street in Raleigh because the marchers "really couldn't see on those buildings."

16. "Collins Decries Curbs by Stores," *NYT,* March 21, 1960; "Incidents Hurt Jacksonville Store Volume," *WWD,* September 1, 1960; "Sit-In Violence Closes Jackson Woolworth Store," *WWD,* May 29, 1963; "Bill Bans Refusal to Sell to Negroes: New Issues Loom," *WWD,* May 23, 1963, all in NRRR, RC.

17. Larry Shields, "War and Peace — Two Faces South," *WWD,* June 21, 1963. "Integration Spur to Sales in South: New Threats Loom," *WWD,* September 23, 1963, both in NRRR, RC. Student marches following King's assassination, during many of which the

participants remained silent or sang nonviolent anthems such as "We Shall Overcome," illustrate well the continuum between early and late 1960s protests. Bob Lynch and Jack Childs, "Negro Riot Brings Curfew in Raleigh," *Raleigh News and Observer*, April 5, 1968, 1, 6B; "Guard Called Out after N.C. Cities Have Violence," *Durham Sun*, April 5, 1968, 1; "Violence Hits State Cities," *Raleigh News and Observer*, April 6, 1968, 7.

18. "Swarm over Downtown Area," *Birmingham News* (*BN*), May 7, 1963, 2; James Spotswood, "Sirens Wail, Horns Blow, Negroes Sing," *BN*, May 7, 1963, 2; "Demonstrations Said Suspended," *BN*, May 8, 1963, 2. "Integration corner" and "collapse" of civil order are from Glen T. Eskew, *But for Birmingham* (Chapel Hill: University of North Carolina Press, 1997), 3, 235, 278.

19. "Tear Gas Routs Birmingham Shoppers," *NYT*, August 16, 1963, NRRR, RC; "Gas Fells Downtown Shoppers," *BN*, August 15, 1963, 1 (a photograph similar to figure 6.6 appears with this article); Marcus A. Jones statement, dated September 1964, 1–2, Loveman's File, Birmingham, Alabama, Police Department Surveillance files, file 1125.7.20, Department of Archives and Manuscripts, Birmingham Public Library (hereafter cited as BPL).

20. "Tear Gas Routs Birmingham Shoppers"; "Birmingham," *Washington Post*, August 16, 1963, A9; "Emergency Facilities Lacking—What If Bomb Had Been Other Type?" *BN*, August 16, 1963, 9. The quotes and information on anti-Semitism and police anticipation of trouble come from the Marcus A. Jones statement dated September 1964, 1–2. For the point that salespeople should have been grateful, see Philip Benjamin, "Negroes' Boycott in Birmingham Cuts Heavily into Retail Sales," *NYT*, May 11, 1963, 9. See also Murray E. Wyche, "Action by Negroes Hurting Stores in Birmingham Area," *WWD*, April 9, 1962, NRRR, RC.

21. "Integration Spur to Sales in South"; "Race Riots Upset Jacksonville Sales," *WWD*, March 27, 1964, both in NRRR, RC.

22. "Integration Spur to Sales in South"; "The Civil Rights Fight—What Does It Do to Business?" *Hardware Merchandiser*, October 1963, 78. Birmingham Area Chamber of Commerce Scrapbooks, file 74.33.1, Department of Archives and Manuscripts, BPL; Jack Patterson, "Business Response to the Negro Movement," *New South*, winter 1966, 71. Southern blacks presumably wielded less "spending power." "Stores See a Sad Sack Santa If Negroes Boycott Holiday," *WWD*, October 2, 1963, NRRR, RC. The Christmas boycott did not take place.

For a sampling of newspaper coverage of northern demonstrations in the late 1950s and early 1960s, see "Woolworth Invites Civil Rights Probe; Actions Continue," *WWD*, March 7, 1960; "Governor Hails Southern Sit-Ins," *NYT*, April 13, 1960; "NAACP Boycott Set for All Sears Cleveland Stores," *WWD*, December 1, 1961; "Pickets Augment Boycott of Two Cleveland Stores," *WWD*, April 15, 1964, all in NRRR, RC.

23. "The Civil Rights Fight," 76, 81; "10 More Negroes Arrested in Sit-Ins," *BN*, April 5, 1963, 2; "Klan Meeting Dull, in Spite of Crosses," *BN*, May 13, 1963, 25; and Eskew, *But for Birmingham*, 390 n. 1. On the evening of the Klan meeting, African American sites were bombed in Birmingham.

24. Untitled July 22, 1963, clipping, *WWD*; "Eye on Integration"; "Bogalusa Pickets Picketed in Turn—Negroes March at Stores—Whites Spur a 'Buy-In,'" *NYT*, April 16, 1965; "Bogalusa Pickets Ignore Radio Plea," *NYT*, April 17, 1965. For other counterpicketing, see "Little Rock Calm in Desegregation," *WWD*, January 30, 1963; Murray Wyche, "Act to Ease Negro Tensions," *WWD*, February 5, 1963, all in NRRR, RC.

25. White counterdemonstrators could have the most chilling effect on downtown commerce when they were not organized. "Sit-In Violence Closes Jackson Woolworth Store"; and Anne Moody, *Coming of Age in Mississippi* (New York: Dell, 1968), 263–75.

26. "Eye on Integration," 1, undated clipping, probably late 1962; Don Giesy, "Chester Retailers Bruised in Civil Rights Rumpus," *WWD*, May 14, 1964; Claude Sitton, "Stores in South Prosper with Integrated Counters," *NYT*, June 6, 1960, 1, all in NRRR, RC. The retail industry described Main Street merchants as hit, bruised, hurt, and suffering. Community studies of civil rights activism have yielded nuanced understandings of divisions among merchants, as well as their shifting alliances with other city leaders. Norrell's examination of Tuskegee captures the conformist pressures within the small-town merchant cohort. Norrell, *Reaping the Whirlwind*, 95–110. Chester would make an excellent case study of how a northern city weathered the storms fostered by civil rights demonstrations.

27. "South's Retailers in Van of Parlays to End Strife," *WWD*, May 16, 1963. See also "Negro Selective Buying Drive Hits Some Cities, Fails in Others," *WWD*, March 29, 1961; "Pickets Protest Lunchroom Closing at Rich's, Knoxville," *WWD*, June 30, 1960; "Savannah Stores End Segregation; Boycott Called Off," *WWD*, July 12, 1961, all in NRRR, RC; and "The Civil Rights Fight," 81.

28. "Incidents Curtail Downtown Atlanta Holiday Selling," *WWD*, December 21, 1960, NRRR, RC; "Retail Losses Cited in Negro Sitdowns"; "Race Riots Upset Jacksonville Sales"; Norrell, *Reaping the Whirlwind*, 101. Gene Roberts, "Negroes Reject Pact in Natchez," *NYT*, October 13, 1965, 33; Martin Waldron, "Natchez Boycott Ends As Negroes Gain Objectives," *NYT*, December 4, 1965; Roy Reed, "Negroes Call Off Pact in Natchez," *NYT*, December 24, 1965, 42. Selective buying was already established among black consumers. For a discussion of pre-Montgomery campaigns of economic retribution, see Weems, *Desegregating the Dollar*, 56–63. In Tuskegee, a year of boycotts closed half of the white businesses by spring of 1958.

29. "Negro Groups Put the Economic Pressure On," *Business Week*, February 27, 1960; "Negroes Said to Constitute 20% of Downtown Shoppers," *WWD*, April 24, 1962; Benjamin, "Negroes' Boycott in Birmingham Cuts Heavily into Retail Sales," 9. "Boycott Rebound Cited in Knoxville Segregation Issue," *WWD*, July 1, 1960; "NAACP Hold in Favor of Store 'Sit-Ins,'" *WWD*, June 27, 1960. See also "Negro Protests Plague Chains; No Solution in Sight," *WWD*, March 21, 1960. Rich's and Davison-Paxon in Atlanta had a 40 percent African American clientele, Philadelphia's Strawbridge & Clothier's was at 25 percent, and Stern's was at 40 percent; Cleveland stores ranged up to 35 percent, those in New Orleans up to 40 percent; Chicago's Carson Pirie Scott had 35 percent, stores in St. Louis ranged from 20 to 40 percent, those in Washington from 50 to 70 percent, and those in Baltimore from 10 to 50 percent. "Negroes Said to Constitute 20% of Downtown Shoppers." All sources in NRRR, RC.

30. "The Civil Rights Fight," 81; see also "Pickets Protest Lunchroom Closing at Rich's, Knoxville."

31. "Negro Groups Put the Economic Pressure On." The chain stores' annual meetings in New York City during the spring of 1960 were dogged by picketing outside and by challenges from stockholders inside the meetings. In response to one such demand by a stockholder and Congress of Racial Equality (CORE) member, W. T. Grant's president read a prepared statement giving the standard explanation that the chains deferred to local custom. "Grant Meeting Picketed on Segregation," *WWD*, April 27, 1960; "Kress in Defense

of Racial Policy," *NYT,* May 18, 1960; "Woolworth Posts Sales Gain, Defends Exclusion of Negroes," *NYT,* May 19, 1960, all in NRRR, RC.

32. It was believed that chains acted more quickly than other organizations. "Negroes Boycott Stores in Capital," *NYT,* March 28, 1958; "Chains Pacing Desegregation in the South," *WWD,* September 10, 1963. Capturing the fluid movement of protestors from store to neighboring store as each one was progressively shut down are "Negroes' Sitdown Hits 2 More Cities"; Sitton, "Negroes' Protest Spreads in South"; and "Negroes Extend Store Picketing," *NYT,* February 11, 1960. All sources in NRRR, RC.

33. I want to thank the members of a panel at the 2000 Organization of American Historians Conference in St. Louis for the opportunity to comment on their work. Responding to and contrasting their papers helped me refine these observations about manipulating the mixed public-private nature of commercial space. The papers include Andrew Sandoval-Strausz, "'The Control of His Own House and of Those Who Enter It': Keepers, Patrons, Prostitutes, Peddlers, and Thieves in the Nineteenth-Century American Hotel"; Jessica Sewell, "From Parlor Meetings to Equality Tea: Domestic and Commercial Hospitality in the California Woman Suffrage Movement"; and Lara Vapnek, "Gender and the Politics of Retail Space in Gilded Age New York."

34. A legal case at Cameron Village in Raleigh, North Carolina, illuminated how the democratic message of retail advertising could erode businesses' private property claims. "Racial Disputes Face Court Test," *NYT,* March 15, 1960, NRRR, RC.

35. "Negro Picket Case in Fla. Top Court," *WWD,* May 10, 1962; Wyche, "Action by Negroes Hurting Stores in Birmingham Area"; Giesy, "Chester Retailers Bruised in Civil Rights Rumpus"; "South's Retailers in Van of Parlays to End Strife"; see also "Planning Problems Mount with Chain Unit Sitdowns," *WWD,* May 10, 1960; and Winona McKennon, "New Orleans Sales Hurt by Local Unrest," *WWD,* September 7, 1960, all in NRRR, RC. On the increase of phone orders during boycotts, see "Incidents Hurt Jacksonville Store Volume."

36. Giesy, "Chester Retailers Bruised in Civil Rights Rumpus"; "Greenville Stores Face Problem on Teen-Age Curfew," *WWD,* July 28, 1960; Wyche, "Act to Ease Negro Tensions"; "Race Riots Upset Jacksonville Sales"; Shields, "War and Peace," all in NRRR, RC. "The Civil Rights Fight," 78.

37. "Incidents Curtail Downtown Atlanta Holiday Selling"; "Boycott Hurts in Nashville," *WWD,* April 15, 1960; Wyche, "Action by Negroes Hurting Stores in Birmingham Area"; Wyche, "Act to Ease Negro Tensions"; Peter Bart, "Advertising: Unorganized Boycotts by Negroes Found," *NYT,* April 18, 1962, all in NRRR, RC. On white-owned businesses in black business districts benefiting from boycotts, see the case of hardware stores in Birmingham in "The Civil Rights Fight." In the black neighborhoods of larger cities, white-owned variety stores and larger establishments often had black employees. Stuart Hanger, "Integration Advances: Negro Employment Found on Rise at Detroit Stores," *WWD,* March 13, 1957, NRRR, RC.

38. Winston-Salem quote from "Negro Protests Plague Chains," 32; see also "Protests Mount: Winston-Salem Stores Facing Boycott Threat," *WWD,* February 29, 1960; and "The Negro Market: Many Stores Fail to Push," NRRR, RC. On Winston-Salem picketing, Barnes interview. On mail order and doing without, see Wyche, "Act to Ease Negro Tensions"; "The Civil Rights Fight," 81 (appliance quote); and Eskew, *But for Birmingham,* 199, 224, 240–41.

39. Shields, "War and Peace"; "Race Strife Forces Jackson to Cancel Christmas Parade," *WWD*, October 24, 1963; "Integration Spur to Sales in South"; Wyche, "Act to Ease Negro Tensions," all in NRRR, RC. "City Takes Another Step in Face Lifting," *BN*, April 9, 1963, 1; "Face-Lifting Begun, Downtown Brighter," *BN*, March 14, 1963, 2. "Christmas Shopping Boycott Launched by CORE in St. Louis," *WWD*, November 20, 1963, NRRR, RC.

40. "Downtown Stores in Jacksonville Hit by Demonstrations," *WWD*, March 26, 1964; McKennon, "New Orleans Sales Hurt by Local Unrest"; "Sit-In Violence Closes Jackson Woolworth Store," all in NRRR, RC. "Ride the Bus Downtown . . . Ride Home Free!" *BN*, May 5, 1963, C-12. Anxieties about integrated buses were exacerbated by the terrifying violence surrounding the 1961 campaign to desegregate interstate bus facilities. "Freedom riders" in several instances in Alabama found their integrated buses attacked and burned.

41. On protests as sidewalk obstructions, see "Negroes in South in Store Sitdown," *NYT*, February 3, 1960; "Virginia Acts to Strengthen Trespass Laws"; Sitton, "Negroes' Protest Spreads in South"; "Bill Bans Refusal to Sell to Negroes"; and "Sit-In Violence Closes Jackson Woolworth Store," all in NRRR, RC.

42. Quote from "South's Retailers in Van of Parlays to End Strife"; "Bogalusa Pickets Ignore Radio Plea." For an example of radio broadcasts (sponsored by Alabama's Attorney General's Office) designed to reassure black shoppers that they would have police protection if they defied a boycott and returned to Tuskegee's white stores, see "Group Set to Aid Tuskegee Negro Business Activity," *WWD*, August 8, 1957. All sources in NRRR, RC.

43. Wyche, "Act to Ease Negro Tensions" (Birmingham); "State St. Store Faces Picketing in Integration Issue," *WWD*, November 5, 1963 (Chicago); "Eye on Integration," 1 (Memphis); "Boycott Rebound Cited in Knoxville Segregation Issue" (stay-away-from-downtown); "Negroes Boycott Hopewell Stores," *WWD*, November 26, 1963 (off limits). See also "Oklahoma City Boycott Begun for Lunchroom Integration," *WWD*, August 24, 1960; Annette Culler, "Negro Boycott Seeks Hiring at Capital Stores," *WWD*, March 18, 1958, 1. All sources in NRRR, RC. The issues inspiring the downtown boycotts, ranging from lunch counter and school integration to employment discrimination, extended far outside the business district itself.

44. "Planning Problems Mount with Chain Unit Sitdowns"; Wyche, "Act to Ease Negro Tensions." Alignments among downtown interests varied from city to city. Membership in, or sympathy with, segregationist or integrationist groups forced retailers and others apart. See Jacoway and Colburn, *Southern Businessmen and Desegregation*. An in-depth comparison of the nature of (and limits to) retailer cooperation during civil rights boycotts to retailer cooperation during urban renewal would be fascinating.

45. Jack Stillman, "Current of Compromise Flows through Tension Here," *BN*, April 14, 1963, A-2; "The Civil Rights Fight," 78; "Sears Considers Expansion in City," *BN*, April 3, 1963, 1; "Eye on Integration"; "Planning Problems Mount with Chain Unit Sitdowns." See essays in Jacoway and Colburn, *Southern Businessmen and Desegregation*, esp. 32, 141, 166; and Patterson, "Business Response to the Negro Movement," 67–74.

46. S. H. Kress & Company *1960 Annual Report*, 3–4, S. H. Kress Annual Reports 1950–1965, file Annual Reports 1949–62/Proxies/Industrial, Historic Corporate Report Collection, Baker Library, Harvard Business School.

47. "Belk's Will Close Birmingham Unit," *WWD*, May 10, 1963, box 2, Belk Bros. Co. file, Resseguie Collection, Baker Library, Harvard University (hereafter cited as RC). Local

officials also drew attention to troublesome long-term shifts in the regional economic base.

48. "Eye on Integration"; Harry Berlfein, "Long, Hot Summer a-Fixin' below the Mason-Dixon," *WWD*, January 13, 1965; "Desegregation Effect Minor in Winston Salem," *WWD*, September 9, 1960, all in NRRR, RC. *DNR* clipping dated May 28, 1964, box 9, Mc-Crory file, RC. Police investigations following the Loveman's bombing uncovered the example of two white women who had left the store's basement lunchroom when they saw African American waitresses. Statement by M. A. Jones, detective, August 19, 1963, 5–6, Loveman's file, Birmingham, Alabama, Police Department Surveillance files, file 1125.7.20, Department of Archives and Manuscripts, BPL.

49. "Central, Los Angeles, California. May 5, 1952 Inspection," 4415 S. Central, Los Angeles, California, 1989.13.3.21, file 10, Kress Archive Collection, National Building Museum, Washington, D.C. "Reports on Lunch Counter Integration in South," *WWD*, June 16, 1960, NRRR, RC.

50. Quotes from "Desegregation Effect Minor in Winston Salem"; see also "Eye on Integration." For examples of media agreeing not to publicize integration, "Houston Stores Drop Negro Ban," *NYT*, August 26, 1960; "4 Dallas Stores Integrate Counters," *WWD*, November 15, 1960; "Nashville Integrates Six Lunch Counters," *NYT*, May 11, 1960; Claude Sitton, "Atlanta Integrates Restaurants Calmly," *NYT*, September 29, 1961; Hedrick Smith, "New Orleans Surprised as Stores Are Integrated," *NYT*, September 13, 1962. All sources in NRRR, RC.

51. Sitton, "Stores in South Prosper with Integrated Counters." A Fairchild News Service survey questioned whether integration was as widespread as the Southern Regional Council study implied. The Fairchild survey agreed that business bounced back after violence lifted. "Reports on Lunch Counter Integration in South"; "Integration Spur to Sales in South." Noncompliance after the Civil Rights Act passed created new problems. Patterson, "Business Response to the Negro Movement," 67–71. New insurance for urban retail investment might be necessary. John C. Melaniphy Jr., "The Changing Retail Market," *NML*, June 1968, 8. See also "Negro Population Growth in Our Largest Cities," *NML*, August 1962, 8; and RERC, *NML*, January 1966.

52. An anecdote from Raleigh illustrated how integration could enhance business in the long term. In May 1963 almost one thousand residents signed a newspaper advertisement pledging to support local businesses that abolished segregation. A local white leader remembered that those who had signed the ad "would get calls saying that, 'Well, Gus Aretakis over on Person Street opened up [integrated] his restaurant, it's hurting his business, we've got to get over there and support him and eat. And we did. And it turned out Gus Aretakis' restaurant was wonderful, we loved it!'" Cyrus King oral history, in "Let Us March On," 18.

53. "Negroes in South in Store Sitdown"; "Negroes Extend Sitdown Protest," *NYT*, February 10, 1960, 21; "Negro Sit-Ins Win in Greensboro, N.C." *NYT*, July 26, 1960, all in NRRR, RC. "Singing Negro Students March Here," *Raleigh News and Observer*, April 6, 1968, 6.

The mass demonstrations finally induced advertisers at the end of 1963 to appeal to the black consumer with focused marketing. Sessions on the topic appeared for the first time in memory at industry conferences. Peter Bart, "Advertising: Negro Market Stirring Interest," *NYT,* November 11, 1963, 51; Peter Bart, "Advertising: Role of Negroes Is Discussed," *NYT,* October 6, 1963, 170. Bart, "Advertising: Unorganized Boycotts by Negroes Found"; Peter Bart, "Advertising: Attitudes of Negro Consumers," *NYT,* October 31, 1962, both in NRRR, RC. In the fall of 1962, when the first black models appeared in television commercials, the pioneering companies received thousands of complaint letters. Peter Bart, "Advertising: Negro Models Getting TV Work," *NYT,* September 7, 1962, 44; and Bart, "Advertising: Role of Negroes Is Discussed," 170.

54. F. W. Smith (district manager), G. W. Etheridge, W. C. Maiden to R. D. Tucker (director, Kress Store Operations), August 1, 1968 memo. Memphis file 6, Kress Archive Collection, National Building Museum. Hill Ferguson to Dewayne N. Morris, June 14, 1962; Ferguson to Gentlemen, April 18, 1963, Newberry file, file 22-36-2-29-7, Jefferson County, Ala., Board of Equalization Appraisal Files, Department of Archives and Manuscripts, BPL.

55. John V. Petrof, "The Effect of Student Boycotts upon the Purchasing Habits of Negro Families in Atlanta, Georgia," *Phylon* (fall 1963): 266–67, 270. Many desegregation agreements themselves arranged for blacks to enter urban commerce in a tightly regulated manner, arriving in small groups, transacting their business, and leaving "quietly." See "Nashville Integrates Six Lunch Counters."

56. On Mississippi coming to New York, Fred Powledge, "Nonviolence vs. Riots," *NYT,* July 25, 1964, 8; on Harlem coming to Memphis, John Herbers, "Paradox in South: Gains in Some Areas Are Offset by Reverses," *NYT,* July 26, 1964, E3. The decade's looting and burning began in the South — in Birmingham on May 12, 1963, in response to bomb explosions at Martin Luther King Jr.'s brother's home and the Gaston Motel — the latter having served as a headquarters for civil rights protestors. "Blasts Rock Home of King's Brother and Gaston Motel," *BN,* May 12, 1963, 1; Eddie Badger, "City Quiet As Troops Stand By," *BN,* May 13, 1963, 1; "Rioters Loot, Burn Store, Wipe Out Woman's Income," *BN,* May 13, 1963. Nine months before King's assassination, the national guard was called to Durham, North Carolina, when a housing protest turned into a destructive rampage downtown. Demonstrators warned officials that "Durham could become 'another Newark, Watts or Vietnam . . . unless something is done.'" "Troops Deployed in Durham, N.C.," *NYT,* July 21, 1967, 28; "Concessions in Durham," *NYT,* July 22, 1967, 11.

57. Thomas A. Johnson, "Economic and Social Differences Separate the Races in Augusta," *NYT,* May 19, 1970, 35; James Wooten, "6 Dead in Augusta Were Shot in Back," *NYT,* May 14, 1970, 1, 33; James Wooten, "Augusta Orders Autopsies on 6; Snipers Open Fire in Riot Area," *NYT,* May 15, 1970, 1, 10. See also Claude Sitton, "Two Negroes Shot in Savannah Riot," *NYT,* July 12, 1963, 8; "Blacks and Police Clash in Florida," *NYT,* November 1, 1969, 19; Douglas Robinson, "Memphis Negroes Dispersed by Gas," *NYT,* November 11, 1969, 1.

58. West Point, Mississippi, found the national spotlight when local politics heated up in 1970 with a black mayoral candidate — antipoverty and civil rights activist John Buffington. A *NYT* reporter prematurely pronounced in August 1970 that for blacks "there is no fear left" on Main Street. Two weeks later, one of Buffington's campaign organizers was fatally shot by a white man in the parking lot of a West Point grocery store. A several-month black boycott of white businesses followed. Earl Caldwell, "Atmosphere in Mississippi Town Has Changed and a Black Runs for Mayor," *NYT,* August 2, 1970, 44; "Negro

Campaigner Slain in Mississippi," *NYT*, August 16, 1970, 49; "White Man in Mississippi Charged in Negro's Slaying," *NYT*, August 18, 1970, 20; "Mississippi White Cleared in Killing," *NYT*, October 12, 1971, 72.

59. Julius Duscha, "Postscript to the Story of Seventh Street," *NYT*, June 2, 1968, Sunday Magazine, 30. For another description of merchants "dragged" from stores by looters, see "Looting Follows Newark Shooting," *NYT*, May 20, 1969, 1. On a furniture dealer who was "trapped" in his store during looting but planned to stay in business and blamed "outsiders" for the violence, see Richard Reeves, "Hatred and Pity Mix in Views of Whites on Newark Negroes," *NYT*, July 22, 1967, 10.

60. John Herbers, "Major Violence Declining, but Small Incidents Rise," *NYT*, September 6, 1970, 1; John Herbers, "Summer's Urban Violence Stirs Fears of Terrorism," *NYT*, September 21, 1971, 1; Jack Rosenthal, "Cities: Why the Summer Was Not as Hot As It Might Have Been," *NYT*, September 7, 1969, E3. Hartford had three riots in two years; Jacksonville had them nearly every summer. Paul L. Montgomery, "Hartford Unrest Is Tied to a Slur," *NYT*, September 3, 1969, 35; Martin Waldron, "Racial Unrest Hits Jacksonville Despite Effort to Ease Tensions," *NYT*, June 21, 1971, 26. On Detroit's complacency, see Jerry M. Flint, "Detroit Leaders Were Optimistic," *NYT*, July 25, 1967, 19. Although 1968 was a watershed year in many respects, it is not entirely clear why historians use it as the endpoint of substantial riot-related violence. Nor is it clear why there have been so few historical studies of the riots, compared to the dozens and dozens of scholarly books on the Civil Rights movement. With a few important exceptions, scholarship on the riots remains close to where it was in the early 1970s, locked into the questions of that era. See especially Sidney Fine, *Violence in the Model City: The Cavanagh Administration, Race Relations, and the Detroit Riot of 1967* (Ann Arbor: University of Michigan Press, 1989); Gerald Horne, *Fire This Time: The Watts Uprising and the 1960s* (Charlottesville: University Press of Virginia, 1995); and Heather Ann Thompson, *Whose Detroit? Politics, Labor, and Race in a Modern American City* (Ithaca, NY: Cornell University Press, 2001). These works introduce new issues of labor, migration, and local politics. An example of the existing periodization of the riots can be found in *Major Problems in American Urban History*, ed. Howard Chudacoff (Lexington, MA: Heath, 1994), 425.

61. Nan Robertson, "Sociologist Blames Anger at Merchants for Ghetto Violence," *NYT*, October 11, 1966, 39. More than 95 percent of the six hundred buildings looted in the Watts riots were retail stores. Frederick D. Sturdivant, "Better Deal for Ghetto Shoppers," *Harvard Business Review* 146, no. 2 (March–April 1968): 131.

62. Anthony Ripley, "Racial Tensions: Terror in Cleveland," *NYT*, July 28, 1968, 136; Thomas A. Johnson, "Angry Cleveland Negroes Curse 'White Devils,'" *NYT*, July 26, 1968, 39; Duscha, "Postscript to the Story of Seventh Street," SM55; Thomas A. Johnson, "Harlem Youths Exhibit Loot, Taken 'to Get Back at Whitey,'" *NYT*, April 8, 1968, 31; lawyer quoted in Michael Knight, "Aid to Consumers Growing in Nation," *NYT*, August 9, 1970, 52. See also Rudy Johnson, "Negroes in Louisville Are Still Tense and Bitter after May 28 Riot That Left 2 Dead," *NYT*, June 17, 1968, 24.

63. Caplovitz and Fogelson quotes from Robertson, "Sociologist Blames Anger at Merchants for Ghetto Violence," 39. Sturdivant, "Better Deal for Ghetto Shoppers," 130–39. On the role of Caplovitz's work in antipoverty programs, see "New and Outstanding," *NYT*, February 15, 1970, 288.

64. "Retailers Rapped on Riots: Unethical . . . Lax in Role," *WWD*, April 19, 1968, 1;

"Miss Furness Links Riots to Swindling of the Poor," *NYT*, April 19, 1968, 16. Failed public relations were pointed out by John V. Petrof, "The Corporate Image of Chain Stores among Ghetto Residents," *Southern Journal of Business* 4, no. 2 (April 1969): 33–34. Compromisers recognized why rioters felt exploited but denied the validity of their complaints. Yes, "many low-income Negroes are probably exploited by white merchants to some degree." But higher prices reflected the special risks of trade in poor neighborhoods and were neither racially based nor greed-inspired. "'Exploitation' of Consumers in Poor Neighborhoods," *NML*, February 1968, 5. Others asserted that the rioters were deliberately destroying stores' credit records. Raymond M. Momboisse, *Store Planning for Riot Survival* (Sacramento, CA: MSM Enterprises, 1968), 26.

65. Stereotype quotes from John A. Hamilton, "The 'Typical Rioter' and Dr. King," *NYT*, April 8, 1968, 46; riffraff thesis described in "Excerpts from a Study to Determine the Characteristics of Negro Rioters," *NYT*, July 28, 1968, 48; and John Herbers, "Study Says Negro Justifies Rioting as Social Protest," *NYT*, July 28, 1968, 1. The studies behind the Kerner report determined that the average rioter usually had a job and was better educated than nonrioters. "'Average' Rioter in Watts Had Job," *NYT*, September 4, 1966, 52.

The contrast between the exploitation and riffraff theories illustrates how arguments about the riots became polarized. Similarly, the options for handling looters seemed to be shooting them or leaving them unchecked. For evidence that the rioters combined political and criminal motivations, see Angus Campbell and Howard Schuman, *Racial Attitudes in Fifteen American Cities*, 3d printing (Ann Arbor: Survey Research Center, Institute for Social Research, University of Michigan, July 1969), 47; and Richard A. Berk and Howard E. Aldrich, "Patterns of Vandalism during Civil Disorders as an Indicator of Selection of Targets," *American Sociological Review* 37, no. 5 (October 1972): 545–46.

66. Duscha, "Postscript to the Story of Seventh Street," SM43; Dan Sullivan, "Flip Wilson Finds Comic Note in Nation's Long, Hot Summer," *NYT*, July 17, 1968, 37.

67. Ward Just, "Laughter, Breaking Glass Sound in Capital," *Durham Herald*, April 6, 1968, 2A; Roy Reed, "Baltimore Negroes Continue Looting; More Troops Sent to Baltimore to Quell Violence," *NYT*, April 9, 1968, 1; Walter Rugaber, "Guard Is Called in Dayton Rioting," *NYT*, September 2, 1966, 40.

An analysis of the gender breakdown among rioters, looters, and arrestees would be relevant to understanding both the menacing image of rioters and the consumer implications. A Detroit survey showed that 40 percent of participants were female, but only 10 percent of arrestees were female, concluding that the police were letting women rioters go free. "Excerpts from a Study to Determine the Characteristics of Negro Rioters," 48.

68. Fred P. Graham, "Police Restraint in Riots," *NYT*, April 13, 1968, 13; Ronald Sullivan, "Eulogy for Negro Killed as Looter," *NYT*, April 16, 1968, 32; Ronald Sullivan, "Negro Is Killed in Trenton," *NYT*, April 10, 1968, 1; Homer Bigart, "Newark Riot Deaths at 21 as Negro Sniping Widens," *NYT*, July 16, 1967, 1; and Johnson, "Negroes in Louisville Are Still Tense and Bitter after May 28 Riot That Left 2 Dead," 24.

69. "Another Opinion: Clark on Shooting Looters," *NYT*, August 18, 1968, E15; "Mayor Daley Orders Chicago's Policemen to Shoot Arsonists and Looters," *NYT*, April 16, 1968, 30; Robert B. Semple Jr., "Clark Criticizes Daley's Order to Shoot Looters," *NYT*, April 18, 1968, 40. Clark also reminded Americans of the nation's history of lynching crimes against African Americans.

70. On merchants shooting at (and sometimes killing) alleged looters, see "Rochester

Beset by New Rioting; White Man Dead," *NYT,* July 26, 1964, 1; and Alfonzo A. Narvaez, "1 Killed, 2 Shot in Camden Riots," *NYT,* August 22, 1971, 22. Retailers and their employees lost their lives too. A man died in the flames of his father's store in a Tallahassee firebombing. An elderly shoemaker was beaten to death trying to defend his store. Cincinnati looters accidentally shot the wife of an African American caretaker as they grabbed his gun. He was defending the jewelry store where he worked. "11 Killed and Sections of Chicago, Washington Burned As Racial Violence Flares in 12 Cities," *Durham Morning Herald,* April 6, 1968, 1A; Jonathan Bean, "'Burn, Baby, Burn': Small Business in the Urban Riots of the 1960s," *Independent Review* 5, no. 2 (fall 2000): 174; "Guard Sent to Cincinnati after 2 Die," *NYT,* April 9, 1968, 37.

71. "Damage in Riots Cost $45-Million," *NYT,* April 13, 1968, 13; John Herbers, "Mood of the Cities: New Stakes for Blacks May Cool Things Off," *NYT,* April 27, 1969, E8. High school student quoted in John Mathews and Ernest Holsendolph, "The Children Write Their Own Postscript," *NYT,* June 2, 1968, SM77. On the specter of "anti-white revenge and destruction," see "Special Research Report: Rioting in City Ghettos — Part II," *NML,* September 1967, 8. Whereas the race riots of the turn of the century chased black businesses from downtown areas into black business districts and residential neighborhoods, in the 1960s the assumption prevailed that the rioters intended to drive white businesses out of black neighborhoods.

72. Winton M. Blount, "A Businessman Looks at Riot and Crime," an address before the National Press Club, Washington, DC, June 27, 1968, 11–12, series II, box 26, binder of COCUSA Publications, 1968 A-N, USCCR; Duscha, "Postscript to the Story of Seventh Street," SM34, SM43. Jonathan Bean uses the rough figure of 75 percent white ownership. He argues that even if the earlier phases of riots targeted white businesses, racial distinctions became immaterial as looting progressed. Bean, "Burn, Baby, Burn," 171–72.

73. Irving Spiegel, "Jews Troubled over Negro Ties," *NYT,* July 8, 1968, 1, 20; Irving Spiegel, "Survey Finds Blacks Own Most Harlem Stores," *NYT,* September 16, 1968, 30. James Baldwin, "Negroes Are Anti-Semitic Because They're Anti-White," *NYT,* April 9, 1967, 26–27, 135–40.

74. "Rochester Beset by New Rioting," 41; Fred Powledge, "In One Part of the City, Looting; In Another, 'Nothing Left to Loot,'" *NYT,* July 26, 1964, 41; "Trouble in New Brunswick," *NYT,* July 18, 1967, 23; Jonathan Randal, "Racial Troubles a Shock to Troy," *NYT,* July 25, 1966, 17; Reeves, "Hatred and Pity Mix in Views of Whites on Newark Negroes," 10. See also William E. Farrell, "Tension Is Rising in Middletown," *NYT,* July 2, 1969, 22; and "Milwaukee Whites Jeer Rights March," *NYT,* August 29, 1967, 23.

It would be illuminating to extend the recent scholarship on northern white resistance during the civil rights years into the riot era. See Arnold Hirsch, "Massive Resistance in the Urban North: Trumbull Park, Chicago, 1953–1966," 522–50; Thomas Sugrue, "Crabgrass-Roots Politics: Race, Rights, and the Reaction against Liberalism in the Urban North, 1940–1964," 551–78; and Gary Gerstle, "Race and the Myth of the Liberal Consensus," 579–86, all in *Journal of American History* 82, no. 2 (September 1995).

75. Duscha, "Postscript to the Story of Seventh Street," SM52. Supporting the conservative critique of the 1960s "riot ideology," Jonathan Bean has an insightful discussion of the small businessman's viewpoint in "Burn, Baby, Burn," 169–70. It was widely rumored that unscrupulous business owners had torched their own properties for insurance money. Horne, *Fire This Time,* 308. On the opinions of white and black people about their

experiences shopping in neighborhood stores, see Campbell and Shuman, *Racial Attitudes,* 43–45.

76. Walter S. Henrion to Roy Wenzlick, November 29, 1967. In Wenzlick's files, no other issue came close to generating the response that the riots did. Wenzlick wrote back to the wife of a real estate broker: "I have been amazed at the response which I have received from this, and it has been rather encouraging to me to find that so many people felt deeply enough about it to write me." Wenzlick to Mrs. James W. Madden, October 5, 1967, both letters in file 14, box 1, series 2, collection sl 574, Roy Wenzlick Papers, Western Historical Manuscript Collection, University of Missouri, St. Louis.

The Real Estate Research Corporation's *NML* devoted numerous articles to race and real estate. Not all topics got the same attention; *NML* editors wondered why Vietnam and the energy crisis had not unnerved investors more. Seven of ten special forum sessions at the U.S. Chamber of Commerce's 1968 annual meeting focused on urban problems. *NML,* February 1968, 5; Blount, "A Businessman Looks at Riot and Crime," 7.

77. Roy Wenzlick, "As I See Current Illusions," *Real Estate Analyst,* August 31, 1967, 365–68. With uncustomary emotion, Wenzlick wrote, "I hate the current thinking which believes we can get rich by credit, get knowledge by trips on marihuana or LSD, acquire skills without study, or develop mastery without apprenticeship" (368). Wenzlick's use of the concept of illusion can be productively compared with other ways of seeing and participating in urban commerce that have been described in this book, such as dream, nightmare, and vision.

78. "Looting in Washington," *NYT,* April 5, 1968, 26. See also "Youth Bands Loot Pittsburgh Stores," *NYT,* June 23, 1968, 32; "Fire Destroys 4 Stores in Downtown Passaic," *NYT,* September 20, 1968, 31; "Violence Erupts in Buffalo Area," *NYT,* April 9, 1968, 1, 18; Donald Janson, "Milwaukee Calm after Negro Riot," *NYT,* August 1, 1967, 1; Joseph Novitski, "Curfew Is Declared in Peekskill after New Outbreak of Violence," *NYT,* October 26, 1968, 74. Martin Waldron, "Curfew Ordered in Most of Miami," *NYT,* August 10, 1968, 28; "Curfew in Natchez Follows Violence," *NYT,* June 3, 1968, 48.

79. "Looting in Washington," 26; "Box Score of Retail Riot Damage," *WWD,* April 10, 1968, 14. "Sales Dip by as Much as 80% in Downtown Memphis Stores," *NYT,* April 12, 1968, 20. Anthony Downs, "Alternative Futures for the American Ghettos," *Appraisal Journal,* October 1968, 526; "11 Killed and Sections of Chicago, Washington Burned As Racial Violence Flares in 12 Cities," *Durham Morning Herald,* April 6, 1968, 1A, 9A; "Guard Sent to Cincinnati after 2 Die," 37. *WWD* published a list of apparel, department, and specialty stores damaged after King's assassination. "Box Score of Retail Riot Damage."

80. Blount, "Smokestacks Are Not Enough," 2; "Detroit Precinct Acts to Curb Fear," *NYT,* December 8, 1968, 141; *Confidential Disaster Control Guides for Members Only* (Washington, DC: Retail Bureau, Metropolitan Washington Board of Trade, April 1968), 2, 5. The national Chamber of Commerce packaged and circulated the Washington guide along with the *Nation's Business* article "If Riots Erupt Again . . ." (*Nation's Business,* March 1968, 2) and two shorter riot plans from Springfield, Ohio, and Pittsburgh. "Guides for Disaster Control and Alert Plans Kit . . . What Local Business Organizations and Community Leaders Can Do before, during and after a Disaster," series II, box 26, binder of COCUSA Publications 1968, A-N, USCCR. Lawrence Van Gelder, "Baseless Rumors of Violence Sweep across the East Coast," *NYT,* July 29, 1967, 11.

81. Momboisse, "Store Planning for Riot Survival," 15, 30. *Confidential Disaster Control*

Guides, 10. "If Riots Erupt Again . . ." The Florida Retail Federation pointed out that "many bombs have been tossed onto one-story buildings." "Center's 19-Point Disaster Program," *Chain Store Age,* August 1968, E16.

82. *Confidential Disaster Control Guides,* 10, 12, 19. See also Momboisse, "Store Planning for Riot Survival," 1. In December 1970 the Retail Bureau's twenty-four-hour Retail Rumor Center was still in place. It is unknown whether business groups in other cities were similarly organized. Isadore Barmash, "Washington Store 'Bargains' Draw Inflation-Wary Shoppers," *NYT,* December 9, 1970, 93.

Sometimes the lockstep actions of a united front smacked of fear and a lack of creative problem-solving. A *WWD* columnist asserted that such was the case the day of Dr. King's funeral, when most retailers closed for at least a few hours, filled store windows with displays of sympathy, and took out ads supporting the mourners. One African American observed of a Fifth Avenue window dedicated to King: " 'Whitey is afraid.' " Samuel Feinberg, "Did Retailers Seek 'Guilt' Edge Security?" *WWD,* April 12, 1968, 1.

83. "New style" from Jerry M. Flint, "Year after Riot, Detroit Is Hopeful Despite Lethargy and Fear," *NYT,* July 23, 1968, 19; William Serrin, "How One Big City Defeated Its Mayor," *NYT,* October 27, 1968, SM138; "If Riots Erupt Again . . ."; on fortress designs, see John Herbers, "Cities Lag in Riot Clean-up despite U.S. Aid Program," *NYT,* November 18, 1969, 29.

84. "DON'T START BOARDING UP YOUR WINDOWS, PULLING OUT YOUR DISPLAYS. DON'T HIT THE PANIC BUTTON!" *Confidential Disaster Control Guides,* 1. On "air of permanency" and aging plywood, see John Herbers, "Cities' Riot Sites Remain Desolate," *NYT,* April 13, 1969, 1, 58. On plywood as symbol and decorating item, see Jerry M. Flint, "Inner-City Decay Causes Business Life to Wither," *NYT,* July 19, 1971, 1.

85. For a projection that downtown shoppers would turn away from cities if "urban unrest" continued, see "The Changing Retail Market," *NML,* June 1968, 7.

86. Robert A. Steele, "The Impact of Civil Disobedience on Property Values," *Appraisal Journal,* July 1968, 346–47. See also Reeves, "Hatred and Pity Mix in Views of Whites on Newark Negroes," 1, 10. On varied investment responses of business, government, and philanthropy to Watts riots, see Horne, *Fire This Time,* 307–21. The Seventh Street article contains interviews with proprietors about their initial attitudes toward continuing business. Duscha, "Postscript to the Story of Seventh Street."

87. David Halberstam, "White Merchants Tense; Many Would Like to Sell Stores," *NYT,* July 22, 1964, 18.

88. These issues would benefit from deeper historical investigation. Insured owners often had to rebuild in order to collect on their policies. Jonathan Bean points out that only limited assistance was offered to victimized small businesses. Bean, "Burn, Baby, Burn," 179–80. U.S. Chamber president Blount suggested that the kinds of businesses vandalized — stores selling liquor, televisions, and groceries — had not mobilized the necessary support for government assistance and that there might have been a different government response if banks had been targeted. Blount, "A Businessman Looks at Riots and Crime," 14.

The place of chain stores in the riots has received less attention than that of small independent stores. Chains possibly played a greater role in Washington unrest, since they anchored the city's riot information network in 1968 and since more chain businesses were destroyed. See Bean, "Burn, Baby, Burn," 169; Horne, *Fire This Time,* 309–10; Petrof, "The

Corporate Image of Chain Stores among Ghetto Residents," 33; "Riot Damage to rtw Stores Fails to Halt Share Trend," *WWD*, April 9, 1968, 18.

89. Jerry M. Flint, "Detroit's Pledge of Change after Riot Is Left Unfulfilled after Three Years," *NYT*, July 23, 1970, 18; on the lingering effect, "If Riots Erupt Again . . . ," 2. On a four-year downswing in downtown D.C. shopping following the riots there, see "Downtown Stores Fight Back," *NYT*, November 5, 1972, F17. See also Isadore Barmash, "Shoppers Brave Cold to Seek Bargains," *NYT*, February 23, 1968, 52.

90. Thomas A. Johnson, "Negroes See Riots Giving Way to Black Activism in the Ghetto," *NYT*, October 21, 1968, 1; Flint, "Detroit's Pledge of Change," 18; Rosenthal, "Cities," E3. Although most blacks disapproved of the violence, they did see "beneficial consequences" in heightened concern among whites to redress inequities. "Excerpts from a Study to Determine the Characteristics of Negro Rioters," 48. On the belief that young African Americans held "extremist" values, had no stake in the existing system, and no reason to respect "traditional" values such as private property, see "Special Research Report: Rioting in City Ghettos — Part II," 7.

91. Herbers, "Cities' Riot Sites Remain Desolate," 58; Herbers, "Mood of the Cities," E8; Flint, "Inner-City Decay Causes Business Life to Wither," 29.

92. Herbers, "Cities' Riot Sites Remain Desolate," 58; Halberstam, "White Harlem Merchants Tense," 18; Flint, "Inner-City Decay Causes Business Life to Wither," 29. Friesma, "Black Control of Central Cities." Many new entrepreneurs feared that if people were finally willing to sell prime commercial real estate to them, then the businesses must not be worth anything.

93. "Woolworth Helps Give Downtown Its Ups," *Nation's Business*, February 1970, 16; Robert Hanley, "Newark since '67 Riots: Hope and Despair," *NYT*, July 12, 1977, 1.

94. "If Riots Erupt Again . . . ," 2. A bullet hitting the sprinkler system had caused the worst damage. According to the article, thousands of businesses also turned to skill-enhancing training programs for workers after riots.

95. The *NML* argued that "white investment in Negro portions of our central cities has virtually ceased during the past two decades," representing an abdication of responsibility. "Special Research Report: Rioting in City Ghettos — Part I," *NML*, August 1967, 7.

96. Morris A. Lieberman, "Today's Appraisal Problems" *NML*, July 1968, 7. One problem was "the tendency for demonstrations of a violent sort to take place in the public street and substantially affect adversely the retail sales made by stores in the commercial area." Little literature existed on the topic, so appraiser Morris Lieberman advised *NML* readers of the need to set aside "personal feelings and test the market." The provocative conduct of "hippie" types also depressed values. Ibid. University communities were downgraded because of campus disorders. RERC, *NML*, June 1969, 4.

97. Steele, "The Impact of Civil Disobedience on Property Values," 346–47. This Kress was the same one inspected in 1952 by the white manager who felt uncomfortable in the store and recommended selling it. In Washington there were allegations that people who purchased businesses shortly after the riots had paid prices based on pre-riot income streams and had been hurt when sales volume did not keep up. Flint, "Inner-City Decay Causes Business Life to Wither," 29.

98. Flint, "Inner-City Decay Causes Business Life to Wither," 29. After the 1968 violence, the pharmacy kept its windows boarded up and closed every night by 5:30. Their suppliers pulled men from delivery routes.

99. Steele wrote that "*people* make value." Steele, "The Impact of Civil Disobedience on Property Values," 351; Hanley, "Newark since '67 Riots," 1; Paul L. Montgomery, "Race Tension Shows Contrasting Pattern in North and South," *NYT,* July 26, 1964, E3.

100. Sturdivant, "Better Deal for Ghetto Shoppers," 130, 136. He modeled the guarantee on protection for the overseas investments of U.S. companies.

101. John Herbers, "U.S. Officials Say Big Riots Are Over," *NYT,* August 24, 1969, 1. See also "'Build, Baby, Build' Is Dr. King's Advice," *NYT,* July 31, 1967, 17.

102. Herbers, "Cities Lag in Riot Clean-Up," 29; Herbers, "Cities' Riot Sites Remain Desolate," 58. It was common to assert that resentment over urban renewal demolitions contributed to the riots. See William Robbins, "Cities Are Left Behind As Middle Class Seeks Breath of Suburban Air," *NYT,* January 6, 1969, 71.

103. On renewal as "inevitably" helping, see S. H. Kress & Co., *1962 Annual Report,* 5, S. H. Kress Annual Reports 1950–1965, file Annual Reports 1949–62/Proxies/Industrial, Historic Corporate Report Collection, Baker Library, Harvard Business School; on New Haven, Samuel Feinberg, "From Where I Sit," *WWD,* November 11, 13, 1963, box 9, Macy's, New Haven, Conn., file, RC; for "death and resurrection," see "Special Research Report: The Life Cycle of Residential Neighborhoods," *NML,* November 1965, 8.

104. "Downtrodden Downtown Downgraded in Downright Downpour of Down-Talk," *WWD,* December 14, 1954, box 9, Louisville, Kentucky, file, RC; "Causes of Long-Run Decline of Many Parts of Large Central Cities," *NML,* November 1972, 5. John T. Metzger has a provocative essay on the rise of real estate thinking in urban policy, which focuses on the emergence and power of decline frameworks, and particularly the contributions to "natural" neighborhood life-cycle theories by RERC and its leading thinkers. See John T. Metzger, "Planned Abandonment: The Neighborhood Life-Cycle Theory and National Urban Policy," *Housing Policy Debate* 11, no. 1 (2000): 7–40.

105. In some communities, such as 125th Street in Harlem, black businesses had complained for decades that they could not get locations on such "Gold Coast" corridors.

106. Sara Rimer, "Watts Organizer Feels Weight of Riots, and History," *NYT,* June 24, 1992, A12. Her father's offices and furniture business had just been burned out in the recent riots. As Los Angeles picked through the debris of its 1992 riots, the nation sadly found a window into the accomplishments of black entrepreneurs since the 1960s.

107. See, for example, the reported comments of the mayor of Charleston, South Carolina (Joe Riley) in the 1990s: "'The downtown belongs to everyone,' he says. 'People need it. They need the eye contact, the human exchange that occurs in the downtowns of our cities. The downtown is the quintessence of the public realm. You cannot replicate this anywhere else.'" Constance E. Beaumont, *Smart States, Better Communities: How State Governments Can Help Citizens Preserve Their Communities* (Washington, DC: National Trust for Historic Preservation, 1996), 191. Beaumont summarized this perspective as the belief that "a community's downtown is its most democratic element," a conviction that underpinned the National Trust for Historic Preservation's Main Street Program, which is discussed in chapter 7.

108. Quoted in Jon Goss, "The 'Magic of the Mall': An Analysis of Form, Function, and Meaning in the Contemporary Retail Built Economy," *Annals of the Association of American Geographers* 83, no. 1 (March 1993): 23. In switching his energies from suburban malls to downtowns, Rouse has much in common with another leading figure in twentieth-century commercial design — architect Victor Gruen. See M. Jeffrey Hardwick, "Creating

a Consumer's Century: Urbanism and Architect Victor Gruen" (Ph.D. diss., Yale University, 2000).

109. The conversion language is from the reporter; Rouse's exact wording is not clear. Michael Demarest, "He Digs Downtown," *Time*, August 24, 1981, 48. David Harvey describes how the 1960s riots led to the Baltimore City Fair and ultimately Harborplace. David Harvey, *The Condition of Postmodernity* (Cambridge, MA: Blackwell Publishers, 1990), 89–90.

CHAPTER 7

1. "Shoppers and Diners in Salt Lake City Flocking to Redeveloped Trolley Barns," *New York Times* (*NYT*), November 12, 1972, 76; Ada Louise Huxtable, "St. Louis and the Crisis of American Cities," *NYT*, June 28, 1964, sec. 2, p. 13. Huxtable pointed out that although some vague historical sense caused the cast-iron commercial fronts of St. Louis's riverfront buildings to be saved in a warehouse for decades, they were buried in landfill when the Mark Twain Highway was constructed. Robert Reinhold, "In St. Louis Even the Old Bricks Are Leaving Town," *NYT*, July 9, 1978, E5. The demand for used brick was greater in the South presumably because of the Sunbelt building boom and the fact that the South had fewer empty brick buildings to salvage at that time.

2. Bernard J. Frieden and Lynne B. Sagalyn, *Downtown, Inc.: How America Rebuilds Cities* (Cambridge, MA: MIT Press, 1989), 5, 87, 174.

3. Surveys of these early districts, including Philadelphia, Providence, New Haven, Norfolk, and Cape May, are included in *Preserving Historic America*, Department of Housing and Urban Development (Washington, DC: U.S. Government Printing Office, 1966). A shift also occurred from saving domestic structures to preserving large-scale urban buildings such as train stations. In the early nineteenth century, historical sensibilities usually focused on people and events and less commonly on structures. Up until the Civil War, except for Independence Hall in Philadelphia, the fledgling organized preservation movement had barely touched cities. Michael Holleran, *Boston's "Changeful Times": Origins of Preservation and Planning in America* (Baltimore: Johns Hopkins University Press, 1998), 85, 90–91.

4. Although pedestrian malls were introduced in the late 1950s, construction hit full stride ten years later. Kent A. Robertson, "Downtown Pedestrian Malls in Sweden and the United States," *Transportation Quarterly*, January 1992, 41.

5. Larry R. Ford, *Cities and Buildings* (Baltimore: Johns Hopkins University Press, 1994), 94; Frieden and Sagalyn, *Downtown, Inc.*, 263–68, 314; Gurney Breckenfeld, "Jim Rouse Shows How to Give Downtown Retailing New Life," *Fortune*, April 10, 1978, 85. Experts expressed concern over the intensity of interest in duplicating little-understood models. Ibid., 91.

6. H. J. Cummins, "The New Face of the Old Market," *Newsday*, October 13, 1991, 17. Other essays describing 1970s Main Street as "doomed," as representing "economic decline": Terry Pindell, "Keene Reborn," *Boston Globe*, March 14, 1999, city ed., magazine sec., 15; Patricia Leigh Brown, "Main Streets Get Street-Wise," *Historic Preservation*, March–April 1979, 29. Kent Robertson pointedly challenges the view that there was a resurgence in downtown retailing during the 1970s, in "Downtown Retail Activity in Large American Cities, 1954–1977," *Geographical Review* 73, no. 3 (July 1983): 323.

7. Ada Louise Huxtable, "The Fall and Rise of Main Street," *NYT*, May 30, 1976, 146.

8. In this chapter the term *historic preservation* denotes the organized, professional preservation movement. *Preservation* refers more loosely to the larger trend to preserve, renovate, reconstruct, replicate, recombine, or sometimes only remember old buildings or building parts (and historical events) in downtown redevelopment. This analysis focuses on understanding the shift toward using historical themes and materials in commercial development, not on the historic preservation field itself. For a similarly broad interpretation of preservation, which also addresses the technical differences among restoration, preservation, rehabilitation, and so forth, see *Preserving Cultural Landscapes in America*, ed. Arnold R. Alanen and Robert Z. Melnick (Baltimore: Johns Hopkins University Press, 2000), 209 n. 3. The same volume contains a useful typology of heritage landscapes, with each category defined partly by the purpose of the sites' presentation to the public: Richard Francaviglia, "Selling Heritage Landscapes," 44–69.

9. Historian David Schuyler provides an incisive critique of how the proponents and allies of New Urbanism have used or misused history in his literature review, "The New Urbanism and the Modern Metropolis," *Urban History* 24, no. 3 (1997): 344–58.

10. Melissa Turner, "Smyrna Restyling Itself, Shooting for 'a Progressive Williamsburg,'" *Atlanta Journal and Constitution*, November 30, 1997, D4; David Harvey, *The Condition of Postmodernity* (Cambridge, MA: Blackwell, 1990), 66–112, esp. 87–88. Promotional materials for the new nostalgic mall described in fig. 7.1, The Streets at Southpoint and Main Street, were inserted into the *Raleigh (N.C.) News and Observer*, March 7, 2002. This new mall had less impact on downtown Durham than on the nearby enclosed regional mall Southgate, which was demolished.

11. These conclusions were based on surveys of 57 cities in the 25,000–50,000 population range. Historic preservation was used in 50 of the sampled cities, and the trust's Main Street Approach was used in 44. Many more cities used the Main Street approach than were formally enrolled in the National Trust's program. Kent Robertson, "Can Small-City Downtowns Remain Viable?" *Journal of the American Planning Association*, summer 1999, 275–76.

12. Jon Teaford, *The Rough Road to Renaissance: Urban Revitalization in America, 1940–1985* (Baltimore: Johns Hopkins University, 1990), 273; the "link to history" quote is in William Severini Kowinski, "A Mall Covers the Waterfront," *NYT*, December 13, 1981, SM27.

13. For an article critiquing the "clean slate" approach to the Inner Harbor while admiring its accomplishments, see Brian Kelly and Roger K. Lewis, "What's Right (and Wrong) about the Inner Harbor," *Planning*, April 1992, 28–32. Ada Louise Huxtable, "Surviving Downtown 'Progress,'" *NYT*, October 20, 1974, 159; Huxtable, "The Fall and Rise of Main Street," 146.

14. M. Christine Boyer, *The City of Collective Memory: Its Historical Imagery and Architectural Entertainments* (Cambridge, MA: MIT Press, 1994), quotations from 67, 420, and 423; see also 416–19, 439, 449–50. The critique of historic preservation was an original inspiration for this wide-ranging book. See the acknowledgments, ix. An interesting contribution to the debates over private control and spatial exclusion also using South Street Seaport as an example is James Defilippis, "From a Public Re-creation to Private Recreation: The Transformation of Public Space in South Street Seaport," *Journal of Urban Affairs* 19, no. 1 (1997): 405–18.

15. Max Page has demonstrated that by 1940 historic preservation was "a partner" in

the destruction of New York City — complementing, facilitating, or cleaning up after development. Max Page, *The Creative Destruction of Manhattan, 1900–1940* (Chicago: University of Chicago Press, 1999), 12, 115, 170, 235, 252, 260. Jon Goss has an especially insightful article investigating, among other themes, the "exploitation" of nostalgia by developers and public officials in their commercial development projects — a middle-class nostalgia for a lost pedestrian-scale community emphasizing human interaction within public spaces. John Goss, "The 'Magic of the Mall': An Analysis of Form, Function, and Meaning in the Contemporary Retail Built Economy," *Annals of the Association of American Geographers* 83, no. 1 (March 1993): 22–25.

Frieden and Sagalyn describe how developers were "ingenious in exploiting the wave of nostalgia that swept the country." They recapitulate the critics of festival marketplaces, with analytical distance. *Downtown, Inc.,* 202. Larry Ford, skeptical of packaged historical environments, still believed in solutions and formulas not too different from the ones currently under way. Ford, *Cities and Buildings.*

16. Barbara Carmen, "Woolworth's Closing Sparks Memories of Days of a Bygone Era," *Columbus (Ohio) Dispatch,* July 22, 1997, 1C. Other news stories capturing the sentiment that nostalgia made good press but did not generate adequate sales include Jennifer Steinhauer, "Woolworth Gives Up on the Five-and-Dime," *NYT,* July 18, 1997, A1; Liz Atwood, "Five-and-Dime Memories," *Baltimore Sun,* July 18, 1997, 1A. On the belief that a dime store "sells as much nostalgia as it does merchandise," see Cynthia Dockrell, "Miles of Aisles Home to Hairnets and Rubber Cement, Five-and-Dimes Offer Value, Service, and a Door into the Past," *Boston Globe,* June 15, 2000, G1.

17. William Fulton, "The Robin Hood of Real Estate," *Planning,* May 1985, 6. Filling the gap between the stereotypes of profit-hungry developers and naive consumers stood the real people who remade real estate — consultants, appraisers, brokers, staff preservationists, merchants, and ordinary shoppers.

18. Geographer Goss was "struck by how little the strategies of the developers seems [*sic*] to consciously affect visitors, and how they seem to ignore even the explicit verbal texts reproducing developer discourse." Jon Goss, "Disquiet on the Waterfront: Reflections on Nostalgia and Utopia in the Urban Archetypes of Festival Marketplaces," *Urban Geography* 17, no. 3 (1996): 241 n. 3. Goss discusses the "modernist critique" of consumers as "passive, sensual, and vulnerable victims." Goss, "The 'Magic of the Mall,'" 19.

19. Kowinski, "A Mall Covers the Waterfront," SM27. Alex Haley, *Roots* (Garden City, NY: Doubleday, 1976).

20. National Trust for Historic Preservation, "The Main Street Approach Script," October 1982, slide 39 entry. This text accompanied a promotional-educational slide show for the Main Street program, a copy of which is available in the Chapin Planning Library, University of North Carolina, Chapel Hill.

21. By the time Kmart sold its last seventy-six Kresge and Jupiter stores to McCrory Corporation in 1987, the stores generated less than 1 percent of Kmart's annual sales figures. Kmart asserted that the variety stores were still profitable. A month before the sale to McCrory's was announced, plans to sell the Kresges to F. W. Woolworth fell through. Jube Shiver Jr., "K Mart Shedding 5-and-Dime Roots with Kresge Stores Sale," *Los Angeles Times,* April 4, 1987, pt. 4, p. 1. Caroline Mayer, "Kresge Being Sold to McCrory; Buyer Is Largest U.S. Operator of Five-and-Dimes," *Washington Post,* April 4, 1987, D10.

22. "How Kresge Became the Top Discounter," *Business Week,* October 24, 1970,

62–63. Between 1962 and 1970, 385 Kmarts opened, achieving a fourfold increase in sales and thus rivaling Woolworth for third place in overall sales (first was Sears, second Penney). Despite the astounding success of Kmart, Kresge stayed in the variety store business. Kresge sales surpassed Woolworth's in 1970 and then overtook J. C. Penney in 1976. "The Problems That Are Upsetting Woolworth's," *Business Week,* June 29, 1974, 73; "J. C. Penney: Getting More from the Same Space," *Business Week,* August 18, 1975, 80–83. "Retailing: The Hot Discounter," *Newsweek,* April 1977, 69. Newberry claimed to be the first large variety chain to enter a regional shopping center. "Whatever Happened to the Dime Store?" *Business Week,* May 3, 1958, 52.

23. Penney operated 1,603 stores in 1947, with 575 located in very small towns (2,500–7,500 population). The company opened its first store off Main Street in 1949. Mary Elizabeth Curry, *Creating an American Institution: The Merchandising Genius of J. C. Penney* (New York: Garland Publishing, 1993), 289. Former Penney president William Batten describes how the mall anchor strategy evolved and put Penney ahead of rivals like Sears. "Oral History—William Batten, July 22, 1986," sec. 2, pp. 5–36; sec. 4, p. 9, courtesy Joan Gosnell, J. C. Penney Company Archives, Plano, Tex. (hereafter cited as JCPCA). See also "JC Penney: An American Legacy," J. C. Penney Co., Inc., 1992, 19, JCPCA; and John McDonald, "How They Minted the New Penney," *Fortune,* July 1967, 110–13, 158–65.

24. Genesco in turn sold the remaining Kress stores to McCrory's in the early 1980s. McCrory's was, according to one analyst, "racing around the country buying up these little variety stores" during that decade. Besides the stores bearing its own name, it operated in the early 1990s as S. H. Kress, G. C. Murphy, H. L. Green, McClellan, and J. J. Newberry. In a typical example, McCrory's bought 130 G. C. Murphy variety stores from Ames Department Stores in 1989, after Ames had owned the chain for only four years. In numbers of variety stores, McCrory's had outstripped Woolworth for lead position by 1987. McCrory's entered bankruptcy court in 1992 and emerged five years later greatly trimmed down but ready to open new stores and reopen old ones. Despite this distinctive history, the McCrory Corporation lurks in Woolworth's shadow. Mark Guidera, "Five-and-Dime's Hard Times," *Baltimore Sun,* December 23, 1994, 9C; Isadore Barmash, "A Kresge-McCrory Reunion," *NYT,* April 4, 1987, sec. 2, p. 33; Carla Lazzareschi, "McCrory's Files Chapter 11," *Los Angeles Times,* February 27, 1992, D1.

25. Analysts felt that W. T. Grant's mistake was that it did not commit to either the J. C. Penney strategy or the Kresge strategy and thus failed in between. "How W. T. Grant Lost $175-Million Last Year," *Business Week,* February 24, 1975, 75; "Woolworth: The Last Stand of the Variety Store," *Business Week,* January 9, 1978, 84.

26. "The Problems That Are Upsetting Woolworth's," 72–73. When Woolworth closed its last 450 variety stores in 1997 and changed its name to Venator, it put its future in specialty retailing such as Lady Footlocker. *Forbes* calculated that Woolworth closed 761 small variety stores between 1965 and 1976 and still had 1,519 units. In 1975 Kmart had 935 stores and Woolco had 253 stores. Paul Gibson, "Time for a New Look," *Forbes,* November 15, 1976, 60.

27. J. S. Roberts, "Why the World's Biggest Woolworth Went Downtown," in Mechlin D. Moore, ed., *Downtown Denver: A Guide to Central City Development,* Urban Land Institute Technical Bulletin no. 54, December 1965, 27; "Woolworth Helps Give Downtown Its Ups," *Nation's Business,* February 1970, 16; Woolworth Corporation, *Who? What? When? Where? How? Annual Report 1991,* 9; Real Estate Research Corporation (RERC),

"Reuse and Appraisal, F. W. Woolworth Store, Willimantic, Connecticut," March 1977, 9, 11. RERC Company Archives, Chicago, Ill. All of the 1976–77 reuse and appraisal reports done by RERC for Woolworth and cited in this chapter were kindly made available to the author by the company. This is not an archive open to researchers.

28. David Hinckley, "Stored Memories Are Lost in America," *New York Daily News,* July 18, 1997, 5. For other examples of Woolworth's close association with downtown, see also Mary Dolan, "Downtown Tampa's Retail Center Declines," *St. Petersburg Times,* February 25, 1988, city ed., 4; Frederic Biddle, "400 Woolworth Stores to Be Closed," *Boston Globe,* October 14, 1993, 41; Richard Greer, "Failure to Change Blamed for Woolworth's Woes," *Atlanta Journal and Constitution,* October 15, 1993, G1; Bob Hohler, "Store Closing Angers Mattapan," *Boston Globe,* October 16, 1993, metro/region sec., 3; "Woolworth to Shut Down 37 Variety Stores," *NYT,* October 24, 1993, sec. 13, p. 4.

29. RERC, *National Market Letter (NML),* April 1970, 6; "The Problems That Are Upsetting Woolworth's," 72–73; "Woolworth Picks a Numbers Man," *Business Week,* March 31, 1975, 20; "J. C. Penney: Getting More from the Same Space," 80; "Woolworth: The Last Stand of the Variety Store," 84–85. In 1960 J. C. Penney's average new store was 30 percent larger than those built in 1950. "J. C. Penney & Co. Annual Report, 1959," n.p., JCPCA; RERC, "Reuse Analysis and Appraisal, F. W. Woolworth Store, Topeka, Kansas," March 1977, 9, 12.

30. RERC had a long-established reputation in the real estate consulting field, partly based on publishing the *NML* since the 1930s but also based on the thousands of reports and studies it performed around the country. The company and its investment newsletter are described in chapter 4.

31. On the choking debt encumbering Kress's parent company, Genesco, see "Genesco May Shed a Bonwit Store," *Business Week,* January 29, 1979, 38. Kress architecture is surveyed by Bernice L. Thomas, *America's 5 and 10 Cent Stores: The Kress Legacy* (New York: John Wiley and Sons, Preservation Press, and the National Building Museum, 1997). A published guide allows a sampling of the Kress records. Susan Wilkerson and Hank Griffith, *A Guide to the Building Records of S. H. Kress & Co. 5–10–25 Cent Stores at the National Building Museum* (Washington, DC: National Building Museum, 1993). For a comprehensive overview of Main Street architecture, see Richard Longstreth, *The Buildings of Main Street* (Washington, DC: Preservation Press, 1987).

32. "Inspection Report by James Parkerson on 12-13-74," January 8, 1975, file 16, 1989.13.3.42, Greenville, Mississippi, Kress Archive Collection, National Building Museum, Washington, D.C.; RERC, "Reuse Analysis and Appraisal, F. W. Woolworth Store, Greenville, South Carolina," March 1977; Springfield Chamber of Commerce, *Shoppers' Paradise: An Experiment in Downtown Revitalization* (Springfield, OR: Springfield Chamber of Commerce, 1957), 5.

33. RERC, "Re-use Analysis and Appraisal, F. W. Woolworth Store, Oneida, New York," March 1977; Woolworth Corporation, *Who? What? When? Where? How?* 6; *Woolworth's First 75 Years: The Story of Everybody's Store, 1879–1954* (New York: William E. Rudge's Sons, 1954), 34.

34. RERC, *NML,* May 1965, 4; RERC, *NML,* April 1960, 6.

35. RERC, *NML,* May 1965, 4; RERC, "Reuse Analysis and Appraisal, F. W. Woolworth Store, Meadville, Pennsylvania," 1977, 11; "Reuse Analysis . . . Greenville, South Carolina," 2; "Reuse Analysis and Appraisal, F. W. Woolworth Store, Port Richmond, New York,"

March 1977, 9, 14, 26–27; "Reuse Analysis and Appraisal, F. W. Woolworth Store, Fond du Lac, Wisconsin," March 1977, 11. The *NML* also distinguished between vacant and "so deteriorated as to be unusable without major alteration." RERC, "Special Research Report: Secondary Strip Stores," *NML*, September 1962, 6.

36. RERC, "Appraisal of F. W. Woolworth Store, Biddeford, Maine," December 1977, 3; "Appraisal of F. W. Woolworth Store, Maynard, Massachusetts," December 1977; "Re-use Analysis . . . Oneida, New York," 13–14; and "Appraisal of F. W. Woolworth Store, Rutland, Vermont," 1977, 4.

37. RERC, "Reuse Analysis and Appraisal, F. W. Woolworth Store, St. Paul, Minnesota," March 1977, 2; "Re-use Analysis . . . Oneida, New York."

38. RERC, "Reuse Analysis and Appraisal, F. W. Woolworth Store, Lawrence, Massachusetts," March 1977, 2. See also "Reuse Analysis . . . Greenville, South Carolina," 13. In Meadville, Pennsylvania, and Greenville, Texas, the Woolworths had closed years before, and those sites were occupied by a CVS and a Perry Brothers Variety Store, respectively. The consultants hoped the current tenants would remain. RERC, "Reuse Analysis . . . Meadville, Pennsylvania," 2; "Reuse Analysis and Appraisal, F. W. Woolworth Store, Greenville, Texas," 1977, 2, 10, 13.

Some evidence suggests that the chains were more effective than independents in finding buyers for their properties. The leading chains usually had key locations and bigger properties. When one chain sold off stores, sometimes others competed to take over multiple units. They had the resources to hire national consultants such as RERC and the perspective to decide whether to use a local broker. RERC, "Reuse Analysis . . . Greenville, South Carolina," 2, 15. W. T. Grant squandered these advantages in a corrupt real estate department. Kickbacks and other illegal practices had saddled the company with long-term leases in weak locations. "How W. T. Grant Lost $175-Million Last Year," 76.

39. In St. Paul, RERC projected that institutional tenants would bring a higher sale price than secondary retail. RERC, "Reuse Analysis . . . St. Paul, Minnesota," 2.

40. The St. Paul site was 967 Payne Avenue, two miles northeast of the downtown. Ibid., 7, 10; RERC "Appraisal of F. W. Woolworth Store, Endicott, New York," 1977, 2; "Reuse Analysis . . . Topeka, Kansas," 3; "Reuse Analysis . . . Port Richmond, New York," 14. *NML* tracked the trend toward nonretail use of former retail space, with conversion rates of 15–20 percent signaling trouble by the early 1960s and worsening by 1970. *NML*, September 1962, 6; RERC, *NML*, October 1970, 5; *NML*, July 1959, 4.

41. RERC, "Reuse Analysis . . . Fond du Lac, Wisconsin," 8–9. The rumors could boost expectations as well, where empty stores were "supposedly rented but not yet occupied." RERC, "Special Research Report: Secondary Strip Stores," 6.

42. RERC, *NML*, July 1959, 3–4; *NML*, April 1963, 7; *NML*, November 1962, 7; *NML*, April 1963; and *NML*, April 1964.

43. RERC, "Appraisal . . . Biddeford, Maine," 4; "Appraisal . . . Rutland, Vermont," 4; RERC, "Reuse Analysis and Appraisal, F. W. Woolworth Store, Allentown, Pennsylvania," March 1977, 9; "Reuse Analysis . . . Fond du Lac, Wisconsin," 12; and "Reuse Analysis . . . Topeka, Kansas," 8; "Re-use Analysis . . . Oneida"; RERC, *NML*, October 1970, 4. For mentions of decline and relative health, see "Appraisal . . . Endicott, New York," 2; "Reuse Analysis . . . Greenville, Texas," 11.

44. RERC, "Reuse Analysis . . . Willimantic, Connecticut," 8–10; "Reuse Analysis . . . Topeka, Kansas," 2, 13; "Reuse Analysis . . . St. Paul, Minnesota," 2, 8; "Appraisal . . . Bid-

deford," 3; "Reuse Analysis . . . Lawrence, Massachusetts," 3; "Appraisal of F. W. Woolworth Store, Taunton, Massachusetts," December 16, 1977, 3.

45. RERC, "Reuse Analysis . . . Willimantic, Connecticut," 11. Other examples from the appraisals addressing demographic and image changes: "Reuse Analysis . . . Topeka, Kansas," 6; "Reuse Analysis . . . St. Paul, Minnesota," 7; "Reuse Analysis and Appraisal, F. W. Woolworth Store, Danbury, Connecticut," March 1977, 10–11, 13; and "Reuse Analysis . . . Greenville, South Carolina," 8.

46. RERC, "Appraisal of . . . Maynard, Massachusetts," 3; "Reuse Analysis and Appraisal, F. W. Woolworth Store, Lebanon, New Hampshire," 1977, 8; "Reuse Analysis . . . Meadville, Pennsylvania," 11; "Appraisal . . . Endicott, New York," 9; "Reuse Analysis . . . Allentown, Pennsylvania," 3; "Reuse Analysis . . . Topeka, Kansas," 14; "Reuse Analysis . . . Danbury, Connecticut," 2, 7; "Reuse Analysis . . . Greenville, Texas," 2; "Appraisal . . . Taunton, Massachusetts," 4; "Reuse Analysis . . . St. Paul, Minnesota," 2; "Appraisal . . . Rutland, Vermont," 4. The assessors filled the reports with "however," "despite," "although," and "nonetheless."

47. "Decay and death" in RERC, "Special Research Report: Secondary Strip Stores," 6. On empty store buildings as "fossils," see Jules Loh, "As 5-and-10-Cent Stores Close, Some Towns Lose Their Anchors," *Los Angeles Times,* March 8, 1992; as "niches," see Dan Wascoe Jr., "Woolworth Exit Another Blow to Budget Shoppers," *Minneapolis Star Tribune,* January 10, 1993, 4D. In the 1970s it was common to hope that a city had already bottomed out and would resume growth. For example, see RERC, "Reuse Analysis . . . Greenville, South Carolina," 8; "Reuse Analysis . . . Danbury, Connecticut," 2, 14.

48. On the shift to family shopping and teenagers, see RERC, *NML,* September 1975, 4; and McDonald, "How They Minted the New Penney," 110, 158.

49. Jennifer Steinhauer, "When Shoppers Walk Away from Pedestrian Malls," *NYT,* November 5, 1996, C1, C4; Ruth Eckdish Knack, "Pedestrian Malls: Twenty Years Later," *Planning,* December 1982, 15, 17; "City Pedestrian Malls Fail to Fulfill Promise of Revitalizing Downtown," *Wall Street Journal,* June 17, 1987, 29; Robertson "Downtown Pedestrian Malls in Sweden and the United States."

50. "You're Not Designing Stores for Women Shoppers," *Chain Store Age,* July 1973, E28–29. Cupino's response to the question "Do you consider yourself a career girl?" is worth quoting in full: "I guess you'd call me that, although I'm no supporter of Women's Liberation, I'm no man-hater. Recently I finished a course on plumbing — I was the only female ever to graduate from it. And now I'd say my major ambition is to obtain an architect's license and become the first female in-house architect that First National, or probably any other chain, has ever had." Ibid.

51. Abbott L. Nelson, "Special Research Report: Downtown Trends," *NML,* August 1972, 5; RERC, *NML,* June 1974, 6; Urban Land Institute, *Downtown Retail Development: Conditions for Success and Project Profiles* (Washington, DC: ULI, 1983), 7–8; RERC, "Reuse Analysis . . . Greenville, South Carolina," 10, 13; "white-collar" quote from RERC, *NML,* September 1975, 3.

52. "It's Get-Tough Time at W. T. Grant," *Business Week,* October 19, 1974, 76; "How W. T. Grant Lost $175-Million Last Year," 74; "Grant's Great Collapse," *Newsweek,* October 13, 1975, 81; Rush Loving Jr., "W. T. Grant's Last Days — As Seen from Store 1192," *Fortune,* April 1976, 110, 114. At the close-out sale for Seattle's downtown Woolworth, "people attacked the merchandise like piranha on a side of beef." Joe Haberstroh, "'Let Us In! Let

Us In! The Rush Is On," *Seattle Times,* November 18, 1993, B1. RERC, "Special Research Report: Secondary Strip Stores," 6.

53. A brilliant response to the "snob view" of Faneuil Hall is Robert Campbell, "Evaluation: Boston's 'Upper of Urbanity,'" *AIA Journal,* June 1981, 24. Kelly and Lewis, "What's Right (and Wrong) about the Inner Harbor," 32; Michael Demarest, "He Digs Downtown," *Time,* August 24, 1981, 44; "James Wilson Rouse," *Fortune,* March 23, 1981, 108.

54. Breckenfeld, "Jim Rouse Shows How to Give Downtown Retailing New Life," 85, 91; "The Shopping Mall Goes Urban," *Business Week,* December 13, 1982, 52. Stephanie Dyer documents that Rouse tried with limited success to help African American entrepreneurs succeed in the Gallery. She focuses on the assertiveness of black consumers in remaking the Gallery into a "black mall" after it was launched to appeal primarily to white suburbanites. Stephanie Dyer, "The Black Mall: Philadelphia's Gallery at Market East and the Racialization of Public Space," paper presented at the First Biennial Urban History Association Conference, Pittsburgh, Pennsylvania, September 27, 2002.

55. Scott Gerloff, "Main Street: The Early Years," *Historic Preservation Forum* 9, no. 3 (spring 1995): 4. Gerloff was one of the first project managers in the Main Street demonstration program. Before starting that position in 1977, he worked for the South Dakota Historic Preservation Center.

56. A 1972 *NML* commentary titled "Future Downtown Improvements" did not mention historic preservation. Nelson, "Special Research Report: Downtown Trends," 7–8.

57. Ada Louise Huxtable, "Design (Good and Bad) Down by the Levee," *NYT,* June 6, 1976, D28; William K. Stevens, "St. Louis Rediscovers Its Past as a New Spirit Rises," *NYT,* July 25, 1977, 24; Huxtable, "St. Louis and the Crisis of American Cities."

58. For "old ladies" quote, see Earl C. Gottschalk Jr., "What's Ahead for Gaslight Square?" *St. Louis Post-Dispatch,* August 6, 1961, *St. Louis Hotels, Taverns, and Restaurants Scrapbook,* 1:113, Scrapbook Collection, Missouri Historical Society, St. Louis, Mo. (hereafter cited as MHS). Sources supporting this view of Gaslight Square as an unlikely success story include the following. On Gaslight Square "rising out of wreckage and decay — like a flower in a dung heap" and flourishing "beyond all expectations," see Andrew Wilson, "Gaslight's Dim Days," *St. Louis Globe-Democrat,* September 28, 1971, *St. Louis Architecture Scrapbook,* 3:44, MHS. On the Gaslight area as being "right on the edge" and known for gay and transvestite bars, see "Oral History Interview with Richard Mutrux, November 21, 1990, by William Fischetti," box 2, Gaslight Square Collection, Western Historical Manuscripts Collection, University of Missouri, St. Louis (hereafter cited as GSC). For an in-depth overview, consult Danny Kathriner, "The Rise and Fall of Gaslight Square," *Gateway Heritage,* fall 2001, 32–43.

59. One tourist captured the nondescript architecture combined with the allure of the interiors: "The shadowy architecture of the buildings, garishly lighted by neon, was a hodgepodge of old and new, of wrought iron exteriors and crystal chandeliers visible through the windows." Fred Kiewit, "Gaslight Square: A Corner of S. Louis Emerges as a Tourist Mecca," *Kansas City Star,* March 11, 1962, *St. Louis Hotels, Taverns, and Restaurants Scrapbook,* 1:135, MHS.

60. Lenny Bruce quote in "Oral History with Jorge Martinez by Milo Gralnick, October 29, 1995," 9, box 2, GSC. For the precise origins of the architectural artifacts, George McCue, "Private Renewal without Federal Aid: Gaslight Square, St. Louis, Mo.," *Historic Preservation,* January 1961, 28. One account of Jimmy Massucci's designs as an "environ-

mental engineer" is in "Gaslight Square Has Seen Its Share of Screwballs," *St. Louis Globe-Democrat,* August 4, 1961, *St. Louis Hotels, Taverns, and Restaurants Scrapbook,* 2:43, MHS.

Dick Mutrux's stories of the area's early years imply that the distinctive assemblage designs incorporating local Victorian-era building parts were identified by some as homosexual, or sometimes just sexualized, aesthetics. He recalled that his first partner in his first saloon venture told him, "My friends are newspaper men, they're drinkers, they don't want this fruit stuff. This is ridiculous, you don't have to put all of the chandeliers around." The partner backed out. Later Dick clashed with his brother Paul, an architect, over the design of their restaurant The Three Fountains. Dick recounted that Paul said, "'This place is going to look like a whore house.' And I said, 'hopefully, hopefully!'" "Oral History Interview with Richard Mutrux," 3–4, 13. On the origins and evolution of assemblage as a twentieth-century artistic movement, see the book published in conjunction with an exhibition at the Museum of Modern Art in New York, William C. Seitz, *The Art of Assemblage* (Garden City, NY: Doubleday, 1961).

61. "Gas Light Era Gone? It's Coming Back Stronger Than in the 'Good Old Days,'" *St. Louis Post-Dispatch,* December 25, 1960, *St. Louis Hotels, Taverns, and Restaurants Scrapbook,* 6:72, MHS. This article looks at the national resurgence of interest in installing historic gaslights and also describes which cities and parts of the country were still using their old ones. On Crystal Palace, "Oral History with Jorge Martinez," 3–4.

62. C. K. Boeschenstein, "Homeland of the Individualists and Non-Conformists, Creative Arts and Saloons of Golden Era," *St. Louis Globe-Democrat,* February 1, 1959, *St. Louis Hotels, Taverns, and Restaurants Scrapbook,* 6:30, MHS.

63. In revealing the role that beatnik and bohemian culture played in St. Louis revitalization around 1960, the story of Gaslight Square also begins to explain the popularity of beat culture outside of literary and intellectual circles, and outside of New York City and San Francisco. Well-dressed suburbanites (whose exposure to and consumption of beat literature and lifestyles still needs to be documented, especially since the beats explicitly rejected so much of suburban values) flocked to the commercial establishments of this edgy neighborhood. For a fascinating story of the coffeehouses in Philadelphia, the reactions of various groups to such establishments and their clientele, and the late 1950s police raids of these businesses, see "Rizzo's Raiders and Beaten Beats," in Marc Stein, *City of Sisterly and Brotherly Loves: Lesbian and Gay Philadelphia, 1945–1972* (Chicago: University of Chicago Press, 2000), 155–76. Two recent works on Greenwich Village as America's quintessential bohemian neighborhood are Christine Stansell, *American Moderns: Bohemian New York and the Creation of a New Century* (New York: Metropolitan Books, 2000); and Ross Wetzsteon, *Republic of Dreams: Greenwich Village, and the American Bohemia, 1910–1960* (New York: Simon and Schuster, 2002).

64. "Oral History with Jorge Martinez," 2.

65. C. K. Boeschenstein, "Gaslight Square Presents New Faces and Plans," *St. Louis Globe-Democrat,* February 28, 1960, *St. Louis Hotels, Taverns, and Restaurants Scrapbook,* 1:71, MHS; McCue, "Private Renewal without Federal Aid," 24.

66. Gottschalk, "What's Ahead for Gaslight Square?"; suburban advantages quote in Earl C. Gottschalk, "Gaslight Square Improvements Planned in Move to Cut Crime," *St. Louis Post-Dispatch,* February 21, 1965, Gaslight Square clippings file, Local History Collection, History and Genealogy Dept., St. Louis Public Library, Main Branch (hereafter cited as GSCF). "Police Declare Gaslight Square to Be One of the City's Safest

Sections," *St. Louis Post-Dispatch,* November 1, 1965, *St. Louis General Scrapbook,* 12:9, MHS. "Gaslight Area Praised as Tourist Attraction," *St. Louis Globe-Democrat,* August 17, 1961, *St. Louis Hotels, Taverns, and Restaurants Scrapbook,* 1:73, MHS. Although the mayor pledged to help the district rebound, and several city departments were in contact with the Gaslight Square Businessman's association, the Square declined as it had risen — without any government help.

67. Jimmy Massucci quoted in Gottschalk, "What's Ahead for Gaslight Square?" See also Munro Roberts III, "'Too Many People': Gaslight Square Seen by Its Former 'King,'" *St. Louis Globe-Democrat,* May 14, 1961, *St. Louis Hotels, Taverns, and Restaurants Scrapbook,* 1:58, MHS; and Kiewit, "Gaslight Square."

68. "Oral History with Jorge Martinez," 4.

69. Charles R. Kelley, "A Plea for Gaslight Square," *St. Louis Post-Dispatch,* October 3, 1965, GSCF; Tom Yarbrough, "New Gaslight Square: 'Just How Square Do We Want to Be?'" *Pictures — St. Louis Post-Dispatch,* October 15, 1972, 12, *St. Louis General Scrapbook,* 17:36F, MHS. On the area remembered as a melting pot experiment, see Carolyn P. Smith, "Gaslight Square: Its Past, Present & Future?" n.d., GSCF.

70. On the impact of the riots, see "Oral History Interview with Richard Mutrux," 9; "Oral Interview . . . with Jack Parker, Conducted by William M. Fischetti on July 19, 1990," box 2, GSC. Mutrux comments on the impact of the riots in Peggy Swanson, "Three Restauranteurs Move Their Fountains," *St. Louis Post-Dispatch,* August 15, 1968, GSCF. Ruins quote from Wilson, "Gaslight's Dim Days." For an analysis of Gaslight's failure, see Dennis R. Judd, "The Gaslight Square Syndrome," *St. Louisian,* April 1977, 59–62.

71. Paul Delaney, "Violence Destroys a Boom in Kansas City's Old Section," *NYT,* April 19, 1977, 16; William Robbins, "Kansas City 'Doorstep' Facing a Major Cleanup," *NYT,* December 16, 1986, A20; "Blast Destroys Two Bars," *NYT,* March 28, 1977, 20.

72. "Institute of Architects Presents Honor Awards for 12 Buildings," *NYT,* July 3, 1966, sec. 8, p. 1.

73. Stuart Rose, "San Francisco's Ghirardelli Square," *Historic Preservation,* October– December 1969, 11–2.; "Old Chocolate Factory Becomes Backdrop for Square," *NYT,* April 17, 1966, sec. 8, p. 1; Vivian Brown, "Factories Converted to Give San Francisco High Spots," *NYT,* July 21, 1968, sec. 8, p. 4; "Waterfront Block Becomes City's Pride," *NYT,* January 23, 1966, sec. 2, p. 27. Although the Roths supported preservation (donating the family's forty-three-room mansion in 1975 to the National Trust for Historic Preservation), Bill Roth had also been deeply involved in San Francisco urban renewal planning.

74. Stuart Rose to Warren M. Lemmon, May 3, 1963, box 1, Advisory Board file, unprocessed collection BANC MSS 82/84c, "Materials relating to Ghirardelli Square, [ca. 1910–1981]," Bancroft Library, University of California, Berkeley (hereafter cited as MGS).

75. William M. Roth, "Ghirardelli Memorandum," January 27, 1963, 1; Karl Kortum to Warren Lemmon, April 6, 1963, 3; Roth noted that the "benches need not be Victorian." Roth to Lemmon, September 2, 1963. All in binder no. 1, box 1, MGS.

76. Karl Kortum to William M. Roth, August 22, 1963, 1–3. On the importance of street furniture and pavement, see Procter Melquist, "Another Ghirardelli Memorandum," July 9, 1962, 6, both in binder no. 1, box 1, MGS. Mellquist's long list of design elements included lights, trash cans, kiosks, benches, balustrades, signs, fountains, plant boxes, drinking fountains, flag poles, and fences.

David Pesonen, a candidate for the job of leading Ghirardelli's conceptual and physical development, asserted that while the initial development proposals obsessed about the site's "character," none demonstrated an understanding of that character. Pesonen agreed that Ghirardelli "should have its face washed, not lifted" and critiqued the renderings of the contracted architects Wurster, Bernardi & Emmons as an "acid bath." Like Kortum, Pesonen worried that Ghirardelli would be "masked by architectural abstractions." An early memorandum from Advisory Board member Proctor Mellquist, editor of *Sunset Magazine,* considered the less desirable but possible option of tearing down many of the site's buildings. (His name is misspelled in various ways in the Ghirardelli records). Pesonen to Lemmon, February 3, 1963, 2, 4; Procter Melquist, "Memorandum: The Ghirardelli Block," June 19, 1962, 1. Although Pesonen did not get the job, Warren Lemmon liked his creativity and initiative. Lemmon to Roth, "Ghirardelli property — David Pesonen," January 10, 1963, 1. All in binder no. 1, box 1, MGS.

77. Kortum to Lemmon, April 6, 1963. Even before the Roths purchased the Ghirardelli property, Kortum argued that its unique historical style would compete favorably with downtown San Francisco, which was becoming "increasingly rigidified and non-special in the grip of international modern architecture." Ghirardelli had a "'just growed' quality." Kortum to Lemmon, "Some Thoughts on Conversion of Ghirardelli Chocolate Factory into Offices/Apartments," March 1, 1962. All in binder no. 1, box 1, MGS.

78. Lawrence Halprin to Roth, "Notes on the Ghirardelli Center," June 27, 1962, 3. Melquist, "Another Ghirardelli Memorandum," 2–3; "Thomas Church #7"; and "Lloyd Flood #9 (formerly chief designer for Edward Stone)," all in binder no. 1, box 1, MGS. Mellquist's carnival concept included tumblers, vaudeville, cafes, and a seal tank.

79. On early-twentieth-century factory design, see Lindy Biggs, *The Rational Factory: Architecture, Technology, and Work in America's Age of Mass Production* (Baltimore: Johns Hopkins University Press, 1996); Betsy Hunter Bradley, *The Works: The Industrial Architecture of the United States* (New York: Oxford University Press, 1999); and Amy E. Slaton, *Reinforced Concrete and the Modernization of American Building, 1900–1930* (Baltimore: Johns Hopkins University Press, 2001). Circa 1919 photographs of the Ghirardelli factory interior and landscaping are available in "D. Ghirardelli Co. Photograph Album of Chocolate Manufacturing Process," Banc Pic 1992.036-ALB (on-line at http://sunsite2 .berkeley.edu/egi-bin/oac/calher/ghirardelli), Bancroft Library, University of California, Berkeley. On tourism to early-twentieth-century factories, see the forthcoming publications of Bill Littman. See also Joel Hoffman's work on the architecture and broader cultural and economic vision of the Cadbury cocoa factory and its industrial village, "Imaging the Industrial Village: Architecture, Art, and Visual Culture in The Garden Community of Bournville, England" (Ph.D. diss., Yale University, 1993).

80. Roth to Lemmon, September 2, 1963, 1, binder no. 1, box 1, MGS.

81. Joseph A. Baird Jr. to Lemmon, April 10, 1963, 1; Lemmon to Roth, "Ghirardelli property — Al Waller development," July 3, 1962; Lemmon to Roth, "American Heritage Wax Museum, Scottsdale, Arizona," February 20, 1963, 1–2; Lemmon to Roth, "Scottsdale Fifth Avenue Shopping Center," February 20, 1963, 1–2. Lemmon to Roth, "Ghirardelli property — Robert Powers (Nut Tree)," January 14, 1963; Mary Cooke, "Personalizing the Shopping Center," *Honolulu Advertiser,* September 12, 1975. In this last article, the Roses took credit for starting the trend of reusing old buildings for commercial purposes. See

also Lemmon to Roth, "Ghirardelli property — Stuart Rose proposal," January 17, 1963. All items are in binder no. 1, box 1, MGS. Roth was very interested in a Western-themed wax museum, but most experts advised Lemmon not to pursue it since wax museums attracted the wrong crowds for a shopping center. Nut Tree was a family-owned investment like Ghirardelli.

82. Melquist, "Memorandum: The Ghirardelli Block," 2, 4.

83. Kortum to Lemmon, April 6, 1963; Kortum to Lemmon, "Some Thoughts on Conversion of Ghirardelli Chocolate Factory into Offices/Apartments," March 1, 1962, 1–2, both in binder no. 1, box 1, MGS.

84. Halprin to Roth, "Notes on the Ghirardelli Center," June 27, 1962, 1, 3; Roth to Lemmon and Mellquist, September 23, 1963, 1; William M. Roth, "Ghirardelli Memorandum," January 27, 1963, 1, all in binder no. 1, box 1, MGS. Roth's inclusion of a question mark after his suggestion for including political meetings indicates that he sought feedback on that matter, in the brainstorming format that dominated these early memos.

85. Kortum to Lemmon, April 6, 1963, binder no. 1, box 1, MGS.

86. David E. Pesonen to Lemmon, February 3, 1963, 2–4, binder no. 1, box 1, MGS. Minutes of Advisory Board Meeting, November 6, 1963, 4–5, Advisory Board file, box 1, MGS. Kortum proposed early on that "purchase of this site for this purpose may well prove a turning point in modern day San Francisco history in that it would blunt, divert and edify the 'high rise' mystique that threatens this part of the city." Kortum to Lemmon, "Some Thoughts on Conversion of Ghirardelli Chocolate Factory into Offices/Apartments." I have not yet been able to evaluate the participation of the architecture firm Wurster, Bernardi & Emmons, but I will do so elsewhere in a fuller account of Ghirardelli Square's development. Some records indicate that the sign was erected in 1923; others suggest that Ghirardelli put it up a decade or so earlier.

87. Another wealthy developer gutted a Del Monte canning factory down the street to create The Cannery, which opened a few years after Ghirardelli Square. Because of this and copycat projects nearby, Ghirardelli Square was seen as a largely local phenomenon and something of a quirk. See Frieden and Sagalyn, *Downtown, Inc.,* 74–75. "Matt De Vito: Mission Control at Rouse," *Chain Store Age Executive,* March 1982, 40.

88. Arnold Gingrich, "The Business Community and Historic Preservation," *Historic Preservation,* October–December 1969, 4; "Shoppers and Diners in Salt Lake City Flocking to Redeveloped Trolley Barns," *NYT,* November 12, 1972, 76; Jon Nordheimer, "Atlanta Brightens Its Cellar," *NYT,* September 11, 1969, 49; Charles Rutheiser, "Making Place in the Nonplace Urban Realm: Notes on the Revitalization of Downtown Atlanta," in *Theorizing the City: The New Anthropology Reader,* ed. Setha M. Low (New Brunswick, NJ: Rutgers University Press, 1999), 325–26. Other cited examples included The Garage in Cambridge, Massachusetts, and an old department store in Lincoln, Nebraska. Phyllis W. Haserot, "Nationwide Development of Downtown Shopping Centers," in *A New Concept: The Downtown Shopping Center,* by Laurence Alexander (New York: Downtown Research and Development Center, 1975), 26.

89. On the local and federal financial assistance required by the Rouse Company and Rouse's Enterprise Development Company marketplaces, especially the $110 million in Urban Development Action Grants, see John T. Metzger, "The Failed Promise of a Festival Marketplace: South Street Seaport in Lower Manhattan," *Planning Perspectives* 16 (2001): 44. The difference between the public-private partnerships of the Rouse festival

concept and the private backing of their precursors appears to be one of the greatest distinctions between the two.

90. John Heller, "How to Fit a Shopping Center into Downtown," in Alexander, *A New Concept*, 8.

91. Kowinski, "A Mall Covers the Waterfront," SM28–29; Brown, "Factories Converted to Give San Francisco High Spots," R8; Cummins, "The New Face of the Old Market," 17.

92. Prior to Faneuil Hall, the Rouse Company had not tried its hand with historical themes, but it had failed in the early 1960s to get the downtown retail redevelopment of Norfolk, Virginia, off the ground, and in the early 1970s it gave up on a downtown shopping mall in Fort Lauderdale, Florida. Frieden and Sagalyn, *Downtown, Inc.*, 113. Later, in many cities by the mid-1980s there was vocal resistance to proposed Rouse marketplaces. St. Petersburg, Florida, voters rejected one such proposal, and Chicago's City Council turned down a Rouse plan for Navy Pier. Some downtown Rouse projects struggled terribly, such as Toledo's Portside and Tampa's Harbor Island. Roger Lowenstein, "Cities, Developers Seek New Approaches As Festival Markets Lose Some Luster," *Wall Street Journal*, December 11, 1986, 35. See also Iver Peterson, "Past and Future Collide in Plan for Albuquerque," *NYT*, February 5, 1985, A14. On Larimer Square, see Kathie Sutin, "The Many Sides of a Successful Square," *St. Louis Post-Dispatch*, February 15, 1972, *St. Louis General Scrapbook*, 17:9, 11, MHS. In Sutin's article the successful developers of places like Ghirardelli and Larimer Squares speculate about the failures of Gaslight and Chicago's Old Town.

93. Ada Louise Huxtable, "Why You Always Win and Lose in Urban Renewal," *NYT*, September 19, 1976, D34. On Faneuil Hall, see Frieden and Sagalyn, *Downtown, Inc.* John T. Metzger looks critically at the long-term failures of festival marketplaces, basing his analysis on a detailed study of South Street Seaport. After initial success, the "economic performance of the festival marketplace concept was weak." Metzger, "The Failed Promise of a Festival Marketplace," 44.

94. Rouse to Honorable Kevin H. White, March 16, 1976, 2 (letter not sent but filed), Faneuil Hall Marketplace file (hereafter cited as FHM), January 1975–June 1976, box 422, James W. Rouse Papers, Columbia Association Archives, Columbia, Md. (hereafter cited as JWRP).

95. Rouse to Roy E. Williams, September 18, 1975, FHM file, January 1975–June 1976, box 422, JWRP. James W. Rouse, "Faneuil Hall Marketplace: Its Special Meaning and Potential for the Rouse Company," September 7, 1976, 1, 2, 4, FHM file, July 1976–December 1976 (2 of 2), box 422, JWRP.

96. Rouse, "Faneuil Hall Marketplace," 7. Leo Molinaro to TRC/ACC Committee, October 18, 1976, FHM file, July 1976–December 1976, box 422, JWRP; Rouse to Warren W. Wilson, "Faneuil Hall Marketplace Shopper Survey," November 2, 1976, file July 1976–December 1976, box 422, JWRP; R. E. Williams to S. P. Cavanaugh et al., "Quincy Market Merchandising," October 26, 1976, FHM file, July 1976–December 1976, box 422, JWRP.

97. Recognizing their commonalities, the Rouse Company sent speakers to many of the first Main Street preservation conferences. Andree Brooks, "Lessons for Main Street from Shopping Centers," *NYT*, December 2, 1979, R6.

98. Mrs. Patrick W. Harrington, "Rochester, New York," *Historic Preservation*, October–December 1969, 25. Michael Holleran has a fascinating discussion of the 1870s preserva-

tion of Boston's Old South meetinghouse — a decision to keep "off the market indefinitely" one of the nation's most valuable parcels of real estate. Holleran, *Boston's "Changeful Times,"* 99–104.

99. Ada Louise Huxtable, "Keeping the There There," *NYT,* May 16, 1971, D21; "Waterfront Block Becomes City's Pride," 119. The model of businesspeople embracing preservation once they are convinced of its economic value is reminiscent of how Progressive era investors took over the Main Street improvement strategies defined by women's clubs in the 1890s. The gendered transition in preservation sensibilities during the 1960s and 1970s would be a fascinating topic for further research.

100. Arthur P. Ziegler Jr., "Pittsburgh, Pennsylvania," *Historic Preservation,* October–December 1969, 30–32. See also Robertson E. Collins, "Jacksonville, Oregon," ibid., 19–21; Harrington, "Rochester, New York," 26. That issue of *Historic Preservation* was devoted to "The Business Community and Historic Preservation." On merchants resisting the preservationists' demand to peel off aluminum siding and neon, see Bradley Skelcher, "Economic Development through Historic Preservation: The Main Street Pilot Project" (Ph.D. diss., Southern Illinois University at Carbondale, 1990), 126.

101. Paul Gibson, "Will the Real Woolworth Please Stand Up?" *Forbes,* May 1, 1978, 58.

102. Undated early 1970 letter from Robert Evans, file 3, 1989.13.3.33, Valdosta, Georgia, Kress Archive Collection, National Building Museum, Washington, D.C. (hereafter cited as KAC). Big-city professionals sometimes could not resist commenting on the spelling of branch correspondence. "We must confess that this is the first time in our lives that we have seen neutral spelled 'Neutrle.'" New York City consulting engineers writing to the San Francisco regional office about a local electrician's evaluation of Webb City, Missouri store, file 12 — General, 1989.13.3.43, Webb City, Missouri, KAC.

103. Herb Lias to F. E. Kerby, April 20, 1968; and "Store Operations: General Customer Evaluation," February 25, 1966, file 12 — General, 1989.13.3.43, Webb City, Missouri, KAC. The store was closed in 1970 and reformatted into a Dart fabric store.

104. Ada Louise Huxtable, "No Time to Joke," *NYT,* May 31, 1970, 16; Wilkerson and Griffith, *A Guide to the Building Records of S. H. Kress & Co.,* 53–54; "Focus: Main Street's Rich Uncle — Uncle Sam," *Women's Wear Daily,* February 15, 1965/6 [date not clear], box 15, file Urban Renewal, Resseguie Collection, Baker Library, Harvard Business School. An insightful discussion of the shift from forward- to backward-looking storefront trends is in Richard Mattson, "Storefront Remodeling on Main Street," *Journal of Cultural Geography* 3, no. 2 (spring–summer 1983): 49–52. On a 1990s Main Street preservation effort that removed widespread 1970s aluminum siding, see Alan Katz, "Greeley Rediscovers Historic Charm," *Denver Post,* May 27, 1996, B1.

105. Joan Horne, "Downtown Mall's a Ball, Y'all" *Memphis Commercial Appeal,* July 14, 1978, 13; A. J. Ellis to Mr. Crocker Graham, July 14, 1978, both in file Memphis, Tennessee, 1989.13.3.65, KAC.

106. Kress new construction encountered changing commercial sensibilities too. In the mid-1960s, Kress opened Variety Fair stores, a busy concept using angles and colors to create a "county fair" atmosphere. The Whirly-Q-Lunchette's "gay" signage included "a Whirly-Q, a disc of red, white and gold swirls in an outward pattern, arranged on a bright red background." Philadelphia's local art commission, opposed to "signs which whirl or revolve," judged the sign to be "aesthetically unacceptable." "Kress to Open Variety Fair

at 1108–14 Market St., Philadelphia, PA," City of Philadelphia to Kress, June 24, 1965. Both sources in files 1 and 2 — General, 1989.13.3.56, Philadelphia, Pennsylvania, KAC.

107. J. C. Spike to Mr. C. L. Thomas and Mr. R. D. Tucker, memo, May 3, 1970; C. L. Thomas to Mr. R. D. Tucker, memo, August 3, 1970; R. A. Chandler to C. L. Thomas, memo, August 7, 1970. Cathy Donelson, "Old Commerce Street Is Gonna Swing," *Montgomery Advertiser-Journal,* June 6, 1971; and "Over 100 Million Dollars in Improvements and Investments on the Way." "Proposed Non-Residential Property Rehabilitation Standards for Court Square Urban Renewal Project, Downtown Montgomery, Alabama." All in file 2 — General, 1989.13.3.2, Montgomery, Alabama, KAC.

108. Skelcher, "Economic Development through Historic Preservation," 1–21. See also Richard Francaviglia, *Main Street Revisited: Time, Space, and Image Building in Small-Town America* (Iowa City: University of Iowa Press, 1996), 51–54. Other cities initiating Main Street preservation before the NTHP included Chillicothe, Ohio, and Woodstock, Illinois. Brown, "Main Streets Get Street-Wise," 30. The director of Corning Market Street Restoration Agency, Inc., cited Historic Savannah and the Small Town Institute in Washington state as inspiration.

109. The trust, for example, played a major role in the creation of federal tax incentives for preservation in 1977. Bradley Skelcher, "What Are the Lessons Learned from the Main Street Pilot Project, 1977–1980," *Small Town,* July–August, 1992, 15–19. Sohyun Park Lee, "From Redevelopment to Preservation: Downtown Planning in Post-War Seattle" (Ph.D. diss., University of Washington, 2001), 17–18, 189–90. As the failures and critiques of urban renewal have disabled that program's ability to unify what political scientists have identified as "progrowth coalitions," historic preservation has become the basis of garnering public support for urban redevelopment (depending on local circumstances). The case of Times Square "reveals how the enormous development project came to be defined in terms of its relatively minor historic preservation component." Alexander J. Reichl, "Historic Preservation and Progrowth Politics in U.S. Cities," *Urban Affairs Review,* March 1997, 513–15.

110. A new Woolworth in downtown Atlanta in 1995 leased its food service to Burger King. "The Business of the City," *Atlanta Journal and Constitution,* January 26, 1995, D4. David Usborne, "Woolworth Disappears from Downtown America," *Independent* (London), July 18, 1997, business sec., 22. Woolworth also began closing the pet departments that loomed large in variety store lore. Parakeets were often the subject of customer nostalgia — ironic, since the birds were a source of distress because they carried a disease sometimes fatal to humans.

111. Davis Bushnell, "Old Woolworth Locales in Varied Stages of Revival," *Boston Globe,* August 30, 1998, 9.

112. For a provocative lament that the postmodern city is so "dominated by corporate values" that "it does not allow for critical perspectives grounded in values formed outside of the marketplace," see Boyer, *City of Collective Memory,* 60–66, esp. 65.

113. John Schmeltzer, "Why Woolworth Died: Variety Stores No Longer Have a Place in America," *Buffalo News,* July 27, 1997, business sec., 21B; Mickey H. Gramig, "No Longer Worth It: Dime Store Demise," *Atlanta Journal and Constitution,* July 18, 1997, business sec., 1F; Guidera, "Five-and-Dime's Hard Times," 9C. See also Ralph Bivins, "Woolworth Store Coming Down for New Parking, Retail Spaces," *Houston Chronicle,*

February 3, 1999, business sec., 1. Barbara Donlon, "Closing of Woolworth's Is Like Losing a Good Friend," *Boston Herald,* August 10, 1997, 47. Sharon Linstedt, "Woolworth Closing to End Tradition: Downtown Patrons Will Miss Regular Trips to the Five-and-Dime Store," *Buffalo News,* July 18, 1997, 1A. In the 1980s and early 1990s, Wall Street looked favorably on Woolworth's aggressive efforts to close stores and reposition itself. But by 1997, the financial world was tired of the "wild ride," which contributed to its good-riddance position when Woolworth closed permanently. Mark Albright, "Last of Woolworth's Stores Will Live On in Memory Only," *St. Petersburg Times,* July 18, 1997, business sec., 1E.

114. John Craddock, "What Will Happen to 5 & 10s?" *St. Petersburg Times,* December 29, 1991, city ed., 1I.

115. Atwood, "Five-and-Dime Memories," 1A; Loh, "As 5-and-10-Cent Stores Close," A3; Tom Wheatley, "Cherokee Street Landmark Closing: Demise of Woolworth's Disappoints Customers," *St. Louis Post-Dispatch,* November 10, 1992, 3A; Guidera, "Five-and-Dime's Hard Times," 9C; RERC, "Reuse Analysis and Appraisal, F. W. Woolworth Store, St. Charles, Missouri," 1977, 14; "Re-use Analysis . . . Oneida, New York." See also "Reuse Analysis . . . Danbury, Connecticut," 13.

116. Goss, "The 'Magic of the Mall,'" 33, crediting the shopper walking habits comment, without quotes, to Joel Garreau, *Edge City: Life on the New Frontier* (New York: Doubleday, 1991), 117–18, 464; Nancy Bartley, "The Counter Community—With the Closing of Woolworth's Lunch Counters, the Regulars Are Wondering Where They'll Go," *Seattle Times,* October 22, 1993, F1; Kara Swisher, "Brother, Can You Spare a Five-and-Dime?" *Washington Post,* October 16, 1993, financial sec., C1.

117. On Woolworth representing a past era of "thrifty values" and "simpler tastes," see "No Time for 5 and Dime," *USA Today,* July 21, 1997, 12A; and "Dimes Have Changed," *Boston Globe,* July 19, 1997, editorial, A14. Some goods seemed to have been available for "a century." Edward R. Silverman, "Woolworth Grows from Its Dime-Store Roots," *Los Angeles Times,* October 22, 1989, D22. On "thingamajigs," see Dick Feagler, "Baubles, Beads of Memory Survive Woolworth's Demise," *Cleveland Plain Dealer,* July 23, 1997, 2A; "The Death of a Dime-Store Chain," *San Francisco Chronicle,* July 19, 1997, A20.

118. Nancy Rivera Brooks, "Woolworth to Lay Off 9,200, Close Stores," *Los Angeles Times,* July 18, 1997, A1; Amy Beth Graves, "Shoppers Saddened by News; Generations of Americans Grew Up Prowling Aisles of Woolworth's," *Columbus (Ohio) Dispatch,* July 18, 1997, 1A; Ada Louise Huxtable, "Remnants of an Era: Two Silent Stores," *NYT,* November 8, 1971, C1, 10. Other articles describing the thrifty and "unassuming" values of the variety store concept, according to which customers bought only what they "needed," and if they overspent it was in nickels: "No Time for 5 and Dime," 12A; Susan Trausch, "The Age of Innocence," *Boston Globe,* October 30, 1993, 11; "Dimes Have Changed," A14. On old-fashioned food, see Katherine Bishop, "Swallowed by Change, a Woolworth's Loses Its Lunch Counter," *NYT,* February 9, 1992, sec. 1, pt. 1, p. 22.

119. Although chain officials and market analysts insisted that these institutions could not generate enough income because of consumer preferences (as in the case of G. Fox at the beginning of this book), the management and profitability of downtown chains (and department stores) in the late twentieth century still awaits scholarly analysis. Anecdotal evidence suggests that many stores at the time of their closing were "often packed with customers" and profitable. Wasco, "Woolworth Exit Another Blow to Budget Shoppers," 4D. See also Gene Amole, "Woolworth Now Memory Candy," *Denver Rocky Mountain*

News, June 13, 2000, 6A; Mark Shaffer, "Facing Life without Woolworth's," *Arizona Republic,* October 23, 1993, A1; Pat Gauen, "Store's Demise Is Symptom of Dying Lifestyle," *St. Louis Post-Dispatch,* January 2, 1992, 1; and Brian Meyer, "Downtown's Store's Sales Top Projections," *Buffalo News,* September 11, 1999, 7A.

120. Dockrell, "Miles of Aisles Home to Hairnets and Rubber Cement," G1; store as window to the past, Carmen, "Woolworth's Closing Sparks Memories of Days of a Bygone Era," 1C; Gramig, "No Longer Worth It," 1F; museum comparison in Linstedt, "Woolworth Closing to End Tradition," 1A.

121. Peterson, "Past and Future Collide in Plan for Albuquerque," A14. On store as time tunnel, Silverman, "Woolworth Grows from Its Dime-Store Roots," D22. Jon Goss analyzes the symbolic and commercial function of history at Honolulu's Aloha Tower Marketplace, a festival marketplace that opened in 1994. Goss, "Disquiet on the Waterfront," 221–41. On movements to commemorate more controversial dimensions of history, see Dolores Hayden, *The Power of Place: Urban Landscapes as Public History* (Cambridge, MA: MIT Press, 1995).

122. Visitor Comment Book 2, December 30, 1997, "Main Street Five-and-Dimes: The Architectural Heritage of the S. H. Kress & Co. Stores," National Building Museum Comment Books, May 1997–March 1998. Courtesy of National Building Museum, Washington, D.C. (hereafter cited as Visitor Comment Book 1 and Visitor Comment Book 2). For many, these sentiments underscored the need for historic preservation and the creative reuse of old commercial buildings.

123. Visitor Comment Book 2, October 27, 1997; Visitor Comment Book 1, September 8, June 16, 1997. In a note to the author regarding the September 8 page, NBM staff noted, "This page was removed from the book because of comments in poor taste." Since nostalgia for segregation became a persistent theme, the staff must have decided later that it was impossible to remove all such comments.

124. Visitor Comment Book 1, July 28, 1997; Visitor Comment Book 2, mid-November 1997; January 25, 1998; Visitor Comment Book 1, June 7, 1997; Visitor Comment Book 2, December 6, 1997; Visitor Comment Book 1, October 1, 1997. Some singled out what they regarded as the degradation of women in store paraphernalia. The uninterpreted photographs of segregated store facilities prompted others to request a more complicated understanding of dime store history before they offered their opinions. See esp. Visitor Comment Book 1, July 6, 1997.

125. Visitor Comment Book 1, early July, mid-July, late June 1997.

126. Visitor Comment Book 1, mid-September 1997 (all punctuation, including ellipses, original); Visitor Comment Book 2, November 12, 1997. Although it did not appear in the visitor comment books, nostalgia among African Americans for the once-thriving black business districts (many destroyed by urban renewal and highway programs) offered yet another decline narrative.

127. Ric Kahn, "He's Well Dressed, but Still a Suspect," *Boston Globe,* March 12, 1995, city weekly, 1; Booth Gunther, "Dozens Revisit 1960 Lunch Demonstration," *Tampa Tribune,* January 19, 1997, Florida/metro, 1. For some of the conflicts arising over Rouse's support for black business and interest in black customers, see Metzger, "The Failed Promise of a Festival Marketplace," 44; and especially Stephanie Kay Dyer, "Markets in the Meadows: Department Stores and Shopping Centers in the Decentralization of Philadelphia, 1920–1980" (Ph.D. diss., University of Pennsylvania, 2000), 334–42. Rouse was a

rare developer in his willingness to raise controversial "social" issues. He often brought up the role commercial development could play in healing the racial rifts of American society. His housing investment programs run through the Enterprise Foundation strove to remedy inequalities. Fulton, "The Robin Hood of Real Estate," 4–10. On race politics and preservation in Atlanta and New Orleans, see Reichl, "Historic Preservation and Progrowth Politics in U.S. Cities."

128. Jon Goss explains that "in evoking the desire for genuine openness of the city, the festival marketplace creates a potential space for an urban politics committed to its general realization." Goss, "Disquiet on the Waterfront," 240.

129. Calvin Trillin, "Thoughts Brought On by Prolonged Exposure to Exposed Brick," quoted in Ruth Rejnis, "Interior Use of Brick Is on the Upswing," NYT, August 28, 1977, sec. 8, p. 1. He observed these similarities even before national developers and architects like James Rouse and Benjamin Thompson spread the genre.

130. For a comparison between 1890s civic improvement groups and 1990s business improvement districts, see Paul Schreiber, "Life after Woolworth," New York Newsday, September 15, 1997, C10. Mike Davis has written a widely read attack on the contemporary obsession with security and control, in City of Quartz: Excavating the Future in Los Angeles (New York: Vintage Books, 1990).

131. Pindell, "Keene Reborn," 15; Eleanor Charles, "A Million-Dollar Baby in a 5-and-10-Cent Store," NYT, November 19, 1995, sec. 9, p. 11; Bill Daley, "Salvation Army Eyes Main Street Building for Thrift Store," Hartford (Conn.) Courant, July 27, 1994, F1; Greg Gatlin, "T. J. Maxx Meets Marshalls," Boston Globe, May 21, 2001, 29; "Ross Dresses Up Old Woolworth's for Grand Opening — Injecting Life into Deteriorating Area," Seattle Times, October 18, 1995, E1; Bill Locey, "Rock (Star) Hunting," Los Angeles Times, March 11, 1999, F46; Frank Green, "Landmark Building to House the Blues," San Diego Union-Tribune, December 8, 2000, C1; Brian Meyer, "Ex-Woolworth Store on Main Eyed as Factory Outlet Mall," Buffalo News, May 28, 1998, 11A; John Rebchook, "Woolworth Site to Get New Life," Denver Rocky Mountain News, January 14, 1999, 1B; John Rebchook, "Blast from the Past," Denver Rocky Mountain News, December 12, 1999, business sec., 12G.

132. "Woolworth's Building Razed," New Orleans Times-Picayune, August 17, 2000, money sec., 1; Steven Jordan, "Office Building in Works," Omaha World-Herald, December 30, 1997, business sec., 21; Ralph Bivins, "Commerce Building Gets New Lease on Life," Houston Chronicle, February 12, 1999, business sec., 2; Ralph Bivins, "Buyer Plans Lofts for Kress Building," Houston Chronicle, May 14, 1998, business sec., 1; Nancy Welsh, "Building Collapses, Closing 2 Streets in Downtown Butler," Pittsburgh Post-Gazette, May 19, 1999, local sec., A12; Chris Burritt, "N.C. Museum Vote Reopens Racial Splits," Atlanta Journal and Constitution, November 4, 2000, 13A.

CONCLUSION

1. The quotation in the chapter title is from the lyrics of "Downtown," a 1964 Grammy Award–winning song. Petula Clark sang "Downtown" in Washington Square Park on November 30, 2002, with off-Broadway performers, to boost morale and promote activity in lower Manhattan following the World Trade Center attacks.

2. Iver Peterson, "Past and Future Collide in Plan for Albuquerque," New York Times, February 5, 1985, A14. For an interesting discussion of the "false gathering spaces" of ur-

ban public life, see Sharon Zukin, "Space and Symbols in an Age of Decline," in *Re-Presenting the City: Ethnicity, Capital, and Culture in the 21st Century Metropolis,* ed. Anthony D. King (London: Macmillan, 1996), 50–54.

3. Michael Sorkin, ed., *Variations on a Theme Park* (New York: Hill and Wang, 1992), xv. Suburban shopping centers have become much more diverse places since the 1960s and even since the 1980s.

4. On the "melting-pot mistake" as a threat to democracy, see Kenneth Jackson, *Crabgrass Frontier: The Suburbanization of the United States* (New York: Oxford University Press, 1985), 217; and Robert Beauregard, *Voices of Decline: The Postwar Fate of US Cities* (Cambridge, MA: Blackwell, 1993), 32.

INDEX

Note: Page numbers in italics refer to illustrations.